BRIDGE CONVENTIONS COMPLETE

by Amalya Kearse

Published by
Devyn Press, Inc.
Louisville, Kentucky

Printed in the United States of America.

Devyn Press, Inc.
3600 Chamberlain Lane, Suite 230
Louisville, KY 40241

ISBN 0-910791-76-7

Contents

Chapter I 22 & 613

RESPONSES TO NOTRUMP OPENING BIDS

Chapter II 91 & 692

RESPONSES AND REBIDS AFTER NATURAL OPENING BIDS IN A SUIT

Chapter III   *149 & 818*

FORCING OPENING BIDS AND RESPONSES

Chapter IV   *283 & 869*

MAKING INQUIRIES

Chapter V   *403 & 932*

COMPETITIVE BIDDING

Chapter VI　　　　　*513 & 1043*

TWO- AND THREE-SUITED OPENING BIDS

Chapter VII   *545 & 1068*

OFFENSIVE PREEMPTIVE CONVENTIONS

Chapter VIII   *555 & 1092*

CONVENTIONS FOR THE DEFENDERS

ACBL GENERAL CONVENTIONS CHART

The conventions listed below must be allowed in all ACBL sanctioned tournament play (other than in events with an upper restriction of 20 or fewer masterpoints and events for which the ACBL conditions of contest state otherwise) and at club-level events with multiple-site overall masterpoint awards. However, Club Managers have full authority to regulate conventions in games conducted solely at their clubs. Conventions listed on the ACBL Limited Convention Chart are marked with an *.

Opening Bids

*1 ♣ artificial forcing opening bid indicating a minimum of 10 HCP (a negative 1 ◊ response may be used)

*1 ◊ may be used as an all-purpose opening bid when played in conjunction with a forcing 1 ♣ (15+ HCP) and 5-card major(s)

1 NT forcing opening bid indicating a balanced or unbalanced hand and a minimum of 16 HCP

2 ♣ artificial opening bid indicating one of:
    *a) a strong hand, balanced or unbalanced
    b) a three suiter with a minimum of 10 HCP

2 ◊ artificial opening bid showing one of:
    a) both majors with a minimum of 10 HCP
    b) a strong hand, balanced or unbalanced
    c) a three suiter with a minimum of 10 HCP

Opening suit bid at the two level or higher indicating the bid suit, another known suit, a minimum of 10 HCP and at least 5-4 distribution in the suits

Opening notrump bid at the two level or higher indicating at least 5-4 distribution in the minors

Opening 3 NT bid indicating
    *a) a solid suit
    b) a broken minor

Opening four-level bid transferring to a known suit

Responses and Rebids

1 ◊ in response to 1 ♣ to deny
    a) a four-card major(s)
    b) a five-card major

1 NT response to a major suit opening bid forcing one round; cannot guarantee game invitational or better values

2 ♣ or 2 ◇ response to 3rd or 4th seat major suit opener asking the quality of opening bid

*Single or higher jump shifts (including into notrump) to indicate a raise or to force to game

Relay systems are not allowed over artificial bids. All other bids are allowed over artificial bids.

All constructive calls made during the second and subsequent rounds of bidding

*Calls that ask for aces, kings, queens, singletons, voids, trump quality and responses thereto

*__Responses and rebids__ after natural notrump including those that have two non-consecutive ranges neither of which exceeds 3 HCP. No conventional responses are allowed over notrump bids with a lower limit of fewer than 10 HCP or with a range of greater than 5 HCP.

*__Responses and rebids__ after opening bids of 2 ♣ or higher (for this classification, by partnership agreement, weak 2 bids must not be fewer than 5 HCP, must be within a range of 7 HCP and the suit must contain at least five cards)

Competitive Auctions

Conventional balancing calls

*Conventional doubles and redoubles

Notrump overcall for

    *a) two suit takeout showing at least 5-4 distribution and at least one known suit

    b) three suit takeout

Jump overcalls into a suit to indicate at least 5-4 distribution in two suits, at least one of which is known

*Cuebid of an opponent's suit

*Defenses to:

    *a) conventional calls

    *b) notrump bids;

    *c) opening bids of 2 ♣ or higher

Disallowed Are

Conventions and/or agreements whose primary purpose is to destroy the opponents' methods

Psyching of artificial opening bids

Psyching of conventional responses to artificial opening bids

Psychic controls

Relay (tell me more) systems

Opening one bids which by partnership agreement could show fewer than eight high-card points. (not applicable to a psych.)

Carding

Dual-message carding strategies are not approved except on each defender's first discard. Only right-side-up or upside-down card ordering strategies are approved. Encrypted signals are not approved.

NOTE: Sponsoring organizations may allow conventions from the SuperChart provided the requested conventions are listed on the Sanction Application, approved by Management, included in all tournament advertising, and posted at the tournament site. Unless all these conditions have been fulfilled, conventions not on the ACBL General Convention Chart **MAY NOT BE ALLOWED.**

ACBL LIMITED CONVENTIONS

(May be used in games with an upper limit of 20 or fewer MPs)

Clubs

Club management shall determine the conventions permitted in club games with an upper limit of 20 or fewer masterpoints.

Local & Higher Events

The sponsoring organization of local and higher rated tournaments may determine the conventions permitted in games with an upper limit of 20 or fewer masterpoints.

Opening bids

A 1♣ opening bid may be both artificial (says nothing about clubs) and forcing (partner must respond at least once), but opener must have at least 10 HCP. A negative 1◊ response may be used.

When a forcing 1♣ opening to show at least 15 HCP is combined with a five-card major opening bid structure, a 1◊ opening may be used to show an opening hand not meeting the requirements for any other opening bid.

A 2♣ opening bid may be artificial and strong. It may be balanced (a hand stronger than a traditional 2 NT opening) or unbalanced (a hand with which you would open a strong two-bid if playing that way). Further bidding will describe the hand.

A 3 NT opening bid may show a hand with a long solid suit (Gambling).

Responses and rebids

A jump shift of one or more levels (into a suit or into notrump) may be used either to force to game or to show a raise of partner's suit.

Any meaning may be given to the responses and rebids after an opening bid of 1 NT. Exception: if the 1 NT opening has a point range which exceeds 5 HCP, or if the 1 NT opening has an agreed lower limit of fewer than 10 HCP, responses and rebids may not be conventional — they must be natural.

Any meaning may be given to the responses to and rebids after an opening bid of 2♣ or higher. Exception: if the opening bid is a weak two-bid with (a) an agreed point range of more than 7 HCP, (b) an agreement that the bid suit can contain fewer than five cards, or (c) an agreement that the hand can contain fewer than 5 HCP, responses and rebids may not be conventional — they must be natural.

Any call may be used to ask partner or to respond to partner about aces, kings, queens, singletons, voids or trump quality with the exceptions noted above.

Competitive auctions

Any meaning may be given to a double or a redouble.

A notrump overcall or jump overcall may be used to show a two-suited hand (at least 5-4 distribution in the two suits). At least one of the suits must be known. The second suit may be known or unknown.

Any meaning may be given to the cuebid of an opponent's suit.

Any meaning may be given to calls used to defend against opponents' conventional calls, notrump bids and opening bids of 2♣ or higher.

Disallowed

Conventions and/or agreements with a primary purpose of destroying the opponents' methods are not allowed (e.g., a bid telling nothing about the bidder's hand, made simply to use up bidding space).

Agreements allowing the partnership to open the bidding at the one level with fewer than 8 HCP are not allowed. This does not preclude a psychic opening bid.

Psyching of artificial opening bids or conventional responses to artificial opening bids is not allowed.

Psychic controls (bids designed to determine whether partner has psyched or to clarify the nature of the psych) are not allowed.

Relay systems (one player tells nothing about his own hand while interrogating partner about his hand through a series of conventional calls) are not allowed.

Carding

A discard (a card played while not following suit) can convey a message to partner. The message can pertain to the length of the discarded suit, to the attitude toward the suit (desire to have partner lead that suit) or to another suit (no information about the discarded suit). A pair may decide to attribute the attitude message (good-bad) to the cards on either a higher-to-lower basis (a higher card is more positive than a lower card) or a lower-to-higher basis (a low card is more positive than a higher card).

A discard may carry more than one message, but only at each defender's first discard of the hand. Dual-message discards are not permitted as second or subsequent discards. Encrypted signals (the order and/or message is based on information known to the other defender but not yet to declarer) are not allowed at any time.

ACBL SUPER CHART

Pre-alerts are required for all conventional methods not permitted on the ACBL General Convention Chart. Descriptions of, and suggested defenses, to such methods must be made available in writing.

This chart applies to:

Vanderbilt Knockout Teams	All sessions
Springold Knockout Teams	All sessions
Women's Knockout Teams	All sessions
Reisinger Board-A-Match Teams	All sessions
Grand National Open Teams	All sessions played at the NABC
All other nationally-rated events with no upper Master Point restrictions	All sessions after the first two qualifying sessions (the ACBL General Convention Chart applies to the first two qualifying sessions)

Allowed:
Any non-destructive convention, treatment or method
Disallowed:
Forcing pass systems
Encrypted signals

Introduction

This classic work by Judge Amalya Kearse, now revised and substantially enlarged, is far more than a simple listing of conventions. Even if you are one of those who like to keep it simple, there are two good reasons why you should read this. One is that the simple conventions which you do favor are explored in depth: Blackwood, that old standby, is given a 15-page essay that includes such vital matters as the distinction between natural and artificial uses of four notrump. And the varieties of Blackwood cover another 15 pages.

The other reason is that your opponents are likely to play some of these against you, especially if you are a duplicate player. You owe it to yourself, your partner and your teammates to have some understanding of modern developments, and be prepared. In many conventional situations the author suggests the appropriate counter-measures available to the opposition.

Even sophisticated experts who think they know it all will find new ideas in these pages. I certainly did, and some discussions with my regular partners will be an inevitable result.

— ALAN TRUSCOTT

Introduction
to First Edition

This is THE book about bridge conventions. I could have guaranteed that statement before I ever read it, because I know Amalya Kearse and the way she works. But more about her later.

What are bridge conventions and who needs to know about them? Duplicate tournament players, of course. But rubber bridge players, too, whether you play in clubs or only socially. It is a great mistake, and it could be an embarrassing one, to say "Oh, we only play a few conventions like Blackwood and Stayman, and I know those."

Do you really know them? If partner answers a 4 NT bid with 5 ♣, how many aces does he have? Did you know he might have all four? Or if partner bids a Stayman 2 ♣ over your opening bid of 1 NT, must you show any four-card major, even one like 5-4-3-2? And if you have two majors, which one should you bid first? And if you deny a major by rebidding 2 ◇, if partner then bids 2 ♡ or 2 ♠ are you required to bid again? Even the most widely used of all conventions may be booby-trapped unless you really understand them.

Blackwood, for example, has such variations as "Key-card" and "Baby Blackwood." "Stayman" is played both "forcing" and "non-forcing." Any time you play with a new partner, or against unfamiliar opponents, you will be at a disadvantage unless you know the answer to questions you might be too embarrassed even to ask.

Some commonly used conventions should be thoroughly understood by you so that you don't suddenly come up against

16

an idea you haven't had time to become familiar with and have no idea how to play against. Some less common conventions are so useful that, if you aren't playing them, you should consider doing so.

More and more players are using 1 ♣ and 2 ♣ openings as their only forcing bids. More and more players are using weak two-bids—which aren't really so weak. Jump bids, which always used to be strong, are not always treated so today. Sometimes the original meaning of a bid has so changed that you would be playing a "convention" if you didn't use it in the new sense. Consider a takeout double as an extreme example. Originally, if you said "Double" it meant that you didn't think the opponent was going to be able to make his contract and therefore you were increasing the penalty he would have to pay if he fell short. Today, however, a takeout double, asking partner to make some bid, is much more common than a penalty double. The original meaning of the bid has become so changed that it has become unconventional and therefore its use is in itself a convention. You would have to announce it as a convention, for example, if you played all doubles for penalties.

These are some of the reasons why what Amalya Kearse has done in this book can be so valuable to you. Also, the way she has done it.

If you haven't already heard of Amalya Kearse, you soon will—either as a brilliant bridge player or a brilliant lawyer. Or both. She is the first black and the second woman ever to become a partner in a major Wall Street law firm—quite an achievement for a young woman in her early thirties. Her bridge career in the tournaments of both the American Contract Bridge League and the American Bridge Association has already been crowned with impressive victories and national titles, even though she is a relative newcomer to big-time bridge.

Thus, this book combines penetrating thought, clarity of

expression and the thoroughness of the kind of research that goes into the preparation of a difficult legal case. It is stripped of non-essentials. You won't find it cluttered with subjects like the "Stripe-tailed Ape" double. There is such a bid, but it isn't a convention, and even if it were you'd have little occasion to want to know more about it.

So, if an opponent says, "I play the XYZ convention" and you can't find it here, tell him to forget it. It doesn't matter if he claims he can explain it in a single sentence—like, "When I bid one heart it means I have exactly seven spades." If it isn't here, it isn't legal.

This book is a must for tournament players and a gold mine for players of all kinds. It is intelligently arranged; you can see what's available to meet situations you may be having trouble with, even if you don't already know the name of the convention you are looking for. And of course it is indexed so that you can find everything you need to know about conventions, both in bidding and in play. Turning a thorough reference work into a fascinating book is quite an accomplishment. Amalya has brought it off.

RICHARD L. FREY

Foreword

In bridge, bidding is a language used to help the partnership to determine where it is going on any given hand. Part of the language may be perfectly straightforward signposts, involving natural bids. Thus, "natural call" is defined by the American Contract Bridge League (ACBL) as a call that suggests itself as the final contract, without giving partner any additional information on the basis of which further action is to be taken. Notrump opening bids, non-forcing raises of partner's suit, and penalty doubles are all examples of natural calls.

Some of the bridge language carries nuances that are not apparent on the face of the words used, although the nuances are related to the call made. Thus, the ACBL defines as "treatments" calls that either indicate a desire to play in the denomination named, or promise or request values in the denomination named, but that also, by agreement, give or request information on which further action can be based. Forcing bids, for example, are treatments. Cue-bids that show or ask about length or high cards in the suit named are treatments.

Conventions, unlike natural calls and treatments, are coded messages. The ACBL defines conventions as calls that, by agreement rather than by logical inference, give or request information unrelated to the denomination named. Transfer bids, for example, are conventions. When decoded they convey a message about a suit other than the one named. Cue-bids that show length in suits other than the one named, are conventions.

Since conventions are largely artificial bids, their use is like asking for or giving directions in a foreign language. If both partners are not speaking the same language, the partnership is not likely to arrive at the right place. They may on occasion end up at a very pleasant spot, but more often than not they will miss their target.

Moreover, the language used by the partnership cannot be a secret language. The opponents are entitled to know the content of each message. They are entitled to know whether a bid contains a coded message; and they may ask the partner of the bidder whether a bid has certain nuances. If the explanation given is not the correct one, the opponents may be awarded redress. Or if the explanation was correct but the player who made the bid had misused the convention and was able to take advantage of the explanation to adjust for his misuse, the partnership may be penalized.

Thus it is essential that the partnership agree on what conventions it will use. And both members of the partnership must understand and remember exactly how the conventions operate, in order to arrive at their proper destination, and in order not to mislead their opponents en route.

The organization of this book is intended to be functional. The conventions described are grouped principally according to the types of hands they describe, or the types of information they seek, or the situations in which they may be used.

Some of the conventions described are more valuable than others. Certain of them may be used with great frequency. Some, such as Stayman and Jacoby Transfers, may be combined and coordinated to great advantage. Some others are extremely complex and highly artificial. If the appropriate circumstances for their use occur infrequently, the agreement to use them may be a bit like learning an entire foreign dialect for a region to be visited once every five years: they may well tax the memory to an extent not warranted by the benefits they produce.

I

Responses to Notrump Opening Bids

Most conventions used in response to opening bids in notrump seek to get the partnership out of notrump and into a suit contract. These conventions fall principally into two categories: first, those by which the responder asks the notrump opener to clarify the distribution of his hand, and second, those by which the responder describes his own hand and at the same time attempts to ensure that the notrump opener will be declarer.

STAYMAN

One of the most widely used conventions in the world is the Stayman convention. It is based on the premise dating back to the days of auction bridge, that after the bidding has been opened in notrump, if the opener and the responder each hold four cards in the same major suit, the hand is likely to fare better in that suit than in notrump.

Fundamentally, therefore, the Stayman convention is designed to allow the partnership to discover whether or not it has an eight-card major suit fit, and if so to escape from notrump into that suit. There are a number of variations and extensions of the Stayman convention designed for other purposes, such as making inquiries about the opener's stoppers for play in notrump, and probing for slam.

Some versions of Stayman, called "Two-Way Stayman," use both a two club response and a two diamond response to a one notrump opening as artificial bids, asking the opener for information about his major suit holdings. It should be recognized that any of these conventions deprives the partnership of the use of the two diamond bid in its natural sense, and blocks potential partnership escape from one notrump at the two level when the responder has a poor hand with a long diamond suit. In addition, use of the two diamond bid as a branch of the Stayman convention precludes its use as any other convention.

See NON-FORCING STAYMAN, FORCING STAYMAN, DOUBLE-BARRELED STAYMAN, SLAM TRY STAYMAN, STAYMAN FOR STOPPERS, STAYMAN OVER A TWO NOTRUMP OPENING, STAYMAN OVER A THREE NOTRUMP OPENING, SHARPLES, MURRAY, AUGUST, FLINT TWO DIAMONDS, WEISSBERGER. *See also* DELAYED STAYMAN, STAYMAN AFTER NOTRUMP OVERCALLS, STAYMAN OVER OPPONENT'S NOTRUMP OVERCALL, JACOBY TRANSFERS and FLINT.

NON-FORCING STAYMAN

In its simplest form the Stayman convention consists of a two club response to an opening bid of one notrump. If the responder holds four hearts or four spades, or four of each, and has enough high cards to invite a game, he bids two clubs. This two club bid asks the opener to bid a four card major suit if he has one, and to bid two diamonds if he has no four card major.

There is a division of opinion as to whether the opener should bid two hearts or two spades when he holds four cards in each major suit. There seems to be little on which to base a preference between the two bids. No matter which major suit opener rebids first, he will always have a chance to show his other major if his first bid did not uncover a fit.

The description of any form of the Stayman convention as "non-forcing" is somewhat misleading. Since the two-club bid has nothing to do with responder's club suit, that bid is always forcing on the opening bidder. The non-forcing aspect of this version of the Stayman convention refers to the fact that if, after the opener answers the two-club bid, the responder bids a new suit on the two level, the opener is not required to bid further.

Thus, using non-forcing Stayman, the following auction is permissible:

Opener	Responder
1 Notrump	2 ♣
2 ♡	2 ♠
Pass	

After the opener has answered the responder's Stayman inquiry, the responder has a variety of bids available to describe his hand. If he has bid two clubs with less than 8 points and a hand such as

♠ Q x x x   ♡ J x x x   ◇ J x x x   ♣ x

he can, of course, pass opener's rebid. Responder can also invite game, force to game, or suggest slam.

Inviting Game

After opener's bid in response to two clubs, if responder makes any bid at the two level, his bid is not forcing, but invites game. For example, opposite a 16 to 18 point one notrump opening responder might hold either of the following hands:

[A] ♠ A J x x   ♡ x x   ◇ Q J x x   ♣ x x x
[B] ♠ K Q x x x   ♡ Q x x   ◇ x x   ♣ x x x

With Hand A, if the opener has bid either two diamonds or two hearts in response to the two club Stayman call, responder would rebid two notrump. This bid invites the opener to bid three notrump if he has a maximum hand. The strength that responder needs for this sequence is the same strength he would have needed to raise the one notrump opening directly to two notrump, i.e., 8 or 9 high card points.

If the responder held Hand B, he would rebid two spades over his partner's two diamond or two heart bid:

Opener	Responder
1 Notrump	2 ♣
2 ◇ or 2 ♡	2 ♠

By using this sequence the responder shows a stronger hand than he would if he had simply bid two spades directly over the one notrump opening.

The opener is invited to raise spades if he has support for the suit, and a maximum notrump opening. With a hand such as

♠ A x x   ♥ Q J x x   ♦ A K x x   ♣ K x

the opener would raise to three spades, allowing the responder to continue to game unless his previous bids were made with less than an 8-point hand.

If, in response to the two club bid, the opener has bid either two hearts or two spades, and the responder holds four or more cards in the suit bid by opener, responder can make his game try by raising opener's suit:

Opener	*Responder*
1 Notrump	2 ♣
2 ♥	3 ♥

Responder might hold a hand such as:

♠ x x x   ♥ A Q x x   ♦ Q x x x   ♣ x x

Forcing to Game

If the responder has a hand worth from 10 to about 14 points he is entitled to force the hand to game. If the opener's bid over two clubs has revealed that the partnership has an eight-card, or longer, major suit fit, the responder may raise to game in that major.

For example, if responder held:

♠ K Q x   ♡ A Q x x   ◇ x x   ♣ J x x x

he would raise a two heart bid by the opener to four hearts. If the opener has bid two diamonds or two spades instead of two hearts, responder would bid three notrump.

After the responder has started a Non-Forcing Stayman sequence with two clubs, if he bids a new major suit on the three level, his bid is forcing to game. Thus, the following sequences are forcing to game:

(A) *Opener*   *Responder*
     1 Notrump   2 ♣
     2 ◇   3 ♡

(B) *Opener*   *Responder*
     1 Notrump   2 ♣
     2 ♠   3 ♡

The three heart bid made by the responder in each of the above examples promises a five-card heart suit and sufficient values for game. Responder might have a hand such as:

♠ K x   ♡ A J x x x   ◇ Q x x   ♣ J x x

In the following auction, the meaning of the three club bid must be agreed upon:

(C) *Opener*   *Responder*
     1 Notrump   2 ♣
     2 ♡   3 ♣ (or 3 ◇)

Some partnerships treat the bid of three of a minor suit in such an auction as weak, and some treat it as strong. If the partnership is using the jumps to three of a minor suit directly in response to the notrump opening as weak bids the three club bid in example (C) should be considered to be forcing to game, and to carry some slam implications. Responder might have one of the following hands:

(D) ♠ x x   ♡ A x x   ◇ K x   ♣ A Q x x x x

(E) ♠ A x x   ♡ K J x x   ◇ x x   ♣ A Q x x

With Hand D the responder would bid three clubs as in auction (C), to make a mild slam try in clubs. With Hand E the responder would bid three clubs en route to showing his support for opener's heart suit, showing interest in a heart slam.

When the Opponents Interfere over the Notrump Opening

If an opponent has doubled the one notrump opening, a two club bid by the responder is not the Stayman convention. In this situation the two club bid, like any other bid at the two level, is an attempt to escape from a penalty, and shows a desire to play in the suit named. (See CONVENTIONS USED OVER AN OPPONENT'S DOUBLE OF A ONE NOTRUMP OPENING.)

If an opponent has overcalled over one notrump, the responder obviously cannot use two clubs as Stayman. He has several choices of action, depending on the nature of his hand. If responder has a weak hand, even with two four-card major suits, he will pass (just as he usually would have done had there been no interference).

If the responder has a hand with 7 or 8 points with a five-card major suit that can be shown at the two level over the overcall, he should bid it. Using standard methods, responder's bid on the two level is not forcing. However, a bid of a new suit on the three level would be forcing. Therefore, if the overcall prevents responder from bidding his suit at the two level, he must either pass or bid two notrump with his 7 or 8 point hand. For example, suppose responder has a hand such as:

♠ x x   ♡ K Q x x x   ♢ x x x   ♣ Q x x

If the notrump opening has been overcalled with two clubs or two diamonds, responder should bid two hearts. However, if the overcall was two spades, responder cannot bid three hearts because his hand is not strong enough; over the two spade overcall responder should bid two notrump. (*See also* LEBENSOHL CONVENTION.)

The two notrump bid by responder is also used when responder has any balanced hand with which he would have invited game without interference. The opener may rebid three notrump if he has a maximum notrump opening and a strong stopper in the suit of the overcall. Opener may, with a maximum, try out a four-card major suit on his way to game in notrump, in case responder has a hand such as:

♠ K J x x   ♡ Q 10 x x   ♢ 10 x   ♣ Q x x

If responder has a hand worth 9 points or better and has one or both four card major suits, he should cue-bid the suit of the overcall. This cue-bid takes the place of the Stayman two club convention, and opener is expected to show a four card major if he has one. For example, suppose North opens one notrump and East overcalls two hearts, and the North and South hands are:

(North) ♠ A K x x   ♡ Q x   ◇ A J x x   ♣ K x x

(South) ♠ Q x x x   ♡ 10 x x   ◇ K x   ♣ A x x x

The bidding should go:

North	East	South	West
1 Notrump	2 ♡	3 ♡	Pass
3 ♠	Pass	4 ♠	

The cue-bid of the overcall is forcing to game, since its use to search for a suit fit does not leave the partnership enough room to make a game try.

Bidding over Doubles of the Stayman Bid

If an opponent should double a Stayman bid for a club lead, the opener should bid normally unless he has reason to believe that the double has given the partnership an opportunity to extract a profitable penalty. For example, holding

[A] ♠ A Q x x   ♡ K x x   ◇ A Q 10 x   ♣ Q x

in the auction

North	East	South	West
1 Notrump	Pass	2 ♣	Double

the opener should make his normal rebid of two spades.

However, if his club and diamond holdings were reversed, and his hand were

[B] ♠ A Q x x   ♡ K x x   ◇ Q x   ♣ A Q 10 x

opener should redouble. The redouble conveys the message to

the responder that opener has a good four card club suit, and if responder is willing, he should play two clubs redoubled. Responder might hold one of the following hands:

[C] ♠ K x x x   ♡ Q J x x x   ♢ A x   ♣ x ·x

[D] ♠ K x x x   ♡ A x   ♢ x x x x   ♣ J x x

With Hand C responder would jump to three hearts over his partner's redouble, showing his interest in game and his disinclination to play in two clubs redoubled. With Hand D, responder would pass the redouble of two clubs. Two clubs redoubled might be the partnership's only makeable game.

If, over the double of two clubs, the opener has only three clubs, he should pass the double around to his partner. For example, if North held

[E] ♠ A Q x x   ♡ Q x   ♢ A Q x x   ♣ K x x

the bidding could start:

North	East	South	West
1 Notrump	Pass	2 ♣	Double
Pass			

If responder has a reasonably strong hand with four clubs, he can redouble for penalties and North can pass. If South has fewer than four clubs, he can bid a suit, over which North will reveal his own four card major suit. For example, South might hold either of the following hands:

[F] ♠ K x   ♡ A x x x x   ♢ J x   ♣ Q 10 x x

[G] ♠ K x x x   ♡ A x x x x   ♢ J x   ♣ x x

If responder held Hand F opposite opener's Hand E, the bidding could go:

North	East	South	West
1 Notrump	Pass	2 ♣	Double
Pass	Pass	Redouble	Pass
Pass	Pass		

If responder held Hand G, the bidding could go:

North	East	South	West
1 Notrump	Pass	2 ♣	Double
Pass	Pass	2 ♡	Pass
2 ♠	Pass	3 ♠	Pass
4 ♠	Pass	Pass	Pass

If responder has no five card suit to bid, he may bid two diamonds to repeat his request that opener show a four card major suit.

FORCING STAYMAN

Like Non-Forcing Stayman, Forcing Stayman is a two club bid in response to a one notrump opening which requests the notrump opener to bid a four-card major suit if he has one. If the opener has no four-card major he must bid two diamonds.

The mechanical difference between Forcing and Non-Forcing Stayman is that, using Forcing Stayman, the opening bidder is not allowed to let the bidding die below the two notrump level. Thus, using forcing Stayman, if the auction starts

Opener	Responder
1 Notrump	2 ♣
2 ♡	2 ♠

the responder's two spade bid is forcing, and the opening bidder is required to bid again. Holding three or four spades the opener would raise spades. Holding only two spades, the opener would bid notrump.

As is the case with Non-Forcing Stayman, the label "Forcing" Stayman is slightly misleading, because the responder is not forced to bid again over the opener's rebid in answer to two clubs. For example, suppose the responder held the following hand:

(A) ♠ x x x x   ♡ Q x x x   ◇ x x x x   ♣ x

If his partner opened the bidding one notrump, responder would bid two clubs, planning to pass whatever the opener rebid, two diamonds, two hearts, or two spades.

The advantage said to result from using Forcing Stayman is that it permits the partnership to explore game and slam possibilities at a low level without the risk that the bidding will die prematurely. Most experts, however, prefer Non-Forcing Stayman, on the theory that they would rather do their exploring at the three level with their good hands, in exchange for being able to rest in peace at the two level with poor hands.

The effect that an agreement to play Forcing Stayman has on the responder is that he must have either a hand such as (A) above, in which he has four cards in each suit that opener could rebid, or a hand worth eight or more points. Thus facing a one notrump opening with a hand such as

(B) ♠ A 10 x x x   ♡ x x   ◇ Q x x x   ♣ x x

the responder should simply bid two spades. If he were to bid two clubs and the opener rebid either two diamonds or two hearts, responder would be too weak to bid two spades, because the opener is forced to bid again over two spades. The partnership could well be overboard in two notrump if the opener's hand were

♠ Q x   ♡ K J x   ◇ A x x   ♣ A Q x x x

or overboard in three spades if opener's hand were

♠ K Q x   ♡ Q J x x   ◇ A J x   ♣ K x x

The agreement to play forcing Stayman places a concealed responsibility on the notrump opener. While it is obvious that when the auction proceeds

Opener	Responder
1 Notrump	2 ♣
2 ◇ (or 2 ♡)	2 ♠

the opener must bid again, what is less apparent is that if the opener has a maximum for his one notrump opening, he must now either bid game or make a forcing bid. The reason is simply that responder may have only an 8-point hand. If he does, he will pass opener's bid of two notrump or three spades. Therefore, if opener has a hand strong enough for game opposite eight points, he must show it by bidding more than he is forced to bid.

Other game invitations and game forcing bids by the responder have the same meanings using Forcing Stayman as they have using Non-Forcing Stayman.

With respect to opponent interference, *see discussion under* NON-FORCING STAYMAN.

DOUBLE-BARRELED STAYMAN

The most prevalent form of Two-Way Stayman, known as Double-Barreled Stayman, is a combination of non-forcing Stayman and game-forcing Stayman. The two club response is used as non-forcing Stayman, and the two diamond response is used as game-forcing Stayman. Both bids start a search for a 4-4 major suit fit.

Using this modification of the Stayman convention the responder would simply bid two clubs with a hand containing one or both four card major suits, and fewer than ten high card points. For example, responder might hold:

♠ K x x x   ♡ K J x x   ◇ x x   ♣ x x x

The rebids by the opener and the responder after the two club call have the same meanings as they would in a Non-Forcing Stayman sequence, with the exception that all of responder's rebids are at best invitational. Responder, having started with a two club bid, has no bids available with which to force the opener to bid a game.

Holding a hand worth ten points or more, the responder will usually bid two diamonds over his partner's one notrump opening, although he is not required to do so.

For tactical reasons, the responder might elect to bid two clubs even with ten or more points, planning to jump to game at his next turn. For example, if responder held

♠ A J x x   ♡ x x x   ◇ x x   ♣ K Q x x

bidding two diamonds would give the responder's left-hand opponent the opportunity to double that bid, asking for a diamond lead. Since responder will be able to place the final contract over whatever his partner rebids, it is to his tactical advantage to start with two clubs rather than two diamonds.

The two diamond response commits the partnership irrevocably to game. Over two diamonds, the opener bids a four card major suit if he has one; he normally bids two notrump if he has no four card major suit. However, opener is allowed to bid three clubs or three diamonds over responder's two diamond bid, if he has a five card suit.

Since the partnership is forced to game when responder bids two diamonds, slam possibilities may be explored at the two- and three-levels; and opener should therefore view any jump by responder to game as denying slam interest.

SLAM-TRY STAYMAN

The Slam-Try version of Two-Way Stayman, like Double-Barreled Stayman, uses both the two club and two diamond responses to ask the opener whether or not he has a four card major suit. The principal difference is that the two diamond response immediately indicates that the responder has slam aspirations. A second difference is that the responder may start with the two club response, and later make a game-forcing bid, just as he can playing simple Forcing or Non-Forcing Stayman.

The use of the two diamond bid as an immediate slam try is intended to alleviate the responder's problems when he has a hand with which the partnership may have a slam if opener's hand is suitable, but with which the partnership may get too high over a standard slam try if the opener's hand is not suitable. The two diamond slam-try allows the partnership to explore slam possibilities at a level which does not put it in jeopardy.

In answer to the two diamond bid, the opener chooses one of a series of bids to describe his hand, specifying how many four card major suits he has, and if he has no four card major, whether he has a minimum or maximum hand.

The complete schedule of responses is as follows:

2 ♡ = Four hearts, fewer than four spades.

2 ♠ = Four spades, fewer than four hearts.

2 NT = No four card major, minimum strength.

3 ♣ = Four hearts and four spades.

3 ◇ = No four card major, maximum strength.

3 ♡ = Five card heart suit.

3 ♠ = Five card spade suit.

For example, suppose responder held the following hand:

[A] ♠ A Q x x   ♡ K x   ◇ Q J x x x   ♣ K x

If the partnership were not using Slam-Try Stayman he wou!
make his normal Stayman bid (two clubs with one-way Stayman
or two diamonds with Double-Barreled Stayman), and woulċ
then want to make a slam try either in spades or in notrump. Ii
opener did not show a four card spade suit, the responder would
want to jump to four notrump:

Opener	*Responder*
1 Notrump	2 ♣
2 ◇	4 Notrump

Responder's bid of four notrump invites the opener to bid a
slam with a maximum one notrump opening. If the opener has a
hand such as

[B] ♠ K J x   ♡ Q x x   ◇ K x x   ♣ A Q J x

he would pass the four notrump bid, but the partnership will be
in jeopardy at the four level if a heart is led.

Using Slam-Try Stayman, however, the responder need not
jump to four notrump because he will already have made his
slam try by bidding two diamonds. With Hand B, opener would
rebid two notrump in answer to the responder's two diamond
bid, showing no four card major suit, and a minimum one notrump opening. Responder can settle into three notrump secure
in the knowledge that he has already made his slam try, and that
his partner knows it:

Opener	*Responder*
1 Notrump	2 ◇
2 Notrump	3 Notrump

Even if the opener's rebid does not reveal his point count, the partnership can avoid going beyond game. For instance:

(C) *Opener*   *Responder*
    1 Notrump   2 ◇
    2 ♡   2 Notrump

(D) *Opener*   *Responder*
    1 Notrump   2 ◇
    2 ♠   3 ♠

The responder's bid of two notrump in auction (C), and his bid of three spades in auction (D), show the equivalent strength of the standard jump to four notrump over a one notrump opening.

If responder held a hand such as

[E]   ♠ A Q x x   ♡ K x   ◇ A J x x x   ♣ J x

and the auction proceeded as in (D) above, the partnership could do most of its cue bidding below the game level. If opener had a hand such as

[F]   ♠ K x x x   ♡ A J x   ◇ Q x x   ♣ A Q x

opposite Hand E, the auction might proceed as follows:

Opener   *Responder*
1 Notrump   2 ◇
2 ♠   3 ♠
4 ♣   4 ◇
4 ♡   5 ♡
6 ♠

STAYMAN FOR STOPPERS

Two-Way Stayman may also be used in a way in which only the two club bid searches for a 4—4 major suit fit. The two diamond bid would then be used to discover whether the partnership has all of the suits sufficiently well stopped to play in notrump.

Using this variation of Two-Way Stayman, the responder would normally reserve his two diamond bid for a hand containing a singleton or a void, such as

[A] ♠ x   ♡ A x x   ◇ K Q x x x   ♣ Q x x x

Responder's two diamond bid asks the notrump opener to bid whichever major suit he has guarded. Suits containing four cards headed by the queen, or three headed by the queen and ten, would be considered minimum sufficient stoppers. If the opener has both major suits guarded he should bid two notrump.

If the opener's rebid in answer to two diamonds is in responder's short suit, responder can settle for game in notrump if his hand is not in the slam range. If the opener does not have the responder's short suit stopped, responder can explore other game, or slam, possibilities.

Indeed, the opener's weakness opposite the responder's short suit strengthens the partnership's slam potential. Opener might have one of the following hands:

[B] ♠ A Q x x   ♡ K J x   ◇ J x x   ♣ A J x

or

[C] ♠ J x x   ♡ K Q x x   ◇ A x x x   ♣ A K

When the opener has Hand B opposite a hand in which the responder is short in spades, such as Hand A, there is probably

41

too much duplication of values to make slam a good proposition. However, when the opener has a hand such as that in [C] with few of its values wasted in the spade suit opposite the responder's singleton, the hands mesh well for slam, even with a total of only 28 high-card points.

When the partnership is using two diamonds to ask for stoppers, the two club Stayman bid can be used as it is used in either Forcing Stayman or Non-Forcing Stayman. In either event, unlike in Double-Barreled Stayman, the responder is able to create game forcing sequences after he has started with a two club response.

STAYMAN OVER A TWO NOTRUMP OPENING

The Stayman convention may be used over an opening bid of two notrump just as easily as it is over an opening bid of one notrump. In simple form, the Stayman bid over a two notrump opening is three clubs, and the responder should have a strong enough hand to play in three notrump if a major suit fit is not found.

In addition, there is at least one two-way variation of Stayman over two notrump openings that uses both the three club response and the three diamond response to ask the opener to bid a four card major suit if he has one. The difference between the three club bid and the three diamond bid is that the latter shows slam interest.*

For example, suppose the responder holds one of the following hands:

[A] ♠ Q x x x   ♥ K x x x   ♦ x x x   ♣ x x

[B] ♠ K Q x x   ♥ x   ♦ x x x x   ♣ A x x x

With Hand A the responder would bid three clubs, planning to raise a major suit rebid by the opener to four, or to bid three notrump if the opener denies holding a four card major. With Hand B, the responder can envision a possible slam if the opener has some holding such as:

*Some partnerships agree to reverse the meanings of the three club and three diamond bids. They prefer to reserve the three club bid as the bid which suggests slam interest, to give the partnership more room to explore when such interest exists.

[C] ♠ A 10 x x   ♡ A x x   ◇ A K x   ♣ K Q x

Therefore, with Hand B, if the partnership has agreed to use this version of Stayman, the responder would bid three diamonds in response to two notrump. Since this bid itself indicates responder's slam interest, responder has no need to make slam tries above the game level which could get the partnership overboard. Using this convention, the following auctions all carry slam implications because responder has started by bidding three diamonds:

(E)	*Opener*	*Responder*
	2 Notrump	3 ◇
	3 ♡	3 Notrump

(F)	*Opener*	*Responder*
	2 Notrump	3 ◇
	3 ♠	4 ♠

(G)	*Opener*	*Responder*
	2 Notrump	3 ◇
	3 ♡	3 ♠

After his first response of three diamonds, any rebid by the responder above the game level shows a hand stronger than that shown in (B) above. Such a bid would invite the opener to bid a slam even with a minimum in high cards, if it is a minimum that is likely to mesh well with responder's hand. For example, responder might hold a hand such as:

[H] ♠ A x x x   ♡ K Q x x   ◇ x x   ♣ Q x x

With Hand H, responder would respond three diamonds to his

44

partner's two notrump opening, and raise opener's rebid, whatever it might be, one level beyond game. For example, either of the following auctions would be possible:

(J) *Opener*   *Responder*
    2 Notrump   3 ◇
    3 ♠   5 ♠

(K) *Opener*   *Responder*
    2 Notrump   3 ◇
    3 Notrump   4 Notrump

Suppose the opener held one of the following hands opposite his partner's slam try in auction (J):

[L] ♠ K Q x x   ♡ A x x   ◇ A Q x x   ♣ A J

[M] ♠ Q J x x   ♡ A x x   ◇ K Q x   ♣ A K J

Hands L and M both contain 20 high-card points. With Hand L, opener would carry on to six spades, on the theory that he could not possibly have a more suitable minimum hand. He has a good trump holding, he has aces, which are invaluable for a slam, and he has tenaces and a ruffing value.

Hand M, however, is not as good. Allowing for the responder to have a good 11-point hand, slam in spades might well be no better than on a finesse, and could be hopeless.

If the opener held one of the following hands opposite the responder's slam try in auction (K), he might drive on to slam in notrump:

[N] ♠ K Q x   ♡ A J x   ◇ A J 10 x   ♣ A J x

[O] ♠ K x   ♡ A J x   ◇ A Q J x x   ♣ A J 10

With either Hand N or Hand O, the opener would bid six no-trump. Hand N will supply fillers for whichever major suit the responder holds. Hand O has a source of tricks of its own.

The agreement to use two-way Stayman over two notrump opening bids requires the partnership to give up the natural use of the three diamond response or other artificial uses of that bid, such as Flint and Jacoby Transfers. Both the Flint and the Jacoby Transfer conventions allow the partnership to rest in three of a major suit after the bidding has been opened with two notrump. To compensate for the loss of the use of these conventions, it is possible to treat the responder's immediate bid of three of a major suit as not forcing:

Opener	Responder
2 Notrump	3 ♡ or 3 ♠
	(not forcing)

This treatment, in turn, may prevent the responder from showing a five card major suit with a game-going hand, and thus from giving the opener a choice of whether to bid game in a major suit rather than in notrump.

For example, suppose responder holds:

[P]   ♠ x x   ♡ Q 10 9 x x   ◇ K 10 x x   ♣ x x

If the partnership has agreed that an immediate bid of three hearts is not forcing, the responder must bid three clubs in response to the two notrump opening. If the opener rebids three spades, responder will be forced to sign off in three notrump, with no way to determine whether or not four hearts would be a better contract.

STAYMAN OVER A THREE NOTRUMP OPENING

The Stayman convention may also be used over opening bids of three notrump. The partnership should take care, however, to discuss whether the bid of four clubs in response to a three notrump opening is Stayman, or is instead the Gerber convention, asking for aces.

There is a great deal to be said for reserving the four club response to three notrump for use as Gerber, and using a response of four diamonds as Stayman. Use of the four diamond bid as Stayman does not in any way impair the opener's ability to respond in a four card major suit. The one drawback to using the four diamond bid as Stayman is that if the opener has no four card major suit, his response will be four notrump. If the responder has a five card heart suit and a poor hand he will not be able to show his suit over this rebid, whereas he might have been able to bid it if he had started with a four club Stayman bid. Of course, if the opener should rebid four spades, the heart suit would have been shut out no matter which suit was used as Stayman.

On balance, it is probably more valuable to use the four club bid as Gerber, giving the opener full room to show his aces, and to use four diamonds as Stayman.

SHARPLES

Responding to a one notrump opening with a hand containing one four card major suit and one or both four card minor suits may present responder with a problem. The Sharples convention is an extension of the Stayman convention that allows the responder to explore first the possibility of a four-four major suit fit, and then the possibility of a four-four minor suit fit.

The responder starts by responding two clubs, Stayman, to his partner's one notrump opening. If the opener does not rebid in responder's four card major suit, responder uses the Sharples convention by leaping to four of his minor suit. If the responder has both four card minors, he jumps to four clubs. The jump to the four level shows a hand at least strong enough to play in four notrump.

In the following sequence:

Opener	Responder
1 Notrump	2 ♣
2 ♡	4 ♣ or 4 ♢

responder might have a hand such as:

[A]   ♠ K Q x x   ♡ x   ♢ A Q x x   ♣ K J x x

or

[B]   ♠ K Q x x   ♡ x x   ♢ A Q x x   ♣ K J x

Responder would jump to four clubs on Hand A, and to four diamonds on Hand B. His four diamond bid denies a four card club suit.

The opening bidder is expected to raise the responder's suit if he has four card support. The opener may raise to the five level or to the six level, depending on the strength of his hand and the location of his high cards. A concentration of the opener's strength in the responder's suits would make his hand more attractive for a jump to slam.

If the opener lacks four card support for the suit that responder has bid at the four-level, opener should bid a new four card suit, if one remains in which responder has not yet denied holding four cards. Lacking such a suit, the opener rebids four notrump with a minimum hand, or five notrump with a maximum.

MURRAY TWO DIAMONDS

The Murray Two Diamond convention is a two diamond response to a one notrump opening that asks the opener to bid his longer major suit. The convention is designed to facilitate responder's bidding of weak, unbalanced hands containing 5—5 or 4—4 in the major suits. Responder might hold a hand such as:

♠ Q x x x x   ♥ J 10 x x x   ♦ x x   ♣ x

The opener is required to rebid his longer major. If he has equal length, he rebids two hearts. If he has no four card major suit, he bids a three card suit.

After the opener has bid two hearts or two spades, the responder will pass if he has a weak hand such as the one above. However, responder may have a strong hand such as:

♠ K J x x   ♥ A x x x   ♦ A J x x   ♣ x

In this event, he may bid two notrump, which requires the opener to bid three of his lowest ranking four card suit. This sequence allows the partnership to determine whether it has a four-four fit in any suit.

AUGUST TWO DIAMONDS

The August Two Diamond convention is similar to the Murray Two Diamond convention, but it is designed to help the responder bid a weak hand containing a four card major suit and a five card minor suit opposite a one notrump opening. The responder might hold a hand such as the following:

♠ Q x x x   ♡ x   ◇ x x x   ♣ K J x x x

As with the Murray convention, the August Two Diamond bid in response to a one notrump opening requires the opening bidder to rebid his longer major suit, or to rebid two hearts with major suits of equal length. If the opener's rebid is not in the major suit held by the responder, the latter will bid his five card minor suit. The minor suit bid is not encouraging, and the opener is required to pass.

If the partnership is using the August convention, the responder may show a hand containing two weak five card minor suits by bidding two clubs (Stayman, in theory) over one notrump, and then bidding three clubs over whatever the opener has rebid to two clubs. The opener will bid three diamonds if he has longer diamonds than clubs, otherwise he will pass.

This use of the two club bid does not impair the partnership's ability to use two clubs to locate its four-four major suit fits. However, it does preclude a strength-showing use of the three-club rebid by the responder.

FLINT TWO DIAMONDS

The Flint Two Diamond convention was designed primarily for use with weak notrump openings. This convention is forcing to three notrump or four of a minor suit, and on the way it searches out stoppers for notrump play.

The responder uses the Flint Two Diamond bid with one of two types of hands. He may have a hand containing a long solid minor suit, such as:

[A] ♠ x x   ♡ x x x   ◇ A K Q x x x   ♣ K x

Or he may have an unbalanced hand with at least four cards in each minor suit, such as:

[B] ♠ K Q x   ♡ x   ◇ A x x x x   ♣ Q x x x

Over the responder's Flint Two Diamond bid, the notrump opener rebids a four card major suit if he has one; otherwise he rebids two notrump. The responder then clarifies which type of hand he has, and at the same time probes for stoppers. If the responder's rebid is three of a minor suit, he shows a hand containing a solid minor suit, although not necessarily the suit he has just bid.

If the responder's solid suit is clubs, he will rebid three clubs; if his solid suit is diamonds, he would still bid three clubs if he had a hand such as [A] above, in which he had a club stopper. A three diamond bid by the responder, therefore, would show a solid diamond suit, and would deny a club stopper. With Hand A the auction would commence as follows:

Opener	Responder
1 Notrump	2 ♦
2 ♡, 2 ♠ or	
2 Notrump	3 ♣

After the responder has made a rebid that shows that he has a solid minor suit, the opener is required to bid three notrump if he has stoppers in all of the unbid suits. If he cannot stop the unbid suits he bids the lowest ranking unbid suit in which he has a stopper. Over opener's bid of a stopper, the responder can either bid three notrump if he now knows that the partnership has all suits stopped, or bid another stopper himself if he has one. If he is unable to do either, the responder must rebid his minor suit. Since this convention is not forcing past four of a minor, the responder should take care not to rebid just four of his suit if he has a game-going hand.

If the responder had a hand with both minor suits, such as Hand B above, he would bid three of a major suit over whatever the opener has bid in response to two clubs. Responder would bid the major suit in which he had the greater concentration of values. Thus with Hand B, the auction would be:

Opener	Responder
1 Notrump	2 ♦
2 ♡, 2 ♠ or	
2 Notrump	3 ♠

The opener now knows that he must have hearts well stopped in order to bid three notrump.

WEISSBERGER

A convention of little utility in the United States, the Weissberger convention was designed to complement a British-style treatment of the Stayman convention, in which the responder's jump rebid to three of a major suit is not forcing In the United States, the following auction would be forcing:

(A)	*Opener*	*Responder*
	1 Notrump	2 ♣
	2 ◇	3 ♡ or 3 ♠

unless the partnership was using DOUBLE-BARRELED STAYMAN, in which a two-diamond bid, forcing to game, also would ask the opener to rebid a four card major suit if he had one.

When the sequence in (A) is not forcing, the Weissberger convention helps the responder to bid hands worth about 10 to 14 points that contain either five spades and five hearts, or five spades and four hearts, and hands worth 8 or 9 points that contain five spades and five hearts. The following would be typical hands with which this convention would be used:

[B]	♠ K x x x x	♡ A J x x	◇ Q x	♣ Q x
[C]	♠ A Q x x x	♡ K Q x x x	◇ x	♣ x x
[D]	♠ K J x x x	♡ Q x x x x	◇ x x	♣ x

The Weissberger convention is used after the responder has tried a two club Stayman bid, and the opener has denied holding a four card major suit. Weissberger is the three diamond bid in the following auction:

(E) *Opener*   *Responder*
     1 Notrump   2 ♣
     2 ◊   3 ◊

The responder's three diamond bid promises a five card spade suit, and either four or five hearts. If the responder has only four hearts, he must have a hand worth ten or more points. Over three diamonds, the opener is expected to bid spades if he has three cards in that suit. If he has a maximum for his one notrump opening, he bids four spades. If he has only a minimum he bids just three spades, which the responder will raise to four if he has a game-going hand such as [B] or [C] above.

If the opener has only two spades with a minimum hand, he will bid his three card heart suit. If he has two spades, with a maximum, he bids three no trump. If the opener has bid three notrump over the Weissberger three diamond bid, the responder will correct to four hearts if he has either Hand C or Hand D above. If the opener has bid three hearts, however, showing a minimum notrump opening, the responder would bid three notrump with Hand A, would bid four hearts with Hand B, and would pass with Hand C.

JACOBY TRANSFERS

Over the years, partnerships have learned that when one partner opens the bidding with one notrump, it is usually advantageous to have him be the declarer at whatever contract the partnership eventually reaches. The notrump bidder almost always has the stronger of the two hands. It is therefore better to have the opening lead come up to his high cards and tenaces, rather than through them. In addition, having the stronger hand concealed sometimes makes it more difficult for the opponents to defend accurately.

One convention designed to make the notrump opener the declarer as often as possible in responder's long major suit is the Jacoby Transfer Bid. (*See also* TEXAS TRANSFERS.)

When one partner opens the bidding with one notrump and the responder has five or more cards in a major suit he may make a Jacoby Transfer by making an artificial bid of two of the suit below the suit he actually holds. This bid requires the notrump bidder to bid the next suit—the suit actually held by the responder.

For example, opposite his partner's one notrump opening bid, the responder might hold:

[A] ♠ K x   ♡ A 10 9 x x   ◇ A x x   ♣ x x x

or

[B] ♠ Q J x x x   ♡ x x   ◇ x x x x   ♣ x x

Using a Jacoby Transfer, in [A] responder would bid two diamonds to show at least a five card heart suit and to ask the opener to bid two hearts. In [B], responder would bid two hearts to show at least a five card spade suit and to ask opener to bid two spades. The responder's bid of two diamonds in [A] says nothing about his diamond suit, and his bid of two hearts in [B] says nothing about his hearts.

After using the Jacoby transfer over the opener's one no-trump bid, the responder has a variety of options available to him depending on the strength and balance of his hand. If he has a very poor hand, such as that in [B], he may simply pass the opener's acceptance of the transfer. If responder has more than seven high card points, assuming that the opening notrump has shown 16 to 18 points, responder can invite game or force to game.

Inviting Game

If North has a middling hand of eight or nine points he may make a bid that invites the notrump bidder to bid a game. If the responder's hand is unbalanced, as, for example:

[A] ♠ x x   ♡ A 10 x x x   ◇ A x x x   ♣ x x

or

[B] ♠ x   ♡ A 10 x x x   ◇ A x x   ♣ x x x x

he should try for game by making a simple raise of his suit:

Opener	*Responder*
1 Notrump	2 ◇
2 ♡	3 ♡

By this sequence of bidding the responder has shown at least a five card heart suit, a singleton or two doubetons on the side, and eight or nine high card points. The opener is invited to bid game if he has a maximum one notrump opening of 17 or 18 points.

If the responder has eight or nine points, but his hand is

well balanced, that is 5-3-3-2, he can make his game try by bidding two notrump. This invites the notrump opener to bid four hearts with a maximum holding (17 or 18 points) and three or more hearts, or to bid three notrump with a maximum and a doubleton heart. The opener may decline the invitation by bidding three hearts or by passing two notrump.

Notice that whether the opener accepts or rejects the invitation, in either hearts or notrump, he will always be the declarer.

Forcing to Game

When the responder's hand is worth ten or more points he may force the hand to game. If he has a six-card suit he may simply bid game after his partner has accepted the transfer.

If the responder has a five card suit and either a singleton or two doubletons, and therefore a side suit of four or more cards, he may give the opener a choice of games by bidding his second suit. Thus, in the following auction:

Opener	*Responder*
1 Notrump	2 ◇
2 ♡	3 ◇

responder has shown at least five hearts and at least four diamonds. He gives the opener a choice of games in hearts, in diamonds, or in notrump.

The responder's three diamond bid should be treated as game forcing, so if the opener now bids just three hearts, the responder must bid again. Probably the responder should bid three notrump unless his hand is more unbalanced than he has indicated. If he has six hearts, he would bid four hearts; if he has five diamonds, he would bid four diamonds.

If the responder's ten point (or stronger) hand is balanced —5-3-3-2—he should make his game force by bidding three notrump. This gives the opener the option of passing if he has just two hearts, or of bidding four hearts if he has more than two.

Opener's Options

When the responder has made a transfer bid, the opener has an obligation to bid his partner's suit. On the great majority of hands, he will simply accept the transfer by bidding that suit at the two level. However, recognizing that with fewer than eight points the responder will pass the opener's acceptance of the transfer, opener may, if he has an especially good hand with a fit for his partner's suit, make his own game invitation.

Suppose the opener held:

♠ K J x x   ♡ A x   ◇ K Q x x   ♣ A x x

If responder transfers to spades over the one notrump opening, the opener should invite game on his own by jumping to three spades. Then the responder, with a hand such as:

♠ Q x x x x   ♡ x x x   ◇ A x x   ♣ x x

—a hand which would not have been strong enough to invite game—can bid the laydown four spade game over the opener's jump to three spades.

When the Opponents Interfere

Jacoby Transfers usually are not used after interference by an opponent. Therefore, if an opponent overcalls over the one

notrump opening, any suit bid by the responder is a natural bid.
For example, if the responder holds

♠ x x ♡ Q J x x x ◇ A x x ♣ x x x

he would have bid two diamonds to transfer to hearts if there
had been no interference. However, if his right hand opponent
overcalls, the transfer may no longer be used, and responder
should simply bid two hearts. Thus the auction might be:

North	East	South	West
1 Notrump	2 ♣	2 ♡	

While Jacoby Transfer bids are normally not used over
doubles of one notrump, there are conventions that use transfers
as well as other escapes over doubles. *See* CONVENTIONS OVER
OPPONENT'S DOUBLE OF ONE NOTRUMP.

If an opponent has overcalled or doubled after the transfer
has been made, for example:

North	East	South	West
1 Notrump	Pass	2 ◇	Double

the opener should not immediately accept the transfer unless he
has at least three cards in his partner's suit. Opener may redouble if he has a reasonably good four-card holding in the suit
doubled.

JACOBY OVER 2 NOTRUMP OPENINGS

Jacoby Transfers may also be used over opening bids of two notrump. The mechanism is the same, except, of course, that the transfer occurs at the three level rather than at the two level.

Opposite a two notrump opening showing 20 to 22 points, for example, the responder might hold any of the following hands:

[A] ♠ Q x x   ♥ K J x x x   ♦ x x   ♣ x x x

[B] ♠ Q x x   ♥ K J x x x x   ♦ x   ♣ x x x

[C] ♠ Q x x x x x   ♥ x x   ♦ x x x   ♣ x x

With Hand A, responder would bid three diamonds, transferring to three hearts. He would follow with a bid of three notrump, giving the opener a choice of games in notrump and hearts. With Hand B, the responder would bid three diamonds and raise the opener's bid of three hearts to four. With Hand C, the responder would bid three hearts, transferring to spades, and would pass his partner's three spade bid.

COORDINATING JACOBY TRANSFERS
WITH STAYMAN

An agreement to use Jacoby Transfers has a hidden benefit, because the transfers mesh quite well with the non-forcing Stayman convention. Use of this combination of conventions facilitates the responder's description of hands containing five cards in one major suit, and four or five cards in the other major suit.

Using Jacoby Transfers, the responder can transfer into his five card major suit and then either pass, invite game, or force to game. As a consequence, sequences in which the responder starts with a Stayman bid of two clubs and then rebids a major suit are no longer needed simply to show five cards in the major suit bid.

When Jacoby Transfers and Stayman are both in use, therefore, the auction

Opener	Responder
1 Notrump	2 ♣
2 ♢	2 ♡ or 2 ♠

can be used to show five cards in the major suit bid by responder, and four cards in the other major suit. The rebid of two of either major suit, as in the above sequence, is not forcing.

Likewise in the sequence

Opener	Responder
1 Notrump	2 ♣
2 ♢	3 ♡ or 3 ♠

the responder shows five cards in the major suit he bids, and four cards in the other major. The three-level bid of a major suit is forcing to game.

If the one notrump opener has three cards in his partner's bid suit, the hand should be played in that suit. If, instead, he has only two cards in the responder's bid suit, he will have three cards in the other major, in which the responder has four. The opener will then have to decide whether the hand should be played in the partnership's 5-2 fit, in its 4-3 fit, or in notrump.

Since the partnership is able to show five-four major suit distributions by starting with the two club Stayman bid, the responder can show that he has five cards in each major suit by transferring into one major and then bidding the other. For example:

(A)	Opener	Responder
	1 Notrump	2 ♦ (transfer)
	2 ♡	2 ♠

By bidding two diamonds the responder has shown a five card heart suit. By next bidding two spades, he has shown, in addition, a five card spade suit. Similarly by using the sequence

(B)	Opener	Responder
	1 Notrump	2 ♡ (transfer)
	2 ♠	3 ♡

the responder first shows a five card spade suit, and then a five card heart suit.

The choice between the sequences shown in (A) and (B) is determined by the strength of the responder's hand. If the responder has a hand that is poor in high cards, he chooses sequence (A), which permits the partnership to play in two spades if the opener has three spades. Sequence (B) shows a stronger hand since it commits the partnership to a higher level. Sequence (B) is forcing to game.

JACOBY FOR THE MINOR SUITS

There are a number of extensions of Jacoby Transfers that are designed to allow the responder to show a long minor suit holding. Two such extensions are described below.

Signing Off

When the responder hears his partner open the bidding with one notrump, and he holds a hand such as:

[A] ♠ x x   ♡ x x   ◇ Q x x   ♣ Q J x x x x

or

[B] ♠ K x x   ♡ x   ◇ J x x x x x x   ♣ x x

it is usually preferable to have the partnership play in three of responder's minor suit rather than in one notrump. To accomplish this it is possible to use a Jacoby-type transfer, in which a bid of two spades asks the opener to bid three clubs and a bid of three clubs asks him to bid three diamonds.

Using this Jacoby extension, the responder would bid two spades with Hand A:

(C)	*Opener*	*Responder*
	1 Notrump	2 ♠
	3 ♣	Pass

With Hand B, responder would bid three clubs:

(D)	*Opener*	*Responder*
	1 Notrump	3 ♣
	3 ◇	Pass

If in either auction (C) or auction (D), the responder had bid again rather than passing, he would have shown a much stronger hand than those set out in (A) and (B), and would have been indicating a mild interest in playing a slam in the suit into which he transferred.

Trying for Slam

An alternative use for the two spade bid is to make an immediate slam try in one or both minor suits. Using this type of variation of the Jacoby Transfer convention, which is also sometimes called minor-suit Stayman, the opener is asked to describe his hand. He is expected to bid a four card minor suit if he has one. If the opener has four cards in each minor suit, he may bid his better *major* suit over responder's two spade bid. Thus, in the auction

Opener	Responder
1 Notrump	2 ♠
3 ♡	

the opener might have a hand such as

[A]   ♠ J x   ♡ A Q x   ◇ K Q x x   ♣ A J x x

If the opening bidder has no four card minor suit he should bid notrump. A two notrump bid would encourage slam exploration, while a three notrump rebid would deny slam interest on opener's part.

One-Suited Slam Try

The factors to be considered in determining whether to encourage responder in exploring for slam, or to try to slow him down, depend on whether responder's two spade bid showed both minor suits or only one. If the partnership has agreed that responder may bid two spades on a hand containing just one long minor suit, rather than both, the opener should rebid two notrump with the maximum point count for his one notrump opening, and should bid three notrump with a minimum.

For example, the opener might hold either of the following hands:

[B]   ♠ A K x x   ♡ 10 9 x   ◇ K J x   ♣ K Q x

[C]   ♠ A K J   ♡ A K x x   ◇ K 9 x   ♣ 10 9 x

After the auction has begun with a two spade response to opener's one notrump bid, the opener would bid three notrump with Hand B, and would bid two notrump with Hand C. The responder's hand might be the following:

[D]   ♠ x x   ♡ Q x   ◇ A Q x x x x   ♣ A x x

With responder holding Hand D opposite opener's Hand B, the auction would be:

Opener	*Responder*
1 Notrump	2 ♠
3 Notrump	Pass

If responder held Hand D opposite opener's Hand C, however, the auction could proceed as follows:

Opener	*Responder*
1 Notrump	2 ♠
2 Notrump	3 ◇ (slam try)
3 ♡ (cue bid)	3 Notrump
6 ◇	(not forcing)

Opener can reason that the responder must have the club suit well controlled, since he was willing to make a slam try without a solid diamond suit, and without the ace and king of hearts and without the ace and king of spades.

Two-Suited Slam Try

If the partnership has agreed that the two spade bid by responder promises at least five cards in one minor suit and at least four cards in the other minor, the opener's choice between the rebids of two notrump and three notrump, holding no four card minor suit, is determined by the location, rather than just the amount, of his high card strength. If his strength is concentrated in the major suits, he would bid three notrump, even with the maximum point count such as in Hand C above, to deny any interest in a slam. If the opener's high cards are instead concentrated in the minor suits, as in Hand B above, the opener should bid two notrump, leaving the partnership more room to probe for slam.

Over the opener's two notrump rebid, if the responder bids three hearts or three spades, he promises at most a singleton in the major suit he bids. If responder rebids four of the same major suit on the next round of the bidding, he shows a void in the suit he bids.

Responder's hand might be:

[E]   ♠ x x   ♡ Q   ◇ A Q x x x   ♣ A x x x x

If responder holds Hand E opposite opener's Hand C,

[C]   ♠ A K J   ♡ A K x x   ◇ K 9 x   ♣ 10 9 x

the auction would proceed:

Opener	Responder
1 Notrump	2 ♠
3 Notrump	Pass

If responder holds Hand E opposite opener's Hand B,

[B]   ♠ A K x x   ♡ 10 9 x   ◇ K J x   ♣ K Q x

the partnership could well reach a slam by the following auction:

Opener	Responder
1 Notrump	2 ♠
2 Notrump	3 ♡ (singleton)
3 ♠ (cue bid)	4 ◇ (suit)
4 ♠ (cue bid)	6 ♣
6 ◇	

After bidding three hearts to show his singleton heart, responder proceeds to bid naturally. The responder knows from opener's two notrump bid that opener has several honor cards in the minor suits. From opener's three spade and four spade bids, respectively, responder knows that opener has the ace and king of spades. However, responder can infer that there is no point in

68

trying for a grand slam since opener apparently does not have the ace of hearts (because he would have bid four hearts to show that card in preference to bidding four spades to show the spade king), and if opener had the ace of hearts as well as the ace and king of spades, he could not have enough minor suit honors to solidify the responder's suits. Therefore, over the four spade cue bid by the opener, responder simply sets the level of the contract at six, and leaves it to opener to choose which minor suit to play in.

TWO NOTRUMP RESPONSE AS A RELAY TO THREE CLUBS

Some partnerships which use the two spade bid as a minor suit slam try use a bid of two notrump as a relay bid to enable the partnership to play in three of a minor suit. For these partnerships, a response of two notrump to a one notrump opening forces the opener to rebid three clubs. If the responder has a weak hand with a long club suit, he passes. If he has instead a weak hand with a long diamond suit, he bids three diamonds, which opener is required to pass.

Some partnerships also allow use of the relay when responder has a three-suited game-going hand with a singleton in one of the major suits. The responder shows this type of hand over opener's forced three club bid by bidding the suit of his singleton. For the auction

Opener	Responder
1 Notrump	2 Notrump
3 ♣	3 ♡

responder might hold, for example,

[A] ♠ Q J x x ♡ x ◇ K x x x ♣ A x x x

or

[B] ♠ A Q x x ♡ x ◇ K x x ♣ K Q x x x

The principal advantage of using the two notrump relay to permit escape into clubs or diamonds with weak hands is that it allows the partnership to use immediate jumps to three clubs or three diamonds directly over the one notrump opening as invitations to game. For a jump to three clubs, for example, responder might have

♠ x x   ♡ J x   ◇ x x x   ♣ A Q 10 x x x

The use of two notrump as a relay also means that the responder can no longer make a natural game invitation in notrump. Instead he must temporize with a two club Stayman bid, and then bid two notrump. Thus, the sequence

Opener	Responder
1 Notrump	2 ♣
2 ♡	2 Notrump

would not guarantee that responder had a four card spade suit, but only that he had enough high card points to try for game.

TEXAS TRANSFERS

Texas Transfers are designed to get the partnership to game in a major suit opposite a one notrump or two notrump opening bid, with the notrump bidder as declarer. The responder must have a major suit of six or more cards, and a hand suitable for game opposite the opening bid.

To make a Texas Transfer, the responder jumps to the four level in the suit below the suit he actually holds. Opposite opener's one notrump opening, for example, responder might hold:

[A] ♠ x ♡ A Q J x x x x ◊ x x ♣ x x x

or

[B] ♠ K 10 9 x x x ♡ K x x ◊ x x x ♣ x

Using a Texas Transfer with Hand A, responder would jump to four diamonds over one notrump, requiring his partner to bid four hearts. With Hand B, the responder would jump to four hearts, requiring the opener to bid four spades. The bid of four diamonds, as on Hand A, has nothing to do with the responder's diamond suit; and the bid of four hearts, as on Hand B, has nothing to do with his hearts.

When the Opponents Interfere

Some partnerships agree to use Texas Transfers even after interference by an opponent, provided the level of interference is not uncomfortably high. The simplest plan is to use Texas Transfers over overcalls through the three spade level, but to agree that if the overcall is made at the four level, all suit bids by the responder are natural.

For example, suppose the auction started as follows:

(A)	North	East	South	West
	1 Notrump	2 ◇	4 ♡	

(B)	North	East	South	West
	1 Notrump	4 ♣	4 ♡	

In Auction A, South's four heart bid would be a transfer to four spades. In Auction B, however, since the overcall was made at the four level, South's four heart bid would be natural.

COMBINING JACOBY TRANSFERS AND TEXAS TRANSFERS

The partnership's use of either Jacoby Transfers or Texas Transfers will enable the transfer of declarership to the strong hand. The value of agreeing to use both of these conventions is that the responder is given more leeway to describe his hand, and can create a variety of slam-going auctions.

When the partnership has agreed to use both Jacoby and Texas Transfers, the responder can use the four level transfer, Texas, to show a minimum game-going hand without slam interest. To show some slight slam interest the responder would transfer at the two level (Jacoby), and then jump to game.

For example, responder might hold either of the following hands facing a one notrump opening bid:

[A] ♠ x x   ♡ K J 10 x x x   ◊ A x x   ♣ x x

[B] ♠ K Q x x x x x   ♡ A J x   ◊ x x   ♣ x

With Hand A, responder wants to bid a game, but has no interest in slam. He would simply jump to four diamonds, requiring the opener to bid four hearts. Hand B, however, could produce a slam if the opener had a suitable hand such as

♠ A x x   ♡ K Q x x   ◊ K x   ♣ A x x x

To make a mild slam suggestion the responder can use the following sequence:

Opener	Responder
1 Notrump	2 ♡
2 ♠	4 ♠

Using this sequence to suggest slam interest has the additional benefit of keeping the level of the bidding low initially, so that the opener, if he had a maximum notrump opening and a good fit with responder's suit, could reveal this immediately by jumping to three spades over the two heart bid. It would then be the responder's responsibility not to content himself with a four spade bid, but to cue-bid towards slam.

Suppose now that the responder held one of the following hands opposite a one notrump opening bid:

[C] ♠ K Q J x x x x   ♥ x   ♦ K Q 10 x   ♣ x

[D] ♠ Q J x   ♥ K Q J x x x   ♦ A x   ♣ K x

With either Hand C or Hand D responder can visualize a slam if his partner has an appropriate hand. When he holds Hand C, responder simply wants to know how many aces his partner holds. When he holds Hand D, he wants to bid a slam if his partner has a maximum one notrump opening.

If the partnership is using both Jacoby and Texas Transfers, the responder will easily be able to find out whatever he needs to know after he transfers. Responder can use a bid of four notrump, after the Texas Transfer, as Blackwood, asking the notrump opener how many aces he has. If responder uses the Jacoby Transfer, he can follow with a bid of four notrump as a quantitative inquiry, rather than an ace-asking bid. Thus, in the auction

Opener	*Responder*
1 Notrump	4 ♥
4 ♠	4 Notrump

the 4 Notrump bid is Blackwood. This is the sequence that responder should adopt with Hand C. In the next auction,

75

Opener	Responder
1 Notrump	2 ♦
2 ♡	4 Notrump

the 4 Notrump bid simply asks the opener to bid six hearts with a 17 or 18 point notrump. This is the sequence that responder should use with Hand D.

If the partnership has agreed to use Jacoby Transfers, but not Texas Transfers, the responder will still have bids at his disposal enabling him to ask about the opener's aces, or to invite him to bid a slam with a maximum hand. The two level transfer followed by the jump to four notrump would still be responder's way of inviting the opener to bid slam with a maximum notrump. To ask about aces, responder would transfer at the two level and then jump to four clubs, which would be the Gerber convention.

The use of a Texas Transfer followed by the bid of four notrump is perhaps an improvement over the use of a Jacoby transfer followed by Gerber, for two reasons. First, if the opener has a good enough hand to jump in responder's suit, the four club bid will be ambiguous:

Opener	Responder
1 Notrump	2 ♡
3 ♠	4 ♣

In this sequence the four club bid could be either a cue bid or Gerber.

Second, even if the responder still has room to jump to four clubs, there may be more useful applications for that bid than just to ask for aces. If Texas is being used, for example, so that four clubs would not be needed to ask for aces, the jump to four clubs could be reserved to show a singleton club, as, for example, with Hand B above. *See* SPLINTER BIDS.

SOUTH AFRICAN TEXAS

There is a psychological danger in using the jump to four hearts as a Texas Transfer bid. The danger is that the notrump bidder will forget that the four heart bid is artificial, and will pass.

A modified version of the Texas Transfers that is designed to minimize this psychological danger is called South African Texas. The South African Texas convention uses a jump to four clubs to require the notrump opener to bid four hearts, and a jump to four diamonds to require the notrump opener to bid four spades.

Since neither jump to four of a minor suit is commonly used as a natural bid, South African Texas serves to jog the notrump opener's memory. The disadvantage of South African Texas is that it precludes the use of the jump to four clubs as the Gerber convention, to ask the notrump bidder how many aces he holds.

With respect to opponent interference, see discussion under TEXAS TRANSFERS.

FLINT

The Flint convention is designed to allow the partnership to play in three of a major suit after the bidding has been opened with two notrump. Unlike the Jacoby Transfer, which will also let the partnership play below the game level after a two notrump opening, the Flint convention does not always transfer declarership to the notrump opener.

Using the Flint convention as it is normally employed, the responder who has a long major suit bids three diamonds in response to his partner's two notrump opening. Over the three diamond bid, the opener is expected to bid three hearts. If the responder's long suit is hearts he will now simply pass; if instead he has a long spade suit, he will bid three spades over the opener's three heart bid. The opener is expected to pass responder's three spade rebid.

Getting to Game

Although the principal aim of the Flint convention is to provide the partnership with a means of stopping short of game, if the notrump opener has a suitable hand he may drive the hand to game anyway. To force to game, the opener should have a hand with which he can visualize a game opposite a hand little better than

[A] ♠ x   ♡ Q x x x x   ◇ x x x   ♣ x x x x
or
[B] ♠ J x x x x   ♡ x x x   ◇ x x   ♣ x x x

Since the opener will not know at the time his partner bids three diamonds which major suit the responder holds, certain precautions may have to be taken to be sure the partnership arrives in game only when there is a good fit, and not when there is no fit. If the opener has the maximum for his two notrump bid and a good four card spade suit, it is safe for him to bid three hearts over three diamonds as he is expected to. If responder's suit is hearts, rather than spades, the partnership will have found its resting place. If responder's suit is spades, he will bid three spades over opener's three heart rebid; and with a hand such as

[C] ♠ K Q x x   ♥ A x   ♦ A Q x x   ♣ A K x

opener will raise to four spades.

However, if the notrump opener has a maximum hand with a good four card heart suit, he cannot simply bid three hearts over three diamonds, for if this is responder's suit, responder will pass. Therefore, if opener has a hand such as

[D] ♠ A x   ♥ A Q x x   ♦ K Q x   ♣ A K x x

he should bid three spades over responders' three diamond bid.

Thus, in the auction

Opener	Responder
2 Notrump	3 ♦
3 ♠	

opener's three spade bid shows a very fine hand containing four good hearts. If responder's suit is hearts, he will bid four hearts; if his suit is spades, he will pass.

If the opener has a maximum two notrump opening with four good hearts and four good spades, he is willing to play game in either major suit. To convey this message the generally prescribed bid is three notrump. Over the three notrump rebid the responder would simply bid four of his suit.

Strategically, however, the better bid to describe a maximum hand with four cards in each major suit is four hearts. If the responder is long in hearts he will pass; if his suit is spades he will bid four spades. The advantage of using the four heart rebid rather than the three notrump bid is that it will allow the stronger hand to be declarer fifty percent of the time.

Notice that except in the sequence just recommended, *i.e.*,

Opener	Responder
2 Notrump	3 ♦
4 ♡	Pass

whenever game is reached after the Flint three diamond bid has been used, the weaker hand becomes the declarer. This is the consequence of the original ambiguity of the three diamond bid, and of the maneuvering the opening bidder must do in order to ensure that game is reached if there is a fit, and avoided if there is no fit.

Showing Diamonds

Although the Flint convention deprives the three diamond bid of its potentially useful natural meaning, it is nevertheless possible for the responder to convey the information that he has a diamond suit. He does this by bidding three diamonds, and then making any rebid other than the minimum bid in a major suit. For example:

(A)	Opener	Responder
	2 Notrump	3 ♦
	3 ♡ or 3 ♠	3 Notrump

(B)   *Opener*   *Responder*
    2 Notrump   3 ♢
    3 ♡ or 3 ♠   4 ♣

In each of the above auctions the responder's three diamond bid has forced the opener to rebid a major suit, but the subsequent rebid by responder of three notrump in (A) and of four clubs in (B) deny long major suit holdings. These rebids show that responder instead has a genuine diamond suit, and suggests that he has interest in a slam.

FLINT THREE CLUBS

If the partners agree, it is also possible to use the Flint convention with three clubs, rather than three diamonds, as the conventional call. The three club bid requests the two notrump opener to bid three diamonds. This sequence allows the partnership to play in a contract of three diamonds, as well as three of a major suit.

If the responder has a long major suit, rather than diamonds, he simply bids three of his major suit over the opener's three diamond rebid. Thus any of the following auctions would be possible:

Opener	Responder
2 Notrump	3 ♣
3 ♦	Pass

Opener	Responder
2 Notrump	3 ♣
3 ♦	3 ♡ or 3 ♠
Pass	

Using the three club bid as the Flint convention means, of course, that the three club bid cannot be used as Stayman to ask the notrump opener if he has a four card major suit. To compensate, the bid of three diamonds would become the Stayman bid. Over this three diamond response, the notrump opener will bid his four card major suit if he has one, or will bid three notrump if he has no four card major.

GLADIATOR

The Gladiator convention is a system of responding to notrump opening bids that is designed to allow the partnership complete flexibility in exploring for slam, trying for game, or stopping at a low part score level. Gladiator is similar to the Flint three club convention, except that Gladiator may be used in response to one notrump, in which case two clubs is the conventional call.

Over the one notrump opening bid the responder's bid of two clubs requires the opener to bid two diamonds. Responder may pass if he has a long diamond suit and a poor hand. If responder bids the minimum number of any suit over opener's two diamond rebid, he shows a weak hand, and the opener should pass.

If the two club bid is used as Gladiator, a two diamond bid is used as a Stayman bid to inquire about the opener's major suit holdings. The two diamond response is forcing to game. The opener's rebids are two hearts with four hearts, two spades with four spades, two notrump with four of neither major suit, and three clubs with four of both.

A direct response of two of a major suit is forcing to game. Opener should raise responder's suit if he has three-card or better support, or bid two notrump without support.

Any jump by responder to the three level over one notrump invites a slam. Opener should raise or bid notrump depending on his fit and his slam interest.

CONOT TWO NOTRUMP

The Conot convention uses a response of two notrump to a one notrump opening bid to ask the opener to bid his longer minor suit. The convention is useful when the responder has a weak two-suiter in the minors, and wants to play in the partnership's better minor suit rather than in one notrump. In addition, the convention can help to uncover a duplication of values for slam purposes, or a duplication of weaknesses for notrump purposes.

The Conot Two Notrump response to one notrump requires the opener to bid three of his longer minor suit, or to bid three clubs if his minors are of equal length. If the responder has a weak hand, he will pass whatever the opener has rebid. Responder may also invite game in the partnership's minor suit by raising the opener's rebid to the four level.

If the responder rebids a major suit over the minor suit that the opener has rebid, he shows a singleton in that major suit. Suppose the opener has one of the following hands:

[A] ♠ K Q J x   ♡ A x x   ◇ 10 x x   ♣ A Q x

[B] ♠ K x x   ♡ K Q J x   ◇ Q x x   ♣ A Q x

[C] ♠ A x x   ♡ A x   ◇ K J x x   ♣ K Q x x

In the auction

Opener	Responder
1 Notrump	2 Notrump
3 ♣	3 ♠

the responder has shown a singleton spade. With Hand A, the opener would bid three notrump, having sufficient spade strength

84

to play that contract opposite responder's singleton. With Hand B, the opener's spade stopper is more anaemic, and he would be better advised to bid four hearts, hoping to find his partner with a three-card heart suit. If responder had only two hearts, he could correct the contract by bidding five clubs. Responder might hold either of the following hands:

[D] ♠ x   ♡ A 10 x   ◇ K x x x x   ♣ K x x x

[E] ♠ x   ♡ A x   ◇ K J x x x   ♣ K x x x x

With Hand C above, the opener can envision a slam after responder has shown a singleton spade. His choice of bids is among (1) four diamonds, which is obviously forcing, but is slightly ambiguous as to whether it shows the ace of diamonds or a genuine suit; (2) four spades, cue bidding the ace; and (3) four notrump, Blackwood. Of the three possibisities, the four notrump bid is probably the least satisfactory on Hand C, since it becomes more difficult to explore for a grand slam.

When the Conot two Notrump response is being used, the partnership must find another way to invite game in notrump. The substitute most commonly employed is a non-forcing Stayman sequence:

Opener	*Responder*
1 Notrump	2 ♣
2 ◇, 2 ♡	
or 2 ♠	2 Notrump

This sequence would no longer promise a four card major suit in the responder's hand, but it would in any event invite game in notrump.

BOLAND

When the bidding proceeds

(A)	*Opener*	*Responder*
	1 Notrump	4 Notrump
or		
(B)	*Opener*	*Responder*
	2 Notrump	4 Notrump

the responder's four notrump bid asks the opener to go on to slam if he has the top of his notrump bid. If the opener does not have the maximum number of high card points, he normally passes.

The Boland convention is used when the opener has better than a minimum notrump opening; it is a method of bidding designed to continue the slam exploration. If the opener has the middle of his notrump range—for example, 17 points using 16 to 18 notrumps, or 16 points using 15 to 17 point notrump openings, or 21 points using 20 to 22 point two notrump openings— the opener bids five of his lowest ranking biddable suit. If opener has no biddable suit he bids five notrump.

If opener has the maximum number of points for his notrump opening, he jumps to six of his lowest ranking biddable suit.

Over the Boland bid by the opener, the responder can raise if opener's bid has disclosed a fit for one of responder's suits, or responder can rebid a biddable four card suit of his own. The bidding of biddable suits up the line by both opener and responder allows the partnership to discover a fitting suit in which slam might be played, or discover that there is no such suit.

What is a "Biddable" Suit?

For the purpose of finding an appropriate trump suit in which to play a slam, a biddable suit is one not worse than four cards headed by the queen and jack. Bidding and raising only suits no worse than Q J x x insures the partnership against playing in a trump suit in which it is normally likely to lose more than one trick.

AUTOMATIC ACES

The Automatic Aces convention is one of the rare conventions in which the first artificial call is made by the notrump opener. The convention is used by the opener to indicate slam interest after a strength-showing three level response to an opening bid of one notrump or two notrump. For example:

(A) *Opener*   *Responder*
    1 Notrump   3 ♡

(B) *Opener*   *Responder*
    2 Notrump   3 ♠

If the opening bidder has no interest in slam, he simply raises his partner's suit to game if he has a fit, or rebids three notrump if there is no fit. If the opening bidder has a fit for the responder's suit and is interested in slam, he reveals this fit and interest by making a bid that tells the responder how many aces he holds. If the partnership is using strong notrumps, the opener must have at least two aces before he is allowed to show slam interest. If the partnership is using weak notrump openings, the opener needs only one ace in order to show slam interest.

The Automatic Aces convention requires the opener to show the number of aces he holds, in a series of steps excluding notrump, counting from the responder's bid as follows:

> First suit step = 2 aces
> Second suit step = 3 aces
> Third suit step = 4 aces

Over a forcing jump to three clubs by the responder, for instance, a bid of three hearts, the second step, would show three aces. Over responder's jump to three hearts, the first step would be three spades, showing two aces, and the second step would be four clubs, showing three aces, etc. Since three notrump is the opener's proper rebid if he has no fit and no slam interest, that bid cannot be used as one of the steps to show aces.

Suppose the auction has started as in (A) above (1 Notrump—3 ♡), and the opener holds one of the following hands:

[C] ♠ K Q x x   ♡ K x x   ◇ A J x x   ♣ K x

[D] ♠ A x   ♡ Q x x x   ◇ A K x x   ♣ K x x

[E] ♠ A K Q x   ♡ A x x   ◇ Q J x   ♣ x x x

With Hand C the opener lacks the requisite two aces, and therefore rebids four hearts. With Hand D, opener would rebid three spades, showing his fit, his two aces, and his slam interest. With Hand E, the opener has a fit for responder's heart suit and has two aces, but he is not terribly interested in slam on account of his lack of control in two suits. With Hand E, therefore, opener would content himself with a four heart bid.

II

Responses and Rebids after a Natural Opening Bid in a Suit

A plurality of the conventions described in this Part fall into the category of strong trump raises. The fact that so many different ways have been devised to make strong trump raises is testimony to the difficulty of exchanging all of the information necessary for sound slam bidding.

The remainder of this Part is devoted to exploratory conventions that seek to solve a variety of problems, including how a responder who is a passed hand can show a fairly good hand without getting the partnership too high, how to show responding hands in the 17 to 18 point range that are normally difficult to describe, how to discover concealed 4-4 or 5-3 fits, and how to respond to weak two bids.

THREE NOTRUMP AS A STRONG
MAJOR SUIT RAISE

In Standard American bidding the jump raise by the responder of his partner's opening bid is treated as a strong bid that is forcing to game. This raise normally shows at least four trumps and a hand worth 13 to 15 points.

When a partnership has agreed to treat the jump raise of a major suit opening bid as not forcing, it needs a replacement bid to show the type of hand on which the strong forcing raise would otherwise have been made. The most common replacement has been the response of three notrump. Using this convention and holding a hand such as

[A] ♠ K Q x x ♡ A x x ◇ K x x ♣ Q x x

the responder would bid three notrump in response to his partner's opening bid of one spade. The partnership is thus forced to game, and bids of other suits en route to four spades have the same meanings as they would have over a forcing raise to three spades.

Some partnerships have not adopted any bid to replace the forcing jump raise, but prefer to proceed by a series of forcing bids eventually ending in game. This procedure runs the risk of responder's misdescribing his hand to the opener. Holding Hand A opposite a one spade opening bid and having no immediate forcing trump raise available to him, the responder would be forced to make a temporizing bid on the two level before raising opener's suit. Certainly a two club response with Hand A does not reveal either responder's long suit or the location of his high card strength.

The use of the three notrump response as a strong raise

precludes the standard, natural use of this bid to show the equivalent of a notrump opening bid. The hands meriting a strong trump raise occur much more frequently, however, and on those rare occasions when the natural use of the three notrump call would have been made, the responder can instead make the temporizing bid on the two level before jumping to three notrump.

JACOBY TWO NOTRUMP

The Jacoby Two Notrump response to an opening bid of one of a major suit is a forcing raise, of unlimited strength. It does not indicate any desire on the responder's part to play the hand in notrump. Rather it supports the opener's suit and requests him to clarify the strength and distribution of his hand.

If the opener has a singleton, he is required to show it by bidding three of that suit. If the opener has a void, he bids four of his void suit. If the opener has no singletons or voids, he describes the strength of his hand. He bids four of his own suit if he has a minimum hand with no slam interest. He bids three of his suit if he has a strong hand, at least one king better than a minimum opening bid. He rebids three notrump if he has a sound opening bid of 14 or 15 points.

For example, the opener's and responder's hands might be:

(Opener)
♠ A x x x x   ♡ x   ◇ K Q x x   ♣ A x x

(Responder)
♠ K Q x x   ♡ x x x x   ◇ A J x   ♣ K x

Over a Jacoby Two Notrump response, the opener would bid three hearts, showing a singleton in that suit. Over three hearts it becomes safe for the responder to use Blackwood to check for aces. Discovering that the opener has two aces, responder reasons that the partnership is unlikely to be worse than a finesse away from slam. The complete auction might be:

Opener	Responder
1 ♠	2 Notrump
3 ♡	4 Notrump
5 ♡	6 ♠

If the responder is a passed hand, his jump to two notrump is not a Jacoby bid, but reverts to its standard meaning, i.e., a balanced notrump-type hand of just under opening strength.

SWISS

The Swiss convention, like the three notrump response as a forcing major suit raise, is used principally by partnerships which have agreed to use limit-jump major raises. Unlike the three notrump response, however, the Swiss convention also allows the responder to describe his hand more precisely in some respect agreed upon by the partnership.

The Swiss convention consists of a jump by responder to four clubs or four diamonds directly over a one heart or one spade opening bid. Both the four club bid and the four diamond bid show a balanced hand with 13 to 15 points and agree on the opener's suit as trumps. Neither bid has any meaning with respect to the responder's minor suit holdings.

The precise meaning of the jump to four clubs and the precise meaning of the jump to four diamonds depend on two factors: first, which ancillary feature (such as good trumps or good controls) the partnership has agreed that the Swiss bid will describe, and second, whether it is the four club bid or the four diamond bid that the partnership has agreed will promise the presence of that feature.

Some partnerships use the Swiss jumps to distinguish between raises made on sound trump suits and raises made on general values but mediocre trumps. Others use the convention to pinpoint hands rich in controls. Still others try to combine these two goals.

See TRUMP SWISS, CONTROL SWISS, TRUMP AND CONTROL SWISS and CONGLOMERATE MAJOR SUIT RAISES.

TRUMP SWISS

The Trump Swiss convention pays tribute to the need for a reasonably solid trump suit in order to make a slam. Holdings of A x x x opposite J x x x are fine for game contracts, but not good enough for slams.

When Trump Swiss is being used, the responder will jump to four clubs to show that his trumps are of high quality. Normally his four club bid will show at least four trumps headed by two of the top three honors, or five trumps headed by at least the ace or the king. For example, holding

♠ K x x   ♡ A Q x x   ♢ Q x x x   ♣ K x

the responder would raise opener's one heart bid to four clubs. With any hand worth a strong raise but not meeting these requirements in the trump suit, the responder would jump to four diamonds.

As hinted above, it is possible for the partnership to agree instead that the four diamond call will show the good trump holding and that the four club bid will show any other strong raise. In principle, however, it is normally more advantageous for the lower ranking response to show the stronger trump holding. This would give the partnership more room to explore slam where the responder's trump holding makes slam seem a more reasonable possibility.

CONTROL SWISS

It is also possible to use the jumps to four of a minor suit to distinguish between a responding hand that is rich in aces and kings and one that is filled with secondary values. When Control Swiss is being used, the responder will jump to four clubs whenever he holds three aces, or two aces and the king of the opener's suit. Lacking these controls as part of his strong raise, the responder will jump instead to four diamonds.

As is true with Trump Swiss, the partnership could agree instead to use the four diamond bid to show three controls, and the four club bid to show the general strength raise. Again, however, using the four club bid to show good controls allows the partnership more room for slam explorations when slam seems more likely.

The Control Swiss convention is most useful in arriving at slams that depend more on long suits and controls than on raw power. However, since there are other ways to determine what aces the partnership holds, Control Swiss seems less valuable than Trump Swiss.

TRUMP AND CONTROL SWISS

Some partnerships attempt to have the responder describe both the quality of his trumps and the possession of controls in a single bid. Using this version of the Swiss convention, a bid of four clubs would show good controls, and a bid of four diamonds would show strong trumps.

As might be expected of a compromise, however, neither the trump feature nor the control feature can be shown with as great accuracy as it can when both jumps to four of a minor are used to distinguish the quality of either feature alone. Thus, opposite a one heart opening bid, the Trump-and-Control Swiss convention is fine when the responder's hand is

[A] ♠ A Q x   ♡ K x x x   ◇ A x x x   ♣ x x
or
[B]   ♠ x x   ♡ K Q x x   ◇ K x x   ♣ A Q x x

With Hand A, the responder would bid four clubs, showing his three controls. With Hand B, he would bid four diamonds showing sound trumps. But the convention is less accurate if the responder holds

[C] ♠ A x x   ♡ K x x x   ◇ K Q x x   ♣ Q x
or
[D] ♠ A x x   ♡ K Q x x   ◇ A x x x   ♣ x x

With Hand C, neither four clubs nor four diamonds is appropriate, while Hand D is suitable for either bid.

SPLINTER RAISES

Splinter raises, like the Swiss convention, make use of bids that otherwise would be used only rarely. Rather than giving information about trump texture or side suit aces and kings, as in the Swiss convention, however, Splinter bids (also called "anti-fragment" bids) allow the responder to show a singleton or a void in a side suit while raising the opener's suit.

A splinter raise is any unusual jump, usually skipping two levels of bidding, into a singleton or void suit. It shows a strong raise in support of the opener's suit. For example, if responder held

[A] ♠ Q x x x   ♡ K J x x   ◇ A Q x x   ♣ x

he would jump to four clubs over his partner's opening bid of one heart or one spade. The opener might hold a hand such as

[B] ♠ A J   ♡ A Q x x x   ◇ K x   ♣ x x x x

Use of splinter bids makes it easier to reach a slam with Hands A and B. The auction might be

Opener	Responder
1 ♡	4 ♣
4 ♠	5 ◇
6 ♡	

The partnership should be sure to discuss whether in the auctions

100

(C) *Opener*   *Responder*
         1 ♠   4 ♡

and

(D) *Opener*   *Responder*
         1 ♡   3 ♠

the responder's bid shows a singleton in the major suit.

If the responder rebids the suit into which he has made the unusual jump, he shows a void in that suit. Thus, in the auction

Opener	*Responder*
1 ♠	4 ◇
4 ♡	5 ◇

the responder promises a 13 to 15 point hand, at least four card spade support, and a void in diamonds. In the bidding of Hands A and B above, therefore, the responder's bid of five diamonds over four spades showed the ace of diamonds but denied a club void, showing the opener that the partnership had a certain club loser.

Partnerships which do not use the Swiss convention can profitably use Splinter raises in combination with standard forcing raises, or with the three notrump response as a forcing raise. Use of these conventions in combination helps to distinguish responder's balanced raises from his distributional raises.

Delayed Splinter Raises

It is also feasible for the responder to use a splinter bid at a later stage in the auction, rather than in immediate response to the opening bid. However, if the unusual jump follows a change of suit by the opener, the responder will be showing support for the opener's second suit rather than his first suit.

For example, the responder might hold:

♠ K x x x   ♡ x   ◇ x x   ♣ A Q J x x x

If his partner opens the bidding with one spade, responder will bid two clubs; responder should delay showing his singleton heart until he has bid his own long suit. If the opener now rebids two spades, responder can jump to four hearts, showing a singleton heart, at least five clubs, and attractive spade support. The auction would therefore proceed:

Opener	Responder
1 ♠	2 ♣
2 ♠	4 ♡

However, if, over the responder's two club response the opener had rebid two diamonds, responder could not jump to four hearts to show his singleton heart, because the jump in this sequence would show diamond support rather than spade support. For the auction

Opener	Responder
1 ♠	2 ♣
2 ◇	4 ♡

responder might have a hand such as

♠ Q x   ♡ x   ◇ K J x x   ♣ A Q x x x x

Splinter Bids by the Opener

Since, as a purely mechanical matter, an unusual jump can be made by either member of the partnership, it is also possible for the opening bidder to make a splinter bid. The opener's splinter bid would be an unusual jump into a singleton and would show support for the suit bid by the responder.

The question of what jumps are unusual, however, is slightly more complex with respect to the opener's bids than it is for responder's bids. Any double jump into a new suit is still, of course, unusual; for example

(A) *Opener*   *Responder*
     1 ◇   1 ♠
     4 ♣ or 4 ♡

(B) *Opener*   *Responder*
     1 ◇   1 ♡
     3 ♠

In auction (A) opener's jump to four clubs or four hearts would show a singleton in the suit in which the jump is made, with a hand worth a game raise in spades. Opener might hold:

    ♠ K Q x x   ♡ A x x   ◇ A K Q x x   ♣ x

In auction (B), opener might have a hand such as

    ♠ x   ♡ A K x x   ◇ K Q J x x   ♣ A Q x

In addition to the obviously unusual jumps, when the opener jumps the bidding in a suit which in he could have made a strong forcing bid without jumping, the jump should be considered unusual, and therefore a splinter bid. For example:

(C)	Opener	Responder
	1 ♣	1 ♠
	2 ♡	

(D)	Opener	Responder
	1 ♠	2 ◇
	3 ♣	

In auction (C), opener has made a reverse bid which shows game possibilities. Although the reverse is not absolutely forcing, it is rarely passed. Therefore the auction

(E)	Opener	Responder
	1 ♣	1 ♠
	3 ♡	

is rarely used simply to force the responder to bid again. Auction (E) therefore, can be used by the opener to show a hand containing a singleton heart and good spade support.

Similarly, in auction (D), the opener's three level bid of a new suit virtually forces the partnership to game, since the responder has shown at least a ten point hand and the opener has shown better than a minimum opening bid. Therefore the auction

(F)	Opener	Responder
	1 ♠	2 ◇
	4 ♣	

can be used to show that the opener has a singleton club and a good diamond support. Opener might have a hand such as

♠ A Q x x x   ♡ A K x   ◊ K J x x   ♣ x

FRAGMENT BIDS

A Fragment Bid is an unusual jump rebid, either by the opener or by the responder, to show a fit with his partner and a singleton or void in the fourth suit. Using fragment bids, say opener opened one spade with a hand such as:

♠ A Q x x   ♡ A K x   ◇ K J x x   ♣ x

If his partner responded two diamonds, the opener would jump to four hearts. Thus in the auction

Opener	*Responder*
1 ♠	2 ◇
4 ♡	

the opener's four heart bid would show some length in hearts, although not usually a biddable suit, a singleton in the unbid suit, clubs, and good support for his partner's diamond suit.

The responder also can make fragment rebids. Unlike splinter raises, however, fragment raises are not available to the responder at his first turn, because fragment bids require the naming of suits held rather than short suits.

Fragment bids by the responder may require detailed discussion by the partnership, because the responder's fragment bid may show shortness in one of the opener's suits. Consider the following two auctions:

(A)	*Opener*	*Responder*
	1 ◇	1 ♡
	1 ♠	4 ◇

(B) *Opener*   *Responder*
     1 ♣   1 ♡
     1 ♠   4 ◇

In auction (A), responder's jump to four diamonds promises shortness in the unbid suit, clubs. In auction (B), all four suits have been bid. Therefore, the jump to four diamonds promises support for opener's last bid suit, and a singleton in his other suit, clubs.

If the fragment bidder rebids the suit in which he has promised shortness, he shows a void. Thus, in the auction

         Opener   *Responder*
          1 ♣   1 ♡
          1 ♠   4 ◇
          4 ♠   5 ♣

the responder's five club bid would show that he is void in clubs.

CONGLOMERATE MAJOR SUIT RAISES

Recognizing that singletons, trump suit solidity, and extra high card values may all be crucial to slam potential, some partnerships have adopted a four-step scheme of strong major suit raises that allows each type of responding hand to be indicated with a single bid. These raises are entirely artificial, and start with the bid which is the next step above the single jump raise of opener's suit (the single jump being used as a limit raise). The complete schedule of responses is as follows:

	Response to 1 ♡ Opening	*Response to 1 ♠ Opening*	*Type of Strong Raise*
First Step	3 ♠	3 Notrump	singleton (not yet identified)
Second Step	3 Notrump	4 ♣	17 to 18 HCP
Third Step	4 ♣	4 ♢	Good trump suit (four cards with at least two of the top three honors, or five cards headed by the ace or king)
Fourth Step	4 ♢	4 ♡	General strong raise (not suitable for any of the above)

For example, suppose responder had one of the following hands opposite a one heart opening:

[A] ♠ x   ♡ A x x x   ◇ Q x x x   ♣ A Q x x

[B] ♠ K x   ♡ A J 10 x   ◇ K J x   ♣ A Q x x

[C] ♠ x x   ♡ A x x x x   ◇ K x x   ♣ A J x

[D] ♠ x x   ♡ A x x x   ◇ K x x x   ♣ K Q x

With Hand A, responder would use the first step, three spades, to show that he has a singleton somewhere, although it need not be in spades. With Hand B, responder would use the second step, three notrump, to show that he has an extremely strong hand in high cards. With Hand C, responder would bid the third step, four clubs, to show his excellent trump support. With Hand D, responder would bid the fourth step, showing a hand worth a game force, but one that is not suitable for any of the other special game raises.

There will, of course, be some hands that fit into more than one of the first three categories of hands, such as a hand with a singleton and extra strength, or a hand with very good trumps and extra strength. Such hands are best dealt with by responder's bidding the cheapest step that is applicable, and later making another move toward slam.

The use of the very first step to show that responder has a singleton somewhere in the hand is designed to allow enough room for opener to find out, below the game level, where the singleton is. Opener makes this inquiry, if he is interested, by bidding the next higher denomination over the singleton-showing response, e.g., by bidding three notrump over responder's three spade bid. Responder then bids the suit of his singleton if he can do so without going past four of the trump suit; otherwise he bids four of the trump suit. His singleton will be clearly identified.

For example, the auction might start

(E)	*Opener*	*Responder*
	1 ♡	3 ♠
	3 Notrump	4 ◇

(F)	*Opener*	*Responder*
	1 ♡	3 ♠
	3 Notrump	4 ♡

In auction (E), opener's three notrump bid, the cheapest bid he can make, asks where responder's singleton is; the four diamond bid shows that the singleton is in diamonds. In auction (F), responder's four heart rebid over three notrump shows that his singleton is in neither clubs nor diamonds, and is therefore in spades. Similarly, if the opening bid were one spade and responder had a hand worth a strong raise, with a singleton club, the bidding could start

Opener	*Responder*
1 ♠	3 Notrump
4 ♣	4 ♠

Here, opener's four club bid, the cheapest bid he could make over the singleton-indicating response, asks where the singleton is, and responder's rebid of four spades says the singleton is in the only suit he cannot actually mention without going past four of the trump suit: clubs.

JUMP SHIFT TO THREE CLUBS

One of the problems with using the Swiss convention, or Splinter bids, or three notrump as a forcing raise is that these conventions all take up a good deal of bidding room. The opener's next chance to bid comes at the four level. Indeed, if he has opened with a one heart bid and his partner jumps to four diamonds, if opener wants to make a slam try he must do so above the game level.

In order to keep the forcing raise at as low a level as possible, while reserving the jump to two notrump for notrump type hands, some partnerships use a jump shift to three clubs as a forcing major suit raise. The jump says nothing about the responder's clubs, and of course the partnerships using this convention cannot use this bid to show the very strong hand with a club suit.

Over the responder's jump to three clubs the opener is expected to rebid three diamonds if he has a singleton or a void anywhere in his hand. If he has no singleton or void, opener should rebid so as to describe his trump holding. His bids are as follows:

3 ♡ shows two of the top three trump honors

3 ♠ shows one of the top three trump honors

3 Notrump shows none of the top three trump honors

After the opener has bid three diamonds, showing that he has a singleton or a void somewhere in the hand, responder can show the quality of his trump support using the same schedule that opener would have used if he had had no singleton or void. After responder has shown how many of the top three trump honors he has, if opener is interested in slam he can identify his singleton, or bid Blackwood.

JUMP SHIFT SHOWING A SINGLETON

It is also possible to use a simple jump shift to show a strong raise of the opening bid, with a singleton in the suit in which the jump is made. This convention is similar to the Splinter bid, but uses a simple jump shift rather than an unusual jump. The use of this convention, which precludes the natural use of the jump shift, is not widespread.

BARON TWO NOTRUMP

Opposite an opening bid of one of a suit, a balanced hand of 17 or 18 points is difficult to describe. It is too strong for a natural three notrump response or rebid, and, being balanced, it does not lend itself well to repeated suit bids.

The Baron Two Notrump convention is a direct response of two notrump to an opening bid of one of a suit. The responder typically has a balanced hand with no singleton or five card suit, worth about 16 to 18 points. The opener is requested to rebid his hand naturally.

Suppose the opener and responder held the following hands:

(Opener)
♠ A Q x x x   ♡ K x x x   ◇ — — —   ♣ K Q x x

(Responder)
♠ K x   ♡ A x x   ◇ K Q x x   ♣ A J x x

Using Baron Two Notrump, the auction might start:

Opener	*Responder*
1 ♠	2 Notrump
3 ♡	3 Notrump

Opener infers that the responder has only two spades because he did not take a preference to three spades, as he would have with three card support. Nor did responder raise hearts as he would have with four-card heart support. Since responder would have bid a five card suit if he had one, he must have exactly two spades, three hearts, four diamonds and four clubs. Opener therefore can easily envision a slam in clubs if responder is not disproportionately laden with diamond values.

Since the Baron Two Notrump response is devoted to very strong hands, an immediate response of three notrump can be used to show a balanced hand of 13 to 15 points.

ONE NOTRUMP FORCING

When the partnership is using five card major suit openings, it may be useful to use the one notrump response as forcing on the opener for one round. The forcing notrump response can help to narrow the ranges of other bids by responder and help him out of otherwise difficult situations.

For example, normally in the auction

(A) *Opener*   *Responder*
    1 ♠   2 ♠

the responder could have anywhere from five to ten points. Some partnerships use the sequence

(B) *Opener*   *Responder*
    1 ♠   1 Notrump
    2 ◇   2 ♠

to show a weaker responding hand than the sequence shown in auction (A). Other partnerships use auction (B) to show a stronger hand than auction (A).

In addition, some partnerships which use five card major suit openings and limit jump raises, use the forcing notrump to start sequences in which the responder shows a hand of limit raise strength, about 10 to 12 points, but only three trumps. Thus in the auction

(C) *Opener*   *Responder*
    1 ♡   1 Notrump
    2 ◇   3 ♡

115

the responder might have a hand such as

♠ x x   ♡ K J x   ◇ A Q x x   ♣ J x x x

This allows the partnership to reserve two-level responses in a new suit for stronger hands.

Use of the forcing one notrump response also enables the responder later to bid a long suit of his own without fear either of being passed in one notrump with an inappropriate hand, or of getting the partnership too high. For example, holding a hand such as

♠ x   ♡ x x   ◇ K J x x x x   ♣ x x x x

responder cannot bid two diamonds directly over an opening of one heart or one spade since this would show a considerably stronger hand, and he is loath to respond one notrump if his partner can pass.

Using the forcing notrump, however, responder could create either of the following non-forcing sequences:

(D) *Opener*   *Responder*
   1 ♠   1 Notrump
   2 ♣   2 ◇

(E) *Opener*   *Responder*
   1 ♠   1 Notrump
   2 ♡   3 ◇

The diamond bids by responder in auctions (D) and (E) are not forcing and not encouraging.

The forcing notrump response may also be useful if the partnership is using a combination of limit jump raises, with a three notrump response substituted as a strong major suit raise, and the Baron two notrump response. Using this combination of

116

conventions leaves the responder no convenient way to respond to a major suit opening bid with a balanced 13 to 15 count and a doubleton in the opener's suit. For example, holding the following hand opposite a one heart opening bid:

♠ A J x   ♡ Q x   ◇ K J x x   ♣ Q J x x

Using standard bidding the responder would have jumped to two notrump over a one heart opening. If he has no other recourse he can temporize with a bid of two clubs, but this risks having the notrump contract played from the wrong side of the table if the opener should rebid notrump. However, if the partnership is using the one notrump response as forcing, the responder may bid one notrump and then jump to three notrump over whatever the opener rebids.

Opener's Rebids

Because forcing notrump responses are used only in conjunction with five card major suit openings, and because the one notrump response may be the start of an escape by responder into a long suit of his own, the opener is not allowed to rebid his suit unless it is at least six cards long. The opener should rebid a four card suit if he can do so consistently with the strength of his hand. If he has no four card suit he must bid a three card suit.

For example, the opener might have any of the following:

[A] ♠ A Q x x x   ♡ K x x x   ◇ x x   ♣ A x

[B] ♠ A Q x x x   ♡ K x   ◇ A J x   ♣ x x x

[C] ♠ A Q x x   ♡ K Q x x x   ◇ A Q   ♣ K x

[D] ♠ A Q x x   ♡ K Q x x x   ◇ x x   ♣ x x

With Hand A the opener has opened with one spade and makes his normal bid of two hearts. With Hand B, however, having no four card suit to rebid, the opener must bid his cheaper three card suit. Here opener rebids two clubs, even though his diamonds are considerably stronger. With Hands C and D opener has started with a one heart bid. Hand C is strong enough to reverse into his four card spade suit over the one notrump response, while with Hand D the opener simply has no adequate rebid. He may well end up playing a 5-1 heart fit.

LIMIT RAISES TO SHOW SINGLETONS

When the partnership is using one notrump as a forcing response to a five-card major suit opening, the responder is able to show a hand worth 10 to 12 points in support of his partner's major by first responding one notrump, and then bidding three of the suit opened. Some partnerships which use the forcing notrump response convention therefore reserve direct limit raise responses for hands containing a singleton in a side suit.

Knowing that the limit raise responder has a singleton somewhere in his hand, the opener may pass if he lacks the strength to bid a game, or he may bid game directly if he has no interest in slam, or he may explore for slam. If opener is interested in slam, he rebids three notrump to ask responder to identify his singleton. Responder normally does so by bidding the suit of the singleton. However, if hearts is the trump suit and responder has a singleton spade, he rebids four hearts over three notrump, to avoid going past four of the trump suit.

Suppose opener and responder have the following hands:

Opener:
♠ K   ♡ A K J x x   ◇ A J x x x   ♣ J x

Responder:
♠ A Q x x x x   ♡ Q 10 x x   ◇ Q x   ♣ x

Using this convention with these hands, one of the pairs on the team which won the 1974 Spingold championship bid a slam that their opponents at the other table did not reach:

119

Opener	Responder
1 ♡	3 ♡
3 Notrump	4 ♣
4 Notrump*	5 ◇
6 ♡	

---

*Blackwood

SHORT SUIT GAME TRIES

From time to time when the opening bidder's major suit has been raised to two by the responder, the opener wants to make a try for game. Since the partnership will rarely have any great surplus of values beyond the 25 to 26 points needed for game, it is useful to determine whether some of the values it has are likely to be wasted.

One convention designed to reveal such a wastage of values is the Short Suit Game Try. Using this convention, the opener's rebid of a new suit at the three level shows a short suit, usually a singleton, and asks the responder to bid a game if his values are principally outside that suit. For example, suppose the opener and responder held these hands:

(Opener)
♠ A K x x x   ♡ K Q x   ◇ x   ♣ K x x x

(Responder)
♠ Q x x   ♡ x x x   ◇ K Q x x   ♣ Q x x

The auction would proceed

Opener	Responder
1 ♠	2 ♠
3 ◇	3 ♠
Pass	

The three diamond rebid by the opener shows his singleton diamond. Since most of responder's values are concentrated in that suit, he signs off in three spades. If the opener had instead rebid three hearts, showing a singleton in that suit, responder would gladly have jumped to four spades.

The partnership should discuss whether or not a rebid of two spades in the auction

Opener	Responder
1 ♡	2 ♡
2 ♠	

shows a short suit. It is probably more useful to reserve this bid as a natural, strength showing bid, especially if the partnership is not using five card major suit openings.

Short Suit Game Tries can be extended to allow the responder to show his own short suit if, in response to the opener's short suit try, the responder still is not sure whether to bid game or settle for three. This gives the opener a chance to reassess his own strength. For example, the auction might start

Opener	Responder
1 ♠	2 ♠
3 ♣	3 ♡

Opener's and responder's hands might be:

(Opener)
♠ A Q x x x   ♡ K x x   ◇ A Q x x   ♣ x

(Responder)
♠ K J x x   ♡ x   ◇ J x x x   ♣ K x x x

With the hand shown, the opener would continue to four spades, not having a great deal of wasted heart values. If instead his diamond ace were the ace of hearts, he would settle for three spades.

The chief disadvantage of short suit game tries is that they

122

are very revealing to the opponents. An opponent may be able to double a Short Suit Game Try to suggest an opening lead or to suggest a suit in which his side might sacrifice. And the early identification of the declarer's short suit may well aid the defenders throughout the hand.

TWO-WAY GAME TRIES

The opener who wants to make a try for game after his major suit opening bid has been raised by responder may have a hand with any of a number of distributions. He may have a singleton. Or he may have a side suit with no singleton but two doubletons. Or he may have neither a singleton nor a side suit.

With a singleton, opener often would like to make a short suit game try. With a side suit opener often would prefer to make a long suit game try. Using standard methods, a partnership must limit itself to one type of game try, for without some sort of converter the two types are largely incompatible.

Two-way game tries are a convention that gives the partnership the ability to make short suit game tries through a direct rebid of a new suit, and to make long suit game tries by way of a relay that converts the new suit rebid into a long suit bid. Using Two way game tries, a simple rebid of the trump suit by the opener is a power game try with neither short suit nor long suit.

Short Suit Tries

If the bidding has started 1 ♠ — 2 ♠, a rebid by the opener of three clubs, three diamonds, or three hearts shows a singleton in the suit bid. If the bidding has begun 1 ♡ — 2 ♡, a rebid of two notrump by the opener shows a singleton spade; a three club or three diamond rebid by opener shows a singleton.

For example, in the auction

Opener	Responder
1 ♡	2 ♡
2 Notrump	4 ♡

opener's two notrump rebid showed a singleton spade.

Responder's four heart bid showed that he had few wasted values in spades.

Long Suit Tries

In order to make a long suit game try, opener uses a relay. He makes the cheapest bid over the raise, forcing responder to bid the next suit. Over responder's forced bid, opener shows his long suit.

If the auction has started 1 ♠ — 2 ♠, opener relays by bidding two notrump, forcing responder to bid three clubs. Over responder's three club bid, opener bids three diamonds with a diamond suit, three hearts with a heart suit, or three spades with a club suit:

Responder	*Opener*
—	1 ♠
2 ♠	2 Notrump (relay)
3 ♣ (forced)	3 ♦ = diamond suit
	3 ♡ = heart suit
	3 ♠ = club suit

If the auction has started 1 ♡ — 2 ♡, two spades is the relay bid; over two spades responder must bid two notrump so that opener can show his long suit naturally:

Responder	*Opener*
—	1 ♡
2 ♡	2 ♠ (relay)
2 Notrump (forced)	3 ♣ = club suit
	3 ♦ = diamond suit
	3 ♡ = heart suit

DRURY

The responder who is a passed hand faces two special problems in describing his hand: first, a simple change of suit is no longer a forcing bid, so he cannot temporize. Second, his partner may well have opened the bidding on a sub-minimum hand, so that any jump response could get the partnership too high.

The Drury convention is a two club response to a third- or fourth-hand opening bid of one of a major suit. The two club response does not necessarily have anything to do with the responder's club suit; it merely asks the opener whether or not he has a full opening bid.

If the opener has a subminimal hand, he rebids two diamonds. If he has full values for his opening, he makes any other appropriate rebid. If opener has a full opening bid and his normal rebid would have been two diamonds, he can either jump to three diamonds, if his hand is very distributional, or he can temporize with a two diamond denial and later either bid diamonds naturally or rebid two notrump.

To use the Drury convention, the responder should have a ten to twelve point hand, and either a tolerance for the opener's suit, or a good six card club suit that he plans to rebid. For example, if the responder held

[A] ♠ K J x x ♡ x x x ◇ A Q x x ♣ J x

opposite a third- or fourth-hand opening bid of one spade, he would bid two clubs, Drury. The opener might hold any of the following hands:

[B] ♠ A Q x x x ♡ J x x ◇ K J ♣ x x x

[C] ♠ A Q x x x ♡ A J x x ◇ K x ♣ x x

[D] ♠ A 10 x x x ♡ A J ◇ K J x x ♣ K x

[E] ♠ A Q x x x ♡ x ◇ K J x x x ♣ A x

After the auction

Opener	Responder
–	Pass
1 ♠	2 ♣

the opener would bid two diamonds with Hand B, having less than a full opening bid. The responder would then sign off at two spades. With Hand C, the opener would make his natural rebid of two hearts. With Hand D he would rebid two diamonds, planning to rebid diamonds naturally at his next turn. With Hand E opener has uneven enough distribution to jump to three diamonds.

The responder might also hold a hand such as

[F] ♠ K x x ♡ K 10 x x ◇ A x x x ♣ Q x

With Hand F opposite Hand C above, the Drury convention makes it easier for the partnership to find his 4 − 4 heart fit. If Drury were not being used, responder would probably have contented himself with a jump raise to three spades.

If responder holds a hand such as

♠ x ♡ x x x ◇ A J x ♣ A J 10 x x x

he would bid two clubs over his partner's one spade opening, and rebid three clubs over whatever the opener rebid:

Responder	Opener
Pass	1 ♠
2 ♣	2 ◇, 2 ♡, 2 ♠
3 ♣	

SNAP (Strong notrump after passing)

The SNAP convention, an acronym for Strong Notrump After Passing, is designed to allow the partnership to play a low level contract when the responder as a passed hand has fair values, and the opener has a poor hand. Using the SNAP convention, the one notrump response by a passed hand shows a relatively balanced hand worth 9 to 12 points.

Unlike the Drury convention, which is used only over an opening bid in a major suit, SNAP may be used over any one-level bid in a suit by the third or fourth seat. The SNAP responder should not bypass a five card major suit in order to bid one notrump.

SNAP may create problems for weaker responding hands, especially when the opening bid has been one spade. The responder may be forced to pass six-point hands, and to bid eight-point hands at the two level in order to preserve the 9 to 12 point range for the one notrump response.

JUMP SHIFT BY PASSED HAND

Some partnerships agree to use jump shifts by passed hands to show support for the opener's suit, plus a long suit in the responder's hand. This convention may be used in conjunction with SNAP or DRURY. For example, the responder might hold:

♠ K x x x   ♡ x x   ◇ x   ♣ A Q J x x x

After passing in first or second seat, the responder would raise a one spade opening bid by his partner by jumping to three clubs. This bid promises spade support, and a long club suit.

The three club bid by responder is forcing on the opener for one round, but does not force the partnership to game. Rather it asks the opener to evaluate his hand in light of the responder's initial pass and subsequent bidding, and to bid a game if he can. In the above auction, if the opener held a hand such as

♠ A 10 x x x   ♡ K x x   ◇ K x x x   ♣ x

with no club fit, he would sign off in three spades.

DELAYED STAYMAN

When the bidding has been opened with one of a suit and the opener rebids in notrump, there is a convention designed to explore whether or not the partnership has an eight card major suit fit. This convention is described as "delayed" Stayman or "checkback" Stayman.

The delayed Stayman bid is a two club bid in response to the opener's one notrump rebid. The "delay", of course, has come in the bidding of notrump, not in the two club major suit probe. A typical auction would be

Opener	*Responder*
1 ◊	1 ♠
1 Notrump	2 ♣

Delayed Stayman can also be used after the opener has made a jump rebid of two notrump.

Using standard methods, the two club rebid by the responder would show a club suit and would not be forcing. Using delayed Stayman, in which the two club bid is artificial and forcing, the partnership can discover whether it has a 5 − 3 spade fit or a 4 − 4 heart fit. For example, in the auction shown above, the opener might have a hand such as

[A] ♠ x x x   ♡ Q J x x   ◊ K Q x x   ♣ A Q

or

[B] ♠ Q x   ♡ Q J x x   ◊ K Q x x   ♣ A x x

The opener's first obligation is to support the responder's spade suit with a three-card holding. With Hand A therefore, the opener should ignore his four card heart suit and bid two spades. With Hand B, having only two spades, opener can show his four hearts. If opener had neither three spades nor four hearts, he would rebid diamonds or notrump.

Responder might have one of the following hands:

[C] ♠ K J 10 x x   ♡ K x x   ◇ A x x   ♣ x x

[D] ♠ K J 10 x x   ♡ A x x x   ◇ A x x   ♣ x

With Hand D, which is strong enough to force to game, the responder cannot take a chance on simply rebidding two hearts over the opener's one notrump rebid, since the two heart bid could be passed. Using standard methods the responder would jump to three hearts over the one notrump rebid.

The use of delayed Stayman allows him to reserve the jump to three hearts for a hand in which he has five spades and five hearts. Thus with Hand D, if the opener has supported spades, as he would with Hand A above, the responder can still show his four card heart suit by bidding three hearts over two spades. Opener can raise to four hearts, and the partnership will play in its 4 — 4 fit rather than its 5 — 3 fit. Playing in spades could be hazardous if one opponent has four spades and the responder is subjected to repeated club leads forcing him to ruff.

NEW MINOR FORCING:
UNBID MINOR AS DELAYED STAYMAN

If the opener has started the auction by bidding one club and has rebid one notrump, and the partnership is using a two club rebid by responder as Delayed Stayman, the responder can no longer retreat from notrump into his partner's first suit, as he would like to do, for example, with

[A] ♠ x   ♡ A x x x x   ◇ x x   ♣ Q 10 x x x

To preserve this escape route, some partnerships elect to "check back" by having the responder bid the unbid minor suit over the opener's notrump rebid. Their forcing auction would thus be

Opener	Responder
1 ♣	1 ♡
1 Notrump	2 ◇

While this solves the responder's problem on Hand A, it makes things more difficult for him when he holds length in the unbid minor suit and has a weak hand. For example

[B] ♠ x   ♡ A x x x x   ◇ Q 10 x x x   ♣ x x

Using the unbid minor suit as a force, the responder cannot rebid two diamonds over the one notrump rebid as in the above auction. However, it is valuable to have a checkback bid available, and it seems more valuable to allow responder to escape into a suit he knows his partner holds, than into one in which his partner may have a doubleton.

TWO CLUBS AS THE ONLY FORCE
AFTER A ONE NOTRUMP REBID

A very useful convention similar to Delayed Stayman in its initial stages uses a two club rebid by the responder as a forcing bid, and as the only forcing bid, after the opener has rebid one notrump. Like Delayed Stayman, the two club bid shows nothing about the responder's clubs. However, unlike Delayed Stayman, which seeks further information as to the opener's major suit holdings, the use of two clubs as the only forcing bid is designed principally to allow the responder to describe his hand with greater precision.

Use of two clubs as the responder's only forcing rebid means that all of his jump suit rebids are merely invitational. This further allows simple suit rebids to be recognized as sign offs. For example, in the auction

Opener	Responder
1 ◇	1 ♠
1 Notrump	

the responder might hold any of the following hands:

[A] ♠ K Q x x x x   ♡ Q x   ◇ x x   ♣ x x x

[B] ♠ A Q J x x x   ♡ x x   ◇ K x x   ♣ x x

[C] ♠ A K x x x x   ♡ Q x   ◇ x x   ♣ A x x

Using standard methods, responder must have a problem with either Hand B or Hand C, depending on whether the partnership has agreed to play responder's jump to three spades over one notrump in the above auction as forcing or only invitational. With Hand B responder wants to invite; with Hand C, he wants to bid a game, either in spades or in notrump.

Using the two club convention, responder can describe Hand C by first rebidding two clubs and then jumping to three spades. Using this sequence to show a forcing hand allows the responder to make an immediate jump rebid in his suit that is only invitational, the ideal rebid with Hand B.

Two-Suited Hands

After responder rebids two clubs over the one notrump rebid, if he bids a new suit or supports the opener's suit, his bid is forcing to game. This use of the two club rebid helps responder to distinguish between forcing and invitational two suited hands.

For example, suppose in the auction

Opener	Responder
1 ♣	1 ♠
1 Notrump	

responder had one of the following hands

[A] ♠ K x x x x   ♡ x   ◇ Q J x x x   ♣ x x

[B] ♠ K J x x x   ♡ x x   ◇ A Q x x x   ♣ x

[C] ♠ K Q x x x   ♡ Q x   ◇ A K x x x   ♣ x

With Hand A the responder would make the standard bid of two diamonds, which is neither forcing nor particularly encouraging. However, using standard methods he would be forced to make the same bid with Hand B, because a jump to three diamonds would be game forcing.

Using two clubs as the only forcing bid, the responder could jump to three diamonds on Hand B, to show a two suited hand with enough strength to invite a game but not enough to force. The auction might be

Opener	Responder
1 ♣	1 ♠
1 Notrump	3 ◇
Pass	

With Hand C, responder would start with the two club rebid and when he rebids his diamond suit the partnership will be forced to game.

Similarly, if the responder has a hand with which he would like to raise opener's suit in a way that forces to game, he rebids two clubs, followed by a bid in the opener's suit:

Opener	Responder
1 ◇	1 ♠
1 Notrump	2 ♣
2 ◇	3 ◇

The responder's three diamond bid in this auction is forcing to game. The availability of this sequence allows responder to invite game by simply jumping in the opener's suit:

Opener	Responder
1 ◇	1 ♠
1 Notrump	3 ◇

Responder might have a hand such as

♠ A x x x x   ♡ K x x   ◇ K x x x   ♣ x

Showing a Singleton

Since, after a two club rebid by the responder over the no-trump rebid, any new suit by responder would be forcing to game, the partnership could agree to use a jump in a new suit to show a singleton. For example:

Opener	Responder
1 ◇	1 ♠
1 Notrump	2 ♣
2 ◇	3 ♡

Since a two heart bid by the responder over two diamonds would have been forcing and shown a genuine heart suit, The jump to three hearts is not needed as a natural bid. Thus the responder shows a singleton heart in a hand such as

♠ K Q x x x   ♡ x   ◇ A J x x   ♣ K x x

or

♠ K Q x x   ♡ x   ◇ A J x x   ♣ K x x x

The opener can now assess his chances of playing in three no-trump opposite responder's known singleton.

Since the jump to three hearts in the auction above shows a singleton, the partnership may play that the jump to four hearts would show a void. Opener would then be able to determine whether the partnership has a duplication of values, or whether the hands mesh well for play in slam.

UNBID MINOR AS THE ONLY FORCE
AFTER A ONE NOTRUMP REBID

As is true with Delayed Stayman, if the opener has started the auction with one club, the responder cannot take a simple preference for clubs over the one notrump rebid if two clubs is a forcing bid. For this reason, some partnerships favoring the concept of using TWO CLUBS AS THE ONLY FORCE after a one notrump rebid, use instead the minor suit as the force.

When the responder has a weak hand and length in the unbid minor suit, he is forced to abandon the idea of giving his partner a chance to choose between this major suit and the unbid minor. For example, with a hand such as

♠ x   ♡ K Q x x x   ◇ Q x x x x   ♣ x x

in the auction

Opener	Responder
1 ♣	1 ♡
1 Notrump	

responder must simply rebid his heart suit.

TWO NOTRUMP FORCING RESPONSE
TO WEAK TWO BIDS

The weak two bid can be a valuable weapon, having both offensive and defensive potential. Its offensive potential is best realized when the bid is used with discipline, within well defined limits as to length and texture of suit, and as to high card strength. However, as a preemptive maneuver, one frequently cannot resist using the bid simply because it seems likely to embarrass the opponents.

The conflicting applications of the weak two bid leads to its use on a wide variety of hand. The response most commonly used to find out what sort of hand the opener has is two notrump.

Normally a two notrump response to an opening weak two bid is played as forcing for one round. The responder generally has a hand worth at least an opening bid with some fit for the opener's suit. The responder is usually not interested primarily in playing the hand in notrump. Rather he asks the opener to describe his hand further.

As to precisely what the opener's rebids promise, there are a variety of practices. Although some partnerships prefer to have the opener rebid three clubs on all minimum hands, the more popular method is to require the opener to rebid his suit with a minimum hand. With a maximum he would bid a side suit in which he had a high card, called a "feature".

For example, suppose opener holds:

[A] ♠ K Q J x x x   ♡ A x x   ◇ J x x   ♣ x
or
[B] ♠ x x x   ♡ x x   ◇ K Q J x x x   ♣ x x

Over a two notrump response, opener would rebid three hearts with Hand A, showing a maximum and a feature. He would simply rebid his suit with Hand B. With a solid suit, such as

[C] ♠ x x   ♡ A K Q J x x   ◇ x x   ♣ x x x

the opener would rebid three notrump.

For other methods of rebidding over a forcing two notrump response, see OGUST REBIDS, MC CABE ADJUNCT. For other uses of the two notrump response to weak two bids, see RELAYS OVER TWO BIDS, TWO RELAYS AND A TRANSFER.

OGUST REBIDS

The Ogust convention systematizes the opener's rebids over the forcing response of two notrump. Choosing one of four steps, the opener describes the strength of his hand and the quality of his suit:

$$3 \clubsuit = \text{weak hand, weak suit}$$
$$3 \diamondsuit = \text{good hand, weak suit}$$
$$3 \heartsuit = \text{weak hand, good suit}$$
$$3 \spadesuit = \text{good hand, good suit}$$

Some partnerships have agreed to reverse the meanings of the three diamond and three heart bids.

The responder might hold the following hand when his partner opens the bidding with two spades:

[A]   ♠ K x x   ♡ A x x x   ◇ A Q x x   ♣ x x

If the opener has a reasonable hand, such as either

[B]   ♠ Q J x x x x   ♡ K x   ◇ x x   ♣ A x x
or
[C]   ♠ A Q J 9 x x   ♡ Q x   ◇ x x   ♣ x x x

game would be a fair proposition.

Using Ogust rebids, opener would rebid three diamonds with Hand B, showing a good hand with a poor suit. Over this bid responder will bid four spades, since he can solidify the spade suit, and opener's side suit high cards may fit well with responder's hand.

With Hand C opener would rebid three hearts, showing a minimum hand in high cards, but a respectable suit. Opener's Hand C opposite responder's Hand A should produce a reasonable play for game.

However, if the opener has a hand such as

[D] ♠ Q J x x x x   ♡ x x x   ◇ x   ♣ Q x x

game is out of the question. With Hand D opener would rebid three clubs, announcing a minimum hand with a ragged suit. Responder would sign off at three spades.

McCABE ADJUNCT

Normally after the opener has made a weak two bid, the responder's bid of a new suit is natural and forcing. If the responder has a weak hand and a long suit, he has no way to play in three of that suit using standard methods. The McCabe Adjunct is a convention that preserves the forcing nature of the change of suit, while giving the partnership a means of playing the hand in responder's long suit at the three level.

Using the McCabe Adjunct, a two notrump response requires the opener to rebid three clubs, whatever his hand may be. The responder may now play in his own long suit, either by passing three clubs if clubs is his suit, or by bidding three of his suit, which the opener must pass.

If the partnership is using a direct raise of the weak two bid suit as preemptive, the McCabe Adjunct may be used constructively. The responder first bids two notrump, forcing the opener to rebid three clubs, then responder retreats to three of the opener's suit. By this sequence of bids, responder invites opener to bid game with a hand containing general strength.

Using the McCabe Adjunct, the responder may get information from the opener by making a simple change of suit. This bid is forcing. With support for the responder's suit—three small cards or a doubleton honor should suffice—the opener should raise the responder's suit, so long as he does not have to go past three notrump to do so. Without support for responder's suit, opener is expected to rebid his suit if he has a minimum hand, or to show a feature with a good hand, or to rebid three notrump with a solid suit.

RELAYS OVER WEAK TWO BIDS

Another method of responding to weak two bids is to use the cheapest bid—either notrump if the opening bid was two spades, or the next higher suit—as a relay bid. A relay is a bid which has no meaning of its own, but simply asks one's partner to describe his hand.

The relay asks the opener to bid a stopper outside of his suit if he has one. If his stopper is in the relay suit, he rebids in notrump. Lacking any stopper, opener rebids his own suit. For example:

Opener	*Responder*
2 ♡	2 ♠ (relay)
2 Notrump	

The two notrump bid by the opener shows a spade stopper. This enables the responder to raise to three notrump with a hand such as

♠ x x　　♡ x x　　♢ A x　　♣ A K Q J x x x

or perhaps with a hand such as

♠ x x x　　♡ K Q x　　♢ A x x x　　♣ A x x

on which the partnership might make exactly nine tricks in whatever contract it plays.

Using this method, the relay bid is the responder's only forcing bid. All other bids by responder, including two notrump when this is not the relay bid, are sign offs. However, if the responder uses a relay and then rebids a new suit, his rebid is forcing.

TWO RELAYS AND A TRANSFER

Another system of responding to weak two bids uses two relays and a transfer. In this system, a single raise of the weak two bid is constructive, inviting the opener to bid game with a maximum hand. The two notrump response is natural and not forcing. Almost all other responses are artificial and forcing for at least one round.

The bid of the cheapest suit is a relay, forcing to game. This bid, i.e., two hearts over a two diamond opening, two spades over a two heart opening, or three clubs over a two spade opening, shows nothing about the suit bid by the responder. It merely asks the opener to bid his lowest ranking feature, whether it be an ace, a king, a singleton or a void. If the opener has a minimum hand and no feature, he rebids his suit.

Suppose opener's and responder's hands were as follows:

(Opener)
♠ A Q x x x x   ♡ x   ◇ Q x x   ♣ J x x

(Responder)
♠ K x x   ♡ J x x x x   ◇ A K x x   ♣ A

Using the game forcing relay, the auction could proceed:

Opener	Responder
2 ♠	3 ♣ (please show
3 ♡ (heart feature)	a feature)
4 ♠ (no interest)	4 ♣ (cue bid)
6 ♠ (interest	5 ◇ (cue bid)
awakened)	

Using this system of responses to weak two bids, the bid of

the second higher ranking suit, i.e., two spades over a two diamond opening, three clubs over a two heart opening, or three diamonds over a two spade opening, is forcing for one round, and is game invitational. Again the responder's bid is a relay, showing nothing about his holding in the suit he has named. This relay asks the opener to show his point count. With a minimum, i.e., 6 to 9 points, the opener rebids his suit. With a maximum, 10 to 12 points he makes the cheapest suit rebid. Thus the auction could go

Opener	Responder
2 ♠	3 ◇ (tell me your
3 ♡ (maximum)	point range)
	4 ♠

Since the simple direct raise of the opener's weak two bid is played as constructive, this system uses a transfer bid to make a preemptive raise. The bid of the suit just below the suit of the weak two bid forces the opener to rebid his suit. Thus with a hand such as

♠ x x x   ♡ Q J x x   ◇ K x   ♣ K Q x x

the responder would bid three diamonds in response to two hearts, forcing the opener to rebid three hearts.

The preemptive transfer raise can be used for jumps as well as simple raises. For example

Opener	Responder
2 ♡	4 ◇
4 ♡	

The responder might have a hand such as

♠ x   ♡ J x x x   ◊ K x x x x   ♣ Q x x

However, this extension of the transfer preempt concept has a twofold disadvantage. First, it informs the opponents that the responder is bidding four hearts preemptively and secondly, it allows them the opportunity to cue bid four hearts. The standard approach of raising directly to four on preemptive hands as well as on very strong hands is tactically much sounder, since it forces the opponents to guess, to their great sorrow if they guess wrongly, whether or not they are being talked out of their own game.

III

Forcing Opening Bids and Responses

Most bidding systems reserve at least one opening as a strong forcing bid, to be used with a hand of game-going or near-game-going strength. A variety of artificial forcing bids are described below, together with the conventional responses used with each. *See* ARTIFICIAL TWO CLUB OPENING, BLUE TEAM CLUB, SCHENKEN CLUB, PRECISION CLUB, ROMAN CLUB, LITTLE ROMAN CLUB, PRO SYSTEM, SCHENKEN TWO DIAMONDS, STAYMAN TWO CLUB AND TWO DIAMOND OPENINGS, MEXICAN TWO DIAMONDS, TAM II TWO CLUBS AND TWO DIAMONDS, BIG DIAMOND SYSTEM, DYNAMIC ONE NOTRUMP.

In standard bidding, opening two-bids are strong and forcing to game. There are a number of conventional methods of responding. *See* TWO NOTRUMP NEGATIVE, HERBERT NEGATIVE, ACE-SHOWING RESPONSES, ACE AND KING SHOWING RESPONSES.

III

TWO NOTRUMP AS A NEGATIVE RESPONSE

The traditional negative response to a strong opening two-bid is two notrump. This response shows a hand worth less than 7 or 8 points, counting high cards plus distribution. For his two notrump response to two hearts, for example, the responder might have either of the following hands:

[A] ♠ x x x   ♡ x x x x   ◇ x x x   ♣ x x x

or

[B] ♠ Q x x x x   ♡ x x   ◇ Q x x   ♣ Q x x

If the responder bids anything other than two notrump in response to the opening two-bid, his response is positive, showing at least 7 or 8 points and usually at least one quick trick (an ace, or two kings, or a king and queen in the same suit). Positive responses include a raise of the opener's suit, a jump in notrump, and the bid of any new suit. If the responder bids a new suit in response to a strong two-bid, he promises at least a five-card suit, headed by no worse than the king, or the queen and jack.

HERBERT NEGATIVE

The Herbert Negative response to a forcing two-bid is the bid of the cheapest suit over the opening bid, for example,

Opener	Responder
2 ♡	2 ♠

The responder's two spade bid shows nothing about his spade suit; it merely says that responder has less than 7 or 8 points in support of the opener's suit.

There are two purposes to using the Herbert negative response. One is that frequently after the bidding has been opened with a strong two-bid the hand will be played in notrump. The use of Herbert enables the strong hand to be declarer. The second purpose of the Herbert Negative is to save room when the bidding has been opened with a strong two-bid in a suit other than spades.

If the responder has a hand with which he would have made a positive response in the cheapest suit, he must jump in that suit to show length and strength. Thus with a hand such as

♠ A Q x x x   ♡ K x   ◇ x x x   ♣ x x x

responder would have to bid three spades in response to the two heart opening bid.

ACE-SHOWING RESPONSES

Ace-showing responses to strong forcing two-bids are designed to show the two-bidder immediately whether or not the responder has any aces, and if so, which ones.

If the responder has no aces he responds two notrump. If he has one ace, he responds in the suit of the ace. For example, suppose responder held one of the following hands in response to a two diamond opening bid:

[A] ♠ K Q x x x   ♡ Q x x   ◇ x x   ♣ x x x

[B] ♠ K x x x x   ♡ A x   ◇ x x x   ♣ x x x

Using ace-showing responses over the two diamond opening, responder would bid two notrump with Hand A, showing that he has no aces. He is not allowed at this point to bid his long strong spade suit, for that would show the ace of spades, and would show nothing else about the spade suit. With Hand B, responder would bid two hearts over the two diamond bid, showing the ace of hearts.

There are at least two methods of showing that the responder has two aces. Using one of these methods, the responder shows his aces one at a time, by first bidding the ace he can show most inexpensively over the opening two-bid, and bidding the second one later. Using this method, if responder held

♠ x x x   ♡ A x x x x   ◇ x x   ♣ A x x

in response to a two-diamond opening, his proper response would be two hearts. Over the opener's rebid, responder must then bid clubs. When responder runs out of aces to bid, he must rebid the minimum number of notrump.

Using an alternative method of showing two aces in the responding hand, the responder would jump to the suit of his lower ranking ace. For example, holding the aces of spades and diamonds, the responder would jump to three diamonds over a two club opening bid, or would jump to four diamonds if the opening bid had been two hearts.

ACE AND KING SHOWING RESPONSES

Some partnerships agree that the responder will show his aces and kings in response to an opening two bid. Some combinations can be shown in one bid; others require more rounds of bidding. With no aces and no kings, the responder bids two notrump; with one king and no aces, he first responds two notrump, and then if his partner makes a bid below the game level, he bids the suit in which he has the king.

If responder has one ace and no kings, he bids the suit in which he has the ace; if he has two kings and no aces, he jumps to three notrump; if he has two aces and no kings, he jumps to four notrump; if he has one ace and one king, he first bids the suit in which he has the ace, and later bids the suit in which he has the king. For example; opener's and responder's hands might be:

(Opener)
♠ K Q J 10 9 x x   ♡ —   ◇ A Q x   ♣ A K Q

(Responder)
♠ A x   ♡ Q x x x x   ◇ K x x   ♣ x x x

The bidding would proceed:

Opener	Responder
2 ♠	3 ♠
4 ♣	4 ◇
7 ♠	

Responder's three spade bid showed the ace of spades; his four diamond bid showed the king of diamonds.

The disadvantage of the responder's showing his aces, or his aces and honors, directly in response to the opening two-bid is that the partnership loses much of its ability to explore for suit fits at a low level of the auction. Since the responder does not get to bid his own suit naturally for the first round or two, hands that have been opened with a strong two-bid usually end up being played in the opener's suit. This is fine if opener's suit is the best place to play; however, sometimes responder's hand will provide a better trump suit.

ARTIFICIAL TWO CLUB OPENING

When the partnership is using strong opening two-bids, a two club bid to show such a hand with a club suit is not a convention. However, many partnerships use weak opening two-bids, and for most of these partnerships the two club bid is the only strong, forcing opening bid.

The strong, artificial two club opening may be made on any of three types of hand. It may be made on a hand worth a forcing strong two-bid in any suit, such as

♠ A K Q J x x   ♡ A K x   ◇ A K x   ♣ x

In many partnerships, the bidding may be opened with two clubs also on a hand that is almost, but not quite, worth a game forcing two-bid. For example, holding

♠ K x   ♡ A K Q x x x x   ◇ A Q x   ♣ x

the bidding could be opened with two clubs if the partnership did not treat that bid as forcing to game.

In addition, many partnerships today have lowered the trational range of the two notrump opening bid to 20 to 22 high card points. These partnerships use a two club opening bid, followed by a rebid of two notrump, to show a hand worth 23 to 24 high card points. The two club opener might have a hand such as

♠ K Q x   ♡ A Q x x   ◇ A Q J x   ♣ A J

To learn which of the above types of hands the opener has for his two club bid, the responder must wait until the opener rebids.

There are several types of responses to the forcing two club bid that can be adopted. Some are designed to show very weak responding hands, some are designed to show how many aces and kings the responder holds, and some are designed simply to help the opener describe his hand.

See TWO DIAMOND NEGATIVE, STEP RESPONSES, CHEAPER MINOR AS A SECOND NEGATIVE, AUTOMATIC TWO DIAMONDS, TWO DIAMONDS AS ONLY POSITIVE RESPONSE, TWO DIAMONDS NEGATIVE AND TWO HEARTS NEUTRAL, ACE-SHOWING RESPONSES, HERBERT SECOND NEGATIVE.

TWO DIAMOND NEGATIVE

Over a strong artificial two club opening bid, the negative response most commonly used is two diamonds. The two diamond response shows nothing with respect to the responder's diamond suit. It simply shows that he has a weak hand, less than about 8 points. The two diamond response to two clubs is the equivalent of the negative two notrump response to a natural strong two-bid.

After the negative two diamond response, many partnerships have agreed that the bidding may end below the game level. Thus either of the following auctions would be possible:

(A)	*Opener*	*Responder*
	2 ♣	2 ♦
	2 Notrump	Pass

(B)	*Opener*	*Responder*
	2 ♣	2 ♦
	2 ♠	2 Notrump
	3 ♠	Pass

If the responder has a genuine diamond suit and a hand strong enough for a positive response, he must show it by jumping to three diamonds. This could be a handicap if the opener's suit is clubs and he has the minimum for his two club bid.

HERBERT SECOND NEGATIVE

In response to a strong artificial two club opening bid, some partnerships attempt to have the responder distinguish between hands that are weak and hands that are in extremis. To achieve this, the responder first makes the negative two diamond response; then over the opener's rebid, he employs the Herbert convention by bidding the cheapest suit over the rebid.

For example, in the auction

Opener	*Responder*
2 ♣	2 ◇
2 ♡	2 ♠

the responder's two diamond bid was negative, showing 0 to 7 points. His two spade bid showed that he was rather closer to 0 than to 7. The two spade bid does not promise length or strength in spades.

This convention has the advantage of keeping the bidding low when the responder has a very weak hand and the opener has either a minimum or a two-suited hand. However, it has the disadvantage of preventing the responder from showing his suit cheaply if it happens to rank next above the opener's suit. For example, suppose responder holds:

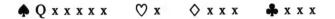

♠ Q x x x x x   ♡ x   ◇ x x x   ♣ x x x

Over his partner's two club opening bid, responder is happy to bid two diamonds. But over a two heart rebid by opener, he would like to be able to bid two spades to show his long spade suit. Using the Herbert convention as a second negative, this responder would have to bid his spades on the three level, without knowing whether or not the opener has a fit. The opener, for example, might hold either of these two hands:

[A] ♠ x   ♡ K Q J 10 x x   ◇ A K x   ♣ A K x

or

[B] ♠ K x x   ♡ A K Q x x x   ◇ A K x   ♣ x

If the opener held Hand A, the partnership could be too high once the responder showed his spade suit at the three level. With Hand B, however, the partnership has a probable game in spades.

CHEAPER MINOR AS A SECOND NEGATIVE

In order to facilitate the showing of a long major suit with a weak hand opposite a strong artificial two club opening bid some partnerships avoid using the Herbert convention as their second negative, and instead substitute a bid of the cheaper minor suit. Using the cheaper minor as a second negative, the responder has comfortable rebids with each of the following hands:

[A] ♠ Q x x x x x   ♡ x   ◇ x x   ♣ x x x x

[B] ♠ Q x x x   ♡ x x   ◇ x x x   ♣ x x x x

After the bidding has started

Opener	Responder
2 ♣	2 ◇
2 ♡	

responder would bid two spades with Hand A, a natural rebid showing a long spade suit. With Hand B responder would make an artificial rebid of three clubs. This bid says nothing about his club suit; it merely says that his weak hand is very weak, and that he did not have a long spade suit he could bid over two hearts.

Most partnerships carry their use of the cheaper minor as a second negative only through three diamonds. Thus, in the auction

Opener	Responder
2 ♣	2 ◇
3 ♣	3 ◇

responder's three diamond bid would be a second negative. But in the auction

Opener	Responder
2 ♣	2 ◇
3 ◇	

responder would have no second negative available.

If the partnership is not using a convention such as Herbert or cheaper minor as a second negative, the responder is forced to rebid two notrump with extremely weak hands. This has the undesirable effect of making the very weak hand the declarer in any notrump contract that might eventually be played.

AUTOMATIC TWO DIAMOND RESPONSE

Some partnerships use the two diamond response to a strong artificial two club opening bid as a waiting bid. When used in this way, the two diamond response neither shows length in the suit, nor gives any information about the strength or weakness of the responder's hand.

The purpose of using the two diamond bid as a relay-type bid is to allow the opening bidder to describe his hand further. The rationale is that after that rebid the responder will have a much better idea of what his hand is worth.

The use of the two diamond bid as a waiting bid also has the effect of making it easier for the opening bidder to complete a description of a two-suited hand if he has one. The drawback, of course, is that while the responder is waiting and relaying, he is not showing opener either the strength or the shape of his hand.

TWO DIAMONDS AS THE ONLY POSITIVE RESPONSE

Some partnerships use the two diamond response to an artificial strong two club opening as the only positive response available to the responder. If the responder makes a bid in any other suit, or if he bids notrump, he shows less than the 7 or so points needed for a positive response.

Using this method, the two diamond response forces the partnership to game. This convention has the advantage of allowing the partnership to explore for slam at the two level. A drawback, however, is that the responder once again makes a bid with very limited meaning, and cannot begin to reveal the contours of his hand until the next round of the bidding.

TWO DIAMONDS NEGATIVE, TWO HEARTS NEUTRAL

A few partnerships use the two diamond response to an artificial two club opening bid as an extreme negative response, and use a two heart response with a hand of any other strength. Any response other than two diamonds or two hearts would be positive and game-forcing.

Using these methods, the two diamond response would be made with about 0 to 3 points—the type of hand with which a HERBERT SECOND NEGATIVE or CHEAPER MINOR SECOND NEGATIVE response might be used. The two heart response is artificial, and shows at least 4 high card points. Two hearts may be bid with a hand not strong enough for a positive response, or with a hand worth a positive response, but with which the responder simply wants to hear opener's rebid before taking any positive action.

Suppose responder held one of the following hands:

[A] ♠ x x   ♡ x x x   ◇ Q x x x   ♣ J x x x

[B] ♠ x x   ♡ x x x   ◇ K Q x x   ♣ J x x x

[C] ♠ x x   ♡ K Q x   ◇ K Q x x   ♣ J x x x

[D] ♠ K x   ♡ K x x   ◇ K x x x   ♣ Q x x x

[E] ♠ K x   ♡ A x x x x   ◇ K x x   ♣ J x x

Using these methods, with Hand A responder would bid two diamonds over two clubs. With Hand B, responder has enough strength to bid two hearts, showing at least a modicum of values. With Hand C, which is worth a positive response, responder would also bid two hearts, temporizing to hear what opener will rebid. With Hand D, however, which has the same point count as Hand C, responder would bid two notrump in response to the two club opening, because if the hand is to be played in notrump, the partnership will surely be better off having the lead come toward responder's hand rather than through it. With Hand E, responder would bid two hearts even though this response does not show his heart suit. However, he does not want to use up a whole level of bidding by jumping to three hearts to make a positive response; therefore he temporizes with a two heart bid.

Over a two diamond response, using these methods, the partnership may agree that a minimum rebid by the opener is not forcing, and that in order to force the responder to bid again the opener must make a jump rebid. This agreement would allow the partnership to play at the two level if both opener and responder had the minimum allowed for their respective bidding. However, it would make it difficult for opener to describe a two-suited hand, since to be sure of having an opportunity to show his second suit he would have to make a jump rebid.

More profitably, the partnership could agree that a minimum rebid by the opener is forcing, and that the jump rebid of a major suit is invitational. This would allow the partnership to stop at the three level whether the opener had a one-suited hand or a two-suited hand. Under this agreement, the following auctions would be possible:

(A)	*Opener*	*Responder*
	2 ♣	2 ◇
	2 ♡	3 ♡
	Pass	

(B)	*Opener*	*Responder*
	2 ♣	2 ◇
	3 ♡	Pass

In auction (A), opener's two heart rebid would show either a hand with which he was no longer interested in bidding game once he found out that responder had at most 3 points, or a two-suited hand. However, his pass of the raise to three hearts indicates that he has the former type of hand. With a two-suited hand opener would either bid game over a raise or show his second suit if responder did not raise.

In auction (B), opener's jump to three hearts shows that he is interested in game if responder has 3 points rather than none, or if responder has as little as a side singleton and three trumps.

If the responder has bid two hearts over the two club opening bid, the partnership will usually reach game. The one sequence by which the partnership can play below game is

Opener	Responder
2 ♣	2 ♡
2 ♠	2 Notrump
3 ♠	Pass

In the auction

Opener	Responder
2 ♣	2 ♡
3 ♡	

opener's three heart bid is forcing. Similarly, in the auction

Opener	Responder
2 ♣	2 ♡
2 Notrump	

opener's two notrump bid may not be passed. Opener has shown 23 to 24 points and responder has shown at least 4 to 7 points. The partnership therefore theoretically has the values to be in game.

ACE-SHOWING RESPONSES TO TWO CLUB OPENINGS

Ace showing responses may be used in conjunction with the strong artificial two club opening bid as well as with strong natural two-bids. Using this convention, the two diamond response is negative, showing no aces and less than 7 or 8 points; a response of two notrump would show a hand with no aces, but one that is worth a positive response.

A bid of two hearts, two spades, three clubs or three diamonds would show the ace of the suit bid. None of these responses promises any length in the suit bid.

There are several methods by which the partnership may choose to have the responder show a hand containing two aces. One method is to have the responder jump to three notrump with any two aces. The theory behind this agreement is that the opener will normally have two aces himself, and will therefore know which two aces the responder holds.

A second method is to jump to three hearts, or three spades or three notrump to show specific pairs of aces, as follows: A jump to three hearts would show aces that do not match either in rank or in color (either clubs and hearts, or diamonds and spades); a jump to three spades would show two aces of the same color (clubs and spades, or diamonds and hearts); a jump to three notrump would show two aces of the same rank (majors or minors).

A third method of showing aces uses the two notrump response as the only bid that says responder has no aces, and thus allows the bid of two diamonds to be made to show the ace of diamonds. All of the other single-ace showing bids described above remain the same. However, to show two aces, the responder would jump to the suit of his lower ranking ace. For these purposes, the spade suit would be deemed to rank below the club suit. Thus, with the aces of spades and clubs, the responder would bid three spades directly over the two club opening; with the aces of clubs and hearts, he would jump to four clubs; with the aces of hearts and spades, he would jump to three hearts, and so forth.

STEP RESPONSES TO TWO CLUB OPENINGS

A convention devised to allow the responder to show both his aces and his kings in a single response to the two club opening is called Step Responses to Two Clubs. Counting each ace as two controls and each king as one control, the responses to the two club opening are as follows:

2 ◇ = 0 or 1 control

2 ♡ = 2 controls (one ace or two kings)

2 ♠ = 3 controls, consisting specifically of one ace and one king

2 Notrump = 3 controls, consisting specifically of three kings

3 ♣ = 4 controls (two aces, or four kings, or one ace and two kings)

3 ◇ = 5 controls (two aces and one king, or one ace and three kings)

The reason underlying the separation of the two types of hands containing three controls is that if the hand is to be played in notrump, the hand with three kings should be the declarer so that the lead will come up to him rather than through him.

Some partnerships use a variation of Step Responses designed to allow the responder show at once whether he has a very weak hand or just a moderately weak hand. Using this variation, a two diamond response to the two club opening would show 0 or 1 control with less than 6 points; a two heart response would show 0 or 1 control, with at least 6 high card points. The other responses would be as follows:

2 ♠ = 2 controls

2 Notrump = 3 kings (3 controls)

3 ♣ = one ace and one king (3 controls)

3 ♦ = 4 controls

BLUE TEAM CLUB

The Blue Team Club system is based on a forcing one club opening bid, with responses showing how many controls the responder has. Opening bids of one of a suit other than clubs are limited to less than a good 17 points. The opening bid style of Blue Team Club is canape, meaning that there is a tendency to bid short suits before long suits.

For example, in the auction

Opener	Responder
1 ♡	2 ♣
2 ◇	2 ♠

The opener's one heart bid could have been made on a four-card suit, and his diamonds are as long as or longer than his hearts. The responder tends to canape also. His two club bid may have been made on as few as three clubs, and his two spade rebid shows a spade suit that is probably longer than his club suit.

Using Blue Team Club, balanced hands worth 16 to 17 points are opened one notrump; balanced hands worth 21 to 22 points are opened two notrump. In addition, there is a bid to show strong three-suited hands: this is the NEAPOLITAN TWO DIAMOND opening, showing a hand containing three four card suits and 17 to 24 points. All other hands worth 17 or more points are opened with one club.

BLUE TEAM ONE CLUB OPENING

There are three types of hands that may be opened with a one club bid. First there are balanced hands that are outside the ranges assigned to the one notrump and two notrump openings. Thus balanced hands worth 18 to 20 points or worth 23 points and up should be opened with one club. The opener's rebid will be in notrump, as follows:

> 18 to 20 points: open one club and rebid the minimum number of notrump
>
> 23 to 24 points: open one club and jump rebid in notrump
>
> 25 to 26 points: open one club and jump to three notrump over a one diamond response

One club may be opened with unbalanced hands worth 17 or more points. These hands may have one or two long suits; or they may have three four card suits if they have more than 24 points. The first rebid with such a hand will be in a suit.

The third type of hand with which a one club opening may be made is a hand with eight or more playing tricks, even if it has less than 17 points. A hand such as

$$\spadesuit \; A \, Q \, J \, x \, x \, x \qquad \heartsuit \; x \qquad \diamondsuit \; x \qquad \clubsuit \; A \, K \, J \, x \, x$$

would qualify for a one club opening.

Responses to One Club

The responder's first bid informs the opener how many controls responder has. Counting each ace as two controls and each king as one, responder shows his strength as follows:

1 ◇ = 0 to 2 controls, less than 6 points

1 ♡ = 0 to 2 controls, 6 or more points

1 ♠ = 3 controls

1 NT = 4 controls

2 ♣ = 5 controls

2 ◇ = 6 controls

2 NT = 7 controls.

The two heart and two spade responses are used to show hands worth 0 to 5 points with a six-card suit headed by two honors. The maximum holding would be K J x x x x. The two heart and two spade responses are not forcing. If the opener has a balanced 18 count without a good fit for the responder's suit he is allowed to pass.

The one diamond response is negative. After the responder has bid one diamond, he is not required to bid again unless the opener makes a jump rebid in a suit.

Responder is, however, required to bid again after he has responded one heart. This response is semi-positive, and could in fact be quite strong in point count, for example:

♠ K Q x   ♡ Q J 10 x x   ◇ Q J x   ♣ K J

This hand contains 15 high card points, but is not worth a full positive response because it has so few controls.

The one heart response forces the partnership to at least two notrump. Responses that show three or more controls force the partnership to game.

When the Opponents Interfere

If an opponent doubles or overcalls over the one club opening bid, adjustments are made in the control showing responses. If the interference is a double, all of the regular responses of one heart and higher remain applicable. However, the double gives the responder two additional calls with which to clarify a negative response. A pass over the double will show 0 to 3 points; a redouble will show 3 to 5 points with values in the club suit; the one diamond bid will show 4 to 5 points with values outside the club suit.

If the opponent overcalls over the one club opening at the one level, the responder will pass with 0 to 5 points—a hand with which he would have responded one diamond had there been no overcall. Responder will double the overcall with six or more points and less than three controls—a hand with which he would have responded one heart had there been no overcall. To show three or more controls, responder bids up the line. The cheapest bid over the overcall shows three controls; the next bid shows four controls, and so forth. For example, if the bidding has gone

North	East	South	West
1 ♣	1 ♠		

and South has

♠ x x x   ♡ A K x x   ◇ x x x   ♣ x x x

he bids one notrump, the cheapest bid, to show that he has three controls.

In bidding up the line over the overcall, however, responses of two of an unbid major suit retain their original meanings. Thus in the auction above, if South bids two hearts over the one spade overcall he does not show six controls even though that is literally the fourth step over the overcall; instead he shows 0 to 5 points with a six-card heart suit headed by two honors. If South had a hand with six controls, his proper response over the one spade overcall would be two spades. If the opponent overcalls one notrump over the one club opening, the responder should pass or bid a long suit with a poor hand. He should double with any hand worth 6 points or more, regardless of the number of controls he holds. If the notrump overcaller retreats into a suit after being doubled, the responder can either pass with a minimum hand, or double for penalties, or bid a new suit, which is forcing. In addition he can show approximately how many controls he has. To show his controls, he bids two notrump with three or four controls, or cue-bids with five or more controls.

If the opponent overcalls over one club at the two level, the responder may double for penalties, or he may pass with a hand that has fewer than three controls, or he may bid a new suit, which is forcing. In addition he may bid two notrump with three or four controls.

SCHENKEN CLUB

The Schenken system is based on a forcing one club opening bid, with natural responses showing that the responder has high card strength. The one club opening normally shows 17 or more high card points, and may be made on one of three types of hands.

The Schenken one club opening may be made on a balanced hand containing 17 to 22 points. If opener has a balanced 16 to 18 point with all suits stopped, he would open with one notrump. However, with a balanced 17 or 18 points and one suit unstopped, the opener bids one club and rebids a suit.

If the opener has a balanced 19 to 20 points he opens one club and rebids one notrump. If he has a balanced 21 to 22 points, he rebids two notrump. If he has a balanced hand with more than 22 points, he opens a SCHENKEN TWO DIAMOND bid.

One club may also be opened with a slightly unbalanced, although not freakish, hand worth 17 or more high card points. With this type of hand the opener will rebid a suit. In addition, a hand may be opened with one club with less than 17 points if it has such great playing strength that game is likely if the responder has a moderately good fit and the right king or queen. For example, holding

♠ A K 10 x x   ♥ A Q J x x x   ♦ x   ♣ x

the opener would bid one club even though the hand contains only 14 high card points.

Using the Schenken system, freakish hands that may produce a slam opposite the right one or two cards in the responder's hand are opened with a SCHENKEN TWO DIAMOND bid.

Responses to One Club

In response to a one club opening, the negative response is one diamond. All other responses are positive and forcing to game. The responder must bid one diamond unless he has at least 9 high card points including at least 1½ quick tricks, i.e., an ace and a king, or an ace and queen in the same suit, or three kings, or a king and queen combination and another king. However, the responder is allowed to make a positive response with only 8 points if those 8 points consist of two aces.

After a one diamond response to the one club opening, a simple non-jump rebid by the opener is not forcing. Thus the auction could go.

Opener	Responder
1 ♣	1 ♢
1 ♠	Pass

If the opener wants to force the responder to bid again he must jump in a suit. Even this jump, however, is not forcing to game; if the opener later rebids his suit, the responder is allowed to pass.

Responses of one heart, one spade, one notrump, two clubs and two diamonds are all positive responses, showing 9 or more points (or possibly two bare aces). These responses are natural, showing the suit in which the responder bids, and are forcing to game.

An alternative treatment is to use the two club response as a semi-positive response, showing 7 or 8 points including one ace or one king. When this treatment is used, the responder promises to rebid over whatever the opener rebids.

Holding a solid or semi-solid six-card suit, with a hand worth a positive response, the responder jumps in his suit. A single jump shows a solid suit, i.e., no worse than A K Q 10 x x or A K Q x x x x. A double jump shows a semi-solid suit, i.e., a suit needing one of the top three honors to be solid. Thus in the auction

Opener	Responder
1 ♣	3 ♠

responder shows a semi-solid spade suit, and at least 1½ quick tricks. If responder had K Q 10 x x x in his suit and nothing outside, his proper response would be one diamond.

When the Opponents Interfere

If an opponent overcalls over the one club opening with any bid up to and including three diamonds, the only ways for the responder to show a positive response are to double or cue-bid. The double is not for penalties, and does not describe the shape of the responder's hand. It simply says he had the strength for a positive response. A cue-bid shows a positive response and first round control of the suit overcalled.

Any bid of a suit over the overcall shows a fair hand, but one not strong enough for a positive response. A notrump bid over the overcall shows two stoppers in the suit overcalled, and some values, but again less than the strength for a positive response.

Suppose North opens with one club and East overcalls one heart, and South has one of the following hands:

[A] ♠ K Q x x x   ♡ x x   ◇ J x x   ♣ x x x

[B] ♠ Q J 10 x x x   ♡ x x   ◇ x x   ♣ x x x

[C] ♠ x x   ♡ K Q 10 x x   ◇ A x x   ♣ Q x x

[D] ♠ A Q x x   ♡ x x   ◇ K Q x x   ♣ x x x

With Hand A, responder would bid one spade over the overcall; however, with Hand B, he should pass because his hand is so weak. With Hand C, responder should pass in the hopes that his partner will reopen with a takeout double which he can pass for penalties. With Hand D, responder should double to show a positive response.

PRECISION CLUB SYSTEM

The Precision Club system is a largely natural system of bidding that uses a forcing one club opening with hands worth 16 points or more, and natural positive responses. Using the Precision system, the bidding is opened with one club much more frequently than it can be in the Schenken or Blue Team club systems in which a minimum of 17 points are required to open one club.

Using the Precision system, all hands worth 16 or more high card points, with one exception, are opened one club. The exception is that balanced hands worth 23 to 24 points are opened two notrump. In addition, hands that are very strong in playing strength may be opened with one club even without 16 points.

Responses to One Club

A one diamond response to a one club opening is negative and shows fewer than 8 high card points. After a one diamond response, a minimum suit rebid by the opener is not forcing. If the opener wishes to force the responder to bid once again, he must jump in a suit.

Other minimum responses to the one club opening, i.e., one heart, one spade, one notrump, two clubs and two diamonds, are positive responses. Each shows 8 or more high card points, and five or more cards in the suit bid. In principle, these bids are forcing to game. However, if the later bidding shows a misfit, and each partner has an absolute minimum, the partnership may stop below game.

After a positive response, a jump shift by the opener shows a solid six-card or longer suit, and at least 19 points. The bid is forcing to game, and fixes the trump suit. Thereafter, bids by the opener or the responder, other than game in the established trump suit, are slam tries. For example, opener's and responder's hands might be:

(Opener)
♠ x x   ♡ A K Q x x x x   ◇ K x   ♣ A K

(Responder)
♠ A K x   ♡ J   ◇ x x x   ♣ Q J x x x x

The bidding could go

Opener	Responder
1 ♣	2 ♣
3 ♡	3 ♠
4 ♣	4 ♠
6 ♡	Pass

Responses in notrump show balanced distribution. The one notrump response shows 8 to 10 high card points; the two notrump response shows 11 to 13 high card points; a three notrump response shows 14 to 15 high card points. As an alternative, the partnership might agree to use the one notrump response to show either the minimum positive response or a response worth 15 or more points. This would enable the opener to describe his hand naturally at a low level; the responder would bid aggressively later in the auction if he had 15 or more points.

When the response to one club has been one notrump, a raise to two notrump by the opener is not forcing. Opener shows a minimum hand, and invites responder to bid game if he has closer to ten points than to eight.

Responses of two of a major suit may be used to show hands containing six-card suits with 4 to 7 high card points. Jumps to the three level by the responder over one club can be used to show seven card suits with four to seven points. (But see UN-USUAL POSITIVE, below.)

Since suit bids in response to a one club opening show at least five cards, and since notrump responses show balanced distribution, the Precision responder has a problem showing a hand worth a positive response if its distribution is 4-4-4-1. There are two alternative methods for dealing with these hands. See IM-POSSIBLE NEGATIVE; UNUSUAL POSITIVE.

When the Opponents Interfere

If the opponents overcall over the one club opening, a pass by the responder is the most negative possible bid, showing 0 to 4 points. The cue-bid is the only action that immediately reveals that the responder has the values for a positive response.

Between the negative pass and the immediately positive cue-bid, there are three avenues open to the responder. If he has a five-card suit and 5 to 8 points, he may bid his suit. If he has a six-card suit and 5 to 8 points, he may jump in his suit. If he has 5 to 8 points but no long suit, responder may double. This double is not for penalties; it simply tells the opener that responder has 5 to 8 points. In addition, some partnerships use the negative double, followed by responder's bid of a new suit as the equivalent of a positive response.

If the opponents make a takeout double rather than an overcall, there are essentially two alternative means of coping with the double. One method is to pass with 0 to 7 points and four or more clubs, or to bid one diamond with 0 to 7 points with fewer than four clubs. All other responses have the same meaning they would have had if there had been no double. A redouble would show 8 or more points with two four card major suits.

An alternative method allows the responder to show a five-card suit with less than the values needed for a positive response. Using this method, the responder will bid freely with a five-card suit and 5 to 8 points. With a hand worth a positive response, he will redouble.

IMPOSSIBLE NEGATIVE

The Impossible Negative is a convention used by a PRECISION CLUB responder to describe a hand worth 8 or more high card points with 4-4-4-1 distribution. Over the one club opening bid the responder bids one diamond, as if he had less than an 8 point hand. However, over the opener's rebid, the responder will jump in a new suit or in notrump to show that he did not really mean his first bid. Hence the term "impossible" negative.

There are two methods by which the singleton can be shown. The simpler is for the responder to jump at his second turn in the suit of his singleton. This shows that he has four cards in each of the other suits. If responder's singleton is in the suit that the opener has rebid, responder jumps in notrump, to avoid giving the impression that he is raising the opener's suit. For example, suppose the responder held the following hand opposite a one club opening:

♠ K x x x   ♡ x   ◊ A Q x x   ♣ Q x x x

The auction could start

Opener	Responder
1 ♣	1 ◊
1 ♡	2 Notrump

or

Opener	Responder
1 ♣	1 ◊
1 ♠	3 ♡

After the responder's jump bid, opener should have a fair idea of where the hand should play. Subsequent bidding will be more or less natural.

An alternative way to show the singleton is for responder to jump in the suit below the singleton. Again, however, a jump to three of the suit bid naturally by opener is a natural raise; a jump to three notrump would show the impossible negative with a singleton in opener's suit. A jump to the suit below openers' suit, therefore, is used to show a singleton in the suit above opener's suit. For example, responder holds one of the following hands:

[A] ♠ A x x x   ♥ x   ♦ J x x x   ♣ K Q x x

[B] ♠ x   ♥ A x x x   ♦ J x x x   ♣ K Q x x

[C] ♠ K Q x x   ♥ J x x x   ♦ A x x x   ♣ x

and the auctions starts as follows:

Opener	Responder
1 ♣	1 ♦
1 ♠	

With Hand A, responder jumps to three diamonds over one spade, showing a singleton heart and four cards in each of the other suits. With Hand B, responder jumps to three notrump, showing a singleton spade. With Hand C, responder jumps to three hearts, showing a singleton in the suit ranking above opener's suit, i.e., clubs.

The advantage of jumping to the suit below the singleton is that the opener can easily make an asking bid by cue-bidding the singleton, to find out how many controls the responder has. For the type of control-showing sequences that are available, *see* UNUSUAL POSITIVE.

187

Unusual Positive

An alternative to the IMPOSSIBLE NEGATIVE for handling game-going 4-4-4-1 responding hands in the PRECISION CLUB system is called the Unusual Positive. It consists of an immediate jump to two hearts, two spades, three clubs or three diamonds to show a hand worth 8 or more points, with a singleton.

As with the Impossible Negative, there are two ways in which the singleton can be pinpointed. The simpler is for the jump to be made in the suit of the singleton. Thus responder's jump to two hearts would show a singleton heart; his jump to three clubs would show a singleton club; etc.

The more sophisticated way of pinpointing the singleton is for responder to jump in the suit below the singleton. Thus, responder's jump to two hearts would show a singleton spade; his jump to three clubs would show a singleton diamond; etc.

Use of either form of the Unusual Positive is, of course, incompatible with the use of these jumps to show long suits with 4 to 7 points.

When the Unusual Positive is used with responder jumping in the suit below the singleton, it enables the opener cheaply to ask responder how many controls he has by bidding the suit of the singleton. Responder shows his controls (ace = two controls, king = one control) in steps. The first step shows 0, 1 or 2 controls; the second step shows 3 controls, and so forth. Thus, in the auction

Opener	Responder
1 ♣	3 ◇
3 ♡	4 ♣

responder's three diamond bid showed a positive response with a singleton heart, and four cards in each of the other suits. Opener's three heart bid asked about controls, and responder's four club response, the third step, showed four controls.

188

PRECISION TRUMP ASKING BIDS

In the Precision system, if the responder makes a positive response and the opener makes a single raise of responder's suit, opener's raise is an Asking Bid. It asks the responder how good his trump suit is. The responder replies in steps, as follows:

First step = none of top three honors, any length

Second step = one of top three honors, five card suit

Third step = two of top three honors, five card suit

Fourth step = one of top three honors, six card suit

Fifth step = two of top three honors, six card suit

Sixth step = all three top honors, any length

Using this method, when opener uses the asking bid, and the responder has, for example, a six card spade suit headed by the ace and queen, the auction would start:

Opener	Responder
1 ♣	1 ♠
2 ♠	3 ♠

An alternative method is for the partnership to agree that responder will use a four-step series of responses, and will show only how many honors he has, not how long his suit is. Using this variation, the first step would show none of the top three honors; the second step would show one of the top three honors; the third step would show two of the top three honors; and the fourth step would show all three honors. If the opener is interested in how long responder's suit is, he can repeat the bid of responder's suit to ask that question. For example:

Opener	Responder
1 ♣	1 ♠
2 ♠	3 ◇
3 ♠	

Responder's three diamond bid shows two of the top three spade honors; opener's three spade rebid asks how long responder's suit is. Responder gives the answer in steps, using the first step to show five cards, the second step to show six cards, and so forth. An advantage of using this alternative method of responding to the trump asking bid is that often the opener is interested only in honor strength, not in length. This method simply uses less space, making it easier for the responder to get on to his next question.

PRECISION CONTROL ASKING BIDS

After the opener has made a trump asking bid, if he bids a new suit it asks the responder about his controls in the new suit. For example, in the auction

Opener	Responder
1 ♣	1 ♡
2 ♡	3 ♣
3 ◇	

opener has learned that responder has 8 or more points, with at least five hearts headed by two of the top three honors. Opener's three diamond rebid asks responder whether he has any sort of control of the diamond suit. Control could take the form of high cards or shortness. Responder answers in steps as follows:

First   step = no control (three or more small cards)

Second step = 3rd round control (queen or doubleton)

Third   step = 2nd round control (king or singleton)

Fourth step = 1st round control (ace or a void)

Fifth   step = 1st and 2nd round control (ace & king, or ace & queen)

With respect to opponent interference with Control Asking Bids, *see discussion under* PRECISION ACE ASKING BIDS.

PRECISION ACE-ASKING BIDS

Using standard Precision bidding, a jump shift by the opener after a positive response shows a solid suit with a 19 point hand. As a modification, the partnership could agree to use the jump shift by the opener as an ace-asking bid. To use this bid the opener will either have a solid suit, or a semi-solid suit, i.e., one that is missing one of the top three honors.

Using this method, the jump shift asks responder two questions: first, whether or not he has the missing trump honor, and second, whether or not he has any aces.

If the responder does not have the missing trump honor, and does not have an ace, he rebids the minimum number of notrump. If he has the missing trump honor but no side ace, he raises opener's suit. If he has one side ace, but not the missing trump honor, he makes a minimum bid in the suit in which he has the ace.

If the responder has two key cards, he must jump to show them, as follows. If he has the missing trump honor and a side suit ace, he jumps in the suit in which he has the ace. If he has two aces, but not the missing trump honor, he jumps in notrump. If he has the missing trump honor and two side aces, he jump raises the opener's suit.

For example, suppose the responder held

♠ A x x x x   ♥ J x x   ♦ x x   ♣ K x x

and the auction started

Opener	Responder
1 ♣	1 ♠
3 ♣	

responder's proper bid would be four spades, showing the ace of spades and the king of clubs.

Note that the opener may have a solid suit, and there may be no missing trump honor. In this event he will be seeking information only about the responder's aces, a fact that responder will not know until later.

After the responder has responded to the opener's ace-asking jump shift, if the opener rebids in a new suit he asks about responder's controls in that suit. Responder will show his controls in steps according to the same schedule used for CONTROL ASKING BIDS (see above).

When the Opponents Interfere

If the opponents overcall over an asking bid, the responder uses a double to show that he would have responded with the first step of the asking bid responses; he uses a pass to show that he would have responded with the second step. To show the third and subsequent steps the responder bids up the line, the cheapest suit over the overcall showing the third step, and so forth.

This method of coping with interference can be used over either the trump suit asking bids or the control asking bids. For example, suppose the bidding had gone

Opener	Responder
1 ♣	2 ♣
3 ♣	3 ♦
3 ♡	

and over the three heart control asking bid the opponent bids three spades. Responder would double with no heart control; he would pass with third round control; he would bid three no-trump with second round control, four clubs with first round control, and four diamonds with first and second round control.

In the above auction, if the opponent had overcalled three spades over the three club bid, which asked about responder's trumps, responder would have used the same method. He would double with none of the top three club honors, that being the first step he would have made without interference, or would pass with a five card suit headed by one of the top three honors. To show the third and succeeding steps, responder would bid up the line:

3 NT = a five card suit headed by two of the top three honors (3rd original step)

4 ♣ = a six card suit headed by one of the top three honors (4th original step)

4 ◇ = a six card suit headed by two of the top three honors (5th original step)

4 ♡ = all three top honors, any length (6th original step)

ROMAN CLUB

The Roman System is a system that attempts to define high card strength and overall distribution with almost every opening bid. There are opening bids that show balanced hands, opening bids that show hands containing long suits, opening bids that show specific two-suited hands, and opening bids that show three-suited hands.

Balanced hands, i.e., 4-4-3-2 or 4-3-3-3, are opened with either a forcing one club bid or with a notrump bid. The one notrump opening shows 17 to 20 points; the two notrump opening shows 23 to 24 points.

Three suited hands, i.e., 4-4-4-1 or 5-4-4-0, are opened with two of a minor suit. The two club opening shows 11 to 16 high card points. The two diamond opening shows 17 to 20 high card points. *See* ROMAN TWO CLUBS and ROMAN TWO DIAMONDS.

Hands with limited playing strength containing at least one long suit, i.e., five cards or more, are opened in a suit other than clubs. The openings of one diamond, one heart and one spade are natural *and forcing.* However, since the Roman system uses the canape style of bidding short suits before long suits, the opening bid of one diamond, one heart or one spade usually does not show the opener's long suit.

The high card strength of the opening one-bids other than one club is not limited nearly so much as it is in the Blue Team, Schenken and Precision Club systems. The one diamond, one heart and one spade openings may range from a meager 12 points to just under the strength of a forcing two bid. The opener's rebid serves to clarify the strength of his hand.

Negative Responses to One Diamond, One Heart or One Spade

The openings of one diamond, one heart and one spade are forcing on the responder for one round. The usual negative response is the bid of the next higher denomination. For example, a response of one heart to a one diamond opening, and a response of one notrump to a one spade opening are negative. In each instance the negative response shows less than 9 points and denies support for the suit the opener has bid.

If the opener rebids one notrump after the negative response, he shows 12 to 14 points with five or more cards in the "negative" suit. If the opener's long suit is the "negative" suit and he has 15 to 17 points, he bids two of that suit. If the opener has a long suit other than the "negative" suit, he bids the minimum number of his suit with 12 to 17 points, or jumps in it with 18 to 21 points.

In addition to the next-suit negative bid, the responder can also make a negative response by raising the opener's bid suit to the two level. The raise shows at least four-card trump support, a doubleton in a side suit, and less than 9 points.

Constructive Responses to One Diamond, One Heart or One Spade

Other responses fall into two categories: constructive responses and positive responses. With a hand worth 9 to 11 points, responder may make a constructive response by making a minimum bid in a suit other than the "negative" suit. If the responder's bid is to be at the two level, he must have at least 10 points. Constructive responses are forcing for one round, but are not forcing to game.

If the responder has 9 to 11 points and a one-suited hand,

he bids and rebids his long suit. With two suits, the responder's bids, like the opener's, are made in the canape style. Therefore, if the responder bids two suits, his second is usually longer than his first.

For example, if responder has the following hand opposite a one diamond opening

[A] ♠ K Q x x   ♥ A J x x x   ♦ x x   ♣ x x

he will respond one spade, showing, for the time being at least, a constructive response. After the opener's rebid, responder will show his heart suit at the minimum level. For example:

Opener	Responder
1 ♦	1 ♠
2 ♦	2 ♥

With a hand worth 9 to 11 points, the responder is not allowed to reverse, i.e., bid a higher ranking suit after bidding a lower ranking suit. Therefore, if instead of hand (A) above responder had

[B] ♠ K Q x x x   ♥ A J x x   ♦ x x   ♣ x x

he could not respond two hearts over one diamond and follow with a spade rebid. With hand (B), responder should simply bid and rebid spades:

Opener	Responder
1 ♦	1 ♠
2 ♦	2 ♠

As a general matter, the responder should be conservative

about making constructive responses. With hands that could create a rebid problem, he should tend to make an initial negative response, planning to bid aggressively at his next turn. For example, suppose opposite a one heart opening responder had

♠ K x x   ♥ A x x   ♦ Q x x x x   ♣ J x

If responder makes the constructive response of two diamonds and opener rebids three clubs (forcing for one round), the responder has no suitable rebid. If he rebids his straggly diamond suit, opener is likely to pass with a singleton; responder cannot take a preference to hearts, in which opener could well have just three cards; and a three notrump rebid could put the partnership on distinctly thin ice. Therefore, with such a hand responder does better to make a negative response first, and raise the opener or bid notrump later.

Positive Responses to One Diamond, One Heart or One Spade

If the responder has 12 or more points, he may make a positive response, forcing the partnership to game. Any notrump response, except one notrump over a one spade opening, is a positive response. One notrump in response to one diamond or one heart shows 12 to 15 points, with all unbid suits stopped. A two notrump response shows 16 to 18 points.

A jump raise of the opener's suit is also a positive response. Because of the canape style of bidding, the responder may not make a jump raise without at lease five cards in the suit opened.

Responder may also make a positive response by jump shifting into a long, strong suit of his own. With a hand worth a positive response but not suitable for notrump or a jump raise or a jump shift, the responder starts by bidding a new suit. He will make it clear at his next turn that this was not just a constructive response, by either reversing or jumping into a long suit. For example, with a hand such as

♠ K Q x x x   ♡ A Q x x   ◇ x x   ♣ Q x

in response to one diamond, responder would bid two hearts. At his next turn he would rebid spades:

Opener	Responder
1 ◇	2 ♡
3 ◇	3 ♠

Responder's three spade bid is a reverse, showing at least twelve points, and longer spades than hearts.

If responder's short suit outranks his long suit, his bidding first the short suit and then the long suit will not be a reverse. In these circumstances, to show a positive responder would make a jump rebid to show a positive response; responder jumps in his longer suit unless that would take him past three notrump, in which event he must jump to three notrump. With

♠ K Q x x   ♡ A Q x x x   ◇ Q x   ♣ x x

responder would respond one spade over the one diamond opening, and follow with a jump to three hearts:

Opener	Responder
1 ◇	1 ♠
2 ◇	3 ♡

After responder has made a constructive or positive response, opener's rebid will clarify the strength of his hand. If opener has 12 to 14 points and just one long suit, he will make the minimum rebid in that suit. This rebid is not forcing if responder has not made a positive response. If opener has 15 to 17 points with one long suit, he makes a jump rebid in his suit. If the responder has made a constructive response, the jump rebid is forcing to game.

If the opener rebids a second suit, that suit is at least five cards long, and his hand is worth 12 to 17 points. This bid of a second suit is forcing on the responder for one round.

Opening Bids of Two Hearts and Two Spades

Applying the canape principle, with two-suited hands, the Roman opener bids his shorter suit first. However, when his shorter suit is clubs, this method cannot be used. Therefore, the Roman system uses opening bids of two hearts and two spades to show 12 to 16 points with at least five cards in the major suit bid, together with a four- or five-card club suit. For example,

♠ A K x x x   ♡ K x x   ◇ x   ♣ K J x x

In response to the opening of two hearts or two spades, the responder may pass, or take a preference to clubs. He may also bid a new suit; such a bid is forcing for one round, and shows either a six-card or longer suit, or a hand worth a slam try. If the responders' hand is of the slam-try variety, he will later jump in clubs or in the opener's major suit. Responder normally will not bid a new suit that is only five cards long, since he has a way to find out whether or not the opener has three-card support for his suit.

A two notrump response to a two heart or two spade opening bid is artificial, and asks the opener to clarify his distribution. If the opener bids three clubs, he shows four clubs, five cards in his major suit, and doubletons in the unbid suits. If opener bids a new suit other than clubs at the three level, he shows three cards in that suit, four clubs, and five cards in the major suit he opened. For example, in the auction

Opener	Responder
2 ♡	2 Notrump
3 ♠	

opener shows 3-5-1-4 distribution. If the opener rebids three notrump over two notrump, he shows five cards in clubs and five in his major suit, with a doubleton and a singleton in the unbid suits. If the opener has five clubs and five of his major suit and a void in one of the other suits, his proper rebids are (a) four clubs holding three cards in the unbid major suit, or (b) four diamonds holding three diamonds. For example, opener's and responder's hands might be

(Opener)
♠ A K x x x   ♡ J x x   ◇ —   ♣ K Q x x x

(Responder)
♠ x x   ♡ A K x x x   ◇ K x x   ♣ J x x

The auction would go

Opener	Responder
2 ♠	2 Notrump
4 ♣	4 ♡

Over the two notrump response, if the opener simply rebids the major suit he has opened, e.g.,

Opener	Responder
2 ♡	2 Notrump
3 ♡	

he shows a six card major suit. He may have four or five clubs; if he rebids clubs after having rebid his major suit he shows a five card club suit.

One Notrump Opening and Responses

The opening bid of one notrump in the Roman system shows a balanced hand with 17 to 20 high card points. With a weak balanced hand, i.e., 0 to 5 points, responder may pass. With a weak unbalanced hand, responder may use GLADIATOR-type responses at the two level.

Holding 0 to 5 points and a five-card or longer suit, responder may respond two clubs to the notrump opening. The two club bid is a relay, forcing opener to rebid two diamonds. Opener is expected to pass any rebid by responder over the forced two diamond bid, but he may raise if he has 20 points and no worse than three-card support for responder's suit, headed by two of the top three honors. If opener's and responder's hands were

(Opener)
♠ K J x   ♡ A K x x   ◇ K x x   ♣ A x x

(Responder)
♠ Q x x x x x   ♡ x x   ◇ x x x   ♣ x x

the auction would be

Opener	Responder
1 Notrump	2 ♣
2 ♢	2 ♠
Pass	

Because the two club bid is used as a relay, a two diamond response to the one notrump opening is used as Stayman, and is forcing to game. Opener rebids a four card major suit if he has one, or bids two notrump if he has none.

If responder has 6 or 7 points and a balanced hand he may invite game by raising to two notrump. If opener elects to accept the invitation, he may either bid three notrump directly, or he may bid three clubs to learn whether or not responder has a four card major suit. However, special responses to the three club inquiry are used in order to allow opener, with his much stronger hand, to be the declarer. If responder has no four-card major suit, he rebids three notrump. If he has a four-card major suit, he bids the suit *below* his four card major. If he has both four hearts and four spades, he rebids three diamonds. Thus the auction could go

Opener	Responder
1 Notrump	2 Notrump
3 ♣	3 ♡
4 ♠	Pass

Responder's three heart rebid promised a four card spade suit, but denied a four card heart suit. If responder had both four card major suits and opener had four spades, the auction could have gone

Opener	*Responder*
1 Notrump	2 Notrump
3 ♣	3 ◇
3 ♠	4 ♠

Opposite the one notrump opening, if responder has a six-card major suit headed by no better than the ace and jack, but no worse than the king and jack, he may jump to three of his suit. After this response bid opener may place the final contract, either by passing, or by raising responder's suit, or by bidding three notrump.

If responder has better than 7 points and has a five-card or longer suit, he may force to game by bidding two hearts, two spades, three clubs or three diamonds. Over these responses opener is required to show his strength and the quality of his support for responder's suit, by the following four steps:

First step = minimum hand, poor support

Second step = minimum hand, good support

Third step = maximum hand, poor support

Fourth step = maximum hand, good support

In this context, good support means no worse than four small cards or three cards headed by the queen.

After opener has shown his strength and his trump support, responder may sign off in three notrump or in game in his suit. Alternatively, responder may bid a new suit to ask about opener's support for that suit. Opener uses a two-step schedule of responses; the first step shows poor support; the second step shows good support. For example, in the auction

Opener	*Responder*
1 Notrump	2 ♠
3 ♢	3 ♡
3 ♠	3 Notrump

opener's three diamond bid showed a maximum one notrump opening, but poor support for responder's spade suit. Responder three heart bid asked about opener's heart holding; opener's three spade bid, the first step, showed that his support for hearts was also poor. Opener's and responder's hands might be

(Opener)
♠ A x   ♡ x x x   ♢ A K Q x   ♣ A K x x

(Responder)
♠ K Q x x x   ♡ K x x x x   ♢ J x   ♣ x

Jumps to four hearts or four spades by responder over the one notrump opening are normal sign offs, showing a long suit and no interest in slam.

If responder has interest in slam and no five-card suit to bid, he may elect to show opener his point count. Thus responder's jumps to four clubs, four diamonds, and to any bid from four notrump through five notrump show responder's exact number of high card points as follows:

$$4 ♣ = 14 \text{ points}$$

$$4 ♢ = 15 \text{ points}$$

$$4 NT = 16 \text{ points}$$

$$5 ♣ = 17 \text{ points}$$

$$5 \diamondsuit = 18 \text{ points}$$
$$5 \heartsuit = 19 \text{ points}$$
$$5 \spadesuit = 20 \text{ points}$$
$$5 \text{ NT} = 21 \text{ points}$$

Over responder's point count showing response, opener may sign off with a minimum bid in notrump, or he may bid a slam. Alternatively, opener may bid his lower ranking four card suit, looking for a 4-4 fit in which to play slam. For example, if opener's and responder's hands were

(Opener.)
♠ K J x   ♡ A Q x x   ◇ K Q x x   ♣ A J

(Responder)
♠ A Q x   ♡ K J x x   ◇ A x   ♣ K x x x

the bidding would go

Opener	Responder
1 Notrump	5 ♣
5 ◇	5 ♡
7 ♡	

Responder's five club response showed 17 high card points. Since opener had 20 points, he had visions of a grand slam, especially if a 4-4 fit could be found.

One Club Opening

A forcing opening bid of one club in the Roman system may be made with any of four types of hands. It may show 12 to 16 points with even distribution, specifically 4-3-3-3 or 4-4-3-2. If the opener has this hand he will usually rebid a major suit or no-trump; or, if responder has made a constructive response, opener may raise responder's suit if he has four card support.

One club may also be opened with a balanced hand worth 21 to 22 points or 25 to 26 points. If opener has one of these hands, his rebid will be a jump in notrump.

The one club opening may also be used with an unbalanced hand of game-forcing strength. If opener has this hand he will make a jump rebid, or other non-minimum rebid, in his suit. One club may also be opened with a two-suited hand that includes at least four clubs, with 17 to 20 points. If opener has this hand, he will rebid clubs.

A one diamond response to one club is negative. This response shows less than 8 high card points, although it may be made with more than 8 points when responder has no four-card major suit and no five-card minor suit.

Constructive Responses to One Club

With a hand worth 8 to 11 points, the responder may make a constructive response. Constructive responses are minimum responses in suits.

When deciding what suit to bid, the responder should prefer a four card major suit to a longer minor suit. For example, with

♠ K x x x ♡ x ◇ A J x x x ♣ J x x

responder would bid one spade over a one club opening, planning to bid diamonds later—a canape series of bids.

If responder has two four card major suits, he should bid

207

one heart, leaving opener room to rebid one spade. If responder has two five-card major suits, he should bid hearts first and then bid spades. With five cards in each minor suit, responder should bid diamonds first and then bid clubs. With a five-card major suit and a five-card minor suit, responder should simply bid and rebid his major suit.

For example, if responder holds

♠ K Q x x x   ♡ x x   ◇ A x x x x   ♣ x

the bidding might go

Opener	Responder
1 ♣	1 ♠
1 Notrump	2 ♠

With the above hand, responder systemically has no way to show his diamond suit without distorting either his strength or his distribution. If he were to respond one spade and follow with a diamond rebid, he would show longer diamonds than spades; if he were to respond two diamonds and follow with a spade rebid, he would show a hand worth a positive response, i.e., more than 12 points.

If responder has no four-card major suit in which to respond to the one club opening, he may bid a minor suit if he has at least 9 points and at least five cards in his suit. Thus, with a hand such as

♠ K x x   ♡ J x x   ◇ x x x   ♣ A Q x x

responder is forced to temporize with a one diamond "negative" response. After the auction has started 1 ♣ — 2 ♣, or 1 ♣ — 2 ◇, therefore, opener can rely on responder to have either 9 points and five cards in the suit bid, or the values for a positive response.

Positive Responses to One Club

If responder has 12 points or more, he may make a positive response. The immediately positive responses are one notrump, two notrump, two hearts and two spades. The notrump responses show balanced or nearly balanced distribution (4-3-3-3, or 4-4-3-2 or 5-3-3-2). One notrump shows 12 to 15 points; two notrump shows 16 or more points.

The response of two hearts or two spades promises a five-card or longer suit; unless the response is followed by a bid of the other major suit, it promises two of the top three honors. For example, holding

♠ J x x   ♡ A Q x x x   ◇ K x x   ♣ A x

responder would jump to two hearts over the one club opening.

If responder has a hand worth a positive response with five cards in each major suit, he responds by jumping in the stronger major and then bidding the other major. For example, if responder has

♠ K x x x x   ♡ K Q x x x   ◇ x   ♣ A x

he will jump to two hearts over one club, and rebid his spade suit.

If responder has five cards in each minor suit, he bids clubs first and then rebids diamonds. Bidding clubs first and then diamonds is the reverse of what responder does with both five-card minor suits and a merely constructive hand.

If responder has a five-card major suit and a five-card minor suit, he bids the minor suit first and then bids his major suit. Initially this sequence is ambiguous because it can be used to show a longer major suit than minor suit; however, the extra minor suit card can be shown later.

If the responder has a five-card or longer suit and a four-card suit, he first responds in the short suit, and then rebids the longer suit. If this short suit ranks higher than his long suit, he will have to make a jump rebid in the long suit to show that his response was positive. Indeed, with respect to any positive response that begins other than with a notrump bid or a jump to two of a major suit, responder's first response is ambiguous; it could be either positive or constructive. Responder's rebid will clarify the strength of his hand. With a positive response, responder's rebid will be either a reverse bid or a jump.

Suppose responder has one of the following hands opposite the one club opening:

[A] ♠ K Q x x x   ♡ A x x   ◇ x   ♣ A x x x

[B] ♠ K Q x x x   ♡ A x   ◇ x   ♣ A x x x x

[C] ♠ K Q x x   ♡ A x x x x   ◇ A x x   ♣ x

With Hand A, responder would bid two clubs, his short suit, and then rebid spades, his long suit. The auction might start

Opener	Responder
1 ♣	2 ♣
2 ◇	2 ♠

Similarly with Hand B, responder would bid two clubs and then rebid his spade suit. In this case responder has an extra club, but his first two bids would be the same as with Hand A.

With Hand C, responder would start with a one spade bid, and then rebid hearts. However, since his short suit outranks his long suit, the non-jump rebid of hearts would show a constructive hand rather than a positive hand; therefore, responder must jump rebid hearts to show his strength. The auction might start

Opener	Responder
1 ♣	1 ♠
1 Notrump	3 ♡

Preemptive Responses to One Club

In addition to the routine negative, constructive and positive responses described above, the responder is allowed to make certain descriptive preemptive responses. These include unencouraging jumps to four of a major suit, weak jumps to three of a major suit or four of a minor suit, and somewhat constructive jumps to three of a minor suit.

If responder holds a six- or seven-card major suit headed by the ace and king, or the king, queen and jack, and has a modicum of outside values, he may jump to four of his suit. For example, holding

[A] ♠ Q x   ♡ K Q J x x x x   ◊ x   ♣ x x x

responder would jump to four hearts over the one club opening.

If responder holds a six- or seven-card club or diamond suit headed by no worse than the ace, king and jack, he may jump to three of his suit. For example, with

[B] ♠ x x   ♡ x x x   ◊ x x   ♣ A K Q x x x

responder would jump to three clubs over the one club opening. Opener would use his best judgment in setting the final contract.

If responder has a weaker hand and a weaker suit than those in (A) and (B) above, he may jump to three hearts, three spades, four clubs or four diamonds. For example, responder might hold

[C] ♠ K J x x x x x   ♡ x   ◇ x x   ♣ x x x

or

[D] ♠ x   ♡ J x x   ◇ K Q 10 x x x x   ♣ x x

With Hand C responder would jump to three spades over the one club opening. With Hand D responder would jump to four diamonds. If opener has a hand such as

♠ A x x   ♡ A x x x   ◇ x x   ♣ A Q x x

he would bid four spades over responder's three spade bid (Hand C), but would pass responder's jump to four diamonds (Hand D).

Rebids When the One Club Opener Has a Minimum Hand Opposite a Negative Response

When the response to the one club opening has been the one diamond negative, opener's first aim with a minimum one club opening (12 to 16 points) is to find a safe home at the one level. Opener therefore bids a four-card major suit if he has one; if he has four cards in both major suits, he rebids one heart. If opener has no four card major suit, he rebids one heart if he has a three-card heart suit; only as a last resort does he rebid one notrump. Thus a one notrump rebid after a one diamond response shows specifically three spades, two hearts, four clubs and four diamonds.

After having made a negative response, responder may pass opener's rebid if he has a very poor hand; however, even with a poor hand, if he has a four-card spade suit that he can show at the one level, he should do so.

If responder has any significant values, he should bid as strongly as seems appropriate at his second turn, since opener is likely to pass any unencouraging sounding rebid. For example, if responder has a hand such as

♠ x   ♡ A 10 9 x x   ◇ Q x x   ♣ x x x x

and the bidding has started

Opener	Responder
1 ♣	1 ◇
1 ♡	

responder should show his maximum negative pointcount, and his good trump support and distribution by jumping to three hearts.

Rebids When the One Club Opener Has a Minimum Hand Opposite a Constructive Response

When opener has a 12 to 16 point balanced hand opposite a constructive response, his first rebid shows whether he has the top (15 to 16) or the bottom (12 to 14) of his range. The rebid may also show one of opener's four card suits. A 15 to 16 point rebid will force the partnership at least to the two notrump level, and frequently the partnership will reach game after such a rebid, either because the hands fit well, or because responder makes a rebid that reveals extra values.

If opener makes a simple raise of responder's suit, he shows a 12 to 14 point hand. If responder's suit was a major, the raise promises four card support; if responder's suit is a minor, which normally promises a five card suit, opener may raise with three card support. If opener has support for responder's suit but has 15 to 16 points, he may not raise immediately, but must temporize with a non-minimum rebid before raising.

If opener rebids one notrump over the constructive response of one heart or one spade, he shows 12 to 14 points; however, if he rebids two notrump over a response of two clubs or two diamonds, he shows 15 to 16 points. If opener rebids a new suit, he shows 15 to 16 points if he has bypassed one notrump, but a minimum if he has not. For example,

(A) *Opener*   *Responder*
        1 ♣   1 ♠
        2 ♦

(B) *Opener*   *Responder*
        1 ♣   2 ♣
        2 ♦

In auction (A), opener's two diamond bid shows 15 to 16 points. Opener might have a hand such as

[C] ♠ Q x   ♡ A K x x   ◇ A Q x x   ♣ x x x
or
[D] ♠ A Q x x   ♡ x x   ◇ Q x x x   ♣ A K x

With Hand D, opener could not raise responder's spade suit because his hand is too strong; therefore he temporized with a two diamond bid, bypassing one notrump.

In auction (B), opener's two diamond bid showed a 12 to 14 point hand, since he did not bypass one notrump in making his rebid. In order to show a maximum hand in auction (B), opener would have had to rebid two notrump.

After opener has clarified his point count opposite a constructive response, the bidding proceeds naturally.

Rebids When the One Club Opener Has a Minimum Hand Opposite a Positive Response

There are three immediately positive types of responses: one notrump, showing a balanced 12 to 15 point hand; two notrump, showing a balanced hand worth more than 15 points; and a jump to two of a major suit, showing a five-card or longer suit headed by two of the top three honors. Opener has a special set of rebids for each of these responses.

After a one notrump response, opener should raise to two notrump with a maximum (15 to 16 points), or rebid a four card suit, preferably a major suit, with a minimum hand. If opener has bid a suit to show 12 to 14 points, responder may rebid two notrump if he has 12 points, giving opener the opportunity to pass if he too has only 12 points. This is the only rebid by responder that can be passed.

If opener has shown a maximum hand by raising to two notrump, responder may bid three clubs as a Stayman-type inquiry for a major suit fit, or he may bid a five-card suit at the three level. For example, in the auction

Opener	Responder
1 ♣	1 Notrump
2 Notrump	3 ♠
4 ♠	

opener has shown 15 to 16 points with his two notrump rebid.

Responder's three spade bid showed a five-card spade suit, and opener's raise to game showed three- or four-card support. Opener might have a hand such as

♠ K x x ♥ A J x x ♦ x x ♣ A K x x

If responder's positive response to the one club opening was two notrump, opener must rebid to show his point count as follows:

$$3 \clubsuit = 12 \text{ to } 13 \text{ points}$$
$$3 \diamondsuit = 14 \text{ points}$$
$$3 \heartsuit = 15 \text{ points}$$
$$3 \spadesuit = 16 \text{ points}$$

After learning opener's point count, responder may sign off in three notrump. Over a three club or three diamond bid by opener, responder may bid three hearts or three spades in search of a major suit fit. Or, over any of opener's point count showing rebids, responder may bid four clubs, a bid that shows slam interest, and asks opener to bid his lower ranking four card suit. Opener and responder thus bid their suits up the line in search of a 4-4 fit.

If opener's and responder's hands were, for example, as follows

(Opener)
♠ A Q ♥ K x x x ♦ Q J x ♣ K x x x

(Responder)
♠ J x   ♡ A Q x x   ◇ A 10 x x   ♣ A Q x

the bidding could go

Opener	Responder
1 ♣	2 Notrump
3 ♡	4 ♣
4 ♡	6 ♡

Opener's three heart rebid showed precisely 15 points; responder, with his good controls, was interested in slam if a 4-4 fit could be found, despite having only 17 points. When opener showed a four-card heart suit, responder bid the slam.

If the positive response to the one club opening was a jump to two hearts or two spades, opener is required to rebid in steps to show his range and the quality of his support for responder's suit as follows:

First   step = minimum hand, poor support

Second step = minimum hand, good support

Third   step = maximum hand, poor support

Fourth step = maximum hand, good support

Over opener's rebid, responder should be able to set the final contract. For example, if opener's and responder's hands were

(Opener)
♠ K x x   ♡ K J x x   ◇ x x x   ♣ A Q x

(Responder)

♠ A Q x x x   ♡ A x   ◇ K Q x   ♣ J x x

the bidding could go

Opener	Responder
1 ♣	2 ♠
3 ♣	4 ♠

Opener's three club rebid, the second step, showed a minimum hand with good spade support. Responder gave up his hopes of a slam on account of opener's minimum, and bid the game in spades rather than notrump based on opener's announced good trump support.

Rebids When the One Club Opener Has a Strong Balanced Hand

When opener has bid one club with a balanced hand worth 21 to 22 or 25 to 26 points, he must jump in notrump over his partner's response. If responder has bid a negative one diamond in response to the one club opening, opener jumps to two notrump with 21 to 22 high card points, or jumps to three notrump with 25 to 26 high card points.

After opener's jump to two notrump over one diamond, if responder has 0 to 3 points, he should pass if he has a balanced hand, or bid three diamonds, three hearts or three spades if he has length in one of those suits. Such a bid by responder is not forcing, but opener may raise if he has a maximum hand and strong support for the suit. A three club bid by responder is a Stayman inquiry for the major suits. It promises 4 to 8 points, and is forcing to game.

After opener's jump to three notrump over one diamond, showing 25 to 26 points, responder may bid game in a long major suit if he has one, or he may bid four clubs as Stayman. Or, if responder has 7 to 8 points, he may try for slam by raising to four notrump. This bid asks opener to bid his lower ranking four card suit, following which the partnership bids its four-card suits up the line in search of a 4-4 fit in which to play a slam.

If the response to the one club opening was constructive, and opener has the strong balanced hand, he makes a single jump in notrump, regardless of whether he has 21 to 22 points, or 25 to 26 points. Thus, over the constructive response of one heart or one spade, opener will rebid two notrump—the partnership is of course forced to game. Over the constructive response of two clubs or two diamonds, opener will jump to three notrump.

After opener's jump rebid in notrump following the constructive response, responder is expected to bid his long suit—whether it be the suit of his initial response or another suit. Over any suit bid by responder, opener must clarify his strength and show his support for the suit responder has just bid. Opener rebids in steps as follows:

First   step = minimum hand (21 to 22), poor support

Second step = minimum hand, good support

Third   step = maximum hand (25 to 26), poor support

Fourth step = maximum hand, good support

If responder thereafter bids a new suit, opener uses a two-step schedule of replies to describe his support for responder's new suit.

Opener and responder might have the following hands:

(Opener)
♠ K Q x   ♡ A K Q x   ◇ A K x x   ♣ A x

(Responder)
♠ A x x x   ♡ x x   ◇ x x   ♣ K Q x x x

The bidding might proceed as follows:

Opener	Responder
1 ♣	1 ♠
2 Notrump	3 ♣
3 ♠	4 ♠
5 ♣	6 ♠
6 Notrump	

With his constructive hand, responder starts by bidding his four-card major suit in response to one club, and over the two no-trump rebid he shows his long suit to find out opener's point count and his club support. Opener's three spade rebid, the third step, showed a maximum point count and poor club support. Hoping to find opener with a four card spade suit, responder bid four spades; opener's five club bid, the second step, showed good spade support. Responder could then jump to six spades, knowing that he had shown only a four-card spade suit by bidding first spades and then clubs. If opener had had four spades he would have passed six spades; as it was, he corrected to six notrump.

Rebids When the One Club Opener Has a Strong Unbalanced Hand

To show a strong unbalanced hand after opening one club, opener must rebid a suit; after a constructive or positive response, he must jump in his suit to show such a hand; after a negative response, any suit rebid at the two level shows such a hand. For example:

(A) *Opener*   *Responder*
     1 ♣   1 ♠
     3 ♡

(B) *Opener*   *Responder*
     1 ♣   1 ♡
     2 ♠

(C) *Opener*   *Responder*
     1 ♣   1 ♢
     2 ♠

(D) *Opener*   *Responder*
     1 ♣   1 ♢
     2 ♢

In auction (A), opener's jump to three hearts shows a hand similar to a traditional forcing two-bid. In auctions (B) and (C), opener's jumps to two spades show the same type of hand as in auction (A). In auction (D), even though opener did not jump, his two diamond bid shows the same type of strong hand, since with a 12 to 16 point type hand, opener is not allowed to go to the two level over a one diamond response.

After a strong suit rebid by opener over any type of response, responder is required to show his support for opener's suit in a series of nine steps, as follows:

First   step = void or small singleton

Second step = two or three small cards

Third   step = singleton ace, king or queen

Fourth   step = two or three cards headed by the ace, king or queen

Fifth   step = four small cards

Sixth   step = four cards headed by the ace, king or queen

Seventh step = three cards headed by two of the top three honors

Eighth step = four cards headed by two of the top three honors

Ninth   step = ace, king and queen

For these purposes the jack is considered a small card. In the auction

Opener	Responder
1 ♣	1 ♡
2 ♠	3 ♠

responder's three spade bid shows that he has four small spades. His hand might be

♠ J 10 x x   ♡ A Q x x   ◇ Q x   ♣ x x x

After responder has shown his support for opener's first bid suit, opener may make either of two further asking bids, depending on whether he bids a higher or lower ranking suit. If he rebids a second suit that ranks higher than his first suit, opener asks responder to show his support for the second suit in the same nine-step series just used. If opener instead bids a second suit that ranks lower than his first suit, he asks responder to show what control he has of the new suit, using a five-step schedule as follows:

First step = no first or second round control

Second step = singleton

Third step = void

Fourth step = king

Fifth step = ace

If opener has two long suits and he wants to know whether or not responder has support for either of them, he must take care to bid his lower suit first. If he bids the higher suit first, his rebid of the lower suit will get him information about responder's control of the suit rather than his support for it.

Consider the following auctions:

(E)	Opener	Responder
	1 ♣	1 ♡
	2 ♠	3 ♡
	4 ◇	

(F)	Opener	Responder
	1 ♣	1 ♡
	3 ♣	3 ◇
	3 ♠	

In auction (E), opener's two spade rebid forces responder to show his spade support; responder's three heart bid shows the ace, king or queen of spades, doubleton or tripleton. Opener's rebid of four diamonds, a lower ranking suit than his first suit, asks about responder's control of diamonds. Opener might have a hand such as

♠ A K 10 x x x x   ♥ A K Q x   ♦ A x   ♣ —

In auction (F), opener's three club bid asked about responder's club support, and responder's three diamond bid showed a singleton or void in clubs. Opener's rebid of three spades asked about spade support. Opener might have a hand such as

♠ A K Q 10 x x   ♥ A K   ♦ —   ♣ K Q J x x

If responder bids three notrump, showing a singleton or void in spades, opener will sign off in four spades.

When the Opponents Interfere

If an opponent makes a takeout double over the one club opening, responder has two ways to show that he would have made a negative response. With less than 8 points and three or more clubs, the responder passes; if the next hand also passes, opener will pass if he has a four-card club suit. If opener has fewer than four clubs, he will seek another resting place, by redoubling with a minimum hand, or by bidding one diamond with a maximum. If the responder has less than 8 points and fewer than three clubs, he will redouble the double, asking the opener to find another suit.

Over the double, a response of one diamond now becomes a constructive response. All other minimum suit responses are constructive, as they would have been without the double. After interference, the constructive response is not forcing, and any rebid by the opener shows a maximum.

With a hand worth a positive response, responder may bid one notrump, two notrump, two hearts or two spades if that is what he would have done had there been no double. In addition, responder may make a positive response by jumping to two diamonds if he has at least a five-card diamond suit headed by two of the top three honors.

With a hand worth a positive response that does not fit any of these specialized responses, the responder must pass, planning to bid later, or to double the opponents for penalties.

If the opponent overcalls over one club instead of doubling, responder's pass is the only negative call. Responder may make any constructive bid at the one or two level, but he should not go to the three level without a strong hand. For example

North	East	South	West
1 ♣	2 ♠	3 ◇	

South's three diamond bid shows a positive response, not a constructive one. As when the interference has been a double, the opener may pass a constructive response if he has a minimum.

When responder has a strong enough hand to make a positive response he has four choices. If he has four good cards in the suit of the overcall, he can double for penalties. If he has a five card suit he may bid it at the three level, jumping if necessary. If he has no five card suit he can bid notrump with a stopper in the overcaller's suit (the minimum number of notrump with 12 to 15, or jump in notrump with 16 or more). If responder has no five card suit and no stopper in the opponent's suit, he may make a cue-bid, asking the opener to bid notrump if he has a stopper.

LITTLE ROMAN CLUB (Arno)

The Little Roman Club System, also called Arno, is similar to the Roman Club system, especially in its two-level opening bids. In the Little Roman System, all one-level openings, including one notrump, are forcing. The opening bid and responding style is canape.

One Club Opening

A forcing one club opening may be made on either of two types of hands. It may show a balanced hand with 12 to 16 points, or a one-suited or two-suited hand worth 17 to 20 points. If opener has a one-suiter, that suit is clubs; if he has a two-suiter, the shorter of the two is clubs.

A response of one diamond is negative, showing less than 10 points. If the opener rebids at the one level he shows a 12 to 16 point balanced hand.

Responses of one heart and one spade are positive, but not forcing to game. While natural, these responses may be made on as few as three cards, with a longer suit held in reserve. After the one heart or one spade response, if opener has a minimum hand he will raise with four-card support, or rebid one notrump if he lacks four-card support. For example, if opener's and responder's hands were

(Opener)
♠ K Q x   ♡ J x x   ◇ A x x   ♣ A x x x

(Responder)
♠ J x   ♡ A Q x   ◇ K Q x x x   ♣ x x x

the auction would go

Opener	Responder
1 ♣	1 ♡
1 Notrump	2 ◇
3 Notrump	

Having a maximum for his one notrump rebid and a fit for diamonds, opener may jump to three notrump over the two diamond bid. If he had had only 12 points, he would have rebid just two notrump.

If opener has 15 or 16 points, his automatic rebid is two clubs. The two club rebid does not promise length in clubs, but merely shows opener's point count. For example, if opener and responder had

(Opener)
♠ K Q x x   ♡ K x x x   ◇ A x x   ♣ A x

(Responder)
♠ J x   ♡ A Q x x   ◇ K Q x x x   ♣ x x

the bidding could go

Opener	Responder
1 ♣	1 ♡
2 ♣	2 ◇
2 ♡	4 ♡

Opener cannot raise responder's heart suit immediately, since that would show 12 to 14 points, and opener has 16. He therefore bids two clubs first, to show his maximum, then supports hearts. Since responder has four hearts, rather than the three

227

he might have, and since he is not interested in slam even opposite a 16 point hand, he jumps to four hearts.

A response of two clubs or two diamonds over the one club opening is also positive, but again, not forcing to game. These responses also may be made on a three-card suit. If opener has 12 to 14 points he rebids a suit at the two level, even a three-card suit if necessary. If he has 15 or 16 points he rebids two notrump.

A one notrump response to one club shows 12 or more points and a balanced hand. This response is forcing to game. If opener has 12 or 13 points, he rebids a suit at the two level. If he has 14 to 16 points he raises to two notrump.

Jumps to two hearts, two spades, three clubs or three diamonds over one club show a long suit, and are forcing to game. These jumps ask opener to describe his strength and his support for opener's suit using one of the following four steps:

First   step = minimum hand, poor support

Second step = minimum hand, good support

Third   step = maximum hand, poor support

Fourth step = maximum hand, good support

If opener has a one-suited or two-suited hand with 17 to 20 points, he must rebid his longest suit one level higher than he would to show a 12 to 16 point hand. For example

Opener	Responder
1 ♣	1 ♡
3 ♣	

With a long club suit opener rebids three clubs; a two club bid would not have given any information with respect to opener's club suit, but would instead have promised 15 to 16 points in a balanced hand.

Openings of One Diamond, One Heart and One Spade

Openings of one diamond, one heart and one spade show 12 to 20 points, and are natural and forcing. The style is strongly canape, and the opening bid may be made in a three-card suit if the hand is worth 15 or more points.

A response in the next higher denomination over a one diamond, one heart or one spade opening is negative, showing 0 to 9 points. Thus a one heart response to a one diamond opening is negative, as is a one notrump response to a one spade opening.

All other suit responses are natural, and may be made on three card suits. A one notrump response to one diamond or one heart shows a balanced hand with 12 or more points. This response is forcing to game.

If opener has a 12 to 16 point hand, he makes a minimum rebid in his long suit. A rebid of one notrump after the negative response of one spade shows that opener has a five card spade suit.

If the one diamond opening is followed by a one notrump rebid by opener, it shows a balanced hand worth 17 to 20 high card points. After the notrump rebid, if responder has made the one heart negative response, a two club bid by responder is a relay, requiring the opener to bid two diamonds and to pass any rebid responder makes thereafter. For example:

Opener	Responder
1 ◇	1 ♡
1 Notrump	2 ♣
2 ◇	2 ♡
Pass	

Forcing One Notrump Opening

A one notrump opening shows either a balanced hand worth 21 to 24 points, or an unbalanced game-going hand. The one notrump opening is forcing. Any rebid by the opener other than in notrump shows the unbalanced hand and is forcing to game.

In response to the one notrump opening, the responder shows how many aces he has, Blackwood style:

$$2 \clubsuit = 0 \text{ aces}$$

$$2 \diamondsuit = 1 \text{ ace}$$

$$2 \heartsuit = 2 \text{ aces}$$

$$2 \spadesuit = 3 \text{ aces}$$

If opener has a balanced hand with 21 to 24 points he will rebid two notrump. Over two notrump, responder may bid three clubs as Stayman. Opener will rebid a four card major suit if he has one, or bid three diamonds if he has no four card major, or will bid three notrump if he has four cards in each major.

If responder rebids three diamonds over the opener's two notrump rebid, he asks opener about his point count. Opener rebids three hearts with 21 to 22 points, or three spades with 23 to 24. For example, opener's and responder's hands might be

(Opener)
♠ K Q x x   ♡ A K x   ◇ A K x   ♣ Q J x

(Responder)
♠ A x x   ♡ x x x   ◇ Q x x   ♣ A x x x

The bidding could go

Opener	Responder
1 Notrump	2 ♡
2 Notrump	3 ◇
3 ♡	3 Notrump

The two heart response showed two aces, but when opener rebid notrump, responder took control of the hand. His three diamond bid asked opener if he had a maximum or a minimum; opener's three heart bid showed 21 to 22 points. Responder therefore settled for three notrump.

After responder has shown his aces in response to the one notrump opening, if opener has an unbalanced hand he will rebid a suit. His bids will follow canape principle of bidding short suits before long suits. For example:

(Opener)
♠ K Q x x ♡ A K ◇ A K Q J x x ♣ x

(Responder)
♠ J x x x x ♡ Q x x ◇ x x ♣ A x x

With the partnership holding these hands the bidding could proceed

Opener	Responder
1 Notrump	2 ◇
2 ♠	3 ♣
3 ◇	3 ♠
6 ♠	

PRO SYSTEM
(Pattern Relay Organized System)

The Pattern Relay Organized, or PRO, system is a relatively natural bidding method that is designed principally to allow the stronger hand on any given deal is to take control of the auction and learn about his partner's strength and distribution. The PRO system uses only a few artificial conventions, although it uses several non-standard treatments.

Among the conventions used by the PRO system are a forcing one club opening bid, a virtually game-forcing one no-trump response to a major suit opening, splinter bids, and the CLARAC slam try. The PRO system is devoted to auctions that do not involve game-forcing openings.

The Relay Principle

Using standard methods, unless opener has started with a strong two-bid type of opening with specialized responses, both opener and responder attempt to describe their strength and distribution as they search for the best contract. The PRO system allows the stronger hand to take control by making non-descriptive, information gathering "relay" bids. The relay is used only by the stronger hand, and only as a rebid; the opening bid or initial response is never a relay.

When used by the responder, the relay is the cheapest new suit rebid that the responder can make when his initial response has not limited his hand. For example, in the auction

(A)	*Opener*	*Responder*
	1 ♣	1 ♠
	2 ♣	2 ◇

responder's one spade response is unlimited; therefore his two diamond bid over two clubs is a relay, asking opener to describe his hand further.

Similarly, in auctions in which responder's initial bid may have limited his hand, opener can sometimes use a non-descriptive type of bid that is designed to get more information from responder.

The major advantage of these relay bids is that they create a forcing situation at a low level of the auction, so that slam prospects may be assessed without getting the partnership out of its depth. In auction (A), for example, the partnership can start its slam investigations at the two level.

A second advantage is that when a forcing relay is available and some other non-jump bid is used instead, the latter bid is logically limited and non-forcing. For example, in the auction

Opener	Responder
1 ◇	1 ♡
2 ◇	3 ♣

responder's one heart response has not limited his hand; he could therefore have bid two hearts over two diamonds as a relay to create a forcing auction. Since he chose instead to bid three clubs, his bid was not forcing. If opener and responder hold, for example

(Opener)
♠ A 10 x   ♡ Q   ◇ A Q x x x x   ♣ J x x

(Responder)
♠ Q J x   ♡ A x x x x   ◇ —   ♣ K x x x

233

opener will pass three clubs, which may be the partnership's last makeable contract.

One Club Opening

The one club opening is forcing, and may be made with two types of hands. One club may be opened with an average hand with a club suit. If opener has this type of hand he will rebid clubs, or raise a suit bid by the responder.

One club may also be opened with a balanced hand worth 17 to 20 high card points. This hand may not include a five card suit other than clubs. If opener has this type of hand he will rebid notrump or a new major suit.

The negative response to the one club opening is one diamond. The one diamond response shows 0 to 6 points. Over the one diamond response opener may bid a four-card major suit if he has one, attempting to find a safe home at the one level.

Responses of one heart and one spade to the one club opening are constructive. If opener rebids one notrump, showing 17 to 20 points, the partnership is forced to game. Over the one notrump rebid, responder may bid two clubs as Stayman.

Opening Bids Other Than One Club

Opening bids are divided into three classes, according to strength. Minimum hands are those worth 13 points or less; intermediate hands are worth 14 to 16 points; strong hands are worth 17 to 20 points.

With minimum hands, the PRO system recommends opening in the highest ranking four-card suit, even if the hand contains a longer lower ranking suit. Thus, opener might hold

[A] ♠ A Q J x   ♡ x x   ◇ J x x x   ♣ K J x

or

[B] ♠ K Q x x   ♡ x   ◇ A Q x x x   ♣ J x x

Both Hand A and Hand B should be opened one spade. Opener shows a minimum hand by rebidding one notrump (unless he has opened one club), or rebidding a lower ranking suit, other than clubs, or making an immediate raise of responder's suit.

Balanced hands of intermediate strength—i.e., 14 to 16 points—are opened one notrump. Unbalanced hands are opened in the long suit. To show the intermediate strength of a hand opened in a suit, opener either rebids his suit, or rebids two clubs if his opening bid was not one club. The two club change of suit by opener is forcing, and does not promise a genuine club suit.

In addition, if responder's response was a two-level limited bid such as in the auction 1 ♠ - 2 ♠ or 1 ♠ - 2 ♡, a two notrump rebid by opener is forcing for one round. The two notrump rebid shows a generally balanced hand.

Reverses by opener are based on distributional playing strength rather than high card power. A reverse promises a concentration of at least ten cards in the two suits. The suit reversed into is usually at least five cards long. For example, with a hand such as

♠ A Q   ♡ A x x x x   ◇ A Q J x x   ♣ x

opener would open with one diamond, and then rebid his heart suit.

Limited Responses to Opening One Bids

One PRO treatment that differs from standard methods is that the two level response in a new suit over an opening bid is not forcing. Thus, the PRO partnership's auction may go

(A) *Opener*   *Responder*
     1 ♠   2 ♡
     Pass

(B) *Opener*   *Responder*
     1 ♠   2 ♢
     Pass

For his two heart bid in auction (A), responder might have

    ♠ x   ♡ K Q x x x x   ♢ x x   ♣ J x x x

This treatment allows the responder to describe a weak hand completely naturally. For example, if responder has a hand such as

    ♠ A x   ♡ x   ♢ Q J x x x   ♣ J 10 x x x

opposite a one spade opening, the bidding might go

    Opener   *Responder*
    1 ♠   2 ♢
    2 Notrump   3 ♣
    Pass

In addition, a jump shift by the responder is not forcing. Except when used by a passed hand, the jump shift shows 10 or 11 points and a solid suit. Opener need not rebid if he has a poor hand, or if the hand is a misfit.

The response of one notrump to a minor suit opening is a limited bid, showing a balanced hand worth 7 to 11 points. Opener is expected to pass with a minimum hand. If he has an intermediate or stronger hand, he may rebid two clubs, which initiates a Stayman type search for a major suit fit.

The response of one spade to a one heart opening bid is also limited to a maximum of 11 points. Since the one notrump response to one heart is used as a very strong forcing response, the one spade response is treated as limited.

Unlimited Responses to Opening One Bids

There are two responses in the PRO system that are used as completely unlimited bids. One is the one notrump response to a major suit opening bid; the other is a major suit response to a minor suit opening bid.

The one notrump response to a one heart or one spade opening immediately announces that responder probably has a game-going hand opposite the opening bid. Having created a forcing situation, this response allows a good deal of low level exploration. If the responder follows his notrump response with a relay bid, the partnership is committed to game. For example, if opener's and responder's hands were

(Opener)
♠ K J x   ♡ K J x x x   ◇ x   ♣ K 10 x x

(Responder)
♠ Q x x x   ♡ Q x   ◇ A x x   ♣ A Q x x

the bidding could go

Opener	Responder
1 ♡	1 Notrump
2 ♣	2 ◇
2 ♠	5 ♣

Responder's two diamond rebid, following his one notrump response, was a relay that was forcing to game. When opener rebid spades as well as clubs, he was marked with at most one diamond. Therefore, responder avoided notrump and bid game in clubs. His leap to the five level denied an interest in probing for slam.

Since a response of one notrump over a minor suit opening shows a hand limited to 11 points, the PRO system uses a major suit response to a minor suit opening to show either a hand worth 12 or more points, or a hand with a five-card or longer suit. Since responder usually has a five-card suit, opener may raise freely with three-card support. Thus, if responder has a hand such as

♠ K 10 x x x   ♡ A x x   ◇ x x   ♣ J x x

and has responded one spade only to hear his partner rebid one notrump, he need not worry about whether to pass or to rebid two spades, since opener has denied three-card support.

CLARAC SLAM TRY

The PRO system incorporates a convention called the CLARAC slam try, which uses a four club bid (or occasionally a three club bid by a responder who has shown a very good hand), to ask about aces, and to initiate further asking bids. The name CLARAC stands for CLub Asking, Respond Aces and Controls.

When the partner of the four club CLARAC bidder has shown a limited hand, the responses to four clubs are as follows: A four diamond bid shows no aces, and denies strong values such as kings or king and queen combinations. A four notrump bid also shows no aces, but promises reasonable king and king-queen values. Responses of four hearts, four spades and five clubs show one ace, plus first or second round control in the suit named. The control shown should be the lowest control held. Thus, a response of four spades would show one ace plus a spade control, and would deny a heart control in addition to the ace promised. The four spade response would not deny a club control.

Responses of five diamonds, five hearts, five spades and six clubs show two aces, plus a second round control in the suit named. For example a hand such as

♠ A x x x   ♡ x   ◇ Q J x x x   ♣ A J x

if previously limited, would respond five hearts to the four club bid. A response of five notrump shows three aces and no other control.

If the partner of the CLARAC four club bidder has shown a good hand rather than a limited hand earlier in the auction, he must hold one ace more than the limited hand to make each of the responses described above, with the possible exception of the four diamond response. Thus, by a good hand, a response of four hearts, four spades or five clubs would show two aces plus control of the suit named; responses of five diamonds, five hearts, five spades or six clubs would show three aces and second round control of the suit named. Responses of six diamonds, six hearts or six spades would show four aces and second round control of the suit named.

If the CLARAC responder has made any bid other than four diamonds, the next suit bid by the four club bidder is an asking bid in that suit. For example, in the auction

(A)	*Opener*	*Responder*
	1 ◇	2 Notrump
	4 ♣	4 ♡
	4 ♠	

opener's four spade bid asks responder about his spade controls. With no control of the asked suit, responder bids the cheapest suit possible; with the king or a singleton, responder makes a minimum bid in notrump. A bid of a new suit by responder, other than the cheapest suit, shows the ace of the asked suit, plus second round control of the suit bid. If responder raises the asked suit, he shows two of the top three honors in that suit, with no other significant controls to show.

For example, in auction (A) shown above, if responder bid five diamonds over opener's four spade asking bid, he would be showing the ace of spades, and second round control of diamonds.

Following the CLARAC responder's answer to the asking bid, the CLARAC bidder may make a further asking bid. This process continues until slam is reached or until a negative response to an asking bid is given.

LEA SYSTEM

The Lea System uses a forcing one club opening to show an opening bid of 12 or more high card points. The responses use a series of six steps to show point count.

The one club opening may be made on all but two types of hands. It may not be made with a weak notrump type of hand. In addition, it may not be made with a hand worth 15 or 16 points, counting high cards plus distribution, with a six card suit; these hands are opened with one of a suit.

In response to a one club opening bid, responder shows his point count as follows:

$$1 \diamondsuit = 0 \text{ to } 5$$
$$1 \heartsuit = 6 \text{ to } 8$$
$$1 \spadesuit = 9 \text{ to } 11$$
$$1 \text{ NT} = 12 \text{ to } 14$$
$$2 \clubsuit = 15 \text{ to } 17$$
$$2 \diamondsuit = 18 \text{ to } 20$$

After a response of one notrump or higher, the partnership is forced to game.

After point count has been shown, rebids show natural suits. For example, suppose opener's and responder's hands were as follows:

(Opener)
♠ K Q x x x   ♡ Q 10 x   ◇ A Q   ♣ A x x

(Responder)

♠ x x   ♡ A K x x x   ◇ x x x x   ♣ x x

Using the Lea system, the auction would go

Opener	Responder
1 ♣	1 ♡
1 ♠	2 ♡
4 ♡	Pass

Responder's one heart response showed nothing about his heart suit, but simply promised 6 to 8 points. Opener's one spade rebid was natural, as was responder's two heart rebid.

SCHENKEN TWO DIAMONDS

The Schenken Two Diamond convention is a forcing opening bid that may be used with two types of hands. It may show a balanced, no-trump-type hand worth 23 points or more. In this event the opener's rebid will be in notrump, and is not forcing if the responder has responded two hearts.

The Schenken two diamond opening may also show a long, strong suit, and a hand with which a slam may be made if the responder has the right honor cards. In this event the opener will rebid a suit, and his rebid is forcing to game.

Showing Aces

The two diamond opening asks responder to show what aces, if any, he holds. The responder bids two hearts to show no aces. With one ace he makes a minimum response other than two hearts. If he has the ace of spades, or clubs or diamonds, he responds by bidding two spades, three clubs or three diamonds, respectively. If he has the ace of hearts, he responds two notrump.

If the responder has two aces he makes a jump response as follows: With touching aces, he jumps in the suit of the higher ranking ace. For these purposes, clubs and spades are considered touching suits, of which clubs is the higher ranking. If responder has non-touching aces, he jumps to three notrump. Thus, over a two diamond opening the responder would show his two aces as follows:

3 ♡ = aces of hearts and diamonds

3 ♠ = aces of spades and hearts

3 Notrump = aces of spades and diamonds, or the
    aces of hearts and clubs

4 ♣ = aces of clubs and spades

4 ◇ = aces of diamonds and clubs

If the responder should be so fortunate as to have three aces in response to the two diamond opening, his proper course is to make a double jump in the suit of his highest ranking ace.

Suppose the opener has a hand such as

♠ A K Q x x x x x   ♡ K Q x   ◇ –   ♣ A x

With this hand opener is assured of game, and if the responder has one or two key cards, the partnership will have a slam. After the hand is opened two diamonds, if responder jumps to three hearts, showing the aces of hearts and diamonds, opener can bid seven spades.

Showing Kings and Queens

After responder has shown his aces, the opener can ask about kings by rebidding the cheapest suit over responder's ace-showing bid. Thus, in the auction

Opener	*Responder*
2 ◇	2 Notrump
3 ♣	

responder has shown the ace of hearts and no other ace. Opener's three club bid asks about responder's kings.

Responder shows his kings in the same manner in which he

showed aces. The cheapest bid shows no kings; all other minimum bids show one king, in the suit bid. With two kings, the responder makes a jump response.

If the opener has the hand shown above,

♠ A K Q x x x x x   ♡ K Q x   ◇ —   ♣ A x

and the two diamond bid has elicited the information that the responder has the ace of hearts and no other ace, the opener can ask about kings. Thus, if the auction goes

Opener	Responder
2 ◇	2 Notrump
3 ♣	4 ♣

responder shows the king of clubs, and opener can now bid seven spades.

STAYMAN TWO CLUB AND TWO DIAMOND OPENINGS

The Stayman Two Club and Two Diamond openings are artificial forcing opening bids designed to enable the opener to show a full range of strong and intermediate hands. The two club opening is used for intermediate hands; the two diamond opening is used for stronger hands.

Two Club Opening

The two club opening is artificial and shows one of three types of hands. It may show a balanced 21 to 22 point hand. If opener has this hand his rebid will be two notrump.

The two club opening may also show a hand with a six-card or longer major suit, and eight to ten playing tricks. If opener has an 8-trick hand, he rebids two of his suit; if he has a 9-trick hand, he rebids three of his suit; if he has a 10-trick hand, he rebids four of his suit.

In addition, the two club opening may show a hand with at least five cards in each major suit, and eight to ten playing tricks. If opener has both major suits, his rebid will be in a minor suit. With an 8-trick hand, opener will rebid three clubs; with a 9-trick hand, he will rebid three diamonds. If opener has a 10-trick hand with 6-6 in the majors, he will rebid four of the minor suit in which he is void.

Suppose opener holds one of the following hands:

[A] ♠ A K Q 10 x x x   ♥ x x   ♦ A J x   ♣ x

[B] ♠ K Q   ♥ A K Q J x x   ♦ x   ♣ K Q J 10

[C] ♠ A K x   ♡ A Q x x x x x   ◇ A K x   ♣ –

[D] ♠ K Q J 10 x   ♡ A K x x x x   ◇ x   ♣ x

With Hand A, opener opens two clubs and rebids two spades, showing an 8-trick hand in spades. With Hand B, he would open two clubs and rebid four hearts, having a 10-trick hand in hearts. With Hand C, however, the opening bid should not be two clubs; it has the playing strength and defensive strength of a strong two-bid, and should be opened two diamonds.

With Hand D, opener should bid two clubs, and rebid three diamonds, showing a 9-trick major two-suiter.

Responses to Two Clubs

In responding to the two club opening, two diamonds is the usual bid; it is a waiting bid to see how the opener describes his hand. Other responses show very specific point count and suit length. Responder bids two of a major suit with a very weak hand—3 to 4 points—and a six-card suit. This response is not forcing.

If responder has a weak hand with a seven-card or longer minor suit, he may bid three of the minor. However, since the two club opening is so heavily major suit oriented, responder may not make the three club or three diamond response if he has as many as three cards in either major. Responder's bid of three clubs or three diamonds is not forcing.

If responder has a weak minor two-suiter, at least six-five, he may respond two notrump. This bid is not forcing. If opener has five cards in each of the major suits he will probably pass. He may rebid three of a minor with three card support. If opener has a good six-card suit, he will bid three of his major.

If responder has a stronger hand with both long minor suits, he may bid three notrump. Opener may pass or bid a three card minor suit.

If responder has a hand with a solid major suit at least five cards long, one that will run opposite a singleton without losing a trick, he may jump to three of his suit. If responder's running suit is a minor, he must jump to four.

Normally, however, responder will have none of these hands, and will bid two diamonds. Over the two diamond response opener has complete flexibility to show whether he has a notrump type hand, a single-suited or two-suited hand, and to show how many tricks he has.

If opener shows a major two-suiter with 8 or 9 playing tricks, responder can sign off in three of a major by taking a simple preference, or he can take his preference at the game level. Alternatively, responder can bid four diamonds, asking opener to bid game in his better suit. If responder bids four clubs over opener's three club or three diamond bid, his bid is Gerber, asking opener how many aces he has.

Two Diamond Opening

The two diamond opening is strong, artificial, and, except in two situations, forcing to game.

It may be made with a strong balanced notrump type hand, or with any other hand that is strong in high cards and defensive strength, and worth a forcing two-bid.

If opener has 23 or more high card points, he will open two diamonds and rebid in notrump. If the response is two hearts, and opener rebids two notrump, he shows 23 to 24 high card points; this rebid is not forcing.

Responses to Two Diamonds

In response to the two diamond opening, responder is expected to show whether or not he has high cards, i.e., aces and kings. The negative response is two hearts. This response has nothing to do with responder's heart suit or his point count; rather it says that he has fewer than two high cards. If responder has as little as two bare kings, he must make some other bid, bidding as naturally as possible.

For example, suppose responder holds one of the following hands in response to a two diamond opening:

[A] ♠ K Q J x x   ♡ Q J x   ◇ Q J x   ♣ Q x

[B] ♠ x x x   ♡ K x x   ◇ K x x x   ♣ x x x

With Hand A, although it has 14 high card points, responder must make the negative response of two hearts to show that he does not have two high cards. With Hand B, which has only 6 high card points, but has two kings, responder must make a positive response. Here, two notrump is best.

If responder bids anything other than two hearts in response to two diamonds the partnership is forced to game. If he responds two hearts, there are two situations in which the partnership may stop below game. One is when the opener rebids two notrump, showing 23 to 24 high card points. The other is when the opener bids a suit over two hearts, and rebids it after responder has made a second negative response. Thus, the following auctions are possible:

(A)   *Opener*   *Responder*
        2 ◇   2 ♡
        2 Notrump   Pass

(B) *Opener*   *Responder*

Opener	Responder
2 ♦	2 ♡
2 ♠	2 Notrump (or 3 ♣ if partnership is using a second negative convention)
3 ♠	Pass

In auction (B), opener might have a hand such as

♠ A K x x x x   ♡ A Q x   ♦ K Q   ♣ A x

With this hand opposite two negative responses, opener has no assurance of making a game. If, however, responder has made a positive response over the two diamond opening, opener would have explored for slam.

MEXICAN TWO DIAMONDS

A part of the Romex System, the Mexican Two Diamond opening shows a relatively balanced hand with 19 to 21 points, and 4 to 6 losers. The two diamond opening normally promises distribution of 4-3-3-3, or 4-4-3-2, or 5-3-3-2; occasionally the opening may be used with 6-3-2-2 or 5-4-2-2 distribution. Typical hands for the two diamond opening would be

[A] ♠ K J x x   ♡ A J x   ◇ K Q x   ♣ A Q x

[B] ♠ A x x   ♡ K J x   ◇ A K J 10 x   ♣ K 10

[C] ♠ A Q   ♡ A Q   ◇ K x x   ♣ K J 10 x x x

The responses to the two diamond opening include transfers and asking bids.

Negative and Invitational Responses

With a hand worth 0 to 4 points, the responder makes a negative response. If he has a long diamond suit he may pass. The other negative responses are two hearts and two spades.

The two heart and two spade responses are transfer bids; they show nothing about the heart or spade suits in responder's hand. If responder has a long suit other than diamonds, his proper response is two hearts. The two heart response forces opener to rebid two spades. If spades is responder's long suit, he may pass. If he has instead a long club suit or a long heart suit, he rebids three clubs or three hearts over the opener's two spade rebid. For example, if responder has a hand such as

♠ x x   ♡ Q x x x x x   ◇ x x   ♣ x x x

the bidding will go

Opener	Responder
2 ◇	2 ♡
2 ♠	3 ♡
Pass	

If responder has 0 to 4 points with no long suit, he responds two spades. This response is also a transfer, and forces the opener to rebid two notrump which responder can pass. This transfer allows the strong hand to be the declarer at notrump.

If responder has 5 or 6 points he is allowed to make a semi-positive response. The semi-positive consists of the initially negative two heart response, followed by some bid other than the three club and three heart sign offs. For example, with a hand such as

♠ J x   ♡ x x x   ◇ Q J 10 x x   ♣ J x x

responder would bid two hearts over the two diamond opening, and over the opener's two spade rebid, responder would rebid two notrump. This sequence invites opener to bid game with a maximum.

If responder has invited game with the sequence

Opener	Responder
2 ◇	2 ♡
2 ♠	2 Notrump

opener may now use three clubs as a Stayman bid to find out whether or not responder has a four-card major suit. In response to three clubs, responder bids a four-card major if he has one, bids thee diamonds if he has neither, or bids three no-trump if he has both four-card majors.

If responder has 5 or 6 points with a long major suit, he invites game by responding two hearts to two diamonds, and then rebidding a suit. To invite game in spades, responder bids three spades over opener's two spade bid; to invite game in hearts, responder bids three diamonds over opener's two spade bid. Note that responder cannot make his game try by bidding three hearts over two spades, since that rebid shows 0 to 4 points. The game invitational sequences, therefore, are

(A)	Opener	Responder
	2 ◇	2 ♡
	2 ♠	2 Notrump

(B)	Opener	Responder
	2 ◇	2 ♡
	2 ♠	3 ♠

(C)	Opener	Responder
	2 ◇	2 ♡
	2 ♠	3 ◇ (showing hearts)

Positive Responses

With a hand worth 7 or more points the responder should make a positive response. Positive responses are forcing to game. There are two types: those that are limited to game-going hands, and those showing slam interest.

With a hand of 7 to 9 points, the responder is interested in game, but not in slam. If he has any balanced hand (4-3-3-3, 4-4-3-2, or 5-3-3-2), or any mildly unbalanced hand (e.g., 5-4-2-2, 4-4-4-1, 5-4-3-1, 5-5-2-1), in the 7 to 9 point range, he makes the initially negative response of two spades. The two spade bid forces the opener to rebid two notrump; when responder makes any rebid over two notrump, the partnership is forced to game.

A rebid of three clubs by responder over opener's forced two notrump rebid is Stayman. Opener bids a four-card major suit if he has one, or bids three diamonds if he has no four card major, or bids three notrump if he has both majors. Thus, the auction could go

Opener	*Responder*
2 ♦	2 ♠
2 Notrump	3 ♣
3 Notrump	4 ♡
Pass	

Over the two notrump rebid, bids by the responder at the three level other than three clubs are natural, and show five-card suits. Thus if responder bids three clubs Stayman and then bids a major suit over the three diamond rebid, he promises five cards in the major suit he bids, and four cards in the other major.

If the responder has a six-card major suit with 7 to 9 points, he jumps to four diamonds or four hearts directly over the two diamond opening. These are Texas Transfer bids. The four diamond bid requires the opener to bid four hearts; responder's jump to four hearts forces opener to bid four spades.

If responder has 10 points or more and a broken six-card suit, he may bid it at the three level directly over the two diamond opening. If the opener has no slam interest, he should raise responder's suit with a fit, or rebid three notrump without a fit.

If opener is interested in a slam after responder's direct three-level response, he may cue-bid an ace. As an alternative, the partnership may agree that the opener will show key cards. Counting each ace, plus the king and queen of the responder's suit as key cards, opener would show how many key cards he had, using the following series of steps:

First   suit step = 0 or 3 key cards

Second suit step = 1 or 4 key cards

Third   suit step = 2 or 5 key cards

In counting steps, notrump is excluded, since that bid is used to deny fit and slam interest. In the auction

Opener	*Responder*
2 ♦	3 ♦
4 ♣	

opener's four club bid is the third step, promising two or five key cards. Opener's and responder's hands might be

(Opener)
♠ K J x x   ♡ K Q x   ♦ A x x   ♣ A Q J

(Responder)
♠ A x   ♡ J x   ♦ K 10 x x x x   ♣ K x x

After opener has shown his key cards, a bid of four notrump by the responder guarantees that the partnership possesses all six keys, and asks opener about his outside kings. If one key card is missing, responder may start cue-bidding in an effort to identify the missing key. With the above hands and auction, responder would know that the partnership is missing two keys, and would simply rebid his diamond suit.

If responder has a 10 point or better hand, either with relatively balanced distribution, or with a solid or semi-solid six-card suit, he may respond two notrump to the two diamond opening. Following the two notrump response a highly specialized sequence may occur.

Bidding After the Two Notrump Response

The two notrump response to the Mexican two diamond opening does not show that responder has any desire to play in notrump. It is a bid that asks opener to specify his point count. Opener answers in three steps:

$$3 \clubsuit = 19 \text{ high card points}$$
$$3 \diamondsuit = 20 \text{ high card points}$$
$$3 \heartsuit = 21 \text{ high card points}$$

If responder now bids the cheapest suit, he asks opener how many aces he has. Opener shows his aces in three steps, Roman style:

First   step = 0 or 3 aces

Second step = 1 or 4 aces

Third   step = 2 aces

If, after either of these inquiries has been answered, the responder rebids three notrump, that sets the final contract. If, instead of bidding three notrump, responder bids a suit, that is his lowest ranking four-card suit, and the partnership should bid four-card suits up the line in search of a fit. For example, if opener and responder hold

(Opener)
♠ A x   ♡ K J x x   ◇ K Q x x   ♣ A K x

(Responder)
♠ K Q x x   ♡ A Q x x   ◇ J x   ♣ x x x

the bidding could go

Opener	Responder
2 ◇	2 Notrump
3 ◇	3 ♡
4 ♣	4 ♡
5 ♡	6 ♡
Pass	

Responder's two notrump bid asked about opener's point count; opener's three diamond bid showed exactly 20 high card points. Responder's three heart bid asked how many aces opener held; the four club bid showed two aces. Then responder's four heart bid showed a suit; opener raised with his four hearts, and the partnership reached its slam.

If responder has 10 or more points and a solid or semi-solid six-card suit, he first responds two notrump over two diamonds, to learn opener's point count; then responder bids four clubs, which is treated as Modified Roman Gerber. The four club bid does not suggest that responder's suit is clubs; his suit is still undisclosed to opener. The four club bid asks opener how many aces he holds. Opener responds according to the following schedule:

4 ◇ = 0 or 3 aces

4 ♡ = 1 or 4 aces

4 ♠ = 2 aces of the same color

4 NT = 2 aces of the same rank

5 ♣ = 2 non-matching aces

Thus, with a hand such as

♠ K Q x x x x   ♡ —   ◇ K Q x x x   ♣ A x

responder can learn whether opener has three aces, and if he does not, whether or not opener has the right two aces for a grand slam.

If responder bids five clubs after opener's ace-showing bid, he asks about kings. If opener's bid was five clubs, five diamonds becomes responder's king-asking bid.

TAM II TWO CLUBS AND TWO DIAMOND OPENINGS

The TAM II Two Club and Two Diamond openings are artificial opening bids showing hands strong enough, or nearly so, to force to game. The two diamond opening is used only with balanced hands worth 22 to 25 high card points. The two club opening may be used with stronger balanced hands, or with unbalanced game-going hands.

Two Club Opening

The TAM II two club opening is forcing to game. It shows either a balanced hand with 26 to 29 high card points, or the equivalent of a strong two-bid in a suit. If opener has the balanced hand he will rebid notrump—the minimum number of notrump with 26 to 27 points, or a single jump in notrump with 28 to 29 points. If opener has instead the strong suit two-bid, he will rebid his suit.

Most of the responder's bids are designed to show opener whether or not responder's high cards fit opener's hand. If responder has less than one quick trick (an ace, or two kings, or a king and queen in the same suit), his proper response is two notrump. If he has one or more quick tricks, he bids the lowest suit in which he holds an ace or a king. For example, with

♠ A J 10 x x x   ♥ x   ♦ K x   ♣ x x x x

responder would bid two diamonds over the two club opening.

If responder has a six-card or longer suit headed by two of the top three honors, he may jump in that suit. For example, to bid three diamonds over two clubs, responder might have

♠ x x   ♡ x x   ◇ K Q x x x x   ♣ x x x

If opener rebids a suit, responder describes his hand further. If responder has fewer than three cards in opener's suit, he either bids a five card suit of his own, or he bids the minimum number of notrump if he has no five card suit. If responder has support for opener's suit he may show it in one of several ways, depending in part on the nature of his first response.

If responder has made an initial negative response of two notrump, he may show support for opener's suit by raising the suit if he has no king. If responder has a king, he may show support for opener's suit by jump shifting into the suit of his king. For example, in the auction

Opener	*Responder*
2 ♣	2 Notrump
3 ◇	4 ♠

responder's two notrump bid showed less than one quick trick; his four spade bid promised diamond support plus the king of spades. Neither of responder's bids has purported to describe his distribution.

If responder has made a positive response to the two club opening, and opener has rebid a suit, responder may show support for opener's suit in one of four ways. If he has no aces or kings in any suit other than the one he bid initially, he may give a simple raise of opener's suit. If responder has the ace or king of opener's suit in addition to the ace or king shown initially, but no ace or king in any unbid suit, he jump raises opener's suit. If responder has support for opener's suit and has an ace or a king in a suit he has not yet shown, he jump shifts into the latter suit. If responder has support for opener's suit

260

and has 1½ to 2 quick tricks in the suit of his initial response, he jumps in his suit.

Suppose the auction has started

Opener	Responder
2 ♣	2 ♦
2 ♡	

and responder has one of the following hands:

[A] ♠ x x x   ♡ x x x   ♦ K Q x x   ♣ x x x

[B] ♠ x x x   ♡ K x x   ♦ K x x x   ♣ x x x

[C] ♠ x x x   ♡ x x x   ♦ K x x x   ♣ K x x

[D] ♠ x x x   ♡ x x x   ♦ A Q x   ♣ x x x x

With Hand A, responder raises hearts to the three level, having no more in aces and kings than he has already shown. With Hand B, responder shows his trump honor by jumping to four hearts. With Hand C, responder shows his king of clubs and his trump support by bidding three clubs. With Hand D, responder has trump support and one and a half quick tricks in the suit of his initial response. Therefore he jumps to four diamonds.

Two Diamond Opening

The TAM II Two Diamond convention uses an opening bid of two diamonds to show a balanced hand worth 22 to 25 high card points. The two diamond opening is forcing for one round, but not necessarily to game. Most of the responses are artificial; they include relays, Stayman, and transfers.

A response of two spades shows a hand with less than 3 high card points. It says nothing about responder's spade suit, but merely describes his point count. Opener may rebid three notrump if he is still optimistic about his prospects in game; otherwise he should rebid two notrump. Any rebid by responder in a suit over opener's two notrump rebid shows a long suit, but is not forward going; opener may nevertheless elect to bid game with a fit for a responder's suit. For example if opener's and responder's hands were

(Opener)
♠ A K x   ♡ A K x x   ◇ A x x x   ♣ A K

(Responder)
♠ x x x   ♡ 10 x x x x   ◇ x x x   ♣ J x

the bidding might go

Opener	Responder
2 ◇	2 ♠
2 Notrump	3 ♡
3 Notrump	

If, instead of the hand shown above, opener had held

♠ A K x   ♡ A K x   ◇ A K Q x x   ♣ Q x

he would have bid four hearts over three hearts in the above auction.

Responses of three clubs and three diamonds over the two diamond opening are Stayman-type bids. The three club bid shows less than 8 points in high cards, and asks opener to bid a four card major suit if he has one. With no four card major opener will rebid three diamonds, over which responder may bid a five card major suit if he has one.

If opener rebids the suit in which responder has four card support and responder has a hand worth a slam try, he may jump to five of the major suit. Opener is requested to bid slam with a maximum. For example, suppose opener's and responder's hands were

(Opener)
♠ A Q x x   ♡ A J   ◇ K Q J x   ♣ A K x

(Responder)
♠ K x x x   ♡ x x x   ◇ A x   ♣ x x x x

The bidding could go

Opener	Responder
2 ◇	3 ♣
3 ♠	5 ♠
6 ♠	Pass

The three diamond response to the two diamond opening shows 8 or more points, and also asks the opener to show a four card major suit if he has one. If opener has no four card major suit, he rebids three notrump with 22 to 23 points; if he has 24 to 25 points, he must either bid a five card minor suit if he has one, or bid four notrump with no five card minor.

If, over the three diamond response, opener rebids a suit in which responder has four card support, responder may raise to game with 8 or 9 points, or invite slam by jumping to five of the major with 10 points, or drive the hand to slam with a good 11 or more points. For example, in the auction

Opener	Responder
2 ◇	3 ◇
3 ♡	5 ♡

responder's five heart bid asks opener to bid a slam if he has an excellent minimum point count, or better. Responder might have either

[A] ♠ x x x ♡ A J x x ◇ J x x ♣ K J x

or

[B] ♠ x x ♡ A J x x ◇ x x ♣ K x x x x

Opener might hold a hand such as

[C] ♠ A x ♡ K Q x x ◇ A K Q x ♣ A x x

or

[D] ♠ K J x ♡ K Q x x ◇ A K Q x ♣ A x

With Hand C opener would continue to slam, having an ideal minimum. This hand should produce a slam opposite either Hand A or Hand B. With Hand D, opener would pass five hearts, having a less attractive minimum.

Note that in the auction

Opener	Responder
2 ◇	3 ◇
3 ♡	4 ♡

responder's four heart bid is not by any means a signoff bid since he has shown 8 or more points (by responding three diamonds), opposite a 22 to 25 point opening. If opener has a maximum, he should move toward slam.

If responder has a five card major suit and 8 or more high card points, he may jump to three of his major suit over the two diamond opening. With a minimum opening, opener rebids three notrump if he has a doubleton in responder's suit; or he raises to game in responder's suit if he has three- or four-card support. If opener has a maximum hand with a doubleton in responder's suit, he rebids four notrump. If opener has a maximum with trump support, he cue-bids his cheapest ace. For example, in the auction

Opener	*Responder*
2 ♢	3 ♡
4 ♣	

opener shows at least three hearts, and 24 to 25 high card points, including the ace of clubs, but excluding the ace of spades, since he bypassed three spades to bid four clubs.

If in response to the two diamond opening responder jumps to four diamonds or four hearts, his bid is a transfer. The jump to four diamonds requires opener to bid four hearts. Responder's jump to four hearts requires opener to rebid four spades.

If responder has a hand that is not suitable for either a Stayman bid or a transfer, or a natural jump to three of a major suit, he may use a response of two hearts as a non-descriptive relay. The two heart response to two diamonds shows nothing about responder's strength or his distribution, but simply asks opener to clarify his point count. Opener rebids two notrump with 22 to 23 high card points, or three notrump with 24 to 25 points. The two heart response is forcing to game.

To use the two heart relay, responder might have a minor suit oriented hand, or he might have a balanced notrump type hand. Responder's use of the relay with a notrump type hand serves to make the stronger hand the declarer in any notrump contract, and to allow minute specification of opener's point count. For example, if responder has a balanced hand he may raise notrump after opener's notrump rebid:

Opener	*Responder*
2 ◇	2 ♡
2 Notrump	4 Notrump

Opener's two notrump rebid showed 22 to 23 high card points. Responder's four notrump rebid showed about 10 points and asked opener to bid slam with 23 points.

Suit rebids by the responder, after opener has clarified his point count over the relay, are natural. Opener should either raise responder's suit or bid a suit of his own. Responder might have a hand such as

[E] ♠ K x x x   ♡ x   ◇ A Q x x   ♣ J x x x

or

[F] ♠ x x   ♡ x   ◇ A x x x x   ♣ Q x x x x

BIG DIAMOND SYSTEM

The Big Diamond System uses a combination of forcing one club and one diamond openings, together with specialized two- and three-level openings, to show general strength and distribution.

A one club opening shows one of two types of hands. It may show a hand with 12 to 16 points including high cards and distribution, with a club suit or a diamond suit, or with an unbiddable heart or spade suit. (Openings of one of a major suit promise five card suits and 12 to 16 points.)

One club may also be opened with a strong balanced hand with 17 to 19, or 22 or more high card points. The Bid Diamond notrump structure is therefore as follows:

14 to 16: open one notrump

17 to 19: open one club, rebid one notrump

20 to 21: open two notrump

22 to 23: open one club, rebid two notrump

24 to 26: open one club, rebid three notrump

27 to 29: open one club, rebid four notrump

Responses to One Club

In response to a one club opening, one diamond is the negative response, usually showing less than 7 points; however, the one diamond negative may be made with up to 10 scattered points. All other minimum suit bids are natural, showing at least four card suits, and are forcing for one round. A response of one heart or one spade shows 7 or more points; a response of two clubs or two diamonds shows 11 or more points with a good suit, usually five cards long.

Responses in notrump show balanced hands. A one notrump response shows 11 to 12 high card points with the major suits stopped, and the minor suits at least partially stopped. The one notrump response is not forcing. Higher notrump bids show stoppers in all suits. A response of two notrump shows 13 to 14 points and is forcing to game; a response of three notrump shows 15 to 16 points; a response of four notrump shows 17 to 18 points.

Responses of two hearts or two spades show 14 or more points with a good suit. Opener either rebids notrump if he has a balanced hand with 17 or more points, or shows his support for opener's suit if he has a 12 to 16 point hand. His support showing bids are as follows:

3 ♣ = singleton or small doubleton

3 ♦ = three small cards, or three cards headed by the jack

3 ♡ = two or three cards headed by the ace, king or queen

3 ♠ = two honors, no worse than the king and jack

In addition, opener may jump to four of responder's suit if he has four trumps headed by an honor, and a side suit singleton.

If opener and responder held the following hands

(Opener)
♠ K x   ♡ A Q J x   ♦ Q 10 x x x   ♣ K x

(Responder)
♠ A Q x x x   ♡ K x x   ♦ K x   ♣ Q J x

the auction would go

Opener	Responder
1 ♣	2 ♠
3 ♡	3 Notrump

Opener's three heart bid, showed two or three spades to an honor. Responder rebid three notrump, expecting opener to correct to four spades if he had three-card support.

Responses to one club at the three level show long semi-solid suits with little outside strength. A jump to three clubs or three diamonds may be made on a six- or seven-card suit; a jump to three hearts or three spades promises a seven-card suit. Responses to one club at the four level show solid seven-card suits with little outside strength.

Openings Above the One Level

Opening bids of two clubs and two diamonds show two-suited hands. See TWO CLUB OPENING FOR MINORS and TWO DIAMOND OPENING FOR MAJORS.

Opening bids of two hearts or two spades show intermediate strength, and are made with one-suited hands. These openings show long, solid or semi-solid suits, with approximately eight playing tricks. A typical hand might be

♠ A K Q 10 x x   ♡ x x   ◇ x x   ♣ A K x

The two heart and two spade openings are not forcing. A two notrump response shows slam interest. All other responses are natural.

An opening bid of three clubs or three diamonds shows 12 to

16 points with a six- or seven-card semi-solid suit. These openings deny possession of a four-card major suit. All responses are natural. A response of three hearts or three spades is forcing and opener should raise with as little as three small cards, or a doubleton honor. For a three diamond opening, for example, opener might have

♠ A x x   ♡ Q x   ◇ A K J x x x x   ♣ x

Over a response of three hearts or three spades, opener should raise to four.

One Diamond Opening

An opening bid of one diamond in the Big Diamond system shows an unbalanced hand worth 17 or more points including distribution. The only negative response is one heart, which usually shows 0 to 7 points; however, the negative response may be made with up to a scattered 9 count.

Responses of one spade, two clubs and two diamonds are natural, showing four card or longer suits, and 8 or more good points. A response of one notrump shows at least a four card heart suit with 8 good points. These responses are forcing to game.

Responses of two hearts and two spades show six-card suits headed by two of the top three honors, with little outside. Responses at the three level show solid six- or seven-card suits with nothing outside.

Rebids by the One Diamond Opener

If responder has bid one heart, showing a weak hand,

270

opener may rebid one spade with a good five-card suit and 17 to 21 points. A rebid of one notrump shows a good heart suit with 17 to 21 points. Rebids of two clubs and two diamonds promise good five card suits, and up to 9 playing tricks. None of these rebids is forcing.

Rebids of two hearts, two spades, three clubs or three diamonds show good suits with 22 points or more. These rebids are forcing for one round, and responder uses a series of steps to show his general strength and his support for opener's suit, as follows:

First step = small doubleton or worse, weak hand

Second step = small doubleton or worse, some high card strength

Third step = three small cards, weak hand

Fourth step = three small cards, some high card strength

Fifth step = good trumps, weak hand

In addition, responder is allowed to jump to game in opener's suit if he has a weak hand with good trumps, and a singleton or void in a side suit.

If opener and responder held the following hands,

(Opener)
♠ A K x   ♡ A K x x x   ◇ Q x   ♣ A K x

(Responder)
♠ J x x   ♡ x x x   ◇ J x x   ♣ J x x x

the bidding could go

Opener	Responder
1 ◇	1 ♡
2 ♡	3 ♣
3 ♡	Pass

If opener jumps to three hearts, three spades, four clubs or four diamonds, he shows a game going hand, and asks responder to show his support for opener's suit in a series of steps as follows:

First   step = void or singleton

Second step = doubleton

Third   step = three small cards

Fourth step = four small cards

Fifth   step = queen

Opener's and responder's hands might be

(Opener)
♠ A x   ♡ A K J x x x x   ◇ A K Q   ♣ x

(Responder)
♠ K x x x x   ♡ x x x   ◇ x x   ♣ A x x

The auction would start

Opener	Responder
1 ◇	1 ♡
3 ♡	4 ♣

Responder's four club bid, the third step, showed three-card heart support.

After responder has shown his holding in opener's suit, opener may ask whether or not responder has control in a side suit. Over the bid of a new suit by opener, responder is required to show his controls by steps as follows:

First   step = queen or worse

Second step = king

Third   step = king and queen

Fourth step = ace

Fifth   step = ace and queen

Sixth   step = ace and king

In the above auction, after opener learned that responder had three-card heart support, he could continue with asking bids in spades and clubs, as follows:

Opener	Responder
1 ♢	1 ♡
3 ♡	4 ♣
4 ♠	5 ♣
6 ♣	6 Notrump
7 ♡	

Opener's four spade asking bid elicits the information that responder has the king of spades. If responder had answered with the first step, denying the king of spades, opener would have persevered in hopes of finding responder with the ace of clubs for the small slam; on the other hand, if responder had answered with the third step, showing the king and queen of spades, opener would have immediately settled for the small slam, since for his initial negative response, responder would not have an ace, a king and a queen. Opener's six club asking bid, looking for the ace of clubs for the grand slam was safe, since if responder answered with the first or second step, the hand could be played in six hearts; and if he answered with the third step, six spades, the hand could be played in six notrump.

After the negative response of one heart to the one diamond opening, if opener rebids two notrump, he shows 22 to 24 points, with one suit, not clubs, unstopped. Responder has a variety of alternatives over two notrump. He may bid three clubs as Stayman; he may bid three diamonds to ask opener to bid his better major suit; or, with a game-going hand, responder may bid a five card or longer major suit.

If responder has bid one spade, one notrump, two clubs or two diamonds in response to the one diamond opening, opener must make a single raise of responder's suit if he has four card support, unless he has a self-supporting suit of his own. Opener's raise of responder's suit would set that as the trump suit, and subsequent bidding could proceed naturally. If opener has his own self-sufficient suit, he jump shifts in it, setting it as the trump suit.

If responder has shown a long solid or semi-solid suit (i.e., by jumping to two of a major or three of any suit), opener's bid of a new suit asks about responder's control of the new suit. Since responder's original response has denied strength outside his own suit, such control as he has will usually be shortness. His responses are as follows:

First   step = void or singleton

Second step = doubleton

Third   step = three small cards

Fourth step = four small cards

Fifth step = queen

If opener's and responder's hands were

(Opener)
♠ K x   ♡ A K x x x x   ◇ K Q x   ♣ A x

(Responder)
♠ A Q x x x x   ♡ x x x x   ◇ J x   ♣ x

the bidding might go

Opener	Responder
1 ◇	2 ♠
3 ♡	4 ◇
6 ♡	

Opener's three heart bid asked about responder's heart control; if responder had shown three small hearts or worse, opener would have settled for game. But with responder having four hearts, slam became a good prospect, and much better in hearts than in spades.

DYNAMIC ONE NOTRUMP

The Dynamic One Notrump opening, an integral part of the Romex system, is a strong opening bid showing a relatively unbalanced hand. The Dynamic Notrump opening can be made on any distribution except 4-3-3-3, 4-4-3-2, or 5-3-3-2. It promises 18 to 21 points, including at least five controls, and has only four or five losers. This one notrump bid is forcing.

The opener may have a one-suited hand such as

♠ A K Q x x x   ♥ A K x   ♦ K x   ♣ x x

or a two suited hand such as

♠ K Q J x x   ♥ A K x x   ♦ A x   ♣ A x

or a three suited hand such as

♠ K Q x x   ♥ A K x x   ♦ A Q x x   ♣ x

Responses to One Notrump

In response to the one notrump opening the responder immediately shows how many controls he has. Counting each ace as two and each king as one, he bids in steps, as follows:

2 ♣ = 0 to 1 control, with 0 to 6 points

2 ♦ = 0 to 1 control with 7 to 15 points

2 ♥ = 2 controls, i.e., one ace or two kings; however, with one ace and less than 6 points, the proper response is two clubs

276

2 ♠ = 3 controls, i.e., one ace and one king, or three kings

2 NT = 4 controls in two suits, i.e., two aces, or an ace king combination and an outside king

3 ♣ = 4 controls in more than two suits, i.e., an ace and two kings all in different suits, or four kings

3 ♢ = 5 controls, i.e., one ace and three kings, or two aces and one king

3 ♡ = 6 controls, i.e., three aces, or two aces and two kings, or one ace and four kings

3 ♠ = 7 controls, i.e., three aces and one king, or two aces and three kings

If responder has fewer than two controls, and has a seven- or eight-card semi-solid major suit, with no void, he may make a natural jump to four of his suit.

Opener's Rebids over Two Club Response

After the responder has shown a very weak hand by bidding two clubs, the opener's first concern, with a minimum hand with poor game prospects, is to find a low level contract to play. If the opener rebids two of a major suit he shows a good five-card or longer suit. If he rebids three of a minor suit, he shows a good six-card or longer suit. If opener rebids four of a major suit he shows that he has game in his own hand.

Opener has available a number of rebids to show major two-suited hands and minor two-suited hands. With both minor suits and a hand with four losers, including at most two quick losers, or a hand with a total of three losers, the opener may rebid two notrump:

Opener	Responder
1 Notrump	2 ♣
2 Notrump	

Opener's distribution could be 5-5 or 5-4 in the minor suits, with the major suits being divided 2-1, 3-1 or 2-2. He might have a hand such as

♠ K J   ♡ K x   ◇ A K 10 x   ♣ A Q 10 x x

With a stronger minor two-suiter, opener may rebid three notrump:

Opener	Responder
1 Notrump	2 ♣
3 Notrump	

The three notrump bid promises at least ten cards in the minor suits, at most three losers, and no more than two quick losers. Opener might have a hand such as

♠ A   ♡ x   ◇ A K x x x x   ♣ A K x x x

If opener has five or more cards in each major suit, he has three descriptive bids available. If he has a four-loser hand, he may jump to three hearts over the two club response, allowing responder to choose a major suit at the three level. If opener has a three-loser hand, he jumps to three spades, requiring responder to state his preference at the four level. Or, if opener

278

has a three loser hand with five cards in each major suit and three cards in a minor suit, he jumps to four of that minor suit.

Opener might have any of the following hands:

[A] ♠ K Q J x x   ♡ A J 10 x x   ◇ K x   ♣ A

[B] ♠ A Q J x x   ♡ A K Q 10 x x   ◇ x   ♣ Q

[C] ♠ A K J 10 x   ♡ K Q J 10 x   ◇ A x x   ♣ —

With Hand A, opener has four losers, and therefore jumps to three hearts. Responder may pass, or take a preference to spades; or if he has a few values, he may bid four of his better major suit. With Hand B, opener has a three-loser hand and no three card minor; he therefore bids three spades. With Hand C, opener rebids four diamonds, showing five cards in each major suit, three diamonds, and a void in clubs.

With a hand that does not fit any of these special rebids, opener rebids two diamonds. The two diamond bid does not mean that opener has diamonds; rather, it is a waiting bid. Opener might have two four-card major suits, or two five-card major suits with a five-loser hand; or he might have a six-card major suit and a four-card major suit, or he might have a long major suit and a long minor suit. His two diamond bid merely suggests that he does not know what to bid, and asks responder to help out.

Over opener's two diamond rebid, responder should bid a major suit if he has one. If responder has a four-card major suit or a weak five-card major suit, he bids two of that suit; if he has a good five-card major suit or a fair six-card major suit, he jumps to three of the major. If responder has no four-card major, he shows a five-card minor suit. If he has neither a five-card minor nor a four-card major, responder bids two no-trump.

If opener's and responder's hands were, for example

(Opener)
♠ A x   ♡ A x x x   ◇ A Q   ♣ K J x x x

(Responder)
♠ K J 10 x x x   ♡ J x   ◇ x x x   ♣ x x

the bidding would start

Opener	Responder
1 Notrump	2 ♣
2 ◇	3 ♠

Opener's Rebids over Two Diamond Response

If responder has bid two diamonds, or higher, in response to the one notrump opening, the partnership is forced to game. The opener's rebids are quite similar to his rebids over a two club response. The rebids that are different are two of a major suit and three of a major suit.

Over a two diamond response, of course, opener cannot use the two diamond waiting bid. Opener will rebid a four- or five-card heart suit whenever he has one, with two exceptions. If he also has a five-card spade suit he will show his spade suit first; if he has a six-card minor suit in addition to his heart suit, he will bid the minor suit first. With a hand such as

♠ A x   ♡ A x x x   ◇ A Q   ♣ K J x x x

opener would rebid two hearts over the two diamond response:

Opener	*Responder*
1 Notrump	2 ◇
2 ♡	

But with one more club and one less spade, opener would rebid his clubs first over the two diamond response.

Similarly, if opener has a four- or five-card spade suit, he will bid it immediately unless he also has a heart suit that is longer than his spade suit, or has a six-card minor suit.

After the two-club response, the jump to three of a major suit showed at least five cards in each major, with three or four losers. However, after a two diamond response, the partnership is forced to game, so the opener can describe his hand in a more leisurely fashion. Thus with five spades and five hearts, he can bid his suits individually, without jumping. After the two diamond response, the jump by opener to three hearts or three spades is reserved to show specifically six cards in the major suit bid, and four cards in the other major.

All other rebids are the same as over the two club response. The two notrump rebid shows a moderately strong minor two-suiter. If the responder has at least one of the top three honors in either diamonds or clubs, he can bid three clubs over the two notrump rebid to ask the opener to describe his major suit distribution. Opener's answers to the three club inquiry are as follows:

3 ◇ = 2-2 in the major suits

3 ♡ = 3-card heart suit

3 ♠ = 3-card spade suit

3 NT = a singleton and doubleton in the majors

Thus, if opener's and responder's hands were

(Opener)
♠ A J 10   ♡ x   ◇ A K Q x x   ♣ A x x x

(Responder)
♠ x   ♡ x x x   ◇ J x x x   ♣ K Q J x x

the auction could go

Opener	Responder
1 Notrump	2 ◇
2 Notrump	3 ♣
3 ♠	4 ♣
4 ♠	6 ♣

Responder's three club bid asked opener to clarify his distribution; opener's three spade bid showed that he had three spades, leaving him with at most one heart. Responder's four club bid set the trump suit. Opener's four spade bid denied the ability to cue-bid four hearts, which he would have done with a heart void. Responder therefore inferred that the partnership had a heart loser, and settled for six clubs.

IV

Making Inquiries

There are few things more frustrating in bridge than having a hand that needs just one or two specific cards from partner to make a slam, and not knowing how to find out whether or not he has them. Sometimes the frustration occurs from the very outset of the hand, and some of the strong forcing opening bid conventions described in Chapter III are designed to elicit the information from the responder at his first turn to bid.

More often, however, the need to locate specific cards occurs after some exchange of information. Almost all of the conventions described below have their application some time after the opening bid, although some can be used as the opening bid itself.

The conventions described below fall into three general categories. The first group consists of conventions that ask partner how many aces, or how many aces and kings, he has. *See* BLACKWOOD, ROMAN BLACKWOOD, KEY CARD BLACKWOOD, BABY BLACKWOOD, GERBER, ROMAN GERBER, KEY CARD GERBER, SUPER GERBER, EXTENDED GERBER, ACE IDENTIFICATION, BLACK AND RED GERBER, FANE FOUR CLUB CONVENTION, ACOL FOUR NOTRUMP OPENING, CULBERTSON FOUR-FIVE NOTRUMP, SAN FRANCISCO, CULWOOD, CLARAC. A second group of conventions asks partner what sort of control he has of specific suits. *See* ASKING BIDS, ROMAN ASKING BIDS, CUL-

BERTSON ASKING BIDS, LEBOVIC ASKING BID, FOUR CLUB ASKING BID, FULWILER ASKING BIDS. *See also* D.I. A third category of conventions asks partner how good his trumps are. *See* GRAND SLAM FORCE, MALOWAN, BARON SLAM TRY, CULBERTSON TRUMP ASKING BIDS, ROMEX TRUMP ASKING BIDS, R/H FOUR NOTRUMP, WANG TRUMP ASKING BIDS.

BLACKWOOD

The Blackwood convention is one of the most widely used in the world. Its widespread acceptance is a tribute to its simplicity. In its basic form, it is a bid of four notrump to ask partner how many aces he has. The responses are as follows:

$$5 \clubsuit = 0 \text{ or } 4 \text{ aces}$$
$$5 \diamondsuit = 1 \text{ ace}$$
$$5 \heartsuit = 2 \text{ aces}$$
$$5 \spadesuit = 3 \text{ aces}$$

Although the five club bid is slightly ambiguous, the Blackwood bidder will normally be able to tell from his hand and from the previous bidding whether his partner has all of the aces or none. *See also* RESPONDING TO BLACKWOOD OVER OPPONENT'S INTERFERENCE, DOPI AND PODI, DEPO.

If, over the response to four notrump, the Blackwood bidder bids five notrump, he normally guarantees that the partnership is in possession of all of the aces, and is asking the responder to tell him how many kings he has. At duplicate bridge, the partnership might choose to agree that the five notrump bid does not guarantee possession of all the aces, since the Blackwood bidder might wish to try for a top score by bidding slam in notrump if the responder had the appropriate number of kings. However, on balance, the partnership is probably better off to agree that five notrump does guarantee all the aces.

Over five notrump, the responder shows his kings as follows:

$$6 \clubsuit = \text{no kings}$$
$$6 \diamondsuit = 1 \text{ king}$$
$$6 \heartsuit = 2 \text{ kings}$$
$$6 \spadesuit = 3 \text{ kings}$$
$$6 \text{ NT} = 4 \text{ kings}$$

The authorities are sharply divided as to the proper bid to show four kings. Several state that the six club bid shows either 0 or 4 kings, apparently on the theory that what is good enough for aces is good enough for kings. The majority, however, state that with four kings, the responder should bid six notrump. The rationale is that there is no need, as there is over four notrump, to conserve space. Since the Blackwood bidder is interested in a grand slam and the partnership has all of the kings, nothing is lost by making the fact quite clear with a bid of six notrump.

Over the five notrump rebid by the Blackwood bidder, the responder has the option, with a suitable hand, of jumping to a grand slam rather than just meekly showing his kings. For example, if he has a hand such as

$\spadesuit$ A x $\heartsuit$ 10 x $\diamondsuit$ Q x $\clubsuit$ A K Q J x x x

and the bidding has gone

Opener	Responder
1 $\spadesuit$	3 $\clubsuit$
3 $\spadesuit$	4 $\spadesuit$
4 Notrump	5 $\heartsuit$
5 Notrump	

responder should bid seven clubs. Once opener has certified that the partnership has all of the aces, responder can almost count thirteen tricks with his running club suit. He should, however, bid seven clubs rather than seven notrump since it is conceivable that he might need to ruff a spade to establish his thirteenth trick. Opener might have a hand such as

♠ K Q 10 9 x x   ♡ A x x   ♢ A x   ♣ x x

On occasion, such as with the hand above, the Blackwood bidder will rebid five notrump not so much to find out about kings, as to reassure the responder that all of the aces are held, just in case he can bid a grand slam upon learning that fact.

Playing in Five Notrump

Sometimes the Blackwood bidder, after hearing the ace-showing response, decides that the hand should not be played in slam, but should be played in five notrump. However, he cannot bid five notrump to play there, because that bid asks responder about his kings.

Assuming that there is a neutral suit higher than the suit of responder's ace-showing response, i.e., one that the responder could not take as a sign-off bid, the Blackwood bidder bids five of that suit. This bid requests the Blackwood responder to bid five notrump, which the Blackwood bidder can pass.

For example, at duplicate bridge, the partnership might try for slam in a minor suit, but need to retreat to notrump if that slam seemed out of reach:

Opener	Responder
1 ♢	3 ♢
4 Notrump	5 ♢
5 ♡	5 Notrump
Pass	

When Blackwood Should Not Be Used

The Blackwood convention is designed principally to help the partnership to stay out of a slam against which the opponents hold too many aces, rather than to help the partnership to reach a slam. The partnership's first tasks are to determine whether or not it has enough tricks and a solid enough trump suit to consider a slam. The use of Blackwood should follow, not precede, the making of these determinations.

Before bidding four notrump, the player should have thought through what he will do over any possible ace-showing response. Once he has embarked on Blackwood, he should bid a slam if the partnership is missing no more than one ace. If he learns that only one ace is missing and stops short of slam, he has misused the Blackwood convention.

A player should not bid Blackwood when the responses will not tell him what he needs to know. For example, if one hand has a small doubleton in a side suit, he needs to know whether his partner has control of that suit for slam purposes. If the owner of the small doubleton uses Blackwood and discovers that the partnership is missing one ace, he will not be able to bid slam with certainty, because the opponents may be able to cash the ace and king of his weak suit.

Blackwood should not be used when the partnership needs to learn specifically which aces it holds rather than just how many aces it holds. Thus, a hand containing a void should rarely bid Blackwood, for unless the partnership has all four aces, he will not know whether or not the essential aces are held. *But see* ROMAN BLACKWOOD.

As between the two partners, the Blackwood bid should be made by the one who has the greater playing strength, or the greater quantity of secondary values. For example, it does little good for a hand such as

♠ A x x x   ♡ K Q x   ◇ K x   ♣ A K x x

to bid Blackwood. Even if the partnership is shown to have all of the aces and kings, what guarantee could this hand have that the partnership had twelve tricks? It is much better for the four notrump bid to come from a hand such as

♠ K Q J x x x   ♡ x   ◇ K Q x x x   ♣ x

When a minor suit has been agreed upon as trumps, the four notrump bidder must be careful that the response to Blackwood cannot embarrass him. For example, if the hand is to be played in clubs, and the Blackwood bidder has only one ace, a response of five diamonds, showing one ace, would have the partnership too high. Similarly, if diamonds are to be the trump suit, and the Blackwood bidder has no aces, a response of five hearts, showing two aces would get the partnership too high.

On occasion, the bidding by the partner of the Blackwood bidder will have been so strong that the embarrassing responses are unlikely to be forthcoming, and Blackwood is really being used in search of a grand slam. In general, however, it is wise not to embark upon Blackwood without at least one ace when diamonds are to be trumps, and two aces if clubs are to be trumps.

When is Four Notrump Not Blackwood?

As simple as the responses to four notrump Blackwood may be, it is sometimes quite difficult to know whether or not a four notrump bid is indeed Blackwood or not. At one end of the scale, it is clear that four notrump is not Blackwood when the four notrump bid is made directly over an opening bid in notrump:

Opener	Responder
2 Notrump	4 Notrump

This four notrump bid is strictly quantitative, asking the opener to bid six notrump with a maximum hand.

At the other end of the scale, it is clear that a jump to four notrump when notrump has never been bid before is Blackwood:

Opener	Responder
1 ♠	3 ♠
4 Notrump	

Here, opener's four notrump bid is clearly Blackwood. But between these two extremes are many difficult cases. For example:

(A)	Opener	Responder
	1 ♠	3 ♣
	3 Notrump	4 Notrump

(B)	Opener	Responder
	1 ♣	1 ♡
	2 Notrump	4 Notrump

(C)	Opener	Responder
	1 Notrump	2 ♣
	2 ♡	4 Notrump

(D)	Opener	Responder
	1 Notrump	3 ♡
	3 Notrump	4 Notrump

Which of the four notrump bids in the above auctions are Blackwood?

There are several key questions that the partner of the four notrump bidder should ask himself in determining whether or not he is being asked to show his aces. The first is whether or not a trump suit has been agreed upon. If a trump suit has definitely been established, four notrump is usually Blackwood. For example, in the auction

Opener	Responder
1 ♡	3 ♡
3 Notrump	4 Notrump

hearts have been established as trumps. Therefore responder's four notrump bid is Blackwood. Similarly, in the auction

Opener	Responder
1 Notrump	3 ♠
4 ◇	4 Notrump

Opener has, by inference, agreed upon spades as trumps; therefore responder's four notrump bid is Blackwood. However, in the auction

Opener	Responder
1 Notrump	3 ♠
3 Notrump	4 Notrump

opener has not agreed on spades as trumps; therefore responder's four notrump bid could be taken as quantitative. However, since responder has no way, absent other conventions, to both establish his suit as trumps and ask about aces, the meaning of his four notrump bid in this auction is still the subject of debate.

When neither partner has supported the other's suit, four

notrump is more often a natural bid than Blackwood. For example:

Opener	Responder
1 ♠	2 ♣
2 ♡	4 ♣
4 Notrump	

Opener's four notrump bid is not Blackwood because no trump suit has been agreed upon. His four notrump bid was a natural bid. However, in the auction

Opener	Responder
1 ♡	3 ◇
3 ♡	4 Notrump

responder's jump to four notrump is Blackwood even though responder has never actually supported hearts. There being no natural meaning to the jump to four notrump when notrump has never before been bid, the bid must be Blackwood.

Another question the partner of the four notrump bidder must ask himself is whether the four notrump bidder has seemed content to play the hand in game. If he has, his four notrump bid is likely to be natural rather than Blackwood. For example:

Opener	Responder
1 Notrump	3 ♣
3 Notrump	4 ◇
4 Notrump	

Since opener was willing to play the hand in three notrump, his partner should not construe his four notrump bid as sudden interest in a slam. Similarly, if four notrump has been bid competitively, there is no reason to interpret it as Blackwood:

North	East	South	West
1 ♡	1 ♠	3 ♡	3 ♠
4 ♡	4 ♠	Pass	Pass
4 Notrump			

Since North was content to play the hand in four hearts, his four notrump bid cannot be Blackwood.

Another revealing question is whether the four notrump bidder has shown a weak hand earlier in the auction. If he has, his four notrump bid is not likely to be Blackwood. For example

Opener	Responder
2 ♠	2 Notrump
3 Notrump	4 Notrump

Responder has made a negative response to the strong two-bid. He is hardly likely to have a hand with which he can profitably ask about aces. More likely responder has a maximum point-count for his negative response, and perhaps one that is worth more than the normal minimum, but is lacking in quick tricks.

However, if responder has made a positive response to the strong two bid, there is no reason he cannot want to use Blackwood:

Opener	Responder
2 ♠	3 ♢
3 Notrump	4 Notrump

Here responder's four notrump bid should be taken as Blackwood.

Yet another question to be asked in assessing whether or not four notrump is Blackwood is whether four notrump was bid at the first genuine opportunity to use Blackwood, and if not, whether the four notrump bidder made a cue-bid apparently attempting to elicit information before bidding four notrump. If the answer to either of those questions is in the affirmative, the four notrump bid is more likely Blackwood than natural. For example

Opener	Responder
1 ♡	3 ♡
3 ♠	4 ♣
4 Notrump	

Opener's four notrump bid is Blackwood even though he did not use the convention at his very first opportunity, over three hearts. He cue-bid first and having received a return cue-bid, bid four notrump. His bid is clearly Blackwood.

Four notrump is also Blackwood if the four notrump bidder has opened with a strong two-bid, or if he has jump-shifted. For example

Opener	Responder
1 ♠	3 ♣
3 Notrump	4 Notrump

Responder's four notrump bid should be considered Blackwood since he made a jump shift response to the opening bid. Having made that response responder has no room to jump to four notrump, and he could well have the type of hand with which it is appropriate to ask for aces.

Four notrump is not Blackwood over an opponent's opening bid of four hearts or four spades. Over these preempts the four notrump bid is needed as a takeout bid. Over an opponent's preempt of four clubs or four diamonds, however, it is a close question as to whether four notrump should be considered to be natural or to be Blackwood.

The key to asking about aces in many of the above auctions in which the partner of the four notrump bidder had already bid notrump, is the use of the GERBER convention. Its use can clarify many otherwise troublesome auctions. *See also* COMBINING JACOBY WITH TEXAS.

Responding to Blackwood with a Void

The question of what the partner of the Blackwood bidder should do about a void divides into two questions: (1) whether or not he should show it, and (2) if so, how.

The void can never be simply counted as an ace and included in the ace-showing response. If the void is to be shown, it will have to be shown in some way out of the mainstream of responses.

The void should not be shown unless the responder has reason to think that it would be valuable for the Blackwood bidder to know about it. For example, a void in the Blackwood bidder's suit is usually not a helpful void. A void in the opponent's suit, however, is normally quite useful.

Another part of the question as to whether the void should be disclosed is whether it can be done without getting the partnership too high. Some partnerships agree, for instance, that a void cannot be shown by one who has opened the bidding or made a jump shift response unless he has two aces. If the Blackwood responder has not opened the bidding or made a jump shift, according to this agreement, he is allowed to show his void even if he has only one ace.

There are several ways in which the partnership could agree to show voids. First, the void could be shown by a jump to the six level, in the suit which the responder would have bid at the five level but for the void. For example, if the responder has one ace his response would have been five diamonds. With one ace and a void, his response would be six diamonds. A jump to six clubs would show no aces and a void, and a jump to six hearts would show two aces and a void.

While this method is precise with respect to the number of Aces held by the responder, it does not always reveal the location of his void. Another convention is designed to help identify which is the suit of the Blackwood responder's void. Using this second convention, the Blackwood responder would jump to six of his void suit unless it ranked higher than the partnership's agreed trump suit. In the latter event the responder would jump to six of the agreed trump suit. For example, if the bidding has gone

Opener	Responder
1 ♡	3 ♡
4 Notrump	6 ♣

using this method responder shows a void in clubs. If he had jumped to six hearts instead of six clubs, he would have been showing a void in spades.

When the trump suit is clubs or diamonds, a jump to six of the trump suit will be ambiguous as to which is the suit of the Blackwood responder's void. Moreover, regardless of what the trump suit is, this method does not allow the Blackwood responder to specify how many aces he has. Thus, in the above auction, responder has pinpointed a club void, but how many aces does he have?

A third method of showing voids requires the Blackwood responder to bid five notrump with two aces and a void, and to jump to the six level with one ace and a void. Using this method the responder will jump to six of his void suit if it ranks below the agreed trump suit, or to six of the trump suit if his void is higher ranking. These methods prevent the Blackwood bidder from asking about kings, but it is probably more valuable for him to know that his partner has two aces and a void, or one ace and a specific void, than to be able to inquire as to kings. Using this way of distinguishing between hands with two aces and hands with one also allows identification of the void suit more often in the situation in which locating the void is more likely to be crucial to a grand slam. When the responder has only one ace the location of the void is more likely to be a cardinal piece of information than it is when he has two aces and a void.

A somewhat similar method of showing voids involves the use of a three-step schedule of Blackwood responses. For example, in the Romex system, aces are shown as follows:

$$5 \clubsuit = 0 \text{ or } 3 \text{ aces}$$
$$5 \diamondsuit = 1 \text{ or } 4 \text{ aces}$$
$$5 \heartsuit = 2 \text{ aces}$$

If the responder has a void and at least one ace his responses will be higher than the five heart response. He will bid five spades if his void is in spades and he has one ace; he will bid five notrump if he has two aces and any void; he will jump to six of his void suit if it ranks below the agreed upon trump suit; or he will jump to six of the trump suit if his void ranks higher. Since responder can pinpoint a spade void when he holds one ace the only ambiguity as to where the void lies is if the trump suit is clubs and responder has a void in diamonds or hearts.

Yet another method of showing voids involves a temporizing bid by the Blackwood responder if he has two or more aces. With at least two aces and a void, the Blackwood responder should understate the number of aces he holds by two (assuming that his response will not land him in the agreed trump suit—if it would, he should respond normally). Thus, with three aces and a void, the response will be five diamonds; with two aces and a void, the response will be five clubs. When the Blackwood bidder returns to five of the trump suit, the responder now bids the suit of his void. The message to the Blackwood bidder is that his partner has two more aces than originally shown, and a void in the suit he has just bid. For example:

Opener	Responder
1 ◇	1 ♡
1 ♠	3 ◇
4 Notrump	5 ♣
5 ◇	6 ♣

Responder's six club bid reveals that he has two aces instead of none, and that he is void in clubs.

Using this method, if the responder has one ace and a void, and wants to be in slam, he can show his void in the following way: if his void suit ranks below the trump suit he jumps to six of the void; if his void suit ranks just above the trump suit he responds five notrump; and if his void suit ranks two suits above the trump suit he jumps to six of the trump suit. For example:

Opener	Responder
1 ◇	1 ♡
1 ♠	3 ◇
4 Notrump	6 ◇

Responder's six diamond bid shows that he has one ace and a

void in the suit ranking two higher than the trump suit, i.e., spades.

Using this method, if the Blackwood responder wants to bid a slam holding no aces and a void, his proper course of action is to respond as if he had three aces. If his desire to be in slam with no aces in his own hand is warranted, his partner will be able to tell that he has overstated the number of aces he holds. The Blackwood bidder in that auction is forced to rebid five notrump so that the responder can show the suit of his void as best he can. If his void ranks lower than the trump suit, he bids six of his void; if it ranks higher he bids six of the trump suit. Thus, the auction might go

Opener	Responder
2 ♣	2 ♠
3 ♡	4 ♡
4 Notrump	5 ♠
5 Notrump	6 ◇
7 ♡	

The opener's and responder's hands might be:

(Opener)
♠ A x   ♡ A K Q x x x   ◇ K x   ♣ A Q x

(Responder)
♠ K Q J 10 x   ♡ J x x x   ◇ —   ♣ K x x x

Suppressing Aces

When the responder to Blackwood has already shown one of his aces, a question arises as to whether he should show it again in responding to four notrump. For example, the Blackwood responder may have opened the bidding with a GAMBLING THREE NOTRUMP, showing a solid suit. Or he may have cue-bid the opponent's suit.

In general, unless the partnership has discussed it, the responder should show all of his aces. However, the more effective partnership agreement is to decline to include the ace of the opponents' suit in the Blackwood response when one member of the partnership has made a point of cue-bidding that suit to show a void.

For example, suppose North holds

♠ —   ♡ K J 10 x x x x   ◇ A Q J x   ♣ K x

and the bidding goes

North	East	South	West
1 ♡	1 ♠	3 ♡	Pass

North should cue-bid three spades, planning to follow with a Blackwood bid. Having taken the time to cue-bid first, the Blackwood bid would ask South to exclude the ace and king of spades from his responses. South might have either

[A] ♠ A x x   ♡ Q x x x   ◇ K x x   ♣ A x x

or

[B] ♠ Q x x   ♡ A x x x   ◇ K x   ♣ A x x x

Similarly, if the partner of the Blackwood bidder has made a cue bid that definitely shows first round control of the opponent's suit, he should exclude this ace from his considerations. If his cue-bid could have been made with less than first round control, however, he should show all of his aces and kings in response to Blackwood.

After a cue-bid by either partner has been followed by Blackwood and the appropriate response given, a rebid of five notrump by the Blackwood bidder asking about kings does not guarantee that the partnership has all four of the aces, but only all of the aces that matter for their suit contract.

ROMAN BLACKWOOD

One modification of the Blackwood convention which compresses the ace-showing responses in order to make room for the exchange of other information is called Roman Blackwood. Using this version, if the partner of the Blackwood bidder has two aces he has a choice of responses. If he feels that he has values he has not yet shown, he can respond five spades; otherwise he responds five hearts. The complete list of responses is as follows:

> 5 ♣ = 0 or 3 aces
> 5 ♦ = 1 or 4 aces
> 5 ♡ = 2 aces without extra values
> 5 ♠ = 2 aces with extra values

For example, suppose the auction has proceeded

Opener	Responder
1 ♣	1 ♦
1 ♠	4 ♡*
4 Notrump	
*singleton heart	

and responder has the following hand:

♠ A Q x x　　♡ x　　♦ A x x x x　　♣ Q x x

Responder has the queen of trumps which in itself qualifies as an extra value; in addition he has the queen of opener's first bid suit. His hand is surely worth a five spade response.

Original Roman Responses

As originally devised, the five heart and five spade responses to Roman Blackwood were slightly different. A five heart response showed two "matching" aces, meaning aces of the same color or rank. There are four pairs of matching aces: clubs and diamonds, clubs and spades, diamonds and hearts, and hearts and spades. A five spade response showed two aces which did not match either in color or in rank. There are two pairs of these: hearts and clubs, and diamonds and spades.

This system of responses was valuable when the Blackwood bidder had one ace and his partner's response was five spades, showing non-matching aces—because the Blackwood bidder could always deduce which ace the partnership was missing. For example, if the Blackwood bidder had the ace of hearts and his partner held non-matching aces, they could only be the aces of diamonds and spades.

However, the five heart response occurred twice as often as the five spade response, and the Blackwood bidder who held one ace had to guess which two aces his partner held. He could always know one, but since there were two ways for that one ace to match another ace, the response was ambiguous.

Blue Team Roman Responses

An alternative method of showing aces is designed, in part, to cure the defect that plagued the original Roman Blackwood responses, and in part to provide the partnership with more room to explore after aces have been announced.

The Blue Team responses to Roman Blackwood are as follows:

5 ♣ = 1 or 4 aces

5 ◇ = 0 or 3 aces

5 ♡ = 2 aces of the same rank

5 ♠ = 2 aces of different ranks and different colors

5 NT = 2 aces of the same color.

Thus, the meanings of the five club and five diamond responses are the reverse of their standard Roman meanings. The rationale for reversing their meanings is that using the cheaper bid to show one ace conserves space when it is more likely to be needed. Further slam exploration is usually unnecessary when the Blackwood response has shown no aces; but it may be warranted if one ace has been shown.

The ambiguity of the original Roman five heart response has been cured by adding a five notrump response to show two specific pairs of aces. In this way the Blackwood bidder who has only one ace will know precisely which two aces his partner has.

This use of the five notrump bid may prevent the Blackwood bidder from inquiring about his partner's kings. This may be a disadvantage, since the number of kings held may be crucial to the determination of whether or not grand slam is a sound proposition. However, the advantage of using the five notrump response in this way is that Blackwood may now be bid by a player who has one ace and a void. If the response shows two aces, he will know whether or not one of the aces is in his void suit.

There does not appear to be any particular magic in maintaining the Rank-Mixed-Color order of responses set out above. The partnership could as easily agree to any ordering of the three groupings.

KEY CARD BLACKWOOD

When slam is to be played in a suit, the king of the trump suit is almost as important a card as any ace. If the partnership is lacking both an ace and the trump king, the slam is likely to be a poor proposition.

One convention intended to help the partnership to determine whether it has the trump king and sufficient aces to be in a slam is called Key Card Blackwood. This convention treats the king of the trump suit as a fifth ace. The responses to the four notrump bid are as follows:

$$5 \clubsuit = 0 \text{ or } 4 \text{ aces}$$

$$5 \diamondsuit = 1 \text{ or } 5 \text{ aces}$$

$$5 \heartsuit = 2 \text{ aces}$$

$$5 \spadesuit = 3 \text{ aces}$$

Use of Key Card Blackwood can help the partnership to bid grand slams that might otherwise be missed, or be bid without certainty that they had a solid trump suit, and to stay out of slams that might otherwise be bid. For example, suppose North held

♠ A Q x x x x   ♡ x   ◇ A K Q x x   ♣ x

and the auction had started as follows:

North	South
1 ♠	3 ♠
4 Notrump	

The king of spades is crucial to the success of the grand slam, and use of Key Card Blackwood responses will reveal whether or not South has that king.

Again, suppose the North and South hands were as follows:

North:
♠ A J x x x x   ♡ A x x   ◇ x   ♣ K Q x

South (opener):
♠ Q x x x   ♡ K Q   ◇ A K Q x x   ♣ A x

Using Key Card Blackwood, the bidding would proceed

(A) | South | North |
|---|---|
| 1 ◇ | 1 ♠ |
| 4 ♠ | 4 Notrump |
| 5 ♡ | 6 ♠ |

Thus the partnership would easily avoid the grand slam.

Five Notrump Rebid

After the response to the four notrump Key Card Blackwood bid has been made, a bid of five notrump confirms that the partnership holds all five "keys". There are a number of ways to use the five notrump bid. The simplest is to ask the responder how many of the remaining kings are held. However, in bidding five notrump, the Blackwood bidder is exploring the prospects of grand slam, and with respect to grand slams, the question is usually not how many kings are held, so much as whether the right kings are held.

For example, North holds:

♠ A Q x x x x   ♡ x   ◇ x   ♣ A Q x x x

and the bidding has started

(B) *North*   *South*
    1 ♠   3 ♠
    4 Notrump   5 ♠
    5 Notrump

South's five spade bid shows three key cards, in this case two aces and the king of spades. North bids five notrump hoping to find out whether the partnership can make a grand slam. He needs to find out only about the king of clubs, however, and has no interest in how many other kings South might have.

The more useful treatment of the five notrump bid, therefore, is to guarantee that the partnership holds all of the aces plus the king of trumps, and to ask the responder to bid a grand slam if he thinks he has a suitable hand. If the responder does not think his hand is good enough to jump to the grand slam, but thinks he has extra values considering his previous bidding, he should make a cue-bid. This will usually show a king. With a hand that is not suitable to bid a grand slam, and that has no values in reserve, the responder would sign off in six of the trump suit.

For example, suppose South held one of the following hands, and the auction had proceeded as in B:

[C] ♠ K x x x   ♡ A K x x   ◇ A x x   ♣ J x

[D] ♠ K J x x   ♡ A J x   ◇ A x x   ♣ x x x

With Hand C South would cue bid six hearts over five notrump, having excellent controls, but not a hand that can guarantee enough tricks for a grand slam. With Hand D, South would simply bid six spades, having nothing in reserve.

However, if South has a hand such as

[E] ♠ K x x x   ♡ A x   ◇ A K Q J x   ♣ x x

and the bidding has started

North	South
1 ♠	3 ◇
4 ♣	4 ♠
4 Notrump	5 ♠
5 Notrump	

South would bid seven spades over five notrump, having a source of tricks in his own hand.

Which Suit is Trump?

The major disadvantage of Key Card Blackwood is that when it is not completely clear which suit has been agreed upon as trumps, there will be doubt as to which king is the key king. For example, in the auction

(F) South	North
1 ♡	2 ♣
3 ♣	3 ♡
4 Notrump	

neither partner will be sure, without specific discussion and agreement, which suit is to be the trump suit. If the responder fails to show the right king, the partnership may miss a laydown slam. On the other hand, if the responder shows the wrong king, the partnership may go down in a slam for lack of enough aces.

The simplest solution to this problem is to adopt the general principle that the last suit bid is considered to be the trump suit for the purposes of responding to Key Card Blackwood. This principle should not apply, however, if the four notrump bidder has responded to the opening bid with a strong jump shift, for example:

(G)	*South*	*North*
	1 ♠	3 ♣
	3 ♠	4 Notrump

North's bid of four notrump in sequence G should fix clubs as the trump suit for the purposes of South's responses. The partnership may yet play the contract in spades, but the key card is the king of clubs. North might hold, for example, either of these hands:

[H] ♠ x ♡ A Q ◇ A K x ♣ A Q J x x x x

[I] ♠ K J x x x ♡ x ◇ K x ♣ A Q x x x

With Hand I, if he can find the opener with three aces and the king of clubs, the responder will bid seven spades.

Instead of adopting the principle that the last suit bid fixes the key card, it is possible to a somewhat more complex set of guidelines, as follows:

(1) If only one suit has been supported, count the king of that suit.

(2) If two suits have been supported, count the king of the suit that was supported by the person who bid four notrump. For example, in Auction F, North should count the king of clubs, not the king of hearts.

(3) If the opening bid was a strong forcing bid such as two clubs, or a Schenken one club opening, count the king of the opener's bid suit. For example:

North	South
2 ♣	2 ♠
3 ♡	3 ♠
4 Notrump	

South should count the king of hearts, not the king of spades.

(4) If the responder made a strong jump shift response to the opening bid, count the king of his suit (as in Auction G).

(5) If none of the four rules stated above applies, count the king of the last bid suit. For example:

North	South
1 ♠	2 ♣
2 ♠	4 Notrump

North should count the king of spades, not the king of clubs.

It is also possible to use Roman type responses to Key Card Blackwood as follows:

$$5 \clubsuit = 0 \text{ or } 3 \text{ aces}$$
$$5 \diamondsuit = 1 \text{ or } 4 \text{ aces}$$
$$5 \heartsuit = 2 \text{ or } 5 \text{ aces}$$

For other conventions focusing on the trump king or on trump suit quality in general, *see* GRAND SLAM FORCE, MALOWAN, BARON SLAM TRY, CULBERTSON TRUMP ASKING BIDS, ROMEX TRUMP ASKING BIDS, RH FOUR NOTRUMP, WANG TRUMP ASKING BIDS.

BABY BLACKWOOD

Occasionally the use of Blackwood will get the partnership to an uncomfortably high contract. Some partnerships have adopted a low level Blackwood bid called Baby Blackwood. As it is normally used the Baby Blackwood convention is a bid of three notrump by the opening bidder after the responder has made a strong forcing raise of the opener's suit. For example,

Opener	Responder
1 ♠	3 ♠
3 Notrump	

Using Baby Blackwood, opener's three notrump bid asks for aces. This three notrump rebid by the opener is rarely put to any other use. But see WANG TRUMP ASKING BIDS.

The Baby Blackwood convention may be extended to have the responder's jump to three notrump over the opening bid of one heart or one spade ask for aces:

Opener	Responder
1 ♡	3 Notrump

This use of the three notrump bid would mean that three notrump could not be used in its natural sense, or as a strong forcing raise of the opener's suit as it is by many partnerships which use limit jump raises.

In addition, it is possible for the responder to use the Baby Blackwood convention by a jump to two notrump over his partner's one heart or one spade opening. When the partnership has agreed to use this version of Baby Blackwood, a series of notrump rebids by the responder can ask opener successively about his kings, queens and jacks:

Opener	*Responder*
1 ♠	2 Notrump ("how many aces?")
3 ♡	3 Notrump ("how many kings?")
4 ♢	4 Notrump ("how many queens?")
5 ♢	5 Notrump ("how many jacks?")

The use of the jump to two notrump as Baby Blackwood precludes use of that response as a natural bid showing a balanced 13 to 15 point hand, or as BARON TWO NOTRUMP or JACOBY TWO NOTRUMP, *q.v.*

RESPONDING TO BLACKWOOD OVER OPPONENT'S INTERFERENCE

When an opponent makes a bid directly over partner's four notrump Blackwood bid, he either usurps one of the bids available to the responder to show his aces, or bids a higher ranking suit than the suit in which the responder would properly have responded. For example:

South	*West*	*North*	*East*
1 ♢	3 ♡	4 Notrump	5 ♡

If South has no aces, or one or two aces, he can no longer make the bid he would have made without interference to show how many aces he has. If he has three aces and bids five spades, his partner cannot be sure, without some conventional understanding, what this bid means.

The standard way of dealing with interference over a Blackwood bid is to double the overcall whenever the size of the prospective penalty seems great enough to warrant abandoning the slam search. When the size of the probable penalty does not seem so attractive, the responder would pass to show that he has no aces, bid the next higher ranking suit over the overcall to show one ace, or bid the second suit above the overcall to show two aces, and so forth. In the above auction, for example, if South thought slam was still worth a try, he would pass to show no aces, bid five spades to show one ace, bid five notrump to show two aces, bid six clubs to show three aces, and bid six diamonds to show all four aces.

For other methods of dealing with opponents who interfere with the responses to Blackwood, *see* DOPI AND PODI, DEPO.

DOPI AND PODI

There are several conventions for bidding over Blackwood interference that do not use the double for penalties, but instead use it as part of a schedule of ace-showing bids. The simplest such convention is called DOPI (pronounced "dopey"). The DOPI convention uses a double to show no aces, a pass to show one ace, the bid of the cheapest suit over the overcall to show two aces, the bid of the second cheapest suit to show three aces, and so forth. The name DOPI might be called an alphanumeric acronym, since the D stands for Double and the P stands for Pass, and the O and I are numerals representing the number of aces held.

It is also possible to use Roman responses to DOPI. Using Roman DOPI, the partner of the Blackwood bidder acts as follows over the interference:

$$Double = 0 \text{ or } 3 \text{ aces}$$

$$Pass = 1 \text{ or } 4 \text{ aces}$$

$$Next \text{ suit} = 2 \text{ aces}$$

A similar convention is called PODI (or DIPO), in which the meanings of the double and the pass are reversed, the pass showing no aces and the double showing one ace. There seems to be little technical reason to prefer DOPI over PODI, or vice versa. However, DOPI is much more widely used, probably for psychological reasons. It seems more natural to double the opponents when there are no aces, making a slam seem more remote.

DEPO

Another Blackwood interference convention, one with a strictly alphabetical acronym, is called DEPO. Using DEPO the responder will double to show no aces, two aces or four aces, and will pass to show one ace or three. Since zero is considered to be an even number, the initials of DEPO stand for Double Even, Pass Odd.

The DEPO convention saves the partnership more room than DOPI or PODI, but has the disadvantage of being ambiguous. Usually the Blackwood bidder should be able to judge from his own hand and from the previous bidding how many aces the responder is showing, but he will not always be able to do so.

In order to retain accuracy as much as possible while saving space when it is most needed, some partnerships use DOPI at the five level, and use DEPO at the six level, where space is usually at a premium.

GERBER

Another ace-asking convention in widespread use is the Gerber convention. The Gerber convention uses a four club bid to ask about aces. One of the great advantages of Gerber is that it may allow the partnership to learn below the game level how many aces it has.

The responses to the Gerber four club bid are as follows:

$$4 \diamondsuit = 0 \text{ or } 4 \text{ aces}$$

$$4 \heartsuit = 1 \text{ ace}$$

$$4 \spadesuit = 2 \text{ aces}$$

$$4 \text{ Notrump} = 3 \text{ aces}$$

Originally, a bid of five clubs was used to show all of the aces. Most partnerships, however, use the four diamond bid to show 0 or 4 aces, just as the five club bid in response to Blackwood shows 0 to 4 aces. The reason is that it saves room, and that the Gerber bidder is unlikely to be unable to determine whether his partner holds all of the aces or none.

Some partnerships use the four club bid as Gerber in all auctions in which a trump suit has been agreed or where no-trump has been bid. For example

(A)	Opener	Responder
	1 ♠	3 ♠
	4 ♣	

(B)	Opener	Responder
	1 ♡	3 ♡
	3 ♠	4 ♣

For these partnerships opener's four club bid in Auction A, and responder's four club bid in Auction B would both be Gerber.

Most experts, however, are unwilling to give up the use of four clubs as a cue-bid. They use Gerber only after notrump has been opened or responded or rebid. These partnerships tend to use Gerber freely in notrump auctions, in any situation in which a four notrump bid could be used in its natural or quantitative sense. For example

(C)	*Opener*	*Responder*
	1 Notrump	4 ♣
(D)	*Opener*	*Responder*
	1 ♢	1 ♠
	2 Notrump	4 ♣
(E)	*Opener*	*Responder*
	1 Notrump	2 ♣
	2 ♡	4 ♣
(F)	*Opener*	*Responder*
	1 ♢	2 Notrump
	4 ♣	

In each of the above auctions, C through F, the four club bid is the Gerber convention.

Further, in notrump auctions, only the partner of the notrump bidder may use the Gerber convention. The rationale is that the player who has shown a balanced hand by bidding notrump is almost never the partner who should ask about aces. Thus in the auctions

(G) *Opener*   *Responder*
      1 Notrump   3 ♡
      4 ♣

(H) *Opener*   *Responder*
      1 Notrump   2 ♦ (slam try)
      2 ♠   3 ♠
      4 ♣

opener's four club bids are cue-bids, not Gerber.

Over three notrump rebids, the four club bid is frequently needed as a natural bid. Some partnerships agree, therefore, that a Gerber bid must be a jump—either to four clubs or to five clubs. For example

(I) *Opener*   *Responder*
      1 ♠   2 ♦
      2 Notrump   4 ♣

(J) *Opener*   *Responder*
      1 ♠   2 ♦
      3 Notrump   4 ♣

In Auction I, responder jumped to four clubs; therefore his bid was Gerber. In Auction J, however, responder's four club bid was not a jump; therefore it is a natural bid, rather than Gerber. If responder wanted to use Gerber over opener's three notrump rebid, he would have to jump to five clubs:

        Opener   *Responder*
        1 ♠   2 ♦
        3 Notrump   5 ♣

Gerber for Kings

As the convention was originally devised, the Gerber bidder asked for kings by bidding the cheapest possible suit, other than the trump suit, over the ace showing response. For example

Opener	Responder
1 ♡	3 ♡
4 ♣	4 ♡
4 ♠	

Opener's four spade bid asked for kings.

To avoid misunderstandings, however, most partnerships agree that in order to ask about kings the Gerber bidder must rebid five clubs over the ace-showing response.

In response to the five club bid, kings are shown as follows:

$$5 \diamondsuit = 0 \text{ kings}$$

$$5 \heartsuit = 1 \text{ king}$$

$$5 \spadesuit = 2 \text{ kings}$$

$$5 \text{ Notrump} = 3 \text{ kings}$$

$$6 \clubsuit = 4 \text{ kings}$$

As is the case with the Blackwood convention, the authorities are not in agreement as to the proper response to show all four kings. Most indicate that a response of five diamonds shows 0 or 4 kings. However, there appears to be little reason why it is not safer to bid six clubs with all of the kings, to avoid any ambiguity.

There are a variety of offshoots of the Gerber convention. *See* ROMAN GERBER, KEY CARD GERBER, SUPER GERBER, ACE IDENTI-

FICATION, BLACK AND RED GERBER, EXTENDED GERBER, CLARAC SLAM TRY, FANE FOUR CLUB CONVENTION.

Interference with Gerber

There are several methods of showing aces after interference by an opponent. *See* RESPONDING TO BLACKWOOD OVER AN OPPONENT'S INTERFERENCE, DOPI AND PODI, DEPO.

GERBER AFTER TWO NOTRUMP AND THREE NOTRUMP OPENINGS

When the bidding has been opened with two notrump—either directly or by way of an artificial two club opening, i.e.,

Opener	Responder
2 ♣	2 ◇
2 Notrump	

—a question arises as to how a genuine club suit may be shown. For example, suppose the bidding is opened with two notrump and the responder has a hand such as

♠ K x x   ♡ x   ◇ Q x x   ♣ K J 10 x x x

A bid of three clubs does not show the club suit because three clubs is normally used as Stayman. Some partnerships use the immediate jump to four clubs as Gerber, and in addition treat a bid of three clubs followed by four clubs as Gerber. These partnerships have no way to bid clubs naturally.

Since it is obviously useful for the responder to be able to check for aces after looking for a major suit fit, a response of three clubs followed by four clubs should be Gerber. There is no reason, moreover, why the responder should not always use this sequence when he wants to bid Gerber. In this way, the immediate jump to four clubs may be reserved to show a club suit. It should not matter that the opener will not know, when responder bids three clubs and then four clubs, whether responder has a four card major suit, or whether his three club bid was just temporizing, paving the way to Gerber.

Over a three notrump opening the question is not so much whether a four club response is natural, as which artificial bid it should be considered to be. Some partnerships use the four club response to a three notrump opening as the Stayman convention; some use it as the Gerber convention. Whichever use four clubs is put to, a four diamond response can be used for the other convention. It seems somewhat preferable to use the four diamond bid as Stayman, and to use four clubs as Gerber, giving the opener maximum room to show the number of aces he holds.

Some partnerships solve this problem by using four clubs as Stayman, and using a jump to five clubs as Gerber.

ROMAN GERBER

A variety of modifications and extensions of the Gerber convention have been devised. Some are patterned after modifications of the Blackwood convention. For example, it is possible to use Roman style responses to Gerber, as follows:

$$4 \diamondsuit = 0 \text{ or } 3 \text{ aces}$$
$$4 \heartsuit = 1 \text{ or } 4 \text{ aces}$$
$$4 \spadesuit = 2 \text{ aces}$$

The Romex system uses a modification of Roman Gerber in which the pairs of aces are identified with greater particularity. The Romex responses are:

$4 \diamondsuit$ = 0 or 3 aces

$4 \heartsuit$ = 1 or 4 aces

$4 \spadesuit$ = 2 aces of the same color

4 NT = 2 aces of the same rank

$5 \clubsuit$ = 2 aces of different colors and different ranks

If the Gerber response is five clubs, five diamonds becomes the king-asking bid.

KEY CARD GERBER

As with Blackwood, the partnership may agree to use Key Card Gerber in which the king of the trump suit is counted as an ace. Using this modification the responses would be

$$4 \diamondsuit = 0 \text{ or } 4 \text{ aces}$$
$$4 \heartsuit = 1 \text{ or } 5 \text{ aces}$$
$$4 \spadesuit = 2 \text{ aces}$$
$$4 \text{ NT} = 3 \text{ aces}$$

See KEYCARD BLACKWOOD.

SUPER GERBER

One drawback to the use of the Gerber convention is that the four club bid cannot be used as a natural bid or as a cue-bid. Super Gerber is a convention that is designed to minimize this drawback. Super Gerber can use any suit bid between four clubs and five clubs, inclusive, depending on the previous bidding, to ask for aces.

Super Gerber is applicable to two situations. It may be used after a three notrump bid, or it may be used after a minor suit is agreed upon as trumps. If one partner has bid three notrump, Super Gerber is the bid of four of the lowest unbid suit. If all four suits have been bid, Super Gerber is a jump to five clubs. For example, in the auction

Opener	Responder
1 ◇	1 ♠
3 Notrump	4 ♣

responder's four club bid is Super Gerber since clubs have never before been bid. However, in the auction

Opener	Responder
1 ♣	1 ◇
3 Notrump	4 ♡

a four club bid by responder over three notrump would be natural rather than Gerber. Therefore, Super Gerber requires that responder bid four hearts, the lowest ranking unbid suit, to ask for aces. In the auction

Opener	Responder
1 ♠	2 ◇
2 ♡	3 ♣
3 Notrump	5 ♣

all of the suits have been bid. Therefore, four clubs would be used as a natural bid. Super Gerber uses a jump to five clubs to ask for aces.

In its second application, Super Gerber is used when a minor suit fit has been established. In this circumstance Super Gerber is a jump to four of the lowest ranking unbid suit. For example

(A)	Opener	Responder
	1 ◇	3 ◇
	4 ♡	

(B)	Opener	Responder
	1 ◇	2 ◇
	4 ♣	

In Auction A, opener's four heart bid, the jump to four of the lowest unbid suit, is Super Gerber. In Auction B, the four club bid is Super Gerber.

(C)	Opener	Responder
	1 ♣	3 ♣
	4 ◇	

(D)	Opener	Responder
	1 ♡	2 ◇
	3 ◇	4 ♠

In Auction C, opener's four diamond bid is Super Gerber. In Auction D, responder's four spade bid is Super Gerber.

Using this facet of Super Gerber, a minor suit is deemed to be agreed upon not only if it is supported, but also if it is rebid by one player. Thus, in the auction

Opener	Responder
1 ♦	1 ♠
3 ♦	4 ♡

responder's four heart bid is Super Gerber. Similarly, in an auction such as

Opener	Responder
1 ♣	2 ♦
2 Notrump	3 ♦
4 ♡	

opener's four heart bid is Super Gerber.

One advantage of Super Gerber over Blackwood when a minor suit is to be trump is that it keeps the auction from bypassing the partnership's game contract when there are not enough aces for slam.

The responses to Super Gerber are the standard series of four steps:

First step = 0 or 4 aces

Second step = 1 ace

Third step = 2 aces

Fourth step = 3 aces

Super Gerber may be used for kings by rebidding the Super Gerber suit. Thus, in the auction

Opener	Responder
1 ♣	2 ◇
2 Notrump	3 ◇
4 ♡	5 ♣
5 ♡	

responder's five club bid, the third step, showed two aces, and opener's five heart bid, repeating the Super Gerber suit, asked about kings.

An ambiguity may arise when five clubs has been used as the Super Gerber bid. Five clubs is used as Super Gerber only when all of the suits have been bid; therefore, if the Super Gerber bidder subsequently rebids six clubs, it may not be clear whether he is bidding clubs naturally, or is asking about kings. For example:

Opener	Responder
1 ♠	2 ◇
2 ♡	3 ♣
3 Notrump	5 ♣
5 ♠	6 ♣

Responder's six club bid is ambiguous.

In a few situations the use of Super Gerber precludes the use of splinter or fragment bids after a minor suit has been agreed. This effect is limited, however, to situations in which the Super Gerber bidder has not bid notrump showing a balanced hand, and where the singleton is in the lowest ranking unbid suit. For example

(E) *Opener*   *Responder*
    1 ♣   3 ♣
    4 ◇

(F) *Opener*   *Responder*
    1 ♣   3 ♣
    4 ♡

In Auction E, opener's four diamond bid would be Super Gerber. But in Auction F, there is no reason why his four heart bid (or a four spade bid) could not be used to show a singleton.

ACE IDENTIFICATION

The Ace Identification convention is an extension of the Gerber convention, used after the responder has shown one or two aces, showing the Gerber bidder that the partnership is missing one ace. After the Gerber response, a bid of four notrump asks for further information, identifying the ace or aces held.

If the response to Gerber has shown one ace, the four notrump bid asks the responder to bid the suit in which he holds the ace. If the response to Gerber has shown two aces, the four notrump bid asks the responder to bid as follows:

> 5 ♣ = two aces of the same color
>
> 5 ♢ = two aces of the same rank
>
> 5 ♡ = two aces of different colors and different ranks

The use of the Ace Identification extension may help the partnership to decide whether or not to bid a slam. If the Gerber bidder has a void, this convention may assist in reaching a grand slam. For example, if South holds

♠ A K Q x   ♡ x x   ♢ K Q x x x x x   ♣ —

and his partner opens the bidding with one notrump, the auction could go

North	South
North	*South*
1 Notrump	2 ♣
2 ♠	4 ♣
4 ♠	4 Notrump
5 ♣	7 ♠

South's four club bid was Gerber, and North showed two aces.
South's four notrump bid asked which two aces North held, and
North's five club bid showed that his aces were the same color.
Knowing that opener had the aces of hearts and diamonds,
South could count thirteen tricks and bid the grand slam. If
North had shown any other two aces, South would have settled
for six spades.

BLACK AND RED GERBER

Another modification of the Gerber convention is designed primarily to solve the problem of how to ask for aces when the agreed suit is clubs. Blackwood might get the partnership too high, while the Gerber convention would be ambiguous. The Black and Red Gerber convention uses a four club bid as Gerber only if a red suit has been agreed upon as trumps. If a black suit has been agreed, the Gerber bid is four diamonds. For example

Opener	Responder
1 ♠	2 ♣
4 ♣	4 ◇

Responder's four diamond bid would be Gerber.

The responses to either Gerber bid are the normal series of four steps:

First	step	= 0 or 4 aces
Second	step	= 1 ace
Third	step	= 2 aces
Fourth	step	= 3 aces

After aces have been shown, a variety of possibilities arise. The Gerber bidder may rebid the Gerber suit to ask for kings. Or he may rebid four notrump to ask his partner to clarify which aces he holds: see ACE IDENTIFICATION. Or he may cue-bid. For example, suppose opener holds the following hand:

♠ x   ♡ A K J x x x   ◇ A   ♣ A Q x x x

The bidding might go

Opener	*Responder*
1 ♡	3 ♡
4 ♣	4 ♡
4 ♠	5 ♣
7 ♡	

Responder's four heart bid showed one ace. Opener cue-bid four spades, hoping to find responder with a club control. When responder was able to cue-bid clubs, opener could bid the grand slam.

FANE FOUR CLUB CONVENTION

The Fane four club convention seeks to determine how many aces the responder holds, and which ones they are. The responder to the four club bid starts by bidding his lowest ranking ace. The responses are as follows:

$$4 \diamondsuit = \text{ace of diamonds}$$
$$4 \heartsuit = \text{ace of hearts}$$
$$4 \spadesuit = \text{ace of spades and no other ace}$$
$$4 \text{ NT} = \text{ace of clubs}$$

If the responder to four clubs has either no aces or four aces, he must bid five clubs.

After the response to four clubs, if the four club bidder rebids five clubs, he asks how many aces are held. The responses are

$$5 \diamondsuit = 1 \text{ ace}$$
$$5 \heartsuit = 2 \text{ aces}$$
$$5 \spadesuit = 3 \text{ aces}$$

After a four spade response to four clubs, showing only the ace of spades, a five club bid can be used as a cue-bid, asking the responder to show his lowest ranking king.

If the player who has bid four clubs and five clubs rebids five notrump, he asks how many kings are held. The responses are

$$6 \clubsuit = 0 \text{ kings}$$
$$6 \diamondsuit = 1 \text{ king}$$
$$6 \heartsuit = 2 \text{ kings}$$
$$6 \spadesuit = 3 \text{ kings}$$
$$6 \text{ NT} = 4 \text{ kings}$$

If the partner of the four club bidder has what he considers to be a useful void, he can show a void and the number of aces he holds by jumping to the five level in response to four clubs:

$$5 \diamondsuit = \text{a void and one ace}$$
$$5 \heartsuit = \text{a void and two aces}$$
$$5 \spadesuit = \text{a void and three aces}$$

In order to sign off, the four club bidder may either bid the agreed trump suit or bid four notrump; his partner is required to pass either of these bids. After a five level response, the four club bidder may sign off by bidding an unbid suit, which asks his partner to return to five notrump.

One of the drawbacks of this convention is that the four club bid cannot be used to initiate a normal cue-bidding sequence. Another, is that the partnership may be at the five level with unsuitable hands before it knows how many aces and what controls, are missing. For example, if opener's and responder's hands were

(Opener)
♠ A K Q J x x   ♡ J x x x   ◇ —   ♣ A K x

(Responder)
♠ 10 x x x   ♡ Q x x   ◇ A K Q x   ♣ Q J

the bidding would go

Opener	Responder
1 ♠	3 ♠
4 ♣	4 ♢ (diamond ace)
5 ♣	5 ♢ (only one ace)
5 ♠	Pass

With these hands five spades is in jeopardy of being set with a heart ruff.

ACOL FOUR NOTRUMP OPENING

The Acol four notrump convention uses an opening bid of four notrump to ask the responder if he has any aces. If he has one ace he is expected to identify it. The proper responses are

$$5 \clubsuit = 0 \text{ aces}$$
$$5 \diamondsuit = \text{ace of diamonds}$$
$$5 \heartsuit = \text{ace of hearts}$$
$$5 \spadesuit = \text{ace of spades}$$
$$6 \clubsuit = \text{ace of clubs}$$

If the responder should be endowed with two aces opposite this opening, his proper response is five notrump.

Probably the most useful type of hand with which to use this convention is one that contains a void, such as

$$\spadesuit \text{ A K Q J x x x} \quad \heartsuit \text{ K Q J x} \quad \diamondsuit - \quad \clubsuit \text{ A K}$$

The Acol four notrump opening can be coordinated with standard Blackwood. An Acol four notrump opening could not, for example, be made with a hand such as

$$\spadesuit \text{ x} \quad \heartsuit \text{ K Q J} \quad \diamondsuit \text{ A K Q J x x x x} \quad \clubsuit \text{ x}$$

because any one-ace-showing response would get the partnership out of its depth. However, with this hand, the opener could start things off with a forcing two-bid, planning to bid Blackwood later.

CULBERTSON FOUR-FIVE NOTRUMP

Normally when the Blackwood convention is used, the four notrump bidder becomes the "captain" of the partnership for the remainder of the auction, and the responder simply does as he is told. The Blackwood bidder may have any of a number of hands, and there is little way that the responder can have enough information to sensibly exercise any judgment.

The Culbertson Four-Five Notrump convention sets certain minimum standards for the bid of four notrump. Thus, the bid gives information to the responder, as well as extracting it from him, and allows both partners to use their judgment in assessing slam prospects.

Using the Culbertson convention, the bid of four notrump guarantees either three aces, or two aces plus the king of a suit genuinely bid by the partnership. A suit that has been cue-bid does not count as a genuinely bid suit.

Responding to Four Notrump

The responses to the four notrump bid are as follows. If the partner of the four notrump bidder has either two aces, or one ace and the kings of all of the suits bid by the partnership, his proper bid is five notrump. Whichever of these two hands the responder has, the partnership is guaranteed that it possesses all four aces.

If the responder either has the kings of all the partnership's suits but no ace, or has the ace of a suit bid by the partnership but does not have all of its kings, he has a choice of responses: he may either bid six of the agreed trump suit, or bid five of one of the partnership's suits, so long as it is not their cheapest suit. Which bid he selects will depend on how he evaluates his hand. For example, North might hold

[A] ♠ K x x x x   ♡ K x x   ◇ A x x   ♣ x x

or

[B] ♠ K x x x x   ♡ K x x   ◇ A x   ♣ K x x

with the auction having proceeded

South	North
1 ◇	1 ♠
3 ♠	4 ◇
4 Notrump	

North is allowed to bid either five spades or six spades in response to four notrump. He knows that the partnership may be missing either one ace, or the king of diamonds. With Hand A he would bid five spades, not being sure that he wants to be in slam. Opener's hand might be

♠ A Q x x   ♡ A x   ◇ Q J x x x   ♣ A x

With Hand B, responder should bid six spades, having extra values.

If the partner of the four notrump bidder has an ace or a void in a suit not genuinely bid by the partnership, but does not have all of the kings in the partnership's suits, his assigned response is five of the suit in which he holds the ace or void. For example, suppose North held:

[C] ♠ K x x x x   ♡ K x   ◇ J x   ♣ A Q x x

and the auction started

South	North
1 ♢	1 ♠
3 ♠	4 ♣
4 Notrump	

The four club bid by North was a cue-bid, and did not promise a suit. Therefore, North's proper response to four notrump is five clubs. If South, holding a hand such as

[D]   ♠ A Q x x   ♡ A x   ♢ K Q x x x   ♣ x x

now signs off in five spades, North can nevertheless carry on to six spades with the Hand C above, having values in reserve.

If the partner of the four notrump bidder has neither an ace nor the kings of all of the partnership's suits, he will normally bid five of the partnership's lowest suit.

None of the above Culbertson responses is absolutely forced upon the responder. Since responder knows that his partner's hand must meet certain minimum requirements to have allowed him to bid four notrump, the responder is free to evaluate his own hand in that light. With one exception, if the responder's overall values are poor, he may choose a response that shows less than he actually holds. The exception is that if he holds two aces, or one ace and the kings of all of the partnership's bid suits, he must act aggressively, bidding at least five notrump. Conversely, if his values probably fit exceptionally well with his partner's hand he may choose to overbid.

If the partner of the four notrump bidder has two aces and a king of a side suit, he is allowed to show this by bidding either five or six of the suit in which he has the king. In the event that he bids five of the suit and his partner has the ace, his partner may infer initially that responder has a void in that suit. However, his next response will clarify that he had instead an especially good hand with useful features in the suit he has bid. For example, if he possesses both the king and queen of this side suit he may bid five to show the king, and then rebid six of the suit to show the queen. For example:

Opener	*Responder*
1 ◇	1 ♡
4 ♡	4 Notrump
5 ♣	5 ♡
6 ♣	

Opener might have a hand such as

♠ A x x ♡ K Q x x ◇ A Q x x ♣ K Q

If he had held the queen of spades instead of the queen of clubs, he would have jumped directly to six clubs instead of bidding first five and then six clubs.

Rebids by the Four Notrump Bidder

If the partner of the four notrump bidder has responded at the five level, a rebid of five notrump by the four notrump bidder guarantees that the partnership has all of the aces. If the response to four notrump has been five notrump, the four notrump bidder may show interest in a grand slam by making any bid other than six of the agreed trump suit. For example, if North holds

♠ A K Q x x x   ♡ A x   ◇ x   ♣ K Q x x

and the auction starts

South	North
1 ◇	2 ♠
3 ♠	4 Notrump
5 Notrump	

North knows from the five notrump response that South has the ace of diamonds and the ace of clubs. But he cannot yet count to thirteen tricks. North therefore cue-bids six clubs over five notrump, hoping that his partner will have a king to cue-bid.

South, for example, might have any of the following hands:

[A]   ♠ J x x   ♡ Q x x   ◇ A Q J x x   ♣ A x

[B]   ♠ x x x x   ♡ K x x   ◇ A Q x x   ♣ A x

[C]   ♠ x x x   ♡ x x x   ◇ A K Q x x   ♣ A x

With Hand A, South would content himself with bidding six spades, having no undisclosed controls to bid. With Hand B, South would cue-bid six hearts over six clubs. And with Hand C, South would cue-bid six diamonds, planning to bid again if necessary to get to the grand slam. North, opposite South's cue-bids with Hands B and C, would need no further information to bid seven spades.

Choice Between Four Notrump and a Cue-Bid

When one is interested in a slam and has the choice between bidding Culbertson four notrump and making a cue-bid, a principal consideration is the frugal use of bidding space. For example, if the bidding starts

Opener	Responder
1 ♣	2 ♡
3 ♡	

responder has room to cue-bid before making the Culbertson four notrump bid. By cue-bidding he may gain valuable information.

On the other hand, if the auction starts

Opener	Responder
1 ♣	1 ♢
1 ♡	4 ♡

there is insufficient room to cue-bid, have partner make a cue-bid in turn, and bid four notrump. In such a situation the Culbertson four notrump bid should be made in preference to the cue-bid, for otherwise partner will infer that the cue-bidder lacked the values required to bid four notrump.

SAN FRANCISCO

The San Francisco convention, like the Culbertson Four-Five Notrump convention, imposes minimum requirements on the four notrump bidder. The San Francisco convention, sometimes called the Warren convention, requires that the four notrump bidder hold at least two aces.

The responder simultaneously shows how many aces and kings he has. Counting each ace as three points and each king as one point, the normal responses are as follows:

5 ♣ = fewer than 3 points (no ace, at most 2 kings)

5 ◇ = 3 points (1 ace and no kings, or 3 kings)

5 ♡ = 4 points (1 ace and 1 king, or 4 kings)

5 ♠ = 5 points (1 ace and 2 kings)

5 NT= 6 points (1 ace and three kings, or 2 aces)

6 ♣ = 7 points (2 aces and 1 king, or 1 ace and 4 kings)

6 ◇ = 8 points (2 aces and 2 kings)

6 ♡ = 9 points (2 aces and 3 kings)

6 ♠ = 10 points (2 aces and 4 kings)

If the four notrump bidder has opened the bidding with a strong two-bid, the responses are altered to reflect the reduced potential of the responding hand. In this event, the five club response shows no points, five diamonds shows one point, five hearts shows two points, and so on.

One drawback to the San Francisco convention is that the responses are much more complicated than those for some other ace-asking conventions. Another defect is that several of the responses are ambiguous since they can be made with more than one combination of aces and kings. Usually the four no-trump bidder will be able to tell which holding responder has, but sometimes he will not.

CULWOOD

The Culwood convention, as its name might imply, is something of a combination of Blackwood and the Culbertson Four-Five Notrump convention. The Culwood convention places the same requirements on the four notrump bidder as does the Culbertson convention, but uses some of the Blackwood responses.

The Culwood four notrump bidder is required to have either three aces, or two aces and the king of a suit bid by himself or his partner. The responses are as follows:

5 ♣ = 0 aces

5 ♦ = 1 ace

5 ♡ = 2 aces

5 ♠ = the partnership has all the aces, and the kings of the bid suits

5 NT = the partnership has all of the aces, and the responder has two of the top three trumps in his own hand.

For example, suppose opener's and responder's hands were the following:

(Opener)
♠ K Q x x   ♡ A Q J x x   ♦ A x   ♣ x x

(Responder)
♠ A J x x x   ♡ K x x   ♦ x   ♣ A K x x

Using the Culwood convention the bidding would start

347

Opener	*Responder*
1 ♡	1 ♠
3 ♠	4 Notrump
5 Notrump	

Opener's five notrump bid promises that the partnership has all of the aces, and that opener has two of the top three trump honors.

EXTENDED GERBER

Extended Gerber is a variation of the Gerber convention in which the responses to the four club bid show how many controls, i.e., aces and kings are held. Thereafter, the four club bidder may ask how many kings and queens are held in any two specific suits.

Asking for Aces and Kings

The Extended Gerber convention starts with a four club bid after notrump has been bid, or after a trump suit has been agreed upon. The four club bid asks partner to announce his controls in accordance with the following schedule:

4 ♢ = 0 or 1 controls, or 5 or 6 controls, or 10 or 11 controls

4 ♡ = 2 or 7 controls

4 ♠ = 3 or 8 controls

4 NT = 4 or 9 controls

Thus, if the bidding has gone

Opener	Responder
1 ♠	3 ♠
4 ♣	4 ♢

responder's four diamond bid shows either 0 or 1 control, or 5 or 6 controls, or 10 or 11 controls. Opener asks for further clarification by bidding the next suit, four hearts. Responder will bid four spades if he has the lower of any pair of controls, i.e., 0, 5 or 10 controls. He will bid four notrump if he holds the upper of any pair of controls, i.e., 1, 6 or 11 controls. Opener should be able to tell from his own hand and from the previous bidding whether his partner has nearly all of the controls (there being a total of twelve in the deck), or virtually no controls, or something in between.

If the response to Extended Gerber has been four diamonds, any four level bid except four hearts is a sign off. If the response to Extended Gerber has been anything other than four diamonds, a bid by the four club bidder of four notrump or four of the trump suit is a sign off.

Signing Off at the Five Level

In order to sign off in five diamonds, five hearts or five spades after the ace and king showing response to Extended Gerber has been given, the four club bidder uses a relay. If the four club bidder bids five clubs, the responder is forced to bid five diamonds. This forced response enables the four club bidder to pass, allowing the partnership to play in five diamonds. Similarly, if the four club bidder rebids five diamonds, the responder is forced to bid five hearts; the forced five heart bid may be passed, or the Extended Gerber bidder may bid five spades as a sign off. For example:

Opener	Responder
1 ◇	1 ♡
1 ♠	3 ♠
4 ♣	4 Notrump
5 ◇	5 ♡
5 ♠	Pass

Responder's four notrump response showed either four or nine controls. If opener had a hand such as

♠ K Q x x   ♡ A x   ◇ K Q J x x x   ♣ x

he would know that responder must have four controls, rather than nine. Unless his controls were specifically the aces of spades and diamonds, slam would be a poor proposition. Therefore opener bid five diamonds, forcing responder to bid five hearts, and to pass opener's five spade sign off.

This somewhat convoluted method of signing off leaves other five level bids free to be used as other asking bids.

Asking for Kings and Queens

After the ace and king asking bids have been completed, the four club bidder may ask his partner how many kings and queens he holds in two specified suits. Counting each king as two points and each queen as one, the responder shows his kings and queens in the designated suits in a series of seven steps. The first step shows no points, the second step shows one point, the third step shows two points, and so forth through the seventh step, which shows all six points in the two suits.

There are six pairs of suits that may be asked about. Each pair is asked about by means of a different five-level bid or series of bids, as follows:

Suits of Inquiry	Asking Bids
spades and hearts	direct five notrump bid
spades and diamonds	direct five spade bid
hearts and diamonds	direct five heart bid

spades and clubs	five club bid, followed by a five spade bid
hearts and clubs	five club bid followed by a five heart bid
diamonds and clubs	five club bid followed by a five notrump bid

For example, in the auction

Opener	*Responder*
1 ♡	3 ♡
4 ♣	4 Notrump (4 or 9 controls)
5 ♣ (relay)	5 ◇ (forced)
5 ♡	6 ♡

opener's five heart bid after the five club relay shows that he did not want to sign off after all, but that he wants to know about responder's kings and queens in hearts and clubs. Responder's six heart bid, the fifth step, shows that he has four points in those suits—i.e., either both kings or one king and both queens. Opener might have a hand such as

♠ A x　　♡ A x x x x　　◇ x　　♣ A K x x x

Responder's four notrump bid has told him that responder has four controls, which must be the ace of diamonds and two kings. Opener uses the five club-five heart asking combination of bids to learn whether his trump suit and side suit are solid.

D.I. ("Declarative Interrogative" or "Declarative Informatory")

The D.I. convention is a general slam exploration bid that lies somewhere between the conventions that ask about aces and kings in bunches, and the conventions that ask about specific controls in individual suits. D.I. is a four notrump bid that is not natural and does not ask how many aces are held, but rather asks partner to show a previously undisclosed feature.

There are several situations in which a four notrump bid cannot be D.I. A jump to four notrump is never D.I. Such a jump is either natural or Blackwood. A bid of four notrump over three notrump is also not D.I. In addition, if four notrump is bid by either the opener or the responder at his first or second turn to bid, it is not D.I. For example

Opener	Responder
4 ♡	4 Notrump

Responder's four notrump bid is Blackwood, not D.I. Similarly in the auction

Opener	Responder
1 ♠	4 ♠
4 Notrump	

opener's four notrump bid is not D.I. but Blackwood.

In its original form, a four notrump D.I. bid promised at least two aces if made by an unlimited hand; it promised at least one ace if bid by a limited hand. For example:

(A)

Opener	Responder
1 ♠	3 ♠
4 ♣	4 ◇
4 Notrump	

(B)

Opener	Responder
1 ♠	2 ◇
2 ♡	4 ◇
4 ♠	4 Notrump

In Auctions A and B the four notrump bids promise at least two aces, since four notrump was bid by a hand that is not yet limited. In the following auction, however,

Opener	Responder
1 ♠	2 ♠
4 ♣	4 ◇
4 ♡	4 Notrump

the four notrump bid does not promise more than one ace since responder has already limited his hand.

In addition, some partnerships agree that in order to bid four notrump as D.I. one must have at least second round control of his own suits and any unbid suits. For example, in Auction A above, opener would promise two aces and no worse than K x or a singleton in clubs and hearts; but he might have three small diamonds.

Responses to D.I.

The D.I. responder may make any of three types of responses: negative, encouraging, or positive. To respond negatively to D.I. the responder simply bids five of the agreed trump suit. For example, if opener has

♠ K J x x x   ♡ A J x x   ◇ Q x   ♣ J x

and the auction goes

Opener	Responder
1 ♠	2 ♣
2 ♡	3 ♠
4 ♠	4 Notrump

opener has no reason to want to encourage responder in his slam interest. Therefore he should respond five spades to responder's four notrump D.I. bid.

To make an encouraging response, the D.I. responder bids a control or value at the five level, below the agreed trump suit. Although this is encouraging, it does not necessarily show extra values. For example, if opener had

♠ A Q x x x   ♡ K Q x x   ◇ x x   ♣ K x

in the above auction, he would bid five clubs in response to the D.I. bid.

Any bid by the D.I. responder higher than five of the trump suit is a positive response. A five notrump response is the strongest of all positive responses. It promises two aces, and maximum strength for the previous bidding. For example, if opener had

♠ A K x x x x   ♡ A K Q x   ◇ x x   ♣ x

he could bid five notrump, having two aces, a six-card suit, and solid hearts.

The weakest positive response is a jump to six of the agreed trump suit. This bid suggests that a grand slam would probably be a poor proposition.

Positive responses, above five of the agreed trump suit, other than a bid of six of the trump suit, show extra values, commit the partnership to a small slam, and encourage exploration of grand slam possibilities. For example, suppose opener had

♠ A K x x x   ♡ K Q x x   ◇ K x   ♣ x x

in the auction

Opener	Responder
1 ♠	2 ♣
2 ♡	3 ♠
4 ♠	4 Notrump
6 ◇	

Opener definitely wants to be in slam, but he cannot bid five no-trump because he has only one ace. He therefore bids six diamonds in order to show a diamond control and extra values. His six diamond bid denies the ability to show a club feature. Responder might have a hand such as

[A] ♠ Q x x x   ♡ A x   ◇ A x x   ♣ A x x x

or

[B] ♠ Q x x x   ♡ A x   ◇ A x x   ♣ A K x x

With Hand A, responder should bid six spades, knowing that the partnership may well have a club loser. With Hand B, responder should bid seven spades. Since the opener has shown extra values including a diamond control, the grand slam rates to be a good proposition.

Rebids

If the four notrump D.I. bidder rebids five notrump, he promises one ace more than he originally guaranteed, and he is asking for further information with an eye on grand slam. Responder may bid a grand slam directly over five notrump if he has extra values such as a solid suit, or extra queens, or well placed doubleton kings. Alternatively, the D.I. responder may encourage by showing a low-ranking feature. If he has no reasons to encourage, he signs off at six of the trump suit.

Blue Team D.I.

As most often used today, the D.I. convention does not place as stringent requirements on the D.I. bidder in terms of the number of aces he holds, or the control of his own suits or the unbid suits. Rather, the convention is used principally as an aid to cue-bidding toward slam.

When used in this way, a four notrump bid in the midst of cue-bidding is a general slam try asking for further information. Some of the adherents of D.I. are fond of saying that D.I. stands for "Do-something Intelligent." Suppose, for example, that North holds

♠ Q   ♡ K J x x x x   ◇ A x x   ♣ A Q x

and opens the bidding with a Precision one club bid, showing at least 16 high card points. Thereafter the bidding proceeds:

North	South
1 ♣	1 ♠
2 ♡	3 ♡
4 ♣	4 ♠
4 Notrump	

North's two heart bid showed his suit; South's one spade bid was natural, as was his raise to three hearts. After opener had cue-bid four clubs and responder had cue-bid four spades, opener bid four notrump as D.I., to enable responder to show a minor suit king if he had one. Using standard methods a four notrump Blackwood bid would be unsatisfactory because there are too many things opener needs to find out. A cue-bid by opener of either minor suit over responder's four spade bid might prevent responder from showing his minor suit control. The D.I. bid therefore gave the partnership the greatest flexibility.

The D.I. bid can also be used to determine whether or not the partnership has two losers in a side suit. For example, if opener's and responder's hands were

(Opener)
♠ — ♡ A x ◊ A K 10 x x x ♣ Q J 10 x x

(Responder)
♠ A K x x x ♡ K x ◊ J x x x ♣ x x

the auction might be

Opener	Responder
1 ◊	1 ♠
3 ♣	4 ◊
4 ♡	4 ♠
4 Notrump	5 ◊
Pass	

Responder's five diamond bid in response to D.I. denied a club control. Therefore slam was out of the question.

The D.I. four notrump bid may also be made in a sequence

that makes it clear that control of a particular suit is crucial. For example

Opener	Responder
1 ◇	2 ♡
3 ♡	4 ♣
4 ◇	4 Notrump

Responder's four notrump bid showed an inability to cue-bid spades. Responder's hand might be

♠ x x   ♡ A K J x x x   ◇ x   ♣ A K Q x

If opener has a hand such as

[A]   ♠ x   ♡ Q x x x   ◇ A K Q x x x   ♣ x x

he will bid six hearts. However, if he has

[B]   ♠ Q J x   ♡ Q x x x   ◇ A K Q J x   ♣ x

which is stronger in high cards, but has no spade control, he must sign off in five hearts.

The problem with this use of D.I. is that if opener has a hand such as

[C]   ♠ K x   ♡ Q x x x   ◇ A K Q x x   ♣ x x

the hand belongs in six notrump from opener's side of the table.

CONTROL ASKING BIDS

Asking bids in general are not widely used. The genuine need to use an asking bid tends to arise fairly infrequently. It is only with relatively freakish hands that one needs to find one particular control in partner's hand, and sometimes that information may be obtained in other ways such as cue-bidding. And because the need to use an asking bid arises infrequently, the agreement to use them places a perhaps unprofitable strain on the memory, as to which bids are asking bids, and what the responses are.

On the other hand there are certain situations in which the use of asking bids seem to make more sense than cue-bidding. Cue-bidding is a cooperative process that normally works well when there is not great disparity between the playing strengths of the two hands. In situations, however, where one hand is known to be much stronger than the other—a fact that is sometimes established at an elevated level of the auction—cue-bidding is less satisfactory. The situations in which asking bids seem *a priori* appropriate include cases in which the hand has been opened with a strong two-bid. After the opening and response, there may not be enough room for the opener to cue-bid all of his treasures in an effort to elicit the one piece of information he needs from his partner. Here the opener is likely to be able to pinpoint his interest with a single bid. And opposite a very strong hand, the needed value may be something that is not susceptible to cue-bidding, such as *third* round control of a suit.

Similarly, when one partner opens with a preemptive bid at the three level or the four level, and the other is interested in slam despite the preemptor's announced weakness, asking bids are more appropriate than cue-bids. The partner of the preemptor should be the captain of the hand, rather than one of the crew.

Asking Bids after Strong Two-Bids

For these reasons some partnerships use new suit bids by the opener as asking bids whenever the bidding has been opened with a strong two-bid; they use new suit bids or jumps by the responder as asking bids when the opening bid has been a high-level preempt. For example, suppose opener has

♠ A K x x x   ♡ A K x x   ◇ A K   ♣ x

and the bidding goes 2 ♠ - 4 ♠, with responder's four spade bid denying first or second round control of any suit. Opener would still like to know if responder has the queen of hearts or a doubleton. Thus some partnerships would treat opener's five heart bid in the auction

Opener	Responder
2 ♠	4 ♠
5 ♡	

as an asking bid in hearts, asking responder to bid six spades with third round control of hearts.

If, in response to the two spade opening bid above, responder had raised to three spades, which the partnership had agreed did not deny first or second round controls, opener would again be hard pressed to get the desired information by cue-bidding, because he needs to know not only about the ace of clubs, but again about third round heart control. Thus some partnerships would use the bid of a new suit at the six-level after Blackwood as an asking bid. For example, in the auction

Opener	Responder
2 ♠	3 ♠
4 Notrump	5 ◇
6 ♡	

361

opener's six heart bid would ask about third round heart control. *See also* ROMAN ASKING BIDS, CULBERTSON ASKING BIDS, LEBOVIC ASKING BID, FOUR CLUB ASKING BID, FULWILER ASKING BIDS.

One drawback to asking bids is that they may reserve a bid that could be put to better use in another way. See, e.g., BARON SLAM TRY. The major disadvantage of asking bids is that they pinpoint the weakness to the defenders as well as to the partnership. Even drowsy defenders will frequently lead the suit of the asking bid, and they will generally be right.

Asking Bids over Preempts

When a player wants to try for a slam opposite a preemptive opening by his partner, he normally has no more than one weak spot in his hand. Some partnerships therefore use asking bids over opening preempts.

In response to an opening preempt at the four level, the bid of any new suit would be an asking bid. The opener should show his control of that suit as follows:

First   step = no first or second round control

Second step = king or singleton

Third   step = ace

Fourth step = singleton ace, ace and king, or a void

For example, if the responder held

♠ A x x   ♡ A K x x x x   ◇ x x   ♣ A x

opposite a four spade opening bid, he would bid five diamonds. Over a five heart response, the first step, responder would sign off at five spades. Over a five spade response, the second step, responder would bid six spades. And over any higher step, responder could bid the grand slam.

When the bidding has been opened with a preempt at the three level, standard practice is to treat any new suit bid by the responder on the three level as forcing. A jump response, therefore, is an idle bid. Some partnerships use the jump response over a three-level preempt as an asking bid.

For example, if responder has

♠ Q J x x x   ♡ A Q x   ◇ A K Q x x   ♣ —

opposite a three heart opening, the bidding could start

Opener	*Responder*
3 ♡	4 ♠

Opener should show his spade control according to the above schedule.

In making one of these asking bids, of course, the asker should take care to have sufficient values that the partnership will not be unduly high if the opener lacks control of the asked suit.

ROMAN ASKING BIDS

In order to reduce the taxing of the memory as to what bids are asking bids, some partnerships use unusual jumps in previously unbid suits to ask about controls. These jumps, called Roman asking bids, may be one level higher than that of a jump shift, as in the auction

Opener	Responder
1 ♦	1 ♡
4 ♣	

Or they may be one level higher than that of a cue-bid, as in the auction

Opener	Responder
1 ♠	3 ♠
5 ♣	

The unusual jump asking bid may be used by the responder as well as the opener. For example

Opener	Responder
1 ♦	1 ♡
1 ♠	4 ♣

The unusual jump asking bid may be used in the suit of an opponent's overcall. For example,

North	East	South	West
1 ♡	2 ♣	4 ♣	

Or it may be used in response to an overcall. For example

North	*East*	*South*	*West*
1 ♠	2 ♣	Pass	3 ♠

Responses to Roman Asking Bids

There are essentially two sets of responses to choose from. The older version uses a series of four steps:

First	step	= no first or second round control
Second	step	= king or singleton
Third	step	= ace or void
Fourth	step	= ace and king

One modern variation would use the fourth step, rather than the third step, to show a void.

Suppose opener and responder had the following hands:

(Opener)
♠ A K Q 10 x x   ♡ A   ◇ A x x x   ♣ K Q

(Responder)
♠ J x x x   ♡ x x x x   ◇ x   ♣ x x x x

Using the above responses the auction would be

Opener	*Responder*
2 ♣	2 ◇ (negative)
2 ♠	3 ♠
5 ◇	5 ♠
6 ♠	

Responder's five spade bid, the second step, showed the king of diamonds or a singleton diamond.

The newer series of responses to Roman asking bids uses a six step schedule designed to clarify the nature of the control. The responses are:

> First   step = no first or second round control
>
> Second step = singleton
>
> Third   step = king
>
> Fourth step = ace
>
> Fifth   step = void
>
> Sixth   step = ace and king

If it is known that the responder cannot be short in the suit asked about, the second and fifth steps are eliminated.

Using these responses with the hands set out above, the auction would have been exactly the same. The responder would have bid five spades over the five diamond asking bid. The difference is that the opener would know that responder had a singleton rather than the king—perhaps a crucial question if the asker is looking for solidification of a suit rather than just control.

A player who makes an asking bid does not guarantee first round control of all of the other suits. Sometimes he makes the asking bid in order to determine whether or not it is safe to use Blackwood. For example, opener might have

♠ A K Q x   ♡ A   ◇ K Q x x x x   ♣ x x

in an auction that starts

Opener	*Responder*
1 ◇	1 ♠

Opener cannot afford to bid Blackwood, because he has a small doubleton club. Therefore, he jumps to four clubs, an unusual jump, to ask responder if he has a club control. If responder bids four diamonds, denying control, opener will settle for four spades. If responder bids anything but four diamonds, opener will bid four notrump Blackwood.

Any partnership using asking bids should be sure to discuss and agree, if Blackwood is to be used after an asking bid response shows an ace, whether that ace is to be included in the Blackwood ace-showing responses.

For alternative uses of unusual jumps, see SPLINTERS, FRAGMENTS.

CULBERTSON ASKING BIDS

A Culbertson asking bid, initially, is any bid of a suit other than trumps at or above the four level after a suit has been raised, or any unusual jump to the three level or higher. If no suit has been raised, an unusual jump by inference agrees on the previous suit as trumps. Examples of Culbertson asking bids are:

(A)	*Opener*	*Responder*
	1 ♠	3 ♠
	4 ◇	

(B)	*Opener*	*Responder*
	1 ♣	1 ♠
	4 ◇	

(C)	*Opener*	*Responder*
	1 ♣	1 ♠
	3 ♠	4 ◇

(D)	*Opener*	*Responder*
	1 ♣	3 ♠

Responses to Culbertson Asking Bids

The responses to Culbertson Asking Bids are intricate, showing both control of the suit asked about, and other controls in addition. First round controls include aces and voids, except when the prescribed response is a notrump bid, in which case only aces are counted. Second round controls are kings or singletons; third round controls are queens or doubletons.

If the responder does not have first or second round control of the asked suit, he signs off with a minimum bid in the agreed trump suit. Or, even if he has first or second round control of the asked suit, if he has no first round control in any other suit, he must sign off.

If the responder has first or second round control of the asked suit, and in addition has two aces, he bids the minimum number of notrump.*

If the responder has first or second round control of the asked suit, and in addition has three aces, he jumps in notrump.

If the responder has first or second round control in the asked suit, and in addition has either one ace or a void, he bids the suit in which he has the ace or void. If his ace is in the agreed trump suit, he must jump in it.

If the responder has a void in the asked suit, and has two aces, he jumps in one of the suits in which he has an ace; if one of his aces is in the trump suit, he must jump in the other suit to avoid confusing his response with that which shows lesser values.

In the auction

Opener	Responder
1 ♠	2 ◇
2 ♠	4 ♡

responder's four heart bid is an asking bid, agreeing on spades as trumps. Suppose opener had one of the following hands:

[A] ♠ A Q 10 x x x ♡ x x ◇ x x ♣ A x x

*An Australian modification to this response is that when the responder holds a singleton in the asked suit and two aces, he jumps in the suit of the lower ranking ace.

[B] ♠ A Q 10 x x x   ♡ x   ◇ x x x   ♣ A x x

[C] ♠ A J 10 x x x   ♡ x   ◇ A x x   ♣ A x x

[D] ♠ A J 10 x x x   ♡ —   ◇ K x x   ♣ K Q x x

[E] ♠ A J 10 x x x   ♡ —   ◇ x x x   ♣ A K x x

[F] ♠ K Q J x x x   ♡ —   ◇ x x x   ♣ K Q J x

With Hand A, in which opener lacks control of hearts, he returns to four spades, the agreed trump suit. With Hand B, opener has control of hearts and has two aces; his proper bid is four notrump. The additional ace in Hand C requires opener to jump to five notrump.

With Hand D, opener must show his heart control and one ace by bidding the suit of the ace. However, since the ace is in the trump suit, and a four spade bid would be negative, opener must jump to five spades. With Hand E, opener must jump to six clubs. With Hand F, opener has control of hearts, but he has no other first round controls; therefore he must sign off with a four spade bid.

Further Asking Bid in the Same Suit

The Culbertson asking bidder may make additional asking bids after the response to the first asking bid. He may ask about the same suit, whether the first response was positive or negative. Or he may ask about a new suit.

If the asking bidder rebids the asked suit after a negative response, he asks the responder to clarify his negative response. If the responder has second round control of the asked suit but has no outside ace, he bids the minimum number of no-trump. If the responder has only third round control of the asked suit but has one or more outside aces, he shows this by bidding an outside ace. If the responder has neither control of the asked suit nor an ace, he bids the minimum number of the trump suit.

Thus, in the auction

Opener	Responder
1 ♠	2 ◇
2 ♠	4 ♡
4 ♠	5 ♡

opener might hold

[A] ♠ A J 10 x x x   ♡ x x   ◇ x x   ♣ A x x

[B] ♠ K Q J x x x   ♡ x   ◇ x x   ♣ K Q J x

[C] ♠ K Q J x x x   ♡ x x   ◇ x x   ♣ K Q J

With Hand A opener would bid six clubs, showing third round control of hearts and the ace of clubs. With Hand B, opener would bid five notrump showing second round control, but no aces. With Hand C, opener would bid five spades, denying both control and aces.

If the asking bidder rebids the asked suit after a positive response, he asks whether his partner has third round control of the asked suit, as well as the first or second round control he has already shown. For example, a singleton, or K x, or K Q x constitutes second and third round control. A singleton ace, or A x, or A Q x constitutes first and third round control.

With no third round control, i.e., holding either A x x (x) or K x x (x), the partner of the asking bidder simply signs off in the agreed trump suit. If he has third round control, he should either bid an undisclosed void, or bid a second round control in another suit; or if he has neither of those features, he should bid the minimum number of notrump. Thus, in the auction

Opener	*Responder*
1 ♠	2 ♦
2 ♠	4 ♡
4 Notrump	5 ♡

opener has shown two aces, plus first or second round control of hearts. Suppose opener's hand is one of the following:

[D] ♠ A J 10 x x x   ♡ K x x   ♦ x x   ♣ A x

[E] ♠ A J 10 x x x   ♡ x   ♦ x x x   ♣ A K x

[F] ♠ A J 10 x x x   ♡ x   ♦ x x x   ♣ A Q x

With Hand D, opener lacks third round control of hearts; therefore he signs off in five spades. With Hand E, opener has third round control of hearts and second round control of clubs. He must bid six clubs. With Hand F, although he has third round control of hearts, he has neither a void nor a side second round control to cue-bid; he must bid five notrump.

Further Asking Bid in a New Suit

If the asking bidder bids a new suit after receiving a positive response to the original asking bid, it asks about second round control of the new suit. If the responder lacks second round control, he signs off in the agreed trump suit. If the responder has second round control, he cue-bids either an undisclosed void, or a second round control in another suit; or if he has neither of those features, he should bid the minimum number of notrump.

If the asking bidder bids a new suit after receiving a negative response to his first asking bid, it is an asking bid in the new suit, and the responses are the same as for the original asking bid. For example, suppose opener has

♠ A J 10 x x x   ♡ x x x   ◇ x   ♣ A x x

The auction would start

Opener	Responder
1 ♠	2 ◇
2 ♠	4 ♡
4 ♠	5 ◇
5 Notrump	

Opener's four spade bid over the four heart asking bid was a negative response. The five diamond bid was a new asking bid, this time in diamonds. Opener's five notrump bid showed first or second round control of diamonds and two aces in addition. If responder had a hand such as

♠ K x x x   ♡ A x   ◇ A 10 x x x x x   ♣ —

he could jump to seven spades over the five notrump bid.

Using Culbertson asking bids, the question as to which should be the suit of the first asking bid is often quite tricky. With the above hand, the responder had no way to make an immediate asking bid in diamonds since no suit had been agreed as trumps, and a jump in diamonds would not have been unusual. Therefore with the above hand, a temporizing asking bid was made in hearts, followed by an asking bid in the real suit of interest.

However, so great is the complexity of these asking bids that when this very hand and this very sequence arose in a 1937 team of four match in Vienna, Josephine Culbertson did not recognize the five diamond bid as an asking bid, and passed. Seven spades was in fact laydown, and was reached at the other table by the Viennese pair—using Culbertson asking bids.

LEBOVIC ASKING BID

The Lebovic Convention is an asking bid designed to deal with the problem of how to determine whether or not the partnership has control of a certain suit when the trump suit is a minor. When a minor suit has been agreed upon, and two other suits have been bid, the Lebovic convention uses a jump in the fourth suit to ask about control in that suit. For example

Opener	Responder
1 ♣	1 ♡
1 ♠	3 ♣
4 ♢	

opener's four diamond bid asks about control of that suit.

The minor suit may be agreed by inference when it has been rebid by one player. For example, in the auction

Opener	Responder
1 ♢	1 ♠
2 ♢	3 ♣
3 ♢	4 ♡

responder's four heart bid agrees on diamonds as trumps, and asks opener about his control of the heart suit. Responder might have a hand such as

♠ A K Q x x x   ♡ x x   ♢ Q x   ♣ A x x

The responses to the Lebovic asking bid are as follows: if the responder has neither first nor second round control of the asked suit, he makes the minimum bid in the trump suit. If the responder has a singleton in the asked suit, he bids six of the trump suit. If the responder has K x or longer in the asked suit, he bids four notrump. If the responder has the ace or a void in the asked suit, he bids five of that suit.

In exceptional cases the Lebovic convention may be extended to auctions in which two suits remain unbid. If one partner has made a strong jump bid, a subsequent jump by the other in a new suit may be used as a Lebovic asking bid, even if another suit also is unbid. For example

Opener	Responder
1 ♣	1 ♠
3 ♣	4 ♡

Responder's four heart bid agrees on clubs, and asks about hearts.

FOUR CLUB ASKING BID

The Four Club Asking Bid convention is a three-stage series of asking bids designed to elicit information about short suits, aces, and trump honors. The convention uses a four club bid as an asking bid in two situations: first, when it is a jump to four clubs, and second, when four clubs is bid immediately after a jump raise in a suit. For example

(A) *Opener*   *Responder*
     1 ♡   3 ♡
     4 ♣

(B) *Opener*   *Responder*
     1 ◇   1 ♡
     2 ♡   4 ♣

The four club bid asks whether partner has a singleton or void anywhere in the hand. If he does, he bids the short suit. Lacking a singleton or void, he bids four of the trump suit.

After the response to the shortness asking bid, if the four club bidder makes the lowest ranking non-trump bid (including notrump), he asks his partner to reveal how many aces he holds. The responses are

First   step = 0 or 4 aces

Second step = 1 ace

Third   step = 2 aces

Fourth step = 3 aces

After the ace showing response, if the four club bidder

bids the lowest ranking non-trump bid, he asks about the quality of partner's trumps. The responses are

First   step = 0 or 3 of the top three honors

Second step = 1 of the top three honors

Third step = 2 of the top three honors

If the auction proceeds as follows

Opener	*Responder*
1 ♠	4 ♣
4 ♡	4 Notrump
5 ◇	5 ♡
5 ♠	

opener's four heart bid showed a singleton heart. Responder's four notrump bid, being the cheapest non-trump bid, asked about aces. Five diamonds by opener showed one ace. Responder's five heart bid, again the cheapest bid, asked about the quality of the trump suit. Opener's five spade bid promised all or none of the top three honors.

FULWILER ASKING BIDS

The Fulwiler Asking Bid is a control asking bid that may be used even at a very low level of the auction. Used after the trump suit has been established, the Fulwiler asking bid is any minimum bid by either opener or responder in another suit. For example

(A) *Opener*
    1 ♠
    3 ◇

                                           Responder
                                           2 ♠

(B) *Opener*
    1 ◇
    2 ♡

                                             Responder
                                         1 ♡
                                         2 ♠

Opener's three diamond bid in A is a Fulwiler asking bid, asking about diamond control. Responder's two spade bid in B asks about opener's spade control.

The responder to the asking bid shows his controls in a series of six steps:

    First   step = no first or second round control

    Second step = singleton

    Third   step = void

    Fourth step = king

    Fifth   step = ace

    Sixth   step = ace and king

The use of such low level bids as asking bids, of course, precludes the use of these bids as natural bids or short suit game tries. When the opener's bid is raised to two, he is more often concerned with whether or not he should bid a game, rather than whether the responder has a particular suit controlled for purposes of a slam.

GRAND SLAM FORCE

The single most important consideration in determining whether or not to bid a grand slam is the solidity of the trump suit. It is even more important than that also important question as to whether the partnership has first round control of all side suits, for sometimes aces are not cashed.

Of the trump quality asking bids, the grand slam force is the most widely used. The use of this convention commits the partnership to at least a small slam. For conventions that may be used in determining whether or not to bid even a small slam, *see* BARON SLAM TRY, CULBERTSON TRUMP ASKING BIDS, ROMEX TRUMP ASKING BIDS, R/H FOUR NOTRUMP, WANG TRUMP ASKING BIDS. *See also* PRECISION CLUB SYSTEM.

In its simple form, the grand slam force is a jump to five notrump after a suit has been agreed on as trump, in which the five notrump bidder asks his partner to bid a grand slam if he has two of the top three trump honors. For example, if responder has a hand such as

♠ A K   ♡ Q 10 x x x x   ◇ K Q 10 x x   ♣ —

and the auction has started

Opener	Responder
1 ♣	1 ♡
3 ♡	4 ♣
4 ◇	

After opener's cue-bid of four diamonds, the only thing of interest to the responder is whether or not his partner has the ace and king of hearts. This is an appropriate hand for the grand slam force.

Before using the grand slam force, however, one must be mindful of certain prerequisites. First, the hand must be able to produce thirteen tricks if the partner of the grand slam force bidder has two of the top three trump honors. Similarly, it is advisable to be sure that the partnership has no side suit losers. Discovery of trump suit solidity is a pyrrhic victory if the grand slam goes down because an opponent cashes an ace, or because the partnership has only twelve tricks.

In order to use the grand slam force, the grand slam force bidder himself must have one of the top three trump honors. Otherwise the partnership could reach a grand slam missing the ace of trumps. Further, since the grand slam force commits the partnership at least to a small slam, the grand slam force bidder should be sure that it will be safe to play at the six level even if his partner has none of the trump honors. For example, if the grand slam force bidder has only the queen of trumps, and his partner turns up with neither the ace nor the king, a small slam is rather iffy.

Which Suit is Trump?

To be effective, both the grand slam force bidder and his partner must be aware what suit has been agreed as trumps. When only one suit has been supported, that suit is trumps. If each partner has supported the other's suit, a five notrump bid will be ambiguous unless the partnership has discussed and agreed on which suit should be deemed trumps. In the absence of specific agreement, the trump suit should probably be deemed to be the suit that was supported second. For example in the auction

Opener	Responder
1 ♡	2 ♣
3 ♣	3 ♡
5 Notrump	

opener's five notrump bid should ask about heart honors. If opener had been interested in club honors he might have been able to jump to five notrump directly over the two club response. In the auction

Opener	Responder
1 ♡	2 ♣
3 ♣	3 ♡
3 ♠	5 Notrump

responder's five notrump bid should ask about hearts.

If no suit has been supported, but the grand slam force bidder has opened with a strong two-bid or its equivalent, or has made a strong jump shift response, his suit should be deemed trumps. If no other rule applies, the last bid suit should be deemed trumps, assuming that the grand slam bidder can be deemed to be supporting that suit. For example,

(A)	Opener	Responder
	1 ♠	3 ♠
	5 Notrump	

(B)	Opener	Responder
	1 ♠	5 Notrump

(C)	Opener	Responder
	1 ♠	3 ♡
	3 ♠	5 Notrump

In Auctions A and B, it is clear that the five notrump bid asks about spades. In Auction C, neither suit has been supported; however, since the grand slam force bidder has made a jump shift response, he should be deemed to be using the grand slam force for his own suit. If he had wanted to use the grand slam force for spades, he could have done so directly over the one spade opening, as in Auction B.

In the Auctions D, E and F none of the five notrump bids is the grand slam force:

(D) *Opener*	*Responder*
1 ♣	1 ♡
2 ♠	3 ♡
3 Notrump	5 Notrump

(E) *Opener*	*Responder*
2 Notrump	3 ♡
3 Notrump	5 Notrump

(F) *Opener*	*Responder*
1 ♢	1 ♠
3 ♠	4 ♣
4 ♠	5 ♠
5 Notrump	

(G) *Opener*	*Responder*
1 ♠	3 ♠
4 ♣	4 ♡
5 ♣	5 ♢
5 Notrump	

In Auction D, no suit has been agreed on, although both partners had opportunities to support each other's suits while forcing to game. Responder's five notrump bid therefore should be construed giving opener a choice among the possible small slam contracts.

In Auction E, the five notrump bid by the responder cannot be a grand slam force because it is virtually impossible that his hand is such that the solidity of the trump suit is his only concern. Responder's five notrump bid gives opener a choice between six hearts and six notrump. In Auction F, opener's five notrump bid cannot be the grand slam force since over four clubs he appeared to be willing to play in four spades. His five notrump bid is therefore a suggestion that the hand be played in six notrump with himself as declarer. He might have the K x of hearts to protect. In Auction G, opener's five notrump bid is ambiguous.

Responses to Five Notrump

If the partner of the grand slam force bidder has two of the top three honors in the trump suit, he should bid a grand slam. However, many partnerships agree that the proper bid with two of the top three honors is always seven *clubs*. If the grand slam force responder can be counted on to bid seven clubs rather than seven of what he has been led to believe is the trump suit, the grand slam force can be used to ask about a suit other than the one in which the grand slam force bidder actually wants to play.

For example, if the responder had a hand such as

♠ K x x   ♥ A K Q J 10 x x   ♦ A x x   ♣ —

and his partner opened one spade, responder would want to be in a grand slam if opener had as little as

♠ A Q x x x   ♡ x   ◇ K x x x x   ♣ x x

But responder does not want the hand played in seven spades, which could be defeated by a 4-1 spade break. The hand should be played in seven hearts, which is a good deal safer. Responder would thus like to establish the solidity of the spade suit and end up in hearts, by means of the following auction:

Opener	Responder
1 ♠	5 Notrump
7 ♣	7 ♡
Pass	

If the partner of the grand slam force bidder does not have two of the top three trump honors, he should attempt to use whatever space there is between five notrump and six of the trump suit to describe just what he does have. Further description could be advantageous because if the partners have between them ten trumps headed by the ace and king, they are unlikely to lose a trump trick; thus the grand slam could be bid even absent the trump queen.

The Culbertson recommended responses to the grand slam force vary according to the trump suit. If spades are trumps, the responses are

     6 ♣ = five spades; no ace, no king

     6 ◇ = four spades headed by the ace or king

     6 ♡ = five spades headed by the ace or king

     6 ♠ = four spades; no ace, no king

If hearts are trumps, the Culbertson responses are

6 ♣ = four hearts headed by the ace or king

6 ◇ = five hearts headed by the ace or king

6 ♡ = four or five hearts; no ace, no king

If diamonds are trumps, the responses are

6 ♣ = five diamonds headed by the ace or king

6 ◇ = any other holding

The principle adopted by most partnerships today as to how to respond holding fewer than two of the top three honors, is the better the suit, the higher the bid. Codifying this principle, the Blue Team responses to the grand slam force are as follows, with spades as trumps

6 ♣ = none of the top three honors

6 ◇ = queen

6 ♡ = no more than four spades by the ace or king

6 ♠ = five spades headed by the ace or king

With hearts as trumps the Blue Team responses are:

6 ♣ = queen or worse

6 ◇ = no more than four hearts headed by the ace or king

6 ♡ = five hearts headed by the ace or king

With diamonds as trumps, the responses are:

6 ♣ = queen or worse

6 ◇ = any number headed by the ace or king

Suppose opener and responder had the following hands:

(Opener)
♠ A Q x x   ♡ A 10 x x x x   ◇ A K   ♣ x

(Responder)
♠ K x   ♡ K x x x   ◇ Q x x   ♣ A J x x

Using the Blue Team responses, the bidding would go

Opener	Responder
1 ♡	3 ♡
3 ♠	4 ♣
4 ◇	4 ♠
5 Notrump	6 ◇
7 ♡	

Some partnerships reverse the meanings of the six-level bids after the five notrump grand slam force bid, so that the cheaper responses show the better trump holdings. This practice has the advantage of allowing the showing first of honor cards, and second of length, since a further asking bid can sometimes be made. For example, in the Romex system, the responses to the grand slam force are

6 ♣ = ace or king

6 ◇ = queen

6 ♡ = none of the top three honors

388

Using these responses the auction might go

Opener	Responder
1 ♠	3 ♠
4 ♣	4 ◇
4 ♡	5 Notrump
6 ♣	6 ◇

Responder's six diamond bid asks opener to bid the grand slam with extra length in his suit.

Triggers Other Than Five Notrump

In order to provide more room for description of fair-to-good trump holdings when a suit other than spades has been agreed on, some partnerships use bids other than five notrump as the grand slam force for other suits. For example, after hearts have been agreed, a jump to five spades can be used as the grand slam force; after diamonds have been agreed, a jump to five hearts can be used as the grand slam force; after clubs have been agreed, a jump to five diamonds can be used as the grand slam force.

Each of these grand slam force triggers allows four steps for description of various trump holdings. The possible four-step gradations would be those described previously for situations in which spades have been agreed on and five notrump is used as the grand slam force.

To use any of these bids as the grand slam force, the bid must be a jump, in order to avoid confusion and interference with ordinary cue-bidding. For example, in the auction

(A) *Opener*   *Responder*
   1 ♠   2 ♣
   3 ♣   3 ♡
   3 ♠   4 ♡
   5 ◇

North's five diamond bid is a simple cue-bid. However, in the auction

(B) *Opener*   *Responder*
   1 ♠   2 ♣
   3 ♣   3 ♡
   5 ◇

North's jump to five diamonds can be used as the grand slam force in clubs. North and South might have hands such as

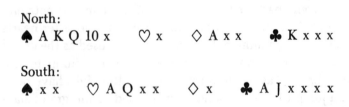

North:
♠ A K Q 10 x   ♡ x   ◇ A x x   ♣ K x x x

South:
♠ x x   ♡ A Q x x   ◇ x   ♣ A J x x x x

If five notrump were used as the grand slam force and South had the above hand, he would have to content himself with a six club response, even though seven is makeable. In auction (B), however, South has room to show that he has one of the top two trump honors plus extra length. Thus, the auction might go

     Opener   *Responder*
      1 ♠   2 ♣
      3 ♣   3 ♡
      5 ◇   6 ♣
      7 ♣

Use of these specific jumps as the grand slam force means, of course, that they cannot be used as splinter or fragment bids. Since splinter or fragment jumps are most frequently used below the game level, however, this seems a modest price to pay for having extra room to show potentially adequate non-maximum trump holdings.

MALOWAN
(Grand Slam Force after Blackwood)

Sometimes the partnership is not able to find out, without using Blackwood, whether or not it has all of the side suits controlled. If Blackwood is used, five notrump cannot be used as the grand slam force, since that bid asks about kings.* In this situation, the Blackwood bidder may usually use the Malowan convention as the grand slam force.

The Malowan convention is a bid of six clubs after the ace-showing response to Blackwood, to ask the Blackwood responser to bid a grand slam if he has two of the top three trump honors. If he does not have two of the top three trump honors, he should again try to use the space between six clubs and six of the trump suit to clarify his trump holding.

If the agreed trump suit is clubs, of course, the Malowan convention does not work. An alternative is for the Blackwood bidder to bid a new suit over the Blackwood response, forcing the Blackwood responder to bid five notrump. Over five notrump, the Blackwood bidder can bid six clubs as the grand slam force.

---

*In the Romex system, a new suit bid after the ace-showing response to Blackwood is used to ask for kings; the five notrump bid is therefore always the grand slam force, whether or not Blackwood has been bid.

BARON SLAM TRY

Sometimes the decision between game and slam, or between a small slam and a grand slam, does not depend on finding partner with two of the top three trump honors, but on finding him with some lesser holding such as one honor, or extra length. The Baron slam try is an invitation to bid slam if the trump suit is "good." The device by which the invitation is issued is a jump to five or six of the suit below the trump suit. For example, if spades is the trump suit, a jump to five hearts would invite a small slam in spades; a jump to six hearts would invite a grand slam in spades.

The partner of the Baron bidder must examine his trump holding in light of the previous auction. If his trumps are no better than he has already suggested, he should decline the invitation. For example, in the auction

Opener	Responder
2 ♣	2 ♦ (negative)
2 ♠	3 ♠
5 ♡	

Responder's trumps might be no better than three small cards. If he has the queen of spades or four small spades, he should accept the invitation. Opener's hand might be

♠ A K x x x x   ♡ x   ♦ A K Q x x   ♣ A

If responder's hand were as "good" as

♠ x x x x   ♡ x x x   ♦ x x x   ♣ x x x

slam would be a fine proposition.

The Baron grand slam try may be made as a non-jump bid after Blackwood has been used. Suppose opener held

♠ K Q x x x   ♡ A 10 x x   ◇ K x x   ♣ x

and the auction proceeded

Opener	Responder
1 ♠	3 ♡
4 ♡	4 Notrump
5 ◇	6 ◇

Responder's six diamond bid, being the suit below the agreed trump suit, invites opener to bid seven hearts with extra trump values. With the hand given, opener should bid the grand slam. He has the ten of trumps, and more importantly, he has four trumps, when he might have raised with only three. Responder is likely to have a six-card heart suit headed by the king. His Blackwood bid has elicited the fact that opener has the ace of trumps; all he needs now is extra length.

CULBERTSON TRUMP ASKING BIDS

Culbertson Trump Asking Bids are usually used in conjunction with CULBERTSON ASKING BIDS. After a four-level response to a Culbertson asking bid, such as

(A) *Opener*   *Responder*
    1 ♣   3 ♠
    4 ♣

(B) *Opener*   *Responder*
    1 ♢   3 ♢
    4 ♣   4 ♡

a bid of four notrump by the asking bidder (responder in Auction A, opener in Auction B) asks about the quality of the trump suit. The partner of the trump asking bidder shows how many of the top three trump honors he has:

        5 ♣ = none of the top three honors

        5 ♢ = 1 of the top three honors

        5 ♡ = 2 of the top three honors

        5 ♠ = all three top honors

If the four notrump bidder rebids five notrump, he asks his partner how many trumps he holds. With the minimum number, considering the previous bidding, the asking bid responder can bid six clubs, and bid one extra step for each additional card held.

If the response to the Culbertson control asking bid was at

the five level, a bid of five notrump by the asking bidder can be used as the trump asking bid. The five notrump bid, however, asks only about trump honors in accordance with the above schedule; there is no way to ask about trump length.

ROMEX TRUMP ASKING BIDS

In the Romex system, a two club opening bid is artificial and is forcing to game. Having established a game force, the opener need not jump in his suit without a special purpose. The Romex system uses a jump rebid after a two club opening as a bid that sets that suit as trumps (at least temporarily), and asks responder how many cards he has in the suit. For example

Opener	*Responder*
2 ♣	2 ◇
3 ♠	

Responder shows his trump length as follows:

> First   step = void or singleton
>
> Second step = doubleton
>
> Third   step = three cards
>
> Fourth step = four or more cards
>
> Fifth   step = singleton ace, king or queen

After receiving a response of the second, third or fourth step, if the opener bids notrump, he asks responder to reveal the number of top trump honors he holds. The responses are

> First   step (♣) = none of the top three honors
>
> Second step (◇) = 1 of the top three honors
>
> Third   step (♡) = 2 of the top three honors
>
> Fourth step (♠) = all three top honors

For example, in the auction

Opener	Responder
2 ♣	2 ◇
3 ♠	4 ◇
4 Notrump	5 ♣

responder's four diamond bid showed three card support for spades; his five club bid showed that he has none of the top spade honors.

If the response to the first trump asking bid was the first or second step, the minimum bid of a new suit by the opener changes the trump suit, and is a trump asking bid in the new suit. The responder shows his length in the new suit in the same way he did to the first trump asking bid:

Opener	Responder
2 ♣	2 ◇
3 ♠	3 Notrump
4 ♣	4 Notrump

Opener's four club bid changes the trump suit to clubs, and asks responder about his length in clubs. Responder's four notrump bid showed four card support for clubs. However, if responder had bid the first or second step in response to the club asking bid, opener could have changed the trump suit again, and made a trump asking bid in a third suit.

THE R/H FOUR NOTRUMP CONVENTION

The R/H four notrump convention uses a non-jump bid of four notrump after a trump suit has been established, to ask about the three top trump honors. This convention is best used after the partnership has had an opportunity to cue-bid first round controls in the side suits.

To show his trump honors, the partner of the four notrump bidder either bids five of the trump suit with none of the top three trump honors, or bids five notrump with all three honors, or bids a non-trump suit with one or two honors, as follows:

Lowest side suit = king or queen

Middle side suit = ace

Highest side suit = any two of the top three honors

Opener's and responder's hands might be

(Opener)
♠ K J x x x   ♡ K x x   ◇ A K Q x x   ♣ —

(Responder)
♠ Q x x x x   ♡ Q J x x   ◇ x   ♣ A K J

The auction would be

Opener	*Responder*
1 ♠	3 ♠
4 ♣	4 ♠ (no red ace
	to cue-bid)
4 Notrump	5 ♣ (king or queen)
5 ♠	

WANG TRUMP ASKING BIDS

Wang trump asking bids use a variety of bids at relatively low levels of the auction to ask about trump honors. The responses are given in three steps as follows:

> First step = none of the top three honors
>
> Second step = one of the top three honors
>
> Third step = two of the top three honors

The bids that can be used as Wang trump asking bids are varied. A three notrump rebid after a strong raise to the three level may be used as a trump asking bid:

Opener	*Responder*
1 ♠	3 ♠
3 Notrump	

Suppose opener has a hand such as

♠ A x x x x   ♡ A K x x   ◇ x   ♣ K Q x

After the auction has started 1 ♠ — 3 ♠, opener wants to ask about aces and about trump honors. If he uses Blackwood first and responder shows two aces, opener can use the grand slam force (six clubs). But if responder shows only one ace, opener has no way to find out whether responder's trumps are good enough for a small slam. Therefore, with this hand the opener uses the trump asking bid first, and follows with four notrump Blackwood:

Opener	Responder
1 ♠	3 ♠
3 Notrump	4 ♡ (two of the top three honors)
4 Notrump	

Similarly, a three notrump rebid after a limit raise could be used as a trump asking bid. The asking bid could also be used by responder if his suit is raised to the three level:

Opener	Responder
1 ◇	1 ♡
3 ♡	3 Notrump

Wang trump asking bids can be used at even lower levels of the auction. For example, when game forcing Stayman is being used, the simple raise of a major suit can be a trump asking bid:

Opener	Responder
1 Notrump	2 ◇
2 ♡	3 ♡

After an inverted minor suit raise, the bid of the cheapest suit may be used as a trump asking bid. For example

Opener	Responder
1 ◇	2 ◇
2 ♡	

The immediate jump raise of a positive response to an artificial forcing one club opening may be used as a trump asking bid. For example

Opener	Responder
1 ♣	1 ♠
3 ♠	

(See PRECISION system, in which a simple raise of a positive suit response is a trump asking bid.)

V

Competitive Bidding

Bidding by the opponents is a double-edged sword. It can be very annoying; some of the best planned auctions become unusable because an opponent has bid—especially when he has preempted.

On the other hand, when the opponents have bid, additional possibilities may facilitate the exchange of information. The opponent's bid may make available a double or a cue bid, or the use of any of a number of conventions designed to allow description of a two-suited hand with one bid.

Conventions for coping with interference with the Blackwood convention have been described above. The conventions described below deal with opposition bidding at somewhat lower levels of the auction.

TAKEOUT DOUBLES

The takeout double is so widely used that most people no longer think of it as a convention, but instead unconsciously accept it as a natural part of bidding. It is nevertheless a convention, since, by agreement, it has a meaning other than the desire to penalize the bidder in the suit he has bid.

A takeout double is a double of a suit bid, usually at a low level of the auction, before the partner of the doubler has made a bid.* Absent agreement, a double of a notrump bid, except in one situation, is always for penalties, never for takeout. The one exception occurs when a one notrump response to an opening bid is doubled. For example:

North	East	South	West
1 ♠	Pass	1 Notrump	Double

West's double in this auction is a takeout double.

A takeout double asks the partner of the doubler to bid one of the unbid suits. The doubler promises strength at least roughly equivalent to that of an opening bid. (See also TAKEOUT DOUBLES OF PREEMPTS.) He suggests that he is short in the suit doubled and has at least three-card support for any other suit that his partner might choose to bid. The doubler also suggests strongly that he has four cards in any unbid major suit. However, what the doubler lacks in distribution can be compensated for by extra high-card strength. For example, a takeout double of a one heart opening bid could be made with either of the following hands:

---

*See also NEGATIVE DOUBLES, RESPONSIVE DOUBLES, COMPETITIVE DOUBLES, DOUBLES FOR SACRIFICE, below.

♠ A Q x x   ♡ x   ◇ K J x x   ♣ J x x x

♠ A K x   ♡ x x   ◇ A K x x   ♣ Q x x x

Because of the modern tendency to use cue-bids as light two-suited takeout bids, the range of the takeout double for some partnerships has increased tremendously. In these partnerships, for any hand that is too strong for a simple overcall, a takeout double must be made. For example:

[A] ♠ A Q x   ♡ A K Q x x x   ◇ x   ♣ A x x

[B] ♠ A K x   ♡ K Q x   ◇ A J x x   ♣ K J x

With Hand A one would double an opening bid, planning to rebid hearts. With Hand B, one would double an opening bid planning to rebid notrump. Thus, in modern practice, there is virtually no upper limit to the strength of the takeout double.

Responses

Unless and until the doubler makes some more revealing rebid, his partner must assume that the takeout doubler has the garden variety, support-for-all-suits type hand, having about the strength of an opening bid. The doubler's partner's possible responses fall into three categories: dutiful, encouraging and enthusiastic.

With a hand worth less than about 9 points, the doubler's partner should make a simple bid in his best suit. (See also HERBERT.) For example, in the auction

North	East	South	West
1 ♡	Double	Pass	

West might have one of the following hands:

[A] ♠ K x x x   ♡ x x x   ◇ J x x x   ♣ K x

[B] ♠ x x x x x   ♡ x x x   ◇ x x   ♣ x x x

[C] ♠ x   ♡ J x x x x x   ◇ x x x   ♣ x x x

With Hands A and B, West should bid one spade. Spades is his best suit and he has less than 9 points.

With Hand C, West should bid two clubs. The partner of the doubler has a duty to bid, and he should not pass the double simply because he has a weak hand, or simply because he has length in the opener's suit. He should pass only if he has good reason to believe he will punish the opponents. When his partner has doubled at the one level, he will need a very good hand and strong trumps to pass the takeout double for penalties. A hand such as the following would suffice to pass a takeout double of one heart:

♠ K x   ♡ A J 10 9 x   ◇ K x x   ♣ x x x

With about 6 to 8 points, the partner of the takeout doubler should make his response even if an opponent bids over the double. For example, in the auction

North	East	South	West
1 ◇	Double	2 ◇	

West should bid two spades with a hand such as

♠ K J x x   ♡ Q x x   ◇ x x x   ♣ J x x

If he has a long suit and can make his bid at the one level, the partner of the double may do so even with less than 6 points. In the auction

North	East	South	West
1 ◇	Double	1 ♡	

West should bid one spade with

♠ Q J x x x   ♡ x x x   ◇ x x   ♣ J x x

If the partner of the doubler has the opponent's suit stopped and has an 8 point hand or better, he may bid notrump. All notrump bids by the partner of the doubler are encouraging; the bid of one notrump therefore may not be made on a poor hand. For example in the auction

North	East	South	West
1 ♠	Double	Pass	

suppose West held one of the following hands:

[D]   ♠ A Q x x   ♡ x x x   ◇ x x x   ♣ x x x

[E]   ♠ K J x x   ♡ J x   ◇ A x x x   ♣ x x x

[F]   ♠ K J x x   ♡ K x   ◇ K Q x   ♣ x x x x

Hand D, although it has a good spade stopper, is not strong enough for the encouraging bid of one notrump. West must therefore bid a suit. Having the same length in all of the unbid suits, he must bid the cheapest. With Hand D, therefore, West should bid two clubs.

With Hand E, West should bid one notrump. This bid describes West's high card strength and his holding in the opponent's suit. Hand F is too strong for the one notrump response, and therefore West must just jump to two notrump. The two notrump bid shows a hand of some 12 to 14 points. This bid is very encouraging, but is not forcing.

If the partner of the doubler has a hand worth about 9 to 12 points, without a secure stopper in the opponent's suit, he should jump in the suit he prefers. For example, over a takeout double of one diamond, he should jump to two hearts with

♠ K x x   ♡ A J x x x   ◇ Q x   ♣ x x x

Like the notrump responses, this response is encouraging, but not forcing.

With a hand worth about 11 or 12 points but with no clear preference as to suits, the partner of the doubler may make a cue-bid of the opponent's suit, asking the doubler to bid his best suit. For example

North	*East*	*South*	*West*
1 ◇	Double	Pass	2 ◇

West might have a hand such as

♠ K x x x   ♡ A J x x   ◇ J x   ♣ Q x x

This cue-bid is highly encouraging, and forces the doubler to bid. However, it is not forcing to game.

If the partner of the doubler has the equivalent of a sound opening bid, he is allowed to become downright enthusiastic. With such a hand he can cue-bid, and follow with forcing bids driving the hand to game.

Doubler's Rebids

If the doubler rebids over a non-forcing response, other than in a competitive auction, he shows a hand stronger than the 12 to 15 points he has already promised. Any bid of a new suit shows a hand that was too strong to make an overcall. Any bid of notrump shows a hand that was too strong for a 16 to 18 point notrump overcall.

If the doubler raises his partner's suit he promises at least four card support. If the response has been a simple suit bid, a single raise by the doubler shows a sound opening bid of about 16 to 19 points. A jump raise would show about 19 to 23 points, or a hand with which the doubler wants to be in game if his partner has as much as four or five points.

For example, in the auction

North	East	South	West
1 ◇	Double	Pass	1 ♡
Pass			

East might hold one of the following hands:

[A] ♠ A Q x x   ♡ K J x x   ◇ x   ♣ K x x x

[B] ♠ A K x   ♡ K x x x   ◇ x   ♣ A Q x x x

[C] ♠ K x x x   ♡ A K x x   ◇ x   ♣ Q x x x

With Hand A, East has a total of 16 points, counting three points for the singleton diamond. He has just enough for a raise to two hearts. Hand B is good enough for a raise to three hearts. With Hand C East should pass.

If the partner of the doubler makes any bid other than a

dutiful response, and thereby shows more than 8 points, the doubler should evaluate his hand to see whether or not the combined hands can reach the 25- or 26-point game level. If the doubler can tell that they do reach that level, he should bid game or force to game. If he still is uncertain whether or not the combined hands reach that level, he should invite game.

After an encouraging response, a change of suit by the doubler is forcing for one round.

STRONG CUE BIDS

For many years the cue-bid of an opponent's opening bid was used as the strongest possible competitive call. It showed the equivalent of a forcing two-bid, promised first or second round control of the suit cue-bid, and was forcing to game.

More modern treatment for the strong cue-bid is to use it with very strong hands with good game prospects, although not to treat it as forcing to game. Second round control of the opponent's suit is not mandatory if the rest of the hand is strong enough. Any of the following hands would be appropriate for a strong cue-bid:

[A] ♠ K x   ♡ A K Q x x x x   ◇ A K   ♣ x x

[B] ♠ K Q J x x x   ♡ —   ◇ A   ♣ A K J x x x

[C] ♠ A K x x   ♡ A K Q J x   ◇ x   ♣ A x x

[D] ♠ K Q 10 x   ♡ A K x   ◇ A Q x x   ♣ A J

The strong cue-bid is forcing on partner, and any change of suit by the cue-bidder is forcing. The partner of the cue-bidder should bid naturally. If the cue-bidder bids the same suit twice, or rebids notrump, or supports his partner's suit below game, he strongly invites game.

For example, with Hand A, West would cue-bid two clubs over South's one club opening bid, and the auction might proceed as follows:

South	West	North	East
1 ♣	2 ♣	Pass	2 ◇
Pass	2 ♡	Pass	2 ♠
Pass	3 ♣		

West has forced East to bid by cue-bidding two clubs. West then showed his heart suit, over which East was forced to bid again. If West had rebid three hearts over East's two spade bid, his bid would not have been forcing. Therefore, having visions of either a three notrump contract or a four heart contract, West cue-bid three clubs, wanting his partner to bid notrump with a club stopper, or to raise to four hearts without a stopper. East might have a hand such as:

♠ Q x x x   ♡ x   ◇ J x x x x   ♣ x x x

or

♠ J x x x   ♡ x   ◇ J x x x x   ♣ Q 10 x

With a hand such as

[B]   ♠ K Q J x x x   ♡ —   ◇ A   ♣ A K J x x x

West would cue-bid over a one diamond or one heart opening bid. The auction might proceed:

South	West	North	East
1 ♡	2 ♡	Pass	3 ◇
Pass	3 ♠	Pass	3 Notrump
Pass	4 ♣	Pass	5 ♣
Pass	6 ♣	Pass	Pass

413

East might have a hand such as

♠ x   ♥ Q J x x   ♦ Q x x x x   ♣ Q x x

With a hand such as

[C] ♠ A K x x   ♥ A K Q J x   ♦ x   ♣ A x x

West would cue-bid two diamonds over a one diamond opening, or two clubs over a one club opening, and the bidding might go

South	West	North	East
1 ♦	2 ♦	Pass	2 ♥
Pass	3 ♥	Pass	Pass

East might hold

♠ x x x   ♥ x x x   ♦ Q x x x x   ♣ x x

With a hand such as

[D] ♠ K Q 10 x   ♥ A K x   ♦ A Q x x   ♣ A J

West would cue-bid over any opening bid by South, and would rebid two notrump. This sequence shows a balanced hand worth about 22 to 24 points.

CUE-BID AS A LIGHT TAKEOUT

It is possible to use an immediate cue-bid of an opponent's opening bid as a weak takeout bid for the other three suits. The cue-bidder might, for example, bid two diamonds over a one diamond opening bid with the following hand:

♠ K x x x   ♡ K x x x   ◇ x   ♣ Q x x x

This use of the cue bid is designed to reserve the takeout double for stronger hands having greater defensive values. It is, more valuable, however, to use the cue-bid to show a two-suited hand.

TWO-SUITED TAKEOUTS—IN PROFILE

Two-suited hands are generally difficult to describe after an opponent has opened the bidding. All too frequently it occurs that either the opponents bid too much too soon for both of the suits to be shown, or everybody passes too soon for both suits to be shown.

Many conventions have been devised to convey in a single competitive bid the information that the bidder has two long suits. Most of these overcalls or cue-bids are intended principally for use as obstructive bids, either to preempt the space in which the opponents wish to exchange information, or to lead to a sacrifice against their contracts. *See* MICHAELS CUE-BID, UPPER SUITS CUE-BIDS, TOP AND BOTTOM CUE-BIDS, COLORFUL CUE-BIDS, UNUSUAL NOTRUMP OVERCALL, UNUSUAL ONE NOTRUMP OVERCALL, ASTRO CUE-BIDS, ROMAN JUMP OVERCALLS, COPENHAGEN, UNUSUAL NOTRUMP & MINORS, TRUSCOTT, SIMPLIFIED TAKEOUT OVER STRONG ARTIFICIAL OPENINGS.

Being designed to hinder the opponents, two-suited takeouts may be made on quite limited high-card values. Their strength should range from about 6 to 10 high card points, with less than two defensive tricks. A hand such as

[A] ♠ K J x x x   ♡ Q 10 x x x   ◇ x x   ♣ x

would be suitable for a non-vulnerable major suit takeout.

Ideally, the two-suited takeout would promise at least five cards in each of the suits shown. If the takeout is for both major suits, however, it is permissible to make the bid with five cards in one major suit and four cards in the other.

Since high level sacrifice is a definite possibility after a two-suited takeout, the texture of the two suits shown by the takeout should be good, for the sake of safety. And such high card strength as there is should be concentrated in the two suits. For example, a hand such as

♠ A   ♡ K x   ◇ J x x x x   ♣ Q x x x x

is inappropriate for a two-suited takeout bid.

In that two-suited takeouts are essentially preemptive in character, it is generally unwise to try to make them do double duty as constructive bids looking for a game or slam. For example, if a two-suited cue-bid or overcall is permissible on a hand such as Hand A above, using it also with a hand such as

[B] ♠ A K J x x   ♡ K Q 10 x x   ◇ K x   ♣ x

makes its range so wide that partner has considerable difficulty in coping with it. He may neglect to try for game when game could be made opposite Hand B. Or he may fail to sacrifice when he should opposite Hand A. Or, opposite Hand B, he may sacrifice when the opponents cannot make their contract.

When to Use

Two-suited cue-bid and overcall conventions are normally used only over the opponent's one-level opening bids, and only in the direct position, as for example:

(A)	*North*	*East*	*or*	(B)	*North*	*East*
	1 ♡	2 ♡			1 ◇	2 ◇

Because most two-suited cue-bid and overcall conventions are fundamentally preemptive devices, they are not needed in the pass-out position:

(C) *North*	*East*	*South*	*West*
1 ♡	Pass	Pass	2 ♡

West is obviously not interested in either preempting or sacrificing. The cue-bid in this position usually means that the cue-bidder has a strong hand, perhaps two-suited, but primarily a hand with which he felt he could not afford to have his partner pass a takeout double. Thus in the Auction C above, the West hand might be

♠ A K Q x x   ♡ —   ◇ K x   ♣ A x x x x x

A special situation deserves attention. When the opponents have bid two suits, the cue-bid of a minor suit bid by either of them should not be used to show a weak two-suiter.

For example, in the auction

North	*East*	*South*	*West*
1 ◇	Pass	1 ♠	2 ◇

West's two diamond bid should simply show a hand worth an overcall, with a long diamond suit. There is no need to use the cue-bid in this situation to show two suits, for when the opponents have bid two suits, a takeout double will call for the other two suits.

If North had opened the bidding with a major suit, however, especially playing five card major suit openings, West's cue-bid would be for takeout, showing a very strong two-suiter:

North	East	South	West
1 ♡	Pass	1 ♠	2 ♡

Conventional two-suited cue-bids or overcalls also are not used when the bidding has been opened with a weak two bid. For example, in the auction

North	East	South	West
2 ♡	3 ♡		

East may have a two-suiter, but the cue-bid suggests primarily that East did not want to risk having West pass a takeout double for penalties. East might have a hand such as

♠ A K Q x x   ♡ —   ◇ K x   ♣ A x x x x x

Responding to the Two-Suited Takeout

The partner of the cue-bidder should, if at all possible, take a preference for one of the cue-bidder's suits. Having a weak hand and two long suits, the cue-bidder is rarely interested in hearing what his partner has to say about a third suit.

Moreover, since the cue-bid is principally an obstructive device, the partner of the cue-bidder should take his preference at an appropriate level. For example:

North	East	South	West
1 ♡	2 ♡	Double	

Suppose East's cue-bid shows a two-suiter in spades and clubs, and West has one of the following hands:

[A]　♠ Q x x x　　♡ 10 x x x　　◇ x x　　♣ K x x

[B] ♠ x x   ♡ Q J x x   ◇ K Q x x   ♣ A x x

With Hand A, West should jump to four spades. The opponents are likely to make four hearts, so a sacrifice is in order. With Hand B, West should simply take his preference by bidding three clubs. The opponents do not seem likely to make a game, so West has no thought of sacrificing.

A Double-Edged Sword

A final word of caution on two-suited bids is in order. These bids are quite useful if they help to take away most of the opponents' bidding room so that they cannot adequately exchange information, or if they lead to a profitable sacrifice.

However, if the side that has made the two-suited bid does not buy the contract, the bid will have become a liability, since it has drawn a blueprint for the declarer as to how the defenders' cards are distributed.

See also DEFENSE AGAINST OPPONENTS' TWO-SUITED CALLS.

MICHAELS CUE-BIDS

The Michaels Cue-bid is usually used as a two-suited takeout bid, although some partnerships use it as a weak three-suited takeout bid. *See* CUE-BID AS A LIGHT TAKEOUT. Over an opponent's minor suit opening bid, the Michaels cue-bid shows both major suits. It promises a total of at least nine cards in those two suits, and preferably ten, with five in each major. See TWO-SUITED TAKEOUTS—IN PROFILE.

For the auction

South	West	North	East
1 ♣	2 ♣		

West might have a hand such as

♠ Q J x x ♡ K J x x ◇ x ♣ x x

Over an opponent's major suit opening bid, the Michaels cue-bid also shows a two suited hand. It promises at least five cards in the unbid major suit, and at least five cards in one of the minor suits. Since the partnership may be forced to the three level to find its fit, the Michaels cue-bid over a major suit opening may be made on a stronger hand.

For example, for the auction

North	East	South	West
Pass	Pass	1 ♡	2 ♡

West might have a hand such as

[A] ♠ K Q x x x ♡ x ◇ x x ♣ K Q x x x

or

[B] ♠ A Q x x x   ♡ x   ◇ x   ♣ Q J 10 x x x

The partner of the Michaels cue-bidder should support his partner's major suit if he can. Any three card support will suffice. If he cannot support the major suit, he may bid two notrump to ask the Michaels bidder to name his minor suit. For example, in the auction

North	East	South	West
1 ♡	2 ♡	Pass	

West might hold either of the following hands:

[C] ♠ K Q x   ♡ K x x x   ◇ Q J x x   ♣ Q x

[D] ♠ x x   ♡ K x x x   ◇ J x   ♣ A x x x x

With Hand C, West would bid two spades. He has spade support, but has no particular desire to play the hand at any higher level, since neither his side nor the opponents seem likely to make very much. With Hand D West cannot support spades, so he bids two notrump to ask his partner which minor suit he has. He expects East will bid three diamonds, in which case West will pass. But if East should bid three clubs, West will be able to bid five clubs to sacrifice against the opponents' probable four heart game.

The Michaels cue-bid is the most flexible of all the two-suited cue-bids (*but see* ROMAN JUMP OVERCALLS). The only two-suited hand it cannot possibly handle, given an appropriate opening bid by the opponents, is the hand with both minor suits. An agreement by the partnership to use Michaels cue-bids in combination with the UNUSUAL NOTRUMP OVERCALL, calling for the lowest unbid suits, would give the partnership the greatest flexibility to show two-suited hands. Using this combination of conventions, the partnership would be able to handle ten of the twelve possible combinations of unbid suits, as shown by the following chart:

Two Suits Held	Opponent's Opening Bid			
	♣	♢	♡	♠
♠ & ♡	Michaels Cue-bid	Michaels Cue-bid	–	–
♠ & ♢	(GAP)	–	Michaels Cue-bid°	–
♠ & ♣	–	(GAP)	Michaels Cue-bid°	–
♡ & ♢	Unusual Notrump	–	–	Michaels Cue-bid°
♡ & ♣	–	Unusual Notrump	–	Michaels Cue-bid°
♢ & ♣	–	–	Unusual Notrump	Unusual Notrump

°Initially ambiguous as to which minor suit held.

UPPER SUITS CUE-BIDS

Some partnerships, disliking the ambiguity of the Michaels cue-bid over a major suit opening bid, use the cue-bid always to show the two highest unbid suits. If the bidding is opened in a minor suit, of course, the suits shown by the cue-bid are the majors. This is the equivalent of the Michaels cue-bid.

If the bidding is opened in a major suit, however, the cue-bid shows specifically the other major suit and diamonds—the two highest unbid suits. The effect of this agreement is that the cue-bidder may never have clubs as his second suit.

The price of certainty, therefore, is a decrease in flexibility. Never being allowed to show a club suit as one of the two suits, there are only three suit combinations that can be shown using Upper Suit cue-bids. For its initial ambiguity, Michaels has the advantage of handling five different combinations, depending on the opponent's opening bid.

For strength and distribution requirements, responses, etc., *see* TWO-SUITED TAKEOUTS—IN PROFILE.

TOP AND BOTTOM CUE-BIDS

The Top and Bottom Cue-bid requires that the cue-bidder's two suits be the highest unbid suit and the lowest unbid suit. If used over all opening suit bids, these cue-bids would have the following meanings:

    1 ♣ — 2 ♣ shows spades and diamonds

    1 ♢ — 2 ♢ shows spades and clubs

    1 ♡ — 2 ♡ shows spades and clubs

    1 ♠ — 2 ♠ shows hearts and clubs

The chief drawback in using this convention over all openings is that the cue-bid may never be made holding both major suits.

In order to preserve the ability to show both major suits, the partnership should agree to use Michaels cue-bids over opponents' minor suit opening bids, and restrict Top and Bottom cue-bids to the opponents' major suit opening bids. The effect of such an agreement would be that the cue-bid could never show a two-suiter that included diamonds.

For strength and distribution requirements, responses, etc., *see* TWO-SUITED TAKEOUTS—IN PROFILE.

COLORFUL CUE-BIDS

Colorful Cue-bids are used over an opponent's opening bid in a major suit. The cue-bidder promises two long suits of the same color, the color opposite that of the opening bid. Thus a cue-bid of two hearts over one heart would show spades and clubs; a cue-bid of two spades over one spade would show hearts and diamonds.

For strength and distribution requirements, responses, etc., *see* TWO-SUITED TAKEOUTS—IN PROFILE.

UNUSUAL NOTRUMP OVERCALL

There are a variety of competitive bidding situations in which, as a matter of logic, a notrump bid cannot signify a desire to play the hand in notrump. As a convention, the Unusual Notrump Overcall is a bid that by agreement, rather than by inference, is a takeout for two suits.

By an unpassed hand, the Unusual Notrump Overcall is a jump to two notrump over an opening bid, to show a two-suited hand. (*See also* UNUSUAL ONE NOTRUMP OVERCALL.) If the opening bid was one heart or one spade, the two notrump bid shows length in both minor suits.

When the opening bid is one club or one diamond, there are two schools of thought as to which suits should be shown. Some partnerships, in recognition of the growing use of five card major suit openings and the consequent frequent openings in a three card minor suit, always use the two notrump overcall to show the minor suits. For these partnerships, the auction

North	East	South	West
1 ◇	2 Notrump		

would show that East has a long club suit and a long diamond suit.

The majority of the partnerships which use The Unusual Notrump convention, however, use it to show length in the two lowest unbid suits. Thus, over a one diamond opening bid a jump to two notrump will show hearts and clubs; over a one club opening bid, a jump to two notrump will show hearts and diamonds. For strength and distribution requirements, responses, etc., *see* TWO-SUITED TAKEOUTS—IN PROFILE.

The partner of the Unusual Notrump overcaller may in

427

turn make an unusual notrump bid. For example, if West has a hand such as

♠ x x   ♡ Q J x   ◇ K x x x   ♣ Q x x x

in an auction such as

North	East	South	West
1 ♠	2 Notrump	4 ♠	

West should bid four notrump. The four notrump bid tells East that West wants to play in five of a minor suit, but that he has no real preference; he asks East to bid his longer suit.

In the absence of special partnership agreement, the Unusual Notrump overcall is not used over the opponent's opening bids at the two level or higher, except over strong forcing two-bids. Thus, consider the following auction:

North	East	South	West
2 ♡	2 Notrump		

If North and South are using strong two-bids, East's two notrump bid is the Unusual Notrump showing at least five cards in each minor suit.

If North and South are using weak two bids, East's two notrump bid is not for takeout, and does not show a two-suited hand. Instead, East simply indicates a desire to play the hand in notrump. He shows a hand worth a one notrump opening bid or overcall.

By a passed hand, the Unusual Notrump overcall can be made at any level, including the one level. For example:

North	East	South	West
Pass	*Pass*	*Pass*	1 ♠
1 Notrump			

Since North did not have a strong enough hand to open the bidding, he cannot show the normal 16 to 18 points with his notrump overcall. His bid, by inference, is unusual. By agreement, the Unusual Notrump overcall at the one level is a two-suited takeout, normally for the two lower unbid suits.

UNUSUAL ONE NOTRUMP OVERCALL

By special agreement the partnership may use Unusual Notrump overcalls at the one level by an unpassed hand, as in the following auction:

North	East	South	West
Pass	1 ♡	1 Notrump	

As to which two suits are shown by South's one notrump bid, this too is a matter for special partnership agreement.

Some partnerships, for example, use the one-level Unusual Notrump to show the highest and lowest ranking unbid suits. If these partnerships are also using Upper Suit Cue-bids, and the jump to two notrump to show the two lowest ranking unbid suits, the addition of the one-level Unusual Notrump gives them complete coverage of all two-suited hands:

Two Suits Held	Opponent's Opening Bid			
	♣	♦	♡	♠
♠ & ♡	Cue-bid	Cue-bid	–	–
♠ & ♦	1 Notrump	–	Cue-bid	–
♠ & ♣	–	1 Notrump	1 Notrump	–
♡ & ♦	2 Notrump	–	–	Cue-bid
♡ & ♣	–	2 Notrump	–	1 Notrump
♦ & ♣	–	–	2 Notrump	2 Notrump

For strength and distribution requirements, responses, etc., *see* TWO-SUITED TAKEOUTS—IN PROFILE.

ASTRO CUE-BID

Astro Cue-bids are used to describe two-suited hands that include one major suit and one minor suit. The cue-bid shows the lower unbid major suit and the lower unbid minor suit. Specific cue-bids show the following two suits:

    1 ♣ — 2 ♣ shows hearts and diamonds

    1 ◇ — 2 ◇ shows hearts and clubs

    1 ♡ — 2 ♡ shows spades and clubs

    1 ♠ — 2 ♠ shows hearts and clubs

Unlike Michaels, Top and Bottom, Upper Suit, and Colorful Cue-bids, and unlike the Unusual Notrump overcall, Astro cue-bids do not suggest that the same length is held in both of the bidder's suits. Astro cue-bids are designed principally to facilitate the description of hands containing a four-card major suit and a five card minor suit; these hands are difficult to describe bidding naturally.

Thus, the Astro cue-bidder promises more cards in the minor suit than in the major suit. He may have, for example, a four-card major suit and a five-card minor suit, or a four-card major suit and a six-card minor suit, or a five-card major suit and a six-card minor suit. Occasionally he may have five or six cards in each suit, but the convention envisions a minor suit that is longer than the major suit. For example, a cue-bid of two diamonds over one diamond, or two spades over one spade, might show

    ♠ x   ♡ K Q x x   ◇ J x   ♣ A J 10 x x x

Because the Astro cue-bid is intended to make it easier to bid a hand in which one of the suits could not be bid as an over-call, the strength of the Astro cue-bid may vary more than it should for other cue-bids such as Michaels. Therefore while the Astro bid may be made on a hand that is worthy only of a pre-empt, it may also be made on hands that have excellent game and slam potential.

ROMAN JUMP OVERCALLS

Roman Jump Overcalls are two-suited bids, showing the suit in which the jump is made, and the next higher unbid suit. For these purposes, clubs are ranked over spades as well as under diamonds. Thus, over a one diamond opening, for example, a jump overcall of two hearts would show hearts and spades, a jump to two spades would show spades and clubs.

This system has the advantage that, with a single convention, there is no combination of suits that cannot be shown, regardless of the suit in which the opening bid was made. Its disadvantage, however, is that it precludes use of single-suited jump overcalls. Weak jump overcalls can be very useful, both defensively in preempting the opponents, and offensively in limiting the weakness with which one-level overcalls will be made. Hands with which weak jump overcalls can be made occur considerably more frequently than hands warranting a two-suited jump overcall.

As with most of the cue-bids discussed in this section, the Roman jump overcall is essentially an obstructive bid. For strength and distribution requirements, responses, etc., *see* TWO-SUITED TAKEOUTS—IN PROFILE.

Strong Two-Suiters

With a strong two suited hand, the Roman system uses a jump to two notrump. The jump to two notrump forces the hand opposite to bid the lowest unbid suit. If the two notrump bidder now bids three notrump, he shows that his two suits still are unbid; the three notrump bid forces his partner to take a preference at the four level. For example:

North	East	South	West
1 ♣	2 Notrump	Pass	3 ♦
Pass	3 Notrump		

East's two notrump bid shows a strong hand with two long suits. West's three diamond bid is forced; West may or may not have length or strength in diamonds. East's three notrump bid shows that he did not have diamonds, and that he therefore has both major suits. West is forced to bid four of his better major. East might have a hand such as

♠ K Q J x x   ♡ A Q J x x x   ◇ x   ♣ x

In the above auction, if East had bid a suit instead of re-bidding three notrump, his bid would have shown the suit that he bid and the suit his partner had been forced to bid:

North	East	South	West
1 ♣	2 Notrump	Pass	3 ♦
Pass	3 ♡ or		
	4 ♡		

East's heart bid means that he has both hearts and diamonds. His three heart bid would be highly invitational, but not forcing.

COPENHAGEN

The Copenhagen convention is a system of jump overcalls designed to show two-suited hands. It uses a jump to two notrump over the opening bid to show the two lowest unbid suits, a jump to three clubs to show the lowest unbid suit and the highest unbid suit, and a jump to three diamonds to show the two highest unbid suits.

This system has the advantage that it can show any two suited hand after an opening bid in any suit. One of its disadvantages is that it necessarily propels the bidding immediately to the three level regardless of which two suits are held. Other conventions sometimes give the partnership a chance to play at the two level. A second disadvantage is that the three-club and three-diamond overcalls cannot be used in their natural senses.

For strength and distribution requirements, responses, etc., *see* TWO-SUITED TAKEOUTS—IN PROFILE.

UNUSUAL NOTRUMP AND MINORS

The unusual Notrump & Minors convention is a part of the Lea System. Using this convention all non-jump notrump and non-jump minor suit overcalls are unusual, showing two-suited hands.

Using this convention, the non-jump notrump overcall shows the lowest ranking unbid suits. A non-jump overcall in clubs shows the lowest ranking unbid suit and the highest ranking unbid suit. A non-jump overcall in diamonds shows the two highest ranking unbid suits. The Unusual Notrump & Minors conventions uses these overcalls over any opening bids, whether in suits or in notrump, and at any level.

When the convention is used over an opponent's notrump opening bid, it arbitrarily assumes that the opponents' suit is clubs, and the other three suits are deemed to be the unbid suits. Some examples:

(A)	*North*		*East*
	1 ♡		2 ♣
(B)	*North*		*East*
	1 ◇		1 Notrump
(C)	*North*		*East*
	1 Notrump		2 ◇
(D)	*North*		*East*
	1 ♣		2 ♣

In Auction A, East's two club overcall shows the lowest and the highest unbid suits, clubs and spades. In Auction D, the two club overcall shows diamonds and spades. In Auction B, the one notrump overcall shows the two lower unbid suits, clubs and hearts. In Auction C, the two diamond overcall shows the major suits.

For strength and distribution requirements, responses, etc., *see* TWO-SUITED TAKEOUTS—IN PROFILE.

TRUSCOTT OVER STRONG
ARTIFICIAL OPENINGS

The Truscott convention is a system of two-suited overcalls used principally over strong artificial club and diamond opening bids. Using the Truscott convention, any non-jump overcall shows the suit overcalled plus the next higher ranking suit. Thus, over an artificial one club opening, West would show the following suits:

South	West
1 ♣	1 ♢ shows diamonds and hearts
1 ♣	1 ♡ shows hearts and spades
1 ♣	1 ♠ shows spades and clubs
1 ♣	2 ♣ shows clubs and diamonds

A double of the artificial opening bid shows the suit doubled and the non-touching suit. Over a Schenken one club opening, for example, a double would show clubs and hearts. A notrump overcall would show the combination of non-touching suits that is not shown by the double of the suit opened. Thus a notrump overcall over one club would show diamonds and spades.

Over a Schenken two diamond opening bid, or over a negative one diamond response to one club, the double would show diamonds and spades, and a notrump overcall would show clubs and hearts.

For strength and distribution recommendations, responses, etc., *see* TWO-SUITED TAKEOUTS—IN PROFILE.

SIMPLIFIED TAKEOUT OVER STRONG ARTIFICIAL OPENINGS

As a defense to an opponent's strong artificial opening bid of one club, many partnerships play a simple combination of two-suited takeout bids. These partnerships use a double to show both major suits, and a one notrump overcall to show both minor suits. This system may also be used against opponents' strong artificial openings of one diamond, two clubs, and two diamonds.

For strength and distribution recommendations, responses, etc., *see* TWO-SUITED TAKEOUTS—IN PROFILE.

EXCLUSION OVERCALLS

If the bidding is opened naturally in a suit and the next player is short in that suit, frequently a takeout double may be made. When an artificial opening bid is made, however, it leaves all four suits unbid, and thus precludes a three-suit takeout double.

To compensate for being deprived of the takeout double over an opponent's artificial opening bid, some partnerships use "exclusion" bids. An exclusion bid is the bid of a short suit promising length in all of the other suits.

For example, suppose North and South are using the Precision Club system, and East and West are using exclusion bids. In the auction

North	*East*	*South*	*West*
1 ♣	1 ♠		

East's one spade bid shows a hand that is short in spades. Had the bidding been opened with a natural one spade bid, East would probably have made a takeout double.

The partner of the exclusion overcaller may respond as he would have to a takeout double of the short suit.

BALANCING TWO CLUB BID (for takeout)

Using standard methods of balancing over an opening bid of one in a suit, all bids in an unbid suit are natural. For example:

North	East	South	West
1 ♠	Pass	Pass	2 ♣

West's two club bid promises length in clubs. A balancing double usually shows close to an opening bid, with support for the unbid suits.

The Roth Stone system uses a balancing bid of two clubs as a forcing takeout. If the bidding has been opened one diamond, one heart, or one spade, the balancing bid of two clubs shows 6 to 9 high card points, with support for the other unbid suits. For example, in the auction

North	East	South	West
1 ♡	Pass	Pass	2 ♣

West might have

[A] ♠ Q x x x   ♡ x x   ◇ A x x x   ♣ x x x

The two club bid is technically forcing for one round; however, the partner of the two club bidder may pass if he has a long club suit, without length in either unbid suit.

The purpose of this use of the two club bid is to provide a takeout bid with weak hands, while reserving the takeout double for hands with at least 10 high card points. The availability of both calls for takeout gives the partner of the balancer a better idea of the partnership's potential. For example, if West

442

were allowed to make a balancing takeout double with both
Hand A above, and a hand such as

[B]   ♠ K x x x   ♡ x x   ◇ A Q 10 x   ♣ A 10 x

East would be hard pressed to know whether he should act aggressively or cautiously with a hand such as

♠ J x x   ♡ A Q x x   ◇ K x   ♣ K J x x

LANDY

It is especially dangerous to overcall over notrump opening bids. The overcaller is bidding largely in the dark, and may find his partner with a weak hand and a singleton in his suit. In contrast, the responder knows the strength of his partner's hand, and knows he has at least two cards in the overcaller's suit. The responder to a notrump opening bid thus has much less difficulty in deciding whether or not to double the overcall in these circumstances than he has over an overcall of a suit opening bid.

Having a two-suited hand greatly increases the safety of overcalling over the notrump bid, because it allows the overcaller's partner to take his choice of suits, thereby decreasing the likelihood of suffering a severe penalty double. The Landy convention is one of several conventions designed to describe two-suited hands over the opponent's one notrump opening. *See also* RIPSTRA, ASTRO, MODIFIED ASTRO, ROTH STONE ASTRO, PINPOINT ASTRO, BROZEL, TWO CLUBS FOR MINORS & TWO DIAMONDS FOR MAJORS, UNUSUAL NOTRUMP & MINORS.

The Landy convention is a two club bid over the opponent's one notrump opening bid to show both major suits. The two club bidder should have at least four cards in each major suit.

The strength needed to overcall varies with the vulnerability. Normally the Landy bidder should have a hand counting to at least 13 total points, counting high cards plus distribution. He might have a hand such as

[A] ♠ A K 10 x   ♡ Q J x x   ◇ A x x   ♣ x x

or

[B] ♠ A Q x x x   ♡ K x x x x   ◇ x x   ♣ x

With a hand that is weak in high cards and not especially freakish in distribution, he should pass:

444

[C] ♠ Q 10 x x x   ♡ A J x x   ◇ x x   ♣ x x

Using Landy, the two club bid does not show anything about the overcaller's club suit; it merely asks his partner to choose his better major suit.

Responses to Landy

Holding four of either major suit, the partner of the Landy bidder should bid that suit. Lacking a four card major, he should bid a three card major. If the partner of the Landy bidder has a very long club suit and no more than two cards in either major suit, he is allowed to pass the two club bid. Similarly, lacking as much as three-card support for a major suit, the partner of the Landy bidder is allowed to bid two diamonds if he has a long diamond suit, for example:

♠ x   ♡ x x   ◇ K J x x x x x   ♣ x x x

In responding to the two club bid with a major suit, a bid at the two level is a simple preference; a bid at the three level invites the Landy bidder to go on to game. In evaluating their hands for game, both the Landy bidder and his partner should be optimistic with very uneven distribution and a concentration of their high cards in the major suits.

For example, in response to the two club bid, West might have one of the following hands:

[A]   ♠ x   ♡ A Q x x x   ◇ x x x   ♣ x x x x

[B]   ♠ x x   ♡ Q x x x x   ◇ K J x   ♣ K Q x

With Hand A West should jump to three hearts. His hand is not robust, but he has excellent trump honors and a singleton in his partner's second suit. A crossruff might well bring in ten tricks.

With Hand B, West should bid just two hearts. Although he has almost twice the high card count he had in Hand A, they are all, except for the queen of hearts, in the wrong places. Kings and queens and jacks do not carry their full weight opposite partner's singletons.

If his partner has taken a simple preference, and the Landy bidder has a very distributional hand with good high cards in his suits, he may try for game by raising the suit his partner has chosen. For example, the Landy bidder should raise two spades to three with

♠ K J x x x   ♡ A Q x x x x   ◇ x   ♣ x

but should pass with a balanced hand such as

♠ K Q x x x   ♡ A Q x x   ◇ K x   ♣ x x

Over Weak Notrumps

The mechanism for the use of the Landy convention is the same over weak notrump openings as it is over strong notrumps, and the strength requirements for the two club overcall are the same. However, over weak notrumps it pays to be more aggressive in trying for game. Thus the Landy convention should be used over weak notrumps even on some balanced hands that would be strong enough to double a strong notrump opening.

If the partner of the Landy bidder has a good fit for one of the major suits and about 9 to 11 points concentrated in the major suits, he should invite game by jumping to three of his major suit. If he has the equivalent of an opening bid and a four card major suit, he should jump to four of the major. With the equivalent of an opening bid but no four-card major suit, for example,

♠ A x x   ♡ K x x   ◇ x x x   ♣ A Q x x

the partner of the Landy bidder should bid two notrump:

447

North	East	South	West
1 Notrump	2 ♣	Pass	2 Notrump

West's two notrump response is forcing on East for one round. If East can bid a five card major suit, West will raise to game. If East bids three diamonds, West will bid three notrump. If East bids three clubs, clubs may well be the partnership's best suit.

With a long solid or semi-solid minor suit and a good hand, the partner of the Landy bidder should bid three of his suit. The Landy bidder will bid again unless he has a very distributional hand with a misfit for his partner's suit.

Positional Considerations

While some partnerships use Landy only in the position directly over the notrump bidder, the convention can be used in both positions. In addition, some partnerships use the two club bid as Landy only if the two club bidder is an unpassed hand. Their reasoning is that a passed hand can double for the major suits without fear that he is showing a hand worth 16 or more points. This frees up the two club bid for use as a natural overcall showing clubs, and allows the partner of the doubler to pass with a moderately good hand that was not strong enough for a penalty double on its own. For example, suppose East had passed, holding

♠ K Q x x   ♡ K J 10 x   ◇ Q x x   ♣ x x

and the bidding proceeded

North	East	South	West
Pass	Pass	1 Notrump	Pass
Pass	Double		

East should be able to double for the major suits rather than bidding two clubs. If West held, for example,

♠ x x   ♡ Q x x   ◇ A x x x   ♣ K Q x x

he could pass for penalties.

RIPSTRA

The Ripstra convention is very similar to the Landy convention, in that it shows at least eight cards in the major suits over the opponent's notrump opening. The difference is that the Ripstra convention uses the two club bid as the takeout bid only when the overcaller's clubs are as strong as, or stronger than, his diamonds; it uses a two diamond bid as the takeout bid when his diamonds are stronger. For example, the Ripstra bidder would overcall two clubs with a hand such as

♠ K J x x   ♡ A Q x x   ◇ x   ♣ K x x x

but he would overcall two diamonds with a hand such as

♠ K Q x x   ♡ A Q x x x   ◇ J x x   ♣ x

The effect of Ripstra, as compared with Landy, is to widen slightly the choices available to the partner of the overcaller. He may more comfortably pass with a weak hand and length in the suit overcalled, since the overcaller is known to have some support for that suit. It is, of course, possible that the sense of added security that this gives will be a false one, for sometimes the Ripstra bidder will have five cards in each major suit and no more than two in the minor suit he is forced to bid. Occasionally, he will have two minor suit singletons.

The use of the Ripstra convention deprives the partnership of the possibility of making a natural two diamond overcall. Considering the marginal advantage of this convention over the Landy convention, the loss of yet another natural overcall is probably too great a price.

ASTRO

The Astro convention over one notrump openings uses a two club overcall to show a two-suited hand in which one suit is hearts and the other suit is a minor. It uses a two diamond overcall to show a two-suited hand in which one suit is spades, and the other may be any of the three remaining suits.

The suit specifically shown by the Astro bidder is called the "anchor" suit. When the Astro bidder's partner has four or more cards in the anchor suit, or has three cards headed by an honor, he is expected to bid that suit. Holding three small cards or worse in the anchor suit, the partner of the Astro bidder will generally bid the cheapest suit. Although this cheapest suit is called the "neutral" suit, it may in fact be the Astro bidder's second suit.

An Astro auction might go as follows:

North	East	South	West
1 Notrump	2 ◇	Pass	2 ♡
Pass	Pass	Pass	

The two diamond bid by East showed spades and another suit. West's two heart bid said nothing about his heart suit; it was simply a neutral bid. East's pass showed that his second suit happened to be hearts.

The strength needed to make an Astro overcall is comparable to that needed for a Landy overcall. However, the responses to Astro may be somewhat different since the Astro bidder's partner does not know which is the Astro bidder's second suit.

If the partner of the Astro bidder has a hand strong enough to warrant a game try and he has a fit for the anchor suit, he may jump in the anchor suit. If he has a hand worth a game try and no fit for the anchor suit, he should bid two notrump.

PINPOINT ASTRO

Pinpoint Astro is a modification of the Astro convention that serves to identify most suit combinations precisely with one bid. The overcalls and the suits shown are as follows:

2 ♣ = hearts and clubs

2 ◇ = hearts and diamonds

2 ♡ = hearts and spades

2 ♠ = spades and a minor suit

See also BROZEL.

For strength and distribution requirements, responses, etc., *see discussion under* LANDY.

ROTH-STONE ASTRO

The Roth Stone System uses a series of overcalls over one no-trump to show specific two-suit combinations as follows:

$$2 \clubsuit = \text{clubs and spades}$$
$$2 \diamondsuit = \text{diamonds and spades}$$
$$3 \clubsuit = \text{clubs and hearts}$$
$$3 \diamondsuit = \text{diamonds and hearts}$$
$$\text{DBL} = \text{hearts and spades}$$

However, if the opening notrump bid was a weak notrump, the double does not promise anything with respect to the major suits holdings, but instead shows at least 15 points.

For strength and distribution requirements for the over-calls, and responses, etc., *see discussion under* LANDY.

MODIFIED ASTRO

A modification of the Astro convention intended to facilitate description of a major suit two-suiter uses the overcalls as follows: a two club bid shows a long heart suit, and it may or may not be accompanied by a long minor suit. A two diamond bid shows spades and a minor suit. A two heart bid shows hearts and spades.

The responses to a two club overcall or a two diamond overcall are as they are for ASTRO. For example, the partner of the two club overcaller should bid hearts if he has four hearts or three hearts headed by an honor. Falling short of these holdings, he should bid two diamonds, the neutral suit. If the overcaller has a one-suited heart hand, he will bid two hearts. If he has hearts and diamonds, he will pass two diamonds. And if he has hearts and clubs, he will bid either two hearts or three clubs, depending on the strength of his hand and the relative strengths of his suits.

The responses to a two heart overcall, which shows specifically both major suits, are almost the same as for LANDY. The exception, of course, is that in order to take a simple preference for hearts, the partner of the overcaller need only pass.

BROZEL

Brozel is a very flexible convention that can allow the partnership to play in any suit at the two level over the opponent's one notrump opening. In exchange, it gives up the ability to double the opponents with a hand equivalent to a strong notrump opening.

Using the Brozel convention, a double shows a one-suited hand of at least average strength. However, this does not mean that a penalty cannot be inflicted; the partner of the ·doubler may pass with a smattering of values.

The doubler might have a hand such as

♠ A x   ♡ K Q J x x x   ◇ x x   ♣ Q x x

and his partner might have

♠ K J x x   ♡ x x   ◇ A J x x   ♣ J x x

If the partner of the Brozel doubler does not have the necessary values to allow him to pass the double, he must bid two clubs. This bid shows nothing about his club suit; it is merely a relay bid to allow the doubler to rebid his long suit, or to pass if his suit was clubs.

The Brozel double can be used either immediately over the opening notrump, or in the pass-out position. In addition the Brozel double can be used after the partner of the notrump opener has made a weak one-suited response:

North	East	South	West
1 Notrump	Pass	2 ♡	Double

West's double of two hearts is not intended either for penalties or for takeout, any more than the double of one notrump would have been. The double simply shows a one-suited hand. The partner of the doubler is again allowed to pass, so long as he holds a few values and good trumps. Otherwise he must bid the next ranking suit, which is a relay to allow the doubler to reveal his suit by passing or bidding.

Two-Suited Hands

Brozel also provides a system of bids to describe two suited hands. The system, which is similar to Pinpoint Astro, pivots principally around the heart suit:

$$2 \clubsuit = \text{hearts and clubs}$$

$$2 \diamondsuit = \text{hearts and diamonds}$$

$$2 \heartsuit = \text{hearts and spades}$$

$$2 \spadesuit = \text{spades and a minor suit}$$

$$2 \text{NT} = \text{both minor suits}$$

If the auction has proceeded

North	East	South	West
1 Notrump	2 ♠	Pass	

West may pass two spades if he has support for spades; if he does not have support for spades he should bid two notrump asking the Brozel bidder to reveal his minor suit.

Two-suited hands may also be shown after the partner of the notrump bidder has made a weak one-suited response. The bid of any suit over the responder's bid shows that suit and the next higher unbid suit. Thus West would bid as follows:

North	East	South	West				
1 Notrump	Pass	2 ♡	2 ♠	=	♠	&	♣
			3 ♣	=	♣	&	◇
			3 ◇	=	◇	&	♠

If West should have a very strong hand in this situation, he may jump in the lower of his touching suits.

Three-Suited Hands

To show a three-suited hand that has good high card strength, the Brozel convention uses a jump to three of the short suit. This bid shows a relatively strong hand, such as

♠ A J 10 x   ♡ K Q x x   ◇ —   ♣ A J x x x

With this hand, the Brozel bidder would jump to three diamonds over one notrump. His partner is requested to set the final contract.

In order to show a three-suited hand after the partner of the notrump bidder has made a weak one-suited response, there are two bids available. A bid of two notrump shows a three-suited hand of moderate strength, and asks partner to choose among the three remaining suits. A cue-bid makes the same request, but shows a stronger hand.

TWO-WAY EXCLUSION BIDS

Some partnerships use what might be called two-way exclusion bids over the opponents' one notrump openings. An exclusion bid is the bid of a short suit, promising length in all of the other suits. Using two-way exclusion bids, a suit overcall has one of two meanings: either the overcaller has that suit, or he is very short in that suit and has the other three suits. Using this convention, West would overcall two hearts over one notrump with either of the following hands:

♠ x x   ♡ K Q J x x x x   ◇ A x   ♣ x x

♠ K Q x x   ♡ x   ◇ A x x x   ♣ K J x x

This convention has the advantage that one can make either a natural overcall, or can make the equivalent of a take-out double even though all four suits are still unbid. The disadvantage, of course, is that the bid is the epitome of ambiguity.

If the partner of the overcaller has fewer than three cards in the suit overcalled, he must assume that the overcaller has length in that suit. Normally the strength of his hand will be such that he is forced to pass. This may occasionally result in the partnership's playing in a 2–1 fit, but not doubled. If the overcall is doubled, either immediately or after the overcaller's partner has passed, the overcaller should redouble if he has bid his short suit rather than a real suit. This will allow the partnership to escape into a more reasonable spot. (*See also* s.o.s. RE-DOUBLES.) Conversely, if the opponents double the overcall of a real long suit, the overcaller must pass.

If the partner of the overcaller has great length in the suit overcalled he will infer that that is the overcaller's short suit. He may nevertheless pass if he has no side four card suit.

If the partner of the overcaller has three or more cards in the suit bid, he usually will not be able to tell whether that is his partner's long suit or his short suit. In these circumstances, the partner of the overcaller should bid his longest suit in case his partner's bid was the exclusion bid. If the overcaller rebids the suit in which he overcalled, he shows that his original bid was not an exclusion bid but a natural bid.

BECKER:
TWO CLUBS FOR MINORS,
TWO DIAMONDS FOR MAJORS

A convention similar to Landy and Ripstra uses only the two diamond overcall to show both major suits. It uses the two club overcall to show length in both minor suits. Use of this convention enables the partnership to play in any suit at the two level. The strength required is the same as that for a Landy bid.

UNUSUAL NOTRUMP AND MINORS
OVER NOTRUMP

A part of the Lea System, this convention consists of three artificial overcalls over the notrump opening, each showing a different pair of suits. An overcall of two clubs shows diamonds and spades; an overcall of two diamonds shows hearts and spades; a two notrump overcall shows diamonds and hearts. Two-suited hands in which one of the long suits is clubs cannot be described using this convention.

For strength and distribution requirements, responses, etc., *see discussion under* LANDY.

NEGATIVE DOUBLES

When the partnership has agreed to use five-card major suit openings, the frequency of their opening the bidding in a minor suit is, of course, increased. One of the hazards of opening the bidding in a minor suit is that it is easier for the opponents to overcall. If the opponent overcalls a minor suit opening with one spade and the responder has a four card heart suit he was planning to bid, the overcall may prove embarrassing.

The Negative Double is a convention that copes with this situation. It is a double of an opponent's overcall for takeout rather than for penalties. The double tells the opener that the responder has some high-card values and support for at least one of the unbid suits, usually the unbid major suit. For example, if the bidding has started

South	West	North	East
1 ♦	1 ♠	Double	Pass

North's double shows at least four hearts, and at least enough strength for him to have responded to the one diamond opening bid had there been no interference. North might have a hand such as

[A] ♠ x x x ♡ A x x x ♦ x x ♣ Q x x x

or

[B] ♠ x x x ♡ K J x x ♦ K x x x ♣ x x

Responder hopes his partner will be able to bid two hearts. If instead he bids two clubs, responder will pass with Hand A, or will correct the contract to two diamonds with Hand B.

After the negative double the opener is expected to bid

the major suit shown by the responder if he has four-card support for that suit. If he has a minimum hand, he will bid just two of the responder's suit. If he has about a trick better than a minimum hand, he should jump in the responder's suit. For example, the opener might have

    [C] ♠ K x   ♡ Q x x x   ◇ A J x x   ♣ A x x

or

    [D] ♠ x x   ♡ A Q x x   ◇ A K x x   ♣ Q x x

After the auction has started

South	*West*	*North*	*East*
1 ◇	1 ♠	Double	Pass

the opener would bid two hearts with Hand C. With Hand D opener would jump to three hearts, just as he would have if the bidding had gone, without interference:

Opener	*Responder*
1 ◇	1 ♡
3 ♡	

Opener's jump to three hearts invites the responder to bid a game if he has extra values; however, it is not forcing. After the responder has made a negative double the only forcing bid available to the opener is a cue-bid of the suit in which the opponent overcalled.

The responder may have a very strong hand and still make a negative double if the overcall has made it difficult for him to bid his hand naturally. For example, responder might hold

    ♠ A x   ♡ K Q x x   ◇ Q x x x x   ♣ A x

If his partner has opened with one diamond and the next hand has overcalled with one spade, the responder has no convenient bid. Therefore he uses a negative double to find out whether or not his partner has four hearts, and plans to force at least to game thereafter.

Although the negative double was originally used primarily by partnerships which had agreed not to open four-card major suits, its use has spread, and it may be useful even if the opener was allowed to open the bidding in a four-card major. For example, using negative doubles, the responder can distinguish between four-card and five-card major suit responses. Suppose the bidding has started

South	West	North	East
1 ♣	1 ♡	1 ♠	

If the partnership is not using negative doubles, North's one spade response could be made on either a four-card suit or a five-card suit. If the partnership is using negative doubles, North's free bid of one spade in the above auction would guarantee a five-card suit since he could have shown a four-card suit by making a negative double.

Many partnerships limit the use of negative doubles to low levels of the bidding, and to auctions in which the responder has been prevented from showing his four-card major suit safely and naturally. However, there is no technical reason why this double cannot be used at quite high levels, and over any combination of openings and overcalls. Of course, the higher the level at which the negative double is made, the stronger the doubler's hand must be, and the more likely opener will pass for penalties.

Suppose, for example, that the bidding goes

North	East	South	West
1 ♠	2 ♡		

and South has a hand such as

♠ K x   ♡ J x x   ◇ A x x x   ♣ K x x x

It is very useful for South to be able to use a negative double to describe his hand. His negative double in this situation shows at least a 10 point hand, since if opener is to bid one of responder's suits it must be at the three level. South also shows that he probably has no five-card suit since he chose to double rather than bidding a suit.

Passing for Penalties: Opener's Duty to Reopen

Use of the immediate double of an overcall as a negative or takeout double means that the responder cannot double the overcall for penalties. Therefore, if North has a hand such as

♠ x x   ♡ A x x   ◇ K J 10 9 x   ♣ Q x x

in an auction such as

South	West	North	East
1 ♠	2 ◇		

North must pass West's two diamond overcall.

The fact that the use of negative doubles may force the responder to pass when otherwise he would have made a penalty double places a heavy obligation on the opening bidder. The opener should make every reasonable effort to keep the bidding open if his lefthand opponent's overcall is passed around to him, especially if he is short in the overcaller's suit. Thus, if the auction goes

South	West	North	East
1 ♠	2 ◇	Pass	Pass

and South holds

[A] ♠ A Q x x x ♡ K x x ◇ x ♣ K x x x

South should reopen the bidding.

One guideline for the opener as to whether or not to reopen is his length in the suit of the overcall. The shorter he is in that suit the more he should strain to keep the bidding open. Conversely, the more cards he has in the overcaller's suit, the less likely it is that his partner has passed with the equivalent of a penalty double, and the more inclined the opener should be to pass. If responder did not pass because he wanted to make a penalty double, he passed because he was weak. In Hand A above, if opener's diamonds and hearts were reversed, he should pass the two diamond overcall.

Once South decides to reopen, he should reopen with a double on any hand with which, if the partnership had not been using negative doubles, he would have been willing to pass an immediate penalty double by his partner. If the opener has a hand with which he would have removed his partner's immediate penalty double, he should keep the bidding open by bidding a suit. In this way, if responder had a hand with which he hoped to penalize the overcaller, he will at least be given another opportunity to bid. Opener and responder might for example have these hands:

(Opener)
♠ A Q x x x x   ♡ x x   ◇ A 10 9 x   ♣ x

(Responder)
♠ J x   ♡ A Q 10 x   ◇ Q x x   ♣ K J x x

With responder precluded from making a penalty double of a two club overcall, the auction might go

North	East	South	West
1 ♠	2 ♣	Pass	Pass
2 ◇	Pass	3 Notrump	

When the responder has made a negative double, the opening bidder has an option to pass for penalties if he has a suitable hand. For example, suppose the opener has a hand such as

♠ A x   ♡ K Q x x x   ◇ K Q 10 9   ♣ x x

and the bidding has gone

North	East	South	West
1 ♡	2 ◇	Double	Pass

The opener has a choice between bidding notrump and passing for penalties.

Thus, a secondary advantage of using negative doubles is that the overcaller may have a penalty inflicted on him from either side. Further, when the opening bidder has the necessary length in the overcaller's suit to allow him to pass the double for penalties, the partner of the overcaller will have had to commit himself before knowing that a penalty is to be sought.

467

Consider West's predicament in the following auction:

North	East	South	West
1 ♠	2 ♣	Double	

If North and South were not using negative doubles, West would know that the double is for penalties, and he might well try to escape into a better suit. However, if South's double is for take-out, West cannot be sure that North and South have any interest in penalizing the overcall. East might after all have such a long or solid suit that North would not have sufficient club length or strength to pass for penalties.

RESPONSIVE DOUBLES

When one's partner has doubled an opening bid for takeout and the responder has raised the opener's suit, one seldom wants to double for penalties. The partnership may find it desirable in this situation to use Responsive Doubles.

A Responsive Double is a takeout double in response to partner's takeout double. For example, in each of the following auctions

(A)	*South*	*West*	*North*	*East*
	1 ♠	Double	2 ♠	Double

(B)	*South*	*West*	*North*	*East*
	1 ◇	Double	3 ◇	Double

East's double of North's raise is a responsive double. The responsive double shows support for at least two of the unbid suits. The double normally denies a five card suit, and shows strength appropriate for play at least at the level to which the responsive doubler invites his partner to bid. For example, in Auction A, East might have a hand such as

♠ x   ♡ Q x x x   ◇ K x x x   ♣ Q x x x

For Auction B, East might have

♠ A J x x   ♡ K J x x   ◇ x x x   ♣ J x

While a cue-bid would describe East's hand pattern in each of the above auctions, it would show a hand stronger in high cards, and might well get the partnership overboard. The responsive double thus allows description on moderate, rather than game-forcing, values.

When the Opponents Have Bid Two Suits

Responsive doubles are usually limited to situations in which the opponents have bid and raised the same suit. However, the partnership may agree to extend the responsive double to a situation in which the responder has bid a new suit over the takeout double. For example:

North	East	South	West
1 ◇	Double	1 ♡	Double

If the partnership has agreed, West may make a responsive double to show spades and clubs. This use of the responsive double, however, makes it somewhat more difficult for East and West to expose a psychic response by South.

When Partner Has Overcalled

Responsive doubles may also be used when the responder has supported the opener's suit after partner has made an overcall. The responsive double over an overcall suggests that the doubler is short in the overcaller's suit, and has length in each of the unbid suits.

For example:

South	West	North	East
1 ♠	2 ♣	2 ♠	Double

East's double invites West to bid one of the unbid suits if he has as much as three-card support. East might have a hand such as

♠ x x　　♡ K J x x x　　◇ K 10 9 x x　　♣ x

COOPERATIVE DOUBLES

A cooperative double is a double that gives the doubler's partner the choice of passing for penalties or bidding on. OPTIONAL DOUBLES and COMPETITIVE DOUBLES are special types of cooperative doubles.

Cooperative doubles are used principally at low levels of the auction. Without special partnership agreement they may be used in situations where the doubler's previous bidding has necessarily limited his hand so that he would not be able to guarantee a penalty. For example:

North	East	South	West
1 ◇	1 ♠	2 ◇	2 ♠
Pass	Pass	Double	

South's two diamond response after the one spade overcall limited his hand. His double of two spades cannot, therefore, be based on massive strength. It suggests to opener that two spades can be defeated if opener is interested in defending; otherwise opener should bid on.

Some partnerships agree, especially playing match point duplicate, that all of their low-level doubles are cooperative doubles. For example, in the auction

North	East	South	West
1 ◇	1 ♡	1 ♠	Pass
2 ◇	2 ♡	Double	

such a partnership would treat South's double as cooperative, and not to be left in by North unless he could contribute substantially to the defense.

A cooperative double may be made even when the partner of the doubler has never bid. For example

North	East	South	West
1 ◇	Pass	Pass	Double
1 ♠	2 ♡	Pass	Pass
Double			

Opener has limited his hand by his failure to redouble at his second turn. His double suggests that he has a very good hand with about 19 or 20 points, and is willing to have South pass with good hearts, or bid any other suit.

COMPETITIVE DOUBLES

From time to time the opponents' overcalls will interfere with the opener's try for game, rather than with the responder's bidding. A convention designed to remedy this situation is called the Competitive Double.

For example, suppose South had a hand such as

♠ K Q x x x   ♡ x   ◇ A Q x x   ♣ K J x

and his partner had raised his one spade opening bid to two. South could make a natural game try by bidding three diamonds; or if the partnership had agreed to use SHORT SUIT GAME TRIES, South could invite game by bidding three hearts.

Suppose, however, that the bidding has gone

(A)	South	West	North	East
	1 ♠	2 ♡	2 ♠	3 ♡

A bid of three spades by South would be merely competitive, and he is deprived of whatever game tries he might have used without competition.

It is in this situation that competitive doubles (also called "maximal overcall" doubles when the opponents have taken up the maximum amount of room with their overcalls) are most useful. However, competitive doubles can be used even when the opponents' bids have not used up all the room for a game try. For example:

(B)	South	West	North	East
	1 ♠	2 ◇	2 ♠	3 ◇

Although opener could still bid three hearts as a game try, if he has good defensive, as well as offensive, strength, he may as well make his game try by doubling. If his partner has an appropriate hand, such as

♠ J 10 x   ♡ x x   ◇ K Q 10 x   ♣ A x x x

he will pass the game-try double for penalties.

The partnership loses little by using the doubles in Auctions A and B as competitive doubles instead of penalty doubles. Opener will rarely have a hand with which to make either a unilateral penalty double, or a cooperative double that his partner is likely to leave in.

Competitive doubles may be made by the responder as well as the opener. Consider the following auction:

South	West	North	East
1 ♠	2 ◇	2 ♠	3 ◇
Pass	Pass		

If North has a hand with which he wants to compete to the three level, he can, of course, bid three spades. However, if he competes with a double he not only conveys this message, but also gives the opener a chance to pass his competitive double for penalties. The North and South hands might be:

(South)
♠ A 10 x x x   ♡ Q x   ◇ K J 10 9   ♣ K J

(North)
♠ J x x   ♡ K J x x   ◇ x x   ♣ A x x x

NEGATIVE SLAM DOUBLES

When the partnership has bid and raised a suit preemptively in a competitive situation, and the opponents have reached a slam, the partnership frequently would like to sacrifice if it cannot defeat the slam. For example:

South	West	North	East
1 ♢	1 ♠	3 ♡	4 ♠
Pass	Pass	5 ♢	Pass
6 ♢			

There are two methods available to help the partnership to determine whether or not it has the two tricks necessary to defeat the slam. They are called Negative Slam Doubles and Positive Slam Doubles. The use of either convention requires the partnership to forego the use of LIGHTNER SLAM DOUBLES in competitive situations such as these.

The Negative Slam double convention requires the person in the first potential sacrifice position ("First Hand"—West in the auction above) to double if he has no defensive tricks against the slam. If First Hand has one or two defensive tricks, he is required to pass. His partner ("Last Hand") now evaluates his defensive potential.

If First Hand has doubled showing no defensive tricks, Last Hand will sacrifice if he has no more than one trick. If Last hand has two tricks, he will pass his partner's double.

If First Hand has passed, showing one or two defensive tricks, Last Hand will pass also if he has one or more tricks. If Last Hand has no defensive tricks, he will double. After Last Hand has doubled, showing no defensive tricks, First Hand will pass if he has two defensive tricks, or will sacrifice if he has only one.

POSITIVE SLAM DOUBLES

When the opponents have reached a slam after an auction in which the defending partnership has bid and raised a suit (see discussion in NEGATIVE SLAM DOUBLES), the partnership may find it advantageous to use Positive Slam doubles in order to determine whether it should sacrifice or should instead try to set the slam.

Positive Slam Doubles are so called because, unlike NEGATIVE SLAM DOUBLES, doubles are made with hands containing one or more defensive tricks, rather than with hands containing no defensive tricks.

Using the Positive Slam Double convention, First Hand doubles if he has two tricks; if he has one or none, he passes. After First Hand has doubled, showing that he expects to defeat the slam in his own hand, Last Hand of course passes.

If First Hand has passed, showing one or no tricks, Last Hand will sacrifice if he has no tricks; he will pass if he has two tricks, and he will double if he has one defensive trick. After Last Hand's double, First Hand will pass if he too has a trick; with no trick First Hand will sacrifice over Last Hand's double.

The Positive Slam Double convention is somewhat simpler and more natural than the Negative Slam Double convention, and has the added advantage of forcing opponents to play their contract doubled more often when they are going down.

JORDAN:
TWO NOTRUMP AS A LIMIT RAISE OVER OPPONENT'S TAKEOUT DOUBLE

When the bidding has been opened with one of a suit and the next hand has passed, the responder's jump to two notrump shows a balanced hand of 13 to 15 points. However, if the intervening hand has made a takeout double and the responder has a balanced 13 to 15 count, he will frequently want to try to penalize the opponents.

Over the takeout double, therefore, the responder will normally redouble with any strong hand. Consequently the jump to two notrump loses its natural meaning.

The most frequent use of the jump to two notrump over the opponent's takeout double is as a limit raise, showing about 9 or 10 points, with three or four card support for partner's suit. For example, after North has opened with one heart and East has made a takeout double, South would jump to two notrump with

♠ x x   ♥ K J x x   ♦ A J x x   ♣ x x x

Use of the jump to two notrump as a limit raise allows the jump raise to three of the opener's suit over the double to be used strictly preemptively. For example:

♠ x   ♥ K J x x x   ♦ J x x x   ♣ x x x

TWO NOTRUMP AS A PREEMPTIVE RAISE OVER DOUBLE OF MINOR SUIT OPENING

The jump to two notrump over the opponent's takeout double can be used to show a hand worth a limit raise of partner's suit when partner has opened the bidding with a minor. Thus responder could make preemptive jumps in opener's suit. However, some partnerships reverse the meanings of the two notrump response and the jump to three of partner's suit. Using this method, in the auction

North	East	South	West
1 ◇	Double	2 Notrump	

South's two notrump bid would show a preemptive raise in diamonds, a hand such as

♠ x x x ♡ x ◇ K J 10 x x x ♣ Q x x

In the auction

North	East	South	West
1 ◇	Double	3 ◇	

South's three diamond bid would show a hand worth a limit raise in diamonds, such as

♠ x x x ♡ K J x ◇ K Q x x ♣ Q x x

The rationale for the reversal of the meanings of these two bids is that when the responder has a limit raise of a minor suit, the partnership may very well belong in three notrump. Using three diamonds as the limit raise accomplishes two things. First, it allows the opener, who has the stronger of the two hands, to be the notrump declarer. And secondly, making opener the declarer will make the doubler, who will have the stronger of the two defensive hands, be the opening leader. His lead will often be made without his knowing which suit his partner prefers, and he will be leading away from strength, rather than toward it.

STAYMAN AFTER NOTRUMP OVERCALLS

The partner of a player who has overcalled one notrump over an opponent's opening bid sometimes wants to find out whether or not his side has a four-four major suit fit. The Stayman convention can be used in response to the notrump overcall. Assuming that the one notrump overcall shows the same strength as a one notrump opening, the partner of the overcaller should have the same strength he would need to use Stayman in response to an opening bid.

There are three ways in which the partnership could agree to use the Stayman convention after notrump overcalls. Standard practice is to use a cue-bid as the Stayman bid:

South	West	North	East
1 ◇	1 Notrump	Pass	2 ◇

East's two diamond bid asks West whether or not he has a four card major. If West has no four card major he rebids two notrump.

An alternative method is to use a two club bid as Stayman, regardless of what the opening bid was. This provides the partnership with somewhat greater offensive flexibility, since the Stayman bidder can proceed just as he would have using nonforcing Stayman in a non-competitive auction. For example, if East held a hand such as

♠ Q x x x x   ♡ x x x x   ◇ x x   ♣ x x

he would like to use Stayman, and pass if his partner bids a four-card major suit. If the two diamond cue-bid must be used as the Stayman bid, West's rebid with no four-card major would

481

be two notrump. With this hand, using only the cue-bid as Stayman, therefore, East would be forced just to bid two spades, giving up on finding a four-four heart fit.

However, if the partnership is using two clubs as Stayman, East can safely bid two clubs to try to find a fit in either major suit. If West does not have a four-card major, his rebid will be two diamonds, and over this East can bid two spades.

The disadvantage of this method is that it leaves the partner of the notrump overcaller one less suit into which he can escape.

A third method of using Stayman when the bidding has been opened with something other than one club, is to play Two-Way Stayman over the overcall. Using this method a two club bid by the partner of the notrump overcaller would be the equivalent of non-forcing Stayman, and a cue-bid of the opponent's suit would be forcing to game.

Having this agreement would give the partner of the over-caller a complete range of bids; he could force to game by cue-bidding; or he could invite game by bidding two clubs and the jumping to three of a five-card major suit; or he could rebid his five-card major suit at the two level with a hand with which he had little interest in game.

STAYMAN OVER OPPONENT'S NOTRUMP OVERCALL

Although seldom adopted, it is possible to use a two club bid as a Stayman-type of convention over an opponent's one notrump overcall. This is most useful when the partnership is using five-card major suit openings and the opening bid has been one club or one diamond. Thus in the auctions

(A)	*North*	*East*	*South*	*West*
	1 ◇	1 Notrump	2 ♣	

(B)	*North*	*East*	*South*	*West*
	1 ♣	1 Notrump	2 ♣	

the partnership could agree to use South's two club bid as Stayman.

The use of two clubs as Stayman in these auctions is similar to using a negative double. It may be the only way South has to bid a hand such as

♠ Q x x x   ♡ K x x x   ◇ Q x x   ♣ x x

LEBENSOHL

When an opponent overcalls over a one notrump opening, the responder frequently has a difficult time bidding his hand appropriately. Many partnerships have not agreed what bids are forcing, or what the responder can do to compete.

The Lebensohl convention is a method for the responder to make competitive and forcing bids after an opponent has overcalled over the one notrump opening. The Lebensohl method uses different methods for overcalls at the two level and at the three-level.

Against One-Suited Overcalls

After a natural overcall at the three level the Lebensohl method is fairly simple. Bids of new suits are forcing to game. A double is negative and promises four cards in any unbid major suit. The double is not forcing to game.

After a natural overcall at the two level, the double by the responder is for penalties. A new suit bid at the two level is competitive and not forward going. A new suit bid at the three level is forcing to game. A cue-bid of the overcaller's suit is also forcing to game and suggests that the responder has no long suit to bid.

If the responder wants to compete, but not force to game, in a suit that ranks below the suit of the overcall, he cannot bid it directly over the overcall, because bidding a new suit at the three level is forcing to game. To play in his suit, the responder must first bid two notrump. The two notrump bid is a relay bid, forcing the opener to bid three clubs. The three club bid permits responder to pass if his long suit is clubs; or to bid another suit, which his partner is normally expected to pass. For example, suppose responder has

♠ K x   ♡ x x x   ◇ J 10 x x x x   ♣ K x

If the opponent overcalled two clubs as a natural bid over the one notrump opening, responder would simply bid two diamonds. If the overcall was two hearts (or two spades), however, the auction would go

North	East	South	West
1 Notrump	2 ♡	2 Notrump	Pass
3 ♣	Pass	3 ◇	Pass
Pass	Pass		

If the responder has a long suit that can be bid at the two level over the overcall, but he has a strong enough hand to invite game, responder can bid two notrump, forcing the opener to bid three clubs, and then bid his suit. The message to opener, since responder did not bid his suit directly over the overcall is that he wants to invite game.

Showing Stoppers

The availability of the two notrump bid as a relay gives the responder added flexibility with game-going hands. Responder has, in effect, two ways to suggest game in notrump, and two ways to look for a major suit fit. For example:

(A)	North	East	South	West
	1 Notrump	2 ♡	3 Notrump	

(B)

North	East	South	West
1 Notrump	2 ♡	2 Notrump	Pass
3 ♣	Pass	3 Notrump	

In both (a) and (b) responder is suggesting that the partnership play three notrump. He should use the two auctions to distinguish between his possible holdings in the overcaller's suit. Tactically it is preferable to use auction (a) to deny a stopper in the overcaller's suit, because it inhibits West from raising his partner's suit. If three notrump becomes the final contract, East will have to guess how good opener's holding is in the suit of the overcall. If responder temporized with a two notrump bid without a stopper, West could more easily raise his partner's suit, solving the lead problem. Auction (b), therefore, should promise a stopper.

The same distinctions can be drawn between the following auctions:

(C)

North	East	South	West
1 Notrump	2 ♡	3 ♡	

(D)

North	East	South	West
1 Notrump	2 ♡	2 Notrump	Pass
3 ♣	Pass	3 ♡	

In both auctions (c) and (d) responder has cue-bid, showing four cards in the unbid major suit and suggested that he has no long suit of his own. Since his partner may not have a matching four card suit, responder should also use these two auctions to show whether or not he has a stopper, in case opener wants to consider notrump. For the sake of consistency, auction (c) should be used to deny a stopper in the overcaller's suit, while auction (d) should promise a stopper.

Against Two-Suited Overcalls

There are many conventional overcalls over one notrump that show two-suited hands. Some, such as Landy and Brozel, show precisely which two suits the overcaller has. Some, such as Astro, specify one suit but not the other. In most respects the Lebensohl convention operates the same way against both types of overcalls.

Against a two-suited overcall in which only one suit is pinpointed, a double is for penalties in that suit. Against a two-suited overcall in which both suits are specified, the double shows the ability to penalize at least one of the suits. For example, against a Landy two club bid, responder would double with

♠ K J x x   ♡ Q x   ♢ K x x x   ♣ x x x

Against either type of overcall, responder's bid of a "new" suit—i.e., not one of the overcaller's known suits—is not forcing if bid at the two level. The bid of a new suit at the three level is forcing to game.

If responder wants to make a non-forcing bid in a suit that cannot be shown at the two level he must first bid two notrump. The two notrump bid is a relay, forcing opener to bid three clubs. Responder can pass three clubs if clubs is his suit; or he can bid his suit over three clubs. For example, suppose the overcall is two diamonds, Ripstra, for the major suits, and responder had a hand such as

♠ K x   ♡ x x   ♢ x x   ♣ Q J x x x x

The auction could go

North	East	South	West
1 Notrump	2 ◇	2 Notrump	Pass
3 ♣	Pass	Pass	Pass

It is in making cue-bids of the opponent's suits that the Lebensohl convention distinguishes between the overcalls that specify the two suits held, and overcalls that identify only one suit. When both of the overcaller's suits are known, two cue bids are available to the responder. When both of the suits are known, and the overcall has been at the two level, the Lebensohl convention uses the cue-bid of the cheaper suit as a non-game-going, competitive bid. Responder should have a hand that is strong enough to play at the three level, but not strong enough to force to game. In the auction above, if responder had cue-bid two hearts, the cheaper of the suits shown by the Ripstra bid, instead of bidding two notrump, he might have had a hand such as

♠ x x   ♡ x   ◇ K J x x x   ♣ Q 10 x x x

The cue-bid of the higher ranking suit specified by the overcall is forcing to game, and shows support for the unbid suits. If responder had cue-bid two spades in the above auction, he might have had a hand such as

♠ x x   ♡ A   ◇ K Q x x x   ♣ K J x x x

When the overcall has identified only one of the overcaller's two suits, there is only one cue-bid available. This cue-bid is forcing to game, and shows supports for all of the other suits.

If the two-suited overcall is made at the three-level and the two suits are identified, e.g., Roth-Stone Astro, the double of the overcall is negative, showing support for the other two suits. The double is not forcing to game. New suit bids are still forcing, and a cue-bid is forcing to game.

TRANSFERS OVER DOUBLES OF
ONE NOTRUMP

When the bidding has been opened with one notrump and the next hand has doubled for penalties, it is standard practice to redouble with good general strength, to pass with either a smattering of values, or no suit to run to, and to bid a suit naturally if possible. It is, however, possible to use transfer bids over the double, or to use a system of artificial bids that give the opener a choice of suits.

The reason most partnerships do not use Jacoby Transfer-type bids over the double of one notrump is that at first glance, transfers seem to reduce the number of avenues of escape. For example, using Jacoby Transfers a two diamond bid would show a heart suit; therefore two diamonds could not be bid naturally.

One convention dealing with this situation uses four-suit two-level transfers. It accomplishes this by the simple expedient of using a redouble to transfer to clubs, a two club bid to transfer to diamonds, a two diamond bid to transfer to hearts, and a two heart bid to transfer to spades.

In addition, a Stayman-type sequence can be used. If the responder wants the opener to bid his better major suit, he first redoubles, transferring temporarily to two clubs. Over opener's bid of two clubs, however, responder will bid two diamonds, asking opener to bid his better major suit.

What the partnership gives up in exchange for these transfers is the ability to redouble for penalties—a small price for the ability to transfer declarership in any suit to the strong hand, and the ability to use Stayman.

REDOUBLES FOR TAKEOUT OVER ONE
NOTRUMP DOUBLED

As an alternative to the standard practice of making "penalty" redoubles of doubles of one notrump openings, some partnerships use the redouble as part of a minor suit escape route. Using this method, a redouble asks the opener to bid his better minor suit. Responder promises at least nine cards in the minor suits. A two diamond bid over the double asks the opener to bid his better major suit. Bids of two hearts and two spades are natural, and have their standard meanings.

In addition, a bid of two clubs shows one long minor suit, but not necessarily clubs. If two clubs gets doubled and responder retreats to two diamonds, his suit was diamonds. Opener should not "correct" to three clubs.

DEFENSE AGAINST OPPONENTS'
TWO-SUITED CALLS

When the opponents have intervened with a cue-bid or overcall that shows a two-suited hand, the partnership should attempt to maximize its chances of extracting a penalty when such a penalty would be severe. The most effective strategy is for the responder to double with a good 9 points or better, and strength in one or both of the suits shown by the opponent.

For example, in the auction

South	West	North	East
1 ♡	2 ♡		

if West's cue-bid shows spades and clubs, North should double with a hand such as

♠ K Q x x   ♡ x x x   ◇ x x   ♣ K J x x

or

♠ Q x x   ♡ x x   ◇ A x x x   ♣ A Q x x

Holding less than the strength necessary to double, the responder can make a single raise of his partner's suit with any hand that would have been worth a free raise after a simple overcall. For example, for the auction

South	West	North	East
1 ◇	2 ◇	3 ◇	

North might hold

♠ K x x   ♡ x x   ◇ A x x x   ♣ x x x x

If responder has a strong offensive hand, the two-suited overcall or cue-bid gives him an excellent weapon, the cue-bid. The responder should make a cue-bid with either a good fit for opener's suit or a powerful suit of his own.

For example, if his partner has opened with one heart and the next hand has cue-bid two hearts, showing spades and diamonds, and North has a hand such as

♠ x x x   ♡ K Q x x   ◇ A x   ♣ A J x x

North may cue-bid three diamonds, the opponents' suit in which he has the greater control. If South had a hand such as

♠ x   ♡ A J x x x   ◇ K x x x   ♣ K Q x

the partnership could reach its slam, since opener would realize that responder has good heart support rather than a self-supporting suit. The entire auction might be

South	West	North	East
1 ♡	2 ♡	3 ◇	Pass
3 ♠	Pass	4 ♣	Pass
5 ♡	Pass	6 ♡	

Cue-bids are very useful tools against two-suited overcalls since there are two suits that may be cue-bid. This method works over any two-suited overcall, so long as the partnership knows which two suits the overcaller shows.

UNUSUAL-OVER-UNUSUAL

The methods described under DEFENSE AGAINST OPPONENTS' TWO-SUITED CALLS can be used over the opponent's jump to two notrump as the Unusual Notrump. An alternative method has been devised to assign precise meanings to the cue-bids of the suits shown by the Unusual Notrump, in an effort to define over-all strength as well as suit length. The meanings assigned are entirely artificial, hence the name "Unusual-over-Unusual".

The Unusual Notrump shows two suits, normally the minor suits, as in the auction

South	West	North	East
1 ♡ or			
1 ♠	2 Notrump		

Unusual-over-Unusual uses a cue-bid in the opponent's lower ranking suit, here clubs, to show a hand with length in the lower of the two suits not shown by the overcall; it uses a cue-bid in the opponent's higher suit to show a hand with length in the higher ranking of those two suits. Whenever the bidding has been opened with a major suit, a club cue-bid would show hearts, and a diamond cue-bid would show spades.

A cue-bid of the minor suit that shows length in the opener's suit promises a hand worth a limit raise or better. Thus in the auction

(A)	North	East	South	West
	1 ♠	2 Notrump	3 ◇	

South's three diamond bid shows at least a limit raise in spades. In the auction

(B) *North*   *East*   *South*   *West*
     1 ♡   2 Notrump   3 ♣

South's three club bid shows at least a limit raise in hearts. In auctions (a) and (b), if North has a hand with which he wishes to be in game opposite as little as a limit raise, he should avoid rebidding his suit at the three level.

A cue-bid that shows the unbid suit—i.e.,

(C) *South*   *West*   *North*   *East*
     1 ♠   2 Notrump   3 ♣

(D) *South*   *West*   *North*   *East*
     1 ♡   2 Notrump   3 ◇

shows that responder has at least five cards in the unbid suit, and a hand worth an invitation to game, but not worth a game force. (Some partnerships instead use the cue-bid to show a game forcing hand, and would treat a simple bid of the suit as not forcing.)

For auction (d) above, North might have a hand such as

[E] ♠ A Q J x x   ♡ x x   ◇ K x x   ♣ x x x

If opener wants to be in game opposite such a hand he should avoid bidding either his suit or the responder's suit at the three level.

Use of the cue-bids to show invitational hands frees the direct bids of the opener's suit and the unbid suit for other uses. A simple raise of opener's suit at the three level is merely competitive:

South   *West*   *North*   *East*
1 ♠   2 Notrump   3 ♠

The free bid of the unbid suit at the three level is forcing to game:

South	West	North	East
1 ♠	2 Notrump	3 ♡	

or

South	West	North	East
1 ♡	2 Notrump	3 ♠	

Having methods to describe both invitational and game forcing hands solves the responder's problem with a hand such as (e) above.

If the bidding has been opened with a minor suit and the Unusual Notrump has been overcalled, promising the two lower unbid suits, the Unusual-over-Unusual convention operates in exactly the same way. For example,

South	West	North	East
1 ◇	2 Notrump	3 ♣	

Here the two notrump bid promises hearts and clubs. The three club cue-bid shows at least a limit raise in the lower suit, diamonds. A cue-bid of three hearts would show at least a five card spade suit and an invitational hand.

Some partnerships use the unusual notrump overcall always to show the minor suits. In this event if the bidding is opened with a minor and the unusual notrump overcall is made, responder should consider that the cue-bids show length in the major suits. The overcaller probably does not have length in either major, and the responder, after all, is hardly likely to want to play in opener's suit when one opponent has five of them. In these circumstances, a cue-bid of three clubs should show hearts, and a cue-bid of three diamonds should show spades.

HERBERT NEGATIVE RESPONSE TO A
TAKEOUT DOUBLE OR ONE-BID

A Herbert Negative is a bid of the cheapest suit in response to partner's action. It may be used in responding to takeout doubles. For example:

South	West	North	East
1 ♡	Double	Pass	1 ♠

Using the Herbert Negative, East's one spade bid shows a very weak hand. The one spade bid shows nothing about East's spade suit; it simply shows a dearth of high cards.

Herbert Negatives may also be used over one-level opening bids. The ROMAN CLUB SYSTEM, for example, uses a response of the cheapest suit as a negative for all opening bids of one of a suit (all of which are forcing in the Roman system). The most advantageous use of the Herbert convention, however, is in responding to very strong opening bids, such as forcing two-bids and strong forcing artificial club bids. It is in this situation that the responder will presumably have least to say about his own suits, at least that his partner is interested in. In other situations, where the opening bid is not so powerful, the Herbert convention is less useful since its use may waste a round of bidding, or its inapplicability may waste a level of bidding.

S.O.S. REDOUBLES

An S.O.S. Redouble is a redouble that asks the redoubler's partner to select another denomination. A redouble is an S.O.S. only when it could not have any other meaning.

The S.O.S. redouble is most often made by the person whose bid has been doubled. For example

South	West	North	East
1 ♣	Double	Pass	Pass
Redouble			

South may have opened with a three-card club suit. His double asks North to choose another suit. However, in the auction

South	West	North	East
1 ♡ or 1 ♠	Double	Pass	Pass
Redouble			

South's redouble shows strength rather than requesting a rescue.

Sometimes a player may deliberately make a bid in a short suit in order to induce a double, so that he may make an S.O.S. redouble to tell his partner that he has the other suits. The most frequent example is a bid over the penalty double of a notrump opening bid:

North	East	South	West
1 Notrump	Double	2 ♣	Pass
Pass	Double	Redouble	

In this sequence, South's bid of two clubs showed a weak hand, one at any rate that was not strong enough to tolerate playing the hand in one notrump doubled. Having announced a weak hand he cannot logically be strong enough to make a penalty redouble of two clubs. Therefore, the North should conclude that the redouble was an S.O.S., asking him to take his choice of the other three suits. In choosing, North should bear in mind that South is likely to have length in diamonds and one major suit rather than in both major suits. If South had four cards in each of the majors, he could have bid two diamonds over the double, and redoubled to ask North to choose between the majors. *See also* TWO-WAY EXCLUSION BIDS.

On occasion the S.O.S. may be issued by the partner of the player who has made the doubled bid. For example

North	East	South	West
1 ♣	Pass	Pass	Double
Pass	Pass	Redouble	

Since South did not have sufficient strength to keep the bidding open, he is unlikely to want to redouble naturally. His redouble should be considered an S.O.S.

KOCK WERNER REDOUBLE

By special agreement the partnership may use S.O.S. redoubles of penalty doubles of overcalls. For example

North	East	South	West
1 ♣	1 ♡	Double	Redouble

Using Kock Werner redoubles, West's redouble asks East to bid any of the other three suits, including the suit bid by the opener.

TAKEOUT DOUBLES OF PREEMPTS

The most common device used against an opponent's preempt is the takeout double. The double asks partner to bid, even with a very weak hand. Of course, if most of partner's strength and his principal length are concentrated in the suit of the preempt, he may pass. (*See also* OPTIONAL DOUBLES.)

Unless the partnership has agreed on some other treatment, the double is for takeout whether it is made immediately over the preempt or in the balancing position. A takeout double may be made over any level of suit preempt through the level of four hearts. Doubles of four spades and higher preempts are normally considered to be for penalties. Over four spades, a four notrump bid is available for takeout.

The higher the preempt, the stronger the doubler's hand should be, to take into account the higher level at which his partner will have to bid. For example, a takeout double of a weak two bid in diamonds might be made with as few as 13 points, while a takeout double of a weak two spade bid promises about 15 points. A takeout double of a three-level preempt promises at least 15 or 16 points.

It is also true that the higher the preempt, the more likely it is that the double will be passed for penalties. This is because it becomes easier and easier to envision setting the contract, and the visions of a large penalty become clearer and clearer.

Balancing Doubles

Because of the somewhat high requirements for an immediate takeout double, the partner in the balancing position may make a takeout double with a somewhat lighter hand. For example, over a three level preempt, the balancing hand needs only about 12 points to make a takeout double.

OPTIONAL DOUBLES

Many players mistakenly call takeout doubles "optional doubles" because the partner of the doubler may opt to pass the double for penalties. This, however, is a misnomer that results from focusing attention on the partner of the doubler rather than on the doubler himself. Even the partner of a takeout doubler may opt to pass if he has an appropriate hand. The nature of an optional double is to be found in the strengths and pattern of the hand of the doubler.

A double of a preemptive bid is an optional double if it shows a good balanced hand that includes a measure of strength in the suit of the preempt. For example, over a three heart opening bid, the following hand is worth an optional double:

♠ A K x x   ♡ A J x   ◇ x x   ♣ A Q x x

The optional double is a type of cooperative double that invites the doubler's partner to pass for penalties. However, being balanced, it promises partner some support for his suit if he should need to remove the double. In general, however, the partner of the doubler is not expected to bid unless he has a good suit and a somewhat unbalanced hand.

Use of optional doubles, of course, precludes the partnership from using takeout doubles over preempts.

WEISS

The Weiss convention uses an optional double of preemptive bids, and a bid of the cheaper minor suit for takeout. *See* OPTIONAL DOUBLE.

The Weiss double invites the partner to pass for penalties. If partner has a long suit and does not wish to pass, the double promises support for his suit.

Using the Weiss convention and holding a hand such as

♠ A Q x x   ♥ x   ♦ K Q x x   ♣ A x x x

over a preemptive opening of three hearts by South, West could not make a takeout double. His proper action would be to bid four clubs for takeout.

The major disadvantage of the Weiss convention is that it precludes use of the takeout double. A second drawback is that when the preempt has been in diamonds or hearts, the use of the cheaper minor suit for takeout uses up valuable bidding room. A workable solution to avoid the loss of bidding space problem is for the partnership to agree to use the Weiss convention only over preempts in spades and clubs.

FISHBEIN

The Fishbein convention is a convention designed to allow the player sitting directly over the preemptive opener to make a penalty double. Thus, using Fishbein, West's double in the following auction would be for penalties:

South	West	North	East
3 ♠	Double		

The Fishbein convention allows the penalty double only by the player sitting over the preemptive bidder. Thus in the above auction, if West and North had both passed over South's preempt, East would not have been allowed to double for penalties. His double in that position would be for takeout.

To compensate for the loss of the use of the double as takeout, the Fishbein convention substitutes the cheapest bid over the preempt as a takeout bid. For example, in the auction

North	East	South	West
3 ♡	3 ♠		

East's three spade bid would not show a long spade suit, any more than a takeout double would have. The three spade bid simply asks West to bid. East might have a hand such as

    ♠ A x x x   ♡ x   ◇ A K x x   ♣ K Q x x

or

    ♠ Q x x   ♡ x   ◇ K Q x x x   ♣ A K x x

However, if East and South had passed in the above auction, a three spade bid by West would be natural.

The Fishbein convention has two principal flaws. The first is that it precludes the natural use of an overcall. The second problem is that the player sitting directly over the preempter must frequently make a decision without any help from his partner. His double would be a unilateral penalty double which his partner may not remove. And with a hand which is short in the suit of the preempt, he must bid to show length in the other suits, rather than doubling. This forecloses all possibility of penalizing the preemptor when the trump strength is not sitting directly over the preemptor.

CHEAPER MINOR TAKEOUT

A convention similar to the Fishbein convention uses a double by the player sitting directly over the preemptor as a penalty double, and uses the bid of the cheaper minor suit for takeout. The cheaper minor is, of course, clubs, unless the preempt has been made in clubs. The rationale for using the cheaper minor as the takeout suit is that frequently it will be desirable to make a natural overcall of three hearts over a three diamond preempt, or of three spades over a three heart preempt. For the strength requirements for the use of this convention, *see discussion under* TAKEOUT DOUBLES OF PREEMPTS.

CLUBS FOR TAKEOUT

A variation of the CHEAPER MINOR TAKEOUT convention is an agreement that the bid for takeout will always be made in clubs. This convention means that even when the preempt was in clubs, the next higher club bid would show a hand worth a takeout double. For the strength requirements for the use of this convention, *see discussion under* TAKEOUT DOUBLES OF PREEMPTS.

NOTRUMP FOR TAKEOUT

Another variation of the Fishbein convention uses the cheapest notrump bid for takeout. This suffers all of the disadvantages of the Fishbein convention. The notrump overcalls are useful as natural, descriptive bids, a two notrump bid showing about 16 to 18 points over a weak two bid, and a three notrump bid showing 18 or more points over a three-level preempt. For the strength requirements for the use of this convention, *see discussion under* TAKEOUT DOUBLES OF PREEMPTS.

TWO-SUITED TAKEOUTS OVER PREEMPTS

A convention designed to show a two-suited hand over a preemptive opening bid in a major suit uses a double for takeout, and a bid of four in a minor suit to show that minor suit and the unbid major suit.

For example, over an opening bid of three spades, a double would show tolerance for all unbid suits; a four club overcall would show hearts and clubs; a four diamond overcall would show hearts and diamonds. This convention can solve some difficult problems.

LEGHORN DIAMOND TAKEOUTS

The Leghorn Diamond system uses a double and a three no-trump bid to show two suited hands over a three-level preemptive opening. The double promises two suits of different rank; the notrump bid promises two suits of the same rank.

For example, over a three heart opening bid, a three notrump overcall would show both minor suits. A double would show spades and an unspecified minor suit. Over a three club preempt, for example, the double would show both major suits, while the three notrump overcall would show diamonds and one of the major suits.

RIPSTRA AGAINST GAMBLING
THREE NOTRUMP

A double of a GAMBLING THREE NOTRUMP bid is strictly for penalties. Since the gambling three notrump bid is almost always based on a long minor suit, the defenders will usually have a large number of major suit cards. If they wish to compete over the three notrump opening, the most effective convention is probably Ripstra.

The Ripstra convention is a minor suit bid used as a takeout for the major suits. The Ripstra bid is made in whichever minor suit is better. For example, if South opens three notrump and West holds

♠ K Q x x x   ♡ K J x x   ◇ K Q   ♣ x x

West would bid four diamonds, Ripstra, asking his partner to bid a major suit.

Use of Ripstra can be quite advantageous on a hand such as this one, where the player sitting over the notrump bidder does not have an ace to lead, and thus may have only one chance to defeat the contract. The Ripstra convention gives the best choices in terms of taking out insurance against a fatal opening lead.

TAKEOUTS AGAINST FOUR-LEVEL PREEMPTS

Doubles of opening bids of four clubs, four diamonds and four hearts are takeout doubles. A double of a four spade preempt is a penalty double.

An overcall of four notrump after an opponent has opened the bidding with four of a major suit is a takeout bid. Standard practice is for the four notrump bid to be used as a minor suit takeout over four hearts since a takeout double could have been made to show spades. A four notrump bid over a four spade preempt would be a three-suited takeout bid. The four notrump bidder might have a hand such as

♠ x   ♡ A Q J x   ◇ A K J x   ♣ A K x x

A bid of four notrump over the opponent's preempt of four of a minor suit is generally considered not to be a takeout bid; it is considered to be either natural or Blackwood.

VI

Two- and Three-Suited Opening Bids

There are a number of conventions by which the opening bid shows that the opener does not have either a balanced hand or a one-suited hand. Some of these conventional openings show two-suited hands. *See* FLANNERY TWO DIAMONDS, FLANNERY TWO HEARTS, TWO DIAMONDS FOR MAJORS, TWO CLUBS FOR MINORS, TWO NOTRUMP FOR MINORS.

Hands containing three biddable suits are difficult to describe. Even if an opponent makes a bid in the short suit, a takeout double only suggests that the doubler has distribution approximating 4-4-4-1; he could easily have 4-4-3-2, or 5-4-3-1, or perhaps even 5-4-2-2 or 4-3-3-3. When the player who has three four-card suits, or two four-card suits and one five card suit, is the opening bidder, the job of describing his hand is formidable.

Some of the conventions described below use a conventional opening bid to show three-suited hands. Some of them can be used with hands that are either 4-4-4-1 or 5-4-4-0. *See* ROMAN TWO CLUBS, ROMAN TWO DIAMONDS. One, Neapolitan Two Diamonds, shows specifically 4-4-4-1 distribution. And one, Precision Two Diamonds, can be used even with a hand that is not always, strictly speaking, three suited, since it was devised to describe a type of hand that otherwise would be systemically impossible to open.

FLANNERY TWO DIAMONDS

The most widely used of the two-suited conventional opening bids is the Flannery convention. Flannery is designed to deal with the dilemma of which major suit to open when holding four spades and five hearts with less than the strength needed for a reverse. If the opening bid is one heart, the partnership might never bid the spade suit even if it is the partnership's best suit. If, for example, responder has three spades and one heart and a weak hand, he may respond one notrump to the one heart opening, and play the hand right there.

If the bidding is opened with one spade, however, and the responder has two or three cards in each major suit the partnership is not likely to end up in its best suit. For example, with three spades and three hearts and a modest hand, responder would raise opener's one spade bid to two, and the partnership would play in its four-three fit rather than its five-three fit. With two spades and two hearts, the responder might eventually take a preference to spades, leaving the partnership in its four-two fit.

The Flannery convention uses a two diamond opening to show a hand worth 11 to 15 high card points, with four spades and five hearts. The four minor suit cards may be distributed in any pattern.

With less than 10 points, responder signs off by bidding two hearts or two spades. If responder has no preference for a major but has a weak hand with six or more diamonds, he may pass the two diamond opening.

Responder may invite game by jumping to three hearts or three spades. In the alternative, responder may invite game by using a conventional two notrump response.

In order to learn more about opener's hand, responder may make the artificial bid of two notrump. This bid asks opener to clarify his minor suit distribution. Opener rebids three clubs with a three-card club suit; he rebids three diamonds with a three-card diamond suit; he jumps to four clubs with a four-card club suit; he jumps to four diamonds with a four-card diamond suit.

If the opener has 4-5-2-2 distribution, he has three possible rebids. With 11 to 13 points, he rebids three hearts; with 14 to 15 points concentrated in the major suits he rebids three spades. With 14 to 15 points with his high cards concentrated largely in the minor suits opener may rebid three notrump.

Opener's rebids may help the partnership to assess game and slam prospects. For example, suppose responder held

♠ K Q x x   ♡ x   ◇ A K J x x   ♣ x x x

Responder would bid two notrump, hoping to hear opener bid three or four diamonds, showing by inference a singleton or a void in clubs. The responder could then use Blackwood to try for slam.

Some partnerships agree that if responder rebids three of a major after opener has shown his minor suit distribution, his bid invites game.

Responses of three of a minor suit ask the opener to rebid three notrump with one of the top three honors in the suit. Responder may use this bid to learn whether or not his own suit is solidified, or to learn whether or not the partnership has a stopper for notrump play. For example, responder could bid three clubs over two diamonds with either of the following hands:

[A] ♠ A x   ♡ x x   ◇ K x x   ♣ A K x x x x
or
[B] ♠ A x   ♡ x x   ◇ A K Q x x x   ♣ x x x

Responder may select a game in one of two ways. He may jump to four hearts or four spades. Or he may jump to four clubs or four diamonds. The latter bids are transfers. The four club bid requires the opener to rebid four hearts; the four diamond bid requires him to rebid four spades.

FLANNERY TWO HEARTS

The Flannery convention can be used with two hearts as the opening bid instead of two diamonds. The two heart opening would show four spades and five hearts.

If the responder has a weak hand and a preference for hearts he will pass the opening bid. Otherwise, all of the responses and rebids are the same as with Flannery Two Diamonds.

Using two hearts as the Flannery bid has three principal effects. First, it makes the Flannery bidder the declarer more often than when he uses the two diamond convention. Second, it frees the two diamond opening for some other use. Many partnerships which use Flannery Two Hearts use the two diamond opening to show three-suited hands. Finally, the use of the two heart bid as Flannery means that it cannot be used as a weak two heart bid.

TWO DIAMOND OPENING FOR MAJORS

As part of the Big Diamond system, a two diamond opening bid may be used to show a hand in the 14 to 16 point range with eight or nine cards in the major suits. The two diamond opening may be made with four-four in the majors, or with five of either major and four of the other. The distributions allowed are 4-4-3-2 and 5-4-2-2.

With a hand worth less than 10 points, responder may take minimum action. With a long diamond suit responder may pass. Responses of two hearts and two spades are preferences, and are not forcing. A response of three clubs shows a weak hand with a club suit; this bid is not forcing.

Responder may invite game with 10 or 11 points by bidding three diamonds, three hearts, or three spades. The jumps to three hearts and three spades show four card support. These are responder's only game invitational bids.

With 12 or more points, responder may force to game by bidding two notrump. This bid does not show a desire to play the hand in notrump; rather, it asks opener for further informamation about his distribution. Opener rebids as follows:

3 ♣ = three clubs, four-four in the majors

3 ◇ = three diamonds, four-four in the majors

3 ♡ = five hearts, two-two in the minors

3 ♠ = five spades, two-two in the minors

3 NT = good 16 points with 5-4-2-2 distribution; the five card suit could be either hearts or spades.

TWO CLUB OPENING FOR MINORS

In the Big Diamond system an opening bid of two clubs shows a 14 to 16 point hand with club and diamond suits. The distribution promised is 4-4-3-2 or 5-4-2-2. The two club opening is not forcing.

With a hand worth less than 10 or 11 points, responder will normally not look for game. He may pass if he has better clubs than diamonds; or he may bid two diamonds with better diamonds than clubs. If responder has a long major suit, he may make a non-forcing bid of two of his suit.

If responder has a hand with which he wants to invite game in a minor suit or notrump, he bids three clubs or three diamonds. If opener has a stopper in one of the major suits he will show it so that responder can decide whether or not the hand can be played in three notrump. This is responder's only way to invite game.

If responder has a game forcing hand with a long major suit, and he wants to know about the quality of opener's holding in that suit, he jumps to three of his suit. This bid is forcing and asks opener to describe his support in a series of steps as follows:

First   step = two small cards

Second step = three small cards

Third   step = two cards headed by the ace, king or queen

Fourth step = three cards headed by the ace, king or queen

If responder wants to force to game or to try for slam, he

can respond two notrump asking opener to clarify his strength and distribution. Opener's rebids are

3 ♣ = five clubs, two-two in the majors

3 ♢ = five diamonds, two-two in the majors

3 ♡ = three hearts, four-four in the minors

3 ♠ = three spades, four-four in the minors

3 NT = good 16 points, 5-4-2-2 distribution; the five-card suit could be either clubs or diamonds

TWO NOTRUMP OPENING FOR MINORS

The Two Notrump Minor Suit convention uses a two notrump opening bid to show a hand with at least five cards in each minor suit. Vulnerable, the two notrump opening shows 14 to 16 points; not vulnerable the opening may be made on 10 to 13 points.

The Two notrump opening promises that the opener's high cards are concentrated in the minor suits, and that the texture of the suits is good. For example

[A] ♠ x x ♡ x ◇ K J 10 x x ♣ K Q J 10 x

[B] ♠ x ♡ x x ◇ A K 10 9 x ♣ A K Q x x

[C] ♠ K x ♡ x ◇ K Q J x x ♣ J 10 9 x x

[D] ♠ x ♡ x x ◇ A K x x x ♣ A Q x x x

Hand A is the minimum hand that may be opened two notrump not vulnerable. Hand B is the maximum that may be opened with two notrump vulnerable. Hands C and D, however, are not appropriate for two notrump openings, Hand C because not all of the high cards are in the minor suits; and Hand D because the minor suits have poor texture.

Responses

If responder has a weak hand, his normal action is to take a preference between clubs and diamonds at the three level. If he has a weak hand with length in the major suits and no three-card or longer minor suit, he is allowed to pass the two notrump opening. If responder has one long major suit and a hand not worth game, he may bid three of his major suit. This bid is not forcing.

With four or more cards in one of the minor suits and a hand with which he wants either to preempt or to play game, responder may jump to four or five of the minor. His jump to the four level is preemptive rather than invitational.

If responder wants to explore for slam, his only recourse is Blackwood, four notrump.

ROMAN TWO DIAMONDS

A Roman Two diamond opening bid shows a hand worth 17 to 20 high card points. It promises either 4-4-4-1 or 5-4-4-0 distribution. The short suit is not identified until the opener rebids.

In order to try for game opposite a two diamond opening, responder needs about a 7 point hand. If responder has less than 7 points, he bids his best suit; if he has no real preference, he bids two hearts. If the suit bid by responder happens to be the opener's singleton, opener will bid the next higher suit, asking the responder to choose again.

If the suit bid by responder is one of opener's four card suits, opener will usually pass. However, if he has a maximum, he might well raise. For example:

♠ A K x x   ♡ A x x x   ◇ x   ♣ A K J x

After this hand is opened with two diamonds, if the responder bids a non-forcing two spades, opener will surely raise.

If responder has 7 or more points, he bids two notrump to make investigations toward game. The notrump response does not suggest that the hand should be played in notrump; it merely asks the opener to bid the suit in which he is short. For example:

Opener	Responder
2 ◇	2 Notrump
3 ♡	

Opener shows a singleton heart.

After learning which suit is opener's short suit, responder can invite a game by bidding one of opener's suits, or can place the hand in game. If the suit in which opener announced shortness is responder's only long suit, responder rebids three no-trump.

When the Opponents Interfere

If an opponent overcalls over the two diamond bid, the responder will pass with a weak hand unless he has some reason to believe he has a fit with one of the opener's suits. If, for example, responder had two suits of his own, at least one of them would fit with opener. In this situation responder may bid his cheaper suit freely.

If responder has a hand that is worth a game try, he should bid two notrump just as he would have had there been no over-call. Or if responder has strong trumps, he can double the over-call for penalties. Opener should not remove the double unless he is void in the overcaller's suit.

ROMAN TWO CLUBS

A Roman Two Club opening shows a hand worth 11 to 16 high card points, and either 4-4-4-1 or 5-4-4-0 distribution. The short suit is not disclosed until the opener rebids.

The responder needs about 10 or 11 points to try for a game. With less he simply tries to find a part-score resting place by bidding his best suit over two clubs. Lacking any substantial preference among his suits, he bids the cheapest. If the suit he bids is one of opener's four card suits opener will usually pass, although he may raise if he has a maximum.

If responder has bid opener's short suit, opener will bid the next higher ranking suit, asking responder to bid his second choice. For example, suppose opener's and responder's hands were as follows:

(Opener)
♠ K J x x   ♡ A K x x   ◇ x   ♣ Q x x x

(Responder)
♠ Q x x   ♡ x x   ◇ A J x x x   ♣ x x x

The bidding would proceed

Opener	Responder
2 ♣	2 ◇
2 ♡	2 ♠
Pass	

Responder bid two diamonds, looking for a fit. Opener's two heart bid showed that diamonds was his short suit. Responder took a preference to spades. Had his spade and heart suits been reversed, he would have passed opener's two heart bid.

With a strong enough hand to try for a game, responder bids two notrump. This response does not signify a desire to play in notrump. It asks the opener to identify his short suit. Opener complies by bidding that suit.

If responder has four or more cards in one of opener's suits, he may either bid a game, or invite game by bidding three of that suit. For example:

Opener	Responder
2 ♣	2 Notrump
3 ♡	3 ♠

If responder's only suit is the opener's short suit, responder signs off with a bid of three notrump. Conceivably if responder has a very long and semi-solid suit he might simply pass opener's short suit bid. For example, if responder had a hand such as

♠ K x   ♡ x x   ◇ A Q J 9 x x   ♣ x x x

the bidding might go

Opener	Responder
2 ♣	2 Notrump
3 ◇	Pass

When the Opponents Interfere

If the opponent overcalls over the two club bid, responder generally passes with a weak balanced hand or a weak one-suited hand. If he has two long suits, he should bid naturally in order to compete, since he knows that opener has four-card support for at least one of his suits.

If responder has a hand worth a game try, he should bid two notrump just as he would have without the overcall. Alternatively, with strong trumps, responder can double the overcall for penalties. Opener should not remove the double unless he is void in the suit of the overcall.

TWO DIAMOND OPENING AS
MINIMUM THREE-SUITER

The ROMAN CLUB SYSTEM is able to devote its two club opening bid to three-suited hands because, using the canape style of bidding, it does not have to open two clubs in order to show a long club suit. It can open any other suit and rebid clubs to show a long club suit. Partnerships not using the canape style usually cannot afford to spend their two club opening on three-suited hands. If the partnership is using a forcing one club opening, it needs a two club opening to show a club suit. If the partnership is not using a forcing one club opening but is using weak two-bids, it needs the two club opening to show a strong forcing hand.

Some of these partnerships, wanting to have a bid that promises a three-suited hand, use a two diamond opening to show a hand of average opening strength, with 5-4-4-0 or 4-4-4-1 distribution.

When two diamonds is used to show the three-suited hand in the 12 to 16 point range, the responder needs about 10 or 11 points in order to try for a game. With less he looks for a safe part score; with more, he forces to game. The mechanics of responding and rebidding are the same as for the ROMAN TWO CLUB and ROMAN TWO DIAMOND openings.

NEAPOLITAN TWO DIAMONDS

The Neapolitan Two Diamond opening, which is part of the Blue Team system, is made with a very strong three-suited hand. The two diamond bid shows 17 to 24 high card points, and its distribution is specifically 4-4-4-1, with the singleton temporarily undisclosed.

Once the two diamond opening has been made, the responder takes charge of the hand. He has a variety of alternatives open to him, depending on what type of hand he has. If he has a very weak hand, in the 0 to 5 point range, and has at least three spades, he bids two spades. The opener will pass if spades is not his singleton; if spades is his singleton, opener will bid two notrump, allowing the responder to choose a suit at the three level.

If the responder has a six-card suit, or has a hand with more than five points he has a choice of relay bids or descriptive bids to ask the opener to describe his hand further.

Responding with a Good Six-Card Suit

If the responder has a six-card suit headed by three honors, or by two of the top three honors, and a hand of about 6 or 7 points, his proper response is two notrump. The two notrump bid does not specify which is the responder's six-card suit, it simply states that he has one, and asks the opener to identify his singleton.

Opener shows his singleton by bidding the suit below the singleton. For example, with a singleton heart the opener would rebid three diamonds. With a singleton club, the opener would rebid three spades.

After opener has identified his singleton, responder bids the minimum number of his suit, with one exception. If the responder's suit is clubs and the opener has bid three spades showing a singleton club, the responder must bid three notrump. After the responder has disclosed his suit, both members of the partnership know whether or not the hand is a misfit.

If the opener's singleton is in the responder's suit, the opener has a choice of actions. If he has a minimum hand he should pass; if the suit in question is clubs and the responder has bid three notrump to show it, the opener may retreat to four clubs. If the opener has a strong hand for his two diamond opening, he may bid three notrump or game in the responder's suit. He uses his judgment as to which contract seems more attainable.

If the opener's singleton is not in the responder's suit, the partnership is committed to game, and may explore for slam. If the opener has a minimum hand and thinks slam is a poor prospect, he simply bids game in the responder's suit.

If the opener thinks that slam is a real possibility, he bids one of his side controls, asking the responder to bid a singleton if he has it. Lacking any singleton, the responder will return to his suit.

For example, suppose the opener has the following hand:

♠ x   ♡ K Q x x   ◇ A x x x   ♣ A K J x

If his partner responds with two notrump, showing a good six card suit, opener must rebid three hearts, showing that his singleton is in spades. If the responder now bids three spades, showing that spades is his six card suit, the opener will pass, since game is unlikely. The auction will have gone

Opener	Responder
2 ♢	2 Notrump
3 ♡	3 ♠
Pass	

If the responder has bid a suit other than spades, however, the opener will have visions of slam. Thus the auction might proceed:

Opener	Responder
2 ♢	2 Notrump
3 ♡	4 ♡
5 ♣	5 ♢
6 ♡	

Opener's five club bid showed the ace of clubs and indicated an interest in slam. It specifically asked the responder to bid a singleton if he had one. Responder's five diamond bid showed a singleton diamond, and opener was able to bid six hearts. If the responder had as little as the queen of clubs, or four spades, he should be able to bring home the slam.

Responding with a Fair Six-Card Suit

If the responder has a hand worth 5 to 6 points containing only a fair six-card suit (as compared with the more solid suit shown by the two notrump response), his proper action is to bid three of his suit. The responder might hold a hand such as

♠ K 10 x x x x   ♡ x x   ♢ Q x x x   ♣ x

If the responder's bid is in the suit in which the opener ha a singleton, the opener will pass if he has a minimum for his two diamond opening. If he has a good maximum, such as

♠ Q ♡ A K x x ♢ A K x x ♣ A Q J x

he may raise the responder to game despite the misfit.

If the opener has four-card support for responder's suit, the partnership is forced to game and opener should assess the prospects for slam. If slam seems out of the question, he should simply bid the game. For example, if the opener has a hand such as

♠ Q x x ♡ A K Q x ♢ x ♣ A K Q x

and the responder has bid three spades, opener will raise to four spades. Since the responder cannot have a hand with which the partnership is certain not to lose a trump trick, slam should not be bid.

If, however, slam is not out of the question, the opener cue-bids his singleton (not the suit below, this time). This cue-bid asks the responder to clarify his hand by showing whether he has the ace or king of trumps, or neither; and if he has the ace or king of trumps, he is asked to reveal whether or not he has a side singleton. The responder conveys this information in three steps, as follows:

First step = no ace or king of trumps

Second step = ace or king of trumps, but no side singleton

Third step = ace or king of trumps and a side singleton

Suppose the opener holds

♠ K x x x ♡ A K x x ◇ x ♣ A K x x

Opener simply wants to know whether the responder has the ace of trumps, for if he has opener can virtually count twelve tricks. The auction might proceed

Opener	Responder
2 ◇	3 ♠
4 ◇	4 ♠ or 4 Notrump
6 ♠	

If responder had bid four hearts over the four diamond cue-bid, showing trumps no better than Q J x x x x, opener would have signed off in four spades. However, when responder shows the ace, opener can confidently bid the slam.

The Two Heart Relay Response

Most frequently in response to the two diamond opening, the responder will have neither a 0 to 5 point hand with spades, nor a 5 to 7 point hand with a fair-to-good six card suit. His proper course of action on all other hands, weak or strong, is to respond two hearts. The two heart response does not show anything about the responder's heart holding or about his strength; it is just a relay bid asking the opener for clarification. The opener's rebids show whether he has a minimum, i.e., 17 to 20 points, or a maximum, i.e., 21 to 24 points; with minor exceptions the opener bids the suit below his singleton.

The complete schedule of opener's rebids over the two heart response is as follows:

2 ♠ = singleton in either major suit, 17 to 20 points

2 NT = singleton club, 17 to 20 points

3 ♣ = singleton diamond, 17 to 20 points

3 ◇ = singleton heart, 21 to 24 points

3 ♡ = singleton spade, 21 to 24 points

3 ♠ = singleton club, 21 to 24 points

3 NT = singleton diamond, 21 to 24 points

If the opener's rebid has been two spades, showing a singleton in one of the major suits and a minimum hand, the responder may make a further relay bid of two notrump to obtain further information. Opener rebids three clubs with a singleton heart, or rebids three diamonds or three hearts with a singleton spade. Opener chooses the three diamond bid when he has 17 or 18 points and a singleton spade, and the three heart bid when he has 19 or 20 points and a singleton spade.

If opener has shown a singleton club or diamond and a minimum hand in response to the two heart relay, or if he has shown a singleton heart and a minimum hand by his responses to the two heart and two notrump relays, the responder can ask opener to narrow his point count range. Responder does this by bidding the suit in which the opener has shown a singleton. The first step by opener shows 17 or 18 points, and the second step shows 19 or 20 points. For example,

(A) *Opener*   *Responder*
        2 ◇   2 ♡
        2 Notrump   3 ♣
        3 ♡

(B)	Opener	Responder
2 ♢	2 ♡
2 ♠	2 Notrump
3 ♣	3 ♡
3 ♠

In Auction A, the two notrump rebid by opener showed a singleton club and a hand worth 17 to 20 points in high cards. Responder's bid of three clubs, opener's singleton, asked whether opener had the top or the bottom of the range he had shown. Opener's three heart rebid, the second step, showed 19 to 20 points.

In Auction (B), the opener's two spade rebid said his singleton was in one of the major suits; his three club rebid over the two notrump relay said his singleton was in hearts. The three heart bid by responder asked opener about his point count; opener's three spade bid, the first step, showed 17 to 18 points.

Usually by this time, if not earlier, the responder can set the final contract. However, if he wants to explore further for a slam after opener has disclosed whether he has the top or the bottom of his 17 to 20 point range, responder can ask the opener precisely how many controls he has. Responder accomplishes this by again bidding the opener's known singleton. Notice that if opener has a singleton spade, he narrows his point range in the process of identifying his singleton. If responder wants to know about opener's controls after the latter has shown a singleton spade, he does so by cue-bidding the singleton spade immediately after it has been shown:

| Opener | Responder
--- | --- | ---
| 2 ♢ | 2 ♡
| 2 ♠ | 2 Notrump
| 3 ♡ | 3 ♠

Since opener's three heart rebid has at once specified a singleton spade and 19 or 20 points, responder need not ask for further clarification of opener's point range. Responder's three spade bid asks about controls.

Counting each ace as two controls and each king as one, the opener shows his controls in a series of five steps. If the opener's first rebid has shown a hand in the 17 to 20 point range, the first step shows four controls:

$$
\begin{array}{llll}
\text{First} & \text{step} & = & \text{four controls} \\
\text{Second} & \text{step} & = & \text{five controls} \\
\text{Third} & \text{step} & = & \text{six controls} \\
\text{Fourth} & \text{step} & = & \text{seven controls} \\
\text{Fifth} & \text{step} & = & \text{eight controls}
\end{array}
$$

For example, in the auction

Opener	Responder
2 ◇	2 ♡
2 ♠	2 Notrump
3 ♣	3 ♡
3 ♠	4 ♡
4 Notrump	

Opener's two spade bid showed 17 to 20 points, with a singleton in one of the major suits; his three club rebid said the singleton was a heart. Responder's three heart bid asked opener to narrow his range; opener's three spade bid showed 17 or 18 points. Responder's four heart bid asked about controls, and opener's four notrump bid, the second step, showed five controls. Opener's hand might be

♠ A K x x   ♡ x   ◇ K Q x x   ♣ K Q x x

If the opener's first response to two hearts has shown a hand in the 21 to 24 point range, the responder can ask about controls directly over the singleton-showing response without first asking for a narrowing of the point count range. Again, opener shows his controls in a series of five steps; this time, however, his first step will show six controls:

> First   step = six controls
>
> Second step = seven controls
>
> Third   step = eight controls
>
> Fourth step = nine controls
>
> Fifth   step = ten controls

For example, in the auction

Opener	*Responder*
2 ◇	2 ♡
3 ◇	3 ♡
3 ♠	

opener's three diamond rebid showed a singleton heart with 21 to 24 points. Responder's three heart bid, therefore, immediately asked about opener's controls. Opener's bid of three spades, the first step, showed six controls. He might have a hand such as

♠ A K Q x   ♡ x   ◇ K Q J x   ♣ A Q x x

After the opener has revealed how many controls he has, if the responder bids opener's singleton yet another time, he asks how many queens opener holds. Using the standard method, opener rebids the first step with no queens, the second step with one queen, the third step with two queens, and so forth. An alternative way of agreeing to show queens is for the opener to bid notrump if he holds no queens, or to bid a suit in which he has a queen; if he has two queens he will bid the less expensive queen.

Suppose the responder held the following hand in response to a two diamond opening:

♠ K Q x   ♡ A x x x x   ◇ A x x   ♣ x x

So long as opener does not have a singleton in one of the major suits, responder can visualize a slam easily, perhaps even a grand slam. His mission is to find out as much as possible about opener's hand. Suppose the auction proceeds:

Opener	Responder
2 ◇	2 ♡
3 ♣	3 ◇
3 ♡	4 ◇

Opener's rebids have shown a 17 to 18 point hand with a singleton diamond. The question now becomes how many controls opener has.

If opener has only four controls, a grand slam will be out of the question; if he has five or six, the grand slam will depend on the opener's holding in the heart suit. If the opener shows six controls, by bidding four notrump in the auction above, responder will know that opener's hand includes the ace of spades, the king of hearts, and the ace and king of clubs. If it also includes the queen of hearts, the grand slam should be laydown.

Using standard step responses to show queens, the complete auction could be

Opener	Responder
2 ♢	2 ♡
3 ♣	3 ♢
3 ♡	4 ♢
4 Notrump	5 ♢
5 ♡	6 ♡

When opener bids five hearts, the first step, to show no queens, responder places the final contract at six hearts.

If the opener had bid five spades in the above auction, showing one queen, responder still would have bid just six hearts, not knowing whether opener's queen was in clubs or hearts. (Use of the alternative queen-showing method would solve this problem, since opener would bid five hearts with the queen of hearts, or six clubs with the queen of clubs and no queen of hearts, or five notrump with no queens.) Over responder's bid of six hearts after opener had shown one queen, if opener's queen is the queen of hearts, opener should, for the first time in the entire auction, exercise his judgment and bid seven hearts, since responder was probing for a grand slam and must have been worried about the queen of trumps.

Notice that the responder has such complete control of the auction, that the opener does not know until responder sets the final contract, here at the six-level, which suit responder wants to play in.

PRECISION TWO DIAMONDS

Using the Precision Club system, the one club opening shows at least 16 points, and opening bids of one of a major suit show at least five cards. Most hands worth less than 16 points that contain no five-card major suit will therefore be opened with one notrump or one diamond; however, hands that are very short in the diamond suit are nearly impossible to bid naturally.

The Precision two diamond opening shows a hand worth 11 to 15 high card points with at most a singleton diamond, and no other suitable opening bid. The most common distributions for this opening are 4-4-1-4 and 4-4-0-5, although two diamonds may also be opened with a hand distributed 4-3-1-5 or 3-4-1-5 if the five card club suit is too weak for a two club opening. For example, opener might have either

[A] ♠ A K x x ♡ A x x x ◇ x ♣ A x x x
or
[B] ♠ A J x ♡ A Q x x ◇ x ♣ K x x x x

With Hand A and Hand B, the proper opening bid is two diamonds. However, with a hand such as

♠ A Q x x ♡ x x x ◇ x ♣ A K x x x

the club suit is strong enough for the hand to be opened two clubs.

Responses

The two diamond bid, even though it shows at most a singleton diamond, is not forcing. The responder is allowed to pass if he has ten points or less with at least six diamonds. If the responder has 0 to 7 points with fewer than six diamonds, he makes a minimum bid in another suit. This response is not forcing.

The only forcing response to a two diamond opening is two notrump. The two notrump response shows at least 8 high card points, but does not show a desire to play in notrump. Rather the two notrump response asks the opener to describe his hand further in terms of its distribution and point count.

Opener rebids over the two notrump response as follows:

3 ♣ shows three spades, four hearts, one diamond and five clubs

3 ◇ shows four spades, three hearts, one diamond and five clubs

3 ♡ shows 4-4-1-4 distribution with 11 to 13 high card points

3 ♠ shows 4-4-1-4 distribution with 14 to 15 high card points

3 Notrump shows 4-4-1-4 distribution with 14 to 15 high card points, including the singleton ace or king of diamonds

4 ♣ shows 4-4-0-5 distribution with 11 to 13 high card points

4 ◇ shows 4-4-0-5 distribution with 14 to 15 high card points

If the opener has rebid three clubs or three diamonds over the two notrump response, responder may bid the cheapest suit to ask opener to specify his point range. The opener's cheapest bid shows 11 to 13 points, and the next cheapest bid shows 14 to 15 points. For example, in the auction

Opener	Responder
2 ♦	2 Notrump
3 ♦	3 ♡
3 ♠	

Opener's three diamond rebid shows 4-3-1-5 distribution, and responder's three heart bid asks how strong opener's hand is. Opener's three spade bid, the cheapest bid, shows 11 to 13 points.

VII

Offensive Preemptive Conventions

Preempts may be made on hands widely varying in strength and distribution. Three of the five conventions described below are transfer preempts, designed to help the partner of the preemptor, when he has a strong hand, to know whether or not to try for slam. *See* FOUR CLUBS AND FOUR DIAMONDS AS STRONG TRANSFERS, FOUR CLUBS AND FOUR DIAMONDS AS WEAK TRANSFERS, FOUR NOTRUMP AS WEAK MINOR PREEMPT. Another convention is sometimes used in aid of the transfer preempts. *See* THREE NOTRUMP AS WEAK MINOR PREEMPT. The Gambling Three Notrump convention is just what its name implies.

NAMYATS:
FOUR CLUBS AND FOUR DIAMONDS
AS STRONG TRANSFERS

Using standard methods, preemptive openings of four of a major suit may be made on a wide variety of hands. For example, four spades might be opened with a hand such as

[A] ♠ A Q J x x x x x   ♡ x   ◇ x x   ♣ x x

Or, opposite a passed hand, four spades might be opened with a hand such as

[B] ♠ A K Q x x x x   ♡ x   ◇ A J x x   ♣ x

With Hand A a slam is a remote possibility. With Hand B, however, even opposite a partner who has passed, slam is possible if responder has either two aces and a doubleton diamond, or one ace and the king of diamonds.

To distinguish the strong major preempts from the weak ones, some partnerships use an opening bid of four clubs to transfer to four hearts, and an opening bid of four diamonds to transfer to four spades. As most frequently used, the openings of four clubs and four diamonds show stronger hands than the direct openings of four hearts and four spades.

After the four club or four diamond openings some partnerships allow the responder to decide which hand should be the declarer. If responder wants to be declarer, he simply bids four of the opener's true suit. If responder wants opener to be declarer, he bids four of the next ranking suit as a relay, transferring back to the opener.

For example, opposite a four diamond opening, showing a good four spade preempt, responder might have either of the following hands:

[C] ♠ x x   ♡ Q x x x   ◇ x x x   ♣ A x x x

[D] ♠ x   ♡ K x x x   ◇ K x x x   ♣ K x x x

With Hand C, responder has no tenaces to protect, so he makes the relay bid of four hearts, telling his partner to bid four spades. With Hand D, however, it is better for the lead to come up to responder's kings rather than through them. Therefore, with Hand D, responder bids four spades.

Although responder's relay, transferring back to opener, does not show slam interest, responder may try for slam over opener's rebid of his suit.

Asking Bid Responses

Some partnerships have agreed to regularize the four club and four diamond openings as much as possible in certain respects, and to use the relay bid (four diamonds over four clubs, or four hearts over four diamonds) as an asking bid rather than just a re-transfer.

Some partnerships agree that the four club and four diamond openings guarantee that the opener does not have two quick losers in more than one suit, and that he does have the king of his trump suit. For example:

[A] ♠ A Q J x x x x   ♡ K x   ◇ x x   ♣ K x

[B] ♠ A K Q J x x x   ♡ K x   ◇ x x   ♣ x x

[C] ♠ A K x x x x x   ♡ K x   ◇ x x x   ♣ x

Hand A is missing the king of trumps; using these methods this hand would be opened with one spade. Hand B has two quick losers in two suits; it too should be opened with one spade rather than four diamonds. Hand C meets all of the requirements for a four diamond opening.

Using these methods, a response in the relay suit asks the opener to identify the suit in which he has two quick losers. Thus, in the auction

Opener	Responder
4 ♣	4 ♦
4 ♠	

Opener shows that he has at least two losing spades.

If opener has no suit in which he has two quick losers he may rebid his suit. However, if his suit is solid, opener may capitalize on the fact that he does not have two quick losers by rebidding four notrump, which is Blackwood. For example, suppose opener's and responder's hands were as follows:

(Opener)
♠ x   ♡ A K Q x x x x x   ◇ K x x   ♣ x

(Responder)
♠ A x x   ♡ x x   ◇ A x x   ♣ A K x x

The bidding could go

Opener	Responder
4 ♣	4 ◇
4 Notrump	5 ♠
5 Notrump	6 ◇
7 Notrump	

FOUR CLUBS AND FOUR DIAMONDS AS WEAK TRANSFERS

Most partnerships which use four club and four diamond openings to show heart and spade preempts, use the four club and four diamond openings to show the stronger preempts. Their rationale is that the lower opening is more desirable with the type of hand that is more likely to produce a slam, leaving the partnership more room to explore, and that the higher opening is more desirable with the more preemptive type hand.

Some partnerships, however, prefer to use the four club and four diamond openings to show the weaker major suit preempts. Their reasoning is that transferring with the weaker hand ensures that the stronger hand will be the declarer. This may have value with respect to the opening lead, and may serve to conceal from the opponents the best line of defense.

GAMBLING THREE NOTRUMP

The Gambling Three Notrump convention is an opening bid of three notrump based on a long solid minor suit. The typical Gambling three notrump opening has at most one stopper outside of the running minor:

♠ x   ♡ Q x x   ◇ A K Q J x x x   ♣ x x

With scattered values, responder should pass. If responder is quite weak, however, or if three notrump is doubled and responder lacks stoppers, he may bid four clubs to escape. The four club bid shows nothing about responder's holding in clubs. If opener's suit is clubs he will pass; if his suit is diamonds, he will bid four diamonds.

If responder wants to play game in a minor suit rather than in notrump, he may jump to five clubs. Again, this club bid does not mean that responder has clubs; he expects opener to pass if clubs is his suit, or to bid five diamonds if diamonds is his suit. Similarly, if responder wants to play in a minor suit slam, he jumps to six clubs. Opener will pass if he has a club suit or bid six diamonds with a diamond suit.

A bid of four of a major suit by the responder is natural, showing a self-sufficient six-card or longer suit. Opener is required to pass.

Responses of four diamonds and four notrump are special responses. Four notrump may be used as Blackwood, with opener's ace-showing responses amended to take into account the fact that the ace of one suit has already been shown by his opening bid. Thus a response of five clubs would show no *additional* aces, and a response of five diamonds would show one additional ace.

A bid of four diamonds may be used to ask the opener to bid his better major suit. Thereafter any bid by responder would be a slam invitation.

A response of five notrump may be used to ask opener to bid a grand slam if he has anything extra—such as an eighth card in his suit, or a king or a queen on the side. Responder might have a hand such as

♠ A J x   ♡ A K x   ◇ x x   ♣ A K x x x

THREE NOTRUMP AS WEAK
MINOR PREEMPT

Some of the partnerships which use four club and four diamond opening bids to show major suit preempts use an opening bid of three notrump to replace the lost four club and four diamond openings. A typical hand might be

♠ x   ♡ x x   ◇ K Q J x x x x x   ♣ J x

In order to pass the three notrump opening, responder must have a relatively strong hand with a high card in each minor suit for safety. In order to retreat from three notrump, responder bids four clubs; opener will pass if his suit is clubs, or will bid four diamonds if diamonds is his suit.

Other responses except four notrump and five notrump may be used as they are over GAMBLING THREE NOTRUMP OPENINGS. Over the three notrump bid as a weak preempt, the four notrump Blackwood bid asks about aces in accordance with the normal schedule of responses. And a jump response to five notrump would be a normal GRAND SLAM FORCE bid, asking opener to bid seven with two of the top three honors in his suit.

FOUR NOTRUMP AS WEAK
MINOR PREEMPT

In order to distinguish a high level minor suit preempt that has a broken suit and no slam interest, from one that has solid values, some partnerships use an opening bid of four notrump as a minor suit preempt. Using this convention, the four notrump opening shows no slam interest, and the hand probably has fewer than five controls, counting aces as two and kings as one.

The four notrump opening might be made on a hand such as

♠ K x   ♡ x   ◇ K Q x x x x x   ♣ x x

The responder is asked to bid five clubs over four notrump. If opener's suit is clubs he will pass; if his suit is diamonds he will bid five diamonds.

The use of the four notrump convention allows the opener to reserve the five club and five diamond openings for hands with solid values such as

♠ A x x   ♡ —   ◇ A K Q x x x x   ♣ x x

VIII

Conventions for the Defenders

There are a number of conventions that are designed to help the side that has not bought, or clearly is not going to buy, the contract. These conventions fall into three general categories: (a) lead-directing doubles that ask the opening leader to start a particular suit; (b) opening lead conventions that lay down rules as to which card should usually be led from a given suit; and (c) signals after the opening lead has been made.

Specific opening lead problems fall into three general groupings. One question is which card should be led from two or more touching honors. *See* ACE FROM ACE-KING, RUSINOW, QUEEN FROM ACE-KING-QUEEN, JOURNALIST HONOR LEADS AGAINST NOTRUMP, JACK TEN OR NINE TO SHOW 0 OR 2 HIGHER HONORS. A second question is which card should be led from a suit headed by one honor or non-touching honors. *See* THIRD BEST LEADS, JOURNALIST SPOT CARD LEADS AGAINST SUIT CONTRACTS, JOURNALIST SPOT CARD LEADS AGAINST NOTRUMP CONTRACTS. A third question is which card should be led from a suit headed by no honors at all. *See* MUD, ROMAN MUD, JOURNALIST LEADS FROM HONORLESS SUITS.

After the opening lead has been made, a defender can attempt, by the order in which he plays his cards, to give his partner an idea of how the hand should be defended. He may try to encourage or discourage the lead of a certain suit. *See* ATTITUDE

SIGNALS, UPSIDE DOWN SIGNALS, ODD-EVEN SIGNALS. Or he may attempt to disclose how many cards he has in a certain suit, perhaps by inference giving his partner information about another suit. *See* COUNT SIGNALS, TRUMP ECHO, FOSTER ECHO, BECHGAARD SIGNALS. Or he may play a certain card in one suit to indicate that he wants a certain other suit led. *See* SUIT PREFERENCE SIGNALS, REVOLVING DISCARDS, ODD-EVEN DISCARDS.

LEAD-DIRECTING DOUBLES

When the opponents are en route to game or slam, they frequently choose to cue-bid suits in which they have some high card strength but not complete control, or to cue-bid short suits in which they have ruffing values but not high cards, or to make asking bids in suits in which they have neither top cards nor prompt ruffing values. And often an opponent may make an artificial response to a control-seeking inquiry, by chance bidding a suit in which he has less than full control.

When an opponent makes such a cue-bid or artificial response or asking bid, the next player may be able to double to suggest to his partner that the suit doubled would be an appropriate opening lead. Such a double is obviously not intended as a penalty double since the opponents are not expected to play the hand in their cue-bid or other artificial bid. However, the doubler should take care that the suit he doubles is one that the opponents cannot play in.

In addition to the information conveyed by the double of such a bid, information is gained when the partner of the opening leader has had an opportunity to make a double but has chosen not to do so. In this situation, the inference is that the suit of the cue-bid is not a lead that is clearly desirable from the point of view of the partner of the opening leader.

The conventional lead directing doubles described below are used after the opponents have arrived in their slam or game contracts. The prudent use of these doubles can be a gold mine. *See* LIGHTNER SLAM DOUBLES, DOUBLES OF THREE NOTRUMP, FISHER DOUBLES.

LIGHTNER SLAM DOUBLES

The double, by the player not on lead, of a slam voluntarily bid by the opponents with the expectation that it will be made rather than as a sacrifice, is not designed primarily to increase the penalty for setting the opponents. Since the opponents usually will not fail by more than one trick, the value of making a pure penalty double is marginal. The more lucrative use of the double is to call for a lead that is likely to set the contract. The Lightner Slam Double is such a double.

The Lightner slam double asks the partner of the doubler to make an aggressive but unusual lead. The opening leader is on no account to make the passive lead of a trump. Nor is he to make the routine lead of a suit bid by either himself or his partner.

The order of priorities usually assigned to the lead possibilities after a Lightner double are these:

(a) If a side suit has been bid by the dummy, the opening lead should be in that suit. If dummy has bid more than one side suit, the opening lead should be in the first side suit bid by dummy.

(b) If dummy has not bid a side suit but declarer has bid a side suit, the opening lead should be in declarer's side suit.

(c) If neither dummy nor declarer has bid a side suit, the opening lead should be in an unbid suit. Usually the opening leader's longest unbid suit is most appropriate, since the doubler generally has a void and wants to ruff the first round of the suit.

For example, in the auction

(A)

North	East	South	West
1 ♣	1 ♠	2 ♡	Pass
4 ♡	Pass	5 ◇	Pass
6 ♡	Doublè	Pass	Pass
Pass			

East's double forbids West to lead East's suit, spades. Instead, West should lead the side suit bid by the dummy, clubs. If the auction has gone,

(B)

North	East	South	West
1 ◇	1 ♡	2 ♡	Pass
3 ♠	Pass	4 Notrump	Pass
5 ♡	Pass	6 ♠	Double
Pass	Pass	Pass	

South, the dummy, has not bid a side suit. He has made a cue-bid showing strength, and probably length in both unbid suits. However, he has not actually bid a side suit. North, the declarer has bid a side suit, diamonds, and West's double calls for a diamond lead.

Suppose that West holds

♠ x   ♡ A K Q x x x   ◇ x   ♣ J x x x x

and the auction has gone

South	West	North	East
1 ♠	2 ♡	3 ♠	Pass
6 ♠	Pass	Pass	Double
Pass	Pass	Pass	

East's double calls for an unusual lead. West is not allowed to lead a heart, which would be a normal lead. Without the double, West might have thought of leading his singleton diamond, attempting to get a ruff. However, East's double cannot be based primarily on the ace of diamonds, because East cannot know that West has a singleton diamond. East's double suggests that he is void in a side suit other than the suit bid by West. Therefore, West should lead a club.

Using Lightner slam doubles places a burden on the partner of the opening leader not to double simply because he thinks he can beat the contract. He should not make a pure penalty double of the slam without considering the effect his double will have on his partner's lead. For example, suppose East has a hand such as

♠ x x   ♡ A K x x x x x   ◇ A x   ♣ x x

and the auction has gone

North	East	South	West
1 ♣	1 ♡	1 ♠	Pass
3 ♣	Pass	4 ♠	Pass
4 Notrump	5 ♡	5 ♠	Pass
6 ♠			

Since neither North nor South made a cue-bid in hearts and since North used Blackwood, East expects to be able to cash two aces to defeat the slam. However, if he doubles, West will lead a club, and the red aces are likely to disappear in a landslide of clubs. Thus, East must pass and forego the slight increase of penalty in order to insure that there is any penalty at all.

The partner of the opening leader must also consider

whether or not his Lightner Slam double may frighten the opponents out of the slam that can be beaten and into one that can be made. If the opponents realize that a ruff will defeat their slam they may be able to neutralize the void by playing in no-trump, or by playing an alternative suit contract from the other side of the table, putting the hand with the void on opening lead.

Further, some partnerships have agreed to restrict their use of Lightner doubles to situations in which they are not obviously considering a sacrifice. In an auction such as

North	East	South	West
1 ♣	2 ♠°	3 ♡	4 ♠
5 ♡	Pass	6 ♡	Pass
Pass	Double		

these partnerships prefer to use the double to help them decide whether or not to sacrifice. *See* NEGATIVE SLAM DOUBLES, POSITIVE SLAM DOUBLES.

Previous Action by the Doubler

When the partner of the opening leader makes a Lightner slam double, the opening leader must consider the meaning of the double in light of the entire previous auction. Suppose, for example, that West has

♠ Q x x   ♡ Q x x x x   ◇ x x x x   ♣ K

and the auction has gone

°Preemptive

South	West	North	East
1 ♠	Pass	3 ♠	Pass
4 Notrump	Pass	5 ♡	Pass
6 ♠	Pass	Pass	Double

East's double calls for an unusual lead, and West's longest suit is hearts; East might be void in hearts. However, West should not lead a heart, because East had an opportunity to double hearts for a heart lead; he did not do so. Therefore, he cannot want a heart lead. East is likely to be void in some suit, so West looks for his next longest suit, diamonds. The whole hand might be:

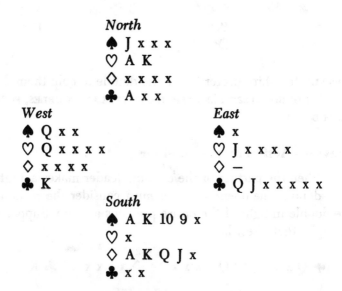

North
♠ J x x x
♡ A K
♢ x x x x
♣ A x x

West
♠ Q x x
♡ Q x x x x
♢ x x x x
♣ K

East
♠ x
♡ J x x x x
♢ —
♣ Q J x x x x x

South
♠ A K 10 9 x
♡ x
♢ A K Q J x
♣ x x

Unless West leads a diamond, he will get his trump trick and nothing more. A diamond lead, however, beats the spade slam.

If the partner of the opening leader has doubled the slam but has also doubled a cue-bid or other artificial bid during the course of the auction, a question is raised as to the meaning of the final double. For example, suppose that in the above auction East had doubled five hearts and then doubled the final contract of six spades. Some players would hold that the message in East's final double is mere emphasis that the slam is sure to be defeated if the suit previously doubled is led. However, the stakes are so much greater than the 50 or 100 point increase in the value of the penalty, that the better view is that the final double said, "Cancel previous message."

Indeed, when the partner of the opening leader has the opportunity to double twice it is sometimes possible for him to remove all guesswork for the opening leader as to which suit should be led. For example, if the bidding has gone

South	West	North	East
2 ♠*	Pass	2 Notrump*	Pass
3 ◇	Pass	4 ◇	Pass
4 ♡	Pass	4 ♠	Pass
4 Notrump	Pass	5 ♣	(?)
6 ◇	Pass	Pass	(?)

If East doubles only the final contract of six diamonds, his double clearly calls for a spade lead—the only obviously genuine side suit bid by the opponents. If East doubles five clubs and does not double the final contract of six diamonds, his double clearly calls for a club lead. Since East can convey either of those messages so unambiguously with one double, if he doubles both five clubs and six diamonds, his final double should ask for a heart lead.

Sometimes the player who will eventually be the opening leader doubles a cue-bid or other artificial bid knowing it can-

---

*Strong two-bid with negative response.

not affect the lead, but hoping that it will assist his partner in the defense. If the opponents have not bid a side suit and his partner doubles the final contract, it asks the opening leader to lead the suit he had doubled.

Lead Directing Doubles of Suit Game Contracts

Lightner doubles may be extended to game contracts bid in power auctions. For example:

North	East	South	West
1 ♠	Pass	3 ♠	Pass
4 ♠	Pass	Pass	Double

West's double is a Lightner double, calling for an unusual lead. But in an auction such as

North	East	South	West
1 ♣	Pass	1 ♡	Pass
1 ♠	Pass	2 ♠	Pass
3 ♠	Pass	4 ♠	Double

West's double suggests that the opponents have overreached and are going down. West probably has strength in dummy's side suit, hearts, but the double does not require an unusual lead.

Which Card to Lead

When leading from a suit that the Lightner doubler is expected to ruff, informing the doubler how many cards the leader holds in the suit is usually unimportant. The opening leader should attempt, therefore, to give his partner a SUIT PREFERENCE SIGNAL. He leads the lowest card he has in the suit to recommend that his partner return the lower ranking side suit; he leads a very high card to recommend the return of the higher ranking side suit; or he leads a middle card to deny any strong preference as between the two side suits.

When the lead directing double is more likely to have been made on power than on a void, and the lead is being made in a suit in which dummy has length, the opening leader should lead the highest card he has in the suit. For example, suppose West has

♠ x x   ♡ J 9 x   ◇ J x x x   ♣ J x x x

and the auction has been

South	West	North	East
1 ♣	Pass	1 ♡	Pass
1 ♠	Pass	3 ♠	Pass
4 ♠	Double	Pass	Pass

West should lead the jack of hearts. East may well have the ace and queen; if he has the ten as well and dummy has the king, the lead of the jack will allow West to hold the lead for another run-through.

DOUBLES OF THREE NOTRUMP

Doubles of three notrump contracts have a variety of meanings depending on the previous auction. These doubles normally do not call for unusual leads unless the previous auction has not tended to suggest which may be the partnership's best suit.

If the doubler has bid a suit, the double normally calls for the lead of his suit. For example:

North	East	South	West
1 ◇	1 ♡	1 Notrump	Pass
3 Notrump	Double		

East's double of three notrump requests a heart lead. East is likely to have a semi-solid suit and a diamond stopper.

If the doubler has not bid a suit but the opening leader has bid a suit, the double calls for the opening leader to lead his own suit. For example:

South	West	North	East
1 ◇	1 ♠	2 ♣	Pass
2 Notrump	Pass	3 Notrump	Double

East's double requests a spade lead. He is likely to have a filler for West's broken suit, plus some high cards that suggest to him that the declarer will not be able to make nine tricks if a spade is led.

If both the doubler and the opening leader have bid suits of their own, there is no logical way to tell definitively which suit the doubler wants led. The partnership should make explicit agreements as to which suit is called for.

If neither the doubler nor the opening leader has bid a suit but dummy has bid a suit, the double calls for the lead of the suit bid by dummy. For example:

North	East	South	West
1 ♡	Pass	1 Notrump	Pass
2 Notrump	Pass	3 Notrump	Pass
Pass	Double		

East's double calls for a heart lead. This principle, however, must not be applied willy nilly. For example if the dummy has rebid his suit, a double of three notrump more likely means that the doubler has a stopper in the suit, and a source of tricks elsewhere. For example if the bidding has gone

North	East	South	West
1 ♣	Pass	1 ♠	Pass
2 ♣	Pass	2 ♡	Pass
3 ♣	Pass	3 Notrump	Pass
Pass	Double		

East's double does not call for a club lead. He might have a hand such as

♠ x x x   ♡ A x x   ♢ K Q J x   ♣ K x x

If the defenders have not bid a suit and dummy has bid a suit by inference, the double should be interpreted to call for the lead of that suit. For example

South	West	North	East
1 Notrump	Pass	2 ♣	Pass
2 ♠	Pass	3 Notrump	Double

Having used two clubs as Stayman ostensibly to learn whether opener has a four card major suit, North appears to have four hearts, since he returned to notrump over South's two spade bid. East may double three notrump, therefore, to ask for a heart lead.

If no suit has been bid by any of the players, there are a variety of meanings that can be ascribed to the double. Most partnerships use the double to show a long running suit; the partner of the doubler is therefore required to lead his shortest and weakest suit. For example, if the auction has gone

South	*West*	*North*	*East*
1 Notrump	Pass	3 Notrump	Double

and West has

♠ Q J 10   ♡ x x   ◇ x x x x   ♣ J 10 9 x

West should lead a heart.

Some partnerships avoid having the opening leader guess which suit to lead by arbitrarily agreeing that the double calls for a specific suit. Some partnerships agree that the double calls for a spade lead; some agree that it calls for a club lead. *See also* FISHER DOUBLES.

FISHER DOUBLES

Fisher doubles assign precise meanings to the double of three notrump after the bidding has been opened one notrump. If the responder has not used a two-club Stayman bid, the double calls for a club lead. If the responder has used Stayman and the two club bid has not been doubled, the double calls for a diamond lead. For example

South	West	North	East
1 Notrump	Pass	2 ♣	Pass
2 ♠	Pass	3 Notrump	Double

Using Fisher doubles, East's double would call for a diamond lead.

ACE FROM ACE-KING

Standard practice is to lead the highest of all honor card sequences, with one exception. The exception is that the king is led from an ace-king combination. This exception creates an ambiguity in the lead of the king: assuming that no revealing cards are tabled in the dummy, the partner of the opening leader frequently does not know whether the king has been led from ace-king or from king-queen.

When the king is led and the third hand has the jack of that suit, he would like to signal encouragement if his partner has led from the king and queen, but not if his partner has led from the king and ace. When the king is led against a suit contract and third hand has a doubleton and the ability to ruff the third round of the suit, he would like to signal encouragement if his partner has led from the king and ace, but not if his partner has led from the king and queen. The ambiguity of the king lead is therefore a serious problem on many hands.

In order to eliminate the ambiguity of the king lead, some partnerships agree to lead the ace from a suit headed by the ace and king. Using this convention, the lead of the king is always from a suit headed by the king and queen (unless the leader has a doubleton).

The drawback to this arrangement is that, against a suit contract, it is frequently advantageous to lead an unsupported ace. Therefore, rather than eliminating all ambiguity, the ace-from-ace-king convention may simply transfer the ambiguity from the king lead to the ace lead. *See* RUSINOW LEADS.

RUSINOW LEADS

Rusinow leads, which are used only against suit contracts, not against notrump, remove the ambiguity of the standard king lead (*see discussion under* ACE FROM ACE-KING) by requiring that the second ranking of touching honors be led. With more than two honor cards in sequence, the second ranking is still led. Thus, from the A K or A K Q, the king would be led; from K Q or K Q J, the queen would be led; from Q J or Q J 10, the jack would be led; from J 10 or J 10 9, the ten would be led; and from 10 9 or 10 9 8, the nine would be led.

Rusinow leads are used only on opening lead, and only in a suit that the leader's partner has not introduced. After the opening lead has been made the highest of touching honors is led. Similarly, if the opening leader is fortunate enough to have touching honors in a suit introduced by his partner, his lead from that suit should be the highest of those honors.

If the honors to be led are doubleton, the order of leading is reversed. Thus, using Rusinow leads, the higher honor is led, followed by the lower in order to show a doubleton.

Rusinow leads are not used against notrump contracts. Against notrump it is more important to exchange information as to the length and general strength of the suit led, than to clarify the ambiguity created by standard king leads.

QUEEN FROM ACE-KING-QUEEN

Some partnerships agree that the queen will be led from suits headed by the ace, king and queen. This convention allows the partner of the leader to encourage when he has the jack in the suit. However, it does not give him sufficient information to allow him to encourage confidently with a doubleton.

JOURNALIST HONOR LEADS AGAINST SUITS

See RUSINOW LEADS.

JOURNALIST HONOR LEADS
AGAINST NOTRUMP

Standard practice against notrump contracts is to lead the highest of touching honors from a complete, or nearly complete, three-card sequence. For example, the king is led from K Q J; the queen is led from Q J 10; the jack is led from J 10 9; the ten is led from 10 9 8.

If the third card in the suit to be led is one pip away from being in sequence with the two top touching honors, the top card is led. For example, the king is led from K Q 10; the queen is led from Q J 9; the jack is led from J 10 8; the 10 is led from 10 9 7.

When the top honor in a suit is one or more cards distant from a sequence headed by an honor, the sequence is called an interior sequence. For example, the jack heads the interior sequence in A J 10 x or K J 10 x. The ten heads the interior sequence in A 10 9 x, or K 10 9 x or Q 10 9 x. Standard practice when leading a suit containing an interior sequence is to lead the second highest card, i.e., the top of the interior sequence. Thus, the jack would be led from A J 10 x or K J 10 x; the ten would be led from A 10 9 x, or K 10 9 x or Q 10 9 x.

The practice of leading the highest of three-card sequences and leading the top of interior sequences creates ambiguities when the jack or the ten is led. Frequently the partner of the leader will have a holding in the suit with which he will wish to continue the suit if it is the top of an interior sequence, but shift to another suit if the jack or ten is the leader's highest card in the suit. For example, suppose the jack of clubs is led by West against a three notrump contract and the dummy and third hand are as follows:

North
♠ A K J x x
♡ A Q J x
♢ x x
♣ x x

Lead: ♣ J

East
♠ x x x
♡ x x x
♢ Q J 10 x
♣ A 9 x

If West has led from K J 10 x x of clubs, East should continue clubs in order to defeat three notrump. On the other hand, if the jack is West's highest club, East should shift to the queen of diamonds in hopes that West has the ace and that the partnership can take four diamond tricks to beat the contract.

Using Journalist methods, the opening lead of the jack denies possession of a higher honor in the suit; the lead of the ten promises possession of the ace, king or queen. In this way the Journalist system eliminates the ambiguity of the standard leads which use both jack and ten leads from interior sequences. In the hand above, in which West led the jack of clubs, a partnership using Journalist leads would have no trouble shifting to a diamond, because the lead of the jack cannot be made from a holding such as K J 10 x, but promises a holding such as J 10 9 x or J 10 8 x. From an interior sequence, such as A J 10 x, A 10 9 x, Q 10 9 x, etc., the ten is led.

In Journalist, the lead of the nine promises either the ten, or no higher honor, or at most a doubleton in the suit. The nine must be led from a holding such as 10 9 8 x or 10 9 7 x because the lead of the ten would promise one of the top three honors in the suit. From three cards headed by the nine, therefore, the nine may not be led; the middle card should be led instead.

The Journalist method of leading against notrump contracts deals not just with the ambiguous jack and ten leads, but assigns a specific message to each honor card lead. Each honor card meaning is designed to make it easier for the leader or his partner to know whether the suit led should be continued or abandoned.

The lead of the ace is usually from a holding such as A K J x x, or A K Q 10 x (x), or A K 10 9 x.

The partner of the leader is requested to unblock a high card in the suit; otherwise he should start a COUNT SIGNAL, playing his lowest card with an odd number of cards, or starting a high-low echo with an even number of cards. For example, if third hand has J x x, he should play the jack on the lead of the ace. If he has 4 3 2, he should play the two to give count. If he has the 10 9 8 x, he should play the 10, followed by the 8 and 9, in case the opening lead was from a suit such as A K Q 7 x.

Using Journalist methods, the lead of the king could be from a suit headed either by the ace and king or the king and queen. The lead of the king asks third hand whether or not he likes the suit. If he likes the suit he encourages by following with a high card; if he prefers another suit, he plays a low card. The opening leader might have length in the suit led, but he might also have just A K x or K Q x and be trying to find his partner's long suit.

The lead of the queen may be made from a suit headed by the Q J 10, or from a suit headed by the K Q 10 9. In the latter event, third hand is requested to play the jack under the queen if he has it. The use of the queen lead to ask partner to unblock the jack avoids the Bath coup situation, in which the declarer, holding A J x in the suit led, plays low on the standard lead of the king. In the standard situation, the opening leader frequently continues the suit into the declarer's ace-jack tenace; or the opening leader sometimes shifts to another suit not knowing that his partner has the jack. The Journalist queen lead solves this problem, because if the partner of the leader does not play the jack under the queen, he does not have it.

JACK, TEN OR NINE TO SHOW 0 OR 2 HIGHER HONORS

Some partnerships use a system of secondary honor card leads against notrump that reduces, but does not eliminate entirely, the ambiguity of the standard jack and ten leads. (*See discussion under* JOURNALIST HONOR LEADS AGAINST NOTRUMP.) They agree that the opening lead of the jack, ten or nine promises that the leader has either two honors higher than the card led, or no higher honors. For example, the jack would be led from A Q J 10 x; the 10 would be led from A J 10 x or K J 10 x; the nine would be led from A 10 9 x, or K 10 9 x, or Q 10 9 x.

While there is obviously an inherent ambiguity, usually the partner of the opening leader can determine whether the leader has two higher honors or none. For example, in the example given above, in which the opening lead was the jack of clubs and the partner of the leader had A 9 x of clubs, it would be clear that the jack was the highest honor held by West in that suit; since he obviously would not lead the jack from K Q J he must have no honors higher than the jack. If West had led the ten of clubs in that example, instead of the jack, and East again held the A 9 x, East could infer that West had led from the K J 10 x (x) of clubs; since West did not have the nine, the ten could not have been from the top of a sequence.

Since the partner of the opening leader will more often than not gain sufficient information from the auction and holdings in dummy and his own hand to infer whether his partner has two honors or no honor higher than the jack, ten or nine he has led, the ambiguity in this conventional system of leading is not a substantial drawback. And in return for the slight ambiguity for the defenders, the lead may make it more difficult for the declarer to determine just where the high cards in the suit led are located.

Some partnerships use these jack, ten and nine leads throughout the hand.

THIRD BEST LEADS

Standard practice is to lead the fourth best card from a suit headed by one honor or non-touching honors. From a three-card suit headed by an honor, it is also standard practice to lead the lowest card. Therefore, the lead of the deuce of a suit (either the actual deuce or the effective deuce, as when the lead is the 4 and third hand can see the 2 and 3 in his own hand or dummy) could be from either a four-card suit or a three-card suit. The difference may be crucial to the defense, as when third hand must decide whether to try to cash another trick in the suit led or to try another suit.

One method devised to help clarify the length of the suit in which a low card is led is to lead the third highest card in the suit. Using this method, and holding Q 8 6 2, for example, the six would be led rather than the two. It will be noted that, using this convention, the lead of a non-deuce does not reveal immediately to the partner of the leader whether the lead is from a three-card suit or a four-card suit. However, the lead of the deuce shows immediately that the lead is not from four cards.

Third-best leads are equally usable against notrump and suit contracts. With respect to fourth-best leads, the partner of the leader usually applies the Rule of Eleven in order to reconstruct the declarer's potential high card holding in the suit led. Using third-best leads, the partner of the leader should apply a Rule of Twelve. Thus, he would subtract the size of the card led from twelve rather than from eleven, to determine how many cards higher than the card led are in the hands other than that of the opening leader.

JOURNALIST SPOT CARD LEADS AGAINST SUIT CONTRACTS

Against suit contracts, Journalist methods distinguish between three-card suits and four-card suits in the same manner that THIRD-BEST leads do. The Journalist method is to lead the third best card from a four-card suit. However, leading the third best card from suits of all lengths would fail to help the partner of the leader to distinguish between four-card and five-card suits, or between five-card and six-card suits.

In order to provide maximum assistance, Journalist applies what it calls the "two-card difference principle". The theory, which is also a basis for using the lead of the JACK, TEN OR NINE TO SHOW ZERO OR TWO HIGHER HONORS, is that it is a great deal easier to fathom which of two holdings the lead is from when the possibilities are two cards apart than when they are one card apart.

Thus, Journalist methods require the lead of the third best card when the suit has an even number of cards in it. The partner of the leader should be able to determine whether the lead is from a doubleton, or a four-card suit or a six-card suit, or an eight-card suit. From suits containing an odd number of cards, Journalist methods use the lead of the lowest card: third best from three, fifth best from five, seventh best from seven.

While there are inherent ambiguities, these leads can be of valuable assistance to the partner of the leader. For example, suppose West leads the deuce of a suit in which North and East have the following holdings:

North

Q 8 x x

Lead: 2

East

A J 9 x

A low card is played from dummy. Using standard methods, East is tempted to play the ace for fear that declarer might have the singleton king. Using Journalist leads, however, West must have either three or five cards in the suit, having led the lowest. Therefore, if declarer has the king of the suit, he has at least one other card with it; East is safe in playing the jack (assuming there are not sufficient discards in other suits for declarer to rid himself of the rest of the suit).

In a similar situation the lead of the non-deuce can help to clarify matters for East. Suppose West leads the three of a suit in which North and East have the following holdings:

North

Q 8 7 5

Lead: 3

East

A J 9

Here again, the auction may lead East to fear that the declarer has a singleton king in the suit led. Using standard methods, West's three could be from a five-card suit. Using Journalist methods, however, if West has a five card suit, declarer's singleton must be the deuce.

When third hand believes that the opening leader has led his fifth best card, he can reconstruct the declarer's potential by applying the Rule of Ten. He subtracts the size of the card led from ten, and the remainder represents the number of cards in

582

his own hand, dummy and declarer's hand that can beat the opening leader's card.

Some partnerships agree to use Journalist spot card leads not only on opening lead, but throughout the hand. These leads are tantamount to COUNT SIGNALS—a high lead from a suit with an even number of cards, and a low lead from a suit with an odd number of cards. Use of these leads during the course of the defense can be quite useful.

JOURNALIST SPOT CARD LEADS AGAINST NOTRUMP

The Journalist method of leading against suit contracts is not carried over into leads against notrump contracts. Against notrump the important goal is to recognize which is the best suit in general for the defense, rather than specifically how many cards the opening leader has in the suit.

Against notrump contracts, therefore, the Journalist method is to lead a low card from a suit that the opening leader wants returned. Usually this suit is headed by one or more honor cards. In general, the lower the card that is led, the more eager the leader is to have the suit returned. For example, from A 10 8 6 3, the correct lead would be the three.

Conversely, when the opening leader has little strength in the suit he starts, and wants some other suit returned, he should lead a high card. For example, against a contract of one notrump, with a hand such as

♠ K J x x ♡ A Q x ◇ 10 8 7 2 ♣ K x

the best lead is probably the eight of diamonds, in order to encourage partner to return another suit in which a tenace is held.

MUD LEADS

Perhaps the most troublesome of all specific leading questions is what to lead from three small cards. The difficulty is that it is impossible to formulate an unvarying rule as to whether it is better to clarify length than strength, or vice versa.

The traditional lead of the top three small cards has the virtue of relieving the leader's partner of any notion that the lead is from a suit headed by an honor. Unfortunately, it also relieves the declarer of any such notion, and, in addition, may deceive the partner of the leader into believing that it is the top of a doubleton.

The lead of a low card from three small cards avoids the confusion as to whether the opening leader has three cards or a doubleton. However, the price of this clarification is the suggestion to the leader's partner that the suit led might be headed by an honor.

One compromise that has been devised is to lead the middle card from a holding of three small cards. When next that suit is played the opening leader will play his highest, and lastly his lowest. This convention is called MUD, an acronym for the order in which the cards are played: Middle, Up, Down.

MUD leads are not used in a suit bid by the partner of the opening leader. In such a suit the opening leader should lead low from three small cards if he has not supported the suit. If he has supported the suit, however, his partner will infer that he has at least three card support, and in that circumstance he should lead his highest card to deny possession of an honor.

Like all compromises, MUD leads are a little bit fishy and a little bit fowl. A system that requires the lead of the same card from, e.g., K 7 3 or 9 7 3 or 7 3 does not give the partner of the leader a great deal of help.

ROMAN MUD

MUD methods may also be used when leading from four small cards. Using this extension, called Roman Mud, the opening leader leads the second highest from his four small cards, then he follows with the highest, then with the third highest and finally plays the lowest. For example, if the suit in which the opening lead is to be made is 8 5 3 2, the five would be led; at his next opportunities the opening leader would play the eight, then the three, then the two.

Roman Mud is easier on the partner of the opening leader than simple MUD is. On the two-card-difference principle, it is easier to recognize a lead as being from a doubleton when the alternative is that it is from four cards, than when the alternative is that it is from three cards. However, the partner of the leader will be at pains to guess whether the lead is from three small or four small cards.

JOURNALIST LEADS FROM
HONORLESS SUITS

Using Journalist leads, the lead of a small card tends to suggest that the suit is headed by an honor. From an honorless suit the opening leader using Journalist methods is allowed to use his judgment as to whether it is more important that his partner be apprised of the length or of the strength of the suit led.

If the leader wants to tell his partner that he has no honor in the suit, he leads the highest card he can afford. In Journalist this is never higher than the eight since the nine would imply possession of the ten.

If the leader wants instead to reveal his length in the suit led, he makes his normal Journalist lead of third best from an even number of cards and the lowest from an odd number of cards.

ATTITUDE SIGNALS

Traditionally, a defender shows interest in having a suit led or continued by playing a high card in that suit. He discourages by playing a low card. For example, if West leads the king of diamonds against a four spade contract and dummy has ◇ Q x x and East has ◇ 9 x, East will play the nine of diamonds if he wants the suit continued so that he may get an immediate ruff. If he does not want to ruff, or if he wants some other suit led first, he will play his lower diamond.

A defender may encourage the lead of a particular suit by playing discouraging cards in the other suits. For example, suppose West leads a club against a three notrump contract, and dummy and East have the following hands:

North
♠ K J
♡ K x x
◇ Q x x x
♣ A J x x

Lead: ♣ 8

East
♠ A Q 10 9
♡ x x x x
◇ x x x
♣ x x

After the lead, declarer cashes four rounds of clubs. East must discard on the third and fourth clubs. He plays his lowest heart and his lowest diamond, to encourage West, if he gets the lead, to play a spade.

If East had held instead

♠ A Q 10 9 8   ♡ x x x   ◇ x x   ♣ x x x

and had to make only one discard on the run of the clubs, he would have thrown the ten of spades to give West the same message.

When a defender plays a high card to encourage his partner to play that suit, he should take care not to be wasteful. For instance, in the above example, if East had ♠ A Q 10 3 2, he could not afford to signal with the ten, for South might have three spades headed by the nine, which would then become a stopper.

When to Show Attitude

In general a defender should signal encouragement or discouragement to his partner's lead of an honor card. The opening lead is the most difficult facet of bridge, and often the opening leader needs a sign from his partner as to whether or not his attack has hit pay dirt.

However, third hand need not encourage just because he has a doubleton, or just because he has a filling card in the suit led. He must consider the hand as a whole. For example, if West leads the king of a side suit of which dummy has Q x x and East has 9 2, East cannot determine whether he will signal encouragement without considering his other suits as well. If East has the J 10 9 8 of trumps, for instance, he is not normally interested in ruffing; he has a natural trump trick, which one ruff will not augment.

If dummy had Q x of the suit led and East had the 9 2, East would have to examine his own and dummy's trumps in order to know whether or not to encourage. If East has the 3 2 of trumps and dummy the 5 4, there is no point in encouraging, because East cannot overruff the dummy.

589

If East, rather than dummy, had the Q x of the suit led, he should not signal with the queen, because the play of that card has a specific meaning. *See* SIGNALS TO SHOW SPECIFIC HONOR CARDS.

Sometimes East will have a filling card for West's lead, but will want West to shift to another suit. Suppose West led the king of diamonds against a three spade contract in the following hand:

> **North**
> ♠ K x x x
> ♡ K x x
> ♢ x x
> ♣ A K 10 x

Lead: ♢ K

> **East**
> ♠ x x
> ♡ A Q J
> ♢ Q 8 5 2
> ♣ x x x x

East should play the two of diamonds at trick one to defeat the three spade contract. He wants West to shift to a heart while West still has the ace of diamonds as an entry for a second heart lead.

Occasionally against a slam contract, rather than encouraging or discouraging, East will want to tell his partner how many cards he holds in the suit led. For example, suppose West leads the king of hearts against a six spade contract, and dummy and East have the following hands:

North
♠ K Q x
♡ Q x x
◇ A Q J x
♣ A J x

Lead: ♡ K

East
♠ x x
♡ J 7 4 2
◇ K x x x
♣ x x x

East has no way of knowing whether a second heart can be cashed, or whether West should shift to a diamond. East should therefore play the seven of hearts to show an even number of hearts. West should recognize that East is giving count rather than attitude, and be able to determine whether or not the second heart can be cashed. From East's point of view declarer might have

♠ A J x x x   ♡ x x   ◇ x   ♣ K Q x x x

in which case a second round of hearts is required to prevent declarer's taking a ruffing finesse in diamonds and discarding his losing heart. Alternatively, declarer might have

♠ A J x x x   ♡ x   ◇ x x   ♣ K Q x x x

in which case a second round of hearts would allow South to discard his losing diamond on the queen of hearts. East's count signal will clarify for West which hand declarer holds.

After the initial stages of the hand, a defender may signal attitude by making a high or low discard in a suit other than the suit led. His first discard in any suit should indicate whether or not he is interested in having that suit led. Again, however, his interest is a relative matter; he should not discard a high card simply to show tolerance for a lead of that suit if he prefers the lead of another suit.

UPSIDE-DOWN SIGNALS

Upside Down signals are attitude signals that reverse the traditional method of showing interest and aversion. To encourage the lead or continuation of a suit using Upside Down signals, the defender plays a low card in the suit; to discourage he plays a high card.

This method has two benefits. First it minimizes the danger that a useful card will be wasted in signaling. Second, it reduces the declarer's ability to falsecard successfully. Suppose for example that West leads the jack of spades in defending against a three notrump contract, and the spade suit is distributed as follows:

> *North*
> ♠ 10 7 6 3

West
♠ J 5

East
♠ K Q 9 2

> *South*
> ♠ A 8 4

East cannot afford to encourage with the nine. Use of Upside Down signals allows him to encourage with a card he can spare.

Suppose West leads the king of hearts against a spade contract and dummy's and East's hearts are as follows:

> *North*
> ♡ 9 8 7

Lead: ♡ K

> *East*
> ♡ 6 5 3

Using standard signals East would play the three of hearts. If declarer has $\heartsuit$ A J 4 2, he should play the four. West then would know whether East started with $\heartsuit$ 6 5 3 or $\heartsuit$ A 3 2 or $\heartsuit$ J 3 2.

Using Upside Down signals, however, East would follow suit with the 6 from 6 5 3, which West would surely read as a high and discouraging card. If East had J 6 5 3 instead, he would play the three to encourage. It is true, of course, that the declarer could still play the four from $\heartsuit$ A 4 2, attempting to persuade West that East's three is a high card. However, if East wants to discourage it is quite likely that he can afford a spot higher than the three.

ODD-EVEN SIGNALS

Odd-even signals, sometimes called Roman signals, are a method of encouraging or discouraging that depends on whether the number of the card played is odd or even, rather than on whether it is high, middle or low. A defender plays an odd numbered card to encourage, or an even numbered card to discourage.

In addition, when an even card is played, the size of the card tends to suggest which of the other suits the defender prefers. For example, if a defender holds ♡ 8 5 2 and wants to encourage the lead or continuation of the heart suit, he plays the five. If he wants to discourage, he has his choice between the eight and the two. He plays the eight if he wants his partner to lead the higher ranking non-trump suit, e.g., spades if clubs or diamonds are trumps; he plays the two if he wants his partner to lead the lower ranking non-trump suit, e.g., diamonds if clubs are trumps.

Just as problems arise with standard signals when "subtle" cards are held (e.g., Q 3 2 in a suit in which partner leads the king), sometimes it will occur that a defender does not have an odd card when he needs it, or an even card when he needs it. In the absence of an odd card with which to encourage, the Odd-Even practice is to play an even card that would call for the more improbable suit preference.

For example, suppose East has the 8 5 doubleton in diamonds against a spade contract, and his partner leads the king of diamonds, promising the ace. East would play the ♢ 5 to encourage continuation of diamonds. If East's doubleton were the ♢ 7 4, he would play the 7 to encourage. However, if East's doubleton were the ♢ 6 2, he would have a slight problem. In this situation, he examines dummy's side suit holdings, clubs and hearts, and issues the more improbable suit preference signal. For example, if dummy has ♣ A K Q x and ♡ K x, East would play the ◇ 2, technically calling for a club shift. However, the club shift is so improbable that West should be able to infer that East simply has no odd numbered cards, but in fact wants to encourage West to continue.

If East has no even cards but wants to discourage, he should tend to discard as he would have if he were not using odd-even discards. Holding 7 5 3, for example, if the partnership is using standard signals East would play the three. If the partnership is using UPSIDE DOWN SIGNALS, East should play the seven.

SIGNALS TO SHOW SPECIFIC HONOR CARDS

When a defender has two or more honors in a suit and can afford to discard one of them, it is standard practice for him to throw the higher honor if his honors are touching. If the top honor is out of sequence with the other(s), he should throw the second highest.

For example, when West leads the king of spades and East has ♠ Q J x, he should play the queen. The play of the queen promises that East has the jack, and enables West to underlead his ace of spades to put East on lead, either to clear the suit without further crashing of honors, or to lead another suit. If East had ♠ J 10 x, his proper play would be the jack, which would deny possession of the queen and promise the ten.

Because of the traditional meaning of the play of the queen under the king, East cannot signal high-low with a doubleton queen, because West will likely place East with the jack and underlead his ace at the second trick. Holding J x, however, East is allowed to throw the jack if he wants a ruff. The rationale is, first, that West is unlikely to have the A K Q of the suit, without which he could not underlead at the second trick, and second, that the Jack is not so valuable a card as the queen.

If West leads a low card against a notrump contract and East has three cards in the suit led headed by a pair of honors, which cannot beat the card played from the dummy, East should throw the higher honor if his honors are touching, and throw the second ranking honor if his honors are not touching. For example, suppose West leads a heart and the dummy's and East's holdings are as follows:

North
♡ A 8

Lead: ♡ 3

East
♡ Q J 4

When the ♡ A is played from the dummy it is standard for East to follow with the queen. This play is in part a signal that East has the jack but not the king, and in part an unblocking of partner's suit. If instead of ♡ Q J 4 East had K 10 4, his proper play would be the ten, which would promise either a higher honor not including the jack, or a sequence headed by the ten.

Similarly, when discarding honor cards on the run of another suit, the ace is played from A K Q, the king from K Q J, the queen from Q J 10, and so forth. If there is a gap in the sequence, the second highest honor is thrown. Thus, the queen is thrown from A Q J, the jack from A J 10 or K J 10, the ten from A 10 9, K 10 9 or Q 10 9.

For example, suppose South has opened the bidding with two notrump which is passed out, and East and dummy have the following hands:

North
♠ x x x x
♡ x x x
♢ Q x x
♣ x x x

Lead: ♠ J

East
♠ K Q 9 x
♡ Q x x
♢ A x x
♣ x x x

West has led the jack of spades, which South ducked once, and then won the second round with the ace. South played the king and jack of diamonds which East ducked, and then a third diamond which East won. When East cashed his third spade, West followed, but when the fourth spade was cashed West discarded the ten of hearts. The discard of the ten denied possession of the jack; therefore East knew that if declarer had the king of hearts he also had the jack, so that a heart lead would only give South a chance to guess the heart position. East therefore exited with a club to force declarer to play hearts from his hand.

See also JOURNALIST HONOR LEADS AGAINST NOTRUMP, *and* FOSTER ECHO.

COUNT SIGNALS

The traditional method of giving count in a suit is to play first a high card followed by a low card with an even number of cards in the suit, and to play a low card followed by a higher card to show an odd number of cards. The reverse method is standard in some countries; and some partnerships use a combination of methods, playing high-low with an even number when following to a suit led by partner, and playing high-low with an odd number of cards if the suit is being led by the declarer or if the suit is being discarded on the run of another suit.

Length signals usually may not be given at the same time that attitude signals are being given. However, count signals may be given after the defender's attitude toward a certain suit has already been shown, by showing the defender's present count. For example, if a defender discards from ♡ 9 8 7 5 4 2 on the run of a suit in which he is void, his first discard should be the two to show disinterest, rather than a higher card to start showing an even number of cards in the suit. Thereafter the defender may show the present number of cards he has in the suit by playing the four—his lowest from his five remaining cards—followed by a higher card. If the defender had started with ♡ 9 8 5 4 2, his first discard would be the two, but his next two discards would be in high-low order to show an even number of cards remaining after the attitude signal. *See also* BECHGAARD SIGNALS.

Count signals should rarely be given in following to the opening lead, when the opening leader more often needs to receive encouragement or discouragement. Similarly, when a new suit is led by a defender, it is frequently more helpful for the other defender to signal his attitude rather than his length, although there are circumstances when length should be shown.

When the declarer attacks a suit, however, it is usually more advantageous to show length than attitude. If it is really desirable for declarer to be playing the suit, it is unlikely that a defender will want to encourage the other defender to lead it. Count signals, however, should not be given when they would help the declarer more than the defense.

Length signals have their greatest utility when the declarer is attempting to establish a long suit in a dummy that has no outside-entries. When one defender has the ace of the suit and needs to hold up only long enough for declarer's supply to be exhausted, he depends on his partner to signal his own length in the suit. For example, suppose the diamond suit were distributed as follows:

North
◇ K Q J 10 7

West　　　　　　　　　　　　*East*
◇ A 4 2　　　　　　　　　　 ◇ 9 6 3

South
◇ 8 5

On the first lead of the suit East would play the three to show an odd number of cards. West would then know that he should win the second round of the suit, either because East has three and South has a doubleton, or because East has a singleton and West cannot exhaust South's supply. If, instead of 9 6 3, East had 6 3, he would play the six on the first round, followed by the three on the second round. West would therefore realize that declarer had three diamonds and could hold up until the third round of the suit.

TRUMP ECHO

In the trump suit, if one defender wants to show his partner how many trumps he has, he does so by playing high-low with an odd number of trumps, and low-high with an even number. The use of the trump echo may be important when the question is whether or not a ruff is available. In order not to give declarer too much information, the trump echo is best reserved for such ruffing situations.

FOSTER ECHO

The Foster Echo is a combination count signal and unblocking play against notrump contracts. When a lead is made, if the third hand either cannot top the card led or cannot top the card played from the dummy, the Foster Echo convention requires him to play his second-highest card in the suit. If third hand has three cards in the suit his next play in the suit will be the highest card; if he has four cards in the suit his next play will be his third highest, followed by his highest, then his lowest.

For example, suppose a heart is led against three notrump, and the dummy and East have the following cards in the suit:

$$\textit{North}$$
$$\heartsuit \text{ A 8}$$

Lead: $\heartsuit$ 5

$$\textit{East}$$
$$\heartsuit \text{ 9 7 3}$$

When the ace is played from dummy, East must follow with the seven. When the suit is next played, East will play the nine, showing that he started with three hearts.

The same principle applies when East started with two honors in the suit led. If his honors are not touching, the effect of using Foster Echos is not different from standard practice. However, if East had $\heartsuit$ J 10 3, for example, using the Foster Echo would require him to follow with the ten rather than the jack; this creates a potential ambiguity, since East would also have played the ten from Q 10 3.

BECHGAARD SIGNALS

Bechgaard Signals are a precise method of discarding from long suits to reveal the length held in those suits. These signals are used to help the other defender to know declarer's length in the various suits. Each requires at least three discards to complete the message.

From a five-card suit, cards are discarded in a delayed echo pattern: for example, first the three, then the four, then the two. From a six-card suit, three cards are discarded in descending order: for example, the four, then the three, then the two. From a seven-card suit, four cards are discarded in a double-echo pattern: for example, the three, then the two, then the five, then the four.

Bechgaard signals are strictly count signals. They should not be used if there is a possibility that attitude should be shown in the suit being discarded.

SUIT PREFERENCE SIGNALS

A suit preference signal is a signal that obviously asks the partner of the signaler to play a specific other suit at his first opportunity. The purpose of the suit preference signal is to eliminate the guesswork as to which suit should be played next. When properly used, suit preference signals do not conflict with attitude signals. Therefore, in order to make a suit preference signal, the defender must play an unusually high card to call for the lead of a higher ranking suit, and an unusually low card to call for the lead of the lower ranking suit.

The suit preference signal never asks for a trump lead, nor for a continuation of the suit led; the choice is strictly between the side suits. For example, on the lead of a diamond against a spade contract, a low suit preference signal would ask for a club lead; a high suit preference signal would ask for a heart lead.

Suit preference signals should not be given in situations in which it is probable that length signals would be more useful. For example, suppose the king of hearts is led against a six spade contract and dummy and East are as follows:

North
♠ K Q x
♡ Q x x
◇ A Q J x
♣ A J x

Lead: ♡ K

East
♠ x x
♡ J 7 6 5 2
◇ K x x
♣ x x x

Obviously the primary question for West is whether or not he can cash the heart ace. Since East has no way of knowing how many hearts West has, his first responsibility is to tell West how many hearts East has. With the above hand, therefore, East's proper play is the two of hearts; this card promises an odd number of hearts; it does not ask West to shift to a club.

To be a suit preference signal, it must be obvious that a mere continuation of the suit led is not being requested. For example, suppose the king of hearts is led against a six spade contract and the dummy and East hands are these:

North
♠ K Q x
♡ x
◇ K Q x x x
♣ x x x

Lead: ♡ K

East
♠ x
♡ Q 10 7 3 2
◇ A x x x
♣ x x x

On the lead of the king of hearts, East would play the queen, an unusually high card in order to induce West to shift to a diamond. However, if East played the seven instead of the queen, this would not be a suit preference signal, but merely an encouraging card asking West to continue the suit. Instead of the hand above, East might have a hand such as

♠ J x x x   ♡ Q 10 7 3 2   ◇ x x   ♣ x x

and want to force dummy to ruff so that his jack of spades cannot be finessed.

Suit preference signals also should not be given where the play of the suit preference card could be mistaken for a signal of a specific honor card holding. For example, West leads the king of diamonds against a three spade contract, and dummy and East have the following hands:

North
♠ A K J x
♡ K x x
◊ x x
♣ J x x x

Lead: ◊ K

East
♠ x x
♡ A Q J
◊ Q 8 5 2
♣ x x x x

East would like to have West shift to a heart at trick two, so that East can return a diamond and West can lead through dummy's ♡ K another time. However, East cannot play the queen of diamonds to ask for a heart shift, because if West does not have the jack of diamonds, he will interpret East's queen as promising the jack. Instead, East must content himself with playing a discouraging two of diamonds, and hoping West will figure out that a heart should be led.

Suit preference signals are most valuable in situations in which a defender is giving, or will give, his partner a ruff, and wants to show where his entry is. For example, suppose West leads a singleton heart against a spade contract, and East has

♠ x x   ♡ A 9 7 5 4 2   ◊ A K x   ♣ x x

East wins the ace of hearts, and should return the nine of hearts, his highest, to show that his re-entry is in the higher ranking of the two side suits.

East can also give a suit preference signal in the situation in which he lacks the ace of the suit of the singleton, but has an entry elsewhere. Suppose the auction has been

North	East	South	West
Pass	1 ♡	1 ♠	2 ♡
2 ♠	Pass	3 ♠	4 ♡
4 ♠	Pass	Pass	Pass

West leads the two of clubs and the dummy and East hands are as follows:

North
♠ 10 7 5
♡ 3 2
♢ 7 4 3
♣ A K Q J 4

Lead: ♣ 2

East
♠ 9 2
♡ K J 10 7 4
♢ A K
♣ 10 8 6 3

West's club deuce is clearly a singleton. If he has a trump entry he will try to reach East for a club ruff. East should attempt to show West that his fast entry is in diamonds by playing the three of clubs. If East had the ace of hearts rather than the ace of diamonds, his proper suit preference signal would be the ten of clubs. Since there can be no question of encouraging or discouraging West in the club suit, and since West cannot have any interest in how many clubs East has, both partners should recognize East's opportunity to make a suit preference signal at trick one.

Suit preference signals may also be used by a defender who is clearing a suit at a notrump contract, to indicate to his partner in which suit he has an entry to his established cards. For example, suppose West leads the four of spades against three notrump and the spade suit is distributed as follows:

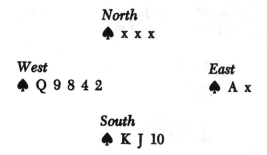

North

♠ x x x

West　　　　　　　　　　　　　*East*

♠ Q 9 8 4 2　　　　　　　　　♠ A x

South

♠ K J 10

East wins and returns a spade, on which South plays the jack, West winning with the queen. West now has a choice of the 9, the 8 or the 2 to return. These cards are equals since the two remaining spades will fall together. West can choose to play the card that best reflects his side entry. If his entry is in hearts, the highest ranking suit, he may lead the nine; if his entry is in clubs, he may lead his lowest spade, the two; if his entry is in diamonds, he may lead his middle card. West may, of course, choose to return a deceptive card in order not to help declarer decide how best to play the hand.

LAVINTHAL SIGNALS:
REVOLVING DISCARDS

Suit preference signals are useful in discarding as well as in leading or following suit.

There are two methods by which suit preference discarding signals may be given. The first is similar to the SUIT PREFERENCE SIGNALS described above, in which the rank of the card played corresponds with the rank of the suit the defender wants led. For example, suppose West leads the three of hearts against three notrump, and the dummy and East hands are as follows:

North
♠ K 8 5
♡ 6
♢ K 10 9 8 4
♣ Q 7 3 2

Lead: ♡ 3

East
♠ 10 7 3
♡ A Q 5
♢ 7 2
♣ J 10 8 6 4

East plays the queen of hearts in order to retain the ace and to lead through South at the crucial time. South leads out the queen, jack and another diamond, West holding up until the third round to try to learn where East's entry lies. Using suit preference discards, East throws the four of clubs on the third round of diamonds, indicating that West should lead the lower ranking of the remaining suits, i.e., hearts. If East held only four

610

clubs, so that he could not afford to discard a club, he could instead have discarded the ten of spades, asking for the higher ranking of the other suits, i.e., hearts.

The other method of making suit preference discards treats the suits as a complete circle, with clubs ranking above spades. Using this method, the discard of a low card in a suit calls for the lead of the next lower ranking suit; the discard of a high card calls for the lead of the next higher ranking suit. Thus, in the hand given above, East would have discarded the ten of clubs to call for the next higher ranking suit (excluding the suit being played by the declarer), i.e., hearts. Again, if East had held only four clubs and therefore could not afford a club discard, he could have thrown the spade three, calling for the suit ranking below spades.

The principal value of these suit preference discards is that they allow a clear signal to be given with a single card, even if the defender cannot afford to release a high card in the suit he wants played. And since the lead of any given suit can be called for in two ways, it is almost always possible for the defender to issue the signal without wasting a card he cannot afford.

ODD-EVEN DISCARDS

The use of odd-even cards for suit preference increases the already considerable flexibility available with Lavinthal and RE-VOLVING DISCARDS. As discussed above (*see* ODD-EVEN SIGNALS), the play of an odd card encourages the lead or continuation of that suit; and the size of an even, discouraging, card indicates which of the side suits the defender prefers.

Therefore, using odd-even discards for suit preference, the defender has three ways in which he can ask for the lead of a specific suit: he can play an odd card in the suit he wants led; or he can play the appropriately high even card from one of the side suits to call for the suit he wants; or he can play the appropriately low even card from the other side suit to call for the suit he wants. If East has, for example, a hand such as

♠ 10 7 2   ♡ A Q 4 3   ◇ 7 3   ♣ K 8 5 2

against a diamond contract, and he wants a heart lead, he has three choices. He can discard the three of hearts. Or he can discard the ten of spades, calling for the higher of the remaining side suits. Or he can discard the two of clubs, calling for the lower of the remaining side suits.

Using "revolving" odd-even discards, in which preferences are shown for touching suits, East would still have three choices. He could still play the three of hearts; or he could play the two of spades to call for the next suit below spades; or he could play the eight of clubs, calling for the next higher suit above clubs.

Supplement of Added Conventions

I

Responses to Notrump Opening Bids

SMOLEN TRANSFERS OVER
NOTRUMP OPENINGS

When the partnership has agreed to use both the STAYMAN and JACOBY TRANSFER conventions over a notrump opening, it is normal for the responder to show a game-going hand with five-four in the major suits by using Stayman. Should the opener rebid two diamonds, the responder will jump in his five-card major. (See COORDINATING JACOBY TRANSFERS WITH STAYMAN.) Using this method, the responder frequently becomes the declarer with his five-card suit as trumps.

A convention designed to make the notrump opening declarer in any major suit game is called the SMOLEN TRANSFER. Using this device, *after a negative two diamond response to his Stayman inquiry,* the responder's jump to three of a major suit shows specifically *four* cards in the suit bid, and five or six cards in the other major.

Thus in the auction

Opener	Responder
1 Notrump	2 ♣
2 ◇	3 ♠

responder shows four spades and five or six hearts. He might have a hand such as

♠ K x x x   ♡ A J x x x   ◇ x   ♣ Q x x

If the opener holds three cards in the responder's long suit, the opener bids game in that suit, becoming the declarer. With only two-card support, the opener bids three notrump.

If the responder holds a six-card major suit, over three notrump he will bid four of the suit below his long major, forcing the opener to bid four of the responder's major. Again, the opener has become the declarer.

See also EXTENDED TEXAS TRANSFERS.

The Smolen convention may also be used in response to an opening bid of two notrump or after opener's rebid of two notrump in the auction

Opener	Responder
2 ♣	2 ◇
2 Notrump	

Using Smolen, responder would rebid three clubs over two notrump, asking opener to bid a four-card major suit if he has one. If opener rebids three diamonds, responder will bid three hearts to show a five-card spade suit, or will bid three spades to show a five-card heart suit. Opener rebids three notrump if he has only two cards in the suit promised by responder or, with three cards, bids responder's suit.

EXTENDED TEXAS TRANSFERS

The Extended TEXAS TRANSFER convention is designed for use when the bidding has been opened with one notrump and responder has six cards in one major suit and four in the other. Though Texas Transfers are normally used directly over the notrump opening, Extended Texas allows responder to transfer into his long major suit at the four level after having used the STAYMAN convention in an unsuccessful effort to locate a four-four fit.

When responder has a four-card major and a six-card major, if the six-card suit is a reasonable one, such as Q J x x x x, it will usually be safer for the partnership to play the hand in the major in which responder has six cards, even if the notrump opener has four cards in the major in which responder has four. With 6-4 in the major suits, therefore, responder generally should not use Stayman to attempt to locate a four-four major suit fit.

If, however, responder's four-card suit is very strong and his six-card suit is very weak, *e.g.*,

♠ A K Q x   ♡ J x x x x x   ◇ x x   ♣ x

the hand may well produce more tricks in responder's four-card major if opener has four or five cards in that suit and has only two weak cards in the major in which responder has six cards. With such a hand, responder may begin by using Stayman; if opener bids two hearts or two spades, responder raises to game in that suit. If opener rebids two diamonds, denying a four-card major, responder may then place the contract in the major in which he has six cards.

Without a special agreement, however, when the bidding has begun

Opener	Responder
1 Notrump	2 ♣
2 ◇	

responder's jump to four hearts or four spades at his second turn would be natural. Thus, though it is often preferable for the notrump opener to be the declarer, in this standard Stayman auction responder would become the declarer.

Use of Extended Texas Transfers allows responder to make a delayed transfer in the above auction. Responder first uses Stayman and, if no four-four fit is found, he can transfer at his second turn, making opener the declarer. The delayed transfer is responder's jump, after opener bids two diamonds, to four of the suit that ranks just below his six-card suit. Thus, in the Extended Texas auction

	Opener	*Responder*
	1 Notrump	2 ♣
	2 ◇	4 ♡
	4 ♠	

responder's four heart bid is a transfer to spades.

See also SMOLEN.

JAC-MAN

The Jac-Man convention is a method of responding to one notrump using a combination of three-level JACOBY TRANSFER bids and TWO-WAY STAYMAN. It is designed principally to help responder to decide in which denomination game should be bid.

Jac-Man uses both the two club response and the two diamond response to one notrump as Stayman-type inquiries. The two club bid is used to initiate game-forcing auctions. The two diamond bid is used to initiate any game invitation in notrump or a minor suit, and game invitations in a major suit if responder does not have a five-card or longer suit.

Other responses permit responder to sign off in any suit or to invite game with a long major suit. Most of the signoffs and invitations use transfer bids.

In order to sign off in hearts or spades, responder simply bids two of his suit. Opener is not invited to bid again. In order to sign off in a minor suit, responder makes a transfer bid: two notrump transfers to three clubs, and three clubs transfers to three diamonds. These transfers are not invitational; opener should simply bid the suit shown by responder.

If responder has a one-suited hand worth an invitation to game in a major suit, he transfers into his suit at the three level. Three diamonds transfers to hearts; three hearts transfers to spades. A three spade bid by responder shows at least five cards in each minor suit and at least 8 high card points.

The complete schedule of responses is thus as follows:

2 ♣	=	Stayman, game-forcing if responder bids again
2 ◊	=	Stayman, game-invitational
2 ♡	=	natural, signoff
2 ♠	=	natural, signoff
2 NT	=	transfer to clubs, signoff
3 ♣	=	transfer to diamonds, signoff
3 ◊	=	transfer to hearts, game-invitational
3 ♡	=	transfer to spades, game-invitational
3 ♠	=	at least 5-5 in the minor suits, 8 or more HCP

After responder's bid of three diamonds or three hearts, if opener has a hand worth accepting the game invitation, he should make a bid other than three of the suit shown by responder's transfer.

The Two Diamond Response

A response of two diamonds is made on a hand worth a game invitation. Responder may have a four-card major but should not have a five-card major. With a five-card major and an invitational hand, he should use the transfer bid.

The two diamond response does not promise a four-card major. This is because a response of two notrump directly over one notrump is a transfer to clubs, and the only way in which responder can invite game in notrump is to temporize with two diamonds and follow with a bid of two notrump.

Over responder's bid of two diamonds, opener should bid a four-card major if he has one. With four cards in each major, he bids two hearts. Neither bid indicates whether opener has maximum or minimum strength.

If opener has no four-card major but has maximum strength, he rebids three notrump. When he has no four-card major and has minimum strength, he may bid three clubs or three diamonds if he has five cards in the suit and a desire to play game when responder has a fitting card in that suit. With a less promising minimum, opener bids two notrump.

For example, in the auction

[A]	*Opener*	*Responder*
	1 Notrump	2 ◇
	3 ♣	

opener might have a hand such as

| ♠ A 10 x | ♡ K Q | ◇ x x x | ♣ A Q x x x |

If responder had

| ♠ J x x | ♡ A x x x | ◇ J x x | ♣ K x x |

he would bid three notrump over three clubs. If his minor suit holdings were reversed, he would pass three clubs. If opener's suit were less substantial, *e.g.*, in a hand such as

| ♠ K J x | ♡ K x | ◇ A Q x | ♣ Q x x x x |

he would simply bid two notrump over two diamonds.

The complete schedule of opener's rebids over two diamonds is:

2 ♡	= four hearts, does not deny four spades
2 ♠	= four spades, fewer than four hearts
2 NT	= no four-card major, minimum
3 ♣	= five clubs, invites game if responder has fit
3 ◇	= five diamonds, invites game if responder has fit
3 NT	= no four-card major, maximum

Over a two heart bid by opener, responder raises hearts if he has four hearts; if he has fewer than four hearts but has four spades, he bids two spades. His two spade bid shows only a four-card suit.

Over either a two heart or a two spade bid by opener, if responder has no four-card major, he bids three clubs or three diamonds if he has a five-card suit. These bids merely invite game; they are not forcing. With neither a four-card major nor a five-card minor, responder rebids two notrump. Opener is invited to bid game with a maximum.

The Two Club Response

If responder has a hand worth a game force but is not sure in what denomination the hand should be played, he begins with a two club response. Two clubs asks opener to bid a four-card major if he has one; without a four-card major, opener must rebid two diamonds. If responder has bid two clubs with a hand such as

♠ x x x x   ♥ Q x x x   ♦ J x x x   ♣ x

he may of course pass opener's rebid. If he makes any rebid, however, the partnership is forced to game.

After opener has rebid two hearts or two spades, showing a four-card major, responder may ask for further information or he may describe his own hand. A rebid of three notrump is a natural signoff. A raise to three of opener's major suit is natural and shows slam interest. Responder's bid of a new suit over two hearts or two spades is also natural and shows a five-card or longer suit.

In order to ask for more information over opener's bid of two hearts or two spades, responder bids two notrump. Thus, if the auction has begun

[B]	*Opener*	*Responder*
	1 Notrump	2 ♣
	2 ♥ or 2 ♠	

responder's rebids are as follows:

2 ♠ (over 2 ♥) = five or more spades
2 NT = asks opener to describe his hand further
3 ♣ = five or more clubs
3 ♦ = five or more diamonds
3 ♥ (over 2 ♥) = heart fit, invites slam exploration
3 ♥ (over 2 ♠) = five or more hearts
3 ♠ (over 2 ♠) = spade fit, invites slam exploration

620

Following responder's two notrump inquiry, opener bids another four-card suit if he has one; otherwise he bids three notrump.

When opener has bid two diamonds, denying a four-card major, responder may bid two hearts to ask opener to describe his distribution further, or he may describe his own hand. If responder has a five-card or longer major, he shows it by means of an artificial bid. He bids two spades to show a heart suit; he bids two notrump to show a spade suit. He jumps to four clubs or four diamonds to show a singleton or void in that minor and at least five cards in each major. In order to show a five-card or longer minor, responder bids three of his suit. Responder's jumps to three hearts or three spades show a singleton or void in that major and at least four cards in each minor.

The complete schedule of responder's rebids after opener has denied a four-card major is thus as follows:

2 ♡ = request for opener to describe his hand further
2 ♠ = five or more hearts
2 NT = five or more spades
3 ♣ = five or more clubs
3 ◇ = five or more diamonds
3 ♡ = singleton or void in hearts, at least four clubs, and at least four diamonds
3 ♠ = singleton or void in spades, at least four clubs, and at least four diamonds
3 NT = natural
4 ♣ = singleton or void in clubs, at least five hearts, and at least five spades
4 ◇ = singleton or void in diamonds, at least five hearts, and at least five spades

Over responder's rebid of two spades, showing length in hearts, or two notrump, showing length in spades, opener bids as follows. If he has three-card support, he raises; he bids four of responder's suit if he has a poor hand, or three with a hand rich in aces and kings. If opener has a doubleton in responder's suit and has a five-card minor, he bids his minor. If responder's suit is hearts and opener's distribution is 3-2-4-4, he bids two notrump with a maximum, or three notrump with a minimum. If responder's suit is spades, and opener's distribution is 2-3-4-4, he may bid three hearts to show a maximum and three notrump to show a minimum.

When opener has denied a four-card major and responder has asked for further information, *i.e.*, the auction has begun

[C]   *Opener*   *Responder*
      1 Notrump   2 ♣
      2 ◊   2 ♡

opener describes his distribution as follows:

    2 ♠   = 3-3-3-4 or 3-3-4-3 distribution
    2 NT = four clubs and four diamonds
    3 ♣   = five clubs
    3 ◊   = five diamonds

If, after this two spade bid by opener, responder is interested in having opener identify his four-card suit, he may bid two notrump. Opener then bids three clubs with four clubs, or three diamonds with four diamonds.

If, over opener's two notrump bid after the auction has begun as in C, responder wants to know opener's precise major suit distribution, he may rebid three clubs. Opener then bids the major in which he has three cards.

See also DOUBLE-BARRELED STAYMAN; TRACER BIDS.

TRACER BIDS

The Tracer Bid is a conventional response to a one notrump opening that is designed principally to help the partnership determine whether the final contract should be three notrump or five of a minor suit. Used when responder has a singleton or void that may make a notrump contract hazardous, the convention also permits exploration for a four-four major suit fit.

The Tracer bid promises a hand worth a game force, but it denies strong slam interest. The most common distribution for the bid is 5-4-3-1; the five-card suit must be a minor. Hands with 4-4-4-1 distribution are also appropriate. The Tracer bid is not made with a hand that contains two five-card or longer suits.

For partnerships that do not use two-level transfer bids, the Tracer bid is two diamonds. For partnerships that use two diamonds as a transfer, the Tracer bid is two spades. In either event, the Tracer bid invites opener to bid two notrump to ask responder to identify his short suit.

Over two notrump, responder bids his short suit at the three level. If he is short in spades, he has two bids available: three spades and three notrump. He bids three spades to say that he has a four-card heart suit; he bids three notrump to say that he has only three hearts. Responder's rebids over opener's two notrump inquiry are thus as follows:

3 ♣	=	singleton or void in clubs
3 ♢	=	singleton or void in diamonds
3 ♡	=	singleton or void in hearts
3 ♠	=	singleton or void in spades, with four hearts
3 NT	=	singleton or void in spades, three hearts

After responder identifies his short suit, the bidding proceeds naturally. When responder has bid three clubs or three diamonds, he usually has five cards in the other minor, with four-three in the major suits. When responder has bid three hearts, his spade length is unspecified. Over any of these bids, opener may bid three notrump with the short suit stopped, or he may bid a four-card major if he has one, seeking a four-four major fit.

Since responder's use of the Tracer bid denies strong slam interest, opener need not bid two notrump if he has all suits well stopped. He may sign off directly over the Tracer bid by bidding three notrump.

Use of the Tracer bid does not interfere with responder's use of two clubs as STAYMAN. In order to explore for a four-four major suit fit with no singleton or with slam interest, responder may still begin by bidding two clubs. Use of Tracer bids does, however, foreclose use of any two-way

Stayman convention. Or, when the partnership has agreed to use JACOBY TRANSFER BIDS, the designation of two spades as a Tracer bid precludes use of that bid as a transfer to clubs or as JACOBY FOR THE MINOR SUITS.

See also DOUBLE-BARRELED STAYMAN; SPLINTERS TO AVOID NOTRUMP; JAC-MAN; TRUSCOTT TWO DIAMONDS.

RELAYS — IN GENERAL

A relay bid is a bid that tells nothing about the bidder's hand but that requires or permits the bidder's partner to describe his hand further. The relay usually is continued by a bid by the relayer — called the "captain" — of the cheapest suit over the disclosure bid of his partner — called the "puppet." The mechanism is thus quite simple. The responses, however, run the gamut in artificiality and degrees of complexity.

Many popular conventions use relays that require relatively simple responses. In the STAYMAN convention, for example, two clubs is a relay asking the opening notrump bidder to describe his hand further. Opener's response in a major suit is a natural bid; his response of two diamonds is artificial. In the more common versions of Stayman, the opener's response ends the relay sequence; further bids by both players are more or less natural. Similarly, in the LEBENSOHL convention, in which a two notrump bid forces a three-club response, the three club bid is a relay, allowing the two notrump bidder to describe his hand relatively naturally. Likewise, in response to a weak two-bid, a two notrump bid that asks opener to show his strength, or his suit texture, or side suit features or singletons, etc., is a relay. Some of the rebids are relatively natural; others are entirely artificial.

Usually the relay bid is a cheap bid, designed to conserve bidding room, but this is not always the case. A BLACKWOOD bid of four notrump, for example, whether bid over four spades or over one spade, is a relay bid that does not describe the Blackwood bidder's hand but merely asks his partner for information.

The relay approach is currently gaining popularity as a means of allowing the partnership to bid accurately at all levels of the auction and over any opening bid or response. A premise of such relay bidding is that, the lower the level of the bidding, the higher the number of different hands that can safely be the basis of a single bid. This is because there remains room for another relay to clarify further which of the various possible holdings, of the type already shown, is actually held. The desire to allow all hand types to be shown at a low level normally will mean that virtually all of the puppet's responses are artificial.

Relays are most useful when one member of the partnership has promised a hand of a certain type, e. g., a notrump-type hand of a certain range, or a hand containing a long suit. Relays enable the partner of such a player, or sometimes even the player himself, to make cheap bids that cause his partner to give a complete description of his hand. Since repeated questioning can be conducted using cheap bids as relays, relays are often conducted in series, one series seeking information as to the puppet's distribution, one seeking information as to his strength, and another asking about his control cards. The order in which these series are pursued may vary according to what type of hand (e. g., balanced or unbalanced, one-suited or multi-suited) has triggered the initiation of the relay sequence, and whether the captain is the partner of the player who caused the relay to be initiated or is the relayer himself. *See, e. g.*, ULTIMATE CLUB.

A number of conventions that use relays are included in this volume. Some of the more venerable ones are mentioned above. Among the newer are EXTENDED LEBENSOHL; FOURTH SUIT FORCING AND ARTIFICIAL; PUPPET STAYMAN; RELAYS AFTER ONE DIAMOND-TWO CLUBS; RELAY BLACKWOOD; SIMPLIFIED RELAY STAYMAN; TRUSCOTT TWO DIAMONDS; ULTIMATE CLUB.

PUPPET STAYMAN

Standard use of the STAYMAN convention usually results in the opening notrump bidder becoming the declarer only after having disclosed his distribution, thereby having given perhaps valuable information to the defenders. The Puppet Stayman convention, used in conjunction with JACOBY TRANSFER BIDS, is a modification of Stayman that is designed principally to allow the requisite disclosures to be made by the responder, whose hand will be tabled as the dummy. A secondary benefit of the convention is that it allows a player to open one notrump with a five-card major suit with less danger of missing a 5-3 fit, because responder may, without himself having a four-card major suit, ask opener if he has a five-card major.

Puppet Stayman uses the two club response to one notrump to initiate a game-invitational search for an eight-card major suit fit. However, rather than asking opener to bid a four-card major suit if he has one, it allows opener to bid a major suit only if it contains five cards. If opener has no five-card major suit, he is required to bid two diamonds.

The two diamond rebid is a relay requiring responder to show his own major suit distribution as follows:

> 2♡ = four spades, fewer than four hearts
>
> 2♠ = four hearts, fewer than four spades
>
> 2NT = four hearts and four spades; invites game
>
> 3♡ = four hearts, four or five spades; forces game
>
> 3♠ = four spades, five hearts; forces game
>
> 3NT = no four card major suit; game strength

Note that in showing a four-card major, responder normally bids the other major (or notrump), in order to allow opener, if he fits the major promised by responder, to become the declarer in that suit. Similarly, in showing 5-4 in the major suits, responder jumps in the suit in which he has four cards, thereby increasing the likelihood that opener will become the declarer, since opener will support the other major with either three or four cards.

After any of responder's above bids, opener places the final contract, bidding game if he wishes to accept the game invitation.

The Puppet two club bid may also be used if responder has simply a very weak hand with length in diamonds. In this event, he will pass a two diamond rebid by opener. If, instead, opener bids two hearts or two spades, responder may bid three diamonds, which opener must pass.

Partnerships that use an immediate response of two notrump to the one notrump opening as an artificial bid, *see*, *e. g.*, TWO NOTRUMP RESPONSE AS RELAY TO THREE CLUBS; BARON TWO NOTRUMP RESPONSE, often use responder's initial two club bid followed by his rebid of two notrump as a game invitation with a balanced hand. To coordinate this style with Puppet Stayman, the partnership may modify Puppet Stayman to allow responder's two heart bid over two diamonds to show *either* four spades or the balanced game try with no four-card major suit. If opener rebids two spades, responder will bid two notrump with the latter hand. If responder has four spades he will either pass or raise.

> (Opener)
> ♠ Q J x   ♡ Q x x x x   ◊ A x   ♣ A K x
>
> (Responder)
> ♠ x x   ♡ x x x   ◊ K J x x x x   ♣ x x

With these hands, the auctions might go

Opener	*Responder*
1 Notrump	2♣
2♡	Pass

Responder intended to pass a two diamond bid by opener, but, having located an eight card major suit fit, he passes.

In an auction that has begun

Opener	*Responder*
1 Notrump	2♣
2◊	2♡

in which responder's two heart bid has shown four spades and a game invitational hand, opener would jump to four spades with a hand such as

> [A]   ♠ K x x x   ♡ A x x x   ◊ A K x   ♣ K x

but he would sign off at two spades with

> [B]   ♠ K x x x   ♡ Q x x   ◊ A K x   ♣ K x x

Responder might have a hand such as

[C]   ♠ Q J x x   ♡ x x x   ◊ Q x x   ♣ A x x

If the partnership is using the modification of Puppet Stayman that gives a two-way meaning to responder's two heart bid, *i. e.*, allows it to show either a four-card spade suit or a game invitation in notrump with no four-card major suit, opener would accept the game invitation with hand [A] by jumping to three spades. Responder is forced to bid a game, either in spades if he has four spades, or in notrump if he has fewer.

FIVE-CARD STAYMAN

The STAYMAN convention, as originally designed, permits the partnership to locate a four-four major suit fit after an opening bid of one notrump. It also allows the partnership to find an eight-card major fit when responder has a five-card major and opener has three-card support. The Five-Card Stayman convention is a device that permits the partnership to locate its eight-card fit when opener has the five-card major and responder has the three-card support.

Responder uses Five-Card Stayman when he has a game-going hand with three cards in one or both major suits and has a singleton or doubleton, *e.g.*,

	♠ Q 10 x	♡ A x x	◇ A x	♣ x x x x x
or	♠ A J x	♡ x	◇ x x x x x	♣ K Q x x

To ask opener whether he has a five-card major, responder jumps to three diamonds directly over one notrump.

In response to three diamonds, opener rebids a five-card major if he has one. In addition, opener should treat a very strong four-card major, *e.g.*, A K J x, as if it were a five-card suit, and bid that suit in response to three diamonds. If opener has no five-card major and no very strong four-card major, he rebids three notrump.

Since opener is to bid a strong four-card major in response to three diamonds, responder may use Five-Card Stayman not only with hands that contain a three-card major but also with hands that contain a weak four-card major. The traditional two club Stayman bid may be reserved for use with at least a reasonable four-card major.

Using Five-Card Stayman, if opener and responder had hands such as

Opener

| ♠ A K J x | ♡ K x x | ◇ x x | ♣ K Q J x |

Responder

| ♠ Q 10 x | ♡ A 10 x | ◇ A x | ♣ x x x x x |

they would bid as follows:

Opener	Responder
1 Notrump	3 ◇
3 ♠	4 ♠

The Five-Card Stayman convention is not used if the one notrump opening has been followed by an overcall. In such an auction, responder's three diamond bid is more useful for other purposes, *e.g.*, as a natural forcing or competitive bid or as part of a transfer convention, such as JACOBY TRANSFERS OVER OVERCALL.

See also PUPPET STAYMAN; BACK-DOOR STAYMAN.

BACK-DOOR STAYMAN

This modification of the STAYMAN convention allows the partnership to locate, in addition to the 4-4 major suit fits located by more traditional Stayman agreements, a 4-3 major suit fit which may provide the only makable game. The mechanism is to have the notrump opener respond to the two club call not by showing a four-card major but by showing a suit in which he is short.

In answer to responder's two club bid, opener bids as follows. If he has no doubleton, *i.e.*, he is 4-3-3-3, he bids at the three level in the suit below his four-card suit. (A three spade bid shows four clubs.) If opener has a doubleton, he bids that suit at the two level; if his doubleton is in clubs, he shows it by bidding two notrump.

Over opener's doubleton-showing bid, responder may ask for further information by making the cheapest bid, *e.g.*,

Opener	Responder
1 Notrump	2♣
2♡ (doubleton)	2♠ (asking further)

Opener completes the description of his distribution as follows. If his shape is 4-4-3-2, he now bids the suit in which he holds three cards, unless that suit is the one in which responder has just made his inquiry. In the latter case, opener shows a tripleton in the asking suit by bidding notrump. In the above auction, over responder's two-spade inquiry, opener's bid of three clubs or three diamonds would show three cards in the suit bid; his bid of two notrump would show three spades. Such a rebid plus his earlier identification of his doubleton reveals to responder the two suits in which opener has four cards.

If opener has opened one notrump with a five-card minor suit, he identifies his long suit as clubs by rebidding the suit in which he has shown a doubleton; or he shows that his five-card suit is diamonds by making the cheapest otherwise meaningless bid. In the above auction, over two spades, a bid by opener of three hearts would show a five-card club suit; a bid of three spades (otherwise meaningless because a bid of two notrump would have shown three spades) would show a five-card diamond suit.

Opener and responder might have the following hands.

(Opener)
♠ K Q x   ♡ A x x   ◊ A J x x x   ♣ Q x

(Responder)
♠ A x x x   ♡ K J x x   ◊ K x   ♣ x x x

Using Back-Door Stayman, the auction would proceed

Opener	Responder
1 Notrump	2♣ ("Where is your shortness?")
2 Notrump ("Clubs")	3♣ ("Where else!")
3 Notrump ("Nowhere")	

Having identified his short suit as clubs, opener rebids three notrump to show that he has five diamonds. Responder will now attempt to guess which of the partnership's two 4-3 major suits fits will give it the better play for game.

SIMPLIFIED RELAY STAYMAN

Simplified Relay Stayman is a system of relays initiated by a two club Stayman-type inquiry in response to a one notrump opening. Responder typically has a hand worth at least a game invitation, although he may use the two club bid with a classic three-suited bust such as

♠ xxxx ♡ xxx ◇ xxxxx ♣ x

Opener responds to the two club inquiry as follows:

2◇ = fewer than four hearts; says nothing about spade length

2♡ = four or more hearts, fewer than four spades

2♠ = four hearts and four spades

After opener's two diamond rebid, all bids by responder below game, other than two hearts, are natural and invite opener to bid game with a maximum. A bid of two hearts by responder is artificial and is forcing to game. The two heart bid does not show anything about responder's hearts but merely asks opener to rebid naturally. If opener has four spades, he bids two spades; if he has a five-card minor suit, he bids it at the three level. If he has neither of the above, he bids two notrump. All bids by responder over two notrump, except a three club bid, are natural. The three club bid, after opener has bid two notrump, asks opener to indicate his precise distribution. He does so as follows:

3◇ = four diamonds, three cards in every other suit

3♡ = four cards in each minor, three hearts, two spades

3♠ = four cards in each minor, three spades, two hearts

3NT = four clubs, three cards in every other suit

After opener has bid two hearts in reply to the two club inquiry, most of responder's bids, other than two spades, are natural and invite game. Responder's bid of two spades is artificial and forcing to game. The bid says nothing about responder's holding in spades. Opener bids three hearts if he has a five-card heart suit, or bids a four-card minor suit if he has one. If he has neither of the above, he rebids two notrump. Responder's bids, over opener's two hearts, of two notrump, three of a minor suit, and three hearts are all natural and invite game in the denomination bid. A jump to three spades, however, is a SPLINTER RAISE of hearts, showing a singleton spade.

After opener has bid two spades, showing four cards in each major, responder's bid of two notrump denies a four-card major and invites opener to bid game in notrump. Responder's bid of three clubs over two spades is artificial, saying nothing about clubs, and asks opener to identify his three-card suit. Opener complies by bidding three diamonds with a tripleton diamond, or three hearts with a tripleton club.

Examples

	Opener	Responder
[A]	1 Notrump	2♣
	2◇	2 Notrump
[B]	1 Notrump	2♣
	2◇	2♡
	2 Notrump	3♣
	3♡	

In auction [A], opener's two diamond bid showed that he did not have a four-card heart suit. Responder's two notrump bid invites game in notrump; responder may or may not have four hearts.

In auction [B], all of responder's bids were relay bids. Opener's sequence has shown that he has two spades, three hearts, four diamonds, and four clubs.

TRUSCOTT TWO DIAMONDS

The Truscott Two Diamond convention uses a two diamond response to a one notrump opening bid to initiate a relay structure by which opener may describe his hand. Responder should have a hand worth a game force. He asks opener first to describe his exact distribution. After each rebid by opener, the cheapest bid by responder is another relay, *i.e.*, an entirely artificial bid that merely asks opener to continue his description. *See* RELAYS — IN GENERAL.

Opener's first rebid shows his general pattern. A bid of two notrump shows 4-3-3-3 distribution, but does not identify the long suit. Over a further relay (3♣) opener bids the suit in which he has four cards.

If opener's first bid is in a suit, he shows either 4-4-3-2 or 5-3-3-2. Assuming that after each of opener's rebids responder continues the relay, opener starts to describe his 4-4-3-2 distributions as follows:

—two of a major followed by three of a minor shows four cards in each suit bid
—two hearts followed by two notrump shows four cards in each major suit
—three diamonds shows four cards in each minor suit.

After opener has revealed the location of his two four-card suits, a further relay by responder asks where opener's doubleton is. Opener reveals this in steps; he bids the first step if his doubleton is in the lower of the suits he has not shown, or bids the second step if his doubleton is in the higher-ranking.

Example:

Opener	Responder
1 Notrump	2 ◊
2 ♡	2 ♠
3 ◊	3 ♡
3 Notrump	

Opener has shown four hearts, four diamonds, and a doubleton spade.

Opener shows 5-3-3-2 distribution as follows. With five hearts, spades, or clubs, he makes the cheapest bid in his long suit. After a further relay by responder, opener bids a major suit or notrump at the three level. The suit he bids shows the location of his doubleton, with the lowest step, *i.e.*, *three hearts;* showing that the doubleton is in the lowest-ranking side suit; three spades shows a doubleton in the middle-ranking side suit; and three notrump shows a doubleton in the highest-ranking side suit.

If opener has 5-3-3-2 with a five-card diamond suit, he shows it and simultaneously reveals the rest of his distribution by jumping to three hearts, three spades, or three notrump directly over the two diamond relay. Again, the suit bid corresponds with the location of the doubleton, with three hearts showing the lowest possible doubleton (clubs) and three notrump showing the highest (spades).

After opener has completed showing his precise distribution, if there is at least one spare bid below three notrump, the cheapest such bid may be used to ask opener whether he has a minimum or a maximum.

If responder does not require a complete description of opener's distribution, he may earlier ask opener about strength by initiating a new relay series. He does this by making a bid that is one step above the normal relay bid.

Example:

Opener	Responder
1 Notrump	2 ◊
3 ♣	3 ♡

Opener has shown five clubs; a three diamond relay would ask where his doubleton is. The three heart bid instead asks about opener's strength. In answer to any such strength inquiry, opener responds in steps, bidding the first step with a minimum, or the second step with a maximum.

If at any stage of these proceedings responder makes a game bid, that becomes the final contract. Opener is not allowed to bid again. If, instead, responder breaks the relay by bidding, below the game level, a suit other than the ones that would ask about opener's distribution or strength, responder designates this as the trump suit and shows a desire to explore for slam.

Example:

Opener	Responder
1 Notrump	2 ◊
2 ♡	3 ♠

Responder has broken the chain of relays that would ask opener about distribution, and he has not bid the next higher step that would have asked opener about his strength. This below-game bid by responder sets the trump suit and now asks opener to describe his "key cards."

There are five key cards: the four aces and the king of the suit responder has set at trumps. Opener shows how many of these controls he has by using Roman Key Card Blackwood-type responses:

first step = 0 or 3 key cards

second step = 1 or 4 key cards

third step = 2 key cards without the queen of the agreed suit

fourth step = 2 key cards with the queen of the agreed suit

If the relays have continued until opener has disclosed his complete distribution and/or his strength, and his last bid has been either three spades or three notrump, if responder wants to explore for slam, he must take care not to bid three notrump or four of a major suit, since any of those bids would end the auction. At this stage, a four club bid by responder requires opener to bid four diamonds; responder may then bid four of a major suit to set that suit as trumps and to require opener to show his key cards in accordance with the above key-card steps. If, instead of bidding a major suit over opener's forced four-diamond bid, responder bids four notrump, he sets clubs as trumps and initiates the same key-card inquiry.

Example:

Opener	Responder
1 Notrump	2 ♢
2 ♠ (= four spades)	2 Notrump
3 ♢ (= four diamonds)	3 ♡
3 ♠ (= two clubs)	4 ♣
4 ♢ (forced)	4 ♡ (trumps)
5 ♢ (= two key cards, plus queen of hearts)	

If Opponents Interfere after Two Diamonds

If the two diamond bid is doubled, a pass shows a weak five-card diamond suit and a redouble shows a good five-card diamond suit; other calls by opener are in accordance with the normal relay scheme. If there is a double of any later relay bid, opener passes to show that he would have bid the cheapest step, or redoubles to show that he would have bid the second step. If any bid by opener is doubled, responder's redouble shows a desire to play the hand there; a pass is a further relay.

If there is an overcall over any relay bid, opener passes if he would have bid the first step, or doubles if he would have bid the second step. If there is an overcall over a bid by opener, responder's double is for penalties, and a pass is a further relay.

The Truscott Two Diamond convention cannot be combined with such conventions as CONFIT or JACOBY TRANSFER BIDS.

GERARD THREE-DIAMOND MINOR SUIT SLAM TRY

The Gerard Three-Diamond Slam Try convention uses an artificial three diamond rebid by a responder who has used STAYMAN in response to a one notrump opening. Over any of opener's responses to Stayman, the three diamond rebid by responder suggests that the partnership may have slam in a minor suit if a fit is found.

Opposite a 15-17 point notrump opening, responder's three diamond bid promises a hand worth at least 14 HCP, with at least one four-card or longer minor. Responder might hold any of the following hands:

[A]	♠ A x x	[B]	♠ x x	[C]	♠ A x
	♡ x		♡ A x x x		♡ K Q x
	◇ K Q x x		◇ A K x x		◇ J 10 x x
	♣ A J x x x		♣ K x x		♣ A K x x

In response to the three-diamond bid, opener describes his distribution. A bid of three hearts promises four clubs and denies four diamonds; a bid of three spades shows four diamonds and denies four clubs. The meaning of opener's rebid of three notrump depends on what opener has shown in response to Stayman. If he has *denied* four-card major, his three notrump bid shows at least four cards in each minor; if he has *promised* a four-card major, and hence cannot have two four-card minors, his three notrump bid shows that he has no four-card minor. Opener's bids of four clubs and four diamonds are natural and show five-card suits.

Opener's complete schedule of rebids over three diamonds is as follows:

3 ♡	= four clubs, with fewer than four diamonds
3 ♠	= four diamonds, with fewer than four clubs
3 NT	= either both minors or neither minor
4 ♣	= five-card club suit
4 ◇	= five-card diamond suit
4 ♡	= six-card club suit
4 ♠	= six-card diamond suit

Responder's Further Rebids

After opener's response to three diamonds, most of responder's rebids are natural. A raise of a minor suit shown by opener promises a fit. The raise indicates, however, that responder's controls or distribution are not sufficient to permit him to take control of the auction. Responder's bid of a minor suit not shown by opener promises five cards in that suit.

Responder's rebids in notrump show varying degrees of slam interest. His non-jump bid in notrump is not forcing and suggests that his slam interest is only mild. A jump to four notrump shows strong slam interest. A jump to five notrump is forcing and asks opener to decide whether the slam should be played in notrump or in a minor. *See also* FIVE NOTRUMP AS CHOICE OF SLAMS.

Responder's bid of the cheaper major suit is ROMAN KEY CARD BLACKWOOD (RKCB). If opener has promised both minors, responder's bid of the cheaper major is RKCB agreeing on clubs, and his bid of the more remote major is RKCB agreeing on diamonds.

Using these methods, if opener and responder held

Opener
♠ K x x   ♡ A J   ◇ K J x x   ♣ K 10 x x
Responder
♠ A x   ♡ K 10 x x   ◇ A x   ♣ Q J x x x

they would bid as follows:

Opener	Responder
1 Notrump	2 ♣
2 ◇	3 ◇
3 Notrump	4 ♡
5 ♣	6 ♣

Since opener showed no four-card major in response to two clubs, his three notrump rebid promises both minor suits. Responder's bid of four hearts agrees on clubs as trumps and asks opener how many of the five key cards (the four aces plus the king of clubs) he has. Opener's five club bid shows two key cards without the queen of trumps.

See also JACOBY FOR THE MINOR SUITS; SHARPLES.

THREE OF OTHER MAJOR AS SLAM TRY

When the bidding has been opened one notrump and the partnership has used the STAYMAN convention and located a four-four major suit fit, if responder knows that the partnership has a total of some 30-32 points, he may want to try for slam. On some hands, a SPLINTER bid, identifying a singleton or void in responder's hand, will be appropriate. On others, responder may need only to find out about opener's aces and can effectively use the GERBER convention. If responder has a balanced hand with good controls, slam may depend on opener's distribution.

When the partnership uses JACOBY TRANSFER BIDS and has agreed that responder will use a transfer bid with any hand that contains a five-card major, *but see* COORDINATING JACOBY TRANSFERS WITH STAYMAN, responder's bid of three of the unbid major after opener has shown a major suit in a Stayman auction, *i.e.*,

[A]	*Opener*	*Responder*		[B]	*Opener*	*Responder*
	1 Notrump	2 ♣			1 Notrump	2 ♣
	2 ♠	3 ♡			2 ♡	3 ♠

his bid of three hearts in auction A and his bid of three spades in auction B, are idle bids.

Some partnerships agree to use an otherwise idle bid of three of the unbid majors as an artificial slam try. The bid initiates a process by which opener is to reveal his distribution and his strength.

When Spades Are Trumps

When the auction has begun as in A, responder's three heart bid over two spades asks opener to identify his doubleton if he has one, or to reveal his point count if he has no doubleton. If opener has a doubleton, he bids one of the first three steps over the asking bid. The first step shows a doubleton club, the second a doubleton diamond, and the third a doubleton heart.

If opener has no doubletons, *i.e.*, he has four spades with 4-3-3-3 distribution, he bids the fourth, fifth, or sixth step to show his precise point count. Thus, opener's rebids after spades have been agreed and responder has bid three hearts are:

3 ♠	=	doubleton club
3 NT	=	doubleton diamond
4 ♣	=	doubleton heart
4 ♢	=	4-3-3-3 distribution, minimum strength
4 ♡	=	4-3-3-3 distribution, medium strength
4 ♠	=	4-3-3-3 distribution, maximum strength

If opener has doubletons in both hearts and one of the minors, he shows his minor-suit doubleton first.

When the partnership has agreed that if opener has both four spades and four hearts he will bid two hearts in response to Stayman, opener's two spade bid denies four hearts. Thus, when opener has bid two spades and later shows a doubleton in clubs or diamonds, his second four-card suit, if he has one, is the other minor. The possibility remains that opener has no second four-card suit but instead has a five-card major with 3-3-2 distribution in the other suits. When the auction has begun

Opener	Responder
1 Notrump	2 ♣
2 ♠	3 ♡
3 ♠ or 3 Notrump	

responder's cheapest bid over three spades or three notrump asks opener to specify whether he has minimum or maximum strength and whether he has a side four-card minor, or a side five-card minor, or a five-card major. Opener's rebids are:

First step	=	minimum strength, side four-card minor
Second step	=	maximum strength, side four-card minor
Third step	=	minimum strength, five-card spade suit
Fourth step	=	maximum strength, five-card spade suit
Fifth step	=	minimum strength, side five-card minor
Sixth step	=	maximum strength, side five-card minor

Some partnerships agree that in response to Stayman, opener will bid two spades with four cards in each major. Within this framework, if opener bids three spades or three notrump over the three heart slam try, showing a doubleton in clubs or diamonds, respectively, opener has not revealed the relative length of hearts and the other minor. Over one of these bids, responder may bid the cheapest suit to request identification of opener's side suit, if any. Opener shows whether he has four-card minor, or a four-card heart suit, or a five-card spade suit, and shows his strength, as follows:

First step   = four cards in other minor, minimum strength
Second step   = four hearts, minimum strength
Third step   = four cards in other minor, maximum strength
Fourth step   = four hearts, maximum strength
Fifth step   = five spades, minimum strength
Sixth step   = five cards in other minor, minimum strength
Seventh step = five cards in other minor, maximum strength
Eighth step   = five spades, maximum

Whether or not opener's two spade bid in response to Stayman denies four hearts, when opener has bid four clubs in response to three hearts, showing a doubleton heart, responder can draw no inferences as to the relative length of opener's minor suit holdings. Responder bids four diamonds to ask opener to reveal his side suit, if any, and whether he is minimum or maximum. Opener rebids as follows:

4 ♡ = four clubs, minimum strength
4 ♠ = four diamonds, minimum strength
4 NT = five spades, minimum strength
5 ♣ = four clubs, maximum strength
5 ◊ = four diamonds, maximum strength
5 ♡ = five spades, maximum strength

If, after any of opener's bids in response to three hearts, responder makes a bid other than the cheapest bid or the cheapest bid in spades, he asks only about opener's strength. In response, opener bids the cheapest step if he has a minimum, or the second step if he has a maximum.

If opener and responder held the following hands

Opener
♠ A J x x   ♡ K Q x   ◊ K x   ♣ K x x x
Responder
♠ K Q 10 x   ♡ x x   ◊ A x x   ♣ A Q x x

the bidding would proceed

Opener	Responder
1 Notrump	2 ♣
2 ♠ (denying 4 hearts)	3 ♡
3 Notrump	4 ♣
4 ♡	6 ♠

644

Opener's three notrump bid shows a doubleton diamond. In response to the four club request for further information, opener bids four hearts to show 4-3-2-4 distribution with maximum strength.

When Hearts Are Trumps

When hearts have been agreed as trumps, responder's slam try will be three spades, and opener will have less room below the game level to describe his hand. Thus, opener will be unable to show his complete pattern; nor will he give as detailed information as to his strength.

When the auction has begun

Opener	Responder
1 Notrump	2 ♣
2 ♡	3 ♠

opener shows his distribution as follows:

3 NT = doubleton club
4 ♣ = doubleton diamond
4 ◇ = doubleton spade
4 ♡ = 3-4-3-3 distribution, minimum strength
4 ♠ = 3-4-3-3 distribution, maximum strength

If the partnership has agreed that with both four spades and four hearts opener will bid two hearts in response to Stayman, responder will be able to draw no inferences, from opener's disclosure of any specific doubleton, as to the relative length of his remaining suits.

If, however, it has agreed that opener's two heart bid denies four spades, more information is available. When opener's two heart bid has denied four spades, his rebid of three notrump or four clubs, showing a doubleton club or a doubleton diamond, respectively, reveals that his side suit, assuming he has only four hearts, is the other minor.

Over any of the doubleton-showing bids, responder may bid four hearts to sign off. However, since he has already shown slam interest, opener is allowed to bid over the signoff with maximum strength principally in aces and kings.

After any of opener's shape-showing bids except four diamonds (showing a doubleton spade), if responder wants to ask about opener's strength, he makes the cheapest bid. If opener has bid four diamonds, responder must bid four spades to inquire. In answer to these inquiries, opener bids the first step with minimum strength, or the second step with a maximum.

The same type of exploration is available after an opening bid of two notrump.

GAME FORCING RELAY

Whereas the TRUSCOTT TWO DIAMOND convention cannot be coordinated with JACOBY TRANSFER BIDS, an alternative system of game-forcing relays in response to a one notrump opening can be used with Jacoby Transfers with some modifications of the latter. The Game Forcing Relay uses the sequence

	Opener	Responder
[A]	1 Notrump	2 ◊
	2 ♡	2 ♠

to initiate a relay, and hence uses the sequence

	Opener	Responder
[B]	1 Notrump	2 ◊
	2 ♡	3 ♠

as a means of substituting for the loss of auction [A] as a transfer sequence.

The two diamond bid by responder says nothing about his diamonds and although it ostensibly transfers to hearts, a rebid of two spades by responder cancels that message and initiates instead the relay sequences.

The first relay chain asks opener to show his distribution. The relays are perpetuated by responder's cheapest bid over a disclosure bid by opener. At any point of the relay auction, if responder bids three notrump (even if that is the cheapest bid) or the non-cheapest game, it is a sign-off. Opener should not bid again. Any bid below game by responder of a suit other than the cheapest also breaks the distribution-showing relay chain and asks opener to begin showing his controls.

Opener's Distribution-Showing Bids

After a Game Forcing Relay has been commenced, using auction [A], opener shows his hand pattern as follows.

> 2NT = four spades, plus another four-card suit
>
> 3 ♣ = four hearts, plus a four or five-card minor suit
>
> 3 ◊ = five diamonds; possibly four clubs
>
> 3 ♡ = four cards in each minor suit, or 4-3-3-3 (any)
>
> 3 ♠ = five clubs, two spades, 3-3 in red suits

3NT = five clubs, two hearts, 3-3 in other suits

4♣ = five clubs, two diamonds, 3-3 in majors

4♢ = five clubs, four diamonds

After opener has bid three hearts, responder may relay again (3♠) to ask for clarification. Opener rebids

3NT = three spades, two hearts, 4-4 in minors

4♣ = two spades, three hearts, 4-4 in minors

4♢ = four spades, 3-3-3 in other suits

4♡ = four hearts, 3-3-3 in other suits

4♠ = four diamonds, 3-3-3 in other suits

4NT = four clubs, 3-3-3 in other suits

After opener has bid three diamonds, showing five diamonds, responder may relay (3♡) to learn the remainder of opener's distribution. Opener bids as follows:

3♠ = two spades, 3-3 in clubs and hearts

3NT = two hearts, 3-3 in black suits

4♣ = two clubs, 3-3 in majors

4♢ = two spades, two hearts, four clubs

After opener has bid three clubs, showing four hearts and a longish minor suit, responder's relay (3♢) asks for further information, which is given in one or two steps:

3♡, then 3 Notrump = three spades, four hearts, four diamonds, two clubs

3♡, then 4♣ = two spades, four hearts, four diamonds, three clubs

3♠ = three spades, four hearts, two diamonds, four clubs

3 Notrump = two spades, four hearts, three diamonds, four clubs

4♣ = two spades, four hearts, five diamonds, two clubs

4♢ = two spades, four hearts, two diamonds, five clubs

647

After opener has bid two notrump, showing four spades and another longish suit, responder's relay (3♣) asks for clarification, which is given in one or two steps:

3◇, then 3♠ = four spades, four hearts, three diamonds, two clubs

3◇, then three notrump = four spades, four hearts, two diamonds, three clubs

3♡, then 3 notrump = four spades, three hearts, four diamonds, two clubs

3♡, then 4♣ = four spades, two hearts, four diamonds, three clubs

3♠ = four spades, three hearts, two diamonds, four clubs

3 Notrump = four spades, two hearts, three diamonds, four clubs

4♣ = four spades, two hearts, five diamonds, two clubs

4◇ = four spades, two hearts, two diamonds, five clubs

Opener's Control-Showing Bids

After opener has shown his exact distribution, the next relay asks about his controls (principally aces and kings). If responder has interrupted the distribution-showing sequences by a suit bid below game, he also has asked opener to show his controls. Opener first shows quantity, then location and quality. His first bid after the control-asking relay shows, in steps, the number of controls: the first step, assuming a 16-18 point notrump range, shows 0-4 controls; each higher step shows one additional control. If the notrump range is 13-15 HCP, the first step shows 0-3 controls.

If opener bids the first step, the next relay asks him exactly how many controls he has. Again he answers in steps, but this time his first step shows the maximum number possible consistent with his prior bid, and each succeeding step shows one fewer.

After opener has shown exactly how many controls he has, the next relay asks where his high cards are located. His answers are, again, in steps, and the steps relate to his suits in order of their known length; if their length is equal, the higher ranking suit is accorded the earlier step. If he has shown for example, four spades, two hearts, three diamonds, and four clubs, the first step would convey information about opener's high cards in spades, the second about his high cards in clubs, the third about his high cards in diamonds, the fourth about his high cards in hearts, the fifth about spades again, the sixth about clubs again, and so forth.

The manner in which the possession of high cards in a suit is signified varies according to whether the suit is known to be a doubleton or not. If it is known to be a doubleton, the indication of an honor is given by bidding the step that relates to the short suit. However, if the suit is not known to be a doubleton, possession of an honor in it is shown by *bypassing* the step that relates to that suit.

Example:

♠ A Q x x   ♡ Q x   ◇ Q J x   ♣ K Q x x

Opener would bypass the first and second steps, since he has the ace of spades (first step suit) and the king of clubs (second step suit). He would bid the third step, since he has neither the ace nor the king of diamonds (third step suit). If instead of the hand shown, opener had the king of diamonds instead of the queen, and the king of hearts instead of that queen, responder would bid the fourth step, since he has the ace or king of his three longest suits, and has the king of his doubleton suit. Bids by opener that accept or decline a second opportunity to make a statement about the same suit tend to give information about high honors not previously shown. The guidelines for showing controls in long (*i.e.*, not doubleton) suits are as follows:

    bid = no ace, no king
    bid, then bid again = no ace, no king, no queen
    bid, then bypass = queen held; no ace, no king
    bypass at first opportunity = ace or king held
    bypass first, bid later = no second top honor
    bypass, then bypass again = two of the three top honors

The guidelines for showing controls in doubleton suits are as follows:

    bid = ace or king held
    bid, then bid again = ace and king held
    bid, then bypass = no second top honor
    bypass = no ace, no king
    bypass, then bypass again = no ace, no king, no queen
    bypass, then bid = queen held; no ace, no king

TWO SPADES QUANTITATIVE

A modification suggested for users of Jacoby Transfer Bids in response to an opening bid of one notrump is to interchange the meanings of the responses of two spades and two notrump. Assuming that the partnership uses a direct raise to two notrump as an invitation to opener to bid three notrump with a maximum *(but see, e. g.,* BARON RESPONSE TO ONE NOTRUMP; TWO NOTRUMP AS RELAY TO THREE CLUBS), the suggestion is to use the two spade response to invite game when opener as a maximum notrump opening.

Over the two spade response, opener would bid two notrump with a minimum, or make a three-level bid if he has a maximum. The precise meaning of such three-level suit bids would be a matter for individual partnership agreement.

The principal advantages of this use of the two spade response are that it is forcing and it allows opener to announce his strength at a lower level than that permitted by standard sequences. Thus, responder need not have merely a game-invitational hand to make the two spade response. Since the response forces opener to bid again, even to sign off, responder may use this response with a strong hand, such as

♠ A x   ♥ K Q x   ♦ A x x x   ♣ K x x x

to learn whether opener has a minimum or a maximum, and then to continue bidding. He could thus explore for a suit fit at the three level when opener has a minimum, with a view to bidding a close slam if a fit is found or ending in three notrump if no fit is found.

REPEATED JACOBY TRANSFERS

An extension of the JACOBY TRANSFER BID principle to the second round of bidding may permit the partnership to explore for game without getting too high and may allow it to land in its best part-score contract. The extension is simply to have responder's second bid, like his first, be an artificial bid that shows the next highest denomination.

Examples:

	Opener	*Responder*
[A]	1 Notrump	2 ♡ (transfer to spades)
	2 ♦	2 Notrump (= four or more clubs)
[B]	1 Notrump	2 ♦ (transfers to hearts)
	2 ♡	3 ♣ (= four or more diamonds)
[C]	1 Notrump	2 ♡ (transfer to spades)
	2 ♠	3 ♦ (= at least 5-5 in the major suits; spades at least as long as hearts)
[D]	1 Notrump	2 ♦ (transfer to hearts)
	2 ♡	3 ♡ (= five or more spades, with longer hearts)
[E]	1 Notrump	2 ♡ (transfer to spades)
	2 ♠	3 ♡ (= six-card spade suit; invites game)
[F]	1 Notrump	2 ♦ (transfer to hearts)
	2 ♡	2 ♠ (= natural two notrump rebid, *i.e.*, 5-3-3-2, game invitation)

Auctions [C] and [D] are game forcing. In the other auctions responder may merely be making a game-try; however his bids are ambiguous, and he may follow with another bid that reveals strength.

After the second transfer, opener should express a preference for one of responder's suits. He should, at the same time, accept or reject the presumed game invitation according to the strength of his hand. He may bid three notrump if he has the side suits stopped and has no fit for responder's major suit. Opener might have the following hands.

[G]	♠ K Q x x	♡ x x	♦ K Q x x	♣ A J x
[H]	♠ K Q x x	♡ A x x	♦ A x	♣ K x x x
[I]	♠ A Q x x	♡ Q x	♦ K Q x x	♣ A x x

If the auction has commenced

Opener	Responder
1 Notrump	2 ◇
2 ♡	2 Notrump

so that responder has shown at least five hearts, at least four clubs, and a hand worth a game invitation, opener should bid three clubs with hand [G], four hearts or cue-bid with hand [H], and three notrump with hand [I].

The repeated Jacoby transfers provide no sequence by which responder may shown an invitational balanced hand with a five-card spade suit, for example,

♠ K Q x x x   ♡ x x   ◇ K x x   ♣ x x x

With such a hand, responder would have to respond with a two club Stayman inquiry over the one notrump opening, and bid spades over opener's rebid.

ONE NOTRUMP OPENER'S REBID AFTER TRANSFER TO CLUBS

Using JACOBY TRANSFERS in response to a one notrump opening, a responder may transfer on hands worth a game force or a game invitation, as well as on hands with which he merely wants to sign off as cheaply as possible in his suit. When the partnership is using a version of Jacoby in which responder bids two spades to transfer to clubs, *see* JACOBY FOR THE MINOR SUITS, it usually has agreed on a method by which opener may indicate whether he has a good hand with a club fit.

Most such partnerships agree that if opener has a hand with which he would reject an invitation to game, he simply bids three clubs over two spades; if he has a better hand, he rebids two notrump. This method keeps the bidding slightly lower on hands on which the partnership is more likely to want to explore.

The reverse treatment, however, has much to recommend it. If opener rebids two notrump when he lacks a fit, responder has the option of playing in two notrump rather than three clubs. Or, if opener rebids three clubs, showing that he would accept an invitation in clubs, additional advantages accrue. First, if responder's hand is sufficiently weak that he wanted to sign off, opener is likely to have a better hand; thus, opener will become the declarer more often when it is likely to be important.

Second, when responder's hand is very weak, the hand may well belong to the opponents. If opener rebids three clubs with a hand worth a game acceptance, the opponents will not learn that responder is weak until he passes. In this auction, only one opponent, responder's left-hand opponent, will have a chance to enter the auction after the partnership's total strength is clarified. Using the more common method, in which opener bids two notrump with a pre-acceptance, responder must bid three clubs to sign off; over this, both opponents, not just one, would have another chance to enter the auction. Thus, having opener bid three clubs with the pre-acceptance has preemptive value.

KANTAR RELAYS AFTER JACOBY TRANSFERS

When the partnership is using JACOBY TRANSFER BIDS in response to a one notrump opening, responder may, after transferring, bid a new suit with a hand worth a game force. Without special agreement, the new-suit bid is somewhat ambiguous. It may be based simply on game-going values and be an effort to find the right game; or it may be made in a quest for slam. It may represent a genuine two-suiter, with each suit having five or more cards; or it may be made on a hand that has no singletons or voids.

On some hands, the ambiguities will not be material. If, for example, opener has three-card or longer support for responder's first suit (the "anchor suit") or has a concentration of strength in the unbid suits, he may simply bid the anchor suit or three notrump, respectively. If, however, opener has two cards in the anchor suit and either has a weak holding in an unbid suit or is interested in slam in responder's second suit, he may need to know which type of hand responder has in order to reach the best contract. The Kantar Relay convention eliminates much of the ambiguity and increases the usefulness of the new-suit bid and of most of the sequences that follow.

When the partnership has agreed to use Kantar Relays, responder should not bid a second suit after having made a Jacoby transfer if his distribution is 5-4-2-2 unless he has slam interest. Thus, opposite a 15-17 point notrump, responder needs at least a good 14 HCP to bid his second suit if his distribution is 5-4-2-2. If he has this semi-balanced hand with less strength, he should simply bid three notrump over opener's acceptance of the transfer. With this understanding, Kantar Relays will, with most two-suiters, give opener a way to ask responder to provide additional information as to his distribution and his strength. Opener normally uses the relay when he is more interested in responder's second suit than his first suit.

Kantar Relays may be used only when responder's suits are not touching suits (*i.e.*, not spades-hearts or hearts-diamonds). The relay bid is the cheapest bid over responder's new-suit bid. If responder's first suit is spades, Kantar Relays may be used when his second suit is either clubs or diamonds. If the anchor suit is hearts, the relays may be used only when responder's second suit is clubs. For example, in the auction

Opener	*Responder*
1 Notrump	2 ♢ (transfer to hearts)
2 ♡	3 ♣

a three diamond bid by opener would ask for further information as to responder's distribution and strength. If, over two hearts, responder had rebid three diamonds, however, a three heart bid by opener would be natural.

In response to the relay, responder describes his pattern and his strength. If responder has two doubletons (and thus has at least 14 HCP), he rebids four notrump. (The three notrump rebid is reserved for use with 5-4-3-1 hands.) With 5-4-3-1 distribution, responder shows his three-card suit (his "fragment"). With five or more cards in each of his suits, responder rebids one of these suits. The two-suited rebids and the fragment-showing rebids are discussed in separate sections below; a recapitulation of all of responder's rebids over the relay is provided at the end.

Responder's Rebids With 5-5-2-1 Distribution

In response to the relay bid, if responder has a genuine two-suiter, *i.e.*, at least five cards in each suit, he rebids one of his suits. If he has minimum strength (9-14 points opposite a 15-17 point notrump), he rebids his first suit. The level at which responder returns to his first suit to show a minimum depends in part on which two suits he has.

When responder's suits are spades and diamonds, he shows minimum strength by bidding four spades. (The three spade bid is reserved for use with 5-4-3-1 hands, as discussed in the next section.)

When responder's suits are spades-clubs or hearts-clubs, thus making the relay bid three diamonds, responder shows his minimum by bidding either three or four of the anchor suit. The bid of three of the anchor suit shows that some of responder's high cards are located in his short suits, thus giving opener an informed option to play in three notrump. Responder's bid of four of the anchor suit over the three diamond relay shows a concentration of high cards in his long suits. In order to bid four of the anchor suit when his second suit is clubs, responder must hold at least two of the six key cards (the six being the four aces plus the kings of responder's long suits). Opposite such a hand, slam remains a possibility despite responder's less-than 15 point hand if opener has fitting honors in responder's suits and good controls in the other two suits.

When responder has at least five-five distribution and a hand worth at least an invitation to slam (*e.g.*, at least a good 14 points opposite a 15-17 point notrump), he rebids his second suit over the relay. For this rebid as well, responder must have at least two key cards.

When responder has shown the genuine two-suiter, opener's bid of four notrump is ROMAN KEY CARD BLACKWOOD. When responder has guaranteed that he has at least two of the six key cards, the modified responses to four notrump are

5 ♣ = two key cards, without the queen of the second suit
5 ◇ = two key cards, with the queen of the second suit
5 ♡ = three key cards
5 ♠ = four key cards

Following one of these responses, opener sets the final contract.

If opener and responder held

Opener
♠ K Q x   ♡ Q x   ◇ A x x   ♣ A x x x x
Responder
♠ x   ♡ A K x x x   ◇ x x   ♣ K J x x x

the bidding, with Kantar Relays, could be

Opener	*Responder*
1 Notrump	2 ◇
2 ♡	3 ♣
3 ◇	4 ♡
4 Notrump	5 ♡
6 ♣	

Responder's four heart bid confirms at least 5-5 in hearts and clubs, and shows a minimum, but with his strength concentrated in his long suits. His five heart bid in response to four notrump shows three key cards. Opener, knowing that one key card is missing, bids six clubs.

Responder's Rebids With 5-4-3-1 Distribution

If responder has only four cards in his second suit and is 3-1 in the unbid suits, he shows his three-card fragment suit in response to the relay. With a minimum, he shows his fragment at the three level; with a maximum, he shows it at the four level. Both four-level fragment bids will be natural; at least one of the three-level bids will have to be artificial.

In order to show a fragment with a maximum, responder simply bids the fragment suit at the four level. Thus, with

♠ K x x   ♡ K Q x x x   ◇ x   ♣ A Q J x

responder would rebid four spades over the three diamond relay. If his diamond and spade holdings were reversed, he would bid four diamonds. After

656

responder has shown a fragment at the four level, opener's bid of four notrump is to play.

In order to show a fragment in the unbid minor suit and minimum strength, responder bids three notrump. Three notrump shows the minor suit fragment no matter which two long suits responder holds.

In order to show a minimum with a fragment in the unbid major suit, responder bids a major suit at the three level. If responder's four-card minor is clubs, making diamonds the relay suit, he will be able to bid this fragment naturally. That is, if the anchor suit is spades he will bid three hearts to show a three-card heart holding; if the anchor suit is hearts, he will bid three spades to show a three-card spade holding. If responder's suits are spades and diamonds, however, making the relay suit hearts, responder must bid three spades to show a fragment in hearts.

If opener bids four notrump after responder has shown a fragment at the three level, his bid is Roman Key Card Blackwood agreeing on responder's fragment suit as trumps. In such an auction, the partnership may agree that there are seven key cards, *i.e.*, the four aces and the kings of the three suits in which responder has more than a singleton.

To summarize, when the auction has begun

Opener	*Responder*
1 Notrump	2 ◇ (transfer to hearts)
2 ♡	3 ♣
3 ◇	

the complete schedule of responder's rebids is as follows:

3 ♡ = at least 5-5 in hearts and clubs, minimum strength, with high cards concentrated in short suits

3 ♠ = three spades, five hearts, four clubs, one diamond, with minimum strength

3 NT = three diamonds, five hearts, four clubs, one spade, with minimum strength

4 ♣ = at least 5-5 in hearts and clubs, maximum strength, with at least two key cards

4 ◇ = three diamonds, five hearts, four clubs, one spade, with maximum strength

4 ♡ = at least 5-5 in hearts and clubs, minimum strength, with high cards concentrated in long suits

4 ♠ = three spades, five hearts, four clubs, one diamond, with maximum strength

4 NT = five hearts, four clubs, two spades, two diamonds, with maximum strength

When the auction has begun

Opener	Responder
1 Notrump	2 ♡ (transfer to spades)
2 ♠	3 ♣
3 ◇	

the complete schedule of responder's rebids is as follows:

3 ♡ = three hearts, five spades, four clubs, one diamond, with minimum strength

3 ♠ = at least 5-5 in spades and clubs, minimum strength, with high cards concentrated in short suits

3 NT = three diamonds, five spades, four clubs, one heart, with minimum strength

4 ♣ = at least 5-5 in spades and clubs, maximum strength, with at least two key cards

4 ◇ = three diamonds, five spades, four clubs, one heart, with maximum strength

4 ♡ = three hearts, five spades, four clubs, one diamond, with maximum strength

4 ♠ = at least 5-5 in spades and clubs, minimum strength, with high cards concentrated in long suits

4 NT = five spades, four clubs, two hearts, two diamonds, with maximum strength

When the auction has begun

Opener	Responder
1 Notrump	2 ♡ (transfer to spades)
2 ♠	3 ◇
3 ♡	

658

the complete schedule of responder's rebids is as follows:

3 ♠ = three hearts, five spades, four diamonds, one club, with
minimum strength

3 NT = three clubs, five spades, four diamonds, one heart, with
minimum strength

4 ♣ = three clubs, five spades, four diamonds, one heart, with
maximum strength

4 ◊ = at least 5-5 in spades and diamonds, maximum strength

4 ♡ = three hearts, five spades, four diamonds, one club, with
maximum strength

4 ♠ = at least 5-5 in spades and diamonds, minimum strength

4 NT = five spades, four diamonds, two hearts, two clubs, with
maximum strength

When responder's suits are spades-hearts or hearts-diamonds, there is
no space between responder's bid of his second suit and opener's return
to the anchor suit. Thus, there is no Kantar Relay in auctions that show
either of these pairs of suits.

See also REPEATED JACOBY TRANSFERS.

CRAWLING STAYMAN

Crawling Stayman is a method of employing NON-FORCING STAYMAN in conjunction with JACOBY TRANSFER BIDS to facilitate escape from one notrump into a playable suit when responder has a weak distributional hand. Whenever responder has a weak hand with a five-card major suit, he simply transfers to his long suit at the two level and passes opener's rebid of the anchor suit. The partnership's ability to show a weak hand with a five-card major in this way allows responder to use Crawling Stayman rebids of two hearts or two spades as escape routes for other weak distributional hands. In addition, responder may use Crawling Stayman to issue certain game invitations.

Responding on a Weak Hand With Four-Four in the Major Suits

The traditional escape from one notrump when the weak responding hand is 4-4-4-1 with shortness in clubs is well known: responder bids two clubs and then passes opener's rebid, whether it be two diamonds, two hearts, or two spades. When responder has four-four in the major suits but instead is short in diamonds rather than clubs, *i.e.*, his precise distribution is 4-4-1-4 or 4-4-0-5, Crawling Stayman allows him to escape into a suit in which the partnership has at least seven cards.

Responder begins by bidding two clubs. If opener rebids two hearts or two spades, responder of course passes. If opener rebids two diamonds, responder bids two hearts. Opener should pass if he has three hearts; if he has only two hearts, however, he must bid again. If opener has two hearts and has three spades, he should rebid two spades. If opener passes two hearts, or if he rebids two spades and responder passes, the partnership will have arrived in a seven-card fit.

If opener has doubletons in both major suits, he rebids two notrump. Responder will then bid three clubs, which opener must pass. The partnership will normally have landed in an eight- or nine-card fit.

Responding on a Weak Hand With Four Hearts and a Five-Card Minor

If responder has a weak hand with four hearts and fewer than four spades, and has a five-card minor, his escape action depends on which minor suit he holds and what opener rebids. If opener rebids two spades, responder will bid three of his minor suit. If the partnership has agreed to use Crawling Stayman, responder's rebid of three clubs or three diamonds over the Stayman response is neither forcing nor invitational.

If opener rebids two diamonds, and responder has five diamonds, he may pass. If, instead, responder has five clubs, he may bid three clubs over two diamonds if his clubs are good and his hearts are weak.

With four reasonably good hearts and five weak clubs, however, responder should bid two hearts over two diamonds. Opener is required to pass if he has three hearts, or to bid again if he has only two. If he has two hearts, he must bid two spades with a three-card spade suit, to cater to the possibility that responder has four-four in the major suits. When opener has only two hearts and three spades, he will usually have at least three clubs. Thus, over two spades, when responder has five clubs he may bid three clubs in order to play in the partnership's presumed eight-card or longer fit.

For example, if the partnership hands were

Opener
♠ A J x   ♡ A x   ◇ K x x x x   ♣ K J x
Responder
♠ x x   ♡ K Q x x   ◇ x x   ♣ 10 x x x x

Crawling Stayman would allow the following auction:

Opener	Responder
1 Notrump	2 ♣
2 ◇	2 ♡
2 ♠	3 ♣
Pass	

Responding on a Weak Hand With Four Spades and a Five-Card Minor

If responder has a weak hand with four spades, fewer than three hearts, and a five-card minor, his rebid will again depend on which minor he holds and what opener rebids. If opener rebids two diamonds, responder may pass with five diamonds. If responder has five clubs, he may bid three clubs over two diamonds.

If opener rebids two hearts, responder bids two spades. Opener passes if he has either four spades and a poor hand for play in spades or three good spades and minimum strength. If opener has only two spades or if he has three weak spades, he must bid again over two spades. He bids two notrump with minimum strength, or three clubs with a maximum. He also bids three clubs if he has three good spades and better than minimum strength.

Over opener's rebid of two notrump, responder will now bid three of his long minor, and opener is required to pass. Over opener's three club bid, responder will pass if his suit is clubs; or he will bid three diamonds if his suit is diamonds, which opener is required to pass.

Inviting Game After Responder's Two Spade Rebid

Though responder's rebid of two spades in the auction

Opener	Responder
1 Notrump	2 ♣
2 ♡	2 ♠

may be made on a weak hand with four spades and a five-card minor, Crawling Stayman allows responder to use this sequence also with two other types of hands: (1) hands with four spades and game-invitational values, and (2) unbalanced hands with five spades, and 7-8 HCP. Typically, the latter type of hand would include a weakish spade suit with which responder would be unsure, after using a Jacoby transfer bid, whether or not to raise to three. *See also* UNBALANCED HEART TRANSFER. Crawling Stayman is useful for the former type of hand if the partnership uses its direct response of two notrump over one notrump for artificial purposes, *e.g.*, as a transfer bid or as part of a minor-suit escape mechanism, *see, e.g.*, TWO NOTRUMP RESPONSE AS A RELAY TO THREE CLUBS. When the direct two notrump response is used artificially, responder must begin by bidding two clubs in order to invite game in notrump; in such a sequence, his bid of two notrump over opener's two heart response to Stayman would not promise four spades. Thus, Crawling Stayman allows responder to rebid two spades if he has an invitational hand with four spades.

In order to accommodate the possibility that responder has one of these more promising types of hands, opener makes a rebid other than those set out in the preceding section if he has both a good spade fit and a good hand. If opener has four spades and less than maximum strength, yet has enough to accept a game invitation if responder has the game-invitational type of hand, he raises responder's two spade bid to three spades. If opener has four spades and a maximum, he makes an artificial bid that reveals his distribution. He bids three diamonds to show a doubleton club; he bids three hearts to show a doubleton diamond.

Thus, the complete schedule of opener's rebids when he has bid two hearts in response to Stayman and responder has rebid two spades is as follows:

Pass	=	four spades or three good spades, minimum
2 NT	=	two spades or three weak spades, minimum
3 ♣	=	two or three spades, maximum
3 ◇	=	four spades, doubleton club, maximum
3 ♡	=	four spades, doubleton diamond, maximum
3 ♠	=	four spades, less than a maximum but worth acceptance of game invitation

Opener's three spade bid is not forcing. If responder has the weak hand with four spades and a five-card minor, he will pass. If he has the weak hand and opener has bid three diamonds or three hearts, responder will bid three spades to sign off. Opener is required to pass responder's three spade bid in this auction. If responder has one of the better hands, of course, he will bid four spades over opener's three diamond, three heart, or three spade bid.

If opener has bid three clubs over two spades, showing a maximum with two or three spades, responder will sign off by passing if he has a weak hand with five clubs, or will sign off by bidding three diamonds if he has a weak hand with five diamonds. If he has the game-invitational hand with four spades, he will bid three notrump. If responder has five spades, he will bid three spades. His three spade bid over three clubs is forcing. If opener has three spades, he will raise to four; if he has only two, he will bid three notrump.

For example, if responder held one of the following hands

[A]	♠ Q x x x	[B]	♠ x x x x	[C]	♠ Q x x x x
	♡ K Q x		♡ x		♡ x
	◇ Q 10 x x		◇ x x x		◇ A Q x x
	♣ x x		♣ Q J x x x		♣ x x x

and opener held

♠ A J 10   ♡ J 10 x x   ◇ K J x   ♣ A K x

the auction would begin

Opener	Responder
1 Notrump	2 ♣
2 ♡	2 ♠
3 ♣	

Opener has shown four hearts, two or three spades, and a maximum notrump opening. With hand A, responder would bid three notrump. With hand B, he would pass; if his minor suits were reversed, he would bid three diamonds, which opener would pass. With hand C, responder would bid three spades, and opener would raise to four.

UNBALANCED HEART TRANSFER

The Unbalanced Heart convention ("UHC") is a modification of responder's rebids following his use of a JACOBY TRANSFER BID to show a heart suit. After the auction has started

Opener	Responder
1 Notrump	2 ◊ (transfer to hearts)
2 ♡	

assuming standard methods, responder has two ways of making a game try. He may rebid two notrump if he has no singleton; if he has a singleton he may raise to three hearts.

The UHC convention is designed to solve responder's problem when he has a game-invitational hand with a side suit singleton but a weak heart suit. A raise to three hearts with a suit such as J x x x x is dangerous since opener might have a holding such as K x.

The convention requires responder to rebid two spades over opener's two heart rebid. The two spade bid promises nothing about spades but says merely that responder has an unbalanced hand with interest in game. Opener may bid notrump without a fit for hearts: he would bid two notrump to reject the game-try, or three notrump to accept.

The availability of the Unbalanced Heart convention enables responder also to distinguish between balanced and unbalanced hands containing a six-card heart suit. With a balanced hand, responder raises opener's two heart bid directly to three. With the unbalanced hand, responder bids three hearts only after having commenced with the two spade bid over two hearts.

A UHC-type convention is not used when responder's long suit is spades. Although it is just as risky to raise to three spades with a spade suit headed by the jack, the hand may be dealt with by eschewing the Jacoby Transfer bid and using STAYMAN instead; responder simply rebids two spades over opener's rebid.

Using the UHC convention and this proposed application of Stayman reduces the partnership's ability to distinguish between responding hands containing 5-4 in the majors from those containing 5-5, and weak 5-5's from strong 5-5's. *See* COORDINATING JACOBY TRANSFERS WITH STAYMAN.

SPLINTERS TO AVOID NOTRUMP

After the bidding has been opened one notrump, there are several devices for locating 4-4 or 5-3 major suit fits, or sometimes 5-4 or 5-3 minor suit fits. Few such mechanisms concentrate on allowing opener to learn just what, if any, singleton responder has. One system for responding uses a number of splinter and mini-splinter-type bids in order to allow opener to evaluate prudently the location of his honor cards.

The system uses several conventions for responder's two-level responses. Two clubs initiates a STAYMAN inquiry. JACOBY TRANSFER BIDS are used for the major suits. The BARON RESPONSE TO ONE NOTRUMP is used on hands with which responder is interested in slam and has no five-card suit. The singleton-showing bids are normally three-level bids at responder's first or second turn.

A jump by responder to three hearts or three spades directly over the one notrump opening shows a singleton in the suit of the jump. It promises at least 10 HCP and at least nine cards in the minor suits.

If responder makes a Jacoby Transfer Bid and then bids a new suit at the three level, he shows a singleton in the suit bid at the three level. This bid is forcing to game.

If responder bids two clubs Stayman and then bids any new suit at the three level, he shows length in the suit he has bid and a singleton in the other suit of the same rank. This bid is forcing to game. If he bids three of a major suit, he shows four cards in that major and a singleton in the other major. If he bids three of a minor suit, he shows five cards in the minor he has bid and a singleton in the other minor.

If responder makes a Baron response of two notrump, which causes the partnership to bid its four-card suits up the line, a jump by responder shows a singleton in the suit in which the jump has been made, and four cards in every other suit, including the suit just bid by opener.

In the following auctions, the last suit bid by responder shows a specific singleton.

	Opener	Responder
[A]	1 Notrump	2♣
	2♦	3♡ (four hearts, singleton spade)
[B]	1 Notrump	3♡ (singleton heart, nine minor suit cards, 10+ HCP)
[C]	1 Notrump	2♡
	2♠	3♦ (singleton diamond)
[D]	1 Notrump	2 Notrump
	3♦	3♡
	3♠	5♣ (singleton club, 4-4-4 in other suits)

If opener has a hand such as

♠ Q x x x   ♡ A K x   ◊ A K x x   ♣ x x

he would consider slam a likely laydown in auction [D], a remote possibility in [B], and worth further exploration in [A]. In [C], notwithstanding the singleton opposite opener's ace and king of diamonds, opener's excellent spade fit makes further consideration of slam worthwhile.

FIVE-CARD TRANSFER STAYMAN (FCTS)

Unless the partnership is using an artificial club system, a hand worth 20-22 HCP containing a five-card major suit is a difficult one with which to choose an effective opening bid. Rather than risk opening with one in the major suit and having responder pass with a useful high card but fewer than six points, most experts open with a bid of two notrump. A responder holding 4-5 points will usually carry on to game over the latter opening. The danger is that the partnership will reach a contract of three notrump which is inferior to four of opener's long major suit.

A convention called FCTS, which stands for Five-Card Transfer Stayman, used in response to an opening bid of two notrump, is designed to permit the partnership to locate any eight-card major suit fit it may have. The convention allows responder to transfer directly over the two notrump opening if he has a five-card major suit of his own or to ask opener whether he has a four- or five-card major suit.

Immediate Transfer by Responder

If responder has a five-card major suit, he may make a transfer bid directly over the two notrump opening bid. A three diamond response transfers to hearts; a three heart response transfers to spades. If responder has five hearts and four spades, he rebids three spades over a three heart rebid by opener after the initial transfer. If responder holds exactly five hearts and exactly three spades, however, he should not transfer directly over the two notrump opening. He will be better able to explore all of the major suit fit possibilities of such a hand by using the FCTS three-club inquiry described below.

A three heart response to two notrump transfers to spades. Opener may, instead of accepting the transfer, bid three notrump if he has two spades and five hearts. Responder may pass this or he may choose to play in one of the majors. He does the latter by bidding, over three notrump, four diamonds to transfer to hearts, or four hearts to transfer to spades. If responder has five spades and four hearts, he should not transfer into spades but should use the three club inquiry in order not to miss a possible 4-4 fit.

The Three Club Inquiry into Opener's Major Suits

The FCTS inquiry into opener's major suit distribution is initiated by responder's bid of three clubs in response to two notrump. Opener replies as follows:

3 ♦ = fewer than four hearts, fewer than five spades
3 ♡ = four or five hearts, fewer than four spades
3 ♠ = five spades
3NT = four hearts and four spades

After opener's three notrump bid, if responder has four cards in either major suit, he commits the partnership to game in that suit. He does this by bidding four of the suit *below* the major suit in which he wishes to play. These transfer bids allow opener to be the declarer in either four hearts or four spades.

After opener's three heart rebid, responder will raise to four with a four-card heart suit and no slam interest. If he has three hearts, he may bid three spades to ask about opener's heart length. Opener now bids three notrump to show four, or four hearts to show five. If responder has fewer than three hearts, he bids three notrump.

After opener's three diamond rebid, responder may bid three hearts to ask about opener's spade length. Opener bids three spades holding three, three notrump with two, or four spades with four.

The Romex version of Stayman also uses the above responses to the three club inquiry. FCTS provides the following additional actions by responder.

After opener's three diamond bid, responder may show his own major suit lengths as follows:

3 ♡ = five spades, four hearts
3 ♠ = five hearts, three spades
4 ♣ = six hearts, four spades
4 ♦ = four hearts, six spades

Examples:

(Opener)
♠ A K J x x   ♡ K x   ♦ A Q x   ♣ A J x

(Responder)
♠ Q x x   ♡ A x x x x   ♦ J x   ♣ x x x

With these hands, using FCTS, the auction would go

Opener	*Responder*
2 Notrump	3 ♣
3 ♠	4 ♣

669

If opener had one more heart and one fewer spade, the auction would go

Opener	Responder
2 Notrump	3♣
3◇	3♠ (= five hearts, three spades)
4♡	Pass

MILES RESPONSES TO TWO NOTRUMP OPENINGS

The Miles method of responding to a two notrump opening is designed to allow responder to show any one-suited, two-suited, or three-suited hand at a safe level, and to distinguish between good and broken suits on hands where he has slam interest. Using this method, all three-level responses are artificial, and all four-level responses are natural.

Three Club Response

The three club response is, ostensibly, the STAYMAN convention. Opener is required to bid a four-card major if he has one or to bid three diamonds if he has none. If he has four cards in each major, he bids three hearts.

After the Stayman rebid by opener, if responder bids four clubs, his bid is the GERBER convention, asking opener how many aces he has. This is the only way in which responder may ask opener for aces. His bids of four notrump are never BLACKWOOD, and bids of four clubs in other sequences have other meanings. Hence, the response of three clubs does not guarantee that responder has a four-card major suit.

If opener has rebid three hearts or three spades, a rebid by responder of four diamonds shows a fit with the suit shown by opener and is a slam try. The four diamond bid does not promise anything about responder's diamond holding.

If opener has rebid three diamonds, a four diamond bid by responder shows that responder's distribution is 4-4-4-1 with a singleton club.

Three-Level Transfers

Responses of three diamonds and three hearts to the two notrump opening are JACOBY TRANSFER BIDS. If responder uses one of these transfers and then bids another suit, his second bid is natural and he shows a two-suited hand containing that suit and the suit into which he earlier transferred. If the new suit is a minor, this sequence shows that responder's major suit is at least as long as his minor suit.

A three spade response to two notrump says nothing about responder's spades, but is also a transfer bid. It simply asks opener to bid three notrump. Responder passes the three notrump bid if he has a hand worth a simple raise. (This sequence is necessary because a bid of three notrump by responder directly over the two notrump opening is also used as a transfer bid.) Responder bids again, after having transferred to three notrump, to show a distributional hand.

Responder's rebid of four clubs over three notrump requires opener to bid four diamonds. Responder promises either a hand with a very good diamond suit, which he will show by next bidding four notrump, or a hand with a long diamond suit and a four-card major. He will show the latter hand by bidding his major suit over four diamonds.

If, over the three notrump rebid by opener, responder bids four notrump, he shows length in both minor suits. If, instead, he bids four diamonds, four hearts, or four spades, he shows a 4-4-4-1 hand, with a singleton in the suit bid.

A three notrump response to the two notrump opening is also artificial, and forces the partnership at least to four notrump. This response requires opener to bid four clubs. Responder promises either a very good club suit, which he will show by next bidding four notrump, or a two-suited hand in which clubs is the longer suit. If responder has the latter hand, he will next bid his second suit.

Four-Level Natural Bids

Responder's immediate jumps to suits at the four level, including clubs, are natural. Each shows a long, but broken, holding in the suit bid.

If responder held the following hands

[A]	♠ A x x	♡ x	◊ K x x x x x	♣ Q x x
[B]	♠ A x x	♡ x x x	◊ K x x	♣ x x x
[C]	♠ A x	♡ x x	◊ K Q x x x x	♣ x x x
[D]	♠ A x x x	♡ x x x	◊ x	♣ K Q x x x

the corresponding auctions would commence

	Opener	*Responder*
[A]	2 Notrump	4 ◊
[B]	2 Notrump	3 ♣
	3 Notrump	Pass
[C]	2 Notrump	3 ♣
	3 Notrump	4 ♣
	4 ◊ (forced)	4 Notrump
[D]	2 Notrump	3 Notrump
	4 ♣	4 ♠

COMBINING JACOBY TRANSFERS AND TEXAS TRANSFERS IN RESPONSE TO TWO NOTRUMP OPENING

Most partnerships that use both JACOBY TRANSFERS and TEXAS TRANSFERS agree that responder will use Texas, the four-level transfer, on hands with which he has no slam interest and that he will use Jacoby, the non-jump transfer, and follow with a bid of his suit at the four level if he has modest slam interest. *See* COMBINING JACOBY TRANSFERS AND TEXAS TRANSFERS. Some partnerships agree to reverse these meanings when the bidding has been opened two notrump.

When the opening bid was two notrump, responder may have a hand that does not justify a slam try, but with which slam could be laydown if opener has the right maximum. Using the reversed meanings of the Jacoby sequence and Texas, responder transfers at the four level to indicate that his hand is worth a slam try; he transfers at the three level when he has a hand that is not worth a slam try.

Opposite responder's non-constructive three-level transfer, opener may simply accept the transfer at the three level, or he may jump to four of the suit shown by the transfer if he has a good fit and a maximum principally in aces and kings. If opener merely accepts the transfer at the three level, responder signs off in four of his suit. If opener has jumped to four, responder may pass if he has a dead minimum, or, with more he may explore further.

After responder's transfer at the four level, indicating slam interest, opener simply accepts the transfer if he has a poor hand for slam, or he makes some other bid to cooperate in the exploration for slam. If opener merely bids four of responder's suit, responder remains free, with strong slam interest, to bid on.

See also MITCHELL ADJUNCT.

MITCHELL ADJUNCT

The Mitchell Adjunct to JACOBY TRANSFER BIDS is a convention used in responding to an opening bid of two notrump. It is designed principally to permit responder to use four clubs as GERBER after he has transferred in his major suit, while also permitting him to show a good two-suited hand with a major suit and clubs without going past four of his major.

Five-Five or Longer Hands

In order to show a good hand with at least five cards in a major suit and at least five diamonds, standard Jacoby transfer sequences are used. *See* JACOBY OVER TWO NOTRUMP OPENINGS. Thus, responder begins by transferring to his major suit (three diamonds transfers to hearts, three hearts transfers to spades), and then rebids four diamonds. Similarly, hands with length in both minor suits are shown by traditional Jacoby methods, *i.e.*, with a response of three spades. *See* JACOBY FOR THE MINOR SUITS.

In order to show a good two-suiter with a major suit and clubs, the Mitchell Adjunct uses an immediate jump response to four of the major suit. Thus, in the auction

Opener	Responder
2 Notrump	4 ♡

responder's four heart bid shows a game-going hand with at least five hearts and at least five clubs. He might have

♠ x x   ♡ K Q x x x   ◇ x   ♣ A x x x x

Responder's jump to four hearts or four spades is not forcing, but it invites opener to explore for slam if he has good controls and fitting honors in responder's long suits.

The complete schedule of responder's slam-invitational two-suited responses and rebids using the Mitchell Adjunct is:

Responder's Two Suits	Responder's Bids and Rebids
spades and hearts	3 ♡ , then 4 ♡
spades and diamonds	3 ♡ , then 4 ◇
spades and clubs	4 ♠ directly
hearts and diamonds	3 ◇ , then 4 ◇
hearts and clubs	4 ♡ directly
diamonds and clubs	3 ♠

When responders transfers to a major suit and then bids four clubs, his four club bid is Gerber.

Over any of responder's two-suited bids at the four level, opener may pass or correct to five clubs. His bid of four notrump is a signoff.

If responder has a hand with which he wants to play slam in a major or clubs, he may jump to five of his major suit. Opener is forced to bid. He may bid six of either of responder's suits; or he may bid five notrump to ask responder to choose the suit.

Use of the Mitchell Adjunct precludes use of TEXAS TRANSFERS in response to two notrump. The convention uses an immediate jump to four diamonds as a natural slam try. An immediate jump to four clubs is a slam try in clubs. In order to use four clubs as Gerber, responder must start with either a transfer bid or three clubs, which is ostensibly STAYMAN. Jumps to five of a minor are natural signoffs. *See also* SUPER GERBER.

Other Distributions

If, in response to Stayman, opener has shown no four-card major, the Mitchell Adjunct also permits responder to show slam interest with a five-card minor suit or with four-four in the minors. Thus, after the auction has begun

Opener	Responder
2 Notrump	3 ♣
3 ◇	

responder's bids of four diamonds, four hearts, and four spades are artificial. Four hearts shows a five-card club suit; four spades shows a five-card diamond suit. Four diamonds shows 4-4 in clubs and diamonds. Opener may sign off after any of these bids by bidding four notrump.

See also MILES RESPONSES TO TWO NOTRUMP OPENINGS; COMBINING JACOBY TRANSFERS AND TEXAS TRANSFERS IN RESPONSE TO TWO NOTRUMP OPENINGS.

MULTICOLORED TRANSFERS AFTER
TWO NOTRUMP OPENING

Multicolored transfers are a system of responding to an opening bid of two notrump that is designed to make it easier for the partnership to reach its minor suit slams. To this end, most of responder's three-level suit bids are two-way bids.

A response of three spades promises length in both minor suits. It says nothing about responder's holding in spades.

A response of three hearts promises long spades. It is a straightforward transfer bid and says nothing about responder's hearts.

A response of three diamonds promises length in either hearts or clubs. Opener should generally bid three hearts. If responder has clubs instead, he will rebid three spades; any other rebid by responder confirms that his long suit is hearts.

A response of three clubs is either a STAYMAN-type inquiry or a long diamond suit. Opener's rebids are as follows.

$3 \diamond$ = fewer than four hearts, says nothing about spades
$3 \heartsuit$ = at least four hearts, fewer than four spades
$3 \spadesuit$ = four hearts and four spades
3NT = three hearts, three spades, two diamonds, five clubs;
    slam interest

After opener's rebid of three diamonds, responder may bid three notrump if he has four hearts, fewer than four spades, and no long diamond suit. Or he may bid three hearts to show four or more spades. Over responder's three heart bid, opener would bid three spades with three or more spades, or three notrump with a doubleton spade. If responder has four spades and opener has bid three spades to show three or more, responder bids three notrump to show exactly four spades, which opener may convert to four spades if he too holds four.

After opener's bid of three diamonds, if responder bids three spades, he shows that he had a long diamond suit rather than a typical Stayman-type hand.

If opener has bid three spades over responder's three club bid, showing both majors, a bid by responder of three notrump shows a long diamond suit and invites opener to explore slam; a bid by responder of four clubs shows diamonds and a stronger hand. Responder's bids of four diamonds and four hearts over opener's three heart bid are transfers to hearts and spades, respectively.

One flaw in this system of responding is that responder cannot show a hand with four spades and five hearts. Another is that it does not seem capable of exploring the possibility that opener may have a five-card major suit. *See, e.g.,* FCTS.

CONFIT

CONFIT is a conventional two diamond response to an opening bid of one notrump. It is made when responder has a balanced hand and sufficient high card points to know that the combined hands hold in the neighborhood of 33 HCP. The convention is designed to disclose whether the partnership has sufficient controls and a good enough fit to make a slam a reasonable proposition. The name CONFIT comes from CONtrols and FIT.

Counting an ace as two controls and a king as one, the deck contains twelve controls. For slam to be a good proposition when the partnership has no more than 33 points and the hands are balanced, the partnership should possess at least ten of the twelve controls. That is, it should not be missing as much as either an ace and a king or three kings.

The CONFIT two diamond response to one notrump asks opener to disclose how many controls he has. In order to use CONFIT opposite a 16-18 point notrump opening, responder should have at least 14 HCP. In addition, he should have at least four controls, and at least one four-card suited headed by no worse than the ace, king, or queen. Other suits, even though containing four cards, are not "biddable" by either opener or responder. Nor may a raise be made with a suit that is not biddable.

In answer to the two diamond inquiry, opener shows his controls according to the following schedule.

$2\heartsuit$ = four or fewer controls
$2\spadesuit$ = five controls
2NT = six controls
$3\clubsuit$ = seven controls
$3\diamondsuit$ = eight or more controls.

After opener's rebid, responder adds the number of controls opener has shown to the number he holds, and if the total is less than ten, he signs off at three notrump. If the total is ten or more, he discloses this to opener, and begins the exploration for a fit, by bidding his cheapest biddable suit. The partnership proceeds to show its biddable suits by bidding up the line until a fit is found. The fit is announced by one partner raising the other's bid. A nonjump raise is made if the raiser has one of the top three honors in the suit; if he has two such honors he jumps in the suit.

For example, if opener and responder have the following hands

    (Opener)
    ♠ K 10 x x   ♡ A x x x   ◇ K x x   ♣ A Q
    (Responder)
    ♠ A J x x   ♡ K x   ◇ A Q x x   ♣ J x x

using CONFIT the auction would proceed

Opener	Responder
1 Notrump	2 ◇
2 Notrump	3 ◇
3 ♡	3 ♠
4 ♠	6 ♠

Opener's two notrump rebid shows six controls, so responder, who has five, knows the partnership has enough controls for slam if it has a fit. Once the spade fit is found, responder bids six.

CONFIT may also be used after an opening bid of two notrump, or after a two notrump rebid following a two club opening. In this event, the control-showing rebids by opener should start with the first step showing six or fewer controls rather than four or fewer.

If the partnership is using transfer bids over one notrump openings, so that a two diamond response is not available for use as CONFIT, the partnership may use as CONFIT the cheapest idle bid, *e.g.*, two spades if that is available.

BARON RESPONSE TO ONE NOTRUMP

The Baron System uses a response of two notrump to a one notrump opening bid to initiate an inquiry into the possibility of slam. Responder should have a hand with which he knows that the partnership's combined assets are in the vicinity of 33 HCP. Opposite a 16-18 point notrump opening, responder might have

♠ K x x x   ♡ Q x   ◇ A K x x   ♣ A x x

The two notrump response asks opener to bid his lowest-ranking four card, or longer, suit, and he and responder bid their four-card suits up the line. When a fit is found, the suit is raised.

See also BARON COROLLARY, ALLEN.

BARON COROLLARY

In an auction that has commenced with a one notrump opening, the Baron Corollary is an artificial three club rebid by responder after a two diamond DOUBLE-BARRELED STAYMAN inquiry has revealed that there is no 4-4 major suit fit. The three club bid enables the partnership to locate a 4-4 minor suit fit.

In the auction

Opener	Responder
1 Notrump	2 ◊ (forcing Stayman)
2 Notrump	

opener's two notrump bid has shown that he has no four-card major suit and no five-card minor. Using the Baron Corollary, a three club bid by responder over two notrump asks opener's precise distribution. Opener answers as follows:

3 ◊ = four diamonds, three cards in every other suit
3 ♡ = three hearts, two spades, four cards in each minor
3 ♠ = three spades, two hearts, four cards in each minor
3NT = four clubs, three cards in every other suit.

See also ALLEN.

ALLEN

The Allen convention after a one notrump opening is designed to allow the partnership to explore for a 4-4 minor suit fit. The convention is employed after opener has responded to a two-club STAYMAN inquiry into his major suit holdings.

If opener has rebid two hearts or two spades in response to the Stayman inquiry, showing that he has four cards in the major bid, the Allen bid consists of a bid of the other major. It asks opener to bid another four-card suit if he has one. If he has no other four-card suit, he bids notrump.

If, over the Stayman inquiry, opener has bid two diamonds, showing no four-card major suit, responder may make the Allen inquiry by bidding three clubs. Opener shows his precise distribution as follows:

3 ◊ = four diamonds, three cards in every other suit.
3 ♡ = two hearts, three spades, four cards in each minor.
3 ♠ = two spades, three hearts, four cards in each minor.
3NT = four clubs, three cards in every other suit.

See also BARON COROLLARY.

Since this convention features rebids by responder in the unbid major suit, the convention is used only in conjuction with JACOBY TRANSFER BIDS. The use of Allen reduces the ability of a partnership using Jacoby transfers to distinguish responding hands that contain 5-4 in the majors from those that contain 5-5, and to distinguish between good and bad 5-5's. *See* COORDINATING JACOBY TRANSFERS WITH STAYMAN.

TWO DIAMOND GAME TRY

The Two Diamond Game Try Convention, which uses a two diamond response to an opening bid of one notrump to initiate responder's invitations to game, is designed to allow the partnership to explore game possibilities and to stop at a low level if game is not to be bid.

Using this mechanism, a response of two clubs is STAYMAN and is to be used only if responder has exactly four cards in a major suit. It is generally not to be used if he has a five-card major. A response of two hearts or two spades to one notrump is a natural sign-off, showing no interest in game.

The two diamond response shows enough strength for game if opener has a maximum or an especially good fit for a particular suit. Opener should envision the game possibilities in each suit on the assumption that responder has five cards in the suit. Responder's suit, if any, is unspecified and opener is required to bid the cheapest denomination in which he would *reject* a game try. If opener bypasses a denomination in making his rebid, it indicates that he would accept a game invitation in the denomination bypassed. Opener's rebids are as follows:

2♡ : rejects game in hearts; says nothing about any other suit or notrump

2♠ : rejects game in spades, accept in hearts; says nothing about the minors or notrump

2NT: rejects game in notrump, accepts in either major suit; says nothing about either minor

3♣ : rejects game in clubs; accepts in notrump or either major; says nothing about diamonds

3♢ : rejects game in diamonds; accepts in every other denomination

3♡ : accepts all game invitations

If opener's rebid is in the denomination in which responder wished to make a game invitation, he passes. If opener's bid shows acceptance of the denomination in which responder is interested, responder simply bids game in that denomination, or if the focus was on a minor suit, more likely in notrump.

For example, if responder holds

♠ K x   ♡ K Q x x x   ♢ x x x   ♣ x x x

he wishes to invite game in hearts. If opener has bid two hearts, rejecting hearts, responder simply passes. If opener has bid something else, indicating his acceptance of a game-try in hearts, responder will jump to four hearts.

If responder is interested in a suit or denomination as to which opener's rebid is noncommittal, responder simply bids the denomination in which he is interested and opener decides whether to reject or accept. For example:

Opener	Responder
1 Notrump	2 ◇
2 ♠	2 Notrump
Pass	

If responder's rebid is in the denomination in which opener has rejected an invitation, it shows that responder had a relatively balanced hand of game-forcing strength. Responder may well have slam aspirations. Thus, in the auction

Opener	Responder
1 Notrump	2 ◇
2 ♡	3 ♡

responder offers a choice of game in hearts or game in notrump.

Since the partnership does not need the direct response of two notrump to invite game in notrump, this response may be used for other purposes as the partnership may agree. *See, e.g.,* BARON RESPONSE TO ONE NOTRUMP.

The use of two diamonds as a game try, of course, means that the partnership cannot use that bid as part of Two-Way Stayman and that it cannot use JACOBY TRANSFER BIDS.

RESPONDING TO NONSTANDARD
NOTRUMP OPENINGS

Using standard methods, the opening bid of one notrump promises 16-18 HCP. Many experienced partnerships have agreed to lower the minimum point requirement by a point and open one notrump with 15+-18 or 15-17 HCP. While obviously the responder to a 15-18 or 15-17 point notrump must keep in mind these ranges when he is considering game or slam, the methods by which he would conduct his exploration opposite a 16-18 point notrump is theoretically as sound opposite these only slightly lighter openings.

When the opening notrump is considerably weaker than 15-17 HCP, however, different considerations come into play and different methods may be superior.

The Weak Notrump: 12-14 HCP

The usual point count range for a weak notrump opening is 12-14 HCP (or 13-15 as in the PRECISION CLUB SYSTEM). Responder's first task is to assess whether the combined assets of the partnership are sufficient to warrant exploration for game. Game should be bid if the partnership has a total of 26 HCP, or 25 with a long suit. If responder has a balanced hand containing 11 HCP or less, he should pass one notrump.

If responder has a hand containing a four-card major suit, he may use the STAYMAN convention if he has the right distribution and sufficient strength to deal with all of opener's possible answers to the Stayman inquiry. *See* NON-FORCING STAYMAN.

When responder has a five-card major suit and a hand worth less than 11 points, he will wish to sign off in two of his suit. With 11 or more, he will wish to explore for, or force to, game. JACOBY TRANSFER BIDS, which are quite valuable in responding to strong notrumps are a less effective tool over weak notrumps. First, although the transfer mechanism is as efficient in permitting the exchange of information for game or slam exploration, the need for such exploration arises less frequently after a weak notrump opening. Since responder needs 11 points to invite game opposite a weak notrump but only 8 or 9 opposite a strong notrump, he will less often have a game invitational hand opposite a weak notrump. These transfers allow opener to be the declarer, which protects the many tenaces one expects to find in a 16-18 point hand from the opening lead. When the opening bid has shown only 12-14 points, there will be fewer high-card holdings that need protecting or concealment. And if game is within contemplation, responder's hand will be about as strong as opener's, thus all but eliminating the theoretical advantage of having the opening lead come up to the opening bidder.

Further, if game is not in view because responder's hand is weak, it is more advantageous for responder to bid his suit naturally and directly over the notrump opening. If an artificial transfer bid is made, the next player has the option of doubling to show length in the artifically bid suit, or bidding the anchor suit for takeout. If the anchor suit is instead bid naturally, the defender's options are reduced. Thus, the natural bid has greater preemptive value than the artificial, lower-ranking transfer bid. If the opening is weak and the responder is weak, the partnership should wish to increase the preemptive effect of its bids, not make it easier for the opponents to enter the auction.

Accordingly, it is recommended that transfer bids not be used in responding to weak notrump openings. A response of two hearts or two spades should be a sign-off, showing a five-card or longer suit, and a hand worth less than 11 points.

A two diamond response may also be used as a sign-off, but is more effectively used as a game-forcing or game-invitational bid. *See, e.g.,* **DOUBLE-BARRELED STAYMAN; TWO DIAMOND GAME TRY.**

THE WOODSON TWO-WAY NOTRUMP

The Woodson Two-Way Notrump convention authorizes an opening bid of one notrump with any balanced hand containing either 10-12 HCP or 16-18 HCP. This device is intended to make it as difficult as possible for the opponents to know whether they should enter the auction.

If responder has 15 or fewer points, he proceeds initially on the premise that opener has the strong notrump and tries for game if he has 8 HCP or more. With 0-7 points and a balanced hand responder should pass the one notrump opening. With 0-7 points and a five-card or longer suit other than clubs, responder bids two of his suit. Opener should not bid again unless he has 18 points and an excellent fit.

If responder has 14-15 HCP or 13 with a five-card suit, he should invite game. If his hand is balanced or his long suit is a minor, he should do so by bidding two notrump. The two notrump bid does not deny a four-card major. Opener should accept the invitation with 11 or more HCP. The best way for opener to accept is to bid three clubs if he has a four-card major suit, initiating a STAYMAN inquiry. If opener has 18 HCP, he should be interested in the possibility of slam and should take care, if he has no four-card major with which he would bid three clubs as Stayman, not simply to rebid three notrump.

If responder has 8 or more points and wishes clarification of opener's strength, responder bids two clubs over the one notrump opening. Opener should respond as follows:

    2 ◊   = 10-12 HCP, fewer than four hearts; says nothing about spade length

    2 ♡   = 10-12 HCP, four hearts, says nothing about spade length

    2 ♠   = 16 HCP, four spades, says nothing about heart length

    2NT = 16 HCP, fewer than four spades; says nothing about heart length

    3 ♣   = 17-18 HCP, and says nothing about major suit length

If responder has 8-13 points and opener has made a rebid showing 10-12 HCP, responder should sign off at the two level. If opener has rebid two diamonds, denying four hearts, responder may bid two hearts with a five-card heart suit, or bid two spades with a four-card or longer spade suit, or bid two notrump with neither holding. If opener has rebid two hearts, responder may pass if he has four hearts; if he has fewer, he may bid two spades if he has four or more spades; if responder has no four-card major, he should rebid two notrump.

None of responder's rebids at the two level is forcing.

If responder has 13-15 points and a five-card major suit, he may invite game over opener's two diamond, or two heart rebid by bidding three of the major suit in which he has five cards.

If opener has rebid two spades in answer to the two club inquiry, showing 16 HCP, responder may pass if he has four spades and a minimum, *i.e.*, 8 or a bad 9 points. With a minimum and fewer than four spades, responder bids two notrump. Opener should not bid again.

If, over any of opener's answers to the two club inquiry, responder bids three diamonds, the bid is forcing to game and asks whether opener has four cards in a major suit as to which his first rebid was noncommittal.

If, in response to the one notrump opening, responder has a hand worth 16 or more points, he should assume initially that opener has the weak hand worth 10-12 HCP. With a balanced hand worth 16 HCP, responder may jump to three notrump with no four-card major suit. With at least one four-card major, he should commence by bidding two clubs, and follow with three diamonds if necessary, to determine whether there is a 4-4 major suit fit.

If responder has 15 or more points and a long major suit he may show it directly over the one notrump opening by jumping to three of his suit if it is five cards long, or to four if it is longer. These direct jumps to three over the one notrump opening are forcing to game.

If opener has the strong notrump opening opposite any of these strong responses, he will explore for slam.

A two club response followed by a three club rebid by responder shows a six-card or longer club suit in a hand whose strength is not sufficient to warrant going to game opposite the strength shown by opener in his rebid over two clubs.

The use of the Woodson Two-Way Notrump makes it difficult for the opponents to know whether they should intervene over the one notrump opening, because opener could have as few points as 10 or as many as 18. Further, since responder would bid two clubs with as few as 8 HCP and would sign off opposite the weak response with as many as 12 or 13, the opponents could have, after such a sign off, a majority of the points or as few as 15. On the other hand, the wide range of the notrump opening reduces the partnership's accuracy in slam bidding in choosing the best game or best part-score, and in staying low on part-score hands. Further, in competition it is more difficult for users of an ambiguous notrump opening to judge when to double the opponents, when to bid a game, and when to compete for a part-score.

If there is a penalty double of the one notrump opening, it is recommended that opener redouble with the weak hand to urge responder to seek an escape. *See also* TRANSFERS OVER DOUBLES OF ONE NOTRUMP.

KAMIKAZE NOTRUMP

The Kamikaze Notrump system uses an opening bid of one notrump in first or second position to show a balanced hand with 10-13 high card points. The hand must not contain a singleton or void; but it may have a six-card suit or even a seven-card suit. It need not have stoppers in any specified number of suits. A Kamikaze one notrump opening would be appropriate with any of the following hands:

[A]	♠ x x x	♡ A K Q	◇ x x x x	♣ J x x
[B]	♠ J x x	♡ K x x	◇ A x x	♣ Q x x x
[C]	♠ Q x	♡ Q x x	◇ K Q	♣ J x x x x x

Responder is required to bid over the Kamikaze notrump if he has fewer than eight high card points. The only convention used in response to the one notrump opening is two clubs as STAYMAN. If responder has a balanced hand worth less than a game invitation, he may bid two clubs planning to pass opener's rebid. If responder has a long suit other than clubs, he may bid it naturally at the two level; this bid is not forcing.

Responder needs 13-14 points to invite game and 15 or more to force to game. He may invite game either by bidding two notrump, or by using Stayman and then bidding a major suit at the three level over opener's rebid. His jumps to three of a major directly over the opening are natural and game-forcing.

If the one notrump opening is doubled, responder's bidding with fewer than 14 points is largely the same as if there had been no interference. If responder has 14 or more points, he is required to redouble.

The Kamikaze system uses opening bids of two hearts and two spades as weak two bids; these openings promise 9-11 HCP and may be made on five-card suits. The system uses an opening bid of two diamonds to show a three-suited hand with 9-11 HCP; the short suit is unspecified. *See* ROMAN TWO DIAMONDS; TWO DIAMOND OPENING AS MINIMUM THREE-SUITER.

The Kamikaze 10-13 point one notrump opening is used only in first and second seats. More traditional notrump ranges, weak or strong according to partnership preference, are used in third or fourth position.

As the Kamikaze system was originally devised, the opening notrump bid showed 9-12 points. The American Contract Bridge League, however, has prohibited the use of any convention in response to an opening notrump bid whose minimum point count may be lower than 10. Thus, in order to minimize the risks associated with a very weak notrump opening, the range of the Kamikaze opening was raised to 10-13 HCP.

The defense recommended by the inventor of the Kamikaze notrump is for opener's left-hand opponent to double the 10-13 point notrump opening if he has 15 or more points, or for opener's right-hand opponent (in the auction 1 Notrump - Pass - Pass - ?) to make a balancing double with 14 or more points. Since the system instructs responder not to pass with fewer than eight points, it may be dangerous to double in the balancing seat with fewer than 14 points. The two-suited defenses agreed to by the non-opening side remain available.

See also WOODSON TWO-WAY NOTRUMP.

II

Responses and Rebids after Natural Opening Bids in a Suit

BERGEN MODIFICATIONS OF JACOBY TWO NOTRUMP

The JACOBY TWO NOTRUMP convention uses a response of two notrump as a forcing raise of an opening bid of one heart or one spade. The original design of rebids permits opener to identify his side-suit singletons on the three level or his side five-card suits on the four level, or to disclose extra strength if his hand is relatively balanced. None of the traditional rebids permits opener to show both his strength and his unbalanced distributional features.

The Bergen modifications to this convention require opener to use the immediate three- and four-level responses to identify types of hands rather than specific singletons or specific side suits. If responder is interested in more precise information after any of these rebids, he generally may obtain it in one of two ways. He may make the cheapest possible rebid, a relay that asks opener to be more specific about the bid he has just made. Or responder may bid one of the three steps just beyond the relay bid as an asking bid about control of a specific suit.

Though there are other variations of the Jacoby two notrump rebids that employ similar two-stage inquiries, *see* MARTEL MODIFICATIONS OF JACOBY TWO NOTRUMP; TWO-PHASE TWO NOTRUMP ASKING BIDS AFTER JACOBY TWO NOTRUMP, the Bergen/Jacoby convention includes an additional feature: it gives the opening bidder the option, over the two notrump response, of not describing his own hand and instead asking for a description of responder's hand.

Opener's Rebids After Responder's Two Notrump

In the Bergen/Jacoby Two Notrump convention, opener's immediate rebids over two notrump show his type of distribution. All but one of these bids also show whether opener's strength is minimum, or a "reasonable" minimum, or better than a reasonable minimum.

A "reasonable" minimum is a hand with at least 12-13 HCP consisting principally of aces and kings, *e.g.*,

[A]	♠ K Q x x x	[B]	♠ A x x x x	[C]	♠ x
	♡ A x x		♡ K Q x x		♡ Q J x x x
	◇ x x		◇ A x		◇ A K x x
	♣ K x x		♣ x x		♣ K x x

A balanced 12- or 13-point hand laden with jacks and queens, *e.g.*,

[D]   ♠ A Q 10 x x   ♡ J x   ◇ Q x x   ♣ K x x does not qualify as a reasonable minimum. Any hand with a singleton or a void is considered better than a minimum if it has at least 13 high card points. Since a hand with 5-3-3-2 distribution should generally be opened one notrump if it contains 15 or 16 HCP, a hand with such distribution is considered better than a minimum if it is stronger than an opening notrump, *i.e.*, it contains 17 or more HCP. Since a hand with a five-card major and 5-4-2-2 distribution, is not normally opened one notrump, a hand with that distribution is considered better than minimum if it contains 15 or more HCP.

In addition to showing opener's strength, the Bergen/Jacoby immediate rebids give a general indication of opener's distribution, though the suit of any shortness or extra length is not specified. The complete schedule of immediate rebids is:

> 3 ♣ = any hand with better than minimum strength and either a singleton, or 5-4-2-2 or 5-3-3-2 distribution
>
> 3 ◇ = any hand with better than minimum strength and a second suit of five or more cards, or any good hand with which opener wants to know more about responder's distribution
>
> 3 ♡ = any hand with a void
>
> 3 ♠ = any hand with minimum strength and a singleton somewhere
>
> 3 NT = any hand with better than minimum strength and six cards in the suit opened
>
> 4 ♣ = a reasonable minimum, with no void or singleton, and with the ace or king of clubs
>
> 4 ◇ = a reasonable minimum, with the ace or king of diamonds, but no ace or king of clubs
>
> 4 ♡ (after 1 ♠ opening) = a reasonable minimum, with the ace or king of hearts, but without the ace or king of either minor suit.
>
> 4 ♡ (after 1 ♡ opening) = signoff, minimum strength
>
> 4 ♠ (after 1 ♠ opening) = signoff, minimum strength

Thus, if opener held one of the hands set out above, he would show at least reasonable minimum values by rebidding four clubs with hand A, four diamonds with hand B, and three clubs with hand C. With hand D, however, an unpromising minimum, opener would bid four spades, a signoff. If one of opener's hearts in hand D were a club or a diamond, he would bid three spades, showing a singleton with a minimum, rather than three clubs which would promise better than a minimum.

Opener's immediate rebids do not identify in which suit he has shortness or extra length. His response of three hearts, which promises a void somewhere, also does not reveal whether he has minimum or better.

694

If responder has no slam aspirations after opener's immediate rebid, he signs off in four of the agreed trump suit. If slam remains a possibility after opener's rebid of three clubs, three hearts, or three spades, responder may ask for further information by bidding the next higher suit, as a relay bid; or he may make make an asking bid in a specific suit.

Relays and Asking Bids After Opener Has Rebid Three Clubs

After opener's rebid of three clubs, showing a hand of better than minimum strength that either is relatively balanced or contains a singleton, responder may make a bid at the three level to ask opener for more information. These bids do not describe responder's hand; they are entirely artificial. The three diamond bid by responder is a relay bid; the other three-level bids are asking bids.

After responder's three diamond relay bid, opener makes a bid at the three level to identify his singleton if he has one. If he has no singleton, he makes a bid on the four level that identifies his cheapest side ace or king. Thus, after the auction has begun

Opener	Responder
1 ♡ or 1 ♠	2 Notrump
3 ♣	3 ◇

opener's rebids are as follows:

3 ♡   = singleton club
3 ♠   = singleton diamond
3 NT = singleton in the other major
4 ♣   = 5-3-3-2 or 5-4-2-2 distribution, with the ace or king of clubs
4 ◇   = 5-3-3-2 or 5-4-2-2 distribution, with the ace or king of diamonds, and with no ace or king of clubs
4 ♡ (after 1 ♠ opening) = 5-3-3-2 or 5-4-2-2 distribution, with the ace or king of hearts, and with no ace or king of either minor suit
4 ♡ (after 1 ♡ opening) = 5-3-3-2 or 5-4-2-2 distribution, no ace or king of either minor suit

Though many of the bids used in responding to responder's inquiries are artificial, this schedule illustrates a Bergen/Jacoby structural principle that provides an aide to memory. Whenever opener is to identify a side suit, be it singleton, void, or long suit, he does so in ascending order: the cheapest of the three bids he uses pinpoints clubs, the next cheapest pinpoints diamonds, and the third pinpoints the unbid major. As discussed below, this principle also guides responder's side-suit asking bids made over opener's three-level shape- and strength-showing rebids.

After opener has responded to a relay bid, responder's bid of a new suit is a cue-bid. Opener is expected, if his hand warrants it, to cue-bid in return.

Though three diamonds is responder's usual action when opener has rebid three clubs, responder may have a highly distributional hand with which he needs only to locate specific controls. If responder makes any other bid at the three level after opener's three clubs, it is a suit-asking bid. This asking bid requires opener to reveal the degree to which he has control of the target suit. The ascending-order principle governs the order of the suits under inquiry. Thus, responder's cheapest bid beyond the relay suit asks about clubs; the second cheapest asks about diamonds; and the third cheapest asks about the unbid major. Accordingly, after opener's three club rebid, responder's asking bids are:

> 3 ♡ = asking bid for club control
> 3 ♠ = asking bid for diamond control
> 3 NT = asking bid for control of major not opened

In response to each suit-asking bid, opener shows his control in the target suit by bidding one of the following steps:

> First step = no control
> Second step = third round control, *i.e.*, queen or doubleton
> Third step = second round control, *i.e.*, king or singleton
> Fourth step = ace

This four-step schedule is used for all responses to suit-asking bids, whether the asking bid follows one of opener's three-level rebids or is a follow-up rebid.

After opener has made his step response, responder may make a further asking bid by bidding another suit. These follow-up asking bids are natural. That is, responder makes his asking bid in the suit which he seeks information. Thus, in the auction

Opener	Responder
1 ♠	2 Notrump
3 ♣	3 Notrump
4 ♠	5 ♣
5 ♠	7 ♠

responder's three notrump bid asks about control in the other major, hearts; opener's four spade bid, the fourth step, shows the ace of hearts. Responder's bid of five clubs asks about control of clubs. Opener shows second round club control by bidding five spades, the third step. For this auction, the partnership hands might be

Opener
♠ K J x x x   ♡ A x x x   ◊ A J x   ♣ x
Responder
♠ A x x x x   ♡ Q J   ◊ —   ♣ A K x x x x

Relays and Asking Bids After Opener Has Rebid Three Hearts

If opener has rebid three hearts, showing a void, responder bids three spades, the cheapest bid, to ask where the void is:

Opener	*Responder*
1 ♡ or 1 ♠	2 Notrump
3 ♡	3 ♠

Opener bids one of the next three steps to identify his void in accordance with the ascending-order principle:

3 NT = void in clubs
4 ♣ = void in diamonds
4 ◊ = void in the other major

In these void-showing sequences, opener has not revealed the high-card strength of his hand. On many hands, however, if opener has the right void, slam will be a good proposition even if he has a minimum in high cards. Suppose opener and responder held

Opener
♠ A x x x x   ♡ K x x x   ◊ —   ♣ A x x x
Responder
♠ K x x x x   ♡ A x   ◊ x x x x   ♣ K Q

Whereas even a small slam would usually fail if opener's minor suits were reversed, responder can envision a laydown grand slam after opener shows a void in diamonds in the following auction:

Opener	Responder
1 ♠	2 Notrump
3 ♡	3 ♠
4 ♣	4 ♡
5 ♣	5 Notrump
6 ♣	7 ♠

Responder's three spade bid asks opener where his void is, and the four club bid shows a diamond void; the four heart and five club bids are cue-bids. Responder's bid of five notrump is the GRAND SLAM FORCE, asking opener to bid seven with two of the top three spade honors. Opener's bid of six clubs shows a very good spade holding, but without two of the top three honors. Responder infers that opener has the ace of spades, since spades headed by no better than the queen could not be considered "very good." Thus, responder knows the partnership has ten spades headed by the ace and king, and he bids the grand slam.

Over opener's three heart rebid, responder may instead make a suit-asking bid. These asking bids are the three steps just above the three spade relay bid:

    3 NT = asking bid for club control
    4 ♣ = asking bid for diamond control
    4 ◇ = asking bid for control of major not opened

Opener responds to any of these inquiries by using one of the four step responses outlined above with respect to the asking bids that follow opener's three club rebid. When opener has rebid three hearts over two notrump, his bid of the fourth step in response to a suit-asking bid shows either the ace or a void.

Relays and Asking Bids After Opener Has Rebid Three Spades

If opener has rebid three spades, showing a singleton somewhere and minimum strength, responder may bid three notrump, the cheapest step, to ask where the singleton is. In accordance with the ascending-order principle, opener responds as follows:

    4 ♣ = singleton club
    4 ◇ = singleton diamond
    4 ♡ = singleton in the major not opened

Instead of bidding three notrump to ask where the singleton is, responder, may, after opener's three spade rebid over two notrump, make a suit-asking bid. These asking bids are:

4 ♣ = asking bid for club control
4 ♢ = asking bid for diamond control
4 ♡ (if opening was 1 ♠) = asking bid about heart control

If the opening bid was one heart, the four heart bid by responder is a signoff. When the opening bid was one heart, responder has no available asking bid with respect to spades.

Opener responds to any of these asking bids by using the customary four-step schedule.

Rebids by Responder After Opener Has Rebid Three Diamonds

After the two notrump response, opener may rebid three diamonds with a two-suited hand, but the three diamond bid does not guarantee such distribution. This bid is used when opener wants to know more about responder's hand.

After opener's three diamond rebid, responder is required to describe his distribution. Certain distributions are not shown, however, for responder is not allowed to rebid past four of the agreed trump suit.

If the opening bid was one spade, and the auction has begun

Opener	Responder
1 ♠	2 Notrump
3 ♢	

responder employs the ascending-order principle to show his distribution as follows:

3 ♡ = doubleton club
3 ♠ = doubleton diamond
3 NT = doubleton in the major not opened
4 ♣ = 4-3-3-3 distribution, better than a minimum
4 ♢ = singleton club, better than a minimum
4 ♡ = singleton diamond, better than a minimum
4 ♠ = 4-3-3-3 distribution, minimum strength

When responder's shape is 4-3-3-3, 13-14 HCP is considered a minimum. He should have 15 or more HCP to rebid four clubs.

If the opening bid were one heart, responder's rebids through four diamonds would be the same. His bid of four hearts, however, would show 4-3-3-3 distribution with minimum strength. After a one heart opening, the only singleton responder can show is in clubs.

Note also that, whether the opening bid is one heart or one spade, responder cannot show a singleton in the other major suit. The partnership should rely on its usual SPLINTER RAISE structure to show the singletons that are not provided for in these schedules. *See, e.g.*, THREE NOTRUMP AS SPLINTER IN OTHER MAJOR.

The Bergen Modifications After Opponent's Double of Two Notrump

When the opponents intervene over the Bergen/Jacoby Two Notrump response, opener's rebids may require some modification. The intervention that causes least immediate difficulty is the double.

If the opponent doubles the two notrump response, most of opener's rebids remain the same. The one difference is that if opener has a minimum hand with 5-3-3-2 distribution, he should redouble. With any other strength or distribution, opener should make his normal shape-showing rebid.

If the doubler's partner bids, responder's double will be for penalties. If responder instead wants to know more about opener's hand, he asks by passing doubler's partner's bid. Opener treats the double as if it were the cheapest bid over whatever bid he has just made, and he gives the requested information in steps. For example, in the auction

North	East	South	West
1 ♡	Pass	2 Notrump	Double
3 ♣	3 ♠	Pass	

opener's three club bid shows a better than minimum hand with either a singleton or a balanced or semi-balanced hand. Responder's pass of three spades asks opener for details. Opener rebids in steps corresponding to the sequence of bids he would have made if, without competition, responder had bid three diamonds over three clubs. Thus,

First step   = singleton club
Second step = singleton diamond
Third step   = singleton in the major not opened
Fourth step = 5-3-3-2 or 5-4-2-2 distribution, with the ace or king of clubs
Fifth step   = 5-3-3-2 or 5-4-2-2 distribution, with the ace or king of diamonds, and with no ace or king of clubs
Sixth step   = 5-3-3-2 or 5-4-2-2 distribution, with no ace or king of either minor suit

If, instead of doubling or passing, responder bids a new suit, it is an asking bid in that suit. Opener shows his control using the customary four-step schedule of responses.

The Bergen Modifications After An Opponent's Three-Level Overcall

If an opponent overcalls at the three level over responder's two notrump bid, the partnership still has a good deal of room for exploration. Though opener can no longer provide the detailed responses that are available without the overcall, his immediate action nonetheless can give some indication of both his strength and his distribution.

With minimum strength and 5-3-3-2 distribution, opener doubles, even if his doubleton is in the suit overcalled. Responder may pass the double or bid three notrump if he has length in the opponent's suit; or he may sign off in four of the major suit opened; or, if he has a very strong hand, he may proceed with slam exploration.

If opener has minimum strength, only a five-card suit, and distribution other than 5-3-3-2, he rebids four of the suit he opened. If he has six cards in his suit, opener should make the cheapest bid possible, other than three notrump, over the overcall. This cheapest-suit rebid, showing a sixth trump, neither promises nor denies extra strength.

With a singleton or void in the opponent's suit and at least a reasonable minimum, opener bids three notrump (assuming the opponent himself has not bid three notrump). If, instead of overcalling, the opponent has cue-bid the suit opened, opener's three notrump rebid shows a singleton in the other major.

If opener has a singleton or void in an unbid suit and at least a reasonable minimum, he may bid the suit in which he is short, so long as (1) it does not go past four of the agreed trump suit, and (2) it is not the bid that shows he has opened with a six-card suit.

Finally, if opener has a good hand with no singleton or void for which a bid is available, and he has opened a five-card suit, he passes the overcall. His pass invites responder to cue-bid if he is interested in slam opposite a relatively balanced hand. Responder is free to sign off in four of the suit opened or to double the overcall for penalties.

For example, if the bidding were opened one spade, opener's calls after a three level overcall over two notrump would be:

Double = 5-3-3-2, minimum

Cheapest suit bid = six cards in suit opened

3 NT = singleton or void in opponent's suit, at least a reasonable minimum, suit length undisclosed

4 ♣ = singleton if not the cheapest suit over the overcall and not the suit of the overcall

4 ◇ = singleton if not the suit of the overcall

4 ♡ = singleton if not the suit of the overcall

4 ♠ = minimum with other than 5-3-3-2

Pass = better than a minimum, five-card suit, no disclosable singleton or void

In the auction

North	East	South	West
1 ♡	Pass	2 Notrump	3 ♠
4 ♣			

North's bid of four clubs, the cheapest available suit bid over the overcall, shows that he has a six-card heart suit. If he had bid three notrump, he would have shown a singleton spade. If he had bid four diamonds, he would have shown a singleton diamond. In this auction, opener has no way to show a singleton club.

On some hands, opener will have more than one feature he wishes to communicate and will have to decide which to describe. If he has both a six-card suit and a singleton or void in the suit overcalled, he should normally bid three notrump, to show his shortness. If he has both a six-card suit and a singleton in an unbid suit, he should normally show his six-card suit.

The Bergen Modifications After An Opponent's Four-Level Overcall

When an opponent has jumped to the four level over responder's two notrump, the partnership has far less room to explore for slam. The available space is allocated as follows.

If the overcall is in the suit that ranks just below the suit opened, only three options are available: double, pass, and a bid of four of the suit opened. Opener's double promises two or more cards in the suit overcalled and suggests that opener does not have a good hand for offense. It suggests that the partnership defend. His bid of four of the suit opened promises a good offensive hand, but does not promise more than minimum high card strength. If opener has slam interest, he passes.

702

These three calls retain their meanings as well if the suit of the overcall is two or three steps below the suit opened. Other options are added.

If the suit of the overcall ranks two below the suit opened (*i.e.*, hearts opened and clubs overcalled, or spades opened and diamonds overcalled), opener has available a bid of the suit that ranks between the two bid suits. He bids this intermediate suit to show that he has opened a six-card suit.

If the opening bid was one spade and the overcall over two notrump was four clubs, opener has two steps available. His bid of four diamonds, the cheaper, shows a six-card spade suit. His bid of four hearts shows a singleton or void in hearts and fewer than six spades.

If the opening bid was one heart and the opponent's overcall over two notrump is four spades, the partnership must decide whether to defend or go at least to the five level. Opener doubles to show a hand that is a minimum for offensive purposes; the double suggests that the partnership defend. If opener has a two-suited hand and slam interest, he bids his second suit. If opener passes, he shows that he has more than a minimum for offensive purposes. Though the pass shows a willingness to play at the five-level, it does not show slam interest.

If opener passes, a double by responder is for penalties. If, over the double, opener bids a new suit, he shows a very good hand with slam interest, and his bid is a cue-bid.

MARTEL MODIFICATIONS OF
JACOBY TWO NOTRUMP

The Martel modifications to opener's rebids after a JACOBY TWO NOTRUMP raise of the opening bid of one heart or one spade are designed to eliminate or minimize opener's revealing rebids when both partners have minimum hands. Martel/Jacoby requires opener to rebid three clubs with any hand of minimum strength, regardless of his distribution.

If opener has extra values, he makes a rebid at the three level to show shortness or a rebid at the four level to show a long side suit. He rebids three diamonds or three of the other major to show a singleton or void in the suit of the rebid, or he rebids three of his own suit to show a singleton or void in clubs. Opener's bids at the four level show five cards in the suit bid.

For example, after an opening bid of one spade, opener's rebids would be as follows:

3 ♣	= minimum strength, any distribution
3 ◇	= singleton or void in diamonds, extra values
3 ♡	= singleton or void in hearts, extra values
3 ♠	= singleton or void in clubs, extra values
3 NT	= balanced hand, extra values
4 ♣	= five-card club suit, extra values
4 ◇	= five-card diamond suit, extra values
4 ♡	= five-card heart suit, extra values

If responder has a minimum for his forcing raise, over opener's three club rebid he may simply sign off in four of the agreed trump suit. This sequence denies the opponents information as to opener's distribution and as to the location of the partnership's controls.

After opener's three club bid, if responder has a sufficiently good hand to be interested in slam even opposite opener's announced minimum, he may bid three diamonds to ask whether opener has a singleton or void, and if so, where it is. In response to the three diamond bid, opener would bid three of his suit to show a balanced hand. His bids of three of the other major, four clubs, and four diamonds would show a singleton or void in the suit bid.

See also BERGEN MODIFICATIONS OF JACOBY TWO NOTRUMP; TWO-PHASE TWO NOTRUMP ASKING BIDS.

TWO-PHASE TWO NOTRUMP ASKING BIDS AFTER JACOBY TWO NOTRUMP

Use of two notrump as an artificial relay bid that asks opener for more information is an integral part of certain conventions such as FLANNERY TWO DIAMONDS, JACOBY TWO NOTRUMP, PRECISION TWO DIAMONDS, and ONE-TWO-THREE TWO-SUITERS. Usually these conventions use the two notrump response to ask opener to disclose whatever is to be revealed of his strength and distribution with a single bid. The Two-Phase Two Notrump Asking Bid convention, adaptable to a variety of bidding situations, instead conducts the inquiry in two stages and permits the delivery of a greater quantity of information when that seems desirable.

Two premises underlie Two-Phase Asking Bids. One is that if two phases of rebids are used, a wider variety of opening hands may be covered. The other is that responder often need not have complete information to make an intelligent decision as to where to play the hand. On many hands, if he knows that opener has a minimum, that knowledge will suffice; or if he knows that opener has no voids or singletons, that information will suffice. Two-Phase Two Notrump Asking Bids thus assign to opener's cheapest rebids the meanings that would be least encouraging; then if responder wishes to know more, he may make a further relay bid.

This technique as it may be applied to the Flannery Two Diamond and FLANNERY TWO HEART conventions is described in EXTENDED FLANNERY; its application to weak two bids is discussed in TWO-PHASE TWO NOTRUMP ASKING BIDS AFTER WEAK TWO BIDS; its use following a three-suited opening bid of two diamonds is described in TWO-PHASE TWO NOTRUMP RESPONSE TO THREE-SUITED OPENINGS. Its use in conjunction with major suit openings when the partnership is using Jacoby two notrump as a forcing raise, is discussed below.

When the partnership has agreed to use the Two-Phase Two Notrump Asking Bid convention as an adjunct to the Jacoby two notrump response, responder's bid of two notrump initiates an inquiry in response to which opener gives the following information as to his shape and strength:

3 ♣ = minimum strength, without shortness in diamonds
3 ◊ = singleton or void in diamonds, strength undisclosed
3 of major opened = extra values, no singleton or void
3 of other major = singleton or void in that suit, plus extra values
3 NT = singleton or void in clubs, plus extra values
4 ♣ = long good club suit, plus extra values
4 ◊ = long good diamond suit, plus extra values

If opener has bid three clubs, responder may bid three diamonds to find out whether opener has a singleton or void in clubs or the unbid major. Opener rebids his suit with no singleton or void; he rebids the other major with shortness in that suit, or three notrump with a singleton or void in clubs.

For alternative schedules of multi-phase rebids by opener over two notrump, *see* BERGEN MODIFICATIONS OF JACOBY TWO NOTRUMP; MARTEL MODIFICATIONS OF JACOBY TWO NOTRUMP.

VALUE SWISS RAISES

One method of making a forcing raise of the opener's major suit with a balanced hand is called Value Swiss Raises. As used in the Aces Scientific System, this convention permits the responder to show trump support suitable for a force to game, and to deny a singleton or a good five-card suit, and to specify the high card strength on which his raise is based.

Holding 12 to a poor 13 high card points, the responder makes a forcing one notrump response, and then follows by jumping to four of the opener's suit. With a good 13 to a bad 14 in high card points, the responder jumps to four diamonds.

With a good 14 to a bad 16 high card points, the responder jumps to four clubs.

With a good 16 to 18 high card points, the responder first bids two notrump, and then follows by jumping in the responder's suit.

For example, if responder had a hand such as

♠ A x x x   ♥ A Q x   ♦ x x   ♣ A x x x

the bidding might begin

Opener	Responder
1♠	4♣

These raises can advantageously be combined with UNBALANCED SWISS RAISES. (See also CONGLOMERATE MAJOR SUIT RAISES, CONTROL SWISS, SPLINTER RAISES, TRUMP SWISS, TRUMP AND CONTROL SWISS.)

UNBALANCED SWISS RAISES

A method of making a forcing raise of the opener's major suit with a singleton (used in coordination with VALUE SWISS RAISES), is called Unbalanced Swiss Raises. If the responder has a singleton somewhere in his hand and holds 10 to 12 points in support of the opener's major suit, he jumps to three of the other major.

With a singleton and 13 to 15 points, the responder jumps to three notrump.

In order to have the responder identify his singleton, the opener makes the cheapest possible bid over the response:

	Opener	Responder
[A]	1 ♠	3 ♡ (10-12)
	3 ♠	

	Opener	Responder
[B]	1 ♡	3 ♠ (10-12)
	3 Notrump	

[C]	1 ♠	3 Notrump (13-15)
	4 ♣	

[D]	1 ♡	3 Notrump (13-15)
	4 ♣	

The opener's three spade bid in auction [A], his three notrump bid in auction [B] and his four club bids in auctions [C] and [D] ask where the responder's singleton is.

The responder shows his singleton by bidding one of the next three steps after the opener's rebid. Two of these steps will be natural suits and show a singleton in those suits; the other step will be either three notrump (in auction [A]) or four of the trump suit (in auctions [B] and [D]) and will show the singleton not shown naturally. Thus, in auction [A], the responder specifies his singleton as follows:

    3NT = singleton heart
    4 ♣ = singleton club
    4 ◊ = singleton diamond

After a three notrump asking bid by the opener as in auction [B], the responder bids as follows:

    4 ♣ = singleton club
    4 ◊ = singleton diamond
    4 ♡ = singleton spade

After the opener's four club bid in auction [C], the responder shows his singleton as follows:

    4 ◊ = singleton diamond
    4 ♡ = singleton heart
    4 ♠ = singleton club

In auction [D], the responder would show his singleton as follows:

    4 ◊ = singleton diamond
    4 ♡ = singleton club
    4 ♠ = singleton spade

(See also CONGLOMERATE MAJOR SUIT RAISES, SPLINTER RAISES.)

INVERTED MINOR RAISES

When the bidding is opened with one of a minor suit, a useful treatment is the reversal of the normal meanings of the immediate raises to two and three of the opener's suit. This treatment, called Inverted Minor Suit Raises, uses the jump raise to three with hands worth no more than 8 points, and reserves the single raise for hands worth 9 or more points. The utility of this reversal of meaning is that it keeps the bidding at a low level to facilitate game and slam exploration on hands where game and slam are realistic possibilities. The method also allows the responder to preempt with hands that are weak.

To make the jump raise to three of the opener's suit, the responder should have at least five-card support to allow for the possibility that the opening was made on a three-card suit. The responder should not have a side four-card major suit, especially when the partnership is using five-card major suit openings. His strength should be such that he is pessimistic about game prospects opposite a normal minimum opening bid. A jump raise to three clubs would be appropriate on either of the following hands:

[A]   ♠ x x   ♡ K x x   ◊ x x x   ♣ K J x x x

[B]   ♠ x x   ♡ x x   ◊ x x   ♣ Q J x x x x

The responder's single raise of the opener's minor suit is made with 9 or more points: it is forcing on the opener for one round. The responder should have at least four-card support, and should not hold a four-card major suit. Any of the following hands would be appropriate for a forcing raise to two clubs:

[C]   ♠ x   ♡ K x x   ◊ Q J x   ♣ K x x x x x

[D]   ♠ A x x   ♡ x x x   ◊ K x x   ♣ Q J x x

[E]   ♠ A Q x   ♡ x x   ◊ A K x x   ♣ A J x x

After the inverted raise to two of his suit, the opener is forced to bid at least once more. If he has a balanced hand of minimum strength he should rebid two notrump. This rebid is not forcing.

The responder will pass if he, too, has a minimum balanced hand such as [D] above, but the responder will rebid three clubs if he has a minimum unbalanced hand such as [C]. The responder's rebid of three clubs is not forcing. Any other suit rebid by the responder promises that the responder had a full opening bid of his own. The partnership is then forced to game.

If the opener has an unbalanced hand, he should rebid a suit. With minimum strength he should simply rebid his original suit. This rebid is not forcing. With better than a minimum hand, the opener should rebid a side suit in which he has a stopper. The responder may then bid either a new suit in which he has a stopper, or notrump if he has both unbid suits guarded. If the responder simply rebids the suit opened, he shows a bare minimum without a stopper in any unbid suit. This rebid is not forcing.

SOLOWAY JUMP SHIFTS

In standard practice, a jump shift response to an opening bid shows a very strong hand with which game is assured, and slam is a likely prospect. The standard jump shift can be made on any of four types of hands:

(1) A good fit for opener's suit
(2) A single long strong suit
(3) A balanced 19 or higher count, or
(4) A strong two-suiter

Soloway jump shifts are similar to traditional jump shifts except that they cannot be made on two-suited hands. In this convention, if the bidding starts

Opener	Responder
1♠	3♦

the responder cannot have a genuine side suit in clubs or hearts. This agreement makes it easier for the responder to describe a very strong hand with support for the opener's suit.

The responder specifies what type of hand he has with his rebid. If he rebids the suit he has jumped in, he has a one-suiter and does not necessarily have support for the opener's suit. If he rebids in notrump, he has a balanced or semi-balanced hand worth at least 18 points. Any other rebid shows a hand with a good fit for the opener's suit.

If the responder bids a new suit on his second turn, he shows a doubleton or a tripleton in the new suit, a good fit for the opener's suit, and a singleton in the suit he has neither bid nor (by agreed inference) supported. For example:

Opener	Responder
1♠	3♦
3♡	4♣

Since the responder is forbidden to make a jump shift with a two-suited hand, his four club bid shows that he intended all along to show support for opener's spades. Since he has bid diamonds and clubs, and by inference has supported spades, he shows a singleton heart.

If the responder has a hand with good support for the opener's suit but has no singleton, he will simply rebid in the opener's suit:

Opener	Responder
1♠	3♦
3♡	3♠

KANTAR RELAYS AFTER ONE HEART
OR ONE SPADE OPENING

When the partnership is using a natural two notrump response to an opening bid of one heart or one spade, it may agree to use Kantar Relays over certain new-suit rebids by opener. The relay, used principally when responder is interested in opener's second suit, allows responder to obtain additional information as to opener's strength and distribution.

The Kantar Relay is responder's bid of three of the cheapest suit after opener's rebid of a new suit:

[A]	*Opener*	*Responder*	[B]	*Opener*	*Responder*
	1 ♡	2 Notrump		1 ♠	2 Notrump
	3 ♣			3 ♣	

[C]	*Opener*	*Responder*
	1 ♠	2 Notrump
	3 ♢	

In each of these auctions, responder may make the cheapest bid over opener's second suit as a relay to ask for more information. Kantar Relays are not used if opener has reversed; nor are they used in either of the following auctions:

[D]	*Opener*	*Responder*	[E]	*Opener*	*Responder*
	1 ♡	2 Notrump		1 ♠	2 Notrump
	3 ♢			3 ♡	

Since a return to opener's first suit is needed as a natural bid, Kantar Relays are usable only when opener's two suits are not touching suits, *i.e.*, not spades-hearts or hearts-diamonds.

When the partnership has agreed to use Kantar Relays after responder's natural two notrump response, opener should not rebid three of a new suit if his distribution is 5-4-2-2 unless he has slam interest. With a semi-balanced hand and less than 17 points, opener should simply rebid three notrump over two notrump.

The general pattern by which opener describes his distribution in response to a Kantar Relay is as follows. If he has two doubletons (and thus has at least 17 HCP), he rebids four notrump. (The three notrump rebid is reserved for use with 5-4-3-1 hands.) With 5-4-3-1 distribution, opener identifies his three-card suit (his "fragment"). With five or more cards in each of his suits, opener rebids one of these suits. The two-suited rebids and the fragment-showing rebids are discussed in separate sections below; a recapitulation of all of opener's rebids over the relay is provided at the end.

Opener's Rebids With 5-5-2-1 Distribution

In response to the relay bid, if opener has a genuine two-suiter, *i.e.*, at least five cards in each suit, he rebids one of his suits. If he has minimum strength, he rebids his first suit. The level at which opener returns to his first suit to show a minimum depends in part on which two suits he has.

When opener's suits are spades and diamonds, he shows minimum strength by bidding four spades. (The three spade bid is reserved for use with 5-4-3-1 hands, as discussed in the next section.)

When opener's suits are spades-clubs or hearts-clubs, thus making the relay bid three diamonds, opener shows his minimum by bidding either three or four of his first suit. Opener's bid of three of his first suit shows that some of his high cards are located in his short suits, thus giving responder useful information for deciding whether to play in three notrump. Opener's bid of four of his first suit over the three diamond relay shows a concentration of high cards in his long suits. Opener's bid of four of his first suit when his second suit is clubs promises at least three of the six key cards (the six being the four aces plus the kings of opener's long suits). Opposite such a hand, slam remains a possibility despite opener's minimum strength if responder has fitting honors in opener's suits and good controls in the other two suits.

When opener has at least five-five distribution and better than a minimum, he rebids his second suit over the relay. For this rebid, as well as for the rebid showing a concentration of his high cards in his long suits, opener should have at least three key cards.

When opener has shown the genuine two-suiter, responder's bid of four notrump is ROMAN KEY CARD BLACKWOOD. When opener has guaranteed that he has at least three of the six key cards, the modified responses to four notrump are

5 ♣ = three key cards, without the queen of the second suit
5 ◇ = three key cards, with the queen of the second suit
5 ♡ = four key cards
5 ♠ = five key cards

Following one of these responses, responder sets the final contract.

If opener and responder held

Opener
♠ K Q x x x   ♡ A x   ◊ x   ♣ A J x x x
Responder
♠ x x   ♡ K Q x x   ◊ A x x   ♣ K Q x x

the bidding, with Kantar Relays, would be

Opener	Responder
1 ♠	2 Notrump
3 ♣	3 ◊
4 ♣	4 Notrump
5 ♣	6 ♣

Opener's four club bid confirms at least 5-5 in spades and clubs, and shows better than a minimum. His five club bid in response to Blackwood shows three key cards, without the queen of clubs. Responder, knowing that one key card is missing, bids six clubs.

Opener's Rebids With 5-4-3-1 Distribution

If opener has only four cards in his second suit and is 3-1 in the unbid suits, he shows his three-card fragment suit in response to the relay. With a minimum, he shows his fragment at the three level; with a maximum, he shows it at the four level. Both four-level fragment bids will be natural; at least one of the three-level bids will have to be artificial.

In order to show a fragment with a maximum, opener simply bids the fragment suit at the four level. Thus, with

♠ A x x   ♡ K Q x x x   ◊ x   ♣ A K J x

opener would rebid four spades over the three diamond relay. If his diamond and spade holdings were reversed, he would bid four diamonds. After opener has shown a fragment at the four level, responder's bid of four notrump is to play.

In order to show a fragment in the unbid minor suit and minimum strength, opener bids three notrump. Three notrump shows the minor suit fragment no matter which two long suits opener holds.

In order to show a minimum with a fragment in the unbid major suit, opener bids a major suit at the three level. If opener's four-card minor is clubs, making diamonds the relay suit, he will be able to bid this fragment naturally. That is, if his first suit is spades he will bid three hearts to show a three-card heart holding; if his first suit is hearts, he will bid three spades to show a three-card spade holding. With the above hand, for example, if opener's spades were x x x instead of A x x, he would rebid three spades over the three diamond relay. If opener's suits are spades and diamonds, making the relay suit hearts, opener must bid three spades to show a fragment in hearts.

If responder bids four notrump after a fragment has been shown at the three level, his bid is Roman Key Card Blackwood.

To summarize, when the auction has begun

Opener	Responder
1 ♡	2 Notrump
3 ♣	3 ◇ (relay)

the complete schedule of opener's rebids is as follows:

3 ♡ = at least 5-5 in hearts and clubs, minimum strength, with high cards concentrated in short suits

3 ♠ = three spades, five hearts, four clubs, one diamond, with minimum strength

3 NT = three diamonds, five hearts, four clubs, one spade, with minimum strength

4 ♣ = at least 5-5 in hearts and clubs, maximum strength, with at least three key cards

4 ◇ = three diamonds, five hearts, four clubs, one spade, with maximum strength

4 ♡ = at least 5-5 in hearts and clubs, minimum strength, high cards concentrated in long suits, with at least three key cards

4 ♠ = three spades, five hearts, four clubs, one diamond, with maximum strength

4 NT = five hearts, four clubs, two spades, two diamonds, with maximum strength

When the auction has begun

Opener	Responder
1 ♠	2 Notrump
3 ♣	3 ◇ (relay)

the complete schedule of opener's rebids is as follows:

3 ♡ = three hearts, five spades, four clubs, one diamond, with minimum strength

3 ♠ = at least 5-5 in spades and clubs, minimum strength, with high cards concentrated in short suits

3 NT = three diamonds, five spades, four clubs, one heart, with minimum strength

4 ♣ = at least 5-5 in spades and clubs, maximum strength, with at least three key cards

4 ◇ = three diamonds, five spades, four clubs, one heart, with maximum strength

4 ♡ = three hearts, five spades, four clubs, one diamond, with maximum strength

4 ♠ = at least 5-5 in spades and clubs, minimum strength, high cards concentrated in long suits, with at least three key cards

4 NT = five spades, four clubs, two hearts, two diamonds, with maximum strength

When the auction has begun

Opener	Responder
1 ♠	2 Notrump
3 ◇	3 ♡ (relay)

the complete schedule of opener's rebids is as follows:

3 ♠ = three hearts, five spades, four diamonds, one club, with minimum strength

3 NT = three clubs, five spades, four diamonds, one heart, with minimum strength

4 ♣ = three clubs, five spades, four diamonds, one heart, with maximum strength

4 ◇ = at least 5-5 in spades and diamonds, maximum strength, with at least three key cards

4 ♡ = three hearts, five spades, four diamonds, one club, with maximum strength

4 ♠ = at least 5-5 in spades and diamonds, minimum strength

4 NT = five spades, four diamonds, two hearts, two clubs, with maximum strength

See also KANTAR RELAYS AFTER JACOBY TRANSFERS.

THREE NOTRUMP LONG SUIT SLAM TRY

The Three Notrump Long Suit Slam Try convention is used principally when the bidding has been opened one heart or one spade, responder has raised to two, and opener has a strong two-suited hand. The convention may also be used when opener's suit has been raised by implication, as when responder is a passed hand and uses DRURY.

The Long Suit Slam Try is a jump to three notrump directly over responder's raise. This rebid shows slam interest and a second suit of at least five cards. Opener's second suit must rank lower than his first suit. A typical hand would be

♠ A K x x x   ♡ x   ◇ A x   ♣ A K x x x

If responder is not interested in slam regardless of what the second suit is, he signs off in four of the agreed suit. If responder is interested in learning the location of the second suit, he bids four clubs. Opener then identifies his second suit as follows:

4 ◇ = club suit
4 ♡ = diamond suit
4 ♠ (after 1 ♠ opening) = heart suit

If responder neither signs off nor bids four clubs, but instead bids a new suit, he shows an extreme concentration of values in the suit he bids. For example, in the auction

Opener	Responder
1 ♠	2 ♠
3 Notrump	

responder would bid four diamonds with a hand such as

♠ Q x x   ♡ x x   ◇ K Q J x x   ♣ x x x

Three notrump may also be used as a Long Suit Slam Try by responder in an auction such as

Opener	Responder
1 ♣	1 ♡
2 ♡	

if the partnership has agreed that a bid by responder of two notrump is forcing.

Assuming that the partnership has agreed that the bid of two notrump after the raise of a major suit is forcing, the Long Suit Slam Try convention gives meaning to an otherwise idle bid. It also permits the partnership to reserve jumps to four of a new suit, after a raise, for use as SPLINTER bids.

THREE NOTRUMP MOVING ALONG

When the partnership has agreed on a major suit and is committed to game, its best means of exploring for a slam is often cue-bidding. The Moving Along Three Notrump convention, a forcing waiting bid, provides an economical method. It is applicable only when a major suit has been agreed as trumps, and it is used principally when the three notrump bidder lacks the wherewithal to make a cue-bid in clubs. The Moving Along three notrump requires the "Mover's" partner to cue-bid his cheapest ace or king.

When a Bid of Three Notrump Is "Moving Along"

Several rules must be borne in mind in order to avoid confusing the Moving Along Three Notrump convention with a natural or other conventional use of three notrump. Three notrump may be Moving Along only if the partnership has bid and raised a major suit and has agreed on a major as trumps, the bidding has reached the three level, the partnership can be interested in slam, and three notrump is not part of another convention. Three notrump cannot be Moving Along when, in light of the prior auction, the partnership cannot be interested in slam. When either partner is a passed hand, the partnership is, for these purposes, deemed to be not interested in slam. Nor can three notrump be Moving Along when the agreed suit is a minor, not a major, or when the major suit has been agreed by a mere preference, not by a raise. Three notrump is also not Moving Along when an opponent has bid a suit, though it may be Moving Along if the opponent has doubled.

When the bidding has suggested that the partnership may have a nine-card or longer major fit, and none of the precluded conditions exists, three notrump is Moving Along.

Examples:

[A]	*Opener*	*Responder*	[B]	*Opener*	*Responder*
	1 ♠	3 ♠ (forcing)		1 ♠	2 ◇
	3 Notrump			3 ◇	3 ♠
				3 Notrump	

[C]	*Opener*	*Responder*	[D]	*Opener*	*Responder*
	1 ♣	1 ♡		1 ♠	3 ♠ (LIMIT)
	3 ♡	3 Notrump		3 Notrump	

In auctions A, B, and C, three notrump is moving along. In auction D, it is not Moving Along because the partnership was not in a game-forcing auction. Though in auctions B and C it is possible that the partnership has only an eight-card fit, it may have nine, and three notrump is Moving Along.

[E]	*Opener*	*Responder*	[F]	*Opener*	*Responder*
	1 ♠	1 Notrump		1 ♠	2 ♦
	2 ♠	3 ♠		3 ♡	3 ♠
	3 Notrump			3 Notrump	

[G]	*Opener*	*Responder*	[H]	*Opener*	*Responder*
	1 ♣	1 ♠		1 ♠	3 Notrump
	2 ♠	3 Notrump			(forcing raise)

In auctions E, F, G, and H, three notrump is not Moving Along: in E, because both opener and responder have limited their hands and cannot be interested in slam; in F, because responder has not raised opener's spades but has merely taken a preference: in both G and H, because three notrump was a jump; and in H, for the additional reason that three notrump is a different convention.

[I]	*North*	*East*	*South*	*West*
	1 ♡	Pass	2 ♡	3 ♦
	3 Notrump			

[J]	*North*	*East*	*South*	*West*
	1 ♡	Pass	3 ♡	Double
	3 Notrump			

In auction I, three notrump is not Moving Along because an opponent has bid a suit. In auction J, however, the opponent has doubled, not bid, and three notrump is Moving Along.

Responses to Moving Along Three Notrump

When three notrump is Moving Along, the bid is forcing and requires the Mover's partner to bid the cheapest non-trump suit in which he has an ace or a king. Using the convention in the auction

[K]		*Opener*	*Responder*
		1 ♡	2 Notrump (heart raise)
		3 ♠	3 Notrump
		4 ♣	

opener bids three spades over the JACOBY TWO NOTRUMP response to show a singleton spade; his bid of four clubs over Moving Along shows the ace or king of clubs. In the auction

	Opener	Responder
	1 ◇	1 ♠
	3 ♣	3 Notrump
	4 ◇	

opener's bid of four diamonds promises control of diamonds and denies the ace and king of clubs.

Moving Along is usually used by a player who, though interested in slam, has neither first nor second round control of the club suit. It may also be used, however, when a player has club control but wants to know whether his partner has a fitting card. For example, in auction K, hearts were agreed as trumps and opener showed a singleton spade. Responder might have bid a Moving Along three notrump with a hand such as

♠ x x x   ♡ A J x x x   ◇ x   ♣ A Q x x

seeking out the club king.

Bypassing Moving Along

The failure to use Moving Along in an auction in which it would have been applicable also has significance. Two understandings might be reached.

One alternative is to agree that when a player, instead of using Moving Along, makes a four-level cue-bid, he promises controls in that suit and in any suit bypassed at the four level but denies control of the next higher suit. For example, over a bid of three spades, a cue-bid of four diamonds would promise controls in both minors, but would deny the ace or king of hearts. A cue-bid instead of four hearts would promise the not only the ace or king of hearts, but also the ace or king of clubs and the ace or king of diamonds. *See also* WILFRED CUE-BIDS; SPIRAL CUE-BIDS; SWEEP CUE-BIDS.

Under the above agreement, when a player has bypassed Moving Along in order to cue-bid, his partner is required to bid the cheapest side suit in which he has a control and the Mover has not shown a control.

Alternatively, a partnership using Moving Along may agree that any four-level cue-bid by a player who bypassed a Moving Along three notrump shows a hand of limited strength and promises a control only in that suit. With a better hand, under this agreement, the player may bid three notrump Moving Along and cue-bid later. Within this framework, a bid fo four of the trump suit without use of either Moving Along three notrump or a cue-bid would indicate a hand with no slam interest whatever.

See also GENERAL INTEREST SLAM TRY; D. I.

GENERAL INTEREST SLAM TRY

The General Interest Slam Try is a convention that facilitates a very mild slam try after the partnership has located an eight-card or longer major suit fit. When the partnership has agreed on spades as trumps, the general interest slam try ("GIST") is a bid of three notrump. When the partnership has agreed on hearts, the GIST is a bid of three spades.

Two conditions must exist for a GIST to be used. First, general interest slam tries are used only in game-forcing auctions. Second, they are used only when the last bid was three of the agreed major. Examples:

[A]	*Opener*	*Responder*
	1 ♠	2 ♦ (game force)
	2 ♠	3 ♠
	3 Notrump	

[B]	*Opener*	*Responder*
	1 ♠	2 Notrump (JACOBY)
	3 ♠	3 Notrump

[C]	*Opener*	*Responder*
	1 ♠	3 ♠ (LIMIT RAISE)
	3 Notrump	

[D]	*Opener*	*Responder*
	1 ♠	2 Notrump (Jacoby)
	3 ◇	3 Notrump

In auctions A and B, the three notrump bids are general interest slam tries. In auction C, opener's three notrump rebid is not a GIST because the partnership was not in a game-forcing auction. In auction D, the three notrump bid is not the general interest try because it did not follow a bid of three of the agreed major.

When three notrump is a GIST, it does not suggest that the partnership play in notrump. Rather, it is a forcing bid that reveals nothing other than that the three notrump bidder has some small interest in slam and that he has less than the full strength with which a slam try would normally be made. The GIST asks partner to make a forward-going bid if he has any slam interest.

For example, after the bidding has begun as in auction A, if opener's hand were

[A] ♠ A K J x x   ♡ A x x   ◇ x x   ♣ J x x

using standard methods, he might reach an unmakeable slam if he cue-bid
four hearts and responder had

♠ x x x   ♡ K x   ◇ A K J x x   ♣ A x x

Or he might fail to reach a laydown slam if he did not cue-bid and responder
had

♠ Q 10 x   ♡ x x   ◇ A K J x x x   ♣ K Q

With hand A, opener may use the general interest slam try by bidding
three notrump over three spades. If responder cue-bids, opener will then
cue-bid his ace of hearts. After such a sequence, responder should not push
to slam if that contract would require from opener a full-strength slam try,
such as a hand containing a good suit, an honor in responder's suit, and
an outside ace.

If the partnership has agreed to use general interest slam tries, a cue-bid
bypassing three notrump shows a full-strength slam try. For example, in
auction A, opener would cue-bid four hearts over three spades if his hand
were

♠ A K J x x x   ♡ A x   ◇ Q x   ♣ x x x

When the partnership has agreed on hearts, the GIST bid is three spades.
Again, the three spade bid can be a GIST only if the auction is forcing to
game and has reached three hearts. Thus, in the auction

[E]   *Opener*   *Responder*
                 1 ♡   2 ◇
                 2 Notrump   3 ♡
                 3 ♠

opener's three spade bid is a GIST.

When the three spade bid is defined as a GIST, a bid of three notrump
by either partner in an auction in which three spades was, or would have
been, a GIST, is used as a cue-bid in spades. For example:

[F]	Opener	Responder
	1 ♡	2 ◇
	2 Notrump	3 ♡
	3 Notrump	

[G]	Opener	Responder
	1 ♡	2 ◇
	2 Notrump	3 ♡
	3 ♠	3 Notrump

In auction F, opener's three notrump bid, bypassing the three spade GIST, is a spade cue-bid, promising a spade control and full strength for the slam try. In auction G, opener's three spade GIST bid shows mild slam interest, and responder's three notrump bid is a cue-bid that shows a control in spades.

See also CHEAP BLACKWOOD; RELAY BLACKWOOD; THREE NOTRUMP MOVING ALONG; D.I.; BABY BLACKWOOD.

WOLFF OVER 2 NOTRUMP REBID

When the opener makes a jump rebid of two notrump after a responder's one-over-one response, the responder with a weak hand may want to play in no more than three of a suit. The Wolff Convention is a three-club bid by responder over the opener's jump to two notrump. This bid asks the opener to bid three of the responder's suit if he has three-card support, a call which the responder can pass:

Opener	Responder
1 ♣	1 ♠
2 Notrump	3 ♣
3 ♠	Pass

If the opener has only two cards in the responder's suit, he is required to bid three diamonds. After a bid of three diamonds, the responder can sign off by bidding three of his original suit, or three of a lower-ranking suit, or four clubs. The responder might have a hand such as

♠ J x x x x x   ♡ x x x   ◇ K x x   ♣ x

However, if the responder rebids three notrump, he reveals that he holds a hand worth a mild slam try in clubs.

STOPLIGHT

The Stoplight convention is based on the use of a three club bid as an artificial, presumably weak, rebid after a game-invitational jump to two notrump. The three club bid, which may be made by either opener or responder after the other has made the invitational jump to two notrump, is used to allow the partnership to play in suit contracts below the game level. The Stoplight three club bid usually says nothing about the bidder's holding in clubs, but merely asks his partner to bid three diamonds.

Auctions Following the Three Club Stoplight

Examples:

	North	South
[A]	1♣	1♠
	2 Notrump	3♣
[B]	1◇	1♡
	1♠	2 Notrump
	3♣	
[C]	Pass	1♠
	2 Notrump	3♣

In each of these auctions, the jump to two notrump invited partner to bid game if he had a maximum. Using Stoplight, the three club bid in each auction is forcing and asks the two notrump bidder to bid three diamonds. The immediate message of the three club bid is that the partnership should probably stop below game.

The three club bidder generally has either a one-suited hand or a weak two-suited hand. If he has the latter, he will show it by passing three diamonds if diamonds is his second suit, or by bidding another suit. Because the three club bidder may well be intending to pass three diamonds, his partner should, with a fit for the known suit, eschew the three diamond call and bid three of the known suit.

For the above auctions, the three club bidder might have the following hands:

[A]	♠ J x x x x x ♡ x	◇ Q x	♣ J x x x
[B]	♠ K Q x x ♡ Q x x	◇ A J x x	♣ x x
[C]	♠ K Q x x x ♡ x	◇ A J x x x	♣ x x

In auction [A], if North rebids three diamonds, South, holding hand [A], will rebid three spades, which North should pass. If North has an especially good fit for spades, *e.g.*,

♠ K Q x   ♡ A Q   ◇ A J x   ♣ K x x x x

he should not take the chance that South will pass three diamonds; rather, North should bid three spades over the three club Stoplight.

In auction [A], if South were to bid three notrump over North's three diamond bid, he would show a hand with long clubs and little more than minimum strength. This sequence indicates a tolerance for three notrump, but a preference to play in four or five clubs. Finally, in auction [A], if South were to bid four spades over either the forced three diamond bid or over a three spade bid, it would deny any slam interest. Using Stoplight, responder's jumps to four of his major suit directly over the two notrump bid carry connotations of slam interest.

In auction [B], over a three diamond bid by South, North, holding hand [B], would bid three hearts.

In auction [C], South's auction over North's three diamond bid would be to pass with hand [C]. In recognition of South's possible pass, North should take care not to make the requested three diamond call if he has a fit for spades. Thus, if North has a hand such as

♠ J 10 x   ♡ K x x   ◇ K x x   ♣ K Q x x

he should bid three spades rather than three diamonds. If he has three spades and four hearts, he should bid three hearts in case his partner has four hearts.

The Stoplight convention is not applicable if the two notrump bid was not a jump.

There are two auctions in which a three club Stoplight bid by opener may conceivably be passed. They are

	North	*South*
[D]	Pass	1 ♣
	2 Notrump	3 ♣
[E]	1 ♣	1 ◇
	1 ♠	2 Notrump
	3 ♣	

In auction [D], South usually has a seven-card club suit, although he could have a weak hand with 5-5 in clubs and spades. North may pass with club support; but if he has spade support, he might bid three diamonds just in case opener has the black two-suited hand.

In auction [E], North might have a hand such as

♠ A J x x   ♡ x   ◊ J x x x   ♣ K Q J 10

and intend to pass the three diamond reply. If South has four-card support for clubs, he may pass. With fewer clubs, he should bid the requested three diamonds.

Other Auctions Over the Jump to Two Notrump

When the auction has begun with two suit bids at the one level and opener has jumped to two notrump, Stoplight uses rebids by responder of three diamonds, three hearts, and three spades as artificial game-forcing bids. The three heart bid shows length in clubs; the three spade bid shows length in diamonds.

The three diamond bid asks opener about his major suit holdings. Specifically, the inquiry is whether opener has (1) an unbid four-card major, (2), a rebiddable major suit of his own, or (3) support for responder's major. (No more than two of these holdings will be possible.) If opener has no such holding, he bids three notrump. If he has both of the two that are possible in light of the previous auction, he bids three hearts. If he has one, he bids the suit that reflects his holding. This last call may be ambiguous as to whether he has one or both.

	Opener	Responder
[F]	1 ♣	1 ♠
	2 Notrump	3 ◊
	3 ♡	
[G]	1 ◊	1 ♠
	2 Notrump	3 ◊
	3 ♠	
[H]	1 ♡	1 ♠
	2 Notrump	3 ◊
	3 ♡	

In [F], opener has shown four hearts; he may have spade support as well. In [G], opener has spade support and no four-card heart suit. In [H], opener has a rebiddable heart suit and may also have spade support.

JACOBY TRANSFERS AFTER TWO NOTRUMP REBID

JACOBY TRANSFERS are commonly used in response to a one notrump opening bid. They may also be used by responder when opener has made a jump rebid of two notrump, *e.g.*:

Opener	Responder
1 ◇	1 ♡
2 Notrump	

After such a rebid, responder's three-level rebid in any suit may be used as a transfer:

3 ♣ = transfer to diamonds
3 ◇ = transfer to hearts
3 ♡ = transfer to spades
3 ♠ = transfer to clubs

The transfers to diamonds, hearts, or spades may be made with weak hands, and responder may pass opener's rebid of the suit shown by the transfer (the ''anchor'' suit). If opener would like to play in game even opposite a weak responding hand, therefore, he should avoid bidding merely three of the anchor suit. If opener bids three of the anchor suit and responder bids again, the partnership is forced to game. Further rebids are natural.

Responder's transfer to clubs, which, if accepted, would take the partnership past three notrump, should indicate at least mild slam interest.

See also WOLFF OVER TWO NOTRUMP REBID; STOPLIGHT; BUCK RELAYS.

BUCK RELAYS

Buck Relays are artificial bids designed to permit responder to show a variety of suit-oriented hands after his partner has opened with one of a major and has raised a ONE NOTRUMP FORCING response to two notrump. With either a weak one-suited hand or a hand worth a slam invitation with both minors, responder rebids three clubs. With a one-suited hand worth a game force after opener's two notrump rebid, responder rebids three diamonds. Both bids are artificial relays; all of the one-suited rebids following the relays show at least six-card suits.

Since the initial response was one notrump, responder cannot have a long spade suit; and if the opening was one heart, he cannot have a long heart suit. Thus, when the opening bid was one heart, responder can have length only in the minor suits; when the opening bid was one spade, he can have length in any of the other three suits.

The Three Club Relay

Responder's three club bid asks opener to bid three diamonds. If opener complies, responder bids three spades to show a good hand with both minor suits. His other actions show weak hands with long suits. He passes with a weak hand with long diamonds, or bids three notrump to show a weak hand with long clubs, or, if the opening bid was one spade, rebids three hearts to show a weak hand with long hearts.

In response to the three club relay, if opener has a hand with good controls and a diamond fit, he may bid three hearts rather than three diamonds. If responder has the weak one-suited diamond hand, he can then safely bid three notrump; if he has the weak hand with hearts, he can pass. If opener has excellent controls with a fit for both diamonds and hearts, *e.g.*,

♠ A 10 x x x   ♡ A J x   ◇ A J x   ♣ A x

he may bid three notrump over three clubs. Over three notrump, responder will pass if he has the diamond hand, bid four hearts if he has the heart hand, or bid four clubs if he has the weak hand with clubs.

If opener has bid three diamonds over three clubs and responder has bid three notrump, showing a weak hand with clubs, opener should pass only with an excellent fit and excellent controls. Without both, he rebids four clubs.

If opener has bid three diamonds over three clubs and responder has bid three spades, showing both minor suits, opener may sign off by bidding three notrump. If instead he bids four of a minor suit, responder's bid of a major suit shows a singleton or void. For example, if the partnership hands were

Opener
♠ A K x x x   ♡ A x x   ◇ Q x   ♣ A J x

Responder
♠ x x   ♡ x   ◇ A x x x x   ♣ K Q x x x

the auction would be

Opener	*Responder*
1 ♠	1 Notrump
2 Notrump	3 ♣
3 ◇	3 ♠
4 ♣	4 ♡
4 ♠	6 ♣

The Three Diamond Relay

After responder's three diamond relay, the partnership is forced to game. This relay, made with a good one-suited hand, forces opener to rebid three hearts. Thereafter, responder identifies his suit as follows:

3 ♠ = club suit
3 NT = diamond suit
4 ♣ = heart suit, with the ace or king of clubs
4 ◇ = heart suit, with the ace or king of diamonds
4 ♡ = heart suit, without slam interest

Over responder's three spade bid, opener may bid three notrump to play. If opener bids four clubs, responder's bid of a new suit shows a singleton or void.

Over responder's three notrump, showing diamonds, opener may pass or bid four diamonds. Again, if responder bids a new suit he shows a singleton or void.

Since responder uses relay bids to show six-card or longer suits, when the bidding has been opened one spade, responder may bid three hearts directly over the two notrump rebid to show a five-card heart suit. If opener has three-card support, he may bid four hearts or he may cue-bid three spades. Over this cue-bid, if responder bids a new suit, it shows a singleton or void. When opener does not have a fit for responder's hearts, he bids three notrump as a signoff. If responder bids a new suit over three notrump, it shows length.

See also JACOBY TRANSFERS AFTER TWO NOTRUMP REBID.

MODIFIED DRURY

The Drury convention allows a responder who is a passed hand but who holds 10-12 points and support for his partner's major suit opening to bid two clubs to ask his partner whether the opening bid was based on full opening strength. As originally designed, the Drury convention required opener to rebid two diamonds if his opening bid was of subminimum strength. Other rebids showed full or extra values.

More modern use of the convention, sometimes called "Reverse Drury," requires that opener rebid his suit if his strength is less than that of a full opening bid. In addition, whereas the original design of Drury allowed responder to show a real club suit, rather than support for opener's major, *e.g.*, a hand such as:

$$\spadesuit \, x \, x \qquad \heartsuit \, x \, x \qquad \diamond \, Q \, x \, x \qquad \clubsuit \, A \, Q \, J \, x \, x \, x$$

by responding two clubs and rebidding three clubs, modern treatment requires responder to jump to three clubs directly with such a hand.

There are two principal advantages of these modifications. First, opener's rebid of two of his major suit, rather than of two diamonds, to show weakness makes it somewhat more difficult for the opponents to enter the auction. Second, the restriction of responder's two club response to hands containing good support for opener's suit allows more efficient slam exploration when opener has better than a minimum opening bid.

Romex Rebids by Opener after a Two-Club Response

Reverse Drury a la Romex has assigned precise meanings to opener's strength-showing rebids after the two club response. Since the two-club response shows 10-12 points, and opener's rebid of something other than two of his suit shows at least a full opening bid, such a sequence commits the partnership to game; the rebids by opener either show or permit responder to show slam interest. The Romex rebids are as follows. Two notrump shows a balanced hand with five cards in the major suit, and 17-18 HCP. A jump to three of opener's major suit is a trump asking bid, calling for responder to show his trump holding as follows:

first step	= three small cards
second step	= three cards headed by the ace, king, or queen
third step	= four small cards
fourth step	= four cards headed by the ace, king, or queen
fifth step	= three or four cards headed by two of the three top honors

Opener's bid of a new suit between two spades and three hearts is a short-suit slam try, promising at most five losers in the hand, but warning responder that his strength in the suit bid is likely to be wasted for slam purposes. Opener's bid of a new suit at the four level shows a second suit at least five cards long, and promises at most five losers in the hand.

Modern Treatment of Responder's Bids other than Two Clubs

In the original Drury convention, all jumps by responder, by definition a passed hand, were treated as preemptive. A more modern treatment is to use responder's jump shifts as SPLINTER RAISES. Thus, in an auction such as

West	East
Pass	1 ♠
3 ◇	

West could show a hand such as

♠ Q x x x   ♡ A K x x   ◇ x   ♣ J x x x

An alternative treatment proposed in Reverse Drury a la Romex uses the jump shift in suits other than clubs to show five cards in the suit bid, four-card support for opener's suit, and a short, but unidentified, side suit. This bid promises game-going strength. Thus, using this method, West in the above auction might hold

♠ Q x x x   ♡ x   ◇ A K x x x   ♣ x x x

Drury in Competition

The Drury convention may profitably be used by responder in competition when the opponent's action is a takeout double or an overcall below the level of two clubs. In either type of auction, use of responder's two club bid as Drury immediately describes his strength and shows that he has at least three-card support for opener's suit. By this means the partnership avoids the risk that responder will be forced either to commit the partnership to the three level on what may be a four-three fit, or to forgo a complete description of his hand until his next turn to bid, when the auction may have reached an uncomfortably high level.

DISTRIBUTIONAL DRURY

Another modification of the DRURY convention allows both opener and responder to describe their distribution. This variation caters to the possibilities (1) that the third-seat opening was made on a four-card suit, and (2) that the presence of singletons may make game a worthwhile proposition even if neither partner has the high card strength of a full opening bid. *See also* MINI-SPLINTERS.

As with the original Drury convention, the trigger is a two club bid by a passed hand in response to an opening bid of one heart or one spade. Using Distributional Drury, responder promises a hand worth a limit raise with at least three-card support for opener's suit. If he has a 10 point hand without support for opener's major and has a long club suit, he bids two notrump with a five-card suit or three clubs with a six-card suit.

Opener's Rebids After Two Clubs

Using Distributional Drury, opener has two rebids that show subminimum openings. These rebids reveal whether he has five cards in the suit opened or only four. When opener has less than a full opening bid, he rebids two diamonds if he has opened a four-card suit, or bids two of his suit if he has opened a five-card suit.

Any other rebid by opener shows a full opening bid (and hence a five-card suit). A rebid of two or three notrump is natural. The three notrump rebid shows a hand with 17-18 HCP, *i.e.*, one too strong for a one notrump opening, with all suits stopped. Opener may pass.

The two notrump rebid shows 12-14 HCP, *i.e.*, less than the strength needed to open one notrump, and promises stoppers in at least two of the side suits. The two notrump bid is not forcing. If responder rebids three of opener's suit, his rebid similarly is not forcing. Responder's bid of a new suit over two notrump shows a singleton or void in that suit and invites game if opener does not have wasted values. If opener rebids just three of his suit, responder may pass.

Opener's non-jump rebid in a new suit other than diamonds is natural; his jump to three diamonds is also natural. These bids are forcing for one round but are not forcing to game. A jump in a new suit other than diamonds shows a singleton or a void.

Opener's jump to three of his suit is forcing to game and shows slam interest. His jump to four of his suit shows the values for game but denies any interest in slam.

Distributional Drury may be coordinated with use of the THREE NOTRUMP LONG SUIT SLAM TRY convention. To use both, the partnership should agree that opener's rebid of two notrump is forcing. Then, over responder's bid of three of opener's suit, which is not forcing, opener would pass with a 12-14 point hand but would bid three notrump with a hand too strong for a one notrump opening. This adjustment will permit opener to jump to three notrump over two clubs with a strong two-suited hand.

Responder's Rebids After Opener Has Shown A Subminimum Opening

After hearing opener's rebid, responder may sign off opposite a subminimum. He signs off by passing opener's rebid of two of his suit or by returning to two of opener's suit over two diamonds.

Alternatively, if opener has opened one spade and rebid two diamonds, showing a subminimum opening and a four-card spade suit, responder may, if he has five hearts and only three spades, try to sign off in an eight-card heart fit. With this hand over two diamonds, responder may bid two hearts. His two heart bid is not forcing. If opener has three or four hearts, he passes; if he has fewer than three hearts, he returns to two spades.

If opener's rebid over two clubs reveals that the partnership has an eight-card fit, responder may try for game even opposite a subminimum opening if he has a maximum and a singleton or void. He invites game by making a splinter bid. *See* SPLINTER RAISES. With one exception, responder splinters simply by making a non-jump bid in a new suit after opener's first rebid. The lone exception is that if opener has opened one spade and rebid two diamonds, responder must jump to three hearts in order to show shortness in hearts.

Responder's splinter auctions are:

[A] | *Opener* | *Responder* |
|---|---|
| — | Pass |
| 1 ♡ | 2 ♣ |
| 2 ◊ or 2 ♡ | 2 ♠, 3 ♣, or 3 ◊ = splinter in suit bid |

[B] | *Opener* | *Responder* |
|---|---|
| — | Pass |
| 1 ♠ | 2 ♣ |
| 2 ◊ or 2 ♠ | 3 ♣, 3 ◊, or 3 ♡ = splinter in suit bid |

If opener has rebid two diamonds, showing a four-card suit, responder's splinter promises four-card support. If opener has rebid his suit, responder may splinter with as little as three-card support. Using Distributional Drury, if opener and responder held

Opener
♠ A x x x x   ♡ x x x   ◇ Q x   ♣ A x x

Responder
♠ K Q x x   ♡ x   ◇ K x x   ♣ K x x x x

they would bid as follows:

Opener	Responder
—	Pass
1♠	2♣
2♠	3♡
4♠	

Use of the above methods does not interfere with the partnership's use of other conventions such as SPLINTER RAISES or SPLIMIT RAISES. Using the latter convention, for example, responder remains able to jump immediately in his short suit if he has no interest in determining in advance whether opener has a four- or five-card suit.

LEBENSOHL AFTER A REVERSE

The Lebensohl concept, which is currently used in a variety of competitive situations, *see* LEBENSOHL; EXTENDED LEBENSOHL, may also be used in uncontested auctions where the partnership feels that there is a need to distinguish between three-level bids that are strength-showing and those that are not. One such application occurs when responder must rebid after opener has made a reverse rebid.

In an auction such as

Opener	Responder
1♦	1♠
2♥	

most modern natural systems treat the two heart bid as forcing for one round. The proper bid for responder when he has a weak hand is a matter for partnership agreement. Some pairs use two notrump as the weak bid; some agree that a rebid of responder's suit shows at least a five-card suit but no extra values; others agree that a return to opener's suit shows no extra values.

The Lebensohl mechanism is a two notrump call that forces partner to bid three clubs. Use of that device by responder is useful in codifying his rebids after the reverse. A return by responder to either of opener's suits after opener's forced three club bid would show extreme weakness. In contrast, a bid by responder of three diamonds or three hearts directly over opener's reverse would be positive calls, committing the partnership to game.

LIMIT RAISES

In "Standard American" bidding, a jump by responder to three of opener's suit is treated as a forcing bid showing at least four-card support for the suit and 13-15 points. More modern methods treat such responses as highly encouraging but not forcing. This "limit raise" still promises at least four trumps, but its strength is limited to 10-12 points, including distribution. For example, a responder holding a hand such as

(Responder)
♠ Q x x x   ♡ x x   ◊ K Q x x   ♣ A x x

jumps to three spades opposite his partner's one spade opening.

When the opening bid has been in a minor suit, responder should bear in mind that a minor suit game, which requires eleven tricks, is a less desirable objective than game in notrump or a major suit. The jump to three of opener's minor suit should deny possession of a four-card major suit. Hence, on the above hand, if the opening bid had been one diamond, responder should bid one spade rather than three diamonds. For alternative methods in raising minor suit openings, *see* INVERTED MINOR RAISES; MINOR SUIT SWISS.

In response to an opening bid of one heart or one spade, the partnership's use of limit raises may be coordinated with the use of a one notrump bid as a forcing response, in order to give opener useful information about either responder's trump length or his shortness in a side suit. *See* ONE NOTRUMP FORCING; LIMIT RAISES TO SHOW SINGLETONS; *see also* FORCING ONE SPADE RESPONSE TO ONE HEART; MATHE ASKING BID.

Opener's Rebids

Opposite responder's limit raise, opener will usually pass with a minimum opening bid but go to game with extra values. With an especially good hand, he may even try for slam. For example:

[A] ♠ A x x x x   ♡ K x   ◊ A x x   ♣ J x x
[B] ♠ A J x x x   ♡ x x x   ◊ A x   ♣ K Q x
[C] ♠ A K x x x x ♡ x   ◊ A x   ♣ K Q x x

With hand [A] opener should pass; opposite the hand shown above for responder, the odds are against his being able to take ten tricks. With hand [B], opener should bid four spades but make no move toward slam. With hand [C], opener may make a slam try by bidding four notrump BLACKWOOD. Six spades would usually be a reasonable proposition whenever responder has an ace. Opposite the hand shown for responder, or opposite a similar hand with the heart and club suits interchanged, slam is a virtual certainty.

For a convention designed to allow opener to make a *game* try after a limit jump raise of a major suit, *see* TWO NOTRUMP AS A LIMIT RAISE.

The Forcing Raise

If the jump to three of opener's suit is used as a limit raise, the partnership usually will find it useful to substitute another bid to show a hand in the 13-15 point range, especially in the major suits. A number of such conventions are available. *See* THREE NOTRUMP AS STRONG MAJOR SUIT RAISE; JACOBY TWO NOTRUMP; SWISS; SPLINTER RAISES; REVERSE SWISS; SUPER SWISS; CONGLOMERATE MAJOR SUIT RAISES; UNBALANCED SWISS; VALUE SWISS, OMNIBUS TWO NOTRUMP.

Limit Raises in Competition

Limit jump raises can be used when the opponents intervene. Thus, in an auction such as

North	East	South	West
1♡	2♣	3♡	

South's three heart bid could show a hand such as

    ♠ Q x x   ♡ A Q x x   ◇ x x x x   ♣ K x

South might also bid three hearts as a limit raise if, instead of overcalling as in the above auction, East had made a takeout double. However, most partnerships that use limit raises prefer to use the jump over a takeout double to show a more preemptive type of raise, perhaps a hand such as

    ♠ x   ♡ A J x x x   ◇ x x x x   ♣ J x x

These partnerships use a bid of two notrump as the limit raise over double. *See* TWO NOTRUMP AS LIMIT RAISE OVER OPPONENT'S TAKEOUT DOUBLE; SPLIMIT RAISES. Indeed, many partnerships prefer to use responder's jump to three of opener's suit as a preemptive bid even when the intervention has been an overcall. These partnerships agree that in order to show a hand worth a limit raise, responder should first cue-bid and then support opener's suit. *See* CUE-BIDS AS RAISE OF OPENING BID.

MATHE ASKING BIDS

The Mathe Asking Bid is a convention that may be used by opener after responder has made a LIMIT RAISE in a major suit. It is designed to ask responder whether he has a singleton and, if he does, where it is. This information enables opener to better assess the partnership's slam prospects.

After responder's limit raise, the Mathe Asking Bid consists of opener's making the cheapest possible bid. Thus, after an auction that has begun 1♡ - 3♡, a three spade rebid by opener would ask responder to identify his singleton if he has one. Responder should rebid as follows.

> 3NT = spade singleton
> 4♣ = club singleton
> 4◇ = diamond singleton
> 4♡ = no singleton

After the auction has begun 1♠ - 3♠, a three notrump rebid by opener is the Mathe Asking Bid. Responder's proper rebids are straightforward: he bids the suit of his singleton at the four level. With no singleton, he bids four spades.

If opener and responder held the following hands

> (Opener)
> ♠ A K x x x x   ♡ x x x   ◇ A Q x   ♣ x
> (Responder)
> ♠ Q x x x   ♡ x   ◇ K x x x   ♣ A x x x

use of these asking bids would lead to the following auction

Opener	Responder
1♠	3♠
3 Notrump	4♡
4 Notrump (Blackwood)	5◇
6♠	

See also FORCING ONE SPADE RESPONSE TO ONE HEART; MINI-SPLINTERS; TWO NOTRUMP AS LIMIT RAISE; LIMIT RAISES TO SHOW SINGLETONS.

TWO NOTRUMP AS LIMIT RAISE OF MAJOR

The traditional method of making a limit major raise in the absence of competitive bidding is for responder to jump to three of opener's suit, *i.e.*, to three hearts over a one heart opening, or to three spades over a one spade opening. After such a jump raise, opener must decide whether or not to bid a game without knowing anything of responder's distribution or the location of his side suit strength.

An alternative method, designed to allow opener to obtain additional information without committing the partnership to game, is to use a two notrump bid by responder as the limit raise of opener's major suit. Following responder's two notrump response, opener may make a "trial bid" in a new suit to ask responder to evaluate his holding in that suit. *See* TRIAL BIDS.

With a high honor or shortness in the suit of opener's trial bid, responder should bid four of the agreed major suit. With three or four small cards in the suit, responder should sign off in three of the agreed major. With intermediate holdings in the trial suit, responder may make a trial bid of his own.

Using two notrump as a limit raise and using trial bids, if opener and responder held

(Opener)
♠ A 10 x x x   ♡ K Q x   ◇ A x x   ♣ x x
(Responder)
♠ Q x x x   ♡ A x x   ◇ J 10 x   ♣ A x x

the bidding might proceed as follows:

Opener	Responder
1 ♠	2 Notrump
3 ◇	3 ♡
4 ♠	Pass

If, instead, responder held

♠ Q x x x   ♡ A x x   ◇ x x x   ♣ A x x

he would sign off in three spades.

TWO CLUBS FOR LIMIT MAJOR RAISE

Partnerships that use natural forcing jump raises of major suit openings need a way to show responding hands worth a limit raise, *i.e.*, one containing support for opener's suit and 9-11 points. *See* LIMIT RAISES. Some agree to describe such a hand by starting with a forcing one notrump response, *see* ONE NOTRUMP FORCING, or to make a limited-strength support-showing jump in a short suit, *see* SPLIMIT RAISES.

Some partnerships agree that when responder has support for opener's major and a hand worth a limit raise, he initially responds two clubs. A two club response is also made on any hand in which that is the natural and traditional response. Responder will clarify which type of hand he has when he rebids.

After a two club response, opener rebids as if the two club bid were natural. If responder has a limit raise in opener's major, he must, at his next turn, make the cheapest possible bid in opener's suit. This applies whether opener has rebid his suit, or has rebid notrump, or has bid a new suit, or has bid three clubs. For example:

[A]	*Opener*	*Responder*	[B]	*Opener*	*Responder*
	1 ♠	2 ♣		1 ♡	2 ♣
	2 ♡	2 ♠		2 Notrump	3 ♡

[C]	*Opener*	*Responder*	[D]	*Opener*	*Responder*
	1 ♠	2 ♣		1 ♡	2 ♣
	2 ♠	3 ♠		3 ♣	3 ♡

In each of these auctions, responder's rebid shows a limit raise in opener's suit.

In contrast, rebids by responder other than the cheapest bid in opener's suit show that responder had a traditional two club response. For example:

[E]	*Opener*	*Responder*	[F]	*Opener*	*Responder*
	1 ♠	2 ♣		1 ♡	2 ♣
	2 ♢	3 ♠		2 ♢	2 Notrump

In E and F, responder's rebid shows that his two club response was natural, not a raise of opener's suit.

When responder has clarified that he has a limit raise, nothing has been disclosed about his club suit. He may be short in clubs or he may be long in clubs, just as he might be if the bidding, using limit raises, had proceeded 1 ♡ - Pass - 3 ♡, or 1 ♠ - Pass - 3 ♠.

One advantage of this convention is that if opener's rebid was a new suit at the two level, the partnership may rest in two of opener's major. For example, if the hands were

Opener
♠ K Q J x x   ♡ Q x x x   ◊ A J   ♣ J x

Responder
♠ A x x   ♡ J x   ◊ Q x x x x   ♣ Q x x

The bidding would begin as in auction A, and opener would pass the two spade rebid. This may be the partnership's highest makeable contract.

See also TWO NOTRUMP AS LIMIT RAISE OF MAJOR; FORCING ONE SPADE RESPONSE TO ONE HEART.

BERGEN MAJOR SUIT RAISES

Bergen Major Suit Raises provide a complete scheme of responses to opening bids of one heart and one spade, generally enabling responder to reveal with a single bid his overall strength and his trump length. Some of the raises are relatively natural, others are artificial.

Raises With Less Than Game-Going Strength

The raise to two of opener's suit shows 6-9 points and precisely three-card support. If responder has more than three trumps, he so indicates by jumping to a suit at the three level. The suit in which he jumps at that level reveals his strength.

The natural jump to three of opener's suit is used preemptively; it shows a hand worth 0-6 points. A jump to three clubs shows 7 to a poor 10 points; a jump to three diamonds shows a hand worth a limit raise, *i.e.,* a good 10 to 12 points. The jumps to three clubs and three diamonds are entirely artificial; neither makes any representation as to responder's minor suit holdings. Each of these three jumps promises at least four-card support for opener's suit.

If responder has a hand worth a good 10 to 12 points but has only three-card support for opener's major, he begins by bidding ONE NOTRUMP FORCING and then, over a new suit rebid by opener, jumps in opener's suit. For example:

[A]	*Opener*	*Responder*	[B]	*Opener*	*Responder*
	1 ♠	1 Notrump		1 ♡	1 Notrump
	2 ♣	3 ♠		3 ♣	4 ♡

Responder's three spade bid in auction A and his four heart bid in auction B promise hands worth a limit raise in the suit opened, with three trumps. If, instead of rebidding a new suit in response to one notrump, opener raises to two notrump, responder's return to three of opener's suit would similarly show 10-12 points with three-card support.

Raises With Game-Going Strength

When the partnership is using Bergen Major Raises, responder's jump to three notrump shows a balanced hand worth a game raise; it promises stoppers in all side suits and only three cards in opener's suit. The three notrump response is not forcing; opener is asked to decide on the basis of his own distribution whether to play in three notrump or four of his major suit. If opener is interested in slam, he may cue-bid.

A jump to three of the other major (1 ♡ - Pass - 3 ♠, or 1 ♠ - Pass - 3 ♡) shows a hand worth a raise to game, with a singleton or void in a side suit. The short suit is not immediately identified.

If opener is interested in learning which is responder's short suit, he inquires by making the next cheapest bid. Responder identifies his short suit in steps; the first step shows clubs, the second shows diamonds, and the third shows the other major. Thus, if the bidding has begun

Opener	Responder
1 ♡	3 ♠
3 Notrump	

responder's rebids have the following meanings:

4 ♣ = singleton or void in clubs
4 ◇ = singleton or void in diamonds
4 ♡ = singleton or void in spades

If the bidding has begun

Opener	Responder
1 ♠	3 ♡
3 ♠	

responder's rebids are:

3 NT = singleton or void in clubs
4 ♣ = singleton or void in diamonds
4 ◇ = singleton or void in hearts

Bergen Major Raises mesh easily with JACOBY TWO NOTRUMP as a strong raise when responder has four trumps, or has a side suit doubleton but no singleton or void, or has more than 15 points. *See also* BERGEN MODIFICATIONS OF JACOBY TWO NOTRUMP; MARTEL MODIFICATIONS OF JACOBY TWO NOTRUMP. Further, since responder's jump to three of the other major shows a singleton or void, the Bergen Raise convention permits the partnership to use responder's jumps to four clubs, four diamonds, or four of the unbid major suit for other purposes. *See, e.g.,* SWISS; TRUMP SWISS; CONTROL SWISS; TRUMP AND CONTROL SWISS. *See also* SUPER SWISS.

Use of Bergen raises means that the partnership cannot use jumps to new suits at the three level as either WEAK JUMP RESPONSES or strong jump shift responses.

Summary

To summarize, when the partnership has agreed to use Bergen Major Raises, the complete schedule of responder's two- and three-level raises is as follows:

> 1 NT, then three or four of opener's suit = 10-12 points with three trumps
>
> 2 of opener's suit = 6-9 points with three trumps
>
> 3 ♣ = 7-10 points, at least four trumps
>
> 3 ◇ = 10-12 points, at least four trumps
>
> 3 of opener's major = 0-6 points, at least four trumps
>
> 3 of other major = 12 or more points, singleton or void somewhere, at least four trumps
>
> 3 NT = 12-15 points, balanced hand, stoppers in all side suits, three-card support for opener's suit

FORCING ONE SPADE RESPONSE TO ONE HEART

Partnerships using five card major suit openings generally agree that a response of one notrump to an opening of one heart or one spade will be forcing for one round. *See* ONE NOTRUMP FORCING. The response by an unpassed hand of one spade after one heart opening is, of course, forcing as a new suit bid by responder. The Forcing One Spade convention reverses these normal meanings of the one spade and one notrump responses.

The forcing one spade response to one heart is made on any hand with which responder would otherwise have responded one notrump forcing. It is an entirely artificial bid; it says nothing about responder's spades.

Opener's rebids are natural. He rebids one notrump with a minimum hand containing a five-card heart suit and no second suit. If opener has six or more hearts, he may rebid his suit. With 17-18 points, and no second suit, opener may rebid two notrump.

After opener's rebid, the auction proceeds naturally. If opener has rebid one notrump and responder has a minimum hand with no six-card suit, responder will pass. With a long suit and no fit for hearts, responder may bid two of his suit. Responder may show a hand worth 10-12 points and containing three hearts by bidding two hearts over opener's one notrump rebid.

Using the forcing one spade convention, the one notrump response to one heart promises that responder has at least four spades. This response is forcing. If the partnership is using a FLANNERY TWO DIAMOND OR TWO HEART OPENING, responder's one notrump response will normally show a five-card spade suit. Opener's rebids are essentially the same as if responder had responded one spade naturally, with the obvious exception that a one notrump rebid is no longer available. Accordingly, with a minimum hand containing two spades, five hearts and three cards in each minor suit, opener is forced to rebid two clubs on his three-card holding.

This convention has many advantages and few theoretical drawbacks. It allows the partnership to play the hand in one notrump, which is not possible using the more usual forcing notrump convention. It also allows the partnership to play in two clubs when responder has a weak hand and a long club suit; using more routine methods, opener often rebids a suit other than clubs over the forcing notrump, thus committing the partnership to the three level if it will play in clubs. Further if opener has a hand worth 17-18 HCP with 5-3-3-2 distribution, his rebid of two notrump after the forcing spade response makes him the declarer, which would not be the case if the response had been the forcing notrump.

For example, if opener and responder held the following hands

(Opener)
♠ A x x   ♡ A K Q x x ◊ x x x   ♣ x x
(Responder)
♠ x x x   ♡ J x   ◊ A x x   ♣ Q 10 x x x

the auction would go

Opener	Responder
1 ♡	1 ♠
1 Notrump	Pass

One notrump is the limit of the hand. Another example:

(Opener)
♠ A Q   ♡ A Q J 10 x ◊ K x x   ♣ Q x x
(Responder)
♠ x x x   ♡ x x   ◊ A Q x x   ♣ A x x x

Using standard methods, it seems highly likely that notrump would first be bid by responder, placing the game contract in jeopardy against a spade lead. Using the forcing one spade response, however, the auction would be

Opener	Responder
1 ♡	1 ♠
2 Notrump	3 Notrump
Pass	

The use of the one spade forcing response also allows responder to show three-card heart support and a hand worth a LIMIT RAISE at the two level rather than, as is usually the case, at the three level. This will occasionally save the partnership from a part-score defeat it might suffer at the three level. Or it may enable opener to explore for game at the three level whereas using other methods he might be compelled to forgo the thought of game.

For example, if opener had a hand such as

♠ x x   ♡ K Q 10 x x ◊ A Q x   ♣ J x x

he would pass a limit raise in the auction

Opener	Responder
1 ♡	1 Notrump
2 ♣	3 ♡

But using the one spade convention, the partnership might agree that opener may ask about a singleton if the auction has begun

Opener	Responder
1 ♡	1 ♠
1 Notrump	2 ♡

The partnership may agree, for example, that a two spade bid now by opener asks responder to show a singleton if he has one, by bidding two notrump with a singleton spade, three clubs or three diamonds with a singleton in the suit bid, or three hearts with no singleton. If responder showed either no singleton or a singleton diamond opposite the bulk of opener's strength, opener would be content to play three hearts. With a black suit singleton, however, game might well be a probability. Responder might hold any of the following hands.

[A] ♠ K x x x ♡ A x x ◇ K x x x ♣ x x

[B] ♠ x ♡ A x x ◇ K x x x x ♣ Q x x x

[C] ♠ Q x x x ♡ A x x ◇ x ♣ K x x x x

[D] ♠ Q x x x ♡ A x x ◇ K x x x x ♣ x

One practical difficulty with this convention is that one or the other member of the partnership may forget that it is being used.

REVERSE FLANNERY BY RESPONDER

When the opening bid has been one club or one diamond, a responder who holds a hand with five spades and four hearts — *i.e.*, major-suit distribution that is the reverse of that shown by a traditional Flannery bid, see FLANNERY TWO DIAMOND OPENING; REVERSE FLANNERY — may have difficulty in rebidding to depict accurately the strength and distribution of his hand.

A convention called Reverse Flannery by Responder permits responder to jump immediately to two hearts over an opening bid of one club or one diamond, to show a hand worth 5-8 HCP, containing five spades and four or five hearts. The two heart response is not forcing. If over the two heart bid opener simply bids two spades, his rebid is not forcing.

In order to show a hand containing five spades and four or five hearts with 9 or more points, responder bids one spade in response to the opening, and then rebids two hearts over opener's rebid. The two heart rebid is forcing for one round, even if opener's rebid was one notrump. If responder's third bid is three hearts, the partnership is forced to game.

When responder has at least five spades and five hearts and a hand worth a game invitation, he responds one spade and then, after opener's rebid, jumps to three hearts. The three heart rebid is not forcing.

For example, responder might have any of the following hands:

[A] ♠ K 10 x x x ♡ A J x x   ◇ x x   ♣ x x

[B] ♠ A K x x x ♡ Q x x x x ◇ x   ♣ x x

[C] ♠ K J x x x ♡ A Q x x   ◇ x x   ♣ A x

After an opening bid of one diamond, responder would jump to two hearts with hand [A]. With hand [B], he would respond one spade, and over a rebid of, for example, one notrump, he would jump to three hearts. If opener's hand were

[D] ♠ x x   ♡ K x x   ◇ A Q x x ♣ K x x

he would pass the nonforcing three heart rebid. With hand [C], responder would respond one spade to the one diamond opening, and over the one notrump rebid bid two hearts, which is forcing for one round.

TWO-SUITED JUMP SHIFT RESPONSES

A responder who has a two-suited hand and not enough points to force to game often cannot show his second suit without overstating the strength of his hand. This is especially so when the partnership has agreed to use a rebid by responder in a new suit as an artificial bid, *see*, *e.g.*, NEW MINOR FORCING.

A convention designed to solve this problem opposite opening bids of one club and one diamond uses jump shift responses to show two-suited hands with less than game-going values. Each jump shift shows five cards in the suit bid and five cards in the next higher unbid suit. A jump to two notrump in response to one club or one diamond also shows a two-suited hand, with the suits ranking just above and just below the suit opened. A jump to three notrump retains its natural meaning.

Three levels of two-suited jump-shift responses are provided. The cheapest jump shifts promise 6-9 points; the intermediate jump shifts promise 9-11 points; the highest jump shifts promise 8-11 points, with three cards in the suit opened.

Opposite an opening bid of one club, responder's jump shift responses show the following two-suiters and point ranges:

2 ◊	=	diamonds and hearts, 6-9 points
2 ♡	=	hearts and spades, 6-9 points
2 ♠	=	spades and diamonds, 6-9 points
2 NT	=	spades and diamonds, 9-11 points
3 ◊	=	diamonds and hearts, 9-11 points
3 ♡	=	hearts and spades, 9-11 points
3 ♠	=	spades and diamonds, with three clubs, 8-11 points
4 ◊	=	diamonds and hearts, with three clubs, 8-11 points
4 ♡	=	hearts and spades, with three clubs, 8-11 points

Opposite an opening bid of one diamond, responder's jump shift responses show the following two-suiters and point ranges:

2 ♡	=	hearts and spades, 6-9 points
2 ♠	=	spades and clubs, 6-9 points
2 NT	=	clubs and hearts, 6-9 points
3 ♣	=	clubs and hearts, 9-11 points
3 ♡	=	hearts and spades, 9-11 points
3 ♠	=	spades and clubs, 9-11 points
4 ♣	=	clubs and hearts, with three diamonds, 8-11 points
4 ♡	=	hearts and spades, with three diamonds, 8-11 points
4 ♠	=	spades and clubs, with three diamonds, 8-11 points

Agreement to use this convention means that the partnership cannot use single jump shift responses to show strong responding hands or as PREEMPTIVE JUMP SHIFT RESPONSES. Nor can it use double or triple jump shift responses either as natural preempts or as conventional bids such as SPLINTER RAISES or MINOR SUIT SWISS.

PREEMPTIVE JUMP SHIFT RESPONSES

In the Roth Stone System, a jump shift response to an opening bid of one in a suit is a preemptive rather than a strong bid. A preemptive jump shift response is made with a hand containing at most 6 HCP and a suit at least six cards long. For example, over an opening bid of one club or one diamond, responder would jump to two hearts with

♠ x x   ♡ Q J 9 x x x   ◊ x   ♣ J x x x

The premise of this treatment is that is is easier to construct forcing auctions to substitute for the loss of the immediate jump shift as a strong bid than it is to deal effectively with a very weak hand containing a long suit. Thus, the preemptive jump shift response avoids having responder making a simple response only to have no appropriate call over a rebid by opener; and it avoids requiring responder to pass a hand which could safely preempt the opponents or which, on occasion, could produce a game opposite excellent support from opener.

For a convention that allows responder to make a jump shift that could be either weak or strong and that allows opener to become the declarer, *see* TRANSFER JUMP SHIFT RESPONSES.

After making a preemptive jump shift response, responder should make no further bids unless forced to do so by opener, or unless opener invites game and responder has a "maximum." Opener should normally take a pessimistic view if he has no length in responder's suit, though he may properly be aggressive with a fit.

Examples:

[A]   ♠ K Q x x   ♡ x   ◊ A K x x   ♣ A Q x x

[B]   ♠ x   ♡ Q x x x   ◊ A K x x x ♣ A Q x

If responder has made a jump to two hearts in response to a one diamond opening, opener should pass with hand [A], game is improbable despite his handsome 18 points. With hand [B], however, opener should jump to four hearts. The game prospects are far greater; but more importantly, the hand may well belong to the opponents, and the four heart rebid will force them to make their assessment at a high level.

Partial Use of Preemptive Jump Shift Responses

Most partnerships that use preemptive jump shift responses do not use them in all situations. Some use them only in competition. For example,

	North	East	South	West
[C]	1♣	Pass	2♠	
[D]	1♣	1♡	2♠	

Under this agreement, South's two spade response would be strong in auction [C], but weak in auction [D].

Some partnerships use weak jump shift responses only if the responder is an unpassed hand. For example:

	North	East	South	West
[E]	1◊	Pass	3♣	
[F]	Pass	Pass	1◊	Pass
	3♣			

Using this agreement, South's three club bid in auction [E] would be preemptive. But North's three club bid in auction [F] would be constructive; having gotten through one whole round of bidding without the opponents uttering a peep, it hardly seems that they need preempting. Hence, it is better to use the jump shift by a passed hand as some sort of invitational bid.

Finally, some partnerships combine these two partial uses of weak jump overcalls. That is, they use them only when the responder is not a passed hand and when there is no competition. In auction [F], if West had overcalled one heart or one spade, these partnerships would treat North's three club bid as preemptive.

TRANSFER RESPONSES

After an opening bid of one in a suit, and especially after a one-spade opening, when responder holds a long suit and a weak hand, the partnership often has difficulty in finding a rational route to its optimum contract. The use of a forcing one notrump response, see ONE NOTRUMP FORCING, is of assistance; but it often does not allow a sufficient exchange of information. The result is that the partnership sometimes lands in the wrong suit, or sometimes lands in the right suit at the wrong level.

A suggested remedy is to have responder use transfer bids. Using this device after a one spade opening, a one notrump response would still be forcing, but would promise either (1) a relatively balanced hand containing 5-9 HCP, no six-card suit in diamonds or hearts, and no good six-card club suit; or (2) a balanced hand worth 10-12 HCP; or (3) a hand worth 10+ HCP with clubs. A response of two spades is a normal raise.

A two club response shows either a five-card or longer diamond suit in a hand worth a genuine two-over-one response in diamonds, or any hand with a six-card or longer diamond suit. A two diamond response shows either a five-card or longer heart suit in a hand worth a genuine two-over-one response in hearts, or a hand of any strength with a six-card heart suit. A response of two hearts shows a balanced hand worth 13-15 HCP, and suggests that the hand be played in notrump. A response of two notrump shows a long club suit in a hand that is either weak, or strong enough for a traditional jump shift response.

Similar methods may be used after a one heart opening.

Examples:

[A] ♠ A K J x x x   ♡ A x x   ◇ x   ♣ A x x
[B] ♠ A K J x x x   ♡ x   ◇ A x x   ♣ A x x

If opener held either of the above hands and opened one spade and received a forcing one notrump response, he would jump to three spades as his rebid. If responder held a hand such as

♠ x   ♡ K Q x x x x   ◇ x x x   ♣ x x x

he would never have had a chance to show his heart suit. Yet opposite hand [A], four hearts is laydown. Opposite hand [B], no game is possible.

Using transfer responses, opener would have been able to assess his hand more accurately. After a two diamond response, showing a heart suit, he would insist on game with hand [A]. He would be duly pessimistic with hand [B].

TRANSFER JUMP SHIFT RESPONSES

A convention designed to ensure that the opening hand will be the declarer when responder has a very weak hand with a long suit, *see*, *e.g.*, PREEMPTIVE JUMP SHIFT RESPONSES, uses two-way transfer bids by the responder. Responder's hand may be worth either 0-6 points, or 17 or more points.

Using this device, responder normally jumps in the suit just below his long suit. If responder's suit is that ranking just above opener's suit, however, responder jumps in the suit that ranks just below opener's suit.

Opener accepts the transfer by bidding responder's promised suit, which responder will pass if he has the weak hand. If opener has a hand with which he would like to play game even opposite 0-6 points, he bids more than the minimum bid in responder's suit.

Responder may also make a transfer jump shift response with a hand worth a traditional strong jump shift. Again he jumps in the unbid suit next below his long suit, but after opener bids the suit shown by responder, responder bids again to show the 17+ point hand.

Examples:

	Opener	*Responder*
[A]	1 ◊	3 ♣
	3 ♡	Pass
[B]	1 ◊	3 ♣
	4 ♡	
[C]	1 ◊	2 ♡
	2 ♠	3 ◊

For auction [A], responder might have a hand such as

$$♠ x \qquad ♡ K J 10 x x x x \qquad ◊ x x \qquad ♣ x x x$$

In auction [B], opener might have as little as

$$♠ A x \qquad ♡ A x x x \qquad ◊ A K x x x \qquad ♣ x x$$

In auction [C], responder might have a hand such as

$$♠ A Q 10 x x \qquad ♡ x \qquad ◊ A J x x \qquad ♣ A Q x$$

See also THREE-LEVEL TRANSFER RESPONSES.

THREE-LEVEL TRANSFER RESPONSES

When a responding hand makes a strong jump to the three level, either as a raise or as a bid in a new suit, there is frequently not enough room for him to describe his hand adequately below the game level. A solution designed to create additional room for needed descriptions and to reduce the point ranges of bids that show strong raises of opener's major suit is to have responder jump in the suit below the one in which he promises length. The forcing and artificial nature of the jump also allows the bids that show jump shifts to be used for *weak* jump shift responses as well.

Jump Shifts, Strong and Weak

This system of responding applies only when the standard strong jump shift would occur at the three level. But *see* TRANSFER JUMP SHIFT RESPONSES. It thus applies only to game forcing jumps showing suits that rank lower than opener's suit. It is not concerned with auctions such as

Opener	Responder
1 ♥	2 ♠

where the natural jump is to the two level and the partnership has the entire three level for its explorations.

The mechanism with respect to jump shifts requires responder to jump to the denomination just below the suit in which he would have made a natural jump shift. Thus, after an opening bid of one diamond, one heart, or one spade, a jump to two notrump transfers to clubs. The two notrump response therefore may not be used for its traditional purpose, *i.e.*, to show 13-15 HCP with all unbid suits stopped. After an opening bid of one heart or one spade, a jump to three clubs transfers to diamonds. After a one spade opening, a jump to three diamonds transfers to three hearts.

These jumps transfers may be made with either an extremely weak hand, *see* PREEMPTIVE JUMP SHIFT RESPONSE, in which case responder should pass opener's bid of responder's promised suit, or with a very strong hand. If the latter, the hand should not be two-suited unless one of the suits is that bid by opener. *See* SOLOWAY JUMP SHIFTS.

Opener should assume that responder has the weak jump shift and should therefore bid the suit promised by responder unless opener has either a hand with a very good fit for responder's suit, or a very good hand with which he would not want to rest in a long weak suit of responder, *e.g.*,

♠ Kx ♡ AQx ◇ AKQJxxx ♣ x

With such a hand, if opener has bid one diamond and responder has jumped to two notrump, showing a long club suit, opener would rather try three notrump than languish in three clubs.

Strong Raises

Transfer jump raises are designed in part to reduce the wide range of strength on which strong major suit raises traditionally have been made. Instead of showing 12-16 points and a balanced hand by jumping to three notrump, *see* THREE NOTRUMP AS STRONG MAJOR SUIT RAISE, or the same range and an unbalanced hand by jumping to four clubs or four diamonds, *see* SPLINTER RAISES, this system of transfer responses limits these jumps to hands worth 15-17 points.

In order to show a strong raise based on 12-14 points, responder would jump to three of the suit below opener's major. Thus, responder would bid three hearts in response to a one spade opening, or three diamonds in response to a one heart opening. These responses say nothing about responder's holding in the suit in which the jump is made, and they do not disclose whether his hand is balanced or unbalanced.

If opener has no slam interest, he simply bids four of his suit. If he wishes to know whether responder has a singleton, he bids three of his suit. Responder will either bid the suit in which he has a singleton, or bid three notrump with no singleton.

Example:

Opener	*Responder*
1♡	3◇
3♡	3♠

Responder's three diamond bid has shown a 12-14 point hand containing four or more hearts. His three spade bid shows a singleton spade.

TRANSFER RESPONSES TO THREE-LEVEL PREEMPTS

The use of transfer responses to opening preempts at the three level may permit the partnership to reach a superior contract in a long suit held by responder. Using these transfers, responder's bid in a new suit indicates that he has length in the next higher unbid suit.

For example, if opener has bid three clubs, a response of three diamonds would show a long heart suit; a response of three spades would show length in diamonds. Responder may have a hand with which he wishes to try for game in his suit. Or he may wish to offer opener a choice of suit contracts. For example:

Opener	Responder
3 ♠	4 ♣
4 ◇	4 ♡

Responder's four club bid showed diamonds; his four heart bid shows hearts as well. Opener should take a preference. If instead of four hearts, responder had bid four spades, he would offer opener a choice between game in spades and game in diamonds.

If opener has a singleton or small doubleton in the suit promised by responder, he should simply bid that suit. Responder may pass this bid. With a better holding in responder's suit, opener should cue-bid a control, *i.e.*, a side ace, king, singleton, or void; or he should rebid his suit with no side controls.

Using standard methods, a new suit bid by responder would be forcing. Thus, the above scheme of responding has the advantage that responder will be able to end the auction in the presence of a known misfit at a lower level than he might do with a standard auction. A disadvantage is that frequently the hand will be played with the preempter as the declarer.

BLUE TEAM FOUR CLUB-FOUR DIAMOND CONVENTION

The Blue Team Four Club-Four Diamond convention is a sequence of bids by responder to make a delayed raise of his partner's major suit opening and while showing his minor suit controls. First-round control may consist of either the ace or a void; second-round control may be either the king or a singleton.

The convention consists of responder's bid of two of a minor suit in response to the opening, followed by his bid of four of a minor suit after opener's rebid. It requires responder to select his two-level response with his focus on the nature and location of his controls rather than on his minor suit lengths. Responder may complete the control-showing sequence only when opener has rebid his suit or has rebid in notrump. The rebid by opener of a new suit cancels operation of the convention.

The information conveyed by responder depends on which minor suit he has bid at the two level and which minor he bids at the four level. His sequences have the following meanings.

2♣ then 4♣	= first or second round control of clubs, but neither first nor second round control of diamonds
2◇ then 4◇	= first or second round control of diamonds, but neither first nor second round control of clubs
2♣ then 4◇	= either first round controls in both clubs and diamonds, or second round controls in both
2◇ then 4♣	= first round control of one of the minors and second round control of the other

For example, for an auction beginning

Opener	Responder
1♡	2♣
2 Notrump	

responder might hold either

[A]	♠ x x	♡ A J x x x	◇ A Q x x	♣ A x
or [B]	♠ x x x	♡ A Q x x	◇ x x	♣ A K x x

In the above auction, responder would rebid four diamonds with hand [A], showing similar controls — *i.e.*, either both first-round or both second-round in the minor suits. With hand [B], he would rebid four clubs, showing first- or second-round control of clubs and no control of diamonds.

OMNIBUS TWO NOTRUMP RESPONSE TO MAJOR OPENING

The Omnibus convention uses a response of two notrump to an opening bid of one heart or one spade to show either a balanced hand with stoppers in the unbid suits and 13-20 HCP, or a strong raise of opener's suit with at least four-card support and 16-18 points including distribution. The convention may be used by partnerships that open four-card majors as well as those that restrict themselves to five-card major openings.

Opener's rebids of suits at the three level after the Omnibus Two Notrump Response are artificial.

Opener's Three Club Bid

Opener's three club rebid shows either interest in a major-suit contract or a better-than-minimum opening bid. The bid does not say anything about opener's clubs. Responder's rebids are also largely artificial.

If responder has a strong notrump-type hand, he bids three diamonds to show 16-18 HCP, or four notrump to show 19-20 HCP. If responder has a notrump-type hand with 13-15 HCP, he is required to disclose whether he has either support for opener's major or four cards in the unbid major. If he has neither, he bids three notrump; if he has both he bids three hearts. The three heart bid will be ambiguous.

If responder has the 16-18 point major suit raise type of hand, he bids at the four level in a suit that does not rank above that of opener. These bids are entirely artificial and show graduations of quality in the 16-18 point raise. The cheapest response, four clubs, shows the best quality hand. The most expensive, *i.e.*, four of opener's suit, shows a minimum hand within the promised range.

Examples:

	Opener	Responder
[A]	1 ♡	2 Notrump
	3 ♣	4 ♡
[B]	1 ♠	2 Notrump
	3 ♣	3 ♡

In auction [A], responder has shown a hand with four or more hearts and about 16 points. In [B], responder has shown 13-15 points, a balanced hand, and four hearts. He may also have support for opener's spades.

Opener's Three Diamond Bid

A three diamond rebid by opener after the Omnibus Two Notrump response shows that opener has three four-card suits. The singleton must be in spades if opener has bid one heart; it must be in clubs if he has opened one spade. If opener has a three-suited hand with the singleton in some other location (*e.g.*, a club singleton and a one heart opening), he should rebid three clubs rather than three diamonds.

Responder may sign off by bidding three notrump over three diamonds. This rebid implies that responder does not have four cards in any of opener's suits.

A three heart bid by responder after opener has rebid three diamonds is artificial. It says nothing about responder's heart holding but rather asks opener to specify his strength. Opener does this by bidding in steps. Each step after the first shows a two-point range:

$$3 \spadesuit \; = 12 \text{ HCP or less}$$
$$3NT = 13\text{-}14 \text{ HCP}$$
$$4 \clubsuit \; = 15\text{-}16 \text{ HCP, etc.}$$

In counting his points, opener is not to include a singleton king, queen, or jack.

Opener's Three Heart and Three Spade Bids

Opener's rebid of three of a major suit over the Omnibus Two Notrump is artificial, but each implies that the suit of the opening bid is five cards long. The three heart rebid shows length in clubs and a minimum hand; the three spade rebid shows length in diamonds and a minimum hand. Thus, in the auction

Opener	Responder
1 ♡	2 Notrump
3 ♠	

opener's three spade bid says nothing about his length in spades, but shows length in diamonds and implies that he has at least five hearts.

REVERSE SWISS

The Reverse Swiss convention is an unusual jump rebid by opener in his own minor suit or in a new suit to show a hand worth a raise to game in responder's suit, based on high-card strength rather than on distribution. Opener jumps in a suit in which he has a high card. For example:

Opener	Responder
1 ◇	1 ♠
4 ♣	

Opener might have a hand such as

♠ A Q x x   ♡ A x   ◇ K Q J x x   ♣ K x

The jump to four clubs, one level higher than a forcing jump shift, is an unusual jump. If responder has made a two-level response, even a single jump by opener may be an unusual jump, as, for example, in the the auction

Opener	Responder
1 ♠	2 ♡
4 ◇	

Using the Reverse Swiss convention, opener's four diamond rebid promises an excellent fit, at least the ace or king of diamonds, and a hand rich in high cards.

Note that if the opening bid is one heart or one spade, opener's jumps in his own suit to the three or four level will not be unusual. After such an opening, only a rebid in a new suit may be used as Reverse Swiss.

Use of this convention is incompatible with opener's use of SPLINTER RAISES. *See also* BLUE TEAM FOUR CLUB-FOUR DIAMOND CONVENTION.

MINOR-SUIT SWISS

When the bidding has been opened one club or one diamond and the partnership is using LIMIT RAISES and not INVERTED MINOR RAISES, a responder who holds a 12-15 point hand with excellent support for opener's suit may have difficulty in adequately describing his hand below the three notrump level. To cater to such hands, there is a convention called Minor-Suit Swiss.

This convention uses jumps to three diamonds or three hearts over a one club opening, and to three hearts or three spades over a one-diamond opening, to show a strong raise of opener's minor. In each case the higher jump, *i.e.*, three hearts over a one club opening, or three spades over a one diamond opening, shows 14-15 points; the lower jump, *i.e.*, to three diamonds over the one club opening or to three hearts over the one diamond opening, shows 12-13 points.

When used thusly to show point count, these jumps do not say anything about responder's holding in the suit in which he jumps. Alternatively the partnership may agree that responder will jump in whichever of the two suits he has securely stopped. Having no stoppers in either, responder would have no way of making a forcing raise and would be required to make a nonjump response in the other minor and await developments.

These Swiss raises are forcing only to three notrump or four of opener's minor suit. If the partnership lacks the necessary stoppers for a three notrump contract, it may be that a minor suit games does not have good prospects when opener and responder each have a 12-13 point hand.

Note that use of the Minor-Suit Swiss convention is incompatible with the partnership's use of these jumps to show either length in the suit bid and a preemptive hand, or a singleton in the suit bid with a constructive hand.

SUPER SWISS

The Super Swiss convention allows responder to use any of four double-jump responses to an opening bid of one heart or one spade to show different features of a game-going raise of opener's suit. The four possible responses are the jump to three notrump, the jumps to four clubs and four diamonds, and the double jump shift in the other major suit.

Super Swiss uses the cheapest of these jumps to show a void; the next cheapest to show a singleton; the third-cheapest to show two or three aces but no singleton or void; and the most expensive to show fewer than two aces with no singleton or void. Thus, after a one heart opening, responder would make his raise as follows:

3♠ = void, location unspecified
3NT = singleton, location unspecified
4♣ = two or three aces, no singleton or void
4◊ = fewer than two aces, no singleton or void

After a one-spade opening, responder would show his raise-type as follows:

3NT = void, location unspecified
4♣ = singleton, location unspecified
4◊ = two or three aces, no singleton or void
4♡ = fewer than two aces, no singleton or void

See also UNBALANCED SWISS; VALUE SWISS; CONGLOMERATE MAJOR RAISES; VOID-VS.-SINGLETON SPLINTER BIDS.

The void-showing and singleton-showing responses do not reveal the location of responder's shortness. After a void-showing raise, opener may inquire as to the location of the void by bidding the next step above the response. Responder bids the suit in which he is void if he can do so without passing four of the trump suit. If he cannot, he bids four of the trump suit. For example:

Opener	Responder
1♠	3 Notrump
4♣	4♠

Responder's return to four spades shows that his void is in clubs.

Similarly, after a singleton-showing raise, opener may make the cheapest bid to ask responder to indicate the suit of his singleton. Responder does so by bidding the suit in which he is short. Since responder may not be able to comply without passing four of the agreed trump suit, opener should be careful that a response showing an unsuitable singleton will not get the partnership out of its depth.

For example, if opener holds

♠ K Q x   ♥ A K J x x   ♦ Q x x x   ♣ x

and the bidding starts

Opener	Responder
1 ♥	3 Notrump (strong raise of
4 ♣	hearts)

responder cannot show a singleton spade or a singleton club without
bypassing four hearts. If he has a hand such as

♠ x   ♥ Q x x x   ♦ J x x x   ♣ A K J x

he will bid four spades to show the singleton spade, and the partnership will reach an unmakable five heart contract. (Of course, on these
hands, even four spades would be jeopardy since the defenders may
well maneuver a diamond ruff.) If opener's spade and diamond
holdings were reversed, the four club inquiry would not be
unreasonable since even if the partnership is missing two aces, a five
heart contract rates to be safe.

THREE NOTRUMP AS SPLINTER IN OTHER MAJOR

Originally, splinter bids were new-suit double jumps that were not used for any natural purpose. Many partnerships using SPLINTER RAISES also began to use jumps to three spades over a one heart opening, and to four hearts over a one spade opening, as splinter bids. These jumps traditionally had been used as preempts and may be useful as such.

In order to preserve the ability to use these bids as natural preempts, some partnerships use a response of three notrump as an immediate forcing raise of opener's major suit with a singleton or void in the other major. After a three notrump response, the partnership may use its customary slam exploration methods.

Use of this convention precludes a partnership agreement to use THREE NOTRUMP AS A STRONG MAJOR SUIT RAISE. It does not conflict, however, with the use of natural forcing raises or with conventions such as JACOBY TWO NOTRUMP.

Three notrump may also be used as a splinter in the other major on the second round of bidding when the partnership has found an eight-card or longer major suit fit in a game-forcing auction. For example:

[A]	*Opener*	*Responder*	[B]	*Opener*	*Responder*
	1 ♡	1 ♠		1 ♠	2 ♡
	3 ♠	3 Notrump		3 ♡	3 Notrump

In both auctions, responder's rebid of three notrump, by agreement, shows a singleton in opener's major suit. For other uses of the three notrump rebid in similar auctions, *see* GENERAL INTEREST SLAM TRY; THREE NOTRUMP MOVING ALONG; CHEAP BLACKWOOD; BABY BLACKWOOD; SWEEP CUE-BIDS.

For other uses of the original jump to three notrump, *see* THREE NOTRUMP AS MINI-SPLINTER RAISE; SUPER SWISS; CONGLOMERATE MAJOR SUIT RAISES.

MINOR CUE-SPLINTER

The Minor Cue-Splinter is a convention designed to facilitate a slam try by responder in hearts when the auction has begun

Opener	Responder
1 ♠	1 Notrump
2 ♡	

and responder has second round spade control, good support for hearts, and first round control of one minor suit, *e.g.*,

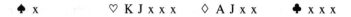

♠ x   ♡ K J x x x   ◇ A J x x   ♣ x x x

When responder has such a hand, the partnership may have a slam if opener has a suitable hand, such as

♠ A x x x x   ♡ A Q x x   ◇ K Q x   ♣ x

or it may be overboard in five if opener has a hand such as

♠ A Q J x x   ♡ Q x x x   ◇ x x x   ♣ A

Using standard methods, responder has no convenient way to show his slam interest below the level of game.

The Minor Cue-Splinter convention uses a jump rebid by responder to four of a minor suit in the above auction to show his interest in a slam in hearts. The four club or four diamond rebid promises the ace of the bid suit, plus at least second round control of spades. The "splinter" portion of the convention's title is recognition that responder's second round control in spades will be a singleton more often than K x.

See also SPLINTER RAISES (Delayed Splinter Raises).

MINI-SPLINTERS

As originally conceived, a splinter bid is a double jump shift showing a hand worth a raise to game in partner's suit, with a singleton or void in the suit of the jump. The double jump shift, *e.g.*, 1 ♡ - Pass - 4 ◊, is a bid that normally would be idle. *See* SPLINTER RAISES; *see also* FRAGMENT BIDS.

In recognition of the fact that distributional values may compensate for the absence of high card strength, many partnerships use shortness-showing bids with less than the high card strength traditionally needed for a game force. Called "Mini-Splinters," these bids may be used either to force game or to invite game, and they may be used not only by responder in support of the opening bid but also by opener in support of responder's suit.

Invitational Mini-Splinters By Responder

Some partnerships agree to use, instead of a double-jump shift, a single jump shift by responder to show a hand worth a limit raise of opener's suit, with a singleton or void in the suit of the jump. *See* LIMIT RAISES. Using the jump shift mini-splinter a responder holding

[A]   ♠ K x x x   ♡ A x x   ◊ x   ♣ Q x x x x

would jump to three diamonds over his partner's opening bid of one spade.

If responder had one more diamond, *e.g.*,

[B]   ♠ K x x x   ♡ A x   ◊ x x   ♣ Q x x x x

he would jump instead to three spades, showing again a limit raise, but denying a singleton. The jump shift mini-splinter is invitational to game if opener has a suitable hand.

Use of single jump shifts as mini-splinters means that the partnership cannot use jump shift responses to show strong responding hands or as PREEMPTIVE JUMP SHIFT RESPONSES. The arguments in favor of mini-splinters are that strong responding hands may be dealt with adequately through a series of forcing bids by responder, and that weak responding hands may be handled by non-forcing bids. Hands containing a singleton and the values for a limit raise are not so easily handled by other means.

The information transmitted by responder's mini-splinter bid with hand A above may be invaluable to opener in assessing the partnership's game prospects. For example, opener might hold

[C]	♠ Q J x x x	♡ K Q	◇ x x x	♣ A J x
[D]	♠ Q J x x x	♡ x x x	◇ K Q x	♣ A J
[E]	♠ Q J x x x	♡ x x	◇ A x x	♣ A J x

With hands C and E, opener would bid four spades, knowing that he has no wasted values in diamonds. With hand D, he would sign off in three spades, staying out of a four spade game that rates to be defeated after a probable heart lead.

Without the ability to use a nonforcing mini-splinter, responder usually will be forced to settle for a less informative jump to three of opener's suit as a limit raise with both hand A and hand B. Opposite hand B, however, opener would not wish to play in game with either hand C or hand E.

See also LIMIT RAISES TO SHOW SINGLETONS; TWO NOTRUMP AS LIMIT RAISE; MATHE ASKING BIDS. For mini-splinters in competition, *see* SPLIMIT RAISES.

Game-Forcing Mini-Splinters By Responder

Though responder's traditional game-forcing raises normally show about 13-15 points in support of opener's suit, and the mini-splinters discussed above, showing limited values, merely invite game, there are many distributional hands on which responder has limited values but wants to take a chance on game notwithstanding his modest high card values. Accordingly, some partnerships agree to designate certain responses as game-forcing mini-splinters.

Opposite an opening bid of one spade, the game-forcing mini-splinter is a jump to three notrump. Opposite an opening bid of one heart, the game-forcing mini-splinter is a jump to three spades. Each of these responses promises support for opener's suit, 10-12 points, and a singleton or void somewhere. The short suit is not specified.

Responder's bid of three notrump in response to one spade, or of three spades in response to one heart, forces game but does not invite exploration for slam. If opener remains interested in slam despite responder's announced limited strength, he may ask where responder's shortness is.

If the opening bid was one spade, opener's shortness-asking bid over three notrump is four clubs. Responder rebids as follows:

    4 ◇ = singleton or void in diamonds
    4 ♡ = singleton or void in hearts
    4 ♠ = singleton or void in clubs

If the opening bid was one heart, opener's shortness-asking bid over the three spade response is three notrump. Responder shows his shortness as follows:

$4 \clubsuit$ = singleton or void in clubs
$4 \diamondsuit$ = singleton or void in diamonds
$4 \heartsuit$ = singleton or void in spades

If responder had a hand such as

[F] ♠ A J x x   ♡ Q x x x   ◊ K x x x   ♣ x

he would jump to three notrump over an opening bid of one spade or to three spades over an opening bid of one heart. Opener would sign off in game with a hand such as

[G] ♠ K x x   ♡ K J x x x   ◊ A x x   ♣ Q x

but would try for slam with

[H] ♠ K x   ♡ A K x x x   ◊ A Q x   ♣ J x x

With hand F opposite hand H, the bidding might go

[I] | Opener | Responder |
|---|---|
| 1 ♡ | 3 ♠ |
| 3 Notrump | 4 ♣ |
| 4 Notrump (BLACKWOOD) | 5 ◊ |
| 6 ♡ | |

This use of the jump to three notrump over a one spade opening and the jump to three spades over a one heart opening permits the partnership to reserve the jumps to new suits at the four level for full-strength splinters or for some other use. *See, e.g.*, SWISS; TRUMP SWISS; CONTROL SWISS; TRUMP AND CONTROL SWISS. Agreement to use the three notrump response to show a mini-splinter hand does, however, preclude use of that response for other conventional purposes, *see, e.g.*, SUPER SWISS; VOID-VS.-SINGLETON SPLINTER BIDS; THREE NOTRUMP AS SPLINTER IN OTHER MAJOR; CONGLOMERATE MAJOR SUIT RAISES.

As discussed in SPLINTER RAISES, opener may make a splinter rebid in raising a suit bid by responder. Most such rebids show game-going values. The partnership may also agree that opener may make a mini-splinter raise.

Thus, after a suit response at the one level, if opener can jump to three of a new suit that ranks above the suit he opened but below the suit bid by responder, the partnership may agree that the auction is merely game-invitational, not game-forcing. In the each of the following auctions,

[J]	*Opener*	*Responder*	[K]	*Opener*	*Responder*
	1 ♣	1 ♡		1 ♣	1 ♠
	3 ◇			3 ♡	

[L]	*Opener*	*Responder*
	1 ◇	1 ♠
	3 ♡	

the final bid shown for opener is a mini-splinter showing a singleton or void in the suit bid, four-card support for responder's suit, and, presumably, less than the high card values needed for a raise to game.

In auction L, for example, opener's hand might be

> ♠ K Q x x   ♡ x   ◇ A K x x x   ♣ x x x

Opposite a mini-splinter, responder may be able to bid a laydown game on minimum values if they are well placed, *e.g.*,

> ♠ A x x x   ♡ x x x   ◇ Q x x   ♣ x x x

With his high cards less well placed, *e.g.*,

> ♠ J x x x   ♡ K Q x   ◇ x   ♣ Q x x x

responder will sign off in three spades. If opener's response is a mini-splinter, responder's bid of three of his suit may be passed.

Since after a mini-splinter rebid opener has another opportunity to bid, the partnership may agree to use opener's mini-splinter followed by a game raise to differentiate between game-raising values. It might agree, for example, that the jump to four shows a singleton and the jump to three followed by a raise to game shows a void. Or it might agree that the jump to three followed by a raise shows a stronger hand than the jump immediately to four.

NONJUMP SPLINTERS

Some partnerships have agreed that in certain auctions a player may make a splinter bid — *i.e.*, a bid showing a singleton in that suit and support for his partner's suit—without jumping. The requirements are that one member of the partnership has not bid more than one suit (although he may have bid notrump), and that the other has bid two of the other suits. In these circumstances, the bid of the fourth suit by the player who has already bid two suits is considered a splinter in support of partner's suit.

Examples:

	Opener	Responder
[A]	1♠	2♦
	2♣	3♥
	3♠	4♣
[B]	1♥	1♠
	3♦	3♠
	4♣	
[C]	1♥	1♠
	1 Notrump	3♦
	3♥	4♣

These partnerships treat the four club bid in each auction as a singleton-showing bid. If the four club bidder instead had bid his partner's suit at his third turn, it would have shown, using this understanding, two losers in the fourth suit.

Although splinter bids originally used otherwise idle bids, *see* SPLINTER RAISES, it is not clear that this convention does not employ a bid that would not otherwise be used. In auctions [A] and [C], responder might wish to bid four clubs because his hand was too strong to sign off in three notrump, even with a misfit.

SWITCHED SPLINTERS

The traditional splinter bid is an unusual jump shift to show support for opener's suit and a singleton or void in the suit of the jump shift. *See, e.g.,* SPLINTER RAISES. "Switched" splinters use an unusual jump shift to show a raise, but the jump is made in the unbid suit that ranks just above the suit of the singleton. For example, after an opening of one heart, responder's switched splinters would be as follows:

3 ♠ = singleton or void in diamonds
4 ♣ = singleton or void in spades
4 ◊ = singleton or void in clubs

The purpose of this switch is to make it more difficult for the defending side to double the suit in which the singleton is held to suggest a sacrifice.

As a practical matter, however, the jump in a suit in which the responder does not have shortness may give even greater assistance to the opposition in the defense of the hand. Thus, the responder's left-hand opponent is given an opportunity to double the suit of the jump shift if he has strength in that suit — a suit in which the responders may expect to take more tricks than they would in a suit in which the responder was short. This information may well be of greater value to the defenders than the ability to double a bid of the short suit, whose location is, in any event, known to them. *See* DOUBLE OF SPLINTER BID TO SHOW ANOTHER SUIT.

VOID-VS.-SINGLETON SPLINTER BIDS

Most splinter bid conventions use a jump shift or double jump shift to show either a singleton or a void without specification of which degree of shortness exists. *See, e.g.,* SPLINTER RAISES; MINI-SPLINTERS; SUPER SWISS. If opener holds the ace of responder's short suit, it may well be useful for him to know whether responder's shortness is a singleton or a void.

The void-vs.-singleton convention, used in response to opening bids of one heart or one spade, is a game-forcing raise of opener's suit using double jumps in notrump and all suits other than opener's to show a side singleton or a void. These four jumps permit responder to specify whether his shortness is a void, and if so, the location of the void. If his shortness is a singleton, its existence, but not its location, is disclosed.

Responder's cheapest double jump shows that he has a singleton; the other double jumps show that he has a void and each indicates the suit of the void. After a one heart opening, responder's double jump shows the following:

    3♠ = side suit singleton, location unspecified
    3NT = void in spades
    4♣ = void in clubs
    4◊ = void in diamonds

After responder's jump to three spades, opener may bid three notrump to inquire as to the location of responder's singleton. Responder's rebid of four clubs or four diamonds shows a singleton in the suit of the rebid; his rebid of four hearts would show a singleton spade.

After a one-spade opening, responder's jumps are as follows:

    3NT = side suit singleton, location unspecified
    3♠ = void in clubs
    4◊ = void in diamonds
    4♡ = void in hearts

After responder's jump to three notrump, opener may ask for identification of the singleton by rebidding four clubs. Responder's rebid of four diamonds or four hearts would show a singleton in the suit of the rebid; a rebid of four spades would show a singleton club.

Opener is, of course, free to forgo asking the location of responder's singleton if he has no interest in slam.

VOID-SHOWING RAISES

The most popular current use for an unusual jump in a new suit or in a suit bid by an opponent is to show support for partner's suit and at most a singleton in the suit of the jump. *See* SPLINTER RAISES; see also SWISS. For example:

	North	East	South	West
[A]	1◇	Pass	1♡	Pass
	4♣			
[B]	1♡	Pass	4♣	
[C]	1♡	2♣	4♣	

In each auction, the four club bid, one level higher than needed to make a forcing bid, is an unusual jump.

Some partnerships agree to use these jumps to show a void in the suit of the jump. Their premise is that the information that the shortness shown is a void rather than a singleton may be of importance to partner in evaluating the prospects for slam. For conventions making provision for responder to show both voids and singletons, *see* SUPER SWISS; VOID-VS.-SINGLETON SPLINTER BIDS. For a convention applicable to auction [C], using the jump cue-bid in a diametrically opposite way, *see* DENIAL JUMP CUE-BID.

The rationale of the void-showing jump — *i.e.*, to promise total control of the suit — can also be extended to hands in which a player's holding in a side suit is the singleton ace.

Following a void-showing raise, if the BLACKWOOD convention is used, the ace of the suit in which the void has been shown should be excluded in showing the number of aces held. This is expecially true if, after a jump has been made on the singleton ace, the partner of the jumper is the Blackwood bidder. *See* EXCLUSION BLACKWOOD.

FOURTH SUIT FORCING AND ARTIFICIAL

Most experienced partnerships agree that most or all of the second-round jump rebids by responder are invitational rather than forcing to game. Thus, for auctions such as

	Opener	*Responder*
[A]	1♣	1♡
	1♠	3♠
[B]	1◊	1♡
	1♠	3♡
[C]	1♣	1♡
	1♠	3♣

responder might hold, respectively,

[A]	♠ K J x x	♡ A Q x x	◊ x x	♣ x x x
[B]	♠ K x	♡ A J 10 9 x x	◊ Q x	♣ x x x
[C]	♠ x	♡ A J x x x	◊ x x x	♣ K Q x x

Such an agreement poses problems when responder wants to force to game with a better hand but one that does not immediately reveal which of two or more possible game — or higher — contracts should be selected. For example, responder might hold

[D]	♠ x x x x	♡ A Q J x x	◊ K x	♣ K x
[E]	♠ K x	♡ A K x x x	◊ x x	♣ K Q x x

With hand [D] in the above auctions, responder knows that a 4-4 spade fit exists; but the hand may play better in notrump than in spades since responder's spades are so weak. With hand [E] in auctions [A] and [C], responder has no idea whether the final contract should be three notrump or five clubs, or perhaps even six clubs.

In order to solve these problems, many partnerships use a bid by responder of the fourth suit as an artificial forcing call. In standard bidding, a bid by responder of the fourth suit is forcing simply as a change of suit by the responder; but there the bid is natural and promises four or more cards in the suit, and it is not forcing to game.

Using Fourth Suit Forcing and Artificial, responder's bid of the fourth suit is forcing to game, unless all four suits have been bid at the one level, and it neither promises nor denies any particular holding in the suit. Opener should not bid notrump without a stopper in the fourth suit.

The Fourth Suit bid asks opener to describe his hand further. If opener has a highly distributional hand, he may show it naturally. For example, after the auction has begun

Opener	Responder
1♣	1♡
1♠	2◇

opener would rebid two spades with a hand such as

[F]　♠ A Q x x x　♡ x　　　◇ x　　　♣ A K x x x

or would rebid three clubs with a hand such as

[G]　♠ A J x x　♡ x　　　◇ x x　　　♣ A K Q x x x

With a less distributional hand, opener should bid notrump if he has a stopper in the fourth suit. If he does not, he should raise opener's first suit if he has three-card support. If opener has neither of the above, he should raise the fourth suit if he has four-card support and if he can do so below three notrump. If he cannot do so without passing three notrump, he should bid three notrump. Even if opener has four small cards in the fourth suit, it is likely that responder has at least a doubleton in the suit and that the opponents cannot take more than four tricks in it at notrump. If opener has none of the above holdings, he should rebid a five-card suit.

If opener has not rebid three notrump, the responder who has used Fourth Suit Forcing must bid again unless the bidding has commenced

Opener	Responder
1♣	1◇
1♡	1♠

In this auction, responder may have a weak hand with four or more spades. If he does have this hand he will likely pass any rebid by opener.

See also EXTENDED PLOB.

FIRST SUIT FORCING

The First Suit Forcing convention is an artificial bid by responder of two of opener's first suit in certain auctions to require opener to describe his hand further. The convention is designed to allow responder to obtain information at a more convenient level of the auction than would be possible using FOURTH SUIT FORCING.

First Suit Forcing is used only in auctions in which responder has made a two-over-one response, opener has made a non-jump rebid in a new suit that ranks lower than his first suit, and the fourth suit cannot be bid without going past two of opener's first suit:

[A]	Opener	Responder	[B]	Opener	Responder
	1 ♠	2 ♦		1 ♠	2 ♣
	2 ♡			2 ♡	

[C]	Opener	Responder
	1 ♡	2 ♣
	2 ♦	

In auctions A and B, responder's fourth-suit-forcing bid would be three of the unbid minor; in C, the fourth-suit bid would be two spades. In all three cases, bidding the fourth suit would take the auction past two of opener's first suit. First Suit Forcing would be applicable to these auctions.

The First Suit Forcing convention uses responder's simple return to opener's first suit as an artificial forcing bid, asking opener to describe his hand further. With this understanding, responder would rebid two spades in auctions A and B, and would rebid two hearts in auction C.

Two benefits are gained in these auctions by having responder make his artificial forcing rebid in opener's first suit rather than in the unbid fourth suit. First, the auction remains lower, giving the partnership more room to explore before game is reached. Second, *opener* may now use the fourth suit as a forcing bid when no natural bid gives a better description of his hand.

For example, if the partnership were using the fourth suit as responder's artificial forcing bid, responder would rebid three diamonds in auction B with a hand such as

♠ K x   ♡ K x x   ◊ J x x   ♣ A K x x x

If opener had a hand such as

♠ A x x x x   ♡ A Q x x   ◇ Q x   ♣ Q x

he would have no good descriptive rebid over three diamonds. He cannot rebid three hearts, for that would promise a five-card suit; he cannot raise clubs; and he lacks a diamond stopper for a three notrump rebid. He would be forced to rebid three spades. Since opener would also rebid three spades with a six-card spade suit, responder would have gained little additional information as to where the hand should be played.

With First Suit Forcing, however, the auction could proceed as follows:

Opener	Responder
1 ♠	2 ♣
2 ♡	2 ♠
3 ◇	3 ♠
3 Notrump	

Opener's rebid of three diamonds provides useful information. His failure to rebid three spades, three hearts, or three clubs indicates that he has two or three diamonds and allows responder to bid three notrump.

The First Suit Forcing convention does not apply if the initial response was in notrump or was a suit at the one level. Nor does it apply if the unbid fourth suit may be bid without bypassing opener's first suit. Thus, in the auction,

Opener	Responder
1 ♠	2 ♣
2 ◇	

the fourth-suit bid would be two hearts, below opener's first suit, and the First suit Forcing convention would not apply.

Use of this convention deprives responder of the ability to make a non-forcing preference to two of opener's suit. Thus, unless the partnership is prepared to agree that its two-over-one responses are forcing at least to two notrump, the First Suit Forcing convention should not be adopted.

TWO-WAY CHECKBACK

The Two-Way Checkback convention, used over opener's one notrump rebid, is designed to permit responder to describe a full range of hands: signoffs, game invitations in any suit or in notrump, game-forcing hands based on high card strength, and game-forcing hands based on distribution. The convention uses responder's rebids of both two clubs and two diamonds as artificial relay bids.

Signoffs and Natural Bids

With one exception, responder uses natural bids to sign off. In order to sign off in hearts or spades, responder simply bids two of that suit. In order to sign off in clubs, responder bids three clubs.

Responder has no natural signoff in diamonds, because two diamonds is used as a relay. In order to sign off in diamonds, responder must rebid an artificial two clubs over one notrump; two clubs is a relay asking opener to bid two diamonds. Over opener's two diamond bid, responder signs off by passing.

In addition to the natural signoffs, responder may make a natural game-forcing bid if his game force is based more on distribution than on high cards. He makes such a game force by jumping to three diamonds, three hearts, or three spades directly over one notrump. If his jump is in the suit he has bid at the one level, he shows a seven-card suit. If he jumps in a new suit, he shows at least 5-5 distribution.

Responder may also issue two relatively natural game invitations. First, his raise of the one notrump rebid to two invites game in notrump. The immediate raise indicates that responder has only four cards in the suit in which he responded. Second, if he has responded one heart, his bid of two spades over one notrump shows four spades; but it also shows that he has only four hearts.

The Two Club Relay for Game-Invitational Hands

Responder's two club rebid over the one notrump rebid is an artificial relay that simply asks opener to rebid two diamonds. It does not make any representation as to responder's club holding. With the exception of the signoff in diamonds, discussed above, the two club relay is used only for hands with which responder wants to invite game.

After use of the two club relay, no rebid by responder below the game level is forcing. His bid of any suit, whether it be opener's, his own, or a new one, invites game in that suit. His bid of two notrump over two diamonds invites game in notrump and shows that he has five cards in the suit he bid at the one level. Thus, the two-level rebid of his suit over two diamonds suggests that he has either a six-card suit or an unbalanced hand. His jump rebid to three of his own major suit is strongly invitational and is usually based on a six-card suit.

If responder has bid a major at the one level, his rebid of two of the other major shows five cards in his first suit and four in the second. In order to show 5-5 in the majors, responder, having bid one spade over the opening bid, jumps to three hearts over opener's two diamonds.

Though the two club relay asks opener to bid two diamonds, opener may ignore this request in one set of circumstances: when he does not want to play in two diamonds, and he has three-card support for the major suit bid by responder at the one level, and he has enough strength to accept a game invitation in responder's major. If all three conditions are met, opener may bypass two diamonds and bid two of responder's major suit; if any of the three conditions is not met, opener must comply with the request to bid two diamonds.

The Two Diamond Relay

Responder's bid of two diamonds over opener's one notrump rebid is forcing to game. Unlike the natural game-forcing jumps that responder can make directly over the one notrump rebid, which are based largely on distributional values, the two diamond bid is based on high cards. Two diamonds is an artificial bid that asks opener to provide further information about his distribution.

Opener's rebids show whether he has three cards in the suit responder bid at the one level, or four cards in an unbid major suit, or a five-card minor suit. He makes the cheapest possible rebid that would show any of these holdings. For example, if the auction has begun

Opener	Responder
1 ◇	1 ♡
1 Notrump	2 ◇

opener's rebid of two hearts would show that he has three hearts; it would not deny four spades or five diamonds. A two spade rebid would show a four-card spade suit that opener had elected to bypass when he rebid one notrump; this rebid would deny three hearts but would not deny five diamonds. If he had neither four spades nor three hearts, opener would bid three clubs or three diamonds to show five cards in that suit, or he would bid two notrump if his distribution were 3-2-4-4.

With the information given by opener's bid over two diamonds, responder is usually able to place the final game contract. His bid of any game contract is a signoff. If he makes any other bid, it invites exploration for slam.

See also DELAYED STAYMAN; TWO CLUBS AS ONLY FORCE AFTER A ONE NOTRUMP REBID; PLOB.

RUBENSOHL WITHOUT COMPETITION

The RUBENSOHL convention, which uses bids ranging from two notrump through three spades as transfers, was originally devised for use by the partner of a player who had doubled or overcalled. Some partnerships agree to extend Rubensohl transfers to uncontested auctions in which opener has rebid two of his suit. This agreement expands responder's ability to make non-forcing bids and his ability to issue natural game invitations.

Using this Rubensohl extension, responder may make a natural bid of a new suit at the two level; if his second suit ranks below his first, his two-level bid is not forcing and not invitational. If responder has a second suit and values worth at least a game invitation, he makes a bid of two notrump or three of a suit, all of which are transfer bids. He bids the denomination below his second suit to transfer into that suit. A transfer into opener's suit suggests that the partnership has a game if opener has better than a minimum for his previous bidding.

For example, in the auction

Opener	Responder
1 ◇	1 ♠
2 ◇	

if responder has a hand such as

♠ K Q x x x   ♡ A K x   ◇ x x   ♣ x x x

using standard methods, he might bid two hearts for lack of a better bid. Though forcing, the bid is not descriptive of his distribution, and opener would be chary of jumping to four hearts with a four-card fit.

Using Rubensohl transfers, responder may bid three clubs on the above hand to invite game if opener has any extra values. If instead he bid two hearts, he would show at least four hearts and a hand not worth a game invitation. To show four hearts and invite game, he would bid three diamonds.

Thus, in the above auction, responder's complete range of rebids would be as follows:

2 ♡	=	at least four hearts, not forcing
2 ♠	=	at least six spades, not forcing
2 NT	=	transfer to clubs, inviting game
3 ♣	=	transfer to diamonds, inviting game
3 ◊	=	transfer to hearts, inviting game; may have only four hearts
3 ♡	=	transfer to spades, inviting game and showing at least six spades
3 ♠	=	transfer to three notrump
3 NT	=	natural signoff

Opener is free to reject the transfer if he does not have a good fit. With such a hand, he may rebid his own suit. If opener accepts the transfer or rebids his own suit, responder is free to pass. Thus, if opener wishes to play in game, he should bid something other than the minimum number of his own suit or the anchor suit.

Note that the availability of transfers also permits responder to transfer to three notrump, thereby permitting opener to become the declarer in that contract.

See also TWO NOTRUMP ASKING GAME TRY.

PLOB

PLOB is a convention used by responder after an opening bid of one club or one diamond, a response of one heart or one spade, and a rebid by opener of one notrump, to obtain additional information. PLOB consists of the bid by responder of the unbid minor suit, and it asks opener to show whether he has three cards in responder's suit and whether he has a minimum or a maximum hand.

In order to use PLOB, responder must have a hand worth a game bid if opener has a maximum, and he should have exactly five cards in the major suit he has bid. He need not have any particular holding in the unbid minor suit (PLOB suit).

In response to PLOB, opener is required to support responder's suit if he has three cards in the suit, by bidding two of the suit with minimum strength, or bidding three with a maximum. With fewer than three cards in responder's suit, opener bids the other major with a minimum, two notrump with a maximum and a stopper in the PLOB suit, or three of the PLOB suit with a maximum but no stopper therein. Opener's rebid of two of the unbid major suit does not say anything about his holding in that suit.

For example, after the auction has begun

Opener	Responder
1♣	1♡
1 Notrump	2♢

opener would bid two hearts with a hand such as

[A] ♠ K J x ♡ x x x ♢ A J x ♣ K J x x

or two notrump with

[B] ♠ K J x ♡ x x ♢ A J x ♣ K Q x x x

or two spades with

[C] ♠ A J x ♡ x x ♢ J x x ♣ A Q x x x

The acronym PLOB was adopted by adherents of this convention, until then known only as "new minor forcing," after one commentator characterized the convention as a "petty little" "odious" bid.

For an alternative schedule of rebids by opener, *see* NEW MINOR FORCING. *See also* EXTENDED PLOB.

After opener bids two of responder's suit, responder may pass if he too has a minimum; or he may raise to three if he wishes to invite opener to bid a game with a "good" minimum. After a bid by opener of two of the other major, responder may sign off at two notrump.

Any other action by responder is forcing to game and suggests interest in slam. For example, in the auction

Opener	Responder
1 ◊	1 ♡
1 Notrump	2 ♣
2 ♡	3 ◊

responder's three diamond bid is game forcing and shows interest in slam. He might have a hand such as

♠ A x   ♡ A K x x x   ◊ K Q x x.   ♣ x x

If opener had a suitable minimum, such as

♠ K x x   ♡ Q x x   ◊ A J x x x   ♣ K x

six diamonds is a good slam.

Hardy Adjunct

The Hardy Adjunct to PLOB assumes that, since responder's use of PLOB promises a game-invitational hand, the partnership is committed to game whenever opener has three cards in responder's suit and maximum strength. Accordingly this convention allows opener to show with a single bid his maximum, his support, and his distribution.

The Adjunct requires the opener who has three-card support and a maximum to jump to three of responder's suit only when he has no side suit doubleton. If opener has a side doubleton, he shows it by bidding at the three level a side suit he has not previously bid in which he has three or four cards.

Example:

Opener	Responder
1 ◊	1 ♡
1 Notrump	2 ♣
3 ♣	

Using the Hardy Adjunct, opener shows three or four clubs, a doubleton spade, and three hearts.

EXTENDED PLOB

The PLOB convention is responder's use of the unbid minor suit, after a one notrump rebid by opener, to require opener to show whether he has three-card support for responder's major suit and whether he has minimum or maximum strength. *See* PLOB. Extended PLOB is designed to evoke similar information after opener has rebid one spade rather than one notrump.

Extended PLOB may be used only when responder's hand is worth at least a game invitation, and only when the auction has begun

		Opener	*Responder*
[A]	1♣	1♡
		1♠	
or	[B]	1♢	1♡
		1♠	

In auction [A], a two diamond bid by responder would be Extended PLOB. In Auction [B], the Extended PLOB bid would be two clubs.

Opener normally rebids as follows:

   2♡ = three hearts, 12-13 HCP
   2♠ = fewer than three hearts, 12-13 HCP
  2NT = fewer than three hearts, 14-15 HCP with a stopper in the
            PLOB suit
   3♡ = three hearts, 14-15 HCP

Opener's rebid of two spades does not indicate that his spade suit is rebiddable, notwithstanding his earlier bid of spades; it is an artificial rebid conveying information only as to his length in hearts and his point count.

If opener bids three of the PLOB suit, he shows fewer than three hearts, 14-15 HCP, and no stopper in the PLOB suit.

If opener has a very distributional hand with fewer than three hearts, he is not limited to the above schedule of rebids. With five spades and six clubs, he may jump to three spades. (Devotees of Extended PLOB recommend opening the bidding one spade with 5-5 in clubs and spades.) With 14 or more HCP and six cards in his minor suit, opener may rebid the suit. With a singleton heart and 16-17 HCP, opener may rebid three notrump.

A rebid by opener showing a minimum may be passed by responder. Any rebid showing 14 or more points is forcing to game.

See also FOURTH SUIT FORCING AND ARTIFICIAL.

CROWHURST

The Crowhurst convention is a delayed Stayman type of inquiry by responder after his partner has opened with one of a suit and rebid one notrump. The convention assumes that opener may rebid one notrump with 12-16 HCP, and a two club rebid by responder asks opener to clarify his strength. The Crowhust bid is always two clubs, even if the opening bid was one club.

After the Crowhurst two club bid, opener rebids two notrump if he has 15-16 points, regardless of his distribution. The two notrump rebid commits the partnership to game. With 12-14 points, opener is to rebid a five-card major suit if he has one; if he does not, he is to show three card support for responder's major suit if he has that holding. If opener has none of the above, he shows an unbid four-card major suit if he has one, or bids two diamonds if he does not.

Examples:

[A]	♠ x x	♡ A K x x x	◊ K J x	♣ A x x
[B]	♠ x x	♡ Q x x x x	◊ K J x	♣ A K x
[C]	♠ x x	♡ K Q J x	◊ K J x	♣ A x x x

In the auction

Opener	Responder
1♡	1♠
1 Notrump	2♣

opener would rebid two notrump with hand [A], or two hearts with hand [B]. With hand [C], he should rebid two diamonds, which does not say anything about his diamond suit but merely says he has fewer than three spades, fewer than five hearts, and fewer than 15 points.

See also PLOB; NEW MINOR FORCING; DELAYED STAYMAN.

RELAYS AFTER ONE DIAMOND-TWO CLUBS

Auctions that begin with a one diamond opening bid and a two club response often present particular difficulties for opener. Rebids above two of his suit may not be, using standing methods, warranted by his strength; yet the length of his diamond suit may not warrant a rebid of the suit. Compromising on either length or strength risks having responder select a contract that takes the chosen bid at face value.

A relay-type series of rebids over the two club response provides a structure for opener to rebid any type of hand and keep the partnership at a manageable level. The special rebids are as follows.

A rebid by opener of two diamonds promises a five-card or longer diamond suit. Opener may also have a four-card major suit; if he does, he has less than the strength needed for a reverse.

A two heart rebid by opener is artificial. It shows a minimum-range opening hand with at most four diamonds; it also promises either four hearts or four spades, or four of each.

A two spade rebid by opener is also artificial. It shows enough strength for a standard reverse and promises at least a five-card diamond suit; it also shows either four hearts, or four spades, or four of each. The two spade bid commits the partnership to game, and the remainder of the auction may proceed naturally.

A rebid of two notrump shows balanced distribution with stoppers in both major suits and enough strength to accept a game invitation.

A rebid of three clubs is natural and forcing, showing extra values either in high cards or in an especially good club fit.

A rebid of three hearts or three spades over the two club response is a splinter bid, showing support for clubs and a singleton in the suit of the jump.

Responder's Rebids

If opener has rebid two diamonds, responder can invite game by bidding two notrump, three clubs, or three diamonds. Any other rebid by responder is game-forcing.

If opener has rebid two hearts, responder can invite game by bidding two notrump or three clubs; or he may force to game by bidding three diamonds or three hearts. All of these rebids by responder are natural.

If responder rebids two spades over opener's two heart rebid, responder's bid is forcing to game, but is entirely artificial. It asks opener to give more information as to his distribution. Opener conveys the following information, in addition to that already conveyed by his two heart bid (*i.e.*, four diamonds and at least one four-card major):

2NT = four spades, three hearts, two clubs; the hearts are weak, or the hand is at the low end of the point range

3♣ = minimum with three clubs

3◇ = four cards in each major and in diamonds; singleton club

3♡ = four hearts, three spades, two clubs; the spades are weak, or the hand is at the low end of the minimum range

3♠ = four hearts, four spades, two clubs; hand is minimum-minimum

3NT = four hearts, four spades, two clubs; hand is a maximum-minimum

After opener's bid of three clubs, showing a minimum hand with three clubs, responder may bid three diamonds to ask opener in which major suit he has four cards. Opener answers by bidding three of that suit.

For example, if opener had

♠ Q x x x   ♡ J x x   ◇ A K x x   ♣ K x

the auction might commence

Opener	Responder
1◇	2♣
2♡	2♠
2 Notrump	

Opener's two heart bid shows at most four diamonds, at least one four-card major suit, and minimum strength. Two notrump in answer to responder's two spade inquiry shows four spades and three weak hearts.

TRIAL BIDS

A "trial bid" is a bid of a new suit by opener as a game try after responder has raised an opening major suit bid from one to two. In the auction

Opener	Responder
1♠	2♠
3♦	

opener's rebid of three diamonds, by partnership agreement, is a bid in a suit in which he needs support in order to make game a reasonable proposition.

Typically the trial bid is made in a suit in which the bidder has at least three cards and at least two losers. In the above auction, opener might have a hand such as

(Opener)
♠ A K x x x x   ♡ x x   ◇ A x x   ♣ K Q

If responder has strength or shortness in the suit of the trial bid, he should accept the game invitation by jumping to four of opener's first bid suit. If he has three or four cards in the suit, without the ace, king, or queen, he should reject the invitation by bidding three of opener's suit. With an intermediate holding, responder may make a return trial bid. Responder might hold

[A]	♠ x x x x	♡ K Q x x	◇ x x x	♣ x x
[B]	♠ x x x x	♡ K Q x x	◇ x	♣ x x x x
[C]	♠ Q x x	♡ A x x x	◇ Q x x	♣ x x x

In the auction shown above, responder should be discouraged and bid three spades with hand [A]; he should be encouraged and bid game in spades with hand [B]; and he should bid three hearts with hand [C] to express his interest but lack of certainty. Opposite the hand shown for opener above, four spades would be a losing proposition on hand [A], an excellent proposition on hand [B], and an acceptable contract on hand [C].

If opener has opened with one spade and responder has raised to two, a trial bid of three hearts may on occasion lead to a four heart contract which will perhaps be superior to four spades. For example, if opener and responder had the following hands:

(Opener)

♠ A 10 9 x x   ♡ K x x x   ◇ x   ♣ A K x

(Responder)

♠ Q x x x   ♡ A x x x   ◇ x x   ♣ x x x

the bidding might go

Opener	Responder
1♠	2♠
3♡	4♡
Pass	

Trial bids are not used when the opening bid has been in a minor suit and responder has raised. Here the bid by opener of a new suit is more likely to be needed to show an interest in playing in notrump than in exploring the fit for a minor suit game. Hence, unless he is making a lead-inhibiting psychic bid, opener's bid of a new suit after his minor suit opening has been raised to two shows strength rather than a suit in which he needs support.

For use of trial bids in conjunction with limit jump raises, *see* TWO NOTRUMP AS LIMIT RAISE. For alternative methods of making game tries, *see* SHORT SUIT GAME TRIES; TWO-WAY GAME TRIES; WEAK SUIT GAME TRIES.

WEAK SUIT GAME TRIES

Like SHORT SUIT GAME TRIES, and TWO-WAY GAME TRIES, Weak Suit Game Tries are designed to help the partnership assess its game prospects after opener's opening bid of one heart or one spade has been raised to two. In such an auction opener's rebid of a new suit shows a weak suit, typically no better than J x x.

This game try asks responder to bid game in the agreed major suit if he has either good strength or shortness in the new suit. After the auction has begun 1♡ - 2♡, for example, an opener holding

♠ x   ♡ A Q J x x   ◇ x x x   ♣ A K x x

could make a weak suit game try by bidding three diamonds.

Responder should bid four hearts with a hand such as

[A]   ♠ K x x   ♡ x x x x   ◇ K Q x x x   ♣ x

or [B]   ♠ K J x x   ♡ x x x x   ◇ x   ♣ Q x x x

However, with

[C]   ♠ K x x x   ♡ K x x x   ◇ Q x x   ♣ x x

responder should bid three hearts since he has little help in diamonds.

See also TRIAL BIDS.

TWO NOTRUMP ASKING GAME TRY

The Two Notrump Asking Game Try convention is a device that enables a player to learn more about his partner's distribution after a certain amount of information has been given naturally. It may be used by opener when his major suit opening has been raised to two.

In several types of auctions, the convention may also be used by responder. When responder has bid a suit and opener has raised, responder may use the two notrump bid to elicit information as to whether opener has a side singleton or void and whether he has maximum or minimum strength. In certain other auctions, responder may use the convention to seek such information after opener has shown a six-card suit or has bid two suits.

Two Notrump Asking By Opener

When an opening bid of one heart or one spade has been raised to two, opener often is not sure whether game will be a good prospect. Using traditional methods, opener simply bids a side suit and asks responder to assess his hand in light of that bid. Using alternative methods, opener may bid a short suit or a weak suit. *See* SHORT SUIT GAME TRIES; TWO-WAY GAME TRIES; WEAK SUIT GAME TRIES; TRIAL BIDS. In all of these methods, opener describes his hand.

The Two Notrump Asking Game Try allows opener instead to obtain further information about the distribution of responder's hand. Responder is asked to show a suit in which he has no more than a doubleton.

If responder has a singleton or void in the unbid major suit, he jumps to four of the agreed suit. With this shortness, responder bids game whether he has minimum or maximum strength. If the agreed suit is spades and he has a doubleton heart, he bids three hearts. When hearts is the agreed suit and responder has a doubleton spade, he is allowed to bid three spades only if he has a maximum; with a minimum, he bids three hearts.

If responder has a doubleton, singleton, or void in a minor suit, he bids three of that minor. If opener returns to three of the agreed suit or bids three notrump and responder has a singleton or void, he bids four of his short suit.

If he has two doubletons, he bids the cheaper. If he has no short suit, he bids three of the agreed suit with a minimum or three notrump with a maximum.

If responder has maximum strength and has a five-card or longer suit headed by two of the top three honors, he jumps to four of his suit if it ranks below the agreed suit. This bid does not reveal where responder's doubleton is, but it does suggest that the side suit will be a source of tricks.

In sum, the most common rebids by responder over two notrump are as follows:

3 of a minor suit = at most a doubleton in that suit
3 of other major = doubleton in that major; if suit opened was spades,
        3 ♡ does not specify strength; if suit opened was
        hearts, 3 ♠ shows maximum strength
3 of trump suit = minimum strength and either 4-3-3-3 or, if hearts
        was opened, perhaps a doubleton spade
3 NT = 4-3-3-3, maximum strength
4 of a new suit = a five-card or longer suit headed by two of the top
        three honors, with maximum strength
4 of trump suit = singleton or void in the other major

After learning that responder has at most a doubleton in a given suit, opener assesses the game prospects. He may settle for three of the agreed suit; or he may bid game in the agreed suit or in notrump.

Responder is allowed to correct three notrump to four of the suit opened. He may also bid game over opener's signoff in three with a doubleton if he has a superb maximum. As indicated above, if responder has a minor suit singleton, he rebids the short suit over opener's three-level rebid.

Using opener's Asking Game Try with

Opener
♠ K Q J x x   ♡ x x   ◇ A K x x   ♣ K x
Responder
♠ A x x   ♡ J x x x   ◇ x x   ♣ Q J x x

opener and responder could reach game by the following auction:

Opener	*Responder*
1 ♠	2 ♠
2 Notrump	3 ◇
4 ♠	

One advantage of using two notrump as a game try asking bid instead is that it gives less useful information to the opponents. Opener reveals nothing about his own hand; and though more is revealed about responder's hand, the information will normally be directly pertinent only to the opening lead since responder's hand will be tabled as the dummy.

The Asking Game Try may be coordinated with other game tries. For example, if the partnership has agreed to use short suit game tries, opener may elect to bid three of a new suit over the raise to show his singleton or void.

Opener may use the Two Notrump Asking Game Try in competition. Two notrump makes the same inquiry regardless of whether the opponents have overcalled or doubled, and regardless of whether the intervention has occurred over the opening bid or the response, so long as the opening bid of one heart or one spade has been raised to two and the bidding is still at the two level.

Responder's Two Notrump Asking After Opener Has Raised

When the auction has been opened with a minor suit, responder has bid a major, and opener has raised responder's major to the two level, the Two Notrump Asking Game Try may be used by responder. Responder may use the convention to invite game, or to determine which game to play, or to explore for slam. Opener should assume initially that responder's two notrump asking bid is merely a game try.

The principal difference between use of this convention by opener and by responder is that any short suit revealed by opener must be either a singleton or a void. Opener does not show doubletons.

If opener has a singleton or void and has four-card support for responder's suit, he jumps to four of his short suit. With only three-card support for responder's suit, opener bids the suit of his singleton or void at the three level. If the agreed suit is hearts and opener has a singleton spade, he is not allowed to bid three spades, which commits the partnership to game, unless he has maximum strength. The short-suit bid of three clubs or three diamonds does not reveal whether opener has minimum or maximum strength. If, over this bid, responder signs off in three of his suit, opener will pass with a minimum but will bid again with a maximum.

If opener has no singleton or void, but has five or six cards in the suit he opened and has three-card support for responder's suit, he rebids three of his suit with minimum strength or bids three notrump with a maximum. Opener's rebid of three of his suit is not forcing. If opener has four-card support, a five-card suit, and no singleton or void, he bids three of responder's suit with a minimum, or jumps to four of the suit he opened with a maximum.

If opener has a balanced hand, i.e., he has neither a five-card or longer suit nor a singleton or void, he signs off in three of responder's suit with a minimum; for his signoff, he may have either three or four cards in responder's suit. If opener has a balanced hand with a maximum, he jumps to four of responder's suit if he has four-card support, or he bids three notrump if he has only three-card support.

Opener's three notrump bid has no significance other than to show a long suit, maximum strength, no singleton or void, and three cards in responder's suit. It does not promise stoppers or honors in the unbid suits.

Opener's complete schedule of rebids is as follows:

> 3 of minor opened = at least a five-card suit, no singleton or void, three-card support, minimum strength
>
> 3 of other minor = singleton or void, three-card support, strength unspecified
>
> 3 of responder's major = no singleton or void, three- or four-card support, minimum strength
>
> 3 ♡ (if responder's suit is spades) = singleton or void, three-card support, strength unspecified
>
> 3 ♠ (if responder's suit is hearts) = singleton or void, three- or four-card support, maximum strength
>
> 3 NT = no singleton or void, three-card support, maximum strength
>
> 4 of minor opened = five-card suit, no singleton or void, four-card support, maximum strength
>
> 4 of other minor = singleton or void, four-card support
>
> 4 of responder's major = no singleton or void, no five-card suit, four-card support, maximum strength
>
> 4 ♡ (if responder's suit is spades) = singleton or void, four-card support

Similar principles may be applied after the bidding has been opened one heart and a response of one spade has been raised to two. After responder's two notrump asking, opener bids three of a minor with a singleton in that suit and only three-card spade support. If responder then signs off in three spades, opener bids again with a maximum. With no singleton, opener would bid three spades with a minimum and either three- or four-card spade support. With no singleton but maximum strength, opener would normally bid three notrump with three spades or four spades with four-card support. If he has only three spades but has either a fair six-card or a very good five-card (*e.g.* K Q J 10 x) heart suit, opener may bid three hearts with a minimum or four hearts with a maximum.

If responder has bid two notrump on a game-invitational hand, planning to contract for game only if opener's response revealed maximum strength, he will sign off below game opposite a bid that does not show a maximum. Thus, he may pass the minimum-showing rebid of three of opener's suit or three of responder's suit. Or, if opener has shown a singleton and has not specified his strength, responder may return to three of the agreed major. If opener has a maximum, he will bid again.

For example, if opener and responder held

Opener
♠ A x x   ♡ A x x x   ◇ x   ♣ K Q J x x
Responder
♠ K J x x x   ♡ x x   ◇ Q x x   ♣ A x x

the bidding would be

Opener	*Responder*
1 ♣	1 ♠
2 ♠	2 Notrump
3 ◇	3 ♠
4 ♣	

If responder has a game-going hand but has bid two notrump in order to determine *which* game should be played, depending not on opener's strength but on his distribution, responder will not know from opener's rebid of three of responder's major or three of the other major whether opener has three-card or four-card support. If opener has rebid three of responder's suit, responder should rebid three notrump in case opener has only three-card support; if opener has four, he will correct to four of the suit. If opener has rebid three of the other major, showing a singleton, responder may bid three notrump with that major securely stopped (*e.g.*, K Q 10 9) or may elect to play game in the possible 4-3 fit. Over three notrump, opener will normally correct to four of responder's suit if he has four-card support.

The Two Notrump Asking Game Try may be used by a responder who is a passed hand. It may also be used in competition so long as responder's suit has been raised and two notrump is still available.

Responder's Two Notrump Asking When Opener Has Bid Two Suits

The Two Notrump Asking Game Try convention may also be used by responder if he has bid one notrump in response to the major suit opening bid and opener has bid the other major at the two level. The meanings of opener's rebids will vary depending on whether he opened with one spade and rebid hearts, or opened with one heart and reversed in spades.

When opener has begun with one spade and rebid two hearts, he should pass two notrump if his distribution is 5-4-2-2 and he has minimum strength. If he has extra strength or unbalanced distribution, his rebids are as follows.

3 ♣	=	five spades, four hearts, singleton or void in clubs, less than a maximum
3 ◊	=	five spades, four hearts, singleton or void in diamonds, less than a maximum
3 ♡	=	five spades and five hearts, short suit undisclosed, minimum
3 ♠	=	six (or five very strong) spades, maximum; forcing
3 NT	=	5-4-2-2 maximum, or 5-4-3-1 with 16-17 HCP
4 ♣	=	five spades and five hearts, with hearts at least as strong as spades, maximum strength
4 ◊	=	five spades and five hearts, with spades stronger, maximum strength
4 ♡	=	five spades and six hearts
4 ♠	=	six self-sufficient spades, with four or five hearts

When the opening bid was one heart and opener has reversed to two spades, his rebids are as follows.

3 ♣	=	four spades, five hearts, singleton or void in clubs
3 ◊	=	four spades, five hearts, singleton or void in diamonds
3 ♡	=	four spades, five hearts, two doubletons, minimum strength
3 ♠	=	four spades and six hearts, short suit undisclosed
3 NT	=	four spades, five hearts, two doubletons, maximum strength
4 ♣	=	five spades, six hearts, with stronger hearts
4 ◊	=	five spades, six hearts, with stronger spades
4 ♡	=	four spades, six or more self-sufficient hearts

Responder's Two Notrump Asking When Opener Has a Six-Card Suit

When opener has rebid two of his suit in an auction that indicates he has a six-card suit, responder's two notrump asking bid again asks him to describe his hand further. Most of his rebids conform to the same standards regardless of what his long suit is. Thus, if opener has a minimum with no singletons, he rebids his suit. If he has a maximum with no singletons, he rebids three notrump. If he has a singleton and it ranks below his long suit, he may bid it even with minimum strength. If he has a singleton that ranks above his long suit, he may not show it unless he has better than minimum strength.

If opener's long suit is spades, his jump to four clubs or four diamonds shows that he has a total of ten cards in spades and that minor. If opener's long suit is hearts, in the auction

	Opener	*Responder*
	1 ♡	1 ♠
	2 ♡	2 Notrump

opener's jump to four clubs or four diamonds shows a void in that suit and precisely three spades.

PUPPET THREE CLUB REBID FOR
MAJOR TWO-SUITERS

When opener has a major two-suiter and his partner persists in bidding notrump, standard bidding sometimes does not permit opener to clarify the length of his suits or the strength of his hand. When the auction begins

Opener	Responder
1 ♠	1 Notrump
2 ♡	2 Notrump

use of the Puppet Three Club Rebid convention will permit opener to indicate whether his major suit distribution is 6-4, 5-5, or 5-4 and to show whether he has the values for game.

With a game-going hand and ten major suit cards, or with five spades, four hearts, and three clubs, opener rebids three clubs over responder's two notrump rebid. The three club bid is artificial and forces responder to rebid three diamonds. Opener's rebids after responder's forced three diamond bid are as follows:

3 ♡ = five hearts, five spades, forcing
3 ♠ = six spades, four hearts, forcing
3 NT = five spades, four hearts, one diamond, and three clubs, with a game-going hand

When opener has bid three hearts or three spades, his minor suit distribution is undisclosed.

Opener's three diamond rebid over two notrump shows five spades, four hearts, three diamonds, and one club. This bid is also forcing to game.

Opener's major suit rebids directly over two notrump are natural and not forcing. Like his rebids after the Puppet three clubs, each shows a total of ten major suit cards: three hearts shows five-five, and three spades shows six spades and four hearts. These direct bids show less than the strength needed for game.

TWO CLUB GAME TRY BY OPENER

The two club game try by opener is designed to ease the rebidding problems of the opening bidder after his partner has responded one notrump. Using this convention, all jump rebids by opener after a one notrump response are forcing to game. If opener wishes merely to invite game, he must rebid two clubs over the one notrump response.

The two club bid does not say anything about opener's holding in clubs. It simply asks responder to clarify his distribution and his support for opener's suit. "Support" means as little as a tripleton, or a doubleton of Q x or better. Use of this convention also allows a responder who has a weak four-card major suit to bypass that suit in responding to a minor suit opening.

If the auction has started

Opener	Responder
1♠	1 Notrump
2♣	

responder's proper rebids are as follows:

    2♦ = no spade support, fewer than four hearts
    2♡ = no spade support, four or more hearts
    2♠ = spade support, says nothing about hearts

If the auction has started with a one heart opening,

Opener	Responder
1♡	1 Notrump
2♣	

responder's proper rebids are

    2♦ = no heart support, fewer than four spades
    2♡ = heart support, says nothing about spades

If the auction has started with a minor suit opening,

Opener	Responder
1♣ or 1♦	1 Notrump
2♣	

responder should bid as follows:

    2♦ = no four-card major
    2♡ = four weak hearts, fewer than four spades
    2♠ = four weak spades; fewer than four hearts

After responder's clarification, opener may pass if responder's bid has discouraged him from proceeding further. Or he may bid again. A bid of three clubs is natural and shows five or more clubs with a weak hand. Any other bid is natural and invites game.

Example:

[A]   ♠ K J 10 x x x   ♡ A K x x   ◇ x   ♣ x x

If responder has bid one notrump in response to the one spade opening, and over two clubs has bid two hearts, denying spade support but showing four or more hearts, opener would pass.

STRONG ONE NOTRUMP RESPONSE

The Strong One Notrump Response convention is used in conjunction with a bidding style that features a strong artificial one club opening, 16-18 HCP one notrump openings, and four-card major suit openings. The convention is a system of responding to the limited (11-15 point) opening bids of one diamond, one heart, and one spade. The one notrump response promises at least 10 points, has no upper limit, and is forcing for one round. No other response to the one diamond, one heart, and one spade openings is forcing.

The one notrump response, which does not promise a balanced hand, asks opener to describe his strength. With 14-15 points opener may reverse, or jump in his own suit or a new suit; or, if he has opened one heart or one spade with 4-3-3-3 distribution, he may rebid two notrump. With 11-13 point hands, opener cannot rebid in notrump and may be forced to rebid a three-card suit to avoid showing greater strength.

SINGLETON AND FEATURE REBIDS
AFTER WEAK TWO-BID

When the partnership is using openings of two hearts and two spades as weak two-bids, a response of two notrump is generally treated as forcing, asking opener for further information. Depending on the partnership's agreement, opener may be asked to show a high card in a side suit, *see* TWO NOTRUMP FORCING RESPONSE TO WEAK TWO-BIDS, or the texture of his suit and the strength of his hand, *see* OGUST REBIDS, or some combination of all of these, *see* ROMEX REBIDS AFTER WEAK TWO-BID.

A method employed by users of the PRECISION CLUB SYSTEM permits responder to seek information either as to opener's side suit high cards, or as to his possession of a singleton. Responder determines which information will be more useful to him on the hand in question, and proceeds as follows.

A two notrump response asks opener to disclose whether or not he has a singleton or void. If he has such shortness, he bids the suit of the shortness; if he has no singleton or void, he rebids three of his suit.

A three club response to the weak two-bid is artificial, saying nothing about responder's holding in clubs, and asks opener to disclose whether or not he has a high honor in a side suit. If opener has such an honor, he bids the suit in which he has it, or bids three notrump if it is in clubs. Otherwise he rebids his suit.

ROMEX REBIDS AFTER WEAK TWO-BID

The Romex system uses a forcing two notrump response to an opening weak two-bid to ask opener to describe his strength and suit texture. The Romex method of responding requires opener to provide somewhat more detailed information than is available using OGUST REBIDS.

The Romex system uses weak two-bids only in the major suits and never when opener has four cards in the other major. After the two notrump response, opener's prescribed rebids are as follows:

three clubs: minimum hand with eight losers

three diamonds: broken suit, seven losers

three of opener's major: semi-solid suit, seven losers

three of other major: maximum hand, six losers

three notrump: six sure tricks, either a solid suit or K Q J 10 x x and a side suit ace

four of a side suit: semi-solid in the suit opened, plus the king of the suit in which the jump is made

See also SINGLETON AND FEATURE REBIDS AFTER WEAK TWO-BIDS.

TWO SPADES ASKING OVER WEAK
TWO BID IN HEARTS

In conjunction with weak two bids, many partnerships use a response of two notrump to ask opener to reveal whether he has a singleton. *See* SINGLETON AND FEATURE REBIDS AFTER WEAK TWO BID. *See also* TWO NOTRUMP RESPONSE TO WEAK TWO BIDS; OGUST REBIDS; MODIFIED OGUST; TWO-PHASE TWO NOTRUMP ASKING BIDS AFTER WEAK TWO BIDS; ROMEX REBIDS AFTER WEAK TWO BID. This works well if the suit opened was spades, for any singleton can be disclosed without going past three spades. It works less well if the suit opened was hearts, for bidding a singleton spade forces the partnership past three hearts.

Rather than forgo the inquiry, some partnerships agree that opposite a weak two bid in hearts, they will reverse the meanings of the two spade response, which is ordinarily natural, and the two notrump response asking for a singleton.

Using this convention, if responder wants to ask opener whether he has a singleton, he bids two spades. Opener responds as follows:

    2 NT = singleton spade
    3 ♣   = singleton club
    3 ◇   = singleton diamond

Responder's two spade bid is entirely artificial and says nothing about his hand. If he has a spade suit that he wishes to show, he responds two notrump.

TWO-PHASE TWO NOTRUMP ASKING BIDS
AFTER WEAK TWO BIDS

The premises underlying two-stage asking bids are discussed and applied in TWO-PHASE TWO NOTRUMP ASKING BIDS AFTER JACOBY TWO NOTRUMP. Application of these principles is further illustrated in EXTENDED FLANNERY and TWO-PHASE TWO NOTRUMP RESPONSE TO THREE-SUITED OPENINGS. Its applications to weak two bids is discussed below.

When the partnership is using weak two bids, it is common to use a two notrump response to ask opener to describe his hand further. Though there are four possible areas of inquiry—strength, suit quality, distribution, and side-suit aces or kings ("features")—most conventions that do not take the rebids beyond the three level allow complete disclosure in one area and only partial disclosure, at best, in a second. For example, if the partnership has agreed that opener should show a side suit feature if he has a maximum, see, e.g., TWO NOTRUMP RESPONSE TO WEAK TWO BIDS, opener's rebid will always reveal his strength; but if he shows a minimum he does not disclose whether or not he has a high card outside of his suit. When this convention is used, opener discloses nothing about his distribution or the quality of his suit. Or if the partnership agreement requires opener to show whether he has a singleton, his singleton-showing rebid does not indicate whether he has minimum or maximum strength, or indeed anything else about his hand. See, e.g., SINGLETON AND FEATURE REBIDS AFTER WEAK TWO BID. The greatest amount of information gained through three-level rebids is provided through use of OGUST REBIDS, with which opener shows both the quality of his suit and the general strength of his hand; he does not, however, disclose anything about his distribution or the location of his high cards. See also ROMEX REBIDS AFTER WEAK TWO BID.

The Two-Phase Two Notrump Asking Bid permits responder to obtain complete information as to two areas of concern. The convention requires opener to make the most discouraging responses at low levels and allows responder to make further inquiry if he remains interested. The partnership may agree whether the two areas are to be strength and features or strength and singletons.

If the partnership agrees that opener is to show strength and features, his rebids over two notrump are as follows:

3 ♣ = minimum hand with a feature somewhere
3 ◊ = no feature; opener's strength is undisclosed
3 ♡ = maximum, with a feature in the lowest unbid suit
3 ♠ = maximum, with a feature in the middle unbid suit
3 NT = maximum, with a feature in the highest unbid suit

If, over three clubs, responder is interested in knowing where opener's feature is, he bids three diamonds to ask. Opener's rebids from three hearts through three notrump show the features in the lowest, middle, and highest unbid suits, respectively. A virtue of the Two-Phase convention is that opener's rebids of three hearts, three spades, and three notrump identify the same three side-suit holdings, respectively, whether bid directly over two notrump (thereby showing extra strength) or in response to a second relay after opener has limited his hand by first bidding three clubs. Thus, only one set of responses for feature identification need be learned and remembered.

If, over opener's three diamond rebid, denying a feature, responder wants to know opener's strength, he inquires by bidding three hearts. Opener rebids three spades with a minimum and three notrump with a maximum. If opener shows a maximum, the quality of his suit is likely to be good since he has no outside ace or king.

If the partnership agrees that instead of showing features in response to two notrump opener should show whether he has a singleton or void, the schedule of rebids would be parallel to that shown above. Thus,

3 ♣	=	minimum hand with a singleton or void somewhere
3 ♢	=	no singleton or void, strength undisclosed
3 ♡	=	maximum, with a singleton or void in the lowest unbid suit
3 ♠	=	maximum, with a singleton or void in the middle unbid suit
3 NT	=	maximum, with a singleton or void in the highest unbid suit

Over the three club rebid, responder may, as above, ask for identification of opener's short suit, and the identifications parallel those set out above. Over the three diamond rebid, responder may bid three hearts to ask about opener's strength. Unlike the sequence when opener is asked about strength and features, his three notrump rebid showing extra strength in this auction does not give rise to an inference that the quality of his suit is good, since, in describing his distribution, he has not denied outside aces or kings.

MODIFIED OGUST

When the bidding is opened with a weak two bid, a two notrump response normally asks opener for more information. The OGUST convention provides a schedule of rebids by which opener describes quality of his hand and his suit. For partnerships whose weak two bids may be made on five-card suits or with hands having a wide variety of distributions, Modified Ogust rebids are needed to allow opener to describe the length of his suit and perhaps the length of his side suits.

Modifications for Weak Two Bids on Five-Card Suits

When the partnership has agreed that a weak bid may be opened with as few as five cards in the suit, the principal information to be conveyed is the length of opener's suit. For a system of rebidding when the opening was two diamonds, *see* BERGEN-COHEN REBIDS AFTER WEAK TWO DIAMOND OPENING. When the opening bid was two hearts or two spades, the following modified OGUST rebids may be used:

    3 ♣ = five-card suit, better than minimum strength
    3 ◊ = five-card suit, minimum strength
    3 ♡ = six-card suit, minimum strength
    3 ♠ = six-card suit, better than minimum strength
    3 NT = solid five- or six-card suit, or a semi-solid five- or six-card
                  suit with an ace or king outside

Three clubs, rather than three diamonds, is used to show the hand with more than minimum strength in order to provide responder with more room to inquire further. Over three clubs, if responder wants to know about the quality of opener's suit, he rebids three diamonds. Opener's rebids over three diamonds are

    3 ♡ = weak suit
    3 ♠ = reasonable suit
    3 NT = good suit

Modifications for Weak Two Bids With Four- or Five-Card Side *Suits*

When the partnership has agreed that a weak two heart or two spade bid may be opened with a four-card or five-card suit on the side, Ogust modifications may use relay principles. *See* RELAYS IN GENERAL. Thus, opener's cheapest rebids will generally show one of two types of hands, leaving responder to make the next cheapest rebid to determine which kind of hand is held.

Opener's Rebids After Two Notrump

Opener's rebid of three clubs shows either a weak hand with a weak suit or a good hand with a good suit. His rebid of three diamonds shows either a good hand with a weak suit or a six-card major suit with a four-card minor. His rebid of three of his own suit promises a weak hand with a good suit. And his rebid of three of the other major shows four cards in that suit and six in the major he opened.

Four-level rebids by opener show six-five distribution. His bid of four of a minor shows five cards in that minor. The meaning of the four heart rebid depends on which major suit was opened. If the opening was two spades, the jump to four hearts shows five hearts and six spades. If the opening was two hearts, the jump to four hearts shows six hearts and five spades.

The complete schedule of opener's rebids is:

$3 \clubsuit$ = weak hand and weak suit, or good hand and good suit, and any distribution

$3 \diamondsuit$ = good hand and weak suit, or six of major opened and either four clubs or four diamonds

3 of major opened = weak hand and good suit

3 of other major = four-cards in that major, with six of major opened

3 NT = solid suit

$4 \clubsuit$ = five clubs, with six of major opened

$4 \diamondsuit$ = five diamonds, with six of major opened

$4 \heartsuit$ (if hearts opened) = six hearts and five spades

$4 \heartsuit$ (if spades opened) = five hearts and six spades

Responder's Relays After Opener's Rebid

After opener has rebid three clubs, responder bids three diamonds to learn which type of hand opener has. Opener rebids his own suit if he has a weak hand and a weak suit. With a good hand and a good suit, opener rebids three notrump if he has no singletons, or he rebids three of the other major if he has a singleton somewhere. Over the latter bid, responder rebids three notrump to have opener identify his singleton. Opener's singleton-showing bids are:

4 ♣ = singleton club
4 ◇ = singleton diamond
4 ♡ (if hearts opened) = singleton spade
4 ♡ (if spades opened) = singleton heart

After opener's three diamond rebid, showing either a good hand with a weak suit or six-four distribution with a side minor suit, responder bids three hearts to ask which hand opener holds. If opener has the six-four hand, he rebids four clubs to show that his side suit is clubs, or four diamonds to show that it is diamonds. If opener has the good hand with a weak suit, he rebids three notrump if he has no singleton, or he rebids three spades with a singleton somewhere. Over three spades, responder may bid three notrump to ask opener to identify his singleton; opener's rebids are the same as those shown above: four of a minor shows a singleton in that suit, and four hearts shows a singleton in the major suit not opened.

After opener's rebid of three of the major he did not open, showing four cards in that suit with six cards in the suit he opened, responder bids four clubs to agree on hearts, or four diamonds to agree on spades.

See also SINGLETON AND FEATURE REBIDS; ROMEX REBIDS; TWO SPADE ASKING BID OVER WEAK TWO BID IN HEARTS; TWO-PHASE TWO NOTRUMP ASKING BIDS.

BERGEN-COHEN REBIDS AFTER WEAK TWO DIAMOND OPENING

Partnerships that use weak two diamond openings freely may need a responding method to determine whether they have a playable major suit fit. Bergen-Cohen rebids after a two notrump response allow opener to disclose whether he has better than minimum strength and whether he has a four-card major or a reasonable three-card major.

Over responder's two notrump, opener rebids three diamonds if he has minimum strength. If his hand also contains a four-card major, it must be an absolute minimum to justify the three diamond rebid.

All of opener's other rebids show better than minimum strength. With no four-card major and no reasonable three-card major, he rebids three notrump. If he has a reasonable three-card major, he rebids three clubs. If opener has a four-card major, he rebids three of the other major. If a major fit is thus located, these rebids allow responder, the stronger hand, to become the declarer.

The complete schedule of opener's rebids over two notrump is as follows:

3 ♣	=	at least one reasonable three-card major, with better than minimum strength
3 ◊	=	minimum strength
3 ♡	=	four spades, five or six diamonds, better than minimum strength
3 ♠	=	four hearts, five or six diamonds, better than minimum strength
3 NT	=	no four-card major, no reasonable three-card major, better than minimum strength

If opener has rebid three diamonds over two notrump, showing minimum strength but not disclosing his major suit holdings, responder may bid a five-card major if he has one. This bid is forcing to game.

After opener's rebid of three clubs, responder's bid of three hearts or three spades is natural and forcing to game. In this auction, in which responder does not stop to inquire which major opener holds, responder's bid promises a self-supporting suit. With a major suit that is not self-supporting, responder may bid three diamonds over three clubs to inquire which major opener holds. Opener's responses are

3 ♡	=	three spades, fewer than three hearts
3 ♠	=	three hearts, fewer than three spades
3 NT	=	three hearts and three spades

Again, if these rebids lead to the discovery of a major suit fit, responder will become the declarer.

See also OGUST; MODIFIED OGUST; SINGLETON AND FEATURE REBIDS; TWO-PHASE TWO NOTRUMP ASKING BIDS.

III

Forcing Opening Bids and Responses

MULTICOLORED TWO DIAMOND
OPENING

The Multicolored Two Diamond convention is an artificial opening bid of two diamonds that promises either a weak two-bid in hearts, a weak two-bid in spades, or a 4-4-4-1 distribution with 17 to 24 high card points. The nature of the opener's hand will be revealed by his rebid.

If the responder has a weak hand with which he would have passed a natural weak two-bid in either major suit, he responds with a bid of two hearts. The opener will pass this bid if he has a weak two-bid in hearts. The opener will rebid two spades if he has a weak two-bid in spades, which of course, the responder will pass.

If the responder has a hand with which he would have passed a two spade opening but would have invited game over a weak two hearts opening, he responds two spades. The opener either passes if spades was his suit, or bids three or four hearts to reject or accept the responder's game invitation.

If the responder has a hand with which he would like to invite game if the opener's suit is spades but not if it is hearts, he jumps to three hearts over two diamonds. The opener either passes if his suit was hearts, or bids three or four spades to reject or accept the responder's game invitation.

For example, if the opener's and the responder's hands are:

(Opener)
♠ K Q J x x x   ♡ x x x   ◇ K x   ♣ x x

(Responder)
♠ x x x x x   ♡ x   ◇ A Q x   ♣ A K x x

the bidding might go

Opener	Responder
2◇	3♡
4♣	

If the opener makes any bid other than one that specifically accepts or rejects the responder's invitation, he shows a strong 4-4-4-1 hand, with a singleton in the next higher suit.

The responder may also bid three clubs or three diamonds over a two-diamond opening as a sign-off. The reason the responder does not simply pass the two diamond opening when he has a weak hand with a long diamond suit is, of course, that the opener may have a strong three-suited hand rather than a weak two-bid type. If the responder jumps to four clubs or four diamonds over two diamonds, he shows a solid suit, and support for hearts and spades.

In order to ask the opener to describe his hand with specificity, the responder may bid two notrump in response to two diamonds. The opener's rebids of three clubs through three spades describe weak two bids as follows:

3♣ = heart suit, maximum strength
3◇ = spade suit, maximum strength
3♡ = heart suit, minimum strength
3♠ = spade suit, minimum strength

If the opener shows maximum strength, the responder's bid of the cheapest suit asks the opener to describe the texture of his suit in two steps; the first step shows a poor suit, and the second step shows a good suit. Thus in the auction

Opener	Responder
2◇	2 Notrump
3◇	3♡
3 Notrump	

the opener has shown a maximum weak two-bid in spades with a good suit.

If the opener has a strong 4-4-4-1 hand and the responder has bid two notrump, the opener's rebid will be as follows:

3NT = singleton club
4♣ = singleton diamond
4◇ = singleton heart
4♡ = singleton spade

The responder may ask for additional information by bidding the opener's singleton. In response to the first bid of his singleton, the opener defines his point count in a series of four steps as follows:

1st step = 17 to 18 high card points
2nd step = 19 to 20 high card points
3rd step = 21 to 22 high card points
4th step = 23 to 24 high card points

If the responder bids the opener's singleton again, the opener shows how many controls he has (ace = 2, king = 1) in a series of five steps. The number of controls shown by the first step depends on whether the opener has shown a hand in the 17 to 20 point range, or one worth 21 to 24 points. If he has the "weaker" hand, the first step shows four controls:

1st step	= 4 controls
2nd step	= 5 controls
3rd step	= 6 controls
4th step	= 7 controls
5th step	= 8 controls

If he has shown 21 to 24 points, the first step shows six controls:

1st step	= 6 controls
2nd step	= 7 controls
3rd step	= 8 controls
4th step	= 9 controls
5th step	= 10 controls

If the responder bids the opener's known singleton a third time, he asks the opener to show how many queens he has. The first step shows no queens; the second shows one, and so forth.

If the opener and the responder had these hands

(Opener)
♠ A J x x   ♡ x   ◊ A K J x   ♣ A J x x

(Responder)
♠ K 10 x x   ♡ A Q x x   ◊ Q x   ♣ K Q x

the auction might proceed as follows:

Opener	Responder
2 ◊	2 Notrump
4 ◊ (singleton ♡)	4 ♡
4 ♠ (17-18)	5 ♡
6 ◊ (7 controls)	6 ♡
6 ♠ (no queen)	Pass

SIMPLIFIED MULTICOLORED TWO DIAMOND OPENING

A simplified version of the MULTICOLORED TWO DIAMOND OPENING uses the two diamond opening to show either a weak two-bid in hearts or spades, or a balanced hand with 21-22 HCP. The opening is forcing for one round.

Responder must assume at the outset that opener has a weak two-bid. If responder has a hand with which he would have passed a natural weak two-bid in either major suit, he responds two hearts. Opener will pass if he has a weak two-bid in hearts, or will rebid two spades if he has a weak two-bid in spades.

If responder has a hand with which he is interested in game if opener has a weak two-bid in hearts but not in spades, responder bids two spades. Opener passes if he has a weak two-bid in spades; if he has the weak two-bid in hearts, he bids three hearts to reject the game invitation, or bids four hearts to accept.

If responder has a hand with which he is interested in game if opener's weak two bid is in spades but not if it is in hearts, responder simply bids two hearts; if opener rebids two spades, responder may raise to invite game in spades.

If responder has a hand with which he is interested in game opposite a weak two-bid in either major suit, he may jump to three hearts over the two diamond opening. Opener will pass if he has a weak two-bid in hearts and wishes to reject the invitation; or he will bid three spades if that is the suit of his weak two-bid and he wishes to reject the game invitation. If he has a weak two-bid but wishes to accept the invitation, opener bids four of his suit.

An alternative means by which responder may show interest in game in either major suit is to use a two notrump response to the two diamond opening for that purpose. If this device is used, opener may reveal his suit and his strength over the two notrump response as follows:

3♣ = maximum weak two-bid in hearts
3♢ = maximum weak two-bid in spades
3♡ = minimum weak two-bid in hearts
3♠ = minimum weak two-bid in spades

The cheaper bids are used to show maximum weak two-bids in order to leave more room for exploration opposite opener's better hands. For alternative responses to the two diamond opening, *see* PENDER TWO BIDS.

If, as his first rebid opposite any response, opener bids notrump, he shows that he has the strong balanced 21-22 point hand rather than a weak two-bid.

Examples:

	(Opener)			
[A]	♠ K Q J x x x	♡ x x	◊ K x x	♣ x x
[B]	♠ A K Q	♡ Q x x x	◊ K Q J x	♣ A x
	(Responder)			
[C]	♠ x	♡ A 10 x x	◊ A x x x	♣ K Q x x

Opposite a two diamond opening, responder would bid two spades with hand [C] since he wishes to invite a game in hearts, but not in spades. If opener had hand [A], responder's two spade response would end the auction, since opener's suit is spades. If opener's major suit holdings were reversed, he would jump to four hearts over two spades.

If opener held hand [B], the auction would begin

Opener	Responder
2 ◊	2 ♠
2 Notrump	

The partnership would then bid according to its usual methods over notrump openings, ideally landing in six diamonds.

The use of the two diamond opening to include a hand with a weak two-bid in a major suit preserves the openings of two hearts and two spades for other purposes. *See also* PENDER TWO BIDS; MINI MULTICOLORED TWO DIAMONDS; CHICO TWO DIAMONDS; COMPREHENSIVE MULTICOLORED TWO-BIDS.

PENDER TWO BIDS

Pender two-bids incorporate a simplified version of the MULTICOLORED TWO DIAMOND OPENING in which the two diamond opening shows either a weak two-bid in a major suit or a strong balanced hand. Opening bids of two hearts, two spades, and two notrump are used to show weakish two-suited hands.

The Two Diamond Opening

The two diamond opening shows either a weak two heart opening or a weak two spade opening, or a blanced hand containing 21-22 HCP. Responder initially must assume that opener has a weak two-bid and should proceed accordingly. For the simpliest prescribed responses and rebids, *see* SIMPLIFIED MULTICOLORED TWO DIAMOND OPENING. Alternatives to the methods there prescribed include:

(1) If responder wishes to preempt opposite a weak two-bid in either major suit, he may jump to three hearts.

(2) If responder has bid two spades, showing interest in a heart game, and opener has a weak two-bid in hearts, opener may rebid three of a minor suit as a transfer to hearts, to allow responder to become the declarer in the final heart contract. Three clubs would transfer with a minimum, and three diamonds would transfer with a maximum.

Example:

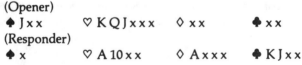

(Opener)
♠ J x x   ♡ K Q J x x x   ◊ x x   ♣ x x
(Responder)
♠ x   ♡ A 10 x x   ◊ A x x x   ♣ K J x x

With these hands the auction would begin

Opener	Responder
2◊	2♠
3♣	

Opener's three club bid shows a minimum and a heart suit. Responder will become the declarer in hearts.

The Two Heart and Two Spade Openings

Opening bids of two in either major suit show two-suited hands, with five cards in the major suit opened and five cards in one of the minor suits. The strength of the bid is below that of an opening bid, normally 8-11 points.

Opposite the opening bid of two hearts or two spades, the only forcing response is two notrump. This response asks opener to bid his minor suit. After opener rebids his minor, a bid by responder in either of opener's suits invites a game; any new suit bid by responder is forcing to game.

Alternative treatments of the two heart and two spade openings are possible. The two heart opening, for example, may be used as FLANNERY TWO HEARTS. The two spade opening may be used to show both minor suits and a hand worth 8-11 points.

The Two Notrump Opening

The opening bid of two notrump shows a hand of 8-11 points with at least five cards in each minor suit. Responses of three clubs and three diamonds are sign-offs. Responses of four clubs and four diamonds are preemptive, but opener is not barred from continuing to game. Major suit responses are natural; at the three level such responses are forcing.

Alternatively, the two notrump opening may be used as a one-suit preemptive bid for any suit. Responder normally bids three clubs to allow opener to show his suit, by passing or correcting. If responder is interested in game or slam in clubs, he must make a response other than three clubs.

MINI-MULTICOLORED TWO DIAMOND OPENING

The simplest version of the MULTICOLORED TWO DIAMOND opening uses the opening bid of two diamonds solely to show a weak two-bid in hearts or spades. This convention allows the partnership to use opening bids of two hearts and two spades for other purposes, such as ACOL TWO-BIDS.

The Mini-Multicolored Two Diamonds Opening is, in theory, forcing. Responder should not pass unless he has a very weak hand with singletons in both major suits and seven or more diamonds.

After the two diamond opening, responder bids two hearts if he has no interest in going higher in either major. If he is interested in going further in spades but not in hearts, he temporizes by responding two hearts; if opener bids two spades, responder may bid again to invite game. If responder is interested in inviting game in hearts but not in spades, he responds two spades.

If responder wishes to know opener's strength and his suit, he responds two notrump, to which opener's scheduled answers are as follows:

> 3♣ = minimum weak two-bid in hearts
> 3◊ = minimum weak two-bid in spades
> 3♡ = maximum weak two-bid in hearts
> 3♠ = maximum weak two-bid in spades.

Theoretically, it would be sounder to have opener show his maximum hands by bidding three clubs or three diamonds. *See* SIMPLIFIED MULTI-COLORED TWO DIAMONDS.

A bid by responder of three clubs or three diamonds directly over the mini-multi two diamond opening is natural, suggesting the suit bid as a possible trump suit, and showing a hand worth an invitation to game in that minor suit.

See also PENDER TWO-BIDS.

CHICO TWO DIAMONDS

The Chico Two Diamond opening is a version of the MULTICOLORED TWO DIAMOND OPENING, promising either a weak two-bid in hearts or spades, or a strong three-suited (4-4-4-1) opening bid with 20 or more points. All other two-level openings are strong.

Responses to the Two-Diamond Opening

Responder must assume at the outset that opener has a weak two-bid in hearts or spades. The response of two hearts is semi-automatic with any weak hand, or with any hand not worth an invitation opposite a weak two-bid in hearts. If responder has a hand worth a game invitation if opener has a weak two-bid in hearts, responder bids two spades.

If opener rebids two notrump over a response of either two hearts or two spades, he shows the strong 4-4-4-1 hand. If the bidding has commenced

Opener	Responder
2◇	2♡
2 Notrump	

responder may bid three clubs to show weakness. This bid does not promise clubs. It is forcing, and opener and responder should proceed to bid their suits up the line until a fit is found. If, over opener's two notrump rebid, responder bids instead three diamonds, three hearts, or three spades, he shows a constructive hand, with length in the suit he has bid. Responder's rebid of three notrump directly over opener's two notrump would show a constructive hand with a long club suit. These three-level rebids by responder are forcing.

If opener has a singleton in the suit shown by responder, he rebids notrump. If he has length in responder's suit, he cue-bids his singleton.

(Opener)
♠ x   ♡ K x x x   ◇ A K Q x   ♣ A K Q x
(Responder)
♠ Q x x   ♡ A J x x x x   ◇ x x   ♣ x x

With these hands, the auction should begin

Opener	Responder
2◇	2♡
2 Notrump	3♡
3♠	

If, directly over the two diamond opening, responder bids two notrump, he asks opener to describe his hand. The two notrump response should not be made unless responder has a willingness to play in three of either major suit opposite a minimum weak two-bid. Opener describes his hand as follows:

3 ♣ = maximum weak two-bid in hearts
3 ◊ = maximum weak two-bid in spades
3 ♡ = minimum weak two-bid in hearts
3 ♠ = minimum weak two-bid in spades
3NT = singleton spade, four cards in every other suit
4 ♣ = singleton club, four cards in every other suit
4 ◊ = singleton diamond, four cards in every other suit
4 ♡ = singleton heart, four cards in every other suit

The Two Club, Two Heart, and Two Spade Openings

Chico uses opening bids of two hearts and two spades to promise good hands with 8-8¾ playing tricks in the Acol style. *See* ACOL TWO BIDS.

An opening bid of two clubs promises either a suit-oriented hand containing nine or more playing tricks, or a balanced hand with 23 or more HCP. With the balanced hand, opener will rebid two notrump with 23-24 points, or three notrump with 25-26 points, etc.

COMPREHENSIVE MULTICOLORED TWO-BIDS

Comprehensive Multicolored Two-Bids are designed to allow the partnership to show either (1) a weak two-bid in a major suit, or (2) an Acol-style two-bid in any suit, or (3) a balanced hand with 22 or more HCP, or (4) a three-suited hand with 19 or more HCP.

An opening bid of two clubs shows either a weak two-bid in hearts, or an ACOL two-bid in clubs, or a balanced hand with 25 or more HCP.

An opening bid of two diamonds shows either a weak two-bid in spades, or an Acol two-bid in diamonds, or a hand with 4-4-4-1 distribution (with the short suit unspecified) with 19 or more points.

An opening bid of two hearts or two spades is an Acol two-bid in the suit bid. For responses to these openings, *see* ACOL TWO-BIDS.

An opening bid of two notrump shows a balanced hand with 22-24 HCP.

Bidding After a Two Club Opening

If, after a two club opening, responder has a hand that is not worth a game invitation opposite a weak two heart bid, he bids two hearts. This response does not indicate that responder has heart support; indeed, he might be void in hearts. If opener has the weak two heart bid, he will pass. If he has the 25 + point balanced hand, he will rebid in notrump. Any other rebid by opener is natural and shows an Acol-type two-bid with clubs as the predominant suit. If opener has, for example,

    [A]   ♠ x   ♡ A K J x   ◊ x x   ♣ A K Q x x x

the auction might begin

Opener	Responder
2♣	2♡
3♡	

If responder has a hand with which he is interested in inviting game if opener has a weak two-bid in hearts, he responds two diamonds to ask opener to clarify his hand. Opener rebids two hearts with the weak two-bid. He rebids two notrump with a balanced hand containing 25 or more HCP. He rebids three notrump with an Acol-type hand containing four hearts and five clubs. Any other rebid is natural and shows an Acol-type two-bid with clubs as the predominant suit.

Opener	Responder
2♣	2♦
2♠	

Opener's sequence of bids has shown a two-suited hand with spades and clubs, with the clubs predominating. He might have a hand such as [A] above with the major suits transposed.

If, over responder's two diamond response, opener has bid two hearts, showing a weak two-bid, a bid of two notrump by responder asks opener to describe his hand further. For methods of rebidding, *see* TWO NOTRUMP FORCING RESPONSE TO WEAK TWO-BIDS; OGUST REBIDS; ROMEX REBIDS AFTER WEAK TWO-BIDS.

Bidding After a Two Diamond Opening

If, after a two diamond opening, responder has a hand that is not worth a game invitation opposite a weak two spade bid, he bids two spades. This response does not show any spade support, and responder may in fact have no spades at all. If opener has the weak two spade hand, he will pass. If he has the 4-4-4-1 hand, he will rebid two notrump. Any other rebid by opener is natural and shows an Acol-type two-bid with diamonds as the predominant suit.

If responder has a hand with which he is interested in inviting game if opener has a weak two-bid in spades, he responds two hearts, asking opener for further information. Opener rebids two spades with the weak two-bid; he rebids two notrump with the 4-4-4-1 hand. He bids three notrump with four spades and five diamonds and an Acol-two type hand. Any other rebid is natural and shows an Acol-type bid with diamonds as the predominant suit.

If opener has rebid two spades over two hearts, showing the weak two-bid, responder may bid two notrump to obtain further information as he would over a weak two heart bid.

If opener has rebid two notrump after the response of two diamonds or two hearts, showing a three-suited hand, responder may bid three clubs to ask opener to identify his short suit. Opener does so by bidding the suit of his singleton at the three level, or bidding three notrump if his short suit is clubs.

Bidding After Interference

If there is an overcall or a double before responder has an opportunity to bid over a two club opening, a double or a redouble means that responder would have bid two diamonds. If the opening bid was two diamonds, the double means that responder would have bid two hearts.

All suit bids by responder are natural and nonforcing; they are made on the assumption that opener had a weak two-bid. If opener has another type of hand, he will bid again.

TARTAN TWO BIDS

Tartan two-bids are multicolored openings of Scottish origin (hence the name) in which an opening bid of two hearts or two spades shows either an Acol two-bid in the suit opened, or a weak two-suited hand that includes the suit opened. Each opening is forcing for one round.

A two heart opening shows either an Acol two-bid with hearts as the predominant suit; or a hand with 5-9 points, at least five hearts, and at least five cards in another, unspecified, suit. The second suit may be spades or a minor.

A two-spade opening shows either an Acol two-bid with spades as the predominant suit; or a hand with 5-9 points, at least five spades, and at least five cards in a minor suit.

In response to either opening, if responder has three-card or longer support for the suit opened, he responds as follows:

    raise to three = 6-10 points
    raise to four   = 11-15 points, no aces
    three notrump = 11-15 points, including at least one ace

Other responses are relays.

Relay Response to Two Heart Opening

A response of two spades to the two heart opening is artificial but nonforcing. It is used for two types of hands. Responder bids two spades if he has 0-5 points, *i.e.*, insufficient values to commit to game opposite an Acol two-bid in hearts. He also bids two spades if he has 6-15 points with fewer than three hearts, *i.e.*, not enough to invite game opposite a weak two-suiter. Responder's bid does not say anything about his holding in spades.

If opener has the weak two-suited hand, and responder has bid two spades, opener will pass if his second suit is spades. (Since a pass may result in the partnership's playing in a 5-0 fit and there is no "checkback," the Tartan Two's in this respect may be said to be out of "kilter.") If opener's second suit is a minor, he will bid it over responder's two spade bid. If opener has an Acol-type hand, he will either rebid his suit, if his hand is one-suited, or jump in a new suit if he is two-suited.

A response of two notrump to the two heart opening is also artificial, but is a stripe of a different color. It is forcing to at least three of opener's major suit and promises either 16+ points or a distributional hand worth a game-force opposite a weak two-suited opening. If opener has the Acol-type hand, he rebids his suit, or jumps in a new suit, or bids three notrump. These rebids are forcing to at least four notrump.

If opener has the weak two-suited hand, he replies to the forcing two notrump response by bidding his second suit. Thereafter, any raise by responder below the game level is forcing to game. Following such a game-forcing raise, opener may bid notrump to show that his major suit is semi-solid, or may bid one of his short suits to show the ace or a void.

Relay Response to Two Spade Opening

As over the two heart opening, responder has available two relay responses to the two spade opening; and the sequences operate similarly.

A response of three clubs is artificial, saying nothing about responder's club holding, but it is not forcing. The three club response shows either 0-5 points, or 6-15 points with fewer than three spades. Opener will pass if he has a weak two-suiter with spades and clubs, or will bid three diamonds if that is his second suit. Any other rebid by opener shows the Acol-type hand.

A response of two notrump to the two spade opening has the same meaning as that discussed above with respect to the two heart opening. The sequences following the two notrump response are also parallel.

MULTICOLORED TWO CLUB OPENING

The Multicolored Two Club Opening, forcing on responder for one round, shows a hand, of intermediate strength, *i.e.*, 16-19 points. The hand either is balanced with 18-19 points, or contains a suit of five or more cards in diamonds, hearts, or spades.

A two diamond response shows 0-6 HCP and denies a five-card major suit. Most other responses are natural and show responder's strength as follows:

2♡ = five or more hearts, 0-4 HCP
2♠ = five or more spades; 0-4 HCP
2NT = 12-14 HCP
3◊ = five or more diamonds, 7-11 HCP
3♡ = five or more hearts, 7-11 HCP
3♠ = five or more spades, 7-11 HCP
3NT = exactly 15 HCP
4NT = BLACKWOOD; responder shows 16 or more HCP

A response of three clubs to the two club opening promises 7-11 points but says nothing about responder's club suit. Rather, it asks opener to bid a four-card or longer major suit if he has one, or to bid three notrump if he does not.

An opening bid of two diamonds promises either a balanced hand with 22 or more HCP, or an unbalanced hand containing nine or more playing tricks. The two diamond opening is forcing.

The chief advantage of the intermediate multicolored two club opening is said to be the limitation of opening bids of one diamond, one heart, and one spade to hands worth 11-15 points. The system appears to leave a gap as to how to open an unbalanced hand with 20-21 points but fewer than nine playing tricks, *e.g.*,

♠ A K Q x x   ♡ x   ◊ A K J x   ♣ K x x

PUPPET TWO CLUBS

The Puppet Two Club convention is designed to allow the partnership to show any of a number of different types of opening bids. Restricting the opening two diamond call, which is artificial and forcing, to strong but always unbalanced hands, the device for showing other types of hands is the forcing opening of two clubs. The two club opening compels responder to bid two diamonds.

After responder has duly complied and bid two diamonds, opener describes his hand by rebidding as follows:

two hearts:	a FLANNERY-type hand: four spades, five hearts; minor suit distribution unspecified; 11-16 points
two spades:	a hand with three four-card suits and a singleton of unspecified location; 17-20 HCP
two notrump:	balanced hand; 23-24 HCP
three clubs:	singleton diamond, four cards in every other suit; 21-24 HCP
three diamonds:	singleton heart, four cards in every other suit; 21-24 HCP
three hearts:	singleton spade, four cards in every other suit; 21-24 HCP
three spades:	singleton club, four cards in every other suit; 21-24 HCP
three notrump:	balanced hand; 25-26 HCP

If opener has rebid two spades, responder may bid two notrump to ask opener in which suit he has the singleton. Opener rebids in the suit below the singleton. Once opener's singleton has been identified, responder may bid the suit of the singleton to obtain more information — as to controls or strength, according to the partnership agreement. *See* NEAPOLITAN TWO DIAMONDS.

If an opponent overcalls before opener has an opportunity to make his rebid, it is recommended that opener pass to show the Flannery-type hand, bid with a three-suited hand, and double with a balanced hand.

TRANSFER POSITIVE RESPONSES TO ARTIFICIAL ONE CLUB OPENING

A modification of the standard positive responses to the artificial and forcing one club opening in the PRECISION CLUB SYSTEM is designed to allow opener to become the declarer on many hands on which responder has made a positive response. An additional advantage is that certain asking bid sequences may be begun one level lower than would ordinarily be the case.

The modification requires that if responder has the strength for a positive response, he must bid the denomination below his five-card suit. Allowing for the use of the one diamond response as a negative bid, the positive response would be

1♡	=	long spades, 9+ points
1♠	=	balanced 9-11 (or 15-16) HCP; transfers to notrump
1NT	=	long clubs, 9+ points
2♣	=	long diamonds, 9+ points
2◇	=	long hearts, 9+ points

If the partnership is using the one heart response as a semipositive, showing 7-8 points, the above schedule may be used, but the positive with long spades would be shown by a two heart bid. An alternative schedule of responder's positive responses that allows use of the one heart response as semipositive and retains the one notrump response as a natural positive, showing a balanced hand, is as follows:

1♠	=	long clubs
2♣	=	long diamonds
2◇	=	long hearts
2♡	=	long spades

If the partnership uses Precision asking bids, opener may initiate such asking sequences by making the cheapest bid in responder's long suit. See PRECISION TRUMP ASKING BIDS; PRECISION CONTROL ASKING BIDS. See also TRANSFER PREEMPTIVE RESPONSES TO ARTIFICIAL ONE CLUB.

TRANSFER PREEMPTIVE RESPONSES TO ARTIFICIAL ONE CLUB

This modification of the standard subpositive responses to the artificial and forcing one club opening in the PRECISION CLUB SYSTEM is intended to allow the opener to become the declarer when responder has a 4-7 point hand and a long suit. The modification requires that responder jump in the suit below his long suit.

Negative, positive, and semipositive responses are shown in the standard fashion. The schedule of preemptive transfer responses is as follows:

two hearts	= six-card spade suit
two spades	= six-card club suit
three clubs	= six- or seven-card diamond suit
three diamonds	= six- or seven-card heart suit

Jumps to higher levels show one additional card in the suit for each level above those shown. For example, a jump to three hearts would promise a seven-card spade suit; jumps to the four level would promise eight-card suits.

Opener may sign off by making a nonjump in responder's long suit, or by bidding notrump. If opener has interest in exploring for game or slam, he may bid a new suit. This bid asks responder if he has an ace. If he has no ace, responder bids notrump. If he has an ace, he bids his cheapest control, *i.e.*, an ace, king, singleton, or void.

In light of the stated possibility that responder will have an ace or a king to cue-bid, it appears that this convention envisions a relaxation of the standard Precision requirement that a preempting responder's high cards be concentrated principally in his suit. The elimination of this requirement will make it substantially more difficult for opener to predict the number of likely losers in responder's long suit.

TRANSPOSED MAJOR RESPONSES TO PRECISION ONE CLUB

In the Precision Club system, a natural positive response to the strong one club opening frequently results in responder's becoming the declarer, with the strong hand exposed in the dummy. A convention intended to make the opening bidder the declarer on such hands transposes the normal suit responses.

A one heart response shows 9 or more points with a five-card or longer suit in spades. A one spade response shows the same strength, with a five-card or longer heart suit.

The inversion of the major suit responses has some drawbacks. It may sometimes result in responder's becoming the declarer when opener has length in the major suit not promised by responder. In addition, if the opponents wish to explore the possibility of a sacrifice, low-level action is less risky than normal. For example, responder's left-hand opponent may make a relatively risk-free double of the artificially bid major to suggest a sacrifice in that suit.

ULTIMATE CLUB

The Ultimate Club System is based on a strong artificial one club opening bid, and the availability of relay sequences in every type of auction. *See* RELAYS — IN GENERAL. Each opening bid at the one or two level is carefully defined in terms of distribution, strength, and controls (ace = 2 controls, king = 1).

In assessing whether a hand is minimum or maximum within the HCP range promised, the partnership tends to count only aces, kings, and queens, ("AKQ points"), generally ignoring jacks. In a balanced hand, three jacks may be deemed the equivalent of one queen. Singleton honors other than the ace are also ignored.

The relay sequences may be used to obtain information as to distribution, strength, and controls. The order in which this information is obtained is tailored to the way in which the auction has begun. If there has been a one club opening and the opening bidder is the relay captain, the puppet usually shows his strength first, his distribution next, and his key cards last. If, in contrast, the bidding has been opened in some other way, and responder is the captain, the puppet will show his distribution first, his strength next, and his key cards last.

When one member of the partnership has reason to believe the hands are in or near the game or slam zone, often an artificial relay sequence will be used.

The One Club Opening

The Ultimate Club System's one club opening bid shows a hand containing at least five controls, and 17 or more HCP if unbalanced or 18 or more HCP if balanced. Hands not meeting these criteria are nevertheless opened one club if they either contain 8 or more controls and are unsuited for a one notrump opening; or are unbalanced and contain 16 HCP with a good six-card or longer suit; or contain 7 controls and a seven-card or longer suit.

In response to the one club opening, responder shows his controls and strength as follows:

- 1 ◊ = negative: 0-2 controls
- 1 ♡ = the strongest immediate positive: 4 controls with at least 10 AKQ points if the hand is balanced, or 5 controls
- 1 ♠ = semipositive: an ace and a king; or an ace and two queens; or two kings and one queen
- 1NT = 3 controls; 9 or more AKQ points if balanced, or 11 or more AKQ points if unbalanced

2♣ = 3 controls; 9 AKQ points unbalanced

2◊ = balanced hand with either 2 controls and 10 or more AKQ points, or 4 controls with 8 AKQ points

2♡ = unbalanced hand with 2 controls and 10 or more AKQ points

After a negative response of one diamond, opener may rebid one heart as a relay bid to ask responder for more specificity. The one heart relay guarantees that opener had more than the minimum necessary for his one club opening. Responder bids over the one heart relay as follows:

1♠ = second negative; at most one king and one queen (one ace, or three queens are also possibilities if the hand is balanced)

1NT = one king and two or three queens

2♣ = one ace or three queens, unbalanced hand

2◊ = an ace and a queen, or two kings, balanced

2♡ = an ace and a queen, or two kings, unbalanced

Opener may, after a one spade second negative response, bid one notrump as another relay. Responder bids as follows:

2♣ = third negative; no more than one king or two queens

2◊ = one king and one queen, or an ace, or three queens, balanced

2♡ = one king and one queen, unbalanced

After responder's third negative bid of two clubs, opener may again relay, by bidding two diamonds. Responder bids as follows:

2♡ = fourth negative; a queen or less

2♠ = one king or two queens, unbalanced

Opener may also relay after responder has made a positive response of one heart, or a semipositive response of one spade. After the one heart response, and a one spade relay by opener, responder would bid as follows:

1NT = 5 controls, balanced hand; or 4 controls, unbalanced hand, and 12+ AKQ points

2♣ = 4 controls, unbalanced hand, 10+ AKQ points

2◊ = 4 controls, balanced hand, 10+ AKQ points

2♡ = 4 controls, unbalanced hand, 8 AKQ points.

After the one spade response and a one notrump relay by opener, responder would bid as follows:

2♣ = an ace and two queens, or two kings and one queen, unbalanced hand

2 ◇ = balanced hand
2 ♡ or higher = an ace and a king, unbalanced hand

The more relays opener embarks on, the better his hand must be. With one exception, the partnership is committed to game as soon as responder makes a relay response that is not negative. The exception is that after a semi-positive one spade response to the opening one-club bid, the partnership may stop at the three level.

Opener may break the chain of relays in order to show his own hand. A simple suit bid by opener other than the cheapest bid is natural and invitational. A jump shift shows a two-suited hand and also is invitational. After a one diamond response, for example, opener's jumps to two spades and higher would show the following two-suited hands:

2 ♠ = spades and diamonds
2NT = clubs and a major suit
3 ♣ = clubs and diamonds
3 ◇ = diamonds and hearts
3 ♡ = hearts and spades

None of these bids is forcing. After the two notrump bid, responder may bid three diamonds to ask opener to bid his major suit.

If the initial response has been one heart or one spade, so that opener could not bid one spade naturally, or if he has conducted a relay by bidding one heart before determining to show his hand naturally, a two spade bid by opener would be nature. His two-suited bids begin with two notrump and have the meanings set forth above; the spade-diamond two suiter is now shown by a bid of three spades.

Numerous additional relay sequences are possible.

Openings of One Diamond, One Heart, and One Spade

Opening bids of one diamond, one heart, and one spade are natural and show less than the strength necessary to open one club. The opening of one diamond shows 11-16 HCP and at least three diamonds; if the hand contains only three diamonds, it will also contain four or five clubs and there will be no other satisfactory opening bid. The openings of one heart and one spade show 11-17 HCP, with four or more cards in the suit opened.

In response to each of these openings, a bid of two diamonds is artificial and invites game; a bid of two clubs is an artificial game-forcing relay.

When responder has commenced the relay by bidding two clubs, the first five step rebids by opener carry the same distributional meanings over all of the above opening bids, giving recognition, of course, to the fact that the principal length promised relates to the suit that has been opened. The rebids are:

$2\Diamond$ = no singleton or void

$2\heartsuit$ = singleton somewhere; likely distribution is 5-4-3-1 or 6-4-2-1; may be 6-5 if hand is minimum and short suit has been opened to avoid reversing

$2\spadesuit$ = singleton somewhere, with distribution of 6-3-3-1, 7-3-2-1, or 7-4-1-1

2NT = void somewhere; distribution is 6-4-3-0, 5-4-4-0, or 5-5-3-0

$3\clubsuit$ = void somewhere; distribution is 7-4-2-0, 7-3-3-0, or 6-5-2-0

Above three clubs, opener's answers to the two club relay diverge, and depend on what suit he opened. After a one diamond opening, opener bids as follows:

$3\Diamond$ = either 5-5-2-1 with length in clubs, or 4-4-4-1 with a singleton club

$3\heartsuit$ = 4-4-4-1, with a singleton heart

$3\spadesuit$ = 4-4-4-1, with a singleton spade, minimum strength

3NT = 4-4-4-1, with a singleton spade, maximum strength

$4\clubsuit$ = six diamonds, five clubs, singletons in hearts and spades; strength unspecified

$4\Diamond$ = five spades, one heart, six diamonds, one club; minimum strength

$4\heartsuit$ = one spade, five hearts, six diamonds, one club; maximum strength

$4\spadesuit$ = five spades, one heart, six diamonds, one club; maximum strength

If the opening was one heart or one spade, opener's bids in answer to the two club relay continue as follows (with principal length in suit opened):

$3\Diamond$ = 5-5-2-1 with length in clubs

$3\heartsuit$ = 5-5-2-1 with length in diamonds

$3\spadesuit$ = (if opening was $1\spadesuit$) five spades, five hearts, one diamond, two clubs; or (if opening was $1\heartsuit$) minimum 4-4-4-1 with singleton diamond

3NT = (if opening was $1\spadesuit$) five spades, five hearts, two diamonds, one club; or (if opening was $1\heartsuit$) maximum 4-4-4-1 with singleton diamond

After opener's answers to the two club inquiry, responder may relay again to obtain further information. For example, after opener has opened in a major suit and rebid two hearts, showing a singleton somewhere in the hand and one of two or three likely distributions, he may provide greater specificity in answer to the further relay, by bidding as follows:

2NT = 6-4-2-1 distribution

3♣ = 5-4-3-1, length in clubs

3◇ = 5-4-3-1, length in diamonds

3♡ = 5-4-3-1, length in the other major suit, one diamond, three clubs

3♠ = 5-4-3-1, length in the other major, three diamonds, one club, minimum strength

3NT = 5-4-3-1, length in the other major, three diamonds, one club, maximum strength

4♣ = (after 1♠ opening) five spades, six hearts, singleton in each minor suit

4◇ = (after 1♠ opened) five spades, six hearts, void in diamonds, two clubs

4♡ = (after 1♠ opened) five spades, six hearts, two diamonds, void in clubs

The One Notrump Opening

The opening bid of one notrump is strong, showing 15-17 HCP and 4-8 controls. The one notrump opening may also be made with as few as 14 HCP if the hand contains a five-card club suit, three spades, three hearts, and two diamonds. If the hand contains a six-card or longer club suit and 17 AKQ points, the proper opening bid is one club rather than one notrump.

The permissible distributions are (a) 4-3-3-3 and 4-4-3-2; (b) 5-3-3-2 if the long suit is other than spades; (c) 5-4-2-2 if the long suit is clubs; and (d) five diamonds and four clubs with a doubleton in each major.

The responding structure uses a two club response as a game-forcing relay. A two diamond response is Stayman and shows a hand worth a game invitation. Responses of two hearts and two spades are natural and nonforcing. A two notrump response is natural and invitational.

Jumps to three clubs and three diamonds are natural sign-offs. Jumps to three hearts and three spades show a singleton in the suit of the jump, and promise length in both minor suits. The major suit jumps are forcing to game.

In answer to the two club relay, opener commences to show his distribution as follows:

2 ◊ = no four-card major; if four diamonds, also four or five clubs
2 ♡ = four or five hearts, fewer than four spades; if four hearts, four cards in a minor suit
2 ♠ = four spades, fewer than four hearts, four cards in a minor suit
2NT = 4-3-3-3 with any long suit but clubs
3 ♣ = four spades, four hearts, two diamonds, three clubs
3 ◊ = four spades, four hearts, three diamonds, two clubs
3 ♡ = two spades, four hearts, two diamonds, five clubs
3 ♠ = four spades, two hearts, two diamonds, five clubs; minimum strength
3NT = four spades, two hearts, two diamonds, five clubs; maximum strength

After any of these, responder may continue the relay sequence to gain further information. Alternatively, he may break the relay to show something of his own distribution. After opener has bid two diamonds, for example, responder may show the following:

2 ♠ = singleton club
2NT = singleton diamond
3 ♣ = singleton heart
3 ◊ = singleton spade
3 ♡ = two suited hand with hearts and a minor suit
3 ♠ = two-suited hand with spades and another suit

After responder has thus bid three hearts or three spades, showing a two-suited hand, opener may make the cheapest bid as a relay to ask responder to indentify his second suit.

After relays by responder have caused opener to show his complete distribution, a continuation of the relay asks opener to show his strength in steps.

The Two-Diamond Opening

The opening bid of two diamonds shows a weak two-bid in either hearts or spades. Many of the responses are natural.

A response of two hearts or two spades may be passed if responder has bid opener's suit; opener should correct if responder has bid the suit in which opener is not long.

A response of two notrump shows at least game-invitational strength and asks opener to describe his side suit features. Responses of three clubs and three diamonds to the two diamond opening are natural and forcing. Rebids by opener over three clubs show opener's suit and his strength as follows:

   3 ◊ = heart suit, minimum strength
   3 ♡ = spade suit, minimum strength
   3 ♠ = heart suit, maximum strength
   3NT = spade suit, maximum strength

Over either the three club or the three diamond response, opener's raise of responder's suit is natural; his bid of four of the other minor suit shows a singleton in that suit and support for responder's suit.

See also MINI-MULTICOLORED TWO DIAMONDS.

Other Two-Level Openings

All other two-level openings show length in clubs. With each a forcing relay response is available.

Opening bids of two hearts and two spades show two-suited hands with length in the suit opened and length in clubs. The clubs should be longer. The hand should contain 14-16 HCP, 10 or more of which should be located in opener's long suits, and 4-7 controls. A response of two notrump starts a relay process.

An opening bid of two notrump shows a balanced hand containing a six-card club suit. The hand should contain 14-16 HCP, 5 or more of which are in the club suit, and 4-7 controls. A response of three hearts or three spades shows a singleton in the suit bid and support for clubs. A response of three diamonds starts a relay process.

An opening bid of two clubs shows either a hand containing a six-card or longer club suit, or one containing five clubs and a four-card major suit. The hand is opened two clubs because of some flaw that makes it unsuitable for an opening of two notrump or two of the major suit. A response of two diamonds is invitational to game and is an artificial relay. If opener has a maximum, the partnership may not stop below three notrump or four of a minor.

UNIVERSAL CLUB SYSTEM

The Universal Club System ("Uni-Club") employs a forcing one club bid both on strong hands worth 17 or more HCP and on hands worth 13-16 points in which the long suit is clubs. The one notrump opening shows 13-16 HCP. Two-level suit openings show either two-suited hands, *see* UNI-CLUB TWO HEART AND TWO SPADE OPENINGS, or three suited hands, *see* UNI-CLUB TWO CLUB AND TWO DIAMOND OPENINGS.

The response of one diamond is artificial and shows either 0-6 points or more than 14 points.

After a one diamond response, opener's rebids other than one heart are natural and show more than 16 points. The one heart rebid is a two-way bid showing either a 16+ point hand with a five-card or longer heart suit, or a minimum hand (12-16 points) with five or more clubs. The one heart rebid is forcing. Thereafter, a bid by opener of the minimum number of clubs shows that his one club opening was a minimum hand with a club suit.

A rebid by opener of the minimum number of clubs after any other response by responder, all of which are natural, shows that the opening hand is a minimum with a club suit.

Responses after Openings of One Diamond, One Heart, and One Spade

After a one diamond opening, a response of two clubs promises either 10-11 HCP and a five-card or longer club suit, or more than 12 HCP with any distribution. If responder rebids three clubs, he shows a minimum hand with clubs. Any other rebid promises more than 12 points, clarifies his distribution, and is forcing to game.

In response to an opening of one heart or one spade, a two club bid by responder is artificial and game-forcing, promising more than 12 HCP. Opener rebids his suit to show a six-card suit. A rebid of two diamonds is artificial and shows that opener has a second suit somewhere. With only five cards in the suit he has opened and no second suit, opener rebids two of the unbid major to show 12-14 points, or two notrump to show 15-16 points.

Over opener's major suit opening, responder may make a strong game raise by jumping directly to four clubs. The four-club bid promises at least four-card support for opener's suit and 13-16 HCP. Responder's jump to three of opener's suit is a LIMIT RAISE.

Over opener's one heart or one spade opening, responder's jump to four diamonds is the Thomas convention, asking opener how many aces he has. *See* THOMAS FOUR DIAMONDS.

KENTUCKY CLUB

The Kentucky Club system uses a forcing one club opening for only two types of hands: balanced hands with 15 or more points, and suit-oriented hands of game-going strength. Other types of hands, with one exception, are begun with natural bids. The system uses one diamond as a positive response, promising at least 6 points.

The One Club Opening and the Responses

The one club opening is made on balanced hands worth 15-19 HCP or more than 22 HCP. With these hands, opener rebids in notrump. The notrump rebids show the following ranges:

One notrump rebid   = 15-17 HCP
Two notrump rebid   = 18-19 HCP
Three notrump rebid   = 23+ HCP

A hand with a five-card suit is considered suitable for a one club opening and notrump rebid only if the distribution is 5-3-3-2 and the five-card suit is a minor. A balanced hand worth 20-22 points is opened two notrump.

An opening bid of one club is also made on a suit-oriented hand worth a force to game. With this type of hand, the one club opener rebids his suit.

A response of one diamond is positive, showing 6 or more points, though responder does not promise a rebid. Since he may respond one diamond with as few as 6 points, he obviously may pass if opener rebids one notrump, showing 15-17. He must of course rebid if opener rebids a suit, showing a game-forcing hand.

Responses of one heart, one spade, two clubs, and two diamonds are natural and weak, showing 0-5 points. The one notrump response is similarly weak and shows both minors; this response asks opener to take a preference if he has the balanced 15-17 point hand.

Responder's higher responses are made on the assumption that opener has a balanced hand with 15-17 points. A response of two notrump shows 9-10 points and invites game in notrump; a response of three notrump shows 10 or more points and is intended as a signoff. The notrump responses are appropriate when responder's hand has tenaces suggesting that it may be profitable to have the opening lead come up to his hand. Without this type of hand, responder should simply bid one diamond, planning to raise opener's anticipated one notrump rebid.

Also on the assumption that opener has a balanced 15-17 point hand, responder may jump to the four level over the one club opening, intending to play game in a major suit. His jumps to four hearts and four spades are natural; the jumps to four clubs and four diamonds are SOUTH AFRICAN TEXAS TRANSFERS.

With a one-suited hand worth a game invitation, responder may jump to the suit below his long suit, as a JACOBY TRANSFER BID.

A summary of the responses:

1 ◇	= positive, showing 6 or more points
1 ♡	= hearts, with 0-5 points
1 ♠	= spades, with 0-5 points
1 NT	= both minor suits, with 0-5 points
2 ♣	= clubs, with 0-5 points
2 ◇	= diamonds, with 0-5 points
2 ♡	= transfer to spades, with 8-9 points
2 ♠	= transfer to clubs, with 8-9 points
2 NT	= 9-10 points, invitational
3 ♣	= transfer to diamonds, with 8-9 points
3 ◇	= transfer to hearts, with 8-9 points
3 NT	= 10 or more points, to play
4 ♣	= transfer to four hearts
4 ◇	= transfer to four spades
4 ♡	= hearts, to play
4 ♠	= spades, to play

The jumps to three of a major may be used to show a hand with both minor suits. Three hearts shows game-invitational strength; three hearts is forcing to game.

Over any of responder's bids, if opener has the suit-oriented game-forcing hand, he will bid his suit. He will not accept a signoff.

Other Opening Bids

An opening bid of one notrump is weak, showing a balanced hand with 12-14 high card points (or 11-14 nonvulnerable). This opening denies a five-card suit.

Opening bids of one diamond, one heart, one spade, and two clubs promise five or more cards in the suit opened. An opening bid of two diamonds shows a three-suited hand worth 11-14 points. The short suit is not specified. *See* TWO DIAMOND OPENING AS MINIMUM THREE-SUITER. A three-suited hand worth more than 14 points should be opened one diamond if one of the suits is diamonds; otherwise it should be opened one spade. Although such one-level openings systemically show five-card suits, the lack of length will likely be offset by the extra high-card strength.

J/W TWO NOTRUMP AS RAISE OF STRONG TWO BID

Opposite a strong natural opening of two hearts or two spades, or opposite a forcing ARTIFICIAL TWO CLUB OPENING and opener's rebid of two hearts or two spades, *e.g.*,

	Opener	Responder
	2 ♣	2 ♦
	2 ♠	

responder normally raises opener's major with support, or rebids two notrump without support. *See* TWO NOTRUMP AS A NEGATIVE RESPONSE. The J/W convention reverses the meanings of these two responses.

This convention requires responder to bid two notrump if he has support for opener's suit and to bid three of the suit without support and without a suit of his own. Thereafter, the bidding may proceed naturally.

This reversal of meanings has two advantages. First, the use of two notrump to show support keeps the bidding lower where, the fit having been found, there is more likely to be slam interest. Second, where there is no fit and the hand will be played in notrump, the strong hand may now become the declarer.

MILES RESPONSES TO TWO CLUB OPENINGS

The traditional method of responding to strong ARTIFICIAL TWO CLUB OPEN-
INGS uses a bid of two notrump as a positive response showing a balanced
hand and a bid of two hearts as a positive response showing a reasonably
good heart suit. The Miles method of responding to strong two club openings reverses the meanings of these two responses. The principal purpose
of this reversal of meanings is to make it easier for responder to describe
the high cards in his own hand. The premise is that the partnership may
more easily assess its slam prospects if the partner having the stronger, and
often more distributional, hand knows which aces or kings are in the weaker
hand.

The Artificial Two Notrump Response

The Miles two notrump response to a strong two club opening is used
to show a hand worth a positive response with a reasonable heart suit. To
be worth a positive response, a hand generally must contain at least 7 or
8 high card points. A reasonable suit is one headed by two of the three
top honors. Using Miles responses, responder would bid two notrump with
a hand such as

♠ K x   ♥ K Q x x x   ♦ x x x   ♣ x x x

The principal purpose of using the two notrump response to show a
positive response in hearts is that it frees up the two heart response for the
more productive uses described below. Another advantage of the two
notrump response is that if opener has a heart fit, he may bid hearts and
the strong hand will become the declarer. A potential disadvantage is that
opener will not be the declarer if the hand is played in notrump.

The Miles convention retains the standard meanings of the responses of
two spades, three clubs, and three diamonds. Each of these bids is natural
and shows a reasonable suit and a hand worth a positive response. Neither
these responses nor the two notrump response should be made with a hand
containing a semi-solid suit. As discussed below, a hand with a semi-solid
suit is indicated by a transfer jump response.

The two diamond response is used as a negative bid. *See* TWO DIAMOND
NEGATIVE. It shows a hand worth less than a standard positive response and
less than a Miles two heart response.

The Miles two heart bid is a positive response, promising a hand with at least a few high cards, and denying a suit as good as K Q x x x. Minimum high-card holdings for this response are:

    6 points consisting precisely of two kings
    7 points that include an ace or two kings
    7 points consisting of a king and two queens
    8 points that include an ace or a king

Except for the restriction that the hand cannot contain a reasonable suit, there is no maximum for the two heart response.

Typical hands worth a two heart response include

[A]	♠ K x x x	[B]	♠ x x x	[C]	♠ A x
	♡ x x		♡ K x x x		♡ J x
	◇ K x x		◇ Q x x		◇ J x x x
	♣ x x x x		♣ Q x x		♣ J x x x x

[D]	♠ x x	[E]	♠ A x x
	♡ K J x x		♡ K x x x x
	◇ J x x x		◇ K x
	♣ Q J x		♣ J x x

Hands that do not qualify for the two heart response include

[F]	♠ x x x	[G]	♠ A x	[H]	♠ K Q x x x
	♡ K x x x		♡ Q x x x		♡ x x
	◇ Q J x		◇ x x x		◇ K x x
	♣ x x x		♣ x x x x		♣ x x x

With hands F and G, responder should respond two diamonds. With hand H, responder should make the standard response of two spades.

After a response of two hearts, opener rebids naturally. If opener bids a suit, responder's bid of a new suit tends to be a cue-bid in support of opener's suit; responder cannot have a good suit of his own since, with such a suit and enough values to bid two hearts, he would have shown his suit instead of bidding two hearts. This principle permits responder to reveal the location of his high cards, thus making it easier for opener to assess the partnership's fit and slam prospects.

The assignment of the above meanings to the two heart response also makes it easier for responder to show distributional support for opener's suit. If opener rebids two spades, responder may jump to four clubs, diamonds, or hearts to show a singleton in that suit plus spade support. *See* SPLINTER RAISES. In contrast, if the partnership were using the more standard two notrump response to show values, opener would have to rebid three spades, and responder would have to jump to the five level to splinter.

In addition, use of Miles responses has an advantage over use of the convention in which responder's two diamond response may be made on either a weak hand or a hand containing values. *See* AUTOMATIC TWO DIAMOND RESPONSE. When Miles responses are being used, a responder who has bid two diamonds may later make a splinter bid in support of opener's suit without incurring the risk that opener will overestimate responder's strength. For example, if responder holds a hand such as

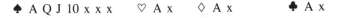

♠ x x x x   ♡ K x x x   ◊ x   ♣ Q J x x

the bidding might begin

Opener	Responder
2 ♣	2 ◊
2 ♠	4 ◊

The four diamond bid is a splinter bid in support of spades. But opener knows, from the failure to respond two hearts, that responder does not have as much as two kings, or a king and two queens, or 7 points that include an ace, or 8 points that include a king. Thus, if opener has a hand such as

♠ A Q J 10 x x x   ♡ A x   ◊ A x   ♣ A x

he knows the possibility of slam is remote.

The artificial use of the two heart response will cause two abnormalities if opener would have rebid hearts over a standard response. First, opener will now have to rebid three hearts to show his suit; thus, the bidding will proceed at a higher level. Second, if the final contract is in hearts, responder will be the declarer. Neither consequence may be serious in light of the fact that the two heart responder must have at least a smattering of values.

Transfer Jumps Showing Semi-Solid Suits

Although the Miles convention largely retains the standard meanings of the natural two spade, three club, and three diamond responses as reasonable hands with reasonably good suits, the convention provides artificial transfer bids for hands in which responder's suit is semi-solid.

In order to show a semi-solid suit, that is, a suit that can normally be played for one loser opposite a singleton, responder makes a jump response to the four level. The jump is made in the suit ranking just below responder's real suit. Thus,

4 ♣ = semi-solid diamond suit
4 ♦ = semi-solid heart suit
4 ♡ = semi-solid spade suit
4 ♠ = semi-solid club suit

The principal purpose of having responder bid the suit below his real suit is to give him an opportunity to show extra values. If no transfer were used and opener wanted to play in game in responder's suit opposite a minimum, opener would sign off by passing. When transfers are used, opener signs off by bidding responder's suit. This gives responder another turn to bid. Responder passes if he has a minimum, but bids again if he has a hand worth a slam try.

See also MARTELSBY RESPONSES TO TWO CLUB OPENINGS.

MARTELSBY RESPONSES TO TWO CLUB OPENINGS

The Martelsby convention allows the partnership to combine two popular methods of responding to ARTIFICIAL TWO CLUB OPENINGS. Using this convention, responder can either show a good suit headed by two of the top three honors or show how many controls he has. *See also* STEP RESPONSES TO TWO CLUB OPENINGS; TWO NOTRUMP AS A NEGATIVE RESPONSE.

The flexibility needed to handle both types of bids is provided by using responder's bid of two spades to show a long good suit somewhere, without specifying the suit. The other responses ranging from two diamonds through three diamonds show how many controls (ace = 2, king = 1) responder has.

The complete schedule of responses is

$2 \diamondsuit$ = 0 or 1 control
$2 \heartsuit$ = 2 controls
$2 \spadesuit$ = five-card suit somewhere, headed by two of the top three honors
2 NT = 3 controls
$3 \clubsuit$ = 4 controls
$3 \diamondsuit$ = 5 controls

After a response of two spades, opener may rebid naturally. If he has a strong two bid in a suit, he rebids his suit. Responder's next bid may identify his long suit. If opener rebids two notrump, responder shows his long suit by transferring into it. *See* JACOBY TRANSFER BIDS.

The partnership may agree that if responder makes a control-showing response he denies possession of a long suit headed by two of the top three honors. In the auction

Opener	Responder
2 ♣	2 ♡
2 Notrump	3 ♢

responder has shown two controls, and his three diamond bid transfers to hearts. Under this agreement, his failure to respond two spades to two clubs would indicate that his heart suit is not headed by two of the top three honors.

See also MILES RESPONSES TO TWO CLUB OPENINGS.

KOKISH RELAY

When a partnership has agreed to use two clubs as its only strong forcing opening bid, *see* ARTIFICIAL TWO CLUB OPENING, it is customary to lower the point count requirements for a two notrump opening to 20-22 HCP and to define the two club opener's two notrump rebid as a hand worth 23-24 points. When the partnership has also agreed to give the two notrump opening an artificial meaning, *see, e.g.*, TWO NOTRUMP AS WEAK MINOR PREEMPT; GAMBLING TWO NOTRUMP; TWO-UNDER PREEMPTS; TWO NOTRUMP OPENING FOR MINORS, this customary way of distinguishing between 20-22 and 23-24 point hands is no longer feasible. Such a partnership may agree to use the Kokish Relay, an artificial two heart rebid by the two club opener, to preserve the ability to show both ranges of balanced hands.

Using the Kokish Relay convention, opener rebids two notrump immediately after a two diamond response to show a balanced hand with 20-22 points. If he has the stronger hand, he rebids two hearts (the Kokish relay) over two diamonds; the two heart bid forces responder to rebid two spades. Over two spades, opener bids two notrump to show his balanced 23-24 point hand.

Both opener's two heart rebid and responder's two spade rebid are artificial. In order to show a strong two bid in hearts, opener would have to rebid three hearts, either over the two diamond response or over responder's forced two spade rebid. One of these sequences may be used to show an absolute game force; the other may be used to show a hand not quite worth a game force. The partnership should agree on which sequence has which meaning.

See also TWO-WAY REBID BY TWO CLUB OPENER.

TWO-WAY REBID BY TWO CLUB OPENER

After a strong artificial opening bid of two clubs and a three notrump rebid by opener, which in most partnerships would show 25-26 HCP, the partnership has little room to explore for the most appropriate game contract. In order to keep the bidding at a lower level when opener has 25 or more points, it has been recommended that opener rebid two hearts with either a strong two-bid in hearts or a balanced hand worth at least 25 HCP.

After the auction has commenced in that fashion, responder may bid two spades to ask opener to disclose which type of hand he has. Opener shows the balanced 25 + point hand by bidding two notrump. Over this rebid, the partnership may use whatever methods it has agreed to use over less strong two notrump openings or rebids.

A three heart rebid shows a one-suited heart hand. A bid of three notrump shows a one-suited hand long in hearts, with sufficient stoppers to make three notrump in opener's own hand. Suit bids at the three level show two-suited hands with hearts and the suit bid.

A rebid by opener of four clubs, four diamonds, or four spades over responder's two spade inquiry may be used to show a strong two-heart bid and to make an asking bid in the suit in which the jump is made. *See, e.g.*, CONTROL ASKING BIDS; KANTAR ASKING BIDS.

SIMPLIFIED MEXICAN TWO DIAMONDS

A simplified version of the MEXICAN TWO DIAMOND CONVENTION uses the two-diamond opening bid to show a 19-20 point hand with balanced distribution (4-3-3-3, 4-4-3-2, 5-3-3-2, or occasionally, 5-4-2-2). The hand must contain a minimum of five controls, with an ace counted as two and a king as one.

The two-level responses to the two diamond opening are artificial and do not say anything about responder's holdings in the suits bid. They are

$2\heartsuit$ = 0-6 HCP
$2\spadesuit$ = 7-13 HCP
2NT = 14 or more HCP

An alternative treatment for the two notrump response is to use it to show either a 14+ point hand, or a worthless hand with a six-card or longer club suit. On the rare occasion on which responder has a worthless hand with a six-card or longer diamond suit, responder may pass the two-diamond opening.

After any of the above responses, opener automatically (with one exception) rebids two notrump. The two notrump rebid is not forcing if responder has bid two hearts. If responder has 5-6 points, however, and a long suit, he should bid again. He should bid three of his long suit unless the partnership is using JACOBY TRANSFER BIDS; in the latter case, responder should transfer into his long suit. Responder's bid of a new suit is not forcing; but if opener has excellent controls and a fit for responder's suit, he may bid game in responder's suit.

The only circumstance in which opener does not automatically rebid two notrump is when the response was two hearts and opener has a strong five-card spade suit, and has one suit unstopped. For example, if opener has

$\spadesuit$ A K Q J x $\heartsuit$ K Q x $\diamondsuit$ A x x $\clubsuit$ x x

he should rebid two spades instead of two notrump. The two spade rebid is not forcing.

After a two spade response to the two diamond opening, the partnership is committed to game. Slam, however, is unlikely unless both opener and responder have maximums and a fit is found. After this response and the two notrump rebid, the partnership may use the methods it normally uses over a two notrump opening.

After a two notrump response using the simplest version of the Mexican responses, the partnership knows the hand is in the slam range. Opener should rebid three notrump and permit the partnership to use the methods it normally employs over a two notrump opening, but one level higher. If, however, the partnership has agreed that responder's two notrump response could be made on a worthless hand with a long club suit, opener should rebid three clubs rather than three notrump. Responder will either pass with the club bust, or will confirm a hand worth 14 or more points by bidding again.

MORGAN TWO DIAMONDS

The Morgan Two Diamond bid is an artificial opening that is forcing for one round but is not forcing to game. The two diamond opening shows a hand of nearly game-forcing strength; it may be balanced or unbalanced. If balanced, the hand must contain 23-24 high card points. If unbalanced, the hand should contain a four-card major suit and a longer suit; the longer suit may be the other major.

If responder wants to learn more about opener's hand, he bids two hearts, an artificial waiting bid. Over two hearts, opener rebids two spades on any unbalanced hand that contains four spades. If opener has four hearts, he bids a suit at the three level. His rebids of three clubs and three diamonds show four hearts plus a long suit in the minor bid; his rebid of three hearts shows four hearts and five spades. The complete schedule of opener's shape-showing rebids over two hearts is as follows:

2 ♠ = four spades and an unidentified five-card or longer suit
2 NT = balanced hand with 23-24 HCP
3 ♣ = five or more clubs and four hearts
3 ◇ = five or more diamonds and four hearts
3 ♡ = four hearts and five spades

After the two heart response and opener's rebid, the auction proceeds with relatively natural bidding. Responder's bid of a suit not yet bid naturally is natural. When opener has bid three clubs, three diamonds, or three hearts, responder's return to opener's other suit at the three level is a signoff.

If opener has rebid two spades and responder has at least four-card support, responder may raise to three spades to invite game or jump to four spades as a signoff. If he has interest in a spade slam, he bids three notrump to show a balanced hand, or he jumps to four clubs, four diamonds, or four hearts to show a singleton or void in the suit of his jump.

If responder has a hand worth slam exploration in a suit other than spades, he may describe his own hand rather than bidding two hearts. Responder's slam interest responses to the two diamond opening are:

2 ♠ = four or more hearts
2 NT = balanced hand
3 ♣ = five or more clubs
3 ◇ = five or more diamonds

After responder has bid two spades, showing at least four hearts, opener's rebids are as follows:

2 NT = 23-24 HCP, balanced, without four hearts
3 ♣ = five or more clubs and four spades
3 ◇ = five or more diamonds and four spades
3 ♡ = four hearts, no singleton
3 ♠ = four hearts and a singleton or void in spades
4 ♣ = four hearts and a singleton or void in clubs
4 ◇ = four hearts and a singleton or void in diamonds

ACOL TWO-BIDS

In the Acol System, opening two-bids in all four suits are strong and forcing. Those in diamonds, hearts, and spades are usually made on unbalanced hands of less than game going strength. The two club opening may be based either on a balanced hand or on an unbalanced game-going hand.

Acol Two Diamonds, Two Hearts, and Two Spades

Opening bids of two diamonds, two hearts, and two spades are strong bids that are forcing for one round. These bids show distributional hands with one or two long suits, and eight or more playing tricks. Typical two-spade openings would be

[A]	♠ A K Q J x x	♡ A x x	◇ x	♣ K Q x
[B]	♠ K Q J 10 x x	♡ x	◇ A Q J 10 x	♣ x

If responder has a hand containing less than one honor trick (one ace, two kings, or a king and queen in the same suit), he makes a negative response of two notrump.

With support of J x x or better for opener's suit, responder raises the opening bid. A raise to three virtually promises at least one ace. A jump raise to four denies an ace.

A response of three notrump shows 11-12 points, principally in intermediate cards rather than aces and kings. Holding 11-12 points with Jxx or better in opener's suit and a side ace, responder should prefer to raise opener's suit to three.

A response in a new suit promises a good suit, usually headed by two of the top three honors. If bid at the two level, the hand may contain as little as one honor trick; a bid at the three level promises 1½ honor tricks. Responder should prefer to raise opener's suit on A x or K x rather than introducing a new suit not headed by at least the king and queen.

The "negative" response of two notrump may also be made on some stronger hands that do not meet the above criteria for raises, responses in a new suit, or the response of three notrump.

Examples:

[C]	♠ K 10 x x x x	♡ J x	◇ x	♣ J x x x
[D]	♠ J x x x	♡ x x x	◇ K Q x	♣ Q x x
[E]	♠ K J x	♡ x x x	◇ x x	♣ K x x x x

If the opening has been two hearts, responder should bid two notrump with each of the above hands.

After a response other than two notrump, the partnership is committed to game. After the negative response of two notrump, neither a simple rebid by opener of his suit nor a non-reverse change of suit is forcing. The following are permissible auctions.

	Opener	Responder
[F]	2♠	2 Notrump
	3♡	Pass
[G]	2♢	2 Notrump
	3♢	Pass
[H]	2♠	2 Notrump
	3♢	3♠
	Pass	

A reverse bid by opener is forcing for one round:

Opener	Responder
2♢	2 Notrump
3♠	

Responder must bid again.

The Acol Two Club Opening

The Acol two club opening is forcing and may be made either on a hand that is balanced and contains at least 23 HCP, or on an unbalanced hand of game-going strength. The negative response is two diamonds.

In order to make a positive response, which is game-forcing, responder needs a fair suit with a queen outside, or a good suit. In response to a two club opening, responder would bid two hearts with either of the following hands:

[I]	♠ x x	♡ K J 10 x x	◇ Q x	♣ J x x x
[J]	♠ x x	♡ A Q x x	◇ J x x x	♣ x x x

Responder should have a slightly better suit than K J 10 x x in order to bid two spades, however, since that response uses up a great deal of space by forcing opener to show his suit, if any, at the three level.

A response of two notrump to two clubs promises at least 8 points including two kings. A response of three notrump promises the equivalent of three kings and a jack.

After the negative response of two diamonds, a rebid by opener of two notrump shows 23-24 HCP and is not forcing. Responder should raise to three notrump if he has as much as 3 points or a five-card suit headed by the queen. A rebid of three notrump by opener over the two diamond response shows 25-26 points, or, in any event, a hand with nine tricks guaranteed.

All other rebids by opener after the two diamond response are forcing to game. Opener's jump to three hearts or three spades establishes that suit as trumps. Responder may then bid a new suit to show the king or a singleton and trump support.

If opener makes a nonjump rebid in a suit, responder may raise without jumping if he has good support (J x x or better) and an ace. With good support and a smattering of high cards but no ace, responder makes a jump raise. Without good support but with a five-card suit of his own, headed by the queen, responder may bid his suit. Lacking the wherewithal to make any of these bids, responder should bid two notrump. He may thereafter raise opener's suit to show support but few high cards.

STRONG TWO DIAMOND OPENING WITH STEP RESPONSES

A system for handling extremely strong hands uses a two diamond opening bid that is virtually game forcing, and a two club opening that is forcing for only one round. *See also* STAYMAN TWO CLUB AND TWO DIAMOND OPENINGS. The low-level responses to both openings show the number of controls (ace = 2, king = 1) held by responder.

The Two Diamond Opening

The two diamond opening shows either a balanced hand containing 23-24 or 27-28 HCP, or an unbalanced hand containing at least five controls and no more than three losers. Except in one auction, the two diamond opening is forcing to game.

Responder usually responds to the two diamond opening by showing his controls in steps as follows:

$2 \heartsuit$ = 0-1 control
$2 \spadesuit$ = 2 controls
2NT = 3 controls
$3 \clubsuit$ = 4 controls
$3 \diamondsuit$ = 5 or more controls

A bid by responder of three hearts or three spades is natural and shows a six-card suit headed by K Q J or K Q 10. It denies any outside ace, king, queen, singleton, or void. A bid by responder of four hearts or four spades is also natural and shows a seven-card suit headed by the king and queen. It denies any outside ace or singleton.

Jumps by responder to four clubs and four diamonds are artificial. Four clubs shows a seven-card heart suit headed by the king and queen. Four diamonds shows a seven-card spade suit headed by the king and queen. Each bid guarantees that responder has a side suit singleton somewhere.

A response of three notrump shows a solid minor suit, with no ace, king, or queen outside.

Examples:

[A]	♠ x x x x	♡ x x	◇ x x x x	♣ x x x
[B]	♠ KQJ10xx	♡ x x	◇ Q x x x	♣ x
[C]	♠ x x	♡ x x x x	◇ A x x	♣ x x x x

Opposite a two diamond opening, responder should bid two hearts with hand [A] since he has no controls. With hand [B], he again bids two hearts because he has only one control; his hand does not meet the criteria for a jump to three spades because it contains a singleton, nor for a jump to four diamonds (which may be bid with a singleton) because he has only a six-card suit. With hand [C], responder bids two spades, showing two controls.

Using this strong two diamond convention, a hand containing 25-26 HCP is opened two notrump. The two notrump opening is forcing to game.

If opener starts with two diamonds and rebids two notrump, he shows the 23-24 point balanced hand. This rebid over a two heart response may be passed. The sequence 2 ◇ - 2 ♡ - 2 Notrump is the only sequence after a two diamond opening that is not forcing to game.

A rebid by opener in a suit announces an unbalanced hand with no more than three losers. This rebid is game-forcing and may be made on a five-card suit. The subsequent bidding proceeds naturally, except that a jump in a new suit is a SPLINTER RAISE, showing a singleton in the suit of the jump and support for the last bid suit. Such a bid may not be made in a suit in which the singleton is the king.

The knowledge that opener has no more than three losers will often enable responder to envision a slam with few high cards. He should expect to take care of one of opener's losers with each ace, king, or queen that he holds in a suit bid by opener. Note that the three-loser requirement does not apply to the balanced hands on which opener rebids in notrump.

Examples:

	Opener	*Responder*
[A]	2 ◇	2 ♠
	3 ♡	4 ♠
	7 ♡	Pass
[B]	2 ◇	2 ♡
	2 ♠	2 Notrump
	3 ♡	

In auction [A], the two hands might be

(Opener)
♠ A x x   ♡ A K Q x x x   ◇ K Q x   ♣ A

(Responder)
♠ x   ♡ x x x x   ◇ A x x x   ♣ x x x x

Responder's two spade bid shows his two controls, and his jump to four spades shows support for opener's hearts and a singleton spade.

Since his singleton cannot be the king, opener knows his two controls can only be the ace of diamonds. Opener can, therefore, confidently bid the grand slam.

If the auction has begun as in [B] above, and responder holds

♠ Q x   ♡ Q x x x   ◊ x x x x   ♣ x x x

he should jump to six spades, since he holds queens in each of opener's long suits. Since opener's rebid in a suit guarantees no more than three losers in his hand, and responder can cover two of them, he jumps to slam. Opener might have

♠ A K x x x x   ♡ A K J x x   ◊ A   ♣ x

The Two Club Opening

Using the above two diamond structure, the partnership may use the two club opening bid as a two-way bid, showing either a balanced hand worth 20+ to 22 HCP, or an unbalanced hand with exactly four or five losers, and at least five controls. The two club opening is forcing for one round. Responder usually shows his controls in steps, as follows:

2◊ = 0-5 HCP, usually no control
2♡ = at least 6 HCP; 0-2 controls, or an ace and a king but no queen
2♠ = 3 controls plus at least one queen
2NT = 4 controls
3♣ = 5 controls
3◊ = 6 controls

Responses of three hearts through four spades have exactly the same meanings that they have over a two diamond opening.

AMBIGUOUS ONE DIAMOND OPENING

The Ambiguous One Diamond convention is a forcing opening bid designed for use in systems featuring weak notrump openings (11-13 HCP) and four-card major suit openings. The one diamond opening promises either a balanced hand containing 16-20 HCP, or a hand containing a five-card or longer diamond suit and at least 16 points including distribution.

All of responder's one-level responses are artificial and forcing. A one heart response shows 0-5 points and denies a six-card or longer suit. The response does not give any indication as to responder's length in hearts. After this response, opener rebids one notrump if he has the balanced hand. Any other rebid is natural, showing the suit bid and a diamond suit.

A response of one spade shows six or more points and asks opener to clarify his hand. The response does not say anything about responder's spade suit and may be made with any distribution. Opener rebids one notrump with a balanced hand containing 16-18 HCP, or two notrump with a balanced hand containing 19-20 HCP. The two notrump rebid commits the partnership to game. Any suit rebid by opener over the one spade response is natural, showing the suit bid and a diamond suit. Subsequent bidding is natural.

A response of one notrump also is artificial. It asks opener to bid his better minor suit at the two level. Responder makes this response with a very weak hand containing at least five clubs and at least five diamonds.

These artificial responses permit the partnership to rest in one notrump when opener has 16-20 points and responder has 0-5, or to play in two of opener's better minor suit when opener has a strong notrump opening and responder has a minor suit bust.

Responses in suits at the two level or higher show weak hands with at least six cards in the suit bid. These responses are neither forcing nor invitational.

In order to show a minimum opening hand (12-15 HCP) with a five-card or longer diamond suit, an opening bid of two diamonds is used. The only forcing response is two hearts. This response says nothing about responder's hearts but merely asks opener to describe his hand further. Other responses to the two diamond opening may be passed.

Hands containing four diamonds and no longer suit are opened either with one notrump (11-13 HCP), or with another four-card suit, or with one club.

STRONG THREE CLUB OPENING

In the Strong Three Club system, the only strong forcing opening bid is three clubs. This opening is forcing to game.

Opening bids of two in any suit are intermediate, promising 19-24 points, including distribution. These openings show length in the suit bid and are not forcing.

Opening bids of one are limited to 18 points.

The author of this convention does not claim that this system is as effective as those normally used, but says that its merit is its extreme simplicity.

IV
Making Inquiries

KICKBACK

When the agreed trump suit is spades, the BLACKWOOD four notrump convention provides a relatively efficient method of asking about aces or key cards. *See* KEY CARD BLACKWOOD; ROMAN KEY CARD BLACKWOOD. When some other suit has been agreed, however, the use of four notrump to ask about key cards may waste room at the four level or may evoke a response that takes the bidding past five of the agreed trump suit.

The Kickback convention conserves useful space by using a bid other than four notrump as the key-card asking bid when the trump suit is other than spades. Precisely which suit is used as the key-card asking bid (the "Kickback suit") is determined by which suit has been agreed as trumps. When trumps have been agreed, the Kickback bid is four of the suit just above the trump suit:

Agreed Trump Suit	Kickback Bid
Clubs	4 ◊
Diamonds	4 ♡
Hearts	4 ♠

This identification of the ace-asking suit is applicable even if that suit has previously been bid by one of the partners, so long as some other suit has been clearly agreed as trumps. For example:

[A]	*Opener*	*Responder*		[B]	*Opener*	*Responder*
	1 ♡	2 ◊			1 ♡	2 Notrump (Jacoby)
	3 ◊	4 ♡			4 ◊	4 ♠

In auction A, responder's jump to four hearts is Kickback. The four-heart bid is not needed as a natural call since three hearts, after responder has made a two-over-one response and opener has raised, would be a game force in hearts. In auction B, responder's JACOBY TWO NOTRUMP response established hearts as trumps; his four spade bid is Kickback.

Kickback may be used even if the opponents have bid. Thus, in the auction

North	East	South	West
1 ♡	1 ♠	2 ♣	2 ♠
3 ♣	Pass	4 ◊	

South's four diamond bid is Kickback. Four diamonds would have been Kickback even if, over three clubs, East had bid three spades.

The partner of the Kickback bidder shows how many key cards he has. The five key cards are the four aces and the king of trumps. In addition, the trump queen may be revealed. The responses to Kickback are steps paralleling the responses to Roman Key Card Blackwood:

First step   = 0 or 3 key cards
Second step = 1 or 4 key cards
Third step   = 2 or 5 key cards, without the queen of trumps
Fourth step = 2 or 5 key cards, with the queen of trumps

The bid of the first or second step does not reveal whether or not the Kickback responder has the queen of trumps. If the Kickback bidder wants to know about the trump queen after one of these responses, he asks by making the cheapest bid other than the trump suit. His partner denies the trump queen by bidding the first step over this queen-asking bid and shows the queen by bidding the second step. For example, in the auction

Opener	Responder
1 ♡	3 ♡ (forcing)
4 ♠	4 Notrump
5 ♣	5 ♡

responder's four notrump bid, the first step, shows none or three of the key cards. Opener's five club bid, the cheapest, asks about the queen of hearts. Responder's bid of five hearts, the second step, promises the queen.

If the Kickback responder has two or five key cards without the queen of trumps but has extra length in that suit, he may treat his extra length as the equivalent of the queen. Thus, if the partnership is using five-card major suit openings and responder has a hand such as

♠ x x   ♡ A x x x x   ◊ A Q x   ♣ K x x

when the auction has begun

Opener	Responder
1 ♡	3 ♡ (forcing)
4 ♠	

responder should bid five hearts, the fourth step, showing two key cards with the trump queen. If the Kickback bidder has K x x x x in hearts, he

871

will not know that the queen is missing; but the partnership nonetheless is not likely to lose a trump trick. If the Kickback bidder has the queen of trumps, he will know that the bid of the fourth step is based on extra length.

After receiving the key card response, the Kickback bidder may bid five of the Kickback suit to explore for a grand slam. This bid indicates that the partnership has all of the aces and no trump losers and asks about side-suit kings.

In response to five of the Kickback suit, the Kickback responder makes the cheapest bid in a side suit of which he has the king. If his cheapest king is the king of the Kickback suit, he bids notrump. If he has no side-suit kings, he rebids the trump suit.

For example:

Opener	Responder
1 ♣	1 ♡
3 ♡	4 ♠
5 ♢	5 ♠
6 ♣	

Responder's four spade bid is Kickback; opener's five diamond bid, the third step, shows two key cards without the queen of hearts. Responder's five spade bid asks about kings; opener's six club bid shows the king of clubs. Since opener would have bid five notrump to show the king of spades, the six club bid denies the king of spades; opener has not revealed whether or not he has the king of diamonds.

When the partnership is using Kickback, the key-card asking bid remains four notrump if the agreed suit is spades. The Kickback bidder uses the Roman Key Card Blackwood responses over four notrump.

Coordination With Splinter Bids

When the partnership has agreed to use Kickback, the jump to the Kickback suit becomes unavailable for use as a SPLINTER bid. The partnership may use four notrump, which would otherwise have been Blackwood, as a splinter bid in the suit that must be used as the Kickback bid. For example, in the auction

Opener	Responder
1 ♡	3 ♡
4 Notrump	

872

since a bid of four spades by opener would have been Kickback, asking for key cards, opener's bid of four notrump may be used to show a singleton or void in spades.

Other splinter bids remain available in their original form. For example,

Opener	Responder
1 ♣	3 ♣
4 ♡	

if the partnership has agreed to use four hearts as a splinter, use of Kickback does not alter this meaning.

See also REDWOOD; CHEAP BLACKWOOD; BABY BLACKWOOD. For other uses of Kickback space conservation principles, *see* GRAND SLAM FORCE (Triggers Other Than Five Notrump).

REDWOOD

The Redwood convention is a variation of KICKBACK that uses bids other than four notrump to ask about key cards, *i.e.*, the four aces and the king of the agreed trump suit. Whereas the Kickback key-card asking bid is always four of the suit just above the trump suit, Redwood may vary the key-card asking bid when the agreed trump suit is a minor.

If no other suits have been bid, the Redwood key-card asking bid is the same as that used in Kickback. That is, four diamonds would ask for aces if the agreed trump suit is clubs; four hearts would ask for aces if the agreed suit is diamonds.

If a suit other than the agreed trump suit has been bid, the Redwood key-card asking bid is a jump to four of the cheapest unbid suit. For example, in the auction

Opener	Responder
1 ♡	2 ◇
3 ◇	

using Redwood, responder would ask about key cards by jumping to four spades. His rebid of four hearts would either be natural or, by agreement, a SPLINTER bid showing a singleton or void in hearts.

If clubs have been agreed as trumps and both diamonds and hearts have been bid along the way, or if diamonds have been agreed and both hearts and spades have been bid, the use of Redwood risks getting the partnership too high. For example, in the auction

Opener	Responder
1 ♣	1 ◇
1 ♡	3 ♣

in order to use Redwood, opener would have to jump to four spades. In such an auction, it would be more efficient to use Kickback, agreeing that the key-card asking bid is the jump to four of the suit just above the agreed trump suit.

The Redwood responder shows how many of the five key cards he has by bidding one of the following steps:

First step   = 0 or 3 key cards
Second step = 1 or 4 key cards
Third step   = 2 or 5 key cards, without the queen of trumps
Fourth step = 2 or 5 key cards, with the queen of trumps

With respect to further inquiries by responder, coordination with splinters, and use of Redwood in competition, see KICKBACK.

See also CHEAP BLACKWOOD; BABY BLACKWOOD.

CHEAP BLACKWOOD

In order to conserve bidding space for slam exploration, many partnerships agree that instead of using four notrump to ask about key cards (the four aces and the king of trumps), they will ask by using a lower ranking bid. *See*, *e.g.*, KICKBACK; REDWOOD. In one such convention, called Cheap Blackwood, the key-card asking bid is the cheapest "meaningless" bid after the partnership has agreed on a trump suit in a game-forcing auction. A meaningless bid is one that has no significance in the partnership's agreed methods, other than perhaps as a cue-bid.

Examples:

		[A]	*Opener*	*Responder*		[B]	*Opener*	*Responder*

[A]
Opener	*Responder*
1 ♠	3 ♠ (forcing)
3 Notrump	

[B]
Opener	*Responder*
1 ◇	2 ♡
3 ♡	3 ♠

[C]
Opener	*Responder*
1 ♠	4 ♣ (SPLINTER)
4 ◇	

[D]
Opener	*Responder*
1 ♠	2 Notrump (JACOBY)
3 ♣	3 ◇

[E]
Opener	*Responder*
1 ♡	3 ♡ (forcing)
3 Notrump	

[F]
Opener	*Responder*
1 ♡	2 ◇
3 ◇	3 ♡

In auctions A, B, and C, the final bid shown is Cheap Blackwood. In auction D, opener's three club bid, though it is the cheapest possible bid after responder's game-forcing artificial raise of spades, is not Cheap Blackwood because it is not meaningless. When the partnership is using the Jacoby Two Notrump convention, opener's three club bid either shows a singleton club or has some other conventional meaning. Responder's three diamond bid, however, if it does not have relay significance, *see*, *e.g.*, BERGEN MODIFICATIONS OF JACOBY TWO NOTRUMP; MARTEL MODIFICATIONS OF JACOBY TWO NOTRUMP; TWO-PHASE TWO NOTRUMP ASKING BIDS, would be Cheap Blackwood.

In auction E, opener's three notrump bid is not Cheap Blackwood because it is not the cheapest bid. In auction F, responder's three heart bid is not Cheap Blackwood because, though it is the cheapest, it is not meaningless; hearts may be the partnership's more appropriate trump suit.

The responses to Cheap Blackwood correspond, in steps, to the responses to ROMAN KEY CARD BLACKWOOD. They are

    First step   = 0 or 3 key cards
    Second step = 1 or 4 key cards
    Third step   = 2 or 5 key cards, without the queen of trumps
    Fourth step = 2 or 5 key cards, with the queen of trumps

If the Cheap Blackwood bidder cannot tell from his own hand whether the response was based on the lesser or the greater number of key cards, he signs off in four of the trump suit. His partner will bid again if the response was based on the greater number.

See also RELAY BLACKWOOD; BABY BLACKWOOD; THREE NOTRUMP MOVING ALONG; GENERAL INTEREST SLAM TRY.

LAST ASKING BIDS

LAST asking bids are slam oriented inquiries over a one notrump opening by a responder who has a one-suited or two-suited hand. LAST is an acronym for *L*eonard *A*sking *S*lam *T*ries. Responder's key-card asking bid when he has shown a one-suited hand with at least a six-card suit is called LAST 6. His key-card asking bid when he has shown a five-five or longer two-suiter is called LAST 55.

LAST 6

LAST 6 is used by responder when he holds a six-card or longer suit in a hand worth slam exploration. To begin, responder jumps to three spades directly over one notrump. The three spade bid is entirely artificial; responder may have any of the four suits.

The three spade bid forces opener to rebid three notrump; responder then bids four of his suit. This rebid by responder sets the trump suit and asks opener how many key cards he holds.

For LAST 6 purposes, there are five key cards: the four aces, plus the king of responder's suit. Over responder's identification of his suit, opener's key card responses use steps corresponding to ROMAN KEY CARD BLACKWOOD responses:

First step   = 0 or 3 key cards
Second step = 1 or 4 key cards
Third step   = 2 or 5 key cards, without the trump queen
Fourth step = 2 or 5 key cards, with the trump queen

Armed with this information, responder usually can set the final contract.
For example, if the partnership hands were

Opener
♠ K x x   ♡ K x   ◊ A x x   ♣ A J x x x
Responder
♠ A x x   ♡ A Q x x x x x   ◊ Q x   ♣ x

the auction would be

Opener	Responder
1 Notrump	3 ♠
3 Notrump	4 ♡
4 ♠	6 ♡

LAST 55 is used when responder has slam interest and two five-card suits. The convention uses JACOBY TRANSFER BIDS and eliminates use of the GERBER ace-asking convention.

With any two-suiter other than both minors, responder begins by transferring to his major suit at the two level (diamonds transfers to hearts; hearts transfers to spades). He then shows his second suit by jumping to it at the four level. He shows a minor two-suiter by jumping to four clubs directly over one notrump. The complete schedule of responder's bids and rebids is thus as follows:

Responder's Two Suits	*Responder's Bids and Rebids*
spades and hearts	2 ♡, then 4 ♡
spades and diamonds	2 ♡, then 4 ◊
spades and clubs	2 ♡, then 4 ♣
hearts and diamonds	2 ◊, then 4 ◊
hearts and clubs	2 ◊, then 4 ♣
diamonds and clubs	4 ♣ directly

As described below, opener's first bid after responder's four-level bid will indicate which of responder's suits opener prefers. In certain circumstances, that bid will also show how many key cards opener has.

Opener's Preference Between Responder's Suits

If the cheapest possible bid over responder's complete identification of his two suits is in one of responder's suits (as is true when responder's suits are touching suits), that bid shows opener's preference for that suit. If the cheapest bid over responder's rebid is not one of responder's suits (*i.e.*, responder's suits are not touching suits), the cheapest bid shows a preference for responder's lower-ranking suit.

For example,

[A] | *Opener* | *Responder* |
|---|---|
| 1 Notrump | 2 ◊ (transfer to hearts) |
| 2 ♡ | 4 ◊ (natural) |
| 4 ♡ | |

[B] | *Opener* | *Responder* |
|---|---|
| 1 Notrump | 2 ♡ (transfer to spades) |
| 2 ♡ | 4 ◊ (natural) |
| 4 ♡ | |

In auction A, opener's bid of four hearts, one of responder's suits, shows a preference for hearts. In auction B, his rebid of four hearts, which is not one of responder's suits, shows a preference for responder's lower bid suit, *i.e.*, diamonds.

If, over responder's four-level bid, opener makes any bid other than the cheapest response, it shows a preference for the suit that would not have been agreed by the cheapest-bid response. Thus, in auction A, if opener preferred diamonds, he would have to show it by bidding something other than four hearts. In auction B, opener's bid of anything other than four hearts would show a preference for spades.

Key Cards Shown By Opener Using LAST 55

When responder has shown two five-card suits, there are six key cards to be considered. They are the four aces, plus the kings of the two suits shown by responder.

Whenever opener's preference requires him to bypass the cheapest bid, he makes a bid that also reveals how many of the six key cards he has. He shows his key cards, plus the queen of the suit for which he has shown a preference, using the following four-step schedule:

> First step above the cheapest suit = 0 or 3 key cards
> Second step above the cheapest suit = 1 or 4 key cards
> Third step above the cheapest suit = 2 or 5 key cards, without the trump queen
> Fourth step above the cheapest suit = 2 or 5 key cards, with the trump queen

No step response is provided for opener to show six key cards since opener cannot have four aces and two kings if the partnership is using standard notrump openings, and responder is unlikely to have slam interest if he has no aces and his suits are headed by queens or wose.

In the auction

[C] *Opener*   *Responder*
    1 Notrump   2 ♡ (transfer to spades)
    2 ♠   4 ♣ (natural)
    4 ♡

responder has shown spades and clubs. A four diamond rebid by opener would have shown a preference for clubs; therefore, four hearts shows a preference for spades. Since four hearts is not the cheapest bid, it also shows how many key cards opener has. As the first step above the cheapest suit, four hearts shows no key cards or 3 key cards.

When opener expresses his preference by bidding the cheapest suit, his bid does not reveal how many key cards he has. In order to ask opener about key cards, responder makes the next cheapest bid. Opener's responses, again by steps, are

First step above the asking suit = 0 or 3 key cards
Second step above the asking suit = 1 or 4 key cards
Third step above the asking suit = 2 or 5 key cards, without the trump queen
Fourth step above the asking suit = 2 or 5 key cards, with the trump queen

Thus, in the auction

[D]	*Opener*	*Responder*
	1 Notrump	2 ♡ (transfer to spades)
	2 ♠	4 ◊ (natural)
	4 ♡	4 ♠ (asking bid)
	5 ◊	

responder has shown spades and diamonds. Opener's four heart bid, the cheapest bid, shows a preference for diamonds and does not give any information about controls. Responder's four spade bid, the cheapest possible over opener's preference bid, asks about key cards. Opener's bid of five diamonds, the third step, shows 2 or 5 key cards and denies the queen of diamonds.

BYZANTINE BLACKWOOD

One complex modern variation of the Blackwood convention is called Byzantine Blackwood. Its principal premise is that an ace-showing response to four notrump may safely be based on a holding in which one ace is replaced by a king, so long as the king is in a "key suit," or "half-key" suit, and there are not more than two key suits.

The trump suit, if one has been agreed upon either specifically or by inference, is a "key suit." In addition, a genuine side suit that has been bid and supported is considered a "key suit," as is any suit bid by a player whose partner's first bid was in notrump.

A "half-key" suit is defined as a genuine suit that has been bid but not supported. When each partner has bid a half-key suit, the suit bid by the four notrump bidder is the half-key suit in which a king may be shown.

Byzantine is initiated by a call of four notrump (but never on the first round of the auction, when such a call is treated as ordinary Blackwood). Byzantine provides two scales of responses: one for use when there is one key suit, and one for use when there are two.

When there is one key suit the responses are:

5 ♣ = 0 or 3 aces; *or* 2 aces plus the key suit king

5 ◇ = 1 or 4 aces; *or* 3 aces plus the key suit king

5 ♡ = 2 aces; *or* the ace, king, and queen of the key suit; *or* the ace-king of the key suit plus the king of the half-key suit

5 ♠ = 2 aces plus the king and queen of the key suit; *or* 3 aces plus the king of the half-key suit

5NT = 3 aces plus the king and queen of the key suit; *or* 4 aces plus the king of the key suit; *or* 2 aces plus the king of a half-key suit (rare)

For example, in the auction,

North	South
1 Notrump	3 ◊
3 Notrump	4 Notrump

there is one key suit, diamonds. If North's hand were

♠ A x x x ♡ A Q x ◊ K x ♣ Q x x x

his response would be five clubs, showing two aces plus the king of diamonds.

When there are two key suits, half-key suits are ignored, and the Byzantine responses are:

5 ♣ = 0 or 3 aces; *or* 2 aces plus a key suit king

5 ◊ = 1 or 4 aces; *or* three aces and a key suit king

5 ♡ = 2 aces; *or* the ace, king and queen of a key suit; *or* 1 ace and both key suit kings

5 ♠ = 2 aces plus the king and queen of a key suit; *or* 2 aces and both key suit kings; *or* 1 ace plus the king and queen of the other key suit

5NT = 3 aces plus the king and queen of a key suit; *or* 3 aces and both key suit kings; *or* 4 aces plus one key suit king; *or* 2 aces plus the king of one key suit and the king and queen of the other; *or* 1 ace and the kings and queens of both key suits.

For example, in the following auction

North	South
1 ♠	2 ♣
3 ♣	3 ♠
4 ♣	4 Notrump

there are two key suits: (1) spades, which have presumably been agreed as trumps, and (2) clubs, which have been bid and supported. If North and South have the following hands

(N) ♠ A K x x x ♡ x x ◊ K x ♣ A x x x

(S) ♠ Q J x x ♡ A ◊ A x ♣ Q J x x x x

North's proper response to Byzantine would be five clubs. South, having two aces himself, will know that North has two aces plus one key king, rather than three aces, and that the grand slam is not a worthwhile proposition, since either the king of trumps or the king of clubs is missing. If North's king of diamonds were the king of clubs, however, his response would be five spades, and South would bid the perfectly-fitting 28-point grand slam (in clubs, for greater probable safety).

Cue-bidding may follow the response to four notrump.

In addition, after a response to four notrump has been made, a bid of five notrump asks for additional high card "features." A king or doubleton king-queen not already shown in response to four notrump counts as one feature; a guarded king-queen combination not already shown counts as two features. The responses are:

6♣ = 0 or 3 features
6◊ = 1 or 4 features
6♡ = 2 features

(See also CULBERTSON FOUR-FIVE NOTRUMP, KEY CARD BLACKWOOD, ROMAN BLACKWOOD.)

SUPER PRECISION ASKING BIDS

In the Super Precision System of bidding, a number of different types of asking bids are used. The opener can ask about the quality of a suit bid by the responder, or about the responder's high card or distributional controls, or about the responder's support for the opener's suit.

Alpha Support Asking Bids

Using what are called Alpha Support Asking Bids, if the opener bids a new suit after a positive response to his one club opening, he is asking the responder about his overall strength and his support for the opener's suit. The responses are:

    1st step = J x x or worse, less than 3 controls
    2nd step = J x x or worse, 3 or more controls
    3rd step = Q x x or better, less than 3 controls
    4th step = Q x x or better, 3 or more controls
    5th step = 4 small cards, 3 or more controls

If the responder has shown support of Q x x or better for the opener's suit, any new suit bids are cue-bids.

If, however, the responder has bid the first or second step, showing J x x or worse in the opener's suit, the opener can ask for further information by bidding a new suit, rebidding his own suit, or bidding two notrump.

If the opener bids a new suit or two notrump, his bid is natural, but requires the responder to bid as follows: he raises opener's suit with J x x or x x x; he jump raises opener's suit with A x or K x; he bids a new suit if he has one; he rebids his own suit if it has six or more cards; he bids notrump with a balanced hand, three notrump with a minimum, or four notrump with a maximum.

If the opener rebids his own suit at the three level after the responder's first response to the Alpha Asking Bid, the responder further defines his support for the opener. If he has shown J x x or worse, he bids as follows:

    1st step = void or singleton
    2nd step = small doubleton
    3rd step = J x x or x x x
    4th step = singleton honor
    5th step = doubleton honor
    6th step = two honors doubleton
    7th step = four small cards (with fewer than three controls)

If the responder has promised Q x x or better, he bids as follows:

    1st step = three or more headed by A J, K J or Q J
    2nd step = Q x x or longer
    3rd step = K x x or longer
    4th step = A x x or longer
    5th step = three or more headed by two of top three honors

If the opener and responder held the following hands

        (Opener)
        ♠ A K J x x x x   ♡ A   ◇ A K Q J x   ♣ —
        (Responder)
        ♠ Q   ♡ K Q x x x   ◇ x x x   ♣ A x x x

the bidding might start:

        Opener   *Responder*
        1♣ (16 + HCP)   1♡ (positive)
        1♠   2♣ (♠ J x x or worse,
                                   3 or more controls)
        3♠   4♡ (singleton honor)

Knowing that responder's singleton honor in opener's suit must be the queen, opener can safely bid the grand slam.

Over Opponents' Interference

For discussion of how to deal with opponent interference with asking bids, see PRECISION ACE ASKING BIDS.

Beta Suit Asking Bids

In order to find out about the responder's holding in opener's suit after a negative response to the one club opening, the opener can jump to two hearts or two spades. The responder bids in 8 steps:

    1st step = 2 or 3 small cards
    2nd step = void or singleton
    3rd step = ace, king or queen singleton or doubleton
    4th step = three cards headed by ace, king or queen
    5th step = four small
    6th step = four headed by ace, king or queen
    7th step = three cards headed by two of top three honors
    8th step = four cards headed by two of top three honors

If the opener and the responder have:

(Opener)
♠ A K J x x x x   ♡ A   ◇ A K Q J x   ♣ —

(Responder)
♠ Q   ♡ x x x x x   ◇ x   ♣ x x x x x x

the auction could be

Opener	Responder
1♣	1◇ (negative)
2♠	3◇
7♠	

Gamma Trump Asking Bids

As in the Precision System, the Super Precision one club opener can ask about the quality of the responder's suit after a positive response, by making an immediate single raise of the responder's suit. The responses are those set out in PRECISION TRUMP ASKING BIDS.

In addition, the opener can make a delayed trump asking bid after he has found out whether the responder has support for the opener's suit. Thus, after a response to support asking bid, the opener's return to the responder's suit below the game level asks about the quality of the responder's suit. The PRECISION TRUMP ASKING BID schedule of responses is used. For example:

Opener	Responder
1♣	1♡
1♠	2♣
2♡	3♣

The opener has asked about spade support, and has learned that the responder has J x x or worse in a hand, with at least three controls. His two heart bid asked about the responder's heart suit; the responder's three club bid, the third step, showed a five-card suit headed by two of the top three honors.

If the opener bids the responder's suit again, below the game level, it is a repeated trump-asking bid. The responder further describes his suit in four steps, which vary according to the number of honors he has previously shown. If no honors were shown, the responder bids:

    1st step = five small cards
    2nd step = five cards headed by the jack
    3rd step = six small cards
    4th step = six cards headed by the jack

If one honor was shown, the responder bids:

 1st step = jack plus ace, king or queen
 2nd step = queen, no jack
 3rd step = king, no jack
 4th step = ace, no jack

If two honors were shown, the responder bids:

 1st step = jack plus two honors
 2nd step = king and queen, but no jack
 3rd step = ace and queen, but no jack
 4th step = ace and king, but no jack

Delta Suit Asking Bids

After a notrump response to a one club opening, the opener can ask about the number of cards and honors the responder has in a specific suit. He asks by jumping in a new suit. The responses are:

 1st step = no honors
 2nd step = doubleton honor
 3rd step = three cards headed by one honor
 4th step = four cards headed by one honor
 5th step = two or three cards headed by two honors
 6th step = four cards headed by two honors

Control Asking Bids

After any step response to an Alpha Support Asking Bid, a direct bid of four clubs by the opener asks the responder to show in steps how many controls he has, unless the responder has bid two clubs (natural) in response to the one-club opening. In the latter event, a four-diamond bid must be used to initiate the control asking bid. Thus in the auction

[A]	Opener	Responder
	1♣	1♠
	2♡	2 Notrump
	4♣	

the opener's four club bid asks about controls. However, in the auction

[B]	Opener	Responder
	1♣	2♣
	2♡	2 Notrump
	4♢	

the opener must bid four diamonds to ask about the responder's controls, since clubs is the responder's suit.

If responder has shown fewer than three controls, his first step shows 0-1 controls (ace = 2, king = 1); the second step shows two controls; and so forth.

If the responder has already shown at least three controls in response to the Alpha Asking Bid, his first step in response to the Control Asking Bid shows three controls.

These control asking bids can be used in other sequences after a trump suit has been agreed upon. To be a control asking bid, the four-club bid (or four-diamond bid as in auction [B]) must be made directly over the response to an Alpha Asking Bid or directly over the agreement on a suit. If any cue-bidding has begun prior to the four club call, four clubs is a cue-bid rather than an asking bid. For example:

Opener	Responder
1♣	1♠
2♡ (Alpha)	3♣ (♡ Q x x or better, fewer than 3 controls)
3◇ (cue-bid)	3♠ (cue-bid)
4♣	

The opener's three diamond bid was a cue-bid; therefore, his four club bid is a cue-bid.

Special Suit Asking Bid

If the one-club opener bids a new suit after making a Control Asking Bid, it is a special asking bid in the new suit.

The responder describes his hand as follows:

```
1st step  = void or singleton
2nd step  = small doubleton
3rd step  = small tripleton
4th step  = any length headed by one of top three honors
5th step  = any length headed by two of top three honors
6th step  = any length headed by all three top honors.
```

For example:

Opener	Responder
1♣	1♡
1♠ (Alpha)	2♡ (♠ Q x x or better
	3+ controls)
4♣ (control ask)	4♡ (4 controls)
5◊ (suit ask)	

The opener's five diamond bid asks about the responder's holding in the diamond suit. The opener's hand might be

♠ A K J x x x   ♡ x   ◊ A K x x   ♠ K x

890

ROMAN KEY CARD BLACKWOOD

The Key Card Blackwood convention recognizes that possession of the king of the agreed trump suit may be as important as possession of any side suit ace. *See* KEY CARD BLACKWOOD. Roman responses to Blackwood compress the ace-showing responses in order to allow the Blackwood responder to convey additional information. *See* ROMAN BLACKWOOD. The Roman Key Card Blackwood ("RKCB") convention combines these considerations and operates on the premise that possession of the queen of the agreed trump suit is the preeminent additional information to be conveyed.

Using RKCB, as in Key Card, there are five key cards, *i.e.*, the four aces and the king of trumps. (For which suit is the agreed trump suit, *see* KEY CARD BLACKWOOD.) The RKCB responses to a Blackwood bid of four notrump (see BLACKWOOD for when four notrump is or is not Blackwood), are as follows:

    5 ♣ = 0 or 3 key cards
    5 ♦ = 1 or 4 key cards
    5 ♡ = 2 or 5 key cards, without the trump queen
    5 ♠ = 2 or 5 key cards, with the trump queen

When the Blackwood responder has shown 0, 1, 3, or 4 key cards, he has not disclosed whether or not he has the trump queen. If the Blackwood bidder wishes to ask about that card, he makes the cheapest possible bid other than a bid in the trump suit over his partner's Blackwood response.

There are several schemes by which the Blackwood responder may proceed. Using the simplest, he may return to the trump suit with no trump queen; bid five notrump with the trump queen and no side king; bid another suit with the trump queen and the king of the suit he bids.

An alternative method allows for the possibility that the Blackwood responder may have the trump queen and more than one side king. Using this alternative, the Blackwood responder answers the trump queen inquiry in steps, with the first step being the suit above that in which the inquiry is made:

    first step   = no trump queen
    second step = trump queen and no side kings
    third step   = trump queen and one side king
    fourth step = trump queen and two side kings
    fifth step   = trump queen and three side kings

Example:

Opener	Responder
1♠	3♠
4 Notrump	5♦
5♥	6♣

The five heart bid asks about the trump queen. Using the first responding method described above, responder's six club bid shows the trump queen and the king of clubs. The bid does not disclose whether he has any other king. Using the second method, the six club bid reveals that responder has the trump queen and one king, but the location of the king is not disclosed.

If the RKCB bidder himself has the queen of the trump suit, obviously he will not need to ask his partner about it. The Blackwood bidder may thus proceed to inquire about his partner's kings immediately after the Blackwood response, whatever it has been.

One king-asking method is for the Blackwood bidder to bid five notrump, and for his partner to respond in the ordinary way. *See* BLACKWOOD. An alternative is for the Blackwood bidder to make the cheapest bid other than the trump suit and other than the one that would ask about the trump queen.

Example:

Opener	Responder
1♠	3♠
4 Notrump	5♣
5♥	

Since a five diamond bid by opener would ask about the trump queen, the five heart bid asks about kings. One method of responding is to sign off in the trump suit with no kings; to bid five notrump with two kings; or, holding one king, to make the cheapest possible bid in the suit in which the king is located. Using this method, the Blackwood responder should not go past six of the agreed suit to show any side kings.

Yet another method of responding to the inquiry about the trump queen combines features of the first two methods described above. This third scheme requires the Blackwood responder to bid the first step if he does not have the trump queen; all other bids show the trump queen and give other information. With the trump queen but no side king, the Blackwood responder either returns to the trump suit or bids five notrump, whichever is cheaper. If he has a side king, he bids the suit of that king if he can do so without going past six of the agreed suit; if he bids six of the agreed suit, he shows the king of a suit that he could not bid more cheaply.

Example:

Opener	Responder
1♣	1♠
2♦	4♦
4 Notrump	5♦
5♡	6♦

Using this method, responder's five diamond bid showed 1 or 4 key cards, and his six diamond bid shows that he has the queen of diamonds and the king of a major suit. A bid, instead, of five spades would have denied the trump queen; a bid of five notrump would have denied any side kings; a bid of six clubs would have shown the trump queen and the king of clubs.

Responses to RKCB With a Void

If the Blackwood responder has a useful void, he may show it in response to four notrump as follows, so long as he does not go past six of the agreed suit.

5NT = 0 or 2 key cards plus a void
6♣   = 1 or 3 key cards, void in clubs
6♦   = 1 or 3 key cards, void in diamonds
6♡   = 1 or 3 key cards, void in hearts
6 of agreed suit = 1 or 3 key cards, plus a void in a higher-ranking suit.

When the Blackwood responder is showing a void, he cannot distinguish between hands that contain the trump queen and those that do not.

Responding to RKCB after Interference

If an opponent has interfered with the RKCB responses by making a five-level overcall in a suit that ranks below the agreed trump suit, the Blackwood responder may show his key cards as follows:

double	= 0 key cards
pass	= 1 or 4 key cards
first step	= 2 key cards, without the trump queen
second step	= 2 key cards, with the trump queen
third step	= 3 key cards

If the overcall is made in a suit that ranks above the agreed suit, or is made at the six or seven level, the DEPO convention should be used. The double would show an even number of key cards; a pass would show an odd number. *See* DEPO.

EXCLUSION BLACKWOOD

Exclusion Blackwood is a device used to determine the number of *useful* aces held by the partnership. It operates when one member of the partnership has shown shortness in a particular suit, by making, *e.g.*, a SPLINTER RAISE, and then uses the BLACKWOOD convention. The partner of the player who has made this sequence of bids must, in showing the number of aces he holds, exclude from consideration the ace of the suit in which the Blackwood bidder has shown shortness.

The player who makes a jump bid to show shortness and follows with Blackwood should take care not to use this sequence unless his shortness is a void rather than a singleton.

Example:

If opener and responder hold

    (Opener)
    ♠ K Q x x   ♡ A K Q x x x   ◊ A x x   ♣ —
    (Responder)
    ♠ J x x x x x x   ♡ x   ◊ x x   ♣ A J x

an Exclusion Blackwood auction would commence

Opener	Responder
1 ♡	1 ♠
4 ♣	4 ♠
4 Notrump	5 ♣

Opener's jump to four clubs shows a strong raise to four spades with at most a singleton club. Thus, in response to Blackwood, responder suppresses his ace of clubs and the partnership avoids bidding a grand slam without the ace of trump.

RELAY BLACKWOOD

This modification of the Blackwood convention uses relay bids after a satisfactory trump fit has been located, to allow one member of the partnership to disclose first, whether or not he has a singleton, and if he does, its location; second, his possession of key cards (*i.e.*, the four aces and the king of the agreed suit); third, his possession of the queen of the agreed suit; and fourth, his side suit kings, if any. The device is most useful when opener has raised responder's suit to the three level (*e.g.*, as in [A] and [B] below), or has jumped in his own suit after a two-over-one response.

Examples:

	Opener	Responder
[A]	1♣	1♠
	3♠	
[B]	1♡	2♣
	3♣	
[C]	1♡	2♦
	3♡	

When the trump suit has been established by opener's jump, as in auctions [A] and [C], the relay is commenced by responder's bid of the cheapest denomination. In [A], a three notrump bid by responder would start the relay. In [C], opener's suit is deemed the trump suit, and a three spade bid by responder would start the relay.

When the trump suit has been established by opener's raise of responder's minor suit to the three level, the relay is commenced by a four club bid. In such an auction, three-level bids by responder are more useful as exploration of possible notrump contracts.

The first relay by responder asks opener whether he has any side-suit singleton; if he has a singleton, his next bid will identify it; if he has no singleton, his next bid will show how many key cards he has. Opener responds in steps. If he has bid two suits, he may identify his singleton by bidding one of two steps. If, as in [C], opener has bid only one suit, he may have any of three singletons, and hence he has three steps in which to identify a singleton. The first step over the relay says that opener has a singleton in the lower (or lowest) unbid suit. The second step shows a singleton in the higher (or next higher) unbid suit. The third step, if there are three suits not bid by opener, shows a singleton in the highest unbid suit.

If opener has no singleton, he proceeds immediately to show his possession of key cards, using ROMAN KEY CARD BLACKWOOD (RKCB), responses. In steps, RKCB responses show

first step   = 0 or 3
second step = 1 or 4
third step   = 2 or 5, without trump queen
fourth step = 2 or 5, with trump queen

Thus opener's bid of the first step above a step that could have shown a singleton shows that he has no singleton and that he has 0 or 3 key cards.

If opener's response to the first relay has shown a singleton, responder may relay again by making the cheapest bid, excluding the trump suit, above opener's singleton-showing bid. This second relay is Roman Key Card Blackwood.

If opener's key-card-showing bids have not disclosed whether or not he has the queen of the trump suit, responder may conduct another relay — again the cheapest bid other than the trump suit, to ask about the trump queen. If opener does not have the trump queen, he returns to the trump suit. If he does have the trump queen, he makes some other bid. The bid he chooses conveys information about his side suit kings as if he were answering a king-asking relay described below.

The king-asking relay may be initiated by responder immediately after the key-card information has been given. If the key-card response has shown whether or not opener has the queen of trump, the normal relay trigger, *i.e.*, the cheapest non-trump bid, is used. If the key-card answer has shown 0, 1, 3, or 4 key cards, and hence has not said anything about the queen of trump, responder may forgo asking about the trump queen and go directly to king-asking by bidding the second-cheapest non-trump bid.

Opener shows his kings either by natural cue-bidding or by making an artificial king response, *i.e.*, a bid of the trump suit, or notrump, or the suit of a known singleton. The cheapest such artificial bid that he can make denies his possession of any unshown side suit king; the most expensive such bid that he can make shows that opener has two kings; and the middle bid shows that he has the king of the relay suit.

Examples:

Opener	Responder
1 ◊	1 ♡
3 ♡	3 ♠
4 ♣	4 ◊
4 ♠	5 ♣
5 Notrump	

In response to the first relay (3 ♠), opener has shown a singleton in the higher ranking unbid suit, *i.e.,* spades. Opener's four spade bid in answer to the next relay (4 ◊) shows one or four key cards. Responder's five club bid asks about kings; if he had wanted to ask about the heart queen, he would have bid four notrump. Opener's five notrump bid shows two side suit kings. Opener's hand might be

♠ x   ♡ A J x x   ◊ K Q J x x   ♣ K Q x

After kings have been shown, it is possible for the relayer to ask about side suit queens. The answers are given in the same fashion as for kings.

THOMAS FOUR DIAMONDS

The Thomas convention is a four diamond response to an opening bid of one heart or one spade that asks opener how many aces he has. The responses to the four diamond ace-asking bid are:

$$4\heartsuit = 0 \text{ or 3 aces}$$
$$4\spadesuit = 1 \text{ ace}$$
$$4NT = 2 \text{ aces}$$
$$5\clubsuit = 4 \text{ aces}$$

If responder wishes to ask opener how many kings he has, he rebids five clubs (or five diamonds if opener has shown all four aces). Opener shows his kings in response to responder's five-club bid as follows:

$$5\diamondsuit = 0 \text{ or 4 kings}$$
$$5\heartsuit = 1 \text{ king}$$
$$5\spadesuit = 2 \text{ kings}$$
$$5NT = 3 \text{ kings}$$

Following opener's king-showing response, responder may bid six clubs to ask opener to bid a grand slam if he has the queen of his suit.

Example:

(Opener)
♠ A J x x x   ♡ K Q x x   ◇ x   ♣ Q x x
(Responder)
♠ K Q x x   ♡ x   ◇ K Q x x x x   ♣ A x

Opener	Responder
1♠	4◇
4♠	Pass

See UNIVERSAL CLUB SYSTEM. *See also* GERBER.

MODIFIED RESPONSES TO GRAND SLAM FORCE

A grand slam force (GSF) bid asks the partner of the GSF bidder to bid a grand slam if he has two of the three top honors in the agreed trump suit. *See* GRAND SLAM FORCE. Lacking two of the three top honors, the responder may nevertheless be able to give useful information as to his possession of one honor and the length of the suit by making any of the possible bids between the GSF trigger and six of the agreed suit.

Meanings other than the traditional ones may be assigned to the GSF responses. In addition, differentiation may be made between holdings that do not include two of the three top honors. One method would be as follows in response to a five notrump trigger when the agreed suit is spades.

6 ♣ (or first step): ace or king of trump suit

6 ♦ (or second step): queen of trump suit

6 ♥ (or third step): none of top three honors, but extra length in light of previous bidding

6 ♠ (or fourth step): none of the top three honors, and no extra length

6 Notrump (or fifth step): two of the three top honors, no extra length

7 ♣ (or sixth step): two of the three top honors, with extra length

The fifth and sixth steps, which may be called positive steps, may assist the GSF bidder in deciding whether to play the grand slam in a minor suit or in notrump, or in deciding in which of two possible suits to play.

If a bid of five notrump is always used as the trigger for the grand slam force, the full range of the four negative responses will not be available unless spades is the agreed trump suit. If the agreed suit is hearts, three steps are available, and the third and fourth steps would be merged. If the agreed suit is diamonds, the second and third and fourth steps would be merged. If the agreed suit is clubs, all four negative steps would be merged. Other GSF triggers may be used, however, (*e.g.*, a jump to five of the suit above the agreed trump suit, *see* GRAND SLAM FORCE), which would give room for all four negative steps to be used.

Another suggested modification of the GSF responses varies the steps according to which suit has been agreed as trumps.

When the agreed suit is clubs, the responses are
    6♣ = at most one of the three top honors in the trump suit
    6◇ = king and queen, or ace and queen of the trump suit
    7♣ = ace and king of the trump suit

When the agreed suit is diamonds, the responses are
    6♣ = at most the queen of the trump suit
    6◇ = ace or king of the trump suit, no extra length
    6♡ = king and queen, or ace and queen of trump suit
    7♣ = ace and king of the trump suit

When the agreed suit is either hearts or spades, the responses are
    6♣ = at best the queen of the trump suit
    6◇ = ace or king of the trump suit, no extra length
    6♡ = ace or king with extra length
    7♣ = two of the three top honors

These modifications for the minor suit responses would allow a player whose partner has preempted in a minor suit (and whose partner would not preempt without at least one of the two top honors) to use the grand slam force with a holding of three small cards. If a responder, opposite a three diamond opening, held

    ♠ A K Q J x x x   ♡ A   ◇ x x x   ♣ A Q

using these methods he would be able to use the GSF, knowing that his partner would not bid seven without both the ace and the king of his suit.

GRAND SLAM ASKING BID

The Grand Slam Asking Bid, not to be confused with the GRAND SLAM FORCE, q. v., is designed to allow the partnership to play its grand slam in the proper denomination when one hand has a long solid suit but no side entries. After the hand containing the long suit has determined that a grand slam should be played, the asking bid consists of a bid of seven of the suit below his long suit. It asks his partner to bid seven of the long suit if he is void in that suit, or to bid seven notrump if he has one or more cards in the suit. If the opener and responder held the following hands,

(Opener)
♠ A x x x x   ♡ A K x x   ◊ —   ♣ A x x x
(Responder)
♠ x   ♡ x   ◊ A K Q x x x x x x   ♣ x

the auction might go

Opener	Responder
1♠	3◊
3♡	4 Notrump
5♣	7♣
7◊	Pass

The Grand Slam Asking Bid should not be used if the suit below the asker's long suit could also be construed as a possible trump suit. Thus, an auction such as

Opener	Responder
1◊	2♠
3♡	4 Notrump
5♠	7♡

may be dangerously ambiguous unless the partnership has agreed that responder may not jump shift with a two-suited hand (*see* SOLOWAY JUMP SHIFTS).

FIVE NOTRUMP AS CHOICE OF SLAMS

When the partnership has conducted slam exploration and knows that a small slam should be bid, but the player who must bid next remains uncertain as to the best denomination for the slam, it may be possible for him to use a bid of five notrump to ask his partner to select the slam. The five notrump bid may be given this meaning only if it has no other natural or conventional use.

In general, five notrump may be used to request partner to choose the denomination of the slam *except* when

- it is bid directly in response to a notrump opening;
- it is bid by the BLACKWOOD bidder after an ace-asking (or key-card asking) four notrump;
- it is a Blackwood response showing two aces and a void;
- it is a forced signoff after Blackwood has been used;
- it is a conventional response to an ace-asking or key-card asking bid, *e.g.*, CULBERTSON FOUR-FIVE NOTRUMP, or CULWOOD;
- it is the GRAND SLAM FORCE after trumps have been clearly agreed;
- it is used as a cue-bid showing a trump honor, *see*, FOUR NOTRUMP AS TRUMP CUE-BID;
- it is bid by a player who has bid four notrump as a general slam invitation;
- it is part of step responses or otherwise agreed responses to a CONTROL ASKING BID or relay bid.

The five notrump choice-of-slams bid is used only to offer a choice between or among small slams. It never invites a grand slam.

Examples:

[A]	Opener	Responder		[B]	Opener	Responder
	1 ♡	2 ♣			1 ◇	3 ◇ (Limit)
	3 ♣	3 ♡			3 ♠	3 Notrump
	4 ♡	5 Notrump			4 ♣	4 ♡
					4 ♠	5 ◇
					5 Notrump	

[C]	Opener	Responder		[D]	Opener	Responder
	1 ♡	1 ♠			2 Notrump	4 ♣ (GERBER)
	2 Notrump	3 ◇			4 Notrump	5 Notrump
	3 Notrump	5 Notrump				

[E]	Opener	Responder	[F]	Opener	Responder
	1 ♣	1 ♠		1 Notrump	5 Notrump
	3 ♠	5 Notrump			

In auctions A, B, C, and D, the five notrump bid may be used to ask partner to decide in which denomination the slam should be played. In A, five notrump is not needed as the grand slam force since the trump suit is not clearly agreed. Use of five notrump to offer a choice of slams in such an auction is plainly preferable.

In auction B, the choice is between diamonds and notrump. In auction C, the choice is among diamonds, notrump, and spades.

In auction D, opener should bid a strong four-card suit at the six level if he has one. If a fit is found, the suit contract may produce one more trick than a notrump contract.

In auction E, five notrump is not choice-of-slam because it is the grand slam force. In F, the five notrump bid is not choice of slam because, while it forces a small slam, it also invites a grand slam.

FIVE OF TRUMP SUIT AS ASKING BID

When a major suit has been agreed as trumps, the bid of five of that suit may have any of a number of meanings, depending on the preceding auction. In many instances, it does not show interest in slam. For example, over an opponent's sacrifice, the bid may be merely an effort to buy the hand. After the partnership has preempted or the opponents have bid strongly, the bid of five of the trump suit may be a sacrifice, or an advance sacrifice. After a response to BLACKWOOD or after five-level cue-bidding, the five-trump bid may be an effort to sign off.

In many auctions, however, the bid of five of the trump suit is a treatment that asks partner to bid a small slam if he has certain specific controls. The bid sometimes focuses on a side suit and sometimes focuses on the trump suit itself. Several ground rules help to establish the suit on which the five-trump bid focuses.

If the opponents have bid a suit and the partnership has not made a control-showing bid in that suit, the five-trump bid asks partner to bid six of the trump suit if he has first or second round control of the opponents' suit. The control-showing bid may be either a cue-bid or a SPLINTER bid.

In other circumstances, the five-trump bid may focus on an unbid suit. If (a) the opponents have not bid a suit, or if they have bid a suit and the partnership has made a control-showing bid in that suit, and (b) there is only one side suit that the partnership has not bid or cue-bid, the bid of five of the trump suit asks partner to bid six of the trump suit if he has first or second round control of the unbid suit.

Finally, in some auctions, the five-trump bid asks about the quality of the trump suit. If (a) the opponents have not bid a suit, or if they have bid a suit and the partnership has made a cue-bid showing control of that suit, and (b) either there is no unbid side suit or there is more than one unbid side suit, the bid of five of the trump suit asks partner to bid six if he has at least two of the three top trump honors.

Examples:

[A]	Opener	Responder		[B]	Opener	Responder
	1 ♠	3 ♠			1 ♡	3 ♡
	4 ♣	4 ◇			5 ♡	
	5 ♠					

[C]	North	East	South	West
	1 ♣	1 ◇	1 ♠	Pass
	3 ♠	Pass	5 ♠	

[D]	North	East	South	West
	1 ♣	1 ♠	2 ♡	Pass
	3 ♡	Pass	3 ♠	Pass
	5 ♡			

In auction A, the partnership has agreed on spades and has cue-bid clubs and diamonds. Opener's five spade bid asks responder to bid six spades if he has first or second round control of hearts. If responder had cue-bid four hearts instead of four diamonds, indicating that he lacked first round control of diamonds, opener's five spade bid would ask responder to bid six spades with second round control of diamonds.

In auction B, there is more than one unbid side suit, and the opponents have not bid. The five heart bid therefore asks responder to bid six hearts with two of the three top heart honors.

In auction C, the opponents have bid diamonds, and neither opener nor responder has cue-bid the suit to show control. The jump to five spades therefore asks about diamond control. In auction D, however, South has shown a control in the opponent's spade suit by his three spade cue-bid; North's five heart bid therefore asks about control of the only unbid suit, diamonds.

In an auction in which a cue-bid of the opponents' suit does not necessarily show a control, the bid of five of the agreed trump suit asks about control of the opponents' suit. For example, when the bidding has begun

North	East	South	West
2 ♠	Double	Pass	3 ♠
Pass	4 ♡	Pass	5 ♡

West's three spade cue-bid was the only available forcing bid; thus, it did not promise spade control. West's five heart bid therefore asks East to bid six hearts with first or second round control of spades.

Care must also be taken not to confuse auctions in which the five-trump bid asks about side-suit control or trump quality with auctions in which the five-trump bid is needed as a general slam try. For example, when the five-trump bidder's partner has shown a very strong hand, it is unlikely that the five-trump bidder needs only to know about the strong hand's holding in trumps. Thus, in an auction such as

Opener	Responder
2 Notrump	3 ♣ (STAYMAN)
3 ♠	5 ♠

responder's five spade bid is a general slam try rather than a specific focus on the trump suit.

See also LACKWOOD; CONTROL ASKING BIDS; TRUMP QUALITY ASKING BIDS; KANTAR ASKING BIDS.

LACKWOOD

A player interested in slam is often awkwardly placed if there is a side suit in which he has neither first nor second round control. In some auctions, he may bid five of the agreed trump suit to ask about the side suit, *see* FIVE OF TRUMP SUIT AS ASKING BID; under some partnership agreements, he may make an asking bid in the side suit, *see* CONTROL ASKING BIDS. When either of these devices is used, the response will indicate the degree to which the asker's partner has control of the suit, but will not give any other information.

The Lackwood convention is used, after a trump suit has been agreed, by a player who (a) lacks first and second round control of a side suit, and (b) has a hand warranting a slam contract if his partner has no worse than second round control of that suit. The Lackwood bidder asks his partner either to sign off immediately if he too lacks control of the problem suit or to make a forward-going bid if he has control. If the partner of the Lackwood bidder has first round control of the problem suit, he so indicates by showing how many key cards he has.

When and How Lackwood Is Used

The Lackwood inquiry is used in three situations. First, if the opening bid was a preempt, the bid of a new suit at the four or five level is Lackwood, asking about control of that suit. Second, if the opponents have bid one, and only one, suit, a bid of five of the trump suit is Lackwood. Third, if a trump suit has been agreed, the opponents have not bid a suit, and there is one, and only one, unbid suit, a bid of five of the trump suit is Lackwood.

For example:

[A]	*Opener*	*Responder*	[B]	*Opener*	*Responder*
	4 ♢	5 ♣		1 ♠	3 ♠
				4 ♣	4 ♢
				5 ♠	

[C]	*North*	*East*	*South*	*West*
	1 ♣	1 ♢	1 ♠	Pass
	3 ♠	Pass	5 ♠	

In auction A, if the four diamond bid is natural, responder's bid of five clubs establishes diamonds as trumps and asks opener about club control. If the four diamond opening is NAMYATS, showing a preempt in spades, responder's five club bid establishes spades as trumps and asks about club control. In the latter situation, since a response of four hearts to a Namyats four diamond opening would be a relay bid, if responder wishes to use Lackwood to ask about control of hearts, he would respond four notrump.

In auction B, the partnership has bid every suit except hearts; the jump to five spades asks about control of hearts. In auction C, the opponents have bid diamonds; the jump to five spades asks about diamond control.

When the bidding has been opened with a preempt of three hearts or three spades, the partnership must take care to distinguish responder's attempts to make a natural signoff in the other major from his attempt to make a Lackwood bid in the other major. After a three heart opening, four spades is the Lackwood bid. If responder wants to play in four spades, he should bid a standard forcing three spades in response to the preempt; when he follows with four spades, his bid is a signoff. If the opening is three spades, a response of four hearts is a signoff in hearts. In order to use Lackwood for hearts over this opening, responder must jump to five hearts.

The Responses to Lackwood

In response to the Lackwood bid, the Lackwood responder returns to the trump suit if he has neither first nor second round control of the target suit. If he has second round control, he bids six of the trump suit.

If the Lackwood responder has first round control, he caters to the possibility that the partnership may have a grand slam by showing how many key cards (four aces plus the king of trumps) he holds. A void also counts as a key card.

The Lackwood responses are made in steps, with one caveat: the trump suit does not count as a step. The responses, excluding the trump suit, are:

First step   = 3 key cards
Second step = 1 or 4 key cards
Third step   = 2 key cards, without the queen of trumps
Fourth step = 2 key cards, with the queen of trumps

Each step guarantees first round control of the problem suit.

The Lackwood convention is particularly useful after an opening four-level preempt of well-defined strength, *e.g.*, ROMEX NAMYATS; KEY CARD NAMYATS RESPONSES.

KEY CARD FOUR CLUBS AFTER PREEMPTS

When the bidding has been opened with a three-level preempt, responder sometimes has slam interest but needs a way to explore without going past game. In order to permit exploration with safety, some partnerships agree to use a four club bid by responder as a bid asking opener about his key cards.

The Key Card Four Club bid establishes opener's suit as trumps and asks opener to show how many key cards he has. For these purposes key cards include all aces and kings. In addition, since possession of the trump suit queen may be crucial, if opener has at least one key card he will indicate also whether or not he has the queen of his suit.

Since a preemptor should not have more than two key cards, the schedule of opener's responses to four clubs is as follows:

4 ◊	=	no aces or kings
4 ♡	=	one key card, without the trump queen
4 ♠	=	one key card, with the trump queen
4 NT	=	two key cards, without the trump queen
5 ♣	=	two key cards, with the trump queen

Opener's bid of four diamonds does not disclose whether or not he has the queen of his suit.

See also ROTH FOUR CLUB ASKING BID AFTER PREEMPTS; CONTROL ASKING BIDS (Asking Bids over Preempts); GERBER; KEY CARD GERBER.

909

SPIRAL CUE-BIDS

The Spiral Cue-Bid (or "spiral scan") is a device employed by the Romex System in the course of slam exploration. It is used after one member of the partnership has responded to a convention such as ROMAN KEY CARD BLACKWOOD ("RKCB"), ROMAN KEY CARD GERBER, or KICKBACK, disclosing his "key cards," *i.e.*, the four aces and the king of the agreed trump suit. The premise is that the key-card response has revealed that the partnership holds all of the key cards, and the goal is disclosure of certain other cards that may be material to a grand slam.

The spiral scan is most useful when one member of the partnership has described his distribution and his strength with a fair amount of precision. The descriptions may have been given through the early use of relays or other conventional bids. The scan then focuses on honors in that partner's long suits. When neither partner has described his distribution, the scans may still be used, though they may be less effective.

Triggering the Spiral Scan

A player asks his partner to make a spiral scan by making a relay bid immediately after the key-card showing response. The relay is the cheapest bid other than a bid in the trump suit. Examples:

[A] *Opener*   *Responder*
     2 ♦ (FLANNERY)   3 ♠ (game force in spades)
     4 ♣   4 Notrump (RKCB)
     5 ♣   5 ♦

[B] *Opener*   *Responder*
     1 ♠   2 ♦
     2 ♥   3 ♦
     3 ♥   4 ♥
     4 Notrump (RKCB)   5 ♥
     5 ♠

[C] *Opener*   *Responder*
     1 ♠   2 ♣
     2 ♦   2 ♥
     3 ♣   4 ♦ (Kickback)
     4 Notrump   5 ♣

In auctions A and B, the last bid shown initiates a spiral scan. In auction C, responder's five club bid is not a relay since it is the agreed trump suit. In order to ask for a spiral scan in this auction, responder would have to bid five diamonds instead of five clubs.

The Ranking of the Cards To Be Shown By the Spiral Cue-bid

The spiral-scan relay bid requires the player who has shown his key cards to survey his hand and show, bidding by steps, what other potentially important cards he holds. The material cards to be scanned are ranked in importance, and the scanner makes a wholesale cue-bid that guarantees that he has (a) the card shown by that step, and (b) all of the cards that would have been shown by any skipped steps. The spiral cue-bid also denies possession of the card that would have been shown by the next step. Note that, though a bid of the trump suit cannot initiate the spiral scan, the scanner does not bypass the trump suit in making his spiral cue-bid. The trump suit counts as a step.

The scanner's first duty is to recognize whether his key-card showing response has revealed whether or not he has the queen of the agreed trump suit. (For these purposes, as for RKCB purposes, extra trump length may be treated as the equivalent of the queen.) If the Blackwood responder has disclosed whether or not he has the trump queen in showing his key cards, the spiral scan does not involve that card. If, however, the Blackwood responder has bid the first or second RKCB step and thus has not made any representation as to that card, the queen of trumps is the first card as to which disclosure must be made.

The general order of importance of the cards to be scanned is

— queen of trumps (if not already disclosed)
— kings of two specific side suits
— queens of those side suits
— jack of trumps
— jacks of the two side suits

The order of the suits in which the kings, queens, and jacks are to be shown by the scanner depends on the prior auction.

If the scanner has defined his own distribution, the cards to be considered are principally kings and queens in the scanner's side suits. In descending order of importance, they are

1. Queen or extra length in the agreed trump suit (if not yet known)
2. King of scanner's longest side suit
3. King of scanner's next longest side suit
4. Queen of scanner's longest side suit
5. Queen of scanner's next longest side suit
6. Jack of the agreed trump suit
7. Jack of scanner's longest side suit
8. Jack of scanner's next longest side suit

For example, in auction A

[A]   *Opener*   *Responder*
       2 ◇ (Flannery)   3 ♠ (game force in spades)
       4 ♣   4 Notrump (RKCB)
       5 ♣   5 ◇

opener has shown four spades, five hearts, and three or four clubs over responder's game-forcing jump to three spades (*see* MODIFIED FLANNERY RESPONSES). After opener's five club response to Roman Key Card Blackwood, responder's five diamond bid, the cheapest non-trump bid, asks opener to disclose other material cards he may hold. Since opener's five club bid, showing zero or three key cards, said nothing about the queen of trumps, the spiral scan in this auction must focus first on the queen of spades, then on the king of the scanner's longest side suit, *i.e.*, hearts, then on the king of his second longest side suit, *i.e.*, clubs, then on the queen of hearts, then on the queen of clubs.

If opener does not have the queen of spades, the card of primary importance, he bids the first step over the five diamond scanning request, *i.e.*, five hearts. If he does have that card, he bids at least the second step. He scans his hand and if he lacks the second most important card, the king of hearts, he bids five spades, the second step. If he has the king of hearts, he skips the second step and looks to see if he has the third most important card, the king of clubs. If he lacks the king of clubs, he bids five notrump, the third step. If he has the king of clubs, along with the queen of trumps and the king of hearts, he looks to see whether he has the fourth most important card, *i.e.*, the queen of hearts. If he lacks that card, he bids the fourth step; if he has it he skips the fourth step. And so on.

Thus, in auction A, if opener held

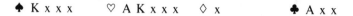

♠ K x x x   ♡ A K x x x   ◇ x   ♣ A x x

he would bid five hearts, the first step because he lacks the queen of trumps.

If he had instead

♠ K Q x x   ♡ A K x x x   ◇ x   ♣ A x x

he would bid five notrump, the third step, showing the queen of trumps
and the king of his longest side suit, but denying the king of his next longest
side suit.

If it is the scanner's partner who has defined his distribution, the side
suit cards to be considered in the scan are the kings and queens in the scanner's partner's side suits. In such an auction, in descending order of importance the scanner would show

    1. Queen or extra length in the agreed trump suit (if not yet known)
    2. King of partner's longest side suit
    3. King of partner's next longest side suit
    4. Queen of partner's longest side suit
    5. Queen of partner's next longest side suit
    6. Jack of the agreed trump suit
    7. Jack of partner's longest side suit
    8. Jack of partner's next longest side suit

If one partner's longest side suit is known but his next longest is not, and
the other partner has bid a suit, the kings and queens of the latter's suit
would be the second suit in focus.

For example, in auction B,

[B]	Opener	Responder
	1 ♠	2 ◇
	2 ♡	3 ◇
	3 ♡	4 ♡
	4 Notrump (RKCB)	5 ♡
	5 ♠	

opener has shown at least five-five in the major suits, and responder's scan
should focus on spades as the principal side suit. Since opener's minor suit
distribution is unknown and responder has shown a suit of his own,
diamonds, responder should focus on diamonds as the second side suit in
which honors are to be shown.

If neither opener nor responder has described his distribution, as in the
auction

[D]

Opener	Responder
1 ♡	3 ♡ (forcing)
4 ♠ (Kickback)	5 ♣
5 ◇	

the cards to be scanned are the unbid suits in descending order of rank.

1. Queen of hearts (trumps) or extra length, if not yet shown
2. King of spades
3. King of diamonds
4. King of clubs
5. Queen of spades
6. Queen of diamonds
7. Queen of clubs
8. Jack of hearts (trumps)
9. Jack of spades
10. Jack of diamonds
11. Jack of clubs

For example, if the partnership hands were

Opener
♠ A x x x x   ♡ K x   ◇ A x   ♣ K Q x x
Responder
♠ K Q x x   ♡ A x x   ◇ K x x   ♣ A x x

the bidding would begin as follows:

[E]

Opener	Responder
1 ♠	3 ♠ (forcing)
4 Notrump	5 ♣
5 ◇	5 ♠

Responder's five club bid shows no key cards or three key cards and does not disclose whether or not he holds the queen of spades. Five diamonds asks for the spiral scan, and since responder holds the queen of trumps, he goes beyond the first step. But on this hand he can bid only the second step, because he lacks the second most important card, the king of hearts.

After hearing any spiral cue-bid response, the relayer may make the cheapest non-trump bid to request a second scan. If the cheapest relay is used, it asks the scanner to resume scanning with the first card that his prior scan did not reach.

For example, in auction E, the five spade bid denied the king of hearts; it said nothing about any less important cards. A five notrump relay would ask responder to begin a new scan with the next most important card, the king of diamonds. If he lacks that card, he bids six clubs, the first step; if he has that card, he looks to see whether he has the next most important card, the king of clubs. If he lacks that card, he bids six diamonds, the second step; if he has that card, he looks to see whether he has the queen of hearts, and so on.

In the Flannery auction A above, suppose opener's response to the scanning request were five hearts, denying the queen of spades:

[A+]	*Opener*	*Responder*
	2 ◇ (FLANNERY)	3 ♠ (game force in spades)
	4 ♣	4 Notrump (RKCB)
	5 ♣	5 ◇
	5 ♡	

If responder held

[1]   ♠ Q J x x x   ♡ A x   ◇ A x   ♣ K Q J x

he would bid five notrump (five spades, the trump suit, would not request a scan), asking opener to show whether he has the most important undisclosed card, *i.e.*, the king of hearts, his longest non-trump suit. Opener might have

♠ A K x x   ♡ K x x x x   ◇ x   ♣ A x x

making the grand slam laydown.

If the relayer has no interest in the first card as to which the scanner has not made disclosure, he may make a "skip-scan" request by skipping to a higher relay (*i.e.*, non-trump) bid. After the five heart spiral cue-bid in auction A+, if responder held

[2]   ♠ Q J x x x   ♡ A   ◇ A x x   ♣ Q x x x

his interest would be not in the king of hearts but in the king of clubs. Thus, he would skip the next relay bid, five notrump, which would ask about the heart king, and bid the next non-trump step, six clubs, to ask about the club king, in order to reach the grand slam if opener holds

♠ A K x x   ♥ x x x x x   ♦ x   ♣ A K x

See also WILFRED CUE-BIDS; SWEEP CUE-BIDS; RELAY BLACKWOOD.

SWEEP CUE-BIDS

The Sweep Cue-Bid convention provides a system for wholesale showing of controls during slam exploration. Principal focus is on side suits, though in some auctions the showing of a side-suit control promises one or more trump honors as well.

Any cue-bid promises "immediate" control of the suit bid. Immediate control means first round control, *i.e.*, the ace or a void, unless first round control has already been shown by one of the partners. In addition, a player who holds the king in a suit that has been bid naturally by his partner is entitled to cue-bid the king as if it were the ace. When first round control has already been shown, immediate control means second round control, *i.e.*, the king or a singleton.

A sweep cue-bid may be a complete sweep or a partial sweep. The complete-sweep cue-bid guarantees immediate control of the suit of the cue-bid plus all of the controls that would have been shown by any intermediate cue-bid. The partial sweep shows control of the suit of the cue-bid plus control of all but one of the intervening side suits. Any sweep cue-bid, whether complete or partial, also denies possession of the card that would have been shown by the next higher cue-bid.

Some cue-bids are not sweeps. Non-sweep cue-bids are made up-the-line. When the cue-bid is not a sweep, it denies a sufficient holding to make any cheaper cue-bid. It neither promises nor denies control of the next higher side suit.

In order to distinguish between complete sweeps, partial sweeps, and non-sweeps, the convention uses certain bids as "waiting bids."

Waiting Bids; Auctions in Which a Cue-Bid May Sweep

Sweep cue-bids are used when the partnership has agreed on a trump suit that contains at least eight cards. Usually the suit agreement has created or occurred in a game-forcing auction. In addition, these cue-bids may be made after responder has made a LIMIT RAISE in opener's major suit or has made an INVERTED MINOR RAISE from one to two. They are also applicable when one partner has made a SHORT SUIT GAME TRY and the other has accepted the invitation.

Typical auctions that provide appropriate foundations for sweep cue-bids include

[A]	*Opener*	*Responder*	[B]	*Opener*	*Responder*
	1 ♡	3 ♡ (limit)		1 ♠	3 ♠ (forcing)

[C]	Opener	Responder		[D]	Opener	Responder
	1 ♣	1 ♡			1 ◇	2 ◇ (inverted)
	3 ♡				3 ♡ (splinter)	

[E]	Opener	Responder		[F]	Opener	Responder
	1 ◇	1 ♠			1 ◇	1 ♡
	2 ♡	3 ♡			2 ♠	3 ♠

[G]	Opener	Responder		[H]	Opener	Responder
	2 ♣	2 ◇			1 ♡	2 Notrump
	2 ♡	3 ♡				(JACOBY)

In all such auctions, sweep cue-bidding would be appropriate.

The convention employs two types of waiting bids. In an auction in which the agreed trump suit is hearts or spades, notrump may be used as a waiting bid. The premise is that once the partnership has located its eight-card or longer major suit fit, it will not play the hand in three notrump. Three notrump cannot, however, be used as a waiting bid if the agreed suit is a minor, as in auction D; in such an auction, it remains a natural bid.

In some auctions, the bid of the trump suit may be a waiting bid. For example, in auction D,

[D]	Opener	Responder
	1 ◇	2 ◇
	3 ♡ (SPLINTER)	

a rebid by responder of four diamonds would be a waiting bid.

A bid of four notrump is also a waiting bid if cue-bidding has begun and has reached the four level. If there has been no cue-bid, four notrump is ROMAN KEY CARD BLACKWOOD. Four notrump would also be Blackwood in the auction

[I]	Opener	Responder
	1 ♠	3 ♠
	4 Notrump	

Complete Sweeps and Partial Sweeps, and the Controls They Show

A complete-sweep cue-bid shows the requisite control of the suit bid plus all intervening controls. Any jump cue-bid is a complete sweep. A jump sweep also promises at least one of the three top honors in the trump suit. It denies a holding sufficient to make the next higher cue-bid.

A non-jump cue-bid that bypasses a waiting bid and does not bypass a suit below the waiting bid is also a complete sweep. For example, in auction B,

[B]	Opener	Responder
	1 ♠	3 ♠

a rebid by opener of three notrump would be a waiting bid. If opener instead bypassed three notrump and bid four clubs, four diamonds, or four hearts, his cue-bid would be a complete sweep cue-bid, promising immediate control of any bypassed side suits and denying sufficient control to make the next higher cue-bid.

A sweep cue-bid may also be made by bidding the trump suit. In auctions E, F, and G, for example, in which opener has shown very strong hands by opening with two clubs, reversing or jump-shifting, responder's raise has set the trump suit in a game-forcing auction; by raising to three, rather than to game, responder asks opener to make a sweep cue-bid. If opener now bids four of the agreed suit, bypassing the three notrump waiting bid, his bid is a sweep. In contrast, in auction A

[A]	Opener	Responder
	1 ♡	3 ♡ (limit)

in which opener has not shown exceptional strength and responder has not invited slam, opener's bid of four hearts would be a signoff.

A cue-bid that bypasses both a waiting bid and the suit just below the waiting bid is a partial sweep. The partial sweep denies immediate control of the suit below the waiting bid. For example, when the auction has begun as in A,

[A]	Opener	Responder
	1 ♡	3 ♡ (limit)

a rebid by opener of four diamonds, bypassing both spades and notrump, would be a partial sweep. It would promise first round control of clubs and diamonds, but would deny control of spades. If opener instead cue-bid four clubs, also a partial sweep, he would deny both first round control of spades (the suit below the waiting bid) and first round control of diamonds (the suit above the cue-bid). Accordingly, in auction A, if opener had a hand such as

♠ A x   ♡ K Q x x x x   ◇ A Q x   ♣ A x

919

his only proper bid would be three spades. A cue-bid of four clubs or four diamonds would be a partial sweep, denying first round control of spades; a bid of four spades would promise second round control of spades (since three spades shows first round control); and four hearts would be a natural signoff.

A cue-bid that does not bypass a waiting bid is not a sweep. It promises immediate control of the suit bid; since non-sweep cue-bids are made up-the-line, such a cue-bid denies immediate control of any bypassed suit and says nothing about any suit not bypassed. Thus, in auction A, a three spade bid by opener, since it would not bypass a waiting bid, would not be a sweep. Since it also would not bypass a side suit, it would say nothing about control of any suit other than spades. In the auction

[J]	Opener	Responder
	1 ♠	3 ♠
	4 ♣	4 ♡

responder's four heart cue-bid similarly is not a sweep because it does not bypass a waiting bid. However, since this four heart cue-bid bypasses four diamonds, it denies first round control of diamonds.

Following a cue-bid, the partner of the cue-bidder must cue-bid in return if he has the necessary immediate control in a suit that can be shown below game. If responder's return cue-bid bypasses a waiting bid, it is a sweep. In the auction

[K]	Opener	Responder
	1 ♣	1 ♡
	2 ♠	3 ♠
	4 ♠	5 ◇

opener's four spade bid, which bypassed three notrump, was a sweep. Responder's five diamond bid, bypassing the four notrump waiting bid, is also a sweep.

When a player bids three notrump as a waiting bid, he indicates insufficient control to cue-bid four clubs. *See also* THREE NOTRUMP MOVING ALONG. In auction K, if opener wanted to initiate cue-bidding but lacked first round control of clubs, he would bid three notrump. The partner of a player who has made a waiting bid is required to cue-bid control of the missing suit if he has it. After a waiting bid, as well as after a cue-bid, if his cue-bid bypasses a waiting bid, it is a sweep.

When hearts is the agreed suit and a three spade bid is available, the use of three notrump as a waiting bid also denies immediate control of spades. In auction A, for example, a bid by opener of three notrump would show control of neither spades nor clubs.

Using Sweep Cue-Bid methods, if opener and responder held

Opener
♠ K J x x x   ♡ A x x   ◇ A J x x   ♣ A
Responder
♠ A Q x x   ♡ K x   ◇ Q x   ♣ x x x x x

they would bid as follows:

[L]

	Opener	Responder
	1♠	3♠ (limit)
	5♣	5♡
	5♠	6♠

Opener's five club jump cue-bid promises first round control of all three side suits, and the ace or king or queen of spades, and second round control of clubs. Responder's five heart bid shows second round control of that suit, opener having shown first round control. Responder's five heart bid denies immediate (here second round) control of diamonds.

See also SPIRAL CUE-BIDS; WILFRED CUE-BIDS.

WILFRED CUE-BIDS

When the trump suit has been agreed and the partners are cue-bidding to assess the prospects for slam, standard methods permit them to show aces and kings in side suits. In such a sequence, the failure to cue-bid a suit usually indicates the absence of the ace or king of that suit. Further, in a standard cue-bidding sequence, a bid of four notrump is ordinarily BLACKWOOD (*but see* D.I.), asking the partner of the four notrump bidder how many aces he has. Using ordinary methods, the partners have no cue-bid available to show the ace or king of the agreed trump suit. *See* FOUR NOTRUMP AS CUE-BID.

Wilfred Cue-Bids allow one member of the partnership to (1) show his trump-suit honors, and (2) show certain combinations of controls by a single bid. The convention is most useful when the partnership has been able to identify the trump suit and establish a game force at a relatively low level of the auction. The cue-bids are used when one of the partners has taken control of the auction, becoming the "captain," and requiring the other partner (the "puppet") to disclose his controls.

Determination of Captaincy

When one of the partners has raised or returned to the other's suit in an auction in which game is forced, the supporting partner becomes the captain. When a player has made a SPLINTER bid in support of his partner's suit, the splinterer yields captaincy of the remaining auction. If the non-splinterer proceeds with a bid other than the trump suit, he assumes captaincy.

Upon one player's assumption of captaincy of the auction, his partner is required to describe his controls. For example:

[A]	*Opener*	*Responder*		[B]	*Opener*	*Responder*
	1 ♠	2 ◇ (game force)			1 ♠	4 ♣ (splinter)
	2 ♡	2 ♠			4 ◇	

In auction A, responder has become captain of the auction by supporting opener's suit in a game-forcing auction. Opener is now required to show his controls. In B, responder has yielded captaincy because of his splinter bid; opener's four diamond cue-bid takes command and requires responder to show his controls.

922

Some of the Wilfred side suit cue-bids are natural, and some are artificial. In order to show a high honor in the trump suit, the convention uses a cue-bid of the denomination just above the trump suit. For example, when diamonds are agreed, a heart cue-bid shows a high trump honor. When spades are the agreed trump suit, the trump cue-bid is notrump. When the agreed trump suit is clubs, diamonds, or hearts, the convention uses a bid in notrump to show a high honor in the suit above the trump suit. Cue-bids in the other side suits are natural.

The meanings of the artificial Wilfred cue-bids are thus as follows:

Agreed Trump Suit	*Artificial Cue-bids*
Clubs	Diamond cue-bid = club honor; notrump bid = diamond control
Diamonds	Heart cue-bid = diamond honor; notrump bid = heart control
Hearts	Spade cue-bid = heart honor notrump bid = spade control
Spades	Notrump bid = spade honor

The controls to be shown by the puppet are normally high cards rather than distributional controls. With respect to side suits, if the puppet has not made a splinter bid, his first cue-bid shows the ace; the second cue-bid shows the king; the third cue-bid shows the queen. If the puppet has splintered, his first cue-bid of his short suit shows a void. These restrictions do not apply to the captain. The captain's first cue-bid of a side suit may be made with either the ace or the king.

When the cue-bid relates to the trump suit, the first cue-bid promises the ace or the king of trumps; the second such cue-bid shows the king or queen of trumps. The Wilfred convention also allows the puppet, in two bids, to show the ace, king, and queen of trumps. If the puppet makes a bid that denies the ability to show the ace or king of trumps, the captain will likely sign off; the puppet then shows a solid trump holding by bidding again over the signoff.

The puppet can deny the requisite trump honor in one of two ways: (1) he bids the trump suit itself, or (2) he makes a side suit cue-bid that does not bypass the trump suit but does bypass the trump cue-bid denomination. For example:

[C]	Opener	Responder	[D]	Opener	Responder
	1 ♠	2 ◇ (game force)		1 ♠	4 ♣ (splinter)
	2 ♡	2 ♠		4 ◇	4 ♠
	2 Notrump	3 ♣			
	3 Notrump				

[E]	Opener	Responder
	1 ♡	3 ♡ (forcing)
	3 Notrump	

In auction C, opener's bid of two notrump shows the ace or king of spades. His bid of three notrump shows a second high spade honor. In auction D, a four spade bid, returning to the trump suit, means that responder has neither the ace nor the king of spades. In auction E, opener's three notrump bid is a cue-bid showing spade control; the bypassing of three spaces shows that opener has neither ace nor-king of hearts.

Wholesale Cue-bids By the Puppet

The Wilfred convention allows the puppet, in some circumstances, to show more than one control with a single bid. This wholesale showing of controls occurs when, following the captain's assumption of control, the puppet makes a cue-bid that bypasses the trump suit. When the puppet makes such a cue-bid, he indicates that his hand contains the requisite controls for the cue-bid actually made and for any bypassed cue-bid. He also indicates that his hand is unsuitable for the next higher cue-bid.

For example, in the auction

[F]	Opener	Responder
	1 ♡	2 ♣ (game force)
	2 ◇	2 ♡
	3 ♠	

opener's cue-bid of three spades, since it bypassed the trump suit, shows all of the controls that would have been shown by lower cue-bids. It shows the ace or king of hearts (which would have been shown by two spades), the ace of spades (which would have been shown by two notrump), the ace of clubs (which would have been shown by three clubs), the ace of diamonds (which would have been shown by three diamonds), and the king or queen of hearts (shown by three spades). The three spade bid denies the ability to cue-bid three notrump to show the king of spades.

In contrast, when the puppet's cue-bid does not bypass the trump suit, his failure to cue-bid an intervening side suit denies possession of the pertinent control of that suit. Thus, in the auction

[G]   *Opener*   *Responder*
                 1 ♠   4 ♣ (SWISS)
                 4 ♡

opener's four heart bid promises the ace of hearts; but since it did not bypass the spade suit it is not a wholesale cue-bid. It indicates that opener lacks the ace of diamonds. Since this cue-bid bypassed neither the trump suit nor the trump cue-bid denomination, it makes no disclosure as to opener's trump suit honors. If the auction were

[H]   *Opener*   *Responder*
                 1 ♠   3 ♠
                 4 ◇

opener's four diamond cue-bid would deny the ace and the king of spades because opener has bypassed notrump, the trump cue-bid denomination. In addition, opener's failure to cue-bid four clubs, since he did not bypass spades, would deny the ace of clubs. Nothing would have been disclosed about his heart holding.

Note that only the puppet may show controls wholesale. The captain's cue-bid of a suit that skips over intervening suits does not promise controls in the intervening suits.

In some auctions, the puppet will eventually have given an obviously complete description of his control of a side suit. For example, if he has splintered and then cue-bid the short suit, he has shown a void; or he may have made cue-bids that promise or deny the ace, king, and queen of a side suit. In these instances, the further cue-bid such a suit would have no natural meaning. The Wilfred convention uses these otherwise meaningless bids to show general pessimism about the hand.

See also SPIRAL CUE-BIDS; SWEEP CUE-BIDS; RELAY BLACKWOOD.

FOUR NOTRUMP AS TRUMP CUE-BID

When a trump suit has been agreed and the partnership is cue-bidding, a bid of four notrump may be assigned any of a number of meanings. It may be Blackwood if the partnership has agreed on a space-saving style that allows a relatively cheap cue-bid in a suit headed by the king to be made before a cue-bid is made in another suit headed by the ace. Or the four notrump bid may simply say, "Tell me more." *See* DI.

It has been suggested that if the partnership agrees that it will always cue-bid suits headed by the ace before cue-bidding suits headed by the king, it may profitably use the four notrump bid for a use other than Blackwood. The use suggested is that the bid of four notrump show either the ace or the king (but not both) of the agreed trump suit. If the partner of the four notrump bidder later bids five notrump, it will promise the other high honor. The four notrump bid would also suggest that the cue-bidding continue.

Example:

Opener	Responder
1♠	3♠
4♣	4♡
4 Notrump	5♣
5♢	5 Notrump
6♠	

Using these methods, opener knows that responder is missing the ace of diamonds. If opener does not have that card, and if over the five diamond bid responder had been unable to bid five notrump to show the other trump honor, opener would content himself with a bid of five spades.

If one player bypasses four notrump in order to cue-bid a suit at the five level, he shows either both the ace and king of trumps or neither. If four notrump is bypassed, a later bid of five notrump by either player shows the queen of trumps.

KANTAR ASKING BIDS

When the partnership knows that it is in the slam zone it may yet need to explore either the quality of its trump suit or the degree to which it can control a side suit. The Kantar method codifies certain bids as trump-asking bids and others as control-asking bids, and prescribes responses for each group.

Trump Asking Bids

In standard bidding, the meaning of a raise to five of the agreed major suit depends on the auction that preceded it. Sometimes it asks about the trump suit; sometimes it asks about a suit bid by the opponents; sometimes it asks about an unbid suit. When the raise to five of the trump suit traditionally has either of the latter two meanings, there is no way to ask specifically about the trump suit quality below the slam level. (Some information may be gained through use of ROMAN KEY CARD BLACKWOOD).

Using the Kantar method, a raise to five of the agreed major suit is always a trump asking bid ("TAB"). If the player who makes the raise to five did not introduce the suit, he denies possession of any of the top honors in the suit, and the partner of the TAB-asker responds as follows. If he has neither the ace nor the king of the suit, he passes. If he has both the ace and the king, he bids the first step above the trump suit. If he has KQJ, KQ10, AQJ, AQ10, or AJ10, he bids two steps above the trump suit. If he has the ace, king, and queen, he jumps to seven clubs. *See also* GRAND SLAM FORCE.

After his partner has bid to show that his trump honors are no worse than AJ10, the TAB-asker may make the next cheapest bid, a relay, asking his partner to show whether he has extra length in the suit. A return to six of the trump suit shows minimum length for the previous bidding; a bid of seven clubs shows maximum length.

Example:

Opener	Responder
1 ◊	1 ♠
2 ♣	3 ♠
5 ♠ (TAB)	5 Notrump (ace and king)
6 ♣ (How long?)	7 ♣ (Longer than promised.)

Opener and responder might have

(Opener)

♠ x x x   ♡ —   ◊ A K x x x   ♣ A K J x x

(Responder)

♠ A K J x x x x   ♡ Q x x   ◊ x x   ♣ x

If responder instead held

♠ Q J 10 x x x x   ♡ A K x   ◊ x   ♣ x x

he would have passed the five spade bid.

If the TAB-asker introduced the agreed major, as in the auction

Opener	*Responder*
1♠	3♠
5♠	

his raise to five does not deny possession of top honors, and his partner responds to the TAB as follows. If he has neither the ace nor the king, he passes unless he has both the queen and the jack. If he has AK, or KJ, or QJ, he bids the first step above the trump suit. If he has the ace and minimum length for his previous bidding, or the king and minimum length, he bids the second step. If he has the ace and extra length or the king and extra length, he bids the third step. If he has KQ or AQ, he bids the fourth step. If he has the ace, king, and queen, he jumps to seven clubs.

If the TAB response was the first step, showing AK, KJ, or QJ, and the TAB-asker is in doubt as to which holding his partner has, he may bid six of a suit in which he cannot wish to play, to ask for clarification. The TAB-responder signs off at six of the agreed major suit if he has QJ or KJ; he bids seven clubs if he has AK.

Side Suit Asking Bids

The Kantar method designates as asking bids ("ABs") each of the following bids in a suit other than that shown by the AB-asker's partner:

> — a jump shift response to a weak two-bid or to a preemptive three-level opening
> — any nonjump change of a suit after partner's opening bid or overcall of four hearts or four spades
> — any jump change of suit at the four or five level when the AB-asker's partner has shown a long suit, in a weak or strong hand

— any nonjump change of suit after partner has shown a very strong suit by bidding four hearts or four spades
— any change of suit after partner has shown a solid suit

In each case the change of suit asks the player who has the long suit to describe his degree of control of the suit his partner has just bid. If the AB-responder has the king of the AB-suit, he bids the cheapest number of notrump. If he does not have the king, he shows his holding by bidding suits in steps:

first step   = two or more quick losers
second step = singleton
third step   = ace
fourth step = singleton ace, or ace and king
fifth step   = void.

The AB-responder must remember, in counting his steps, that a notrump bid shows specifically the king and is not a step.

Example:

Opener	Responder
2♠	4♡
5♣	6♡

Opener shows a singleton heart. The two hands might be

(Opener)
♠ Q J 10 x x x   ♡ x   ◇ K Q x x   ♣ x x
(Responder)
♠ A K x x   ♡ x x x   ◇ —   ♣ A K Q J 10 x

Responder would have passed a bid of four spades if opener had made that bid, showing at least two quick losers in hearts. If opener had shown first-round control of hearts, responder would have bid a grand slam.

DIET TABS

Diet TABs are a streamlined system of responding to Trump Asking Bids (TABs), designed to reduce the amount of space needed for the responder to a TAB to show his trump holding, strength, and key cards. (The five key cards are the four aces and the king of the trump suit.)

Presumably this convention will assist the partnership in reaching good thin slams and gain them their just desserts. Diet is an acronym for "Detailed Itemization Establishing Trumps."

The use of TABS and the precise trigger for a TAB is either a systemic matter, *see, e. g.*, PRECISION TRUMP ASKING BIDS, or a question of partnership understanding, *see, e.g.*, KANTAR ASKING BIDS. Once a TAB has made, the Dietetic responses are made in five steps.

first step: shows a minimum hand; promises either the queen of trumps, or extra length in trumps, or both

second step: shows maximum strength; says nothing about trump length or quality

third step: minimum strength; no queen of trumps and no extra length; shows 0 or 3 key cards

fourth step: minimum strength; no queen of trumps and no extra length; shows 1 or 4 key cards

fifth step: minimum strength; no queen of trumps and no extra length; shows 2 or 5 key cards

After a bid of the first or second step, the TAB-asker may seek further information by means of relay bids, *i.e.*, the TAB-asker's cheapest non-trump bid over the step response. After a response of the first-step, a relay asks about key cards. The responses are by steps as in ROMAN KEY CARD BLACKWOOD.

After a second-step response to the TAB, showing a maximum but giving no other information, the TAB-asker's relay asks about the trump queen and the key cards. The responses are by steps

first step   = queen or extra length in trumps

second step = no queen of trumps and no extra length; 0 or 3 key cards

third step   = no queen of trumps and no extra length; 1 or 4 key cards

fourth step = no queen of trumps and no extra length; 2 or 5 key cards

After a bid of the first step showing the trump queen or extra length, the TAB-asker may once more relay, this time asking about key cards. The responses are

first step   = 0 or 3 key cards
second step = 1 or 4 key cards
third step   = 2 or 5 key cards

Example:

Opener	Responder
1♠	2♣
2 Notrump	3♠ (TAB, by agreement, setting spades as trumps)
4♣	4◇ (asks about trumps)
4♡	4♠ (asks about key cards)
4 Notrump	6♠

Opener and responder might have

(Opener)

♠ A Q x x x   ♡ A J   ◇ Q x x   ♣ A x x

(Responder)

♠ K x x   ♡ K Q x x   ◇ K x   ♣ K Q x x

Opener's four-club bid following the TAB showed that he had maximum strength; his four-heart bid showed that he had the queen of spades or extra length in spades; and his four notrump bid showed 0 or 3 key cards.

V
Competitive Bidding

SUPPORT DOUBLES

Interference by the opponents in the opening side's auction often impedes opener and responder in their efforts to determine their optimum denomination or level. At the same time, if the opening side is willing to give up its ability to make low-level penalty doubles, the intervention provides an otherwise unavailable call with which opener or responder may give differentiated information to the other. The most common example, of course, is the NEGATIVE DOUBLE.

A device used by some partnerships to allow opener to show support for responder's suit notwithstanding an intervening overcall and to differentiate between good and mediocre holdings in the suit is called the Support Double. The Support Double does not seek to penalize the overcaller but merely says that opener wishes to raise responder's suit to the two level with a holding of only three trumps. Using this method, a direct raise to two of responder's suit promises four-card support.

Holding a hand with which he would like to make a penalty double, opener is forced either to bid notrump, or to pass hoping that responder will reopen with a takeout double which opener can pass for penalties.

For example, in the auction

North	East	South	West
1 ◊	Pass	1 ♡	2 ♣
Double			

North's double promises three-card heart support. He might have

♠ A Q x x   ♡ Q x x   ◊ K J x x   ♣ J x

Support doubles are used only if it is possible for opener to bid two of responder's suit. Thus, a double of a jump overcall over the response remains a penalty double. *See also* RENEGATIVE DOUBLES.

Opener's support double is not forcing. With an appropriate hand, responder may pass the double for penalties.

Support Redoubles

The same principles may be applied when opener's right-hand opponent has doubled.

North	East	South	West
1 ♣	Pass	1 ♡	Double
Redouble			

Using support redoubles in such an auction, opener redoubles to show three-card support for responder's suit; his bid of two of the suit would promise four-card support.

So long as a bid of two of responder's suit is available, support doubles and redoubles may also be used over an opponent's cue-bid or notrump overcall; they may be used even if both opponents have bid. For example

North	East	South	West
1 ♣	Pass	1 ♠	1 Notrump
Double			

North	East	South	West
1 ♣	1 ◇	1 ♠	2 ♣
Double			

North	East	South	West
1 ♣	1 ◇	1 ♠	Double
Redouble			

RENEGATIVE DOUBLE

The renegative double is a double by the opening bidder after a suit has been overcalled by his left-hand opponent and has been raised to two or three by his right-hand opponent after responder's NEGATIVE DOUBLE. Using this convention in the auctions

	North	East	South	West
[A]	1◇	1♠ or 2♠	Double	3♠
	Double			
[B]	1◇	1♡	Double	2♡
	Double			
[C]	1◇	1♡	Double	3♡
	Double			

North's double is "renegative."

The renegative double enables opener to show strength while assigning more precise meanings his three- and four-level bids. The meaning of the double varies according to the precision with which the negative double has disclosed responder's length in any unbid major suit and the level at which opener can rebid.

If, as in auction C, the double has disclosed precisely how many cards responder holds in any unbid major and opener cannot support the suit at the two level because of the level of right-hand opponent's bid, the double promises four-card support for responder's suit. The double is invitational to game. If, as in auction B, opener can bid one or both of the unbid major suits at the two level, the double shows strength but denies four cards in any unbid major.

If, as in auction A, responder's negative double has not disclosed his precise length in the unbid major suit, opener's double shows high-card strength and denies four-card support for the unbid major(s). It does, however, suggest that opener has three-card support. With fewer than three cards in responder's major, opener would tend to rebid his own suit, or to make a WESTERN CUE-BID seeking a notrump contract, or to pass, hoping that responder will be able to reopen with a double so that opener can then pass for penalties.

These treatments for the double allow opener to make nonjump bids in order to compete with hands not worth a game invitation, and to make jump raises with hands whose merit lies more in distribution than in high card strength.

Whenever opener has passed the raise of the overcall and responder has precisely disclosed his major suit length, responder will try to reopen with a double in case opener wishes to pass for penalties. If opener has passed and responder has not precisely defined his unbid major suit length responder will reopen with a rebid of his suit if it contains five or more cards, or will otherwise try to reopen with a double.

Suppose opener holds

[D]   ♠ Q J 10 x   ♡ A K   ◊ A K x x x   ♣ x x

In auction [A] above, responder's double of the one spade overcall may be based on a four- or five-card heart suit. Opener has no heart fit but has a strong hand. He passes, hoping responder will reopen with a double so he can pass for penalties.

In auction [B], responder's spade suit must contain exactly four cards. Since opener can bid spades at the two level, he jumps to three spades to invite to game. In this auction a double would deny four spades.

In auction [C], responder's double has the same precise meaning. Since, however, opener cannot bid at the two level, a three spade bid would be merely competitive. Thus, his game invitation must take the form of a Renegative Double.

See also COMPETITIVE DOUBLES.

WESTERN CUE-BIDS

A Western cue-bid is a cue-bid of a suit bid by an opponent to ask about stoppers for play in notrump. In the auction

North	East	South	West
1♣	1♠	2♡	Pass
3♣	Pass	3♠	

South's three spade bid traditionally would show a high card in spades. As a Western cue-bid, it asks North to bid three notrump if he holds a spade stopper. South might have a hand such as

♠ x x x   ♡ A K Q J x   ◊ Q J x   ♣ x x

SPLIMIT RAISES

The traditional use of a jump shift by responder over an opponent's takeout double is to show a weak one-suited hand. "Splimit" bids use these jump shifts instead to show a hand worth 9-11 points with three- or four-card support for opener's suit, and with a singleton or void in the suit bid. The name "splimit" is a combination of "SPLInter," the common term for a singleton-showing bid, and "LIMIT" raise. *See* LIMIT RAISES; MINI-SPLINTERS.

When the partnership has agreed to use splimit raises over an intervening double, a response of two notrump over the double promises a limit raise of opener's suit but denies a side suit singleton. *See* TWO NOTRUMP AS LIMIT RAISE OVER OPPONENT'S TAKEOUT DOUBLE.

If South holds

♠ Q x x   ♡ K x x x   ◊ x   ♣ K x x x x

and the auction has started

North	East	South	West
1♡	Double		

he would bid three diamonds to show 9-11 points in support of hearts, and at most a singleton diamond. In such an auction opener would have a reasonable basis for bidding four hearts with a hand such as

[A]   ♠ K x   ♡ A J x x x   ◊ J x x   ♣ A x x

but would pass with a hand having apparently wasted diamond values:

[B]   ♠ A x   ♡ A J x x x   ◊ K Q x   ♣ x x x

CUE-BID AS RAISE BY RESPONDER

Many partnerships that use LIMIT RAISES of opener's suit to show a hand with 10-12 points prefer not to use such limit bids in competition. Their view is that it is more useful for responder to be able to make a preemptive jump, raising the level of the bidding when he is weaker. Thus, after an overcall over a one-spade opening bid, responder would jump to three spades on a hand such as

♠ J 10 x x x   ♡ x   ◇ K x x   ♣ x x x x

In order to show the hand worth a limit raise after an overcall, responder must make a cue-bid of the suit of the overcall. The cue-bid does not promise any control of the suit overcalled, nor any particular length or shortness. It merely forces opener to bid again. If, after opener's rebid, responder simply makes the cheapest possible bid in opener's suit, he shows a limit raise.

For an analogous convention if the intervention is a takeout double, *see* TWO NOTRUMP AS LIMIT RAISE OVER OPPONENT'S TAKEOUT DOUBLE.

KANTAR CUE-BIDS

Kantar Cue-Bids are designed to help a responder show a three-suited hand of intermediate strength over an opponent's overcall. Using this convention, responder makes a non-jump bid in the opponent's suit to show a singleton or void in that suit, at least four cards in the other three suits, and at least 8-9 points.

In response to the Kantar cue-bid, opener can decide in what denomination to play the hand. If he has a hand with which he would accept a game invitation, he should take care not to make a non-jump rebid. Thus, in the auction

North	East	South	West
1 ♢	1 ♡	2 ♡	Pass
2 ♠	Pass		

North's two spade bid may be passed. If responder has more than the 9 points he has announced, he may bid again.

See also CUE-BID AS RAISE BY RESPONDER; NEGATIVE DOUBLES; SPLINTER RAISES; MICHAELS JUMP CUE-BID BY RESPONDER.

UNUSUAL-OVER-MICHAELS

The UNUSUAL-OVER-UNUSUAL convention is helpful when an opponent has made an UNUSUAL NOTRUMP OVERCALL because it enables responder to show economically either of the suits not promised by the opponent's takeout while indicating whether he is interested in game or is merely competing. The partnership may agree to use similar conventional methods, generically entitled "Unusual-Over-Michaels," after other two-suited takeouts. Since the focus is, in large part, on whether or not responder wishes to force to game, Unusual-Over-Michaels is not applicable, without explicit partnership agreement, if responder is a passed hand.

"Unusual" Over a Cue-Bid that Identifies Both Suits

The partnership may most easily exchange information if the two-suited cue-bid is of the type that precisely identifies both suits, *e.g.*, MICHAELS CUE-BIDS over an opening bid of one club or one diamond, TOP AND BOTTOM CUE-BIDS, and UPPER SUIT TAKEOUTS. The partnership's focus will then be squarely on the other two suits as potentially playable suits: the suit opened, and the unbid suit not promised by the opponent's cue-bid.

Since the opponent's two suits are known, two cue-bids are available. Responder uses one cue-bid to show support for his partner's suit, and the other cue-bid to show length in the other suit not promised by the opponent. Each cue-bid shows enough strength to force to game. Alternatively, the partnership may agree that the cue-bid shows at least the strength of a LIMIT RAISE but not necessarily enough to force to game.

Using Unusual-Over-Michaels, responder makes the cheaper cue-bid to show a good hand with length in the lower of the two potentially playable suits. He uses the more remote cue-bid to show a good hand with length in the higher of the two potentially playable suits. For example, if the opening bid were one diamond and the two diamond cue-bid showed top and bottom, *i.e.*, spades and clubs, responder's bid of two spades, the cheaper cue-bid, would show length in diamonds, the lower of the potentially playable suits; his cue-bid of three clubs would show at least five hearts. If the two diamond cue-bid instead showed hearts and spades, responder's cue-bid of two hearts, the cheaper, would show length in clubs and his cue-bid of two spades would show length in diamonds.

Responder's bid of opener's suit, or of the unbid suit not promised by the opponent, or of notrump, is natural and not forcing. A double promises defensive strength, with length in at least one of the opponent's suits; it suggests defending.

The complete schedule of responder's suit-showing bids when both of the opponent's suits have been identified is as follows:

After an opening bid of one club or one diamond, and a cue-bid promising both major suits:

    2♡ = club suit (or support), game-forcing
    2♠ = diamond suit (or support), game-forcing
    3♣ = club suit (or support), not forcing
    3◇ = diamond suit (or support), not forcing

After 1♡ - 2♡, promising spades and clubs:

    2♠ = diamond suit, game-forcing
    3♣ = heart support, game-forcing
    3◇ = diamond suit, not forcing
    3♡ = heart support, not forcing

After 1♡ - 2♡, promising spades and diamonds:

    2♠ = club suit, game-forcing
    3♣ = club suit, not forcing
    3◇ = heart support, game-forcing
    3♡ = heart support, not forcing

After 1♠ - 2♠, promising hearts and diamonds:

    3♣ = club suit, not forcing
    3◇ = club suit, game-forcing
    3♡ = spade support, game-forcing
    3♠ = spade support, not forcing

After 1♠ - 2♠, promising hearts and clubs:

    3♣ = diamond suit, game-forcing
    3◇ = diamond suit, not forcing
    3♡ = spade support, game-forcing
    3♠ = spade support, not forcing

Over a major suit opening, a Michaels cue-bid shows the other major suit but does not specify which minor suit is held. With only one suit identified, only one cue-bid is available. In order to permit responder to cover all of the possibilities in these circumstances, Unusual-Over-Michaels uses a bid of two notrump artificially.

Some of responder's bids are the same whether the auction has begun 1♠ - 2♠ or 1♡ - 2♡. In both, responder's bids of three of the suit opened show competitive raises; these bids show less than 10 points and are not forcing.

In both auctions, responder's bids of three clubs and three diamonds show hands with a long diamond suit; three clubs is game-forcing, while three diamonds is merely competitive. Over responder's three club bid, opener may rebid his own suit if he has extra length; or he may bid three notrump with a stopper in the opponent's known suit; or he may cue-bid the opponent's suit, suggesting that responder bid three notrump with a stopper. If none of these actions seems appropriate, opener may bid three diamonds as a waiting bid; responder must bid again since his three club bid created a game force.

Responder's bids to show either club length or better than minimum support for opener's suit vary depending on whether the opening was one heart or one spade.

If the bidding has started 1♡ - 2♡, responder bids two spades to show a club suit. He may have either a hand with which he merely wants to compete or a hand worth a force to game. Responder bids two notrump to show a hand worth a limit raise or better in hearts.

The complete schedule of responses after 1♡ - 2♡, in which the opponent has shown spades and an unspecified minor, is:

2♠	=	club suit, either competitive or game-going
2 NT	=	heart support, 10-12 or more points
3♣	=	diamond suit, game-forcing
3◇	=	diamond suit, competitive
3♡	=	heart support, competitive

After responder's two notrump bid, showing heart support, opener rebids three of his suit if he wishes to sign off opposite a limit raise. If responder has better than a limit raise, he will bid on. After any of the other responses, opener's rebid of three of his major suit is constructive, showing no desire to play in responder's minor suit if responder has merely a competitive hand. This rebid over two spades, two notrump, or three diamonds is not forcing.

After responder's bid of two spades, showing clubs, opener bids three clubs if he wants to play there opposite a hand of merely competitive strength. He may bid two notrump if he has the unbid suits stopped and wants to suggest playing in notrump. Or he may bid three diamonds or three spades to show a stopper in that suit, or make a constructive rebid of his own suit. His bids of two notrump and his own suit are invitational but not forcing.

If the bidding has begun 1♠ - 2♠, responder bids two notrump to show a club suit. He may have either competitive or game-forcing strength. In order to show a limit raise or better in spades, responder bids three hearts. Thus, when the opening bid was one spade and the cue-bid has promised hearts and an unspecified minor, responder's rebids are:

2 NT	=	club suit, either competitive or game-going
3♣	=	diamond suit, game-forcing
3◇	=	diamond suit, competitive
3♡	=	spade support, 10-12 or more points
3♠	=	spade support, competitive

After responder's three heart bid, showing at least a limit raise in spades, opener may bid three spades to sign off if he does not want to play in game opposite just a limit raise. If responder has better than a limit raise, he will bid again.

After responder's bid of two notrump, showing clubs, opener bids three clubs if he wants to play there opposite a hand of merely competitive strength. If he has a hand worth a game invitation opposite a merely competitive bid, he may bid three diamonds or three hearts to show a stopper in the suit he bids, or rebid his own suit. Opener's rebid of his suit, though constructive, is not forcing.

See also DEFENSE AGAINST OPPONENTS' TWO-SUITED CALLS.

MICHAELS JUMP CUE-BID BY RESPONDER

Responder's Michaels is a convention designed principally to improve responder's ability, following his partner's one club opening and a one diamond overcall, to show a hand with at least five hearts and at least five spades and enough strength to invite game. The convention uses a jump cue-bid of three diamonds to describe such a hand. A cue-bid of two diamonds retains its ordinary meaning. A jump cue-bid of four diamonds promises a sufficiently good major two-suiter to play in four hearts or four spades opposite a doubleton.

Using Responder's Michaels, responder jumps to three diamonds over the overcall to show five cards in each major and nine or more high card points. He might have

♠ Q J x x x   ♡ A Q x x x   ◇ x x   ♣ x

Responder's jump cue-bid of four diamonds shows a major two-suiter in a hand worth a force to game based more on distribution than on high cards. Each of his suits should be strong enough to play opposite a doubleton. *E.g.*,

♠ Q J 10 9 x   ♡ A 10 9 x x x   ◇ x   ♣ x

After the jump cue-bid of three diamonds, opener bids one of the majors if he has three-card or longer support. If he has a hand worth acceptance of a game invitation, he bids four of the suit; otherwise, he bids three of the suit. Opener's bid of three hearts or three spades is not forcing.

With no fit for a major, opener may rebid three notrump if he has a hand such as

♠ x x   ♡ J x   ◇ A Q x   ♣ A K J 10 x x

When the partnership is using this convention, if responder has five-five in the major suits with 5-8 points, he simply bids one spade over one diamond. Later, if opener has not raised sades and the level of the auction is not inconvenient, responder may rebid hearts. This sequence shows responder's distribution and his less-than-game-invitational strength.

See also SPLINTER RAISES; BERGEN JUMP CUE-BID AS TRANSFER TO THREE NOTRUMP; ANDERSON CUE-BIDS; MANDELL JUMP CUE-BID; DENIAL JUMP CUE-BID.

NEGATIVE FREE BIDS AND POSITIVE DOUBLES

In order to increase responder's ability to show a good suit after an opponent's overcall, some partnerships have agreed that a free bid by responder does not promise the standard minimum of 11 or 12 points. Because these free bids may be made on weaker hands, they do not force opener to bid again. They are called "negative" free bids in recognition of their nonforcing nature; they are, however, intended to be constructive bids, showing good suits.

For example, in the auction

North	East	South	West
1 ◊	1 ♠	2 ♡	Pass

South might have a hand such as

♠ xx   ♡ KQxxxx   ◊ Qxx   ♣ xx

All strong actions by responder are commenced by doubling. The double does not promise or deny any particular shape, but it does commit the partnership to game.

After responder's negative free bid, opener may bid on if he has a fitting hand, or he may pass. In the above auction, North might have

[A]   ♠ xxxx   ♡ Ax   ◊ AKxxx   ♣ KQ

or [B]   ♠ xxxx   ♡ Jx   ◊ AKxx   ♣ KQx

With hand [A], opener would raise to three hearts, knowing that although responder's hand is weak, his suit is good. Responder, having a useful doubleton in spades and the queen of opener's suit would bid four hearts. With hand [B], opener would pass the nonforcing two heart bid, but would be willing to compete to three hearts over further bids by the opponents.

CAPP OVER OPPONENT'S DOUBLE OF
MAJOR SUIT OPENING

The Cappelletti convention over an opponent's double of an opening bid of one heart or one spade (sometimes called "CAPP/1MX" for short) permits responder to compete effectively with hands containing two cards in opener's suit. The convention centers on the artificial use of a one notrump response.

After the auction has begun

North	East	South	West
1♡ or 1♠	Double		

South's responses are given the following meanings:

1NT: transfers to two clubs; promises either a good six-card or longer club suit, or a doubleton in opener's major with 7-9 points

2♣: transfers to two diamonds; promises a good diamond suit with less than 10 points

2◇: shows a balanced hand with 7-9 points and three cards in opener's major

After the one notrump response and a two club rebid by opener, responder will pass with the long-club hand. If opener has a hand such as

♠ x x   ♡ A K J x x x   ◇ A x x x   ♣ x

he should not accept the transfer to two clubs but should rebid his suit.

After a two club rebid by opener, if responder bids two of opener's suit he shows two-card support and 7-9 points. If responder instead bids two diamonds over two clubs, he again shows a doubleton in opener's suit and 7-9 points, but he also shows that he has a five-card diamond suit. If the opening bid was one spade, and responder rebids two hearts in the auction

North	East	South	West
1♠	Double	1 Notrump	Pass
2♣	Pass	2♡	

responder shows a five-card heart suit, a doubleton spade, and 7-9 points.

The use of the 1NT and two club bids as transfers allows opener to choose between responder's promised five-card suit and his own, knowing that responder has two-card support for the latter. The transfers gain a further advantage in that if the final contract is in clubs or diamonds, opener will be declarer and the doubler will be the opening leader.

Using the CAPP/1MX convention, responder's direct raises of opener's suit have the following meanings:

raise to two = 4-6 points

raise to three = preemptive, premised on distribution rather than high-card strength; promises four-card support for opener's major

jump to two notrump = a LIMIT RAISE or better.

See TWO NOTRUMP AS LIMIT RAISE OVER DOUBLE. A jump to three of a minor suit may be used to show a hand worth 7-9 points with four cards in opener's suit, length in the minor suit bid, and a singleton elsewhere. Such an agreement would permit the partnership to limit the scope of the jump to three of a major. *See also* SPLIMIT RAISES.

OSTOT: TRANSFERS OVER OPPONENT'S TAKEOUT DOUBLE

When one member of the partnership has opened the bidding and the next player has made a takeout double, responder sometimes has difficulty in bidding when he has a hand worth a game invitation and a long suit that ranks lower than the suit opened. If he merely bids two of his suit, which is not forcing, the bidding may be passed out. If he redoubles to show a reasonable hand, the auction may have proceeded to an uncomfortably high level by his next turn to bid.

A convention called OSTOT (a pseudo-acronym for *O*ne of a *S*uit — *T*ake*O*ut double — *T*ransfers) is designed for use over a takeout double when responder's long suit ranks lower than opener's suit. Over the double, one-level responses in a suit remain natural and forcing, but responses of one notrump and two-level non-jump responses in a new suit are transfers. The response of one notrump transfers to clubs; a non-jump response of two of any new suit promises the next higher suit.

A response in two of the suit below the suit bid by opener, (*e.g.*, 1 ♠ - Double - 2 ♡) transfers to opener's suit and promises a hand worth a single raise, including some defensive strength. With a hand worth a raise but without defense, responder raises opener's suit by bidding it naturally (*e.g.*, 1 ♠ - Double - 2 ♠). This bifurcated way of raising opener's suit to the two level may be used regardless of what suit is opened.

For example, if the bidding has been opened with one heart, responder's OSTOT bids over a takeout double would have the following meanings:

1 ♠	=	natural and forcing
1 NT	=	transfer to clubs
2 ♣	=	transfer to diamonds
2 ◇	=	transfer to hearts, with defensive values
2 ♡	=	natural and not forcing, without defensive values

Use of transfer responses permits responder to show his suit immediately over the takeout double without fear of having opener pass. Over opener's acceptance of the transfer, responder will pass if he has a weak hand but will bid again with a stronger hand.

Opener should presume that responder has a weak hand and should usually bid two of the suit shown by the transfer. He need not always do so, however. He may jump in responder's suit with a fit. This jump is preemptive; responder will bid again if he has a game-invitational hand. Or opener may rebid his own suit if it is long and strong and he has a void or singleton in responder's suit; with a ragged suit, however, it is usually more prudent to accept the transfer even with extreme shortness in responder's suit. If opener has a two-suiter, he may rebid his second suit; unless this new-suit bid is a reverse or a jump-shift, it is not forcing.

See also CAPP OVER OPPONENT'S DOUBLE OF MAJOR SUIT OPENING; TRANSFER RESPONSES.

PARKING LOT REDOUBLES

The Parking Lot Redouble is a convention that permits the partner of the opening bidder or overcaller to take temporary control of the auction, over an opponent's takeout double, in order to convey a precise bit of information about his hand. The only initial message of the redouble is that the redoubler believes he has an important fact to describe.

The availability of the redouble facilitates distinctions between raises made with weak trump holdings and those made with support headed by the ace or king. It also facilitates lead-directing bids in other suits when the support is weak.

The Redouble and Rebids

The redouble requires opener/overcaller, assuming the next hand passes, to make the cheapest possible bid. Thereafter, his partner, referred to here as the "advancer," clarifies his hand. Examples:

[A]	North	East	Advancer	West
	1 ♡	Double	Redouble	Pass

[B]	North	East	South	Advancer
	1 ◇	1 ♠	Double	Redouble
	1 Notrump			

In auction A, the Parking Lot redouble forces the opener to bid one spade, permitting advancer to describe his hand. In auction B, the redouble does not force the overcaller to bid once North has rebid; the advancer is assured of another turn. In both auctions, advancer's next bid will indicate the nature of his hand.

After the redouble, the advancer's bid of notrump or a new suit is natural and suggests a final resting place. Neither rebid is forcing.

Advancer's return to his partner's suit is a non-forcing raise with none of the three top honors in the suit. Raises that promise high honors in his partner's suit are made by a variety of calls without an initial redouble.

Advancer's Actions Other Than Redouble

In the Parking Lot convention, all of the advancer's bids other than redouble are given new meanings. Virtually all of them promise support for his partner's suit.

The advancer's immediate bid of any suit other than his partner's is forcing and lead-directing. The bid may be in a new suit or in the opponent's suit; it may be a jump or a non-jump. Whatever the suit and whatever the level, it promises support for his partner's suit and suggests that partner lead the suit bid by the advancer. The lead-directing bid may prove invaluable if opener/overcaller is on lead against the final contract and his suit is broken, *e.g.*, A Q 10 x x rather than semi-solid, *e.g.*, K Q J 10 x. The new-suit bid may be a jump if advancer wishes to preempt while he makes his lead-directing, support-showing bid.

Advancer's immediate bid of notrump, whether jump or non-jump, is also a raise of his partner's suit. A jump to two notrump shows a hand worth at least a limit raise. Any other bid of notrump shows support for partner's suit headed by the queen. Note that if the advancer wishes to suggest notrump as a final contract, he must begin by redoubling.

Advancer's immediate natural raise of his partner's suit promises the ace or the king of the suit. The raise may be a jump or a non-jump; neither is forcing. In order to make a raise without any of the top three honors in partner's suit, advancer redoubles and then raises.

In summary, the advancer shows the quality of his support for his partner's suit as follows:

Headed by the ace or king: immediate natural raise
Headed by the queen: immediate notrump bid other than a jump to two notrump
None of the three top honors: redouble, then raise
9-11 points with any support: immediate jump to 2 NT

See also ROSENKRANZ DOUBLE.

952

NEGATIVE DOUBLE AFTER ONE NOTRUMP OPENING

When an opponent has overcalled opener's one notrump opening and the opening side is using a LEBENSOHL-type convention, in which a bid of two notrump by responder forces opener to bid three clubs, responder has no natural means of bidding a competitive two notrump.

A solution to his problem is to use the NEGATIVE DOUBLE as a competitive device over the overcall. This double does not signify an offer to penalize the overcaller, but merely promises a balanced hand with 7-8 HCP. Opener may pass for penalties if he has a particularly strong holding in overcaller's suit. More frequently, he will bid over the double. Opener and responder may bid their suits naturally until a fit is located.

Example:

(North)
♠ KQxx   ♡ Ax   ◇ KQxx   ♣ Kxx
(South)
♠ xx   ♡ Jxx   ◇ Axxx   ♣ Qxxx

If there is a two heart overcall, the auction might go as follows:

North	East	South	West
1 Notrump	2♡	Double	Pass
2♠	Pass	3♣	Pass
3◇	Pass	Pass	Pass

JACOBY TRANSFERS OVER OPPONENT'S OVERCALL

JACOBY TRANSFERS are commonly used in response to a one notrump opening bid when there has been no intervening bid. Many partnerships use similar transfers after an opponent has overcalled two hearts or two spades. Transfers enable responder to sign off cheaply if he has a weak hand or to explore for slam with a good hand.

Under this extension of the Jacoby Transfer convention, a two spade bid by responder after a two heart overcall is a natural signoff, showing spades. His other bids are transfers. Calls of two notrump and three clubs transfer to clubs and diamonds, respectively. A bid of three diamonds transfers to the unbid major suit. The complete schedule of responder's bids is as follows:

2 ♠ (over heart overcall) = spades, weak
2 NT = transfer to clubs, strength unspecified
3 ♣ = transfer to diamonds, strength unspecified
3 ◊ (over heart overcall) = transfer to spades, invitational or strong
3 ◊ (over spade overcall) = transfer to hearts, weak or strong
3 of opponent's major = Stayman
3 of unbid major = both minor suits, with slam interest

Responder's double of the overcall is negative, but he shows a balanced hand that is suited to defense. He should have three or four cards in the other major. The cue-bid of the opponent's suit, which strongly suggests that responder has four cards in the other major, also suggests that responder has a singleton or void in the overcalled suit.

If responder has transferred with a weak or invitational hand, he will pass opener's bid of the anchor suit. If he has a strong hand, he will bid again. If the overcall was two hearts and responder has bid three diamonds, showing at least an invitational hand in spades, opener should make a bid other than three spades if he wants to accept the invitation.

If the overcall was two spades, and the above schedule of responses has been adopted, responder will have no way of making a game invitation in hearts. Accordingly, the partnership may decide to use responder's three heart bid to show an invitational hand in hearts, rather than a strong minor two-suiter.

See also LEBENSOHL; LEBENSOHL WITH TRANSFERS; TRANSFER RESPONSES TO NOTRUMP OVERCALLS; TRANSFERS OVER DOUBLE OF ONE NOTRUMP OVERCALL; ONE NOTRUMP OPENER'S REBID AFTER TRANSFER TO CLUBS.

STOPPER-SHOWING PASSES

When a STAYMAN two club bid is doubled to direct a lead, the partnership should have a way, if it fails to locate a major suit fit, to communicate whether the club suit is sufficiently stopped for play in notrump. One method uses a pass to promise a stopper and immediate calls other than redouble to deny a stopper.

If opener has four or five good clubs, he may redouble. His redouble denies a four-card major. With clubs at least as good as Q x x but not strong enough for a redouble, opener must pass. His pass does not disclose whether or not he has a four-card major. Following the pass, responder may redouble in order to ask opener to bid a four-card major if he has one. The auction may then proceed as if there had been no interference.

If his club holding is weaker than Q x x , opener bids immediately over the double of two clubs. His bid is the response he would have made to the Stayman inquiry without interference.

See also LEAD REDIRECTING REDOUBLES.

LEAD REDIRECTING REDOUBLES

When the partnership methods include conventions such as JACOBY TRANSFER BIDS, TEXAS TRANSFER BIDS, and STAYMAN over its opening notrumps, or artificial openings such as NAMYATS, use of the convention gives an opponent an opportunity to make a LEAD DIRECTING DOUBLE of the artificial bid. The partnership may agree on a system of coping with these doubles that on many hands can, if it seems advisable, place the doubler on opening lead.

After the Double of a Jacoby Transfer Bid

The lead redirecting redouble is most easily used when the opponent has doubled a transfer bid, for there is no doubt as to the identity of responder's suit (the "anchor" suit). Under standard methods, a redouble of the double of a Jacoby transfer bid would suggest that the hand be played in the artificial suit. The Redirecting Redouble suggests instead that opener has a holding in the artificial suit that needs no protection, *e.g.*, x x x or A x x, and that the hand should be played in responder's suit with responder as declarer.

The redouble thus implies a fit and asks responder to bid the anchor suit. If he would have passed opener's two-level acceptance of the transfer, responder simply bids his suit at the two level. This two-level bid is not forcing. If responder would have invited game in his suit, he invites over the redouble by bidding three of the suit. If he would have bid game, he bids four of the suit.

If responder has a game-going hand with slam interest, he may cue-bid. If opener too has interest in slam, he may cue-bid in return; if he lacks slam interest, he should bid notrump in order to allow responder to make the first bid in the anchor suit and become the declarer. This notrump bid is not a suggestion that the hand be played in notrump since opener has already suggested, by redoubling, that the hand be played in responder's suit.

If opener has a holding in the artificial suit that he wishes to protect, such as K J x , and has at least three cards in responder's suit, he may accept the transfer by bidding responder's suit over the double. If opener has neither a fit for responder's suit nor a tenace position in the artificial suit, he may pass. The pass is forcing.

The pass asks responder to redouble if he would have been able to pass a standard penalty redouble; if responder cannot redouble, he should make his normal bid. If responder does redouble, opener remains free to bid if he has a hand that is not suitable for playing in the artificial suit.

After the Double of a Texas Transfer Bid

When an opponent has doubled a Texas transfer bid, similar methods may be adopted. Opener should redouble if he has a good fit for responder's suit and no holding in the doubled suit that he needs to protect. He should bid four of responder's suit if he has a holding in the doubled suit that does need protection.

If opener has neither a vulnerable holding in the doubled suit nor a particularly good fit for responder's suit, he should pass. Responder will normally bid his suit. If, however, responder has shortness rather than tenaces in the doubled suit, he may redouble to force opener to bid the anchor suit.

After the Double of a Stayman Bid

After an opponent has doubled a Stayman two club bid, it is less easy to redirect the lead since responder's major suit, if he has only one, is not identified. Nonetheless, the lead may be redirected on many hands if the following precise meanings are given to opener's pass and redouble and his other rebids are redefined.

Opener's pass, which is forcing, asks responder to redouble if he has a hand with which he would have passed a penalty redouble. The pass does not disclose whether or not opener has a four-card major. If responder would not have passed a penalty redouble, he makes whatever bid he would have made if opener had made a standard redouble.

Opener's redouble is similar to a COOPERATIVE DOUBLE. Responder is encouraged to pass if he has length in clubs; without such length, responder should bid. Opener's redouble denies a four-card major.

Opener's rebid of two diamonds promises four hearts; it does not deny four spades. Over two diamonds, if responder has four hearts, he may bid hearts and become the declarer. He bids hearts at the level to which he would have raised if opener had made a natural two heart rebid in an unobstructed auction. Thus, he bids three hearts to invite game, or four hearts to play in game; if he would have passed a natural two heart bid by opener, he simply bids two hearts to sign off.

Opener's rebid of two hearts denies four hearts and shows four spades. Again, if responder has four spades, he bids spades at the same level at which he would have bid them if opener had made a natural two spade rebid in an auction with no double.

Opener's rebid of two spades is a catchall bid that denies a four-card major and denies a sufficient club holding to warrant either a cooperative redouble or a pass suggesting that responder redouble.

Lead redirecting redoubles and passes may also be used when the opening bid is a Namyats four clubs, showing a preempt in hearts, or four diamonds, showing a preempt in spades. After the opponent's double, responder bids four of the anchor suit if he has a tenace, *e.g.*, A Q or K x, in the suit doubled. Without such a tenace, responder either passes or redoubles.

The redouble shows a reasonable hand and allows opener to become the declarer. Both responder's immediate bid of the anchor suit and his redouble suggest a willingness to continue to the five level if the opponents bid, but they do not show interest in slam. In order to show interest in slam, responder must bid the suit between the suit opened and the suit promised, *i.e.*, four diamonds if the opening was four clubs, or four hearts if the opening was four diamonds.

If responder has a hand with which he is interested neither in slam nor in competing at the five level, he passes the double. Over the pass, opener normally bids his suit. If, however, he is short in the suit opened and would be content to have that suit led through his hand, he may redouble to force responder to bid the anchor suit.

See also STOPPER-SHOWING PASSES.

BERGEN OVER DOUBLES OF ONE NOTRUMP

The Bergen method for dealing with an opponent's double of a one notrump opening bid is designed to permit the partnership to reach its most appropriate contract after a competitive type of double, such as BROZEL, and to escape cheaply after a penalty double.

Defense Against Competitive Doubles

If the opponent's double promises competitive values, *i.e.*, one or two long suits rather than a wealth of high cards, the Bergen convention retains the partnership's normal methods of responding. Thus, whether the partnership had agreed to use natural responses, or TWO-WAY STAYMAN, or JACOBY TRANSFERS, or any other convention, responder's bids would remain the same as if there had been no double.

Using the Bergen convention, the partnership may define the redouble of a competitive double in any of a number of ways. It may agree that responder will redouble to show at least 6-7 HCP and a balanced hand. This double would suggest that opener has a good chance of making one notrump doubled if the opponents pass, and that the partnership should consider doubling the opponents for penalties if they bid. This use of the redouble should commit the partnership to buying the contract or doubling the opponents. Thus, in auctions such as

[A]	*North*	*East*	*South*	*West*
	1 Notrump	Double	Redouble	2 ♣
	Pass	Pass	?	

[B]	*North*	*East*	*South*	*West*
	1 Notrump	Double	Redouble	2 ♣
	Pass	2 ♡	Pass	Pass
	?			

the partnership must either double or bid again. In auction A, opener's pass of two clubs is forcing; in auction B, responder's pass of two hearts is forcing.

As an alternative to the penalty redouble, the partnership could agree to use the redouble of a competitive double in a way that describes a hand that it cannot easily describe using its ordinary methods. It might agree, for example, that the redouble shows a weak hand with both minor suits. Or it might agree that the redouble shows a 6-7 point hand with a singleton or void in one of the major suits.

When the opponent's double does not expressly promise one or two long suits, over which the doubler's partner is expected to bid, but instead expressly seeks to penalize the opening side, the Bergen convention uses a number of calls for artificial escape routes. Using these methods, responder can show one-suited or two-suited hands and can indicate whether he has a very weak or a game-invitational hand.

If responder has a weak hand with long spades, he bids two spades. This bid is not invitational. Opener is required to pass.

If responder has a weak hand with any other long suit, or if he has a one-suited hand that is worth a game invitation, he begins by redoubling. The redouble forces opener to bid two clubs. If responder has a weak hand, he passes if clubs is his suit, or he rebids two of his suit. His bid of two diamonds or two hearts after he has redoubled is neither forcing nor invitational. Opener is required to pass. If, instead, responder has a hand worth a game invitation, after opener has bid two clubs responder bids two spades if that is his suit or, if he has a different suit, he bids his suit at the three level. Thus, if responder had a hand such as

♠ x x x   ♡ K Q x x x   ◊ K x x   ♣ x x

the auction might begin

North	East	South	West
1 Notrump	Double	Redouble	Pass
2 ♣	Pass or 2 ♠	3 ♡	

If responder has a hand that is weak defensively but has a six-card or longer suit, he may jump to three of his suit directly over the double. Thus, he would jump to three hearts with

♠ x x x   ♡ K J x x x x   ◊ x   ♣ x x x

If responder has a two-suited hand, he bids the cheaper of his suits at the two level directly over the penalty double. Thus, his response of two clubs shows clubs and any other suit; his response of two diamonds shows diamonds and either hearts or spades; and his response of two hearts shows both major suits.

The complete schedule of responder's calls after a penalty double is

Redouble = relay, forcing opener to bid 2 ♣
2 ♣ = clubs and an unspecified second suit
2 ◇ = diamonds and a major suit
2 ♡ = hearts and spades
2 ♠ = spades, signoff
3 ♣ = clubs, preemptive
3 ◇ = diamonds, preemptive
3 ♡ = hearts, preemptive
3 ♠ = spades, preemptive

After responder has shown a two-suiter by bidding two clubs, two diamonds, or two hearts, opener may pass if he has a fit for the suit responder has bid; if he has an especially good fit, he may raise. Without a fit for responder's cheaper suit, opener bids the next higher suit to allow responder to pass if that is his suit or to bid again. If responder's first bid is doubled, a redouble by opener asks responder to bid his other suit.

See also TRANSFERS OVER DOUBLES OF ONE NOTRUMP; REDOUBLES FOR TAKEOUT OVER ONE NOTRUMP DOUBLED.

RAISE AS TAKEOUT OVER NOTRUMP OVERCALL

When the partnership is using five-card major suit openings and the bidding has been opened with one club or one diamond, responder is often at a loss to know how to compete effectively over an intervening overcall of one notrump. Using standard methods, a double is for penalties, and any bid in a new suit shows a five-card or longer suit.

An effective device to increase responder's ability to compete is to allow him to use the raise to two of opener's minor not as a natural bid but as a takeout call for the other suits. For example, if South holds

$$\spadesuit \text{ K J x x} \qquad \heartsuit \text{ K x x x} \qquad \diamond \text{ Q x x} \qquad \clubsuit \text{ x x}$$

and the bidding has started

North	East	South	West
1♣ or 1◇	1 Notrump	?	

South's most effective means of competing will be to bid two of opener's minor to ask opener to bid a four-card major.

Use of this convention means that responder cannot make a natural raise to two of opener's minor suit. However, this seems a small price to pay since such a raise would have little preemptive effect. *See also* STAYMAN OVER OPPONENT'S NOTRUMP OVERCALL.

JUMP OVERCALLS

Using traditional methods, a jump overcall, *i.e.*, an overcall at a level one higher than necessary, shows a strong hand. Normally the overcaller would have at least six or seven cards in the suit of the overcall and about 15-17 HCP. A hand worth a strong jump overcall in spades would be

♠ A Q J 10 x x   ♡ A x   ◇ A Q x   ♣ x x

The partner of the jump overcaller normally should strain to bid with even a smattering of high cards. He should prefer to raise overcaller's suit if it is a major or try to bid notrump if overcaller has bid a minor. New suit bids by overcaller's partner are forcing.

The frequency with which such a hand arises after right-hand opponent has opened the bidding is low, however, and experts today prefer to use the jump overcall for different purposes. Some use it to show a two-suited hand. *See, e.g.*, ROMAN JUMP OVERCALLS. Others use what are termed intermediate jump overcalls, promising a good six-card suit and a hand of approxmiately opening strength, *e.g.*,

♠ K Q J x x x   ♡ A x x   ◇ K x   ♣ x x

Most commonly, however, the jump overcall is currently used as a weak, natural, one-suited hand.

Weak Jump Overcall

The weak jump overcall is intended to preempt the opponents. The bid should be based on a six- or seven-card suit in a hand of about 5-10 HCP. Most of the high cards should be concentrated in the long suit. The level of the preempt should be governed by the vulnerability and the playing strength of the hand. Not vulnerable, the preempt should be made at a level at which the overcaller is within three tricks of his contract; if vulnerable, overcaller should have within two tricks of his contract. For example, a player who holds

♠ K Q J 9 x x x   ♡ x x   ◇ x x x   ♣ x

could jump to three spades over an opponent's bid if he were not vulnerable; he should bid only two spades if vulnerable.

Overcaller's partner (the "advancer") should take into account the criteria for the weak jump overcall in determining what action he should take. He may raise preemptively if he has a few cards in the suit of the overcall and has little defensive strength. In considering whether to double for penalties, the advancer should not count on his partner for any defensive tricks.

As an aid to constructive bidding by advancer after a preemptive jump overcall, some partnerships have agreed that after such an overcall at the two level, a two notrump bid by advancer is forcing. Over this, Ogust-style rebids may be used. *See* OGUST REBIDS AFTER WEAK JUMP OVERCALLS.

If a weak jump overcall at the two level has been doubled, the advancer may, if the partnership has so agreed, use a two notrump bid to initiate an escape from the overcaller's suit. *See* EXTENDED LEBENSOHL.

ANDERSON CUE-BIDS

The Anderson cue-bid is a nonjump, or single-jump, or double-jump cue-bid by the player to the left of the opening bidder, to show a hand with one long suit, usually headed by the AKQ or AKJ. These cue-bids are made only directly over the opening bid. If the player to the right of opener wishes to show a long strong suit, he may only bid his suit naturally. Likewise, if the player to opener's left lacks the required suit texture or length, he may only bid his suit naturally. *See* WEAK JUMP OVERCALLS.

The principal goal of the Anderson cue-bid is to allow a three notrump contract to be reached when the cue-bidder has a solid or semi-solid suit and the cue-bidder's partner has stoppers in three suits, and to make cue-bidder's partner the declarer.

The nonjump cue-bid (*e.g.*, 1♠ - 2♠) promises a six- or seven-card suit headed by at least the ace, king, and jack, and shows no outside strength, *e.g.*,

$$\spadesuit \, xx \qquad \heartsuit \, xx \qquad \diamondsuit \, xx \qquad \clubsuit \, AKQxxxx$$

or ♠ x   ♡ AKQxxx   ◊ xx   ♣ xxxx

Facing the nonjump or single-jump cue-bid, the cue-bidder's partner knows that any suit in which he holds the ace, or the king, or both the queen and jack is not his partner's long suit. If he has good stoppers in three suits, he may bid three notrump. If the cue-bidder's partner has two suits unstopped, he bids the suit above the cue-bid to allow the cue-bidder to pass if that is his suit or to correct to his long suit.

A double-jump cue-bid (*e.g.* 1◊ - 4◊) promises an eight-card major suit and a hand containing 1½ to 2 defensive tricks. Since the partnership cannot play in three notrump, the quality of the cue-bidder's suit is less important, and the suit may be headed by any two of the top three honors. An appropriate hand for a jump to four diamonds over one diamond would be

♠ AKxxxxxx   ♡ x   ◊ xx   ♣ Kx

Lacking the requisite defensive holding, the player to the left of the opener should simply jump in his suit. For example, holding

♠ x   ♡ KQJxxxxx   ◊ Qx   ♣ xx

the player to the left of opener would jump to four hearts.

OGUST REBIDS AFTER WEAK JUMP OVERCALLS

After a weak jump overcall at the two level, the partner of the overcaller may have a hand with which game would be a reasonable prospect if overcaller has a good suit or maximum strength. Some partnerships treat a two notrump bid by the overcaller's partner as a forcing bid, requiring overcaller to describe his hand further using an Ogust-type schedule of responses, *e.g.*,

3 ♣ : weak hand, weak suit
3 ◊ : weak hand, good suit
3 ♡ : good hand, weak suit
3 ♠ : good hand, good suit

See JUMP OVERCALLS; OGUST REBIDS.

MANDELL JUMP CUE-BID

The Mandell Jump Cue-Bid is a jump bid in an opponent's suit to show that the cue-bidder has a hand worth a preemptive jump to the same level, in a suit that ranks higher than the suit of the cue-bid, and that he has about one defensive trick more than is traditionally recommended.

East hands:

[A]	♠ K Q J 9 x x x	♡ x x	◊ x	♣ Q x x
[B]	♠ K Q J 9 x x x	♡ x x	◊ x	♣ A x x
[C]	♠ x	♡ A K J x x x x	◊ x	♣ Q x x x
[D]	♠ x	♡ A K J x x x x	◊ x	♣ A J x x

Following North's opening bid of, for example, one diamond, East would make the natural preemptive bid of three spades with hand [A]. But with hand [B], which has a defensive trick outside of the semi-solid spade suit, East would instead jump to three diamonds.

The three diamond bid does not identify East's suit except to say that it ranks higher than diamonds. West makes a bid in the suit next above the cue-bid — here hearts — in order to find the cue-bidder's suit. The cue-bidder passes if his partner has bid his suit, or corrects if he has not.

With hand [C], East would jump to four hearts as a preempt over any opening bid by North. With hand [D], East would make a jump cue-bid of four of the opener's suit if it were clubs or diamonds. But if North has opened with one spade, the transfer preempt is not available because opener's suit ranks higher than that of the preemptor.

See also ANDERSON CUE-BID; DENIAL JUMP CUE-BID.

DENIAL JUMP CUE-BID

The Denial Jump Cue-Bid is a jump in a suit that has been bid by an opponent, showing a game-forcing hand and at least two quick losers in the opponent's suit. A nonjump cue-bid promises first- or second-round control of the suit. The denial jump cue-bid may be made in a variety of auctions in which the cue-bidder has an interest in slam.

Examples:

	North	East	South	West
[A]	Pass	1◇	2♣	2♡
	2♠	4♣		
[B]	1♠	3♠		

In auction [A] East might have a hand such as

♠ —　　♡ A Q x x　　◇ A K Q x x x x　　♣ x x

In auction [B], East might have a hand such as

♠ x x　　♡ A K Q J x x　　◇ A K J x　　♣ A

If West has a singleton or void in spades, a small or grand slam becomes a reasonable proposition.

See also CUE-BIDS AS RAISES OF OVERCALLS; MANDELL TRANSFER PREEMPT.

BERGEN JUMP CUE-BID AS TRANSFER
TO THREE NOTRUMP

The Bergen Jump Cue-Bid is a convention that allows responder to ask opener, whose bid has been overcalled at the one level, to bid three notrump regardless of opener's holding in the suit of the overcall. The goal of the cue-bid is to cause the opponent who overcalled to become the opening leader, thereby forcing the defenders to lead away from, rather than up to, their presumed strength.

The jump cue-bid promises a hand worth a raise to game and a stopper in the opponent's suit. It also promises balanced distribution and denies four cards in any unbid major suit. For example, after a one diamond opening and a one heart overcall,

[A]	North	East	South	West
	1 ◇	1 ♡	3 ♡	

responder might jump to three hearts with a hand such as

♠ A x	♡ A x x	◇ K x x x x	♣ Q x x

Bergen jump cue-bids are not applicable in the following auctions:

[B]	North	East	South	West
	1 ♣	1 ♡	1 ♠	Pass
	3 ♡			

[C]	North	East	South	West
	1 ♣	Pass	1 ♡	1 ♠
	3 ♠			

In auction B, North has no need to make a Bergen jump cue-bid; the over-caller will be on lead if North becomes the declarer. The jump to three of the suit bid by one's left-hand opponent may more profitably be used as a SPLINTER RAISE or MINI-SPLINTER, showing a singleton or void in the op-ponent's suit and support for partner's suit. In auction C, North's jump cue-bid of three spades is not a Bergen cue-bid because the overcall followed the response, not the opening bid.

In defense against a Bergen Jump Cue-Bid, the overcaller's partner should try to make a call that indicates whether or not it is safe for the overcaller to lead his suit. Thus, overcaller's partner should make a lead-directing double if he has any of the top four honors in the overcaller's suit, even if only a singleton; he should also double if he has as many as four cards in the suit, even if they are not headed by an honor. A pass indicates the absence of any help for the overcaller's suit.

See also WESTERN CUE-BID; ANDERSON CUE-BIDS; DENIAL JUMP CUE-BID; MICHAELS CUE-BID BY RESPONDER.

STAID: TRANSFERS OVER PARTNER'S TAKEOUT DOUBLE

A convention called "STAID" (a pseudo-acronym for *Senior Transfers After 1-level Doubles*) is designed to make it easier for a player who has a hand worth a game invitation or a game force to respond to his partner's takeout double. The convention uses cue-bids and single-jump responses by the doubler's partner (the "advancer") as transfers.

After his partner's takeout double, advancer's non-jump bid in any new suit is natural. These bids show no interest in game. His bids in notrump also are natural.

Advancer's Transfers

In order to invite game or force to game in a suit, advancer makes a non-jump cue-bid of opener's suit or a single jump in a new suit. Each of these bids, except the jump in the suit just below opener's suit, is a transfer to the next higher unbid suit. After a double of a one heart opening, for example, advancer's cue-bid of two hearts transfers to spades; the jump to two spades transfers to clubs; and the jump to three clubs transfers to diamonds.

Advancer would cue-bid two hearts with hands such as

[A]	♠ A J x x	[B]	♠ A J x x x	[C]	♠ K Q x x
	♡ J x x		♡ x x		♡ J x x
	◊ K x		◊ A J x x		◊ A x x x x
	♣ J x x x		♣ x x		♣ x

If, over the cue-bid, doubler rebid two spades, declining the game invitation, advancer would pass with hand A; he would continue to game, however, with hand B and would bid three diamonds, showing his second suit, with hand C. Advancer's bid of a new suit after a minimum rebid by doubler is forcing for one round, but it is not forcing to game.

In response to the double, advancer's jump in the suit next below the suit opened is also artificial. It denies a four-card major suit, denies a minor suit worth bidding, and asks doubler to bid notrump if he has a stopper in the suit opened. Thus, advancer's jump to three diamonds over a double of one heart might be made on a hand such as

♠ A Q x   ♡ x x x   ◊ J x x x   ♣ A K x

After a transfer bid, doubler may simply make the minimum bid in advancer's suit if he wishes to decline a game invitation; if he wishes to accept the game invitation, he should make some other bid. He may accept by bidding a new suit, or by bidding notrump, or by jumping in advancer's suit. All of these bids, if not game bids, are forcing to game. Doubler's jump directly to game denies slam interest.

In many auctions, doubler can make either of two jumps in advancer's suit without going beyond the game level. *E.g.*,

[A]	*North*	*East*	*South*	*West*
	1 ◇	Double	Pass	2 ◇

[B]	*North*	*East*	*South*	*West*
	1 ♠	Double	Pass	3 ♣

In auction A, for example, doubler can jump to three or four hearts over advancer's two diamond transfer to hearts. In auction B, the doubler can jump to four or five diamonds over three clubs.

When the doubler has available a jump in advancer's suit below game, that jump is game-forcing and shows slam interest, but it denies a singleton or void in opener's suit. Following such a jump, advancer should cue-bid a control if possible. With a hand having both slam potential and a singleton or void in opener's suit, the doubler should cue-bid. A jump cue-bid promises a void.

Only when the auction has begun with one spade and advancer has bid three diamonds to transfer to hearts is doubler unable to make a jump raise of advancer's suit below game. In this auction, doubler's cue-bid again shows slam interest, but it does not promise a singleton or void in opener's suit.

Doubler's rebid of two notrump over the transfer is natural and forcing to game. A jump by doubler to three notrump indicates that his takeout double was off-shape; three notrump is intended as a signoff. Doubler's bid of a new suit is also natural and game-forcing; it indicates a one-suited hand that was too strong for a simple overcall. Following doubler's new suit bid, the advancer's cue-bid of the suit opened shows a full stopper.

If doubler cue-bids opener's suit after the advancer's transfer, he promises one of two types of hands. He may, as indicated above, have a hand worth a slam try; or he may have a hand with which he is interested in playing game in notrump but which has only a partial stopper in opener's suit.

A jump cue-bid by the advancer shows one of two types of hands. He has either a hand worth a preempt in the suit just above the suit opened, or a hand worth a slam try in one of the other unbid suits. Doubler normally makes the minimum bid in the suit next above the cue-bid; he must make some other bid if he would have bid over a natural preempt in that suit.

If, over doubler's minimum bid in the suit above the cue-bid, advancer now bids a new suit, he suggests that this new suit is playable opposite a singleton or doubleton, and he asks doubler to cue-bid a control in an effort to reach slam. For example, in the auction

North	East	South	West
1 ◊	Double	Pass	3 ◊
Pass	3 ♡	Pass	

advancer would pass with a hand such as

♠ x x   ♡ Q J x x x x   ◊ x x   ♣ Q x x

but would continue by bidding four clubs with

♠ x   ♡ x x   ◊ A x x x   ♣ K Q J 10 x x

Higher jumps by advancer are natural. The double jump to the suit ranking just above opener's suit shows a solid suit. The other double jumps are preemptive.

See also FORCING NOTRUMP RESPONSE TO TAKEOUT DOUBLE.

FORCING NOTRUMP RESPONSE TO TAKEOUT DOUBLE

The standard constructive responses to a takeout double are a jump in a new suit, showing 9 or more points and at least a four-card suit; a bid in notrump, showing 8-11 points and a stopper in opener's suit; and a cue-bid, showing 12 or more points. On occasion, the doubler's partner (called the "advancer") has a hand whose high-card strength is worth a constructive response but whose distribution or high-card location makes the hand unsuitable for any particular standard response. Or the advancer may have a hand that is appropriate for two types of constructive response, and he will have no way to guess which will serve the partnership better.

For example:

[A] ♠ K x x   ♡ x x x x   ◊ A x x   ♣ Q x x

[B] ♠ K x x x   ♡ x x x   ◊ A Q x x x   ♣ x

If his partner has doubled a one heart opening, the advancer has no suitable bid with hand [A]. He is too weak to cue-bid; he has no good suit into which to jump; he has no heart stopper for notrump. With hand [B], advancer has two possible constructive bids: a jump to two spades and a jump to three diamonds. The former risks landing the partnership in a 4-3 fit; the latter risks having it miss a 4-4 fit.

A suggestion designed to deal with these problems is to have the advancer's bid of one notrump over the double be forcing and to make no promise as to length or stoppers in the opener's suit. The forcing notrump bid shows at least 8 HCP with no suitable alternative bid. Following the one notrump bid, doubler may bid the unbid major suit if he has four cards in it, or he may make another bid.

Use of this convention can clarify advancer's other constructive bids. Thus, a cue-bid may be deemed unequivocally forcing to game; a jump may promise a five-card suit; a jump in a minor suit may deny possession of a four-card major suit; and so forth.

CUE-BID AS RAISE OF OVERCALL

Using standard methods, a cue-bid in opener's suit by the partner of a player who has overcalled, for example

North	East	South	West
1◇	1♠	Pass	2◇

promises a game-going hand but suggests uncertainty as to what game contract should be played. Further, traditionally a simple raise of the overcaller's suit is meant to be mildly encouraging, and a jump raise is meant to be strongly encouraging.

Most expert players have abandoned these traditional treatments in order to allow the overcaller's partner (the "advancer") to raise the overcaller's suit freely, the better to obstruct the bidding of the opening side when the overcaller's side has a paucity of high cards. Modern methods treat any raise as preemptive rather than constructive. A jump raise tends to be based on distributional values rather than on high cards.

For example, in the above auction a bid by West of three spades might show a hand such as

♠ Qxxxx   ♡ xxx   ◇ x   ♣ Kxxx

Using these methods, in order to show a hand with which he wishes to invite the overcaller to bid game, the advancer must make a cue-bid. Two methods of cue-bidding are in vogue.

One variation uses a nonjump cue-bid to initiate all sequences in which advancer has a hand worth at least a LIMIT RAISE of overcaller's suit. In response to the cue-bid, the overcaller should rebid his suit with a minimum hand. With better than a minimum he may rebid in a new suit or jump in his suit if it is a good suit. If advancer bids a new suit after he has cue-bid, he shows a good six-card or longer suit of his own; such a nonjump is forcing for one round but is not forcing to game.

An alternative method uses a jump cue-bid to show specifically a limit raise in overcaller's suit. This has the virtue of immediately clarifying the advancer's hand. *See also* DENIAL JUMP CUE-BID.

RUBENS ADVANCES

The term "advancer" is used to refer to the partner of a player who has made an overcall. Rubens Advances are a system of bidding that allows the advancer to show either a new suit or a constructive raise of the overcaller's suit. It is designed to allow advancer to make a forcing bid when he has a new suit and a forward-going hand, or in many instances, to show his suit although he has a weak hand. The system is designed to conserve bidding space when either overcaller or advancer is likely to have a constructive hand.

Some of advancer's responses to the overcall are natural, and some are transfer bids. The character of advancer's bid in this respect is determined by the amount of space taken up by the overcall. The guiding principles are as follows:

(I) If the suit of the overcall ranks just above the suit of the opening bid, the bid of a new suit by advancer is a natural and forcing bid; a cue-bid by advancer is a constructive raise of overcaller's suit. For purposes of Rubens Advances, clubs are deemed to rank just above spades. Thus, in the auction

North	East	South	West
1 ◇	1 ♡	Pass	?

West's bid of one spade would show length in spades; his bid of two clubs would show length in clubs. Each of these advances would be forcing for one round. West's cue-bid of two diamonds would "transfer" to hearts and thus show a hand worth at least a LIMIT RAISE of overcaller's heart suit.

(II) If overcaller's suit ranks just below opener's suit, advancer's bid of opener's suit and of the next ranking suit are transfer bids, promising length in the suit ranking just above that bid by advancer. For example, in the auction

North	East	South	West
1 ♡	2 ◇	Pass	?

West's cue-bid of two hearts would transfer to spades; his bid of two spades would transfer to clubs. A bid of three clubs would transfer to diamonds, showing at least a limit raise of overcaller's diamond suit.

(III) If overcaller's suit and opener's suit are non-touching (i.e., one player has bid hearts and the other has bid clubs; or one has bid diamonds and the other has bid spades), advancer's cheapest bid of an unbid suit is natural and forcing; his cue-bid of opener's suit is a transfer to the next higher suit; and his bid in the other unbid suit is a constructive raise of overcaller's suit. Example:

North	East	South	West
1♣	1♡	Pass	?

West's bid of one spade would be natural; his bid of two clubs would transfer to diamonds; his bid of two diamonds would transfer to hearts, showing a limit raise or better.

Note that in all three schemes, advancer makes his limit raise in overcaller's suit by bidding the suit that ranks just *under* overcaller's suit, regardless of whether that is opener's suit or an unbid suit. Note also that whenever advancer can bid a new suit over the overcall but below the level of a cue-bid, that new suit bid is natural. The cue-bid always shows length in the next higher suit, whether that suit is overcaller's suit or an unbid suit.

Opening Bid	Overcall	Advance	
1♣	1♢	1♡ =	natural and forcing
		1♠ =	natural and forcing
		2♣ =	raise of diamonds
1♣	1♡	1♠ =	natural and forcing
		2♣ =	transfer to diamonds
		2♢ =	raise of hearts
1♣	1♠	2♣ =	transfer to diamonds
		2♢ =	transfer to hearts
		2♡ =	raise of spades
1♢	1♡	1♠ =	natural and forcing
		2♣ =	natural and forcing
		2♢ =	raise of hearts
1♢	1♠	2♣ =	natural and forcing
		2♢ =	transfer to hearts
		2♡ =	raise of spades
1♢	2♣	2♢ =	transfer to hearts
		2♡ =	transfer to spades
		2♠ =	raise of clubs
1♡	1♠	2♣ =	natural and forcing
		2♢ =	natural and forcing
		2♡ =	raise of spades
1♡	2♣	2♢ =	natural and forcing
		2♡ =	transfer to spades
		2♠ =	raise of clubs

1♡	2◇	2♡ =	transfer to spades
		2♠ =	transfer to clubs
		3♣ =	raise of diamonds
1♠	2♣	2◇ =	natural and forcing
		2♡ =	natural and forcing
		2♠ =	raise of clubs
1♠	2◇	2♡ =	natural and forcing
		2♠ =	transfer to clubs
		3◇ =	raise of diamonds
1♠	2♡	2♠ =	transfer to clubs
		3♣ =	transfer to diamonds
		3◇ =	raise of hearts

If advancer's bid is a transfer bid and overcaller bids the long suit promised by advancer, advancer may pass if he has a weak hand; or he may bid again if his hand is forward-going. For example, if the auction has started

North	East	South	West
1♠	2◇	Pass	2♠

West's two spade bid is a transfer showing long clubs. He might have any of the following hands:

[A]	♠ x	♡ x x	◇ K x x x	♣ K J 10 x x x
[B]	♠ x	♡ x x	◇ A Q x x	♣ K Q x x x x
[C]	♠ x	♡ A x	◇ A x x x	♣ K J 10 x x x

If overcaller merely accepted the transfer by bidding three clubs, West would pass with hand [A], or bid three diamonds as a game try with hands [B] and [C].

See also RUBENSOHL.

FOUR CLUB RESPONSE TO THREE NOTRUMP OVERCALL

When an opponent's preempt has taken up a great deal of bidding space, a double or an overcall may have to be used on any of a number of disparate hands. Thus, over a three-level preempt in spades, a three notrump overcall might be made with any of the following hands.

[A] ♠ K Q x   ♡ A   ◇ A K Q x x x x   ♣ Q X

[B] ♠ Q J 10 x   ♡ A K x   ◇ K Q 10 x   ♣ A K

[C] ♠ Q J x x   ♡ A x   ◇ K x   ♣ A K J 10 x

Hand [A] may be described as a hand on which three notrump should be gambled. Such a gamble may be taken with a major suit as well as with a minor. Hand [B] is a balanced powerhouse. Hand [C] is balanced, but is a "stretch" for three notrump.

If responder holds a balanced hand containing about 11 HCP, he would be interested in bidding a slam opposite the powerhouse, but probably not opposite a stretch or a gamble.

A convention designed to allow overcaller's partner (the "advancer") to determine which type of hand overcaller holds uses a four club bid to ask just that question. The four club bid by advancer says nothing about advancer's club suit.

Overcaller bids four notrump to show the balanced "stretch;" he cue-bids opener's suit to show the true powerhouse; and he bids a new suit to show the gambling type of notrump overcall.

TRANSFER RESPONSES TO NOTRUMP OVERCALLS

Extension of JACOBY TRANSFER BIDS to auctions in which there has been a notrump overcall permits the overcaller's partner (called the "advancer") to use much of the standard structure for responding to notrump openings. Transfers may be used after a one notrump overcall or after a two notrump overcall of a weak two-bid.

After a Two Notrump Overcall of a Weak Two-Bid

The following method has been recommended for advancer's transfers when the opening bid was a weak two-bid and his partner has overcalled two notrump.

Any bid by advancer at the three level in an unbid suit transfers to the next higher unbid suit. Thus, after a two heart opening and a two notrump overcall,

> 3♣ = diamonds
> 3◇ = spades
> 3♠ = clubs

A cue-bid by advancer initiates a STAYMAN-type inquiry.

After a One Notrump Overcall

The above method may also be used, one level lower, after a one-level opening and a one notrump overcall.

An alternative method for using transfers after a one notrump overcall has been suggested. Using this alternative, responder makes a two club bid as Stayman regardless of the suit of the opening bid. Other two-level suit bids transfer as follows:

- 2◇ : transfers to hearts unless the opening bid was one heart; after a one heart opening, transfers to clubs
- 2♡ : transfers to spades unless the opening bid was one spade; after a one spade opening, transfers to clubs
- 2♠ : transfers to diamonds unless the opening bid was one diamond; after a one diamond opening, transfers to clubs

TRANSFERS OVER DOUBLE OF ONE NOTRUMP OVERCALL

When a one notrump overcall has been doubled for penalties, the overcaller's partner (the "advancer") should normally pass with a balanced hand, even a very weak one. If he has a weak distributional hand, it will be useful for him to be able to use a transfer bid so that the opening lead will come to, and not through, the strong hand, and so that the strong hand will remain undisclosed.

A system of transfers similar to those that may be used by responder to escape from a double of opener's one notrump, *see* TRANSFERS OVER DOUBLE OF ONE NOTRUMP OPENING, is as follows:

redouble: transfers to clubs
2♣:   transfers to diamonds
2◇:   transfers to hearts
2♡:   transfers to spades

If the opening bid was in a minor suit, a transfer to that minor should be accepted at face value since many minor suit openings are based on three-card suits. Thus, in the auction

North	East	South	West
1◇	1 Notrump	Double	2♣
Pass	?		

East should bid two diamonds. West may easily have two or three more cards in that suit than does opener.

In addition, if overcaller's partner has a weak hand with two long suits other than opener's suit, he may use the redouble to initiate a sequence by which he shows both of his suits. After the redouble and overcaller's bid of two clubs, advancer's rebids show the suit bid and the next higher unbid suit. After a one club opening, for example, advancer would show his two-suited hands as follows after overcaller's two club bid:

2◇ = diamonds and hearts
2♡ = hearts and spades
2♠ = spades and diamonds

MODIFIED LEBENSOHL

The LEBENSOHL convention allows the partner of a player who has opened one notrump to cope with an intervening overcall by bidding two notrump to force opener to bid three clubs. This sequence permits responder, to *inter alia*, explore for 4-4 major suit fits and to know whether at least one member of the partnership has a stopper in the overcaller's suit.

A modification of the meanings of certain auctions taken by responder will permit the partnership both to use "Stayman" to find a 4-4 major fit and to reach three notrump intelligently when neither member has a full stopper but each has a partial stopper (*i.e.*, Q x x or J x x). The bids or sequences taken by responder are as follows:

Direct cue-bid of overcaller's suit = Stayman, with no stopper

Two notrump, followed by cue-bid after opener's forced three clubs = Stayman with a partial stopper

Two notrump, followed by three notrump after opener's forced three clubs = Stayman with a full stopper.

Direct bid of three notrump = full stopper; no interest in unbid major

If responder has a hand worth 10 points or more but lacks a full stopper in the overcaller's suit, he bids three of a minor suit. Opener may bid three notrump with a stopper in the overcalled suit, or may cue-bid that suit with a partial stopper.

Examples:

(Opener)

| ♠ Q x x | ♡ K Q x | ◇ A x x | ♣ A J x x |

(Responder)

| ♠ J x x | ♡ A x x x | ◇ K Q J x | ♣ x x |

Using these methods the bidding might go

North	East	South	West
1 Notrump	2 ♠	2 Notrump	Pass
3 ♣	Pass	3 ♠	Pass
3 Notrump			

If instead of the above hand responder had

♠ J x x	♡ A x x	◇ K Q J x	♣ x x x

the auction would go

North	East	South	West
1 Notrump	2 ♠	3 ◇	Pass
3 ♠	Pass	3 Notrump	

See also RUBENSOHL.

LEBENSOHL WITH TRANSFERS

A variation of the LEBENSOHL convention can be combined with transfer bids in a way that enables the partnership to explore for game after a major suit overcall when responder has either an invitational hand with a five-card major suit, or a long minor, or a strong two-suited hand. To use Lebensohl with transfers, the instruction conveyed by the two notrump response is altered slightly; in addition, the partnership loses the ability to have responder make a natural forcing bid of three clubs or three hearts directly over the overcall.

After an overcall of two spades responder's bids have the following meanings:

    2NT: asks opener to bid three of his better minor
    3♣ : weak hand with long clubs, sign-off
    3◇ : transfer to hearts, game-invitational
    3♡ : strong minor two-suiter
    3♠ : Stayman (with or without a stopper, according to partnership agreement—*See* LEBENSOHL, MODIFIED LEBENSOHL)
    3NT: to play; promises or denies a stopper according to partnership agreement

After an overcall of two hearts, responder bids as follows:

    2NT: asks opener to bid three of his better minor
    3♣ : weak hand with long clubs, sign-off
    3◇ : Stayman with a stopper
    3♡ : transfer to spades, at least game invitational
    3♠ : strong minor two-suiter
    3NT: to play; promises or denies a stopper according to partnership agreement

In either sequence, after opener has bid his better minor over responder's two notrump, responder may pass. Responder might have a hand such as

    ♠ x   ♡ x x   ◇ K x x x x ♣ x x x x x

If responder has a weak hand with a diamond suit of ◇ A J x x x x or better he bids two notrump, and if opener bids three clubs, responder corrects to three diamonds; if opener bids three diamonds, responder may bid three notrump.

After a transfer bid by responder, which shows a hand worth at least an invitation to game, opener may decline the invitation by bidding three of responder's suit, or accept by bidding four or by cue-

!

bidding. With a maximum, and a lack of desire to play in responder's suit, and with the overcaller's suit appropriately stopped, opener may rebid three notrump over the transfer bid.

Examples:

Responder might have a hand such as

[A]	♠ x x x	♡ K Q x x x	◊ K x x	♣ x x
or [B]	♠ x	♡ K Q x x x x	◊ K Q x x	♣ x x

Opener might have

[C]	♠ K x	♡ J x x	◊ A x x	♣ A K Q x x
or [D]	♠ Q x x	♡ A x	◊ A J x x	♣ K J x x

After a two spade overcall, responder would bid three diamonds on both hand [A] and hand [B], transferring to hearts. Opener, with hand [C], would accept the game invitation by jumping to game over three diamonds. With hand [D], opener would bid just three hearts. If responder's hand were [A], he would pass; if he had hand [B], he would raise to game over opener's three hearts.

See also RUBENSOHL.

Advanced Lebensohl

An alternative method of combining Lebensohl with transfers, called Advanced Lebensohl and applicable over both major- and minor-suit overcalls, uses game-invitational transfer bids for all three suits not shown by the overcall. Transfers to suits other than clubs are made by means of bids at the three level. Advanced Lebensohl uses the two notrump response to transfer to clubs. The two notrump response is also used with a weak hand with a long diamond or heart suit, or a hand with four cards in an unbid major suit and a stopper in the opponent's suit, or a hand worth a raise to three notrump with a stopper in the opponent's suit.

If responder bids any suit at the two level other than the one shown by the overcall, his bid is natural and not forcing. For example, if the opponent's suit is not spades, responder bids two spades to sign off. In order to sign off in diamonds or hearts, assuming that he is unable to bid the suit at the two level, responder begins by bidding two notrump and then signs off at three of his suit over opener's rebid. After any of responder's signoffs, opener should not bid again.

In order to invite game in a suit other than that shown by the overcall and other than clubs, responder makes a transfer bid by bidding three of the suit just below his long suit. Thus, if the overcall were two spades, responder would transfer to diamonds by bidding three clubs or transfer to hearts by bidding three diamonds. If the overcall were two hearts, responder would transfer to diamonds by bidding three clubs or to spades by bidding three hearts. Opposite responder's game invitation, if opener has a hand suitable for game he should make a rebid other than three of responder's promised suit.

In order to sign off or invite game in clubs, responder begins by bidding two notrump. Though responder could instead have one of the other types of hand mentioned above, opener must assume initially that responder has a game invitation in clubs. Thus, opener rebids three clubs if he has a hand with which he wants to reject such an invitation. If he would accept the invitation, opener must bid three diamonds. The requirement that opener bid three diamonds on any hand with which he would accept an invitation in clubs caters to the possibility that responder instead has a weak hand with diamonds or hearts.

If responder has the weak hand with clubs, he passes opener's three club rebid or bids four clubs over three diamonds. If responder has the game-invitational hand in clubs, he passes opener's three club rebid. With a game-forcing hand, or with an invitational hand opposite opener's three diamond rebid, responder may cue-bid the opponent's suit, bid game in clubs, or bid three notrump. The cue-bid tends to deny a stopper; three notrump promises a stopper but does not confirm a club suit. With a game-forcing or invitational hand, responder must take care not to bid three diamonds, three hearts, or four clubs, however, since those bids are signoffs.

Responder may also force to game without showing a long suit. If he bids two notrump and follows with three of the suit just below the opponent's suit, his sequence is STAYMAN and promises a stopper in the opponent's suit. If, having bid two notrump, responder follows with three notrump, he denies a four-card major, shows game-going values, and promises a stopper.

If responder jumps to three notrump directly over the overcall, he shows game values but denies a stopper in the opponent's suit. If he bypasses two notrump and directly bids three of the suit just below the opponent's suit, his bid is Stayman without a stopper.

Finally, if responder has a hand worth a slam try with one or both minor suits, he jumps to three spades over the overcall. His three spade bid has this meaning regardless of what suit was shown by the overcall.

A summary of responder's bids over two diamonds, two hearts, or two spades, is as follows.

After a natural two diamond overcall, or an overcall promising diamonds and an unspecified second suit, responder's bids are:

2 ♡ = hearts, signoff
2 ♠ = spades, signoff
2 NT = weak hand with clubs; or game-invitational hand with clubs; or Stayman with a stopper; or notrump game raise with a stopper
3 ♣ = Stayman, without a diamond stopper
3 ♢ = transfer to hearts, at least a game invitation
3 ♡ = transfer to spades, at least a game invitation
3 ♠ = slam try in clubs
3 NT = signoff without a diamond stopper

After a natural two heart overcall, or an overcall promising hearts and an unspecified second suit, responder's bids are:

2 ♠ = natural, signoff
2 NT = weak hand with clubs or diamonds; or game-invitational hand with clubs; or Stayman with a stopper; or notrump game raise with a stopper
3 ♣ = transfer to diamonds, at least a game invitation
3 ♢ = Stayman without a heart stopper
3 ♡ = transfer to spades, at least a game invitation
3 ♠ = slam try in one or both minors
3 NT = signoff without a heart stopper

After a natural two spade overcall, or an overcall promising spades and an unspecified second suit, responder's bids are:

2 NT = weak hand with clubs, diamonds, or hearts; or game-invitational hand with clubs; or Stayman with a stopper; or notrump game raise with a stopper
3 ♣ = transfer to diamonds, at least a game invitation
3 ♢ = transfer to hearts, at least a game invitation
3 ♡ = Stayman, without a spade stopper
3 ♠ = slam try in one or both minors
3 NT = signoff without a spade stopper

Note that the meanings assigned the three-level cue-bids are effective whether the opponent's overcall is entirely natural or also promises a second unspecified suit. If the opponents use artificial overcalls that show suits ranking higher than the bid, (*see, e.g.*, ASTRO, in which 2♣ = hearts and another suit, and 2◊ = spades and another suit; SAHARA, in which 2♣ = spades and another suit; UNI-CLUB DEFENSE TO ONE NOTRUMP, in which 2◊ = diamonds and a major), responder will, of course, have available an additional cue-bid at the two level. The partnership may agree as to what meaning to ascribe to the additional cue-bid.

If responder has bid an Advanced Lebensohl two notrump and the overcaller's partner raises the overcall, opener may take any of a number of actions. He may bid three an unbid major with four cards in the suit; or, with length in both minor suits and a stopper in the opponents' suit, he may bid three notrump. Or he may make a penalty double. If opener's hand is unsuitable for any of the above actions, he passes. Over any of these calls by opener, responder may, if he has a weak hand with which he was planning to sign off, bid his suit.

If opener passes the raise of the overcall, responder may double for penalties, or he may bid three of an unbid major to show a four-card suit, a longer minor suit, and a stopper in the suit of the overcall. Or he may bid three notrump to show a one-loser club suit, without a stopper in the suit overcalled.

STAYMANSOHL

The Staymansohl modification of LEBENSOHL revises the meanings of responder's direct and delayed bids in order to permit the partnership to compete more effectively when its one notrump opening has been overcalled with two hearts or two spades and the overcaller's partner raises. Staymansohl requires responder to disclose immediately, when he has a game-going hand, whether he has four cards in the other major.

The traditional Lebensohl method, when responder has a game-going hand, causes responder to specify immediately whether he has a stopper in the suit overcalled. Since the two notrump bid serves both to show a stopper (when followed by notrump or a cue-bid) and to begin a signoff (when followed by a new suit or a pass), its use delays disclosure of what type of hand responder has. Responder may have values worth a game force with four cards in the unbid major; or he may have such values without four cards in the unbid major; or he may have a weak hand with a long suit in which he wishes to sign off. Given the ambiguity, if the auction begins

North	East	South	West
1 Notrump	2 ♠	2 Notrump	3 ♠

it would plainly be risky for opener to double three spades for penalties; and if he passes, the opponents may well escape a penalty even when the opening side has strength but no fit, for responder will have at his disposal only two calls, double and three notrump, to indicate whether or not he has a four-card major. Since the double must be assigned one of these meanings, responder will not be able to double for penalties.

The Staymansohl modification, used over a two heart or two spade overcall, focuses immediately on whether or not responder has four cards in the unbid major. Responder's bid of two notrump denies four cards in the unbid major. Both his direct cue-bid and his direct bid of three notrump promise the four-card major. The cue-bid denies a stopper in the suit overcalled; three notrump promises a stopper.

Though the two notrump response indicates immediately that responder does not have a four-card major, it does not reveal whether responder has a stopper in the opponent's suit. At his next turn, assuming there is room, responder may, when he has the game-going hand, bid three notrump with a stopper or cue-bid to deny a stopper.

To summarize, responder's bids and sequences show:

Direct cue-bid = four-card major, no stopper
Direct bid of three notrump = four-card major, promises a stopper
Two notrump, then cue-bid = no four-card major, no stopper
Two notrump, then three notrump = no four-card major, promises a
    stopper

The two notrump response, as in the original Lebensohl convention, requires opener to rebid three clubs. The Staymansohl modification leaves responder free, assuming the overcaller's partner does not raise, to sign off in a long suit after opener's forced three club rebid. If overcaller's partner raises over two notrump, opener still must pass, unsure whether responder's two notrump bid was the start of a game raise or start of a signoff. Using Staymansohl, however, if responder has the good hand, he can double for penalties.

YAS: "YET ANOTHER SOHL"

The "YAS" modification of LEBENSOHL, like Lebensohl, uses an artificial two notrump response following an opponent's overcall over a one notrump opening. Unlike Lebensohl, however, YAS (an acronym for "Yet Another Sohl") does not force opener to bid three clubs but rather invites him to indicate principally whether he has a stopper in the suit overcalled, and secondarily whether he has four cards in any unbid major suit.

Over the YAS two notrump response, opener bids three clubs to show a stopper in the opponent's suit. Without such a stopper he shows four cards in an unbid major by bidding that suit. If the overcall was two clubs or two diamonds and opener has four cards in each major, he bids three hearts.

When opener has neither a stopper in the opponent's suit nor four cards in an unbid major, if the opponent's suit is a major opener should cue-bid if he has a partial stopper. If opener has neither the necessary stopper in the suit overcalled nor four cards in an unbid major, he bids three diamonds.

The complete schedule of opener's rebids over two notrump is:

3 ♣ = full stopper in opponent's suit; does not deny four cards in any unbid major

3 ◇ (after an overcall in a minor) = less than a full stopper in opponent's suit, and fewer than four cards in either major suit

3 ◇ (after an overcall in a major) = less than a partial stopper in opponent's suit, and fewer than four cards in the unbid major

3 ♡ (after heart overcall) = partial heart stopper and fewer than four spades

3 ♡ (after overcall in a suit other than hearts) = four hearts, with less than a full stopper in opponent's suit; does not deny four spades

3 ♠ (after spade overcall) = partial spade stopper and fewer than four hearts

3 ♠ (after overcall in a suit other than spades) = four spades, with less than a full stopper in opponent's suit; denies four hearts

If opener has rebid three clubs, showing a stopper in the opponent's suit, responder may bid three diamonds to ask opener whether he has a four-card major. Opener rebids three notrump if he has no four-card major. If the opponent's suit is a minor and opener has rebid three hearts, responder's bid of three spades shows a four-card spade suit.

If the opponent's suit is a major, a direct cue-bid by responder, bypassing two notrump, shows a partial stopper in the opponent's suit and denies four cards in the other major. If responder bids two notrump and then makes a cue-bid, he shows a partial stopper and promises four cards in the other major. If the overcall was two spades, responder's bid of two notrump followed by three hearts shows a game-forcing hand with a five-card heart suit.

Responder's other calls directly over the overcall are natural. A double is for penalties. A non-jump bid in a new suit is competitive and not forcing. A jump to three of a new suit is natural and forcing to game.

See also ADVANCED LEBENSOHL; LEBENSOHL WITH TRANSFERS; MODIFIED LEBENSOHL; STAYMANSOHL.

EXTENDED LEBENSOHL

The LEBENSOHL convention, initially devised as a method for responder to compete after an overcall over his partner's one notrump opening, uses a response of two notrump to force opener to bid three clubs. This device has profitably been extended to several other bidding contexts. A variety of competitive situations are considered below. *See also* LEBENSOHL AFTER A REVERSE; MCCABE ADJUNCT.

Responding to a Weak Two-Bid After an Intervening Double

After an auction has begun

North	East	South	West
2♡	Double		

some partnerships treat a two notrump bid by South as a Lebensohl-type bid, requiring North to bid three clubs. The three club bid may be passed by South, as with a hand such as

♠ K x x	♡ x	◇ x x	♣ K J 10 x x x x

A bid of a new suit by South over three clubs would show a long weak suit and should be passed.

Using this convention, South's bid of a new suit directly over the double is generally treated as lead-directing rather than constructive. If West passes such a bid, North should retreat to three hearts, for which South presumably has tolerance.

This type of treatment may be further extended to an auction in which a weak JUMP OVERCALL has been made at the two level. The partner of the overcaller may use the two notrump call to force the overcaller to bid three clubs.

Responding to the Double of a Weak Two-Bid

The Lebensohl extension may also be valuable to the side that did not open the bidding. After the auction has started

North	East	South	West
2♡	Double	Pass	

some partnerships treat a two notrump bid by West as Lebensohl, requiring East to bid three clubs. This treatment allows the doubler's partner to make bids that distinguish between good and subminimum hands.

After the double, any bid by West at the three level promises a minimum of 7-8 points, e.g., a hand such as

♠ x x x   ♡ Q x   ♢ K Q x x x   ♣ J x x

Holding less, he would start instead with two notrump. Over East's forced bid of three clubs, West will pass if he has a hand such as

♠ x x x   ♡ x x x   ♢ x x   ♣ Q x x x x

or bid a new suit if his long suit is not clubs.

A suit bid by the doubler's partner at the two level is weak; a jump to three of a suit is forcing. If he bids two notrump and, over three clubs, bids a suit that he could have bid at the two level, he shows at least 7-8 points and a fair suit. This sequence invites the doubler to bid a game.

If the doubler's partner has 10 or more points, the use of Extended Lebensohl gives him two routes to show his values. He may, for example, show his values by making a direct cue-bid or a direct bid of three notrump; or he may show the same point count by making his cue-bid or bidding three notrump only after first having bid two notrump. The precise information conveyed by the route chosen is a matter for partnership agreement. For example, the partnership might agree that a bid of two notrump followed by three notrump would show ten or more points but only a partial stopper in opener's suit. Or it might agree that such a sequence shows four cards in the unbid major suit, whereas a direct jump to three notrump would deny such a holding. Some partnerships agree that if the doubler's partner jumps directly to four of a major suit he shows a strong suit with a side suit singleton or void, but that if he jumps to four of a major only after having bid two notrump, he denies such side suit shortness.

If the doubler has a very strong balanced hand or an unbalanced hand with a long good suit, he should ignore his partner's demand that he bid three clubs, lest that be his partner's suit and the partnership languish right there.

Examples:

[A]   ♠ A K x   ♡ A Q   ♢ K Q J x x   ♣ A Q x

[B]   ♠ A K Q J x x   ♡ x x   ♢ A x x   ♣ A x

With both hands, the doubler has doubled because his hand was too strong for a simple overcall. If his partner bids two notrump in response to his double, he should bid three notrump if he has hand [A], or bid three spades if he has hand [B].

Responding to a Suit Opening After an Overcall

A Lebensohl extension may also be used to increase responder's ability to respond to an opening bid of one in a suit after an intervening overcall at the one or two level. Called the Ring Two Notrump, this application preserves responder's ability to make strength-showing free bids and negative doubles, but permits him also to compete safely with a hand that would be worth no more than a weak jump shift response. *See* PREEMPTIVE JUMP SHIFT RESPONSE; NEGATIVE FREE BIDS AND POSITIVE DOUBLES.

In auctions such as

	North	East	South	West
[A]	1 ◊	1 ♡	2 Notrump	
[B]	1 ♡	2 ♠	2 Notrump	
[C]	1 ♠	2 ◊	2 Notrump	

South's two notrump bid asks opener to bid three clubs. South will pass three clubs if he has a hand such as

♠ x x	♡ x	◊ x x x	♣ K J x x x x x

or he will sign off by bidding a new suit to show length in that suit and a very weak hand.

After opener has bid three clubs, responder's bid of three of opener's suit shows a LIMIT RAISE of that suit with stoppers in the suit of the overcall. If the opening bid was one club, responder shows a limit raise by rebidding three notrump over three clubs. He may show a balanced hand of game-forcing strength by cue-bidding the suit of the overcall after opener has rebid three clubs. If the overcall was in clubs, responder shows this balanced game-going hand by rebidding three notrump.

If opener has a hand with which he would prefer not to rest in three clubs opposite the hand shown above, he must make a bid other than three clubs over responder's two notrump call. *See* PREEMPTIVE JUMP SHIFT RESPONSE; *see also* RUBENSOHL.

Rebids by Opener over Intervention

In many competitive auctions, opener is faced with a choice between foregoing effective competition for a part-score contract, and over-bidding, thereby risking that responder will carry on to an unmakable game. A Lebensohl extension called Mouse Two Notrump allows opener to distinguish between bids based on sound values and those that are strictly competitive or based on distributional values.

The convention may be applied in any auction in which opener's right-hand opponent has bid at the two level. The Mouse Two Notrump in such an auction asks responder to bid three clubs. Following the three club bid, opener may rebid his suit or support the suit shown by responder. By this sequence opener promises sound values for his ascent to the three level.

Holding values that are more distributional, opener bids at the three level directly over right-hand opponent's intervention. The direct bid bespeaks more a desire to compete than a desire to explore for game.

For example, in the auction

North	East	South	West
1 ◊	Pass	1 ♡	2 ♣
?			

North might have either

[A] ♠ A x x   ♡ ẋ   ◊ A K Q x x x x   ♣ K x

or [B] ♠ A Q x   ♡ Q x   ◊ A K x x x   ♣ A x x

Using standard methods, opener would likely bid three notrump with either hand. Using the Mouse Convention, he would, with hand [A], bid three notrump directly over the two club overcall. With hand [B], he would bid two notrump first then rebid three notrump after South's three club bid. The slower route to three notrump promises a more balanced hand and more high cards. With this knowledge, South may more safely rebid a six-card heart suit after the delayed three notrump bid but will be wary of doing so after the direct bid.

RUBENSOHL

The Rubensohl convention uses a combination of Rubens-type Advances and a variation of the Lebensohl convention to enable either responder or the partner of a player who has overcalled or doubled to compete effectively with both weak and constructive hands. *See* LEBENSOHL; RUBENS ADVANCES.

Rubensohl may be used by responder after an opening bid of one notrump or one in a suit, or by the partner of the overcaller (the "advancer") when a responder has so responded as to interfere with a planned Rubens Advance.

After a One Notrump Opening

If an opening bid of one notrump has been overcalled, responder may use Rubensohl to transfer into a long suit he holds, or to show a four-card major suit, or to deny a four-card major while disclosing whether or not he has a stopper in the suit of the overcall. All of responder's bids from two notrump through three spades are artificial.

Unlike Lebensohl, the two notrump bid does not ask opener to bid three clubs as a relay. Rather it asks opener to bid clubs because responder shows length in clubs, unless the suit overcalled was clubs. With the exception of the denomination that ranks just below overcaller's suit, bids by responder from two notrump through three hearts are transfer bids. For example after the auction has commenced

North	East	South	West
1 Notrump	2 ♡		

a bid by South of two notrump transfers to three clubs; three clubs transfers to three diamonds; and three hearts transfers to three spades. After opener has bid the suit responder has promised by his transfer bid, responder may pass if he merely wished to compete, or may bid again with a more constructive hand.

The bid by responder of the denomination just below overcaller's suit (*e.g.*, two notrump after a two club overcall; three hearts after a two-spade overcall) announces that responder has four cards in a major suit (other than a major bid by the overcaller). This bid is forcing to game.

A bid by responder of three spades says nothing about spades, regardless of what the overcall has been, but shows a game-going hand without a four-card major, without a good five-card minor, and without a stopper in the overcaller's suit. It asks opener to bid notrump with a stopper.

997

Responder's bid of three notrump directly over the overcall promises a stopper.

See also LEBENSOHL WITH TRANSFERS; MODIFIED LEBENSOHL.

After a Weak Jump Overcall

Responder may also use Rubensohl after his partner has opened with one of a suit and there has been a weak jump overcall to the two level. Responder must, of course, have sufficient strength to carry the partnership to the three level opposite a minimum one-of-a-suit opening, but the mechanism operates just as it would have after a one notrump and two-level overcall. For example, in the auction

North	East	South	West
1 ◇	2 ♠		

responder may bid two notrump to transfer to clubs, three clubs to transfer to diamonds, and three diamonds to transfer to hearts. After any of these transfers, if responder bids three notrump he shows a stopper in overcaller's suit; if instead he cue-bids, he asks opener to bid three notrump with a stopper.

If, opposite a transfer bid by responder, opener has a hand with which he would not wish to rest in three of responder's suit, he should bid something other than three of that suit. *See, e.g.,* PREEMPTIVE JUMP SHIFT RESPONSES; *see also* EXTENDED LEBENSOHL.

After a One-Level Overcall

Rubensohl may be used by responder after a one-level overcall also. Here, it is a *one* notrump bid that initiates the series of transfer bids. To use Rubensohl at this level, the partnership must, of course, recognize that it gives up the ability to play in one notrump.

See also EXTENDED LEBENSOHL.

By Advancer after Responder Has Raised

The partnership of the overcaller may use Rubens Advances if responder has passed over the overcall. If the responder has raised opener's suit, and the suit bid and raised ranks just above overcaller's suit, so that only one bid has been eliminated from advancer's arsenal, the Rubens Advances may be used with a minimum of adjustment.

For example, in the auction

North	East	South	West
1◊	2♣	2◊	

West may double to say that he would have bid two diamonds, and
the remainder of his bids remain as they were. *See* RUBENS ADVANCES
for the meanings of West's other bids. When the raise has used up
more space, however, the sequences become more complicated.

Rubensohl may be used by advancer in all sequences in which
responder has raised. Advancer's transfers begin, as usual, with the
two notrump bid.

GOOD-BAD TWO NOTRUMP

The Good-Bad Two Notrump convention is a device used in competitive auctions to distinguish a hand that is constructive from one that is merely competitive. In the auctions to which the convention is applicable, the two notrump bid is artificial and shows the weaker hand; a direct bid, bypassing two notrump, shows the stronger hand.

When Two Notrump Can Be Good-Bad

Two affirmative conditions must be present for the Good-Bad convention to be applicable. First, the auction must be at the two level. Second, the bidder's right hand opponent must just have bid, doubled, or redoubled.

In addition, several sets of conditions must be absent for the convention to apply. First, a two notrump bid cannot be Good-Bad when the bid plainly has some other significance, *e.g.,*

— it is needed as a natural bid, or it is an UNUSUAL NOTRUMP; or
— it has another meaning as part of some other convention, *see, e.g.,* LEBENSOHL, or as a previously agreed defense to a convention used by the opponents, *see, e.g.,* UNUSUAL OVER MICHAELS.

Second, the two notrump bid is not Good-Bad when the partnership's strength has been fairly well defined, *e.g.,*

— the partnership's prior auction has established a game-force; or
— the partnership has shown that it is very weak, while the opponents have shown great strength; or
— one member of the partnership has made a preemptive jump overcall; or
— the opponents have doubled for penalties.

Third, the Good-Bad two notrump convention is not used when certain opening bids have been made, to wit,

— an opening bid in notrump by either side, or
— a weak two bid by either side, or
— an opponent's strong forcing one club opening.

Finally, the convention is not used when the partnership has bid and raised a suit.

The following are examples of auctions in which the two notrump bid can be Good-Bad.

[A]	*North*	*East*	*South*	*West*
	1 ♣	1 ♠	Pass	2 ♠
	2 Notrump			

[B]	*North*	*East*	*South*	*West*
	1 ♣	1 ♠	Double	2 ♠
	2 Notrump			

[C]	*North*	*East*	*South*	*West*
	1 ♠	2 ♦	2 ♠	2 Notrump

[D]	*North*	*East*	*South*	*West*
	1 ♣	Pass	1 ♠	2 ♡
	2 Notrump			

Bidding After a Good-Bad Two Notrump

The Good-Bad two notrump bid is artificial and asks the bidder's partner to bid three clubs. If one member of the partnership has bid clubs, and the two notrump bidder simply wishes to compete to three clubs, he may pass his partner's bid. Thus, in auction A, North may have a hand such as

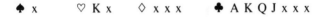

♠ x   ♡ K x   ◇ x x x   ♣ A K Q J x x x

If the two notrump bidder wishes to compete in some other suit, he bids that suit over his partner's three club bid. For example, in auction B, North might have either a long club suit or a heart fit.

Similarly, in auction C, West may have either

♠ x x   ♡ A x x   ◇ x x   ♣ Q J x x x x

or

♠ x x x   ♡ A x x   ◇ Q x x x   ♣ J x x

With the first hand, West plans to pass three clubs. With the second, he plans to bid three diamonds over three clubs. By making the delayed raise, West shows that he has minimum values for his raise. With one more king in each hand, West would not bid two notrump; he would instead bid three clubs directly with the first hand, and three diamonds directly with the second.

The partner of the Good-Bad two notrump bidder is expected to bid three clubs, but he is not required to do so if he has extra strength or has a clear bid other than three clubs. For example, in auction D, if South held

♠ K Q J 10 x x ♡ x x ◇ Q x x x ♣ x

he should bid three spades, not three clubs, over two notrump.

See also RUBENSOHL; SCRAMBLING TWO NOTRUMP.

SCRAMBLING TWO NOTRUMP

Scrambling Two Notrump is a convention designed to permit the partnership to find its best suit after the opponents have arrived at two of a major suit and one partner has made an overcall or a double. The convention is used when the overcaller/doubler's partner (the "advancer") has no suit good enough to bid and hence is not sure in which suit the partnership should play.

The convention is used only after the opponents have arrived in two of a major suit. It is not used when the opponents' suit is a minor, in order to preserve the opportunity to play at the two level.

The Scrambling Two Notrump bid is artificial. It does not suggest that the partnership play in notrump; rather, it asks the overcaller/doubler to bid a suit.

Auctions in Which Two Notrump Would Be Scrambling

The most common circumstance in which the Scrambling Two Notrump is used is an auction in which an opponent's opening bid of one heart or one spade has been raised to two and the raise has been followed by a takeout double. For example

	North	*East*	*South*	*West*
[A]	1 ♠	Pass	2 ♠	Double
	Pass			

	North	*East*	*South*	*West*
[B]	1 ♠	Pass	2 ♠	Pass
	Pass	Double	Pass	

	North	*East*	*South*	*West*
[C]	1 ♡	Pass	2 ♡	Pass
	Pass	Double	Pass	

In each of these auctions, a two notrump bid by the advancer (East in auction A, West in auctions B and C) would be Scrambling. Thus, the convention may be used opposite a direct takeout double, as in auction A; or opposite a balancing takeout double, as in auctions B and C. Similarly, the two notrump bid by West in the following auction is Scrambling:

[D]	*North*	*East*	*South*	*West*
	1 ♣	Pass	1 ♡	Pass
	2 ♡	Double	Pass	2 Notrump

The Scrambling Two Notrump bid may also be used in any other type of auction in which the opponents have arrived at two hearts or two spades and the advancer's partner has doubled. Thus, it may be used opposite a NEGATIVE DOUBLE, as in auction E, or a RESPONSIVE DOUBLE, as in auctions F and G:

[E]	*North*	*East*	*South*	*West*
	1 ◇	1 ♠	Double (Negative)	2 ♠
	2 Notrump			

[F]	*North*	*East*	*South*	*West*
	1 ♠	Double	2 ♠	Double
	Pass	2 Notrump		(Responsive)

[G]	*North*	*East*	*South*	*West*
	1 ♡	2 ♣	2 ♡	Double
	Pass	2 Notrump		(Responsive)

See also GOOD-BAD TWO NOTRUMP. Scrambling Two Notrump may even be used opposite a COOPERATIVE DOUBLE, as in auction H, or a penalty double, as in auction I:

[H]	*North*	*East*	*South*	*West*
	1 ♣	1 ♠	2 ♣	2 ♠
	Pass	Pass	Double	Pass
	2 Notrump			

[I]	*North*	*East*	*South*	*West*
	1 ♠	Pass	Pass	2 ♡
	2 ♠	Double	Pass	2 Notrump

The convention may be used in other auctions as well. The common denominator is a prior auction making it highly unlikely that the two notrump bid was meant to suggest a notrump contract. Thus, two notrump would be Scrambling in

[J]	*North*	*East*	*South*	*West*
	1 ♡	2 ◇	Pass	Pass
	2 ♡	Pass	Pass	2 Notrump

But two notrump would be natural, not Scrambling, in

[K]	*North*	*East*	*South*	*West*
	1 ♡	2 ◇	Pass	2 Notrump

The Scrambling Two Notrump bid is made when the advancer has no long or good suit to bid in response to his partner's call. In auction A, for example,

[A]	*North*	*East*	*South*	*West*
	1 ♠	Pass	2 ♠	Double
	Pass			

East would bid two notrump with either

    ♠ x x   ♡ J x x x   ◇ A Q x x   ♣ K x x

or

    ♠ x x x x   ♡ K x x   ◇ Q x x   ♣ A x x

However, with a hand such as

    ♠ x x   ♡ K x x   ◇ Q x x x x   ♣ A x x

he should bid three diamonds.

Bidding After Two Notrump

When the opponents' suit is hearts, as, for example, in auctions C and G, the two notrump bid shows clubs and diamonds. The advancer's partner should bid his longer minor; if they are the same length, he should bid the stronger.

When the opponents' suit is spades, advancer's two notrump bid may be based on support for all three of the other suits or for only two. His partner should bid his lower ranking four-card suit. Advancer will pass if he fits that suit, or he will bid his cheapest four-card suit.

For example, if East and West held

East
♠ x x   ♡ A x x   ◇ J x x x   ♣ A x x x
West
♠ Q x   ♡ K x x x   ◇ A Q x x   ♣ J x x

the auction might be as follows:

North	*East*	*South*	*West*
1 ♠	Pass	2 ♠	Pass
Pass	Double	Pass	2 Notrump
3 ♣	Pass	3 ◇	Pass
Pass	Pass		

See also RUBENSOHL: GOOD-BAD TWO NOTRUMP.

SCHLEIFER: CUE-BIDS OF MAJOR SUIT WEAK TWO BIDS

The Schleifer convention is designed to permit a player who has a good hand with length in both minor suits to compete over an opponent's opening weak two bid in a major suit. The convention uses a cue-bid of opener's suit to show a constructive hand with at least five clubs and at least five diamonds. For example, over an opening bid of either two hearts or two spades, the cue-bidder might have

[A]		[B]		[C]	
♠	x x	♠	A K	♠	x
♡	x	♡	x	♡	x
◇	A K x x x	◇	Q J x x x	◇	A Q x x x
♣	A K x x x	♣	K x x x x	♣	K Q x x x x

Over the Schleifer cue-bid, the cue-bidder's partner ("advancer") should bid four of whichever minor suit he prefers if he has a weak hand. If he has a hand worth 9-10 points or more, with stoppers in the major suits, *e.g.*,

♠ Q J x x   ♡ K J x   ◇ K 10 x   ♣ x x x

he may try three notrump. If he has a 9-10 point hand without a stopper in the suit opened, the advancer should generally opt for game in his better minor suit.

Advancer's bid of three or four of the unbid major suit is natural, promising a seven-card suit or a very good six-card suit. The bid of three spades in the auction

North	East	South	West
2 ♡	3 ♡	Pass	3 ♠

is not forcing. The cue-bidder is free to pass but may raise to four spades with an appropriate hand.

See also LEAPING MICHAELS.

LEAPING MICHAELS

The MICHAELS CUE-BID is a non-jump bid in a suit opened by an opponent, showing a two-suited hand. Typically, this cue-bid shows a weak hand, and when the suit opened was hearts or spades, the cue-bid does not specify which minor suit the cue-bidder holds. The Leaping Michaels convention also shows a two-suited hand. In contrast to Michaels, however, Leaping Michaels uses an overcall rather than a cue-bid, is a jump rather than a non-jump, identifies precisely which two suits are held, and promises a game-going hand rather than a weak one.

Leaping Michaels is used only over an opponent's opening weak two bid in hearts or spades. The convention uses a jump overcall of four clubs or four diamonds to show at least five cards in the minor suit bid and at least five cards in the unbid major. *See also* TWO-SUITED TAKEOUTS OVER PREEMPTS.

The Leaping Michaels overcaller promises a hand worth a game force. His overcall is forcing.

The convention uses a cue-bid of the opponent's opening to show a strong hand with both minor suits. *See also* SCHLEIFER. Thus, after an opponent's major-suit weak two bid, any combination of strong two-suited hands can be shown with a single bid.

"Liberalized" Leaping Michaels

A variation called "Liberalized Leaping Michaels" allows the overcalls of four clubs and four diamonds to be made with weaker hands. Using this modification, the overcaller again promises at least five cards in the minor suit bid and at least five cards in the unbid major; but he may have as little as 9 or 10 points. For example, after an opponent's opening bid of two hearts, a four club overcall could be made with

$$\spadesuit \text{ A x x x x} \qquad \heartsuit \text{ x} \qquad \diamondsuit \text{ x x} \qquad \clubsuit \text{ K Q x x x}$$

In Liberalized Leaping Michaels, the overcall of four clubs or four diamonds is not forcing. The overcaller's partner should bid four of the promised major if at all feasible.

Using this less constructive version of the convention, a player who has a very strong two-suiter should make a cue-bid rather than the four-level overcall in order to ensure that game will be reached. Though the cue-bid ostensibly promises both minor suits, the cue-bidder will clarify at his next turn that he had the minor-major two-suiter and a hand too strong for the liberalized jump overcall.

CAPPELLETTI CUE-BIDS

Cappelletti Cue-Bids are designed for use when the opponents have bid two suits. Each cue-bid shows length in both unbid suits. The cheaper cue-bid shows greater length in the lower-ranking unbid suit, while the more remote cue-bid shows greater length in the higher-ranking unbid suit.

For example, in the auction

North	East	South	West
1 ◇	Pass	1 ♠	2 ◇

West's two diamond bid promises clubs and hearts, with longer clubs. He might have

♠ x x   ♡ K Q x x   ◇ x   ♣ A J 10 x x x

If he bid two spades instead, he would promise longer hearts than clubs, *e.g.*,

♠ x   ♡ A Q x x x x   ◇ x   ♣ K 10 9 x x

If the auction were

North	East	South	West
1 ♡	Pass	2 ◇	

West's cue-bid of two hearts, the cheaper cue-bid, would show longer clubs than spades; his cue-bid of three diamonds would show longer spades than clubs.

If his suits were the same length, West would make a TAKEOUT DOUBLE or use the UNUSUAL NOTRUMP.

See also HESS CUE-BIDS. For possible actions by the partner of the cue-bidder, *see* TWO-SUITED TAKEOUTS—IN PROFILE.

HESS CUE-BIDS

Hess Cue-Bids, used in auctions in which the opponents have bid two suits, are made with two-suited hands in which the two suits are of unequal length. The cue-bid of the opponents' lower-ranking suit shows greater length in the higher-ranking unbid suit. The cue-bid of the opponents' higher-ranking suit shows greater length in the lower-ranking unbid suit. Thus, in the auction

North	East	South	West
1 ♦	Pass	1 ♠	

a bid of two diamonds by West would show longer hearts than clubs, while a cue-bid of two spades would show longer clubs than hearts. For a convention that would reverse the meanings of the cue-bids in this auction, *see* CAPPELLETTI CUE-BIDS.

In the auction

North	East	South	West
1 ♡	Pass	2 ♦	

West's bid of two hearts would show longer clubs than spades; a cue-bid of three diamonds would show longer spades than clubs.

The Hess Cue-Bid may be used when the suits are six-five, six-four, or five-four. With two suits of equal length, a TAKEOUT DOUBLE or the UNUSUAL NOTRUMP is preferred. The cue-bid typically is made on a hand that has little defensive strength. With a good defensive hand, a takeout double is preferred.

For possible actions by the partner of the cue-bidder, *see* TWO-SUITED TAKEOUTS—IN PROFILE.

SCHRAMM ADJUNCT TO TWO-SUITED TAKEOUTS

Many partnerships use two-suited takeouts in which one of the suits, usually a major, is identified, and the other, usually a minor, is initially unidentified, *see, e.g.*, MICHAELS CUE-BIDS; BROZEL. In order to learn which minor the cue-bidder (or overcaller) has, his partner (the "advancer") bids two notrump.

The Schramm Adjunct is designed to provide greater definition for the advancer's two notrump response and for the cue-bidder's rebids. The greater precision assists when, for example, the advancer may wish to sign off in one of the minors but has game interest in the other, or when the cue-bidder has extra length in his major suit.

The schedule of advancer's responses is as follows:

    3 ♣ = signoff in cue-bidder's minor; cue-bidder passes if his suit is clubs, or bids three diamonds if it is diamonds
    3 ◇ = signoff if cue-bidder's suit is diamonds; forcing for one round if his suit is clubs
    3 of cue-bidder's major = semi-preemptive
    3 of other major = natural and non-forcing

Advancer's two notrump response remains a request for cue-bidder to identify his minor suit. In the Schramm Adjunct, this response shows a hand worth a game invitation. The cue-bidder rebids three of his minor if he has a minimum, but avoids this bid if he has extra values. Other possible rebids are

    3 of his known major = a six-card, rather than a five-card, suit
    3 of other major = club suit with maximum strength
    3 NT = diamond suit with maximum strength

ROSENKRANZ DOUBLE

The Rosenkranz Double is a device used to allow the partner of a player who has overcalled to specify whether his raise of the overcall is made with or without a high honor in overcaller's suit. Overcaller's possession of this information may assist in the defense if the opening side buys the contract.

The double is used after there has been an opening one-bid, an overcall, and a call other than pass by the responder, e.g.,

North	East	South	West
1◇	1♠	2♣	

Using the Rosenkranz Double, West's double of two clubs would not indicate a desire to penalize the opponents. Rather it would promise a high honor in the overcaller's suit, here, the ace, king, or queen of spades. A bid of two spades by West would show spade support but would deny possession of any of the top three honors.

Analogous action may be taken if responder has made a negative double of the overcall. In that event, a redouble promises support for the overcall headed by the ace, king, or queen.

The Rosenkranz Double may be used even after responder has raised opener's suit. This use of the convention would be inconsistent with the use of "responsive" doubles after an overcall.

See RESPONSIVE DOUBLES.

GARDENER ONE NOTRUMP OVERCALL

The Gardener notrump overcall is a two-way overcall of one notrump that promises either a 16-18 point relatively balanced hand, or a weak hand with one long suit. The convention is used principally by partnerships that use strong JUMP OVERCALLS and that hence have no other convenient way of entering the auction with a weak hand and a long suit. Some such partnerships use the one notrump overcall solely to show a weak hand with a long suit. This one-way device is known as the Comic Notrump.

Using the Gardener convention, the overcaller's partner may bid two clubs to learn which type of hand his partner holds. Overcaller rebids two notrump if he has the 16-18 point hand and otherwise rebids his suit.

CRASH

The CRASH convention is based on a series of two-suited overcalls in defense against a strong, artificial one club opening. The system is designed not only to facilitate preemption of the opening side, but also to forestall effective counter-measures because the overcaller's two suits are not precisely identified.

Overcalls of one diamond, one heart, and one notrump are artificial and show that the overcaller has a two-suited hand containing one of two specific pairs of suits.

- 1 ◊ = two suits of the same color, *i.e.*, **either both red suits or both black suits**
- 1 ♡ = two suits of the same rank, *i.e.*, **either both majors or both minors**
- 1NT = two suits both of which either have rounded tops (*i.e.*, **clubs and hearts**), or pointed tops (*i.e.*, **diamonds and spades**)

The name CRASH comes from the mnemonic device reflecting the pertinent characteristic of the suit pairs announced by the one diamond, one heart, and one notrump bids. In that order, the overcalls show Color, RAnk, and SHape.

These two-suited overcalls are particularly difficult for the opening side to counter because only the overcaller knows which two suits he has. Thus, no sure cue-bid is available.

Using CRASH, an overcall of one spade is natural, but is made entirely for its preemptive effect. Thus, it may be made with a very weak hand and a spade suit as short and weak as K J 10 x.

A double of the one club opening shows a very strong hand, itself worth a strong notrump opening or a strong JUMP OVERCALL. The purport of the double is that the hand may belong to the doubler's side rather than to opener's side.

Overcalls above the one level are natural one-suiters and are intended to be preemptive.

Responding to CRASH

Responder's goal is to assess the offensive potential of the opening side and the highest level to which he may safely preempt. Having done so, he selects what suit he will bid based on inferences as to which pair of suits his partner is likely to hold and on the knowledge that if he selects a suit in which his partner does not have length, partner will correct as cheaply as possible to a suit he does have.

For example, suppose East has overcalled one diamond over the one club opening, showing two suits of the same color, and West has either

| [A] | ♠ K J x x x | ♡ x | ◇ Q J x x | ♣ x x x |
| or [B] | ♠ K J x x x | ♡ x x | ◇ x | ♣ K Q x x x |

If West holds hand [A], he knows he has a fit for one of overcaller's suits; if not vulnerable, West should jump to three diamonds. If East has the black suits, he will correct by bidding three spades. If West holds hand [B] after the same overcall by East, he will infer that East probably holds the red suits; since the hands probably fit poorly, he bids one heart.

If East instead has overcalled one heart, showing either both majors or both minors, West can safely preempt on both hand [A] and hand [B]. He might bid three diamonds on [A] and four spades on [B].

If East has overcalled one notrump, showing either clubs and hearts or diamonds and spades, West should bid a safe two clubs with hand [A] but may jump to four spades with hand [B].

Variations

Some partnerships have retained the principal concept of CRASH, *i.e.*, bidding to show two possible pairs of suits without disclosing which pair is held, but have altered the calls by which the two-suited hands are shown. The modification uses a double of the one club opening not to show a strong hand, but as one of the two-suited takeouts.

One such variation uses the following scheme:

Double: two suits of the same color
1 Notrump: two suits of the same rank
1 diamond: two suits of the same shape

Using this modification, the partnership is able to make natural overcalls of both one spade and one heart.

Some partnerships have extended the modification in order to allow use of CRASH also after a negative response of one diamond. In such an auction, the double and one notrump calls would retain their previous meanings, and a one heart bid would show two suits of the same shape.

SUPER CRASH

The CRASH convention uses overcalls of one diamond, one heart, and one notrump to show various two-suited hands over an opponent's strong one club opening. The one diamond bid shows two suits of the same color (both blacks or both reds); one heart shows two suits of the same rank (both majors or both minors); one notrump shows two suits of the same shape (rounded tops, *i.e.*, clubs and hearts, or pointed tops, *i.e.*, diamonds and spades). The Super Crash modification allows an intervenor to describe one-suited and three-suited hands as well as two-suited hands.

Super Crash retains the original Crash meanings of the one diamond and one heart overcalls but redefines the one notrump overcall. In addition, it introduces two new calls: three clubs, to show a three-suited hand, and two spades to show a two-suited hand with either clubs and hearts or diamonds and spades.

With this definition of the two spade overcall, the non-jump overcall in notrump is available to show a one-suited hand. In response to the notrump overcall, the partner of the overcaller normally bids two clubs. Overcaller passes if his suit is clubs, or bids his suit if it is other than clubs.

All of the above overcalls are made with relatively weak hands. If the intervenor has a stronger hand, he may make a jump overcall; each jump overcall shows the same suit combinations that would have been shown by a non-jump overcall in the same denomination. While the jump overcalls show greater playing strength, they do not normally show a wealth of high cards. With any hand rich in high cards, Super Crash requires the intervenor to begin by doubling. The doubler describes his distribution at his next turn.

If the one club opening was made by the intervenor's left-hand opponent, and responder has made the bid that the intervenor had planned to make, a double shows the intervention associated with the denomination the opponent has bid. For example, if the response were one diamond, a double would show the same pairs of suits as a one diamond overcall *i.e.*, both red suits or both black suits. If the response were one notrump, the double would show a one-suited hand. If the response were two clubs, the double would show a three-suited hand.

Super Crash is used only on the first round of the auction, thereafter, all calls revert to their standard meanings.

See also TRUSCOTT OVER STRONG ARTIFICIAL OPENINGS; SIMPLIFIED TAKEOUT OVER STRONG ARTIFICIAL OPENINGS; CLIFF OVER STRONG ONE CLUB OPENINGS.

CLIFF OVER STRONG ONE CLUB OPENINGS

Several conventions have been devised to permit the non-opening side to compete with weak hands when the bidding has been opened with a strong one club bid. *See, e.g.*, CRASH; SUPER CRASH; TRUSCOTT DEFENSE TO ARTIFICIAL OPENINGS. Since these conventions may be used when the overcaller has a weak hand, the overcaller normally must bid a second time in order to show a strong hand.

The Cliff defense to an opponent's strong one club opening permits the overcaller to describe a strong hand with his first bid. The convention uses overcalls of one diamond, one heart, and two clubs as transfers, showing the suit just above the suit bid. Jumps to two diamonds and two notrump show two-suited hands: two diamonds shows length in both major suits, and two notrump shows length in both minor suits. An overcall of one spade is used to show a strong hand that contains four spades but no longer suit. The complete schedule of conventional responses is as follows:

1 ◇	=	long heart suit
1 ♡	=	long spade suit
1 ♠	=	four-card spade suit, no longer suit, and a hand good enough to warrant entering the auction over a strong club opening
2 ♣	=	long diamond suit
2 ◇	=	long heart suit and long spade suit
2 NT	=	long club suit and long diamond suit

All of these bids show hands worth some 16 or more points, including distribution. For example, if North opens one club and East holds

[A]
♠ x x
♡ A K x x x x
◇ A x
♣ K J x

[B]
♠ x
♡ K Q x x
◇ A K Q x x x
♣ x x

[C]
♠ A J x x x
♡ A K Q x x
◇ x x
♣ x

[D]
♠ A J x x
♡ x
◇ A K x x
♣ K Q x x

East bids one diamond with hand A, two clubs with hand B, two diamonds with hand C, and one spade with hand D.

The Cliff convention does not alter the traditional meanings of jumps to two hearts and two spades, which are natural and preemptive. The calls of double and one notrump may retain whatever meaning the partnership had previously assigned them, *e.g.*, as weak takeouts for the majors and minors, respectively, *see* SIMPLIFIED TAKEOUT OVER STRONG ARTIFICIAL OPENINGS.

DARE

The DARE (an acronym for Defense Against Really Everything) convention is designed to enable partnerships using artificial one-club openings to counteract an opponent's interference over one club. The responder's immediate action revolves around the suit of the intervenor's overcall; or if the intervention has been a double, the pivotal suit is deemed to be clubs.

After an overcall, if responder has a hand worth a positive response, he takes one of the following actions.

double = at least four cards in the suit of the overcall; does not deny possession of a second suit

nonjump in new suit = five cards in suit bid; does not deny possession of a second suit

nonjump in notrump = singleton or void in the suit of the overcall

jump in a new suit = two-suited hand (5-5 or longer); the two suits are those *other than* that of the overcall and that in which the jump is made

double-jump in a new suit = a one-suited hand; shows the suit bid

jump in notrump = balanced hand with double stopper in the suit of the overcall

jump cue-bid = at least six cards in the suit of the overcall; denies possession of a second suit

nonjump cue-bid = any hand worth a positive response that does not meet the requirements for one of the above responses.

These responses work best if the opponent's intervention occurs at the one level. If a two-level or higher overcall is made, responder may well have to forgo the jump responses and begin instead with one of the other responses.

Examples:

	North	East	South	West
[A]	1♣	1◇	1 Notrump	
[B]	1♣	1♠	3♠	
[C]	1♣	1♠	2♠	

Responder might have the following hands for the above auctions:

[A] ♠ Q x x x   ♡ A x x x   ◇ x   ♣ K Q x x
[B] ♠ A Q x x x x ♡ x   ◇ K x x   ♣ x x x
[C] ♠ A Q x x x x ♡ x   ◇ K x x x ♣ x x

With hand [C], responder may either double or cue-bid.

If the intervention has taken the form of a one notrump overcall, responder shows his positive response as follows. He doubles with a balanced or semi-balanced hand. He bids a suit at the two level with a one-suited hand. Bids of two notrump through three spades show two-suited hands as follows:

    2NT = clubs and diamonds
    3♣ = clubs and a major suit
    3◇ = hearts and spades
    3♡ = diamonds and spades
    3♠ = diamonds and hearts

After the three club response, opener can bid three diamonds to ask responder to identify his long major suit. Responder does so by bidding the *other* major.

DEFENSE AGAINST PRECISION ONE DIAMOND OPENING

In the PRECISION CLUB SYSTEM, the opening bid of one diamond is an ambiguous bid because of its "catchall" nature. If opener's hand has 12-15 points but is not suitable for a 13-15 HCP one notrump bid, and does not contain a five-card major suit, and does not contain a six-card club suit, the opening bid will usually be one diamond. The bid says little about opener's diamond suit and he may well have but two small cards in the suit. Opener might have, for example, any of the following hands:

[A]	♠ A x	♡ A x x	◇ A K x x x x	♣ x x
[B]	♠ A x x x	♡ K Q x x	◇ x x	♣ A x x
[C]	♠ K Q	♡ A J x x	◇ x x	♣ K x x x x

In order to enable the nonopening side to compete effectively after a Precision one diamond opening, the following mechanism has been suggested for action by opener's left-hand opponent.

double = balanced hand with 16 or more HCP; diamond stopper
one heart = artificial takeout for all suits but diamonds
one spade = natural overcall
one notrump = an overcall in hearts
two clubs = natural overcall
two diamonds = natural overcall
jump overcall in any suit = preemptive

The double to promise a hand worth a strong notrump opening containing a diamond stopper enables doubler's partner to pass for penalties with a smattering of strength and a fair diamond holding. After the double, if either opener or responder runs to one of a major suit, a pass by either doubler or his partner is forcing; the opening side is not to be allowed to play in one heart or one spade undoubled.

If responder passes the double of one diamond and doubler's partner lacks the values to pass for penalties, responder may bid one heart or one spade on a four-card suit. These bids do not promise any high-card strength. Or if doubler's partner has a hand with which he would have passed a 16-18 point opening bid of one notrump, he bids one notrump over the double.

Bidding after a One Heart Overcall

The one heart overcall is a takeout bid for spades, hearts, and clubs. Overcall's partner (called the "advancer") should bid as he would in response to a takeout double of one diamond, except that he may pass if he has a very weak hand with a preference for hearts. *See* TAKEOUT DOUBLES. Bids in spades, hearts, and clubs are natural.

A bid of two diamonds is a forcing cue-bid. If advancer has long diamonds and no other suit, he must bid one notrump if his hand is weak; he may jump to three diamonds (natural) with a hand worth a game invitation.

Bidding after a One Notrump Overcall

The one notrump overcall promises length in hearts. It is not forcing. Advancer's only forcing bid is two diamonds.

Advancer may pass if he has no fit for hearts and no long suit of his own and considers that passing one notrump is preferable to bidding on.

Advancer may bid two hearts to sign off. This bid does not promise any strength. To obtain further information, advancer may bid two clubs, which asks overcaller to bid another suit if he has one. Overcaller may pass with a club suit, bid diamonds or spades to show those suits, or rebid two hearts to show a one-suited hand.

A nonjump bid in a new suit by the advancer, other than two clubs, is merely an effort to improve the contract; it is not constructive. A jump bid by advancer in a new suit is invitational but nonforcing.

CRASH OVER NOTRUMP

An extension of the CRASH convention, which originally was designed for preemptive interference with artificial one club openings, may be used for constructive bidding over an opponent's one notrump opening. *See* CRASH.

Using CRASH over notrump, a double by the opening bidder's left-hand opponent, so long as he is an unpassed hand, is a penalty double. Overcalls of two hearts and two spades are natural and show one-suited hands. The artificial calls are (1) two clubs, (2) two diamonds, and (3) two notrump by opener's LHO as an unpassed hand. Since a player who is either a passed hand or is the notrump opener's right-hand opponent is unlikely to want to make a penalty double, a double by that player, rather than the two notrump bid, shows a two-suiter.

Each artificial call shows a pair of suits sharing a particular characteristic.

    2♣ = two suits of the same color, *i.e.*, either both red suits or both black suits

    2◇ = two suits of the same rank, *i.e.*, either both majors or both minors

    2NT if bid by an unpassed hand in direct position (or double by a passed hand or an unpassed hand in the balancing position) = two suits both of which either have rounded tops (*i.e.*, clubs and hearts), or pointed tops (*i.e.*, diamonds and spades)

After a two-suited overcall, overcaller's partner (called the "advancer") assumes that his hand fits poorly with overcaller's unless he has one suit in each of the possible pairs of suits shown by overcaller's bid, and he bids one of overcaller's presumed suits. Advancer bids the suit he has chosen at as low a level as possible if he has no desire to make a game invitation, or makes a higher bid if he has game interest.

For example, if advancer holds

    ♠ A x x x   ♡ x x   ◇ x   ♣ A x x x x x

and the overcall has been two clubs, showing two suits of the same color, advancer should assume his partner has hearts and diamonds. He should therefore bid a discouraging two hearts. If overcaller corrects to two spades, advancer will jump to four spades. If the overcall has been either two diamonds, showing suits of the same rank, or two notrump, showing suits of the same shape, advancer should jump to four spades. In either case, if overcaller does not have length in spades, he will have a club suit and will correct to five clubs.

If the auction has started either

	North	East	South	West
[A]	1 Notrump	Pass	Pass	2 Notrump
or [B]	Pass	Pass	Pass	1 Notrump
	2 Notrump			

the two notrump call does not show a two-suited hand. In [A], in order to show a hand with two suits of the same shape, West, since he is in the balancing position, would double. Similarly, in auction [B], North, since he is a passed hand, would use a double, rather than the two notrump bid, to show two suits of the same shape.

MODIFIED PINPOINT ASTRO

A modification of the PINPOINT ASTRO convention which is itself a modification of ASTRO, is designed to facilitate one-suited overcalls in major suits. Used principally against strong notrump openings, this convention uses a double to promise a two-suited hand including spades. Bids of two hearts and two spades are natural and do not suggest possession of a second suit.

The complete schedule of overcalls is as follows:

    2♣ = clubs and hearts
    2◊ = diamonds and hearts
    2♡ = hearts
    2♠ = spades
    double = spades and a second suit (unidentified)

The partner of the doubler may, if his hand is suitable, pass for penalties. If he chooses to bid and has no fit in spades, he may bid two clubs to ask doubler to pass with a club suit or correct with a red suit.

Most partnerships employing this convention agree to use it only against strong notrump openings, since against weak notrumps the double is more useful as a penalty double.

SAHARA

The Sahara convention is a system for intervention over an opponent's one notrump opening. It is designed to convey immediate information as to whether the intervenor has a one-suited, two-suited, or three-suited hand.

One-suiters are bid naturally, using bids from two hearts through three diamonds:

  2 ♡ = hearts, with no other long suit
  2 ♠ = spades, with no other long suit
  3 ♣ = clubs, with no other long suit
  3 ◇ = diamonds, with no other long suit

The immediate identification of the intervenor's suit helps his partner (the "advancer") to determine whether to compete against further bidding by the opening side.

Two- and three-suited hands are shown by doubling or by making an artificial bid at the two level. The two-suited calls provide at least partial identification of the suits held. The three-suited call, a bid of two diamonds, does not reveal which is the overcaller's short suit. The artificial calls are:

  Double = hearts and a minor suit
  2 ♣   = spades and any other suit
  2 ◇   = any three-suited hand
  2 NT = clubs and diamonds

In response to a double or a two club bid, if the advancer does not have a fit for his partner's major suit, he makes the cheapest bid (two clubs over the double; two diamonds over two clubs) in order to allow the intervenor to show his other suit. Except when the intervenor's suits are spades and clubs or the minors, Sahara thus permits the partnership to play in either of intervenor's suits at the two level.

In response to a two diamond overcall, which shows a three-suiter, the advancer may, if he has a weak hand with length in hearts, begin a signoff by bidding two hearts. Overcaller will pass if hearts is one of his suits, or will bid two spades if he has a singleton or void in hearts. If the overcaller has rebid two spades, the advancer will pass if he has a spade fit or will bid three of his better minor if he does not. If the advancer has a hand worth at least an invitation to game, he bids two notrump in response to two diamonds. Over two notrump, overcaller is required to identify his singleton or void.

See also BROZEL; CAPPELLETTI OVER NOTRUMP; VROOM; UNI-CLUB DEFENSE AGAINST ONE NOTRUMP; MODIFIED PINPOINT ASTRO.

CAPPELLETTI OVER NOTRUMP

Cappelletti Over Notrump is a system of showing one-suited or two-suited hands over an opponent's opening bid of one notrump. Overcaller's two-level bids are largely artificial and have the following meanings:

2 ♣	= any one-suited hand
2 ◇	= hearts and spades
2 ♡	= hearts and a minor suit
2 ♠	= spades and a minor suit
2 NT	= clubs and diamonds

These two-level overcalls are normally made with hands worth less than 15 points. With a stronger hand, especially a one-suiter, a double should be preferred. With a strong two-suited hand, especially a major-minor two-suiter, the intervenor may, if he would prefer that his partner not pass the double of one notrump, elect to bid two notrump instead of doubling. Though this bid ostensibly promises both minor suits, the overcaller's rebid of a major suit will reveal that he has instead a hand that was too strong for a double or a simple overcall of two hearts or two spades.

Responses and Rebids After Two Clubs

After a two club overcall, the overcaller's partner (the "advancer") usually bids two diamonds in order to learn what overcaller's suit is. The overcaller will bid his suit if it is not diamonds; if it is diamonds, he will pass. If overcaller has six clubs and four diamonds, he may show this distribution by rebidding two notrump over the advancer's two diamond response.

If the advancer has a long suit of his own, he need not respond two diamonds. If he has a reasonable six-card club suit, he may pass two clubs. If he has a reasonable five-card or longer major suit, he may bid two of that suit.

If the advancer has a balanced hand with a good 11 points or more and support for all four suits, he may bid two notrump. This response invites the overcaller to bid game with a maximum.

If the two club overcall is doubled, a redouble by the advancer promises at least 7 high card points, plus support for all suits. Overcaller is invited to compete at the three level.

Responses After Two Diamonds or Two of a Major

If the overcaller has bid two diamonds, promising both major suits, the advancer normally bids two of the major in which he has greater length. If the advancer has a very good long diamond suit, he may pass two diamonds. If he has a long good club suit, he may bid three clubs. If the advancer has length in both clubs and diamonds, he may bid two notrump to ask overcaller to choose a minor.

If the advancer has four or more cards in one of the major suits, he may, instead of signing off in two of that suit, jump to three of the suit preemptively. If the advancer has a hand worth a game invitation, he bids two notrump; though this bid ostensibly promises only the minor suits, at his next turn the advancer will reveal his major-suit game invitation by bidding three of the major.

If the overcall was two hearts or two spades, and the advancer has a fit for the suit bid, he passes with 0-7 points, or raises to three with 8-9 points. A two notrump bid by advancer asks overcaller to identify his minor suit. After opener's rebid, if the advancer bids three of overcaller's major suit, he shows a hand worth 10-12 points and invites game in the major.

Other Uses of the Convention

The Cappelletti conventional overcalls may be used both directly over the one notrump opening and in the balancing position. In addition, the partnership may agree that in the balancing position a double shows a four-card major suit plus a longer minor suit.

The convention may also be used over openings of two notrump and three notrump, including a GAMBLING THREE NOTRUMP OPENING or a GAMBLING TWO NOTRUMP OPENING.

The partnership may also agree to use Cappelletti after one partner has opened the bidding with one club or one diamond and an opponent has overcalled one notrump. Under such an agreement, in the auction

North	East	South	West
1 ◇	1 Notrump	?	

South's two-level bids would have the meanings set out above. Two clubs, for example, would show a hand with one long suit; two diamonds would show both major suits, *see also* STAYMAN OVER OPPONENT'S NOTRUMP OVERCALL; and two of a major would show five cards in that major plus a five-card minor suit. All such bids would indicate that South has a weak hand, for with a hand worth 8 or more points, he should normally double for penalties.

See also LANDY; RIPSTRA; ASTRO; BERGEN OVER TWO NOTRUMP; BROZEL; VROOM; UNI-CLUB DEFENSE AGAINST ONE NOTRUMP; SAHARA.

VROOM

The Vroom convention is a system of two-suited overcalls for defensive bidding against a strong notrump opening. The system also allows the overcaller to show one-suited hands containing a long major suit. The methods are as follows:

> double = a heart one-suiter; or a two-suiter with hearts and a minor suit
>
> two clubs = a spade one-suiter; or a two-suiter with spades and a minor suit
>
> two diamonds = the LANDY convention, with at least 5-4 in the majors
>
> two hearts = four hearts and a long (usually six-card) minor
>
> two spades = four spades and a long (usually six-card) minor
>
> two notrump = length in both minors

Bids at the three level are natural.

After a double, the doubler's partner may, with a forward-going hand, bid two notrump to ask doubler to bid his minor suit if he has the two-suited hand. If doubler's partner has a weak hand, he may simply bid two clubs. Doubler will pass if his second suit is clubs, bid two diamonds if it is diamonds, or bid two hearts if he has the one-suiter.

Vroom is less useful against weak notrump openings since against such openings there is often a desire to double for penalties.

See also LANDY; RIPSTRA; BECKER; ASTRO; MODIFIED ASTRO; PINPOINT ASTRO; MODIFIED PINPOINT ASTRO; BROZEL.

UNI-CLUB DEFENSE AGAINST ONE NOTRUMP

The UNI-CLUB system of competing against an opponent's opening bid of one notrump is designed to allow a defender to show a two-suited hand or a three-suited hand. In most instances at least one of the suits held by the bidder is unspecified. The overcalls over one notrump show the following:

    2♣ = clubs plus another, unspecified, suit
    2◇ = diamonds plus a major suit
    2♡ = hearts and spades
    2♠ = a three-suiter with spades as one of the suits and the other
         two suits unspecified
    3♣ = a three-suiter without spades

In each case the overcaller should have at least five cards in the suit he has bid. If his partner has a fit for that suit he may pass or raise; if he has no fit, he may bid the next higher denomination to ask overcaller to show another suit. For example, a bid of two diamonds over two clubs asks overcaller to pass with diamonds or to bid his major suit if he has clubs and a major; two hearts over a two-diamond overcall asks opener to pass if he had diamonds and hearts, or to bid two spades if he has diamonds and spades; a two notrump bid over a two spade overcall asks the overcall to bid the cheaper of his remaining suits.

Rather than accepting one of overcaller's suits, the partner of the overcaller may instead bid a six-card or longer suit of his own.

The Uni-Club system uses a double of a one notrump opening to show a one-suited hand, similar to the Brozel convention. The partner of the overcaller normally bids two clubs to allow the overcaller to show his suit, but with a suitable hand he may pass for penalties. *See* BROZEL.

UNI-CLUB DEFENSE AGAINST WEAK RESPONSES
TO ONE NOTRUMP

When the opening bid has been one notrump and the responder has signed off in two of a suit, the side that did not open often has enough strength to compete effectively at the two or three level. The Uni-Club defense to an auction such as

	North	East	South	West
[A]	1 Notrump	Pass	2♡ (Natural)	
or [B]	1 Notrump	Pass	2♣	Pass
	2♡	Pass	Pass	

allows a defender to compete as follows. With a one-suited hand, West may double. His partner makes the cheapest suit bid in order to allow him to show his suit; or his partner may, with a suitable hand, pass for penalties.

With a two-suited hand, West bids the cheaper of his suits; his partner, if he has no fit for the suit bid, bids on to locate the overcaller's second suit.

With a three-suited hand, the defender bids two notrump and his partner simply takes a preference.

If, in auction [A], West and North pass, East may compete in the above manner.

1031

GATES ADJUNCT: DOUBLES OF ONE NOTRUMP BY PASSED HAND

The Gates Adjunct is a convention that assigns a specific meaning to the double of a one notrump opening when the doubler has previously passed, making it ''impossible'' that the double is intended to be for penalties. The precise meaning to be assigned will depend on what other takeout bids, if any, the partnership has agreed to use. In general, the passed-hand double will be used to take the place of the bid that is used as an artificial takeout.

If the partnership uses the LANDY convention, in which two clubs is a takeout bid for the major suits, the double may be used to show clubs. If the partnership has agreed that all of its bids over the opponents' notrump openings are natural, the double may be used as a takeout bid for both major suits.

If the partnership uses a convention in which both two clubs and two diamonds are takeout bids, *see, e.g.*, ASTRO, BECKER, CAPPELLETTI OVER NOTRUMP, RIPSTRA, the double may be used to show a one-suited hand in which the long suit is either clubs or diamonds. The partner of the doubler should generally bid two clubs; the doubler will pass if his suit is clubs, or will bid two diamonds.

The Gates Adjunct is not used when the partnership has agreed to use a convention in which the double has its own artificial significance, *e.g.*, BROZEL or SAHARA.

BERGEN OVER TWO NOTRUMP

The Bergen-Cohen methods provide for one-suited and two-suited overcalls over an opponent's opening bid of two notrump. The conventional calls may also be used after an opponent has opened with one notrump and responder has made an invitational raise to two notrump.

Bergen Over Two Notrump uses a double to show a one-suited hand. The doubler's partner must bid three clubs. If clubs is the doubler's suit, he passes; if he has a different suit, he bids it.

With a two-suited hand, the cheaper suit is bid first, and the other is usually not fully identified. The two-suited overcalls are

3 ♣ = clubs and any other suit
3 ◊ = diamonds and a major suit
3 ♡ = hearts and spades

Each of these calls suggests a hand with extreme distributional values, given the great strength shown by the opening side.

The overcaller's partner should pass if he has a fit with the suit bid. Without a fit and with better support for the higher ranking suits, he bids the next higher ranking suit to allow the overcaller to pass if that is his suit or to bid again.

If an overcall is doubled, a redouble by the overcaller's partner is an S.O.S. REDOUBLE, asking the overcaller to bid his other suit.

See also BROZEL; CAPPELLETTI OVER NOTRUMP; VROOM; UNI-CLUB DEFENSE AGAINST ONE NOTRUMP; SAHARA.

BALANCING NEGATIVE DOUBLE

The Balancing Negative Double is designed for use when responder has a hand with about 7-9 high card points and no suit worth bidding over his right-hand opponent's takeout double. Using this method, responder passes the double and allows his left-hand opponent to bid; if LHO's bid is followed by two passes, responder's double is negative, suggesting shortness in the suit bid by LHO and support for the unbid suits. For example, in the auction

North	East	South	West
1 ♣	Double	Pass	1 ♠
Pass	Pass	Double	

South might have a hand such as

♠ K x   ♡ Q x x x   ◊ x x x x   ♣ Q x x

When the partnership has agreed that responder's reopening double in such an auction is negative, greater definition may be given to responder's other actions. His bid of a new suit directly over the double will promise a five-card suit. His bid of a new suit in the balancing position after he has passed the double will indicate that he has only a four-card suit. Thus, if responder had the above hand in the auction

North	East	South	West
1 ♣	Double	Pass	1 ◊
Pass	Pass		

he would balance with a one heart bid since he lacks support for spades.

Responder's raises of opener's suit and his bids of notrump directly over the double retain their ordinary meanings.

BALANCING FISHBEIN

The original FISHBEIN convention consisted of the cheapest suit bid over an opponent's opening preempt to ask partner to bid. The use of this artificial suit bid was designed to allow the player sitting over the preempter to make a penalty double of the preempt.

The Fishbein concept has been extended to the quite different situation in which an opponent's opening bid of one in a suit has been followed by two passes. And the goal of using a Fishbein bid for takeout in these circumstances is quite different. The Balancing Fishbein convention is used to provide a comprehensive and more precise structure for balancing calls. The complete structure is as follows.

The Fishbein balancing bid, *i.e.*, the bid of the suit next above opener's suit, is a takeout bid that promises 13-15 HCP. It also promises either shortness in opener's suit, or a stopper in opener's suit, or a good five-card or longer suit. The Fishbein bid says nothing about the balancer's length in the suit bid.

Example:

North	East	South	West
1 ◊	Pass	Pass	1 ♡

West's one heart bid does not promise hearts but merely indicates he has one of the three types of hands listed above.

A balancing double shows either 8-12 HCP and support for all of the unbid suits, or 16 or more HCP with any distribution. Therefore, if the doubler rebids one notrump or a nonjump two notrump, he shows 16-18 HCP and a balanced hand. If instead he jumps in notrump he shows more than 21 HCP.

A balancing bid of one notrump shows 9-12 HCP with a stopper in opener's suit. A balancing jump to two notrump shows 19-21 HCP and a balanced hand. A balancing jump to three notrump is a gambling bid based on a long running suit.

A bid of a new suit other than the cheapest suit (*i.e.*, other than the Fishbein bid) is a natural bid showing fewer than 13 HCP. The texture of the suit need not be good.

A jump bid in the suit next above opener's suit (*i.e.*, the Fishbein suit) is, except when the opening bid was one spade, a natural bid showing fewer than 13 HCP. The texture of the suit need not be good.

A jump cue-bid promises a solid suit somewhere and asks the balancer's partner to bid three notrump with a stopper in opener's suit.

A nonjump cue-bid or a jump in a suit other than the one next above opener's suit shows a good two-suited hand. When the opening bid was one spade, a jump to three clubs also shows a two-suiter. The length of the suits shown must be 5-4 or longer.

The general structure of these bids is that the cue-bid usually shows the two next higher suits, and the jump shows the suit in which the jump is made and the next higher unbid suit. Thus after a one club opening the balancing cue-bid and jumps would show the following

    2♣ = diamonds and hearts
    2♦ = natural
    2♥ = hearts and spades
    2♠ = spades and diamonds

After a one diamond opening

    2♦ = hearts and spades
    2♥ = natural
    2♠ = spades and clubs
    3♣ = clubs and hearts

After a one heart opening

    2♥ = spades and clubs
    2♠ = natural
    3♣ = clubs and diamonds
    3♦ = diamonds and spades

After a one spade opening

    2♠ = clubs and hearts
    3♣ = clubs and diamonds
    3♦ = diamonds and hearts
    3♥ = natural

Note that the bidding after a one spade opening follow a slightly different pattern. The use of the jump to three clubs, and not the jump in hearts, to show a two-suiter is designed to avoid the balancer's partner having to express his preference at the four level.

Examples:

	North	East	South	West
[A]	1♥	Pass	Pass	1♠
	Pass			
[B]	1♦	Pass	Pass	3♣
	Pass			

[C]	1♣	Pass	Pass	1 Notrump
	Pass			
[D]	1♠	Pass	Pass	Double

If in auction [A], East has a hand such as

♠ KJxxx   ♡ xx   ◊ AQxx   ♣ xx

he should bid two spades. West's one spade bid shows 13-15 points but does not guarantee spade length. If West has support for East's spades he will raise to three spades with a minimum and to four spades with a maximum. If instead he has a hand such as

♠ Qx   ♡ QJ10x   ◊ Kxxx   ♣ AJx

he will rebid two notrump.

In auction [B] West's three club bid shows a good two-suiter with at least 5-4 in clubs and hearts. If East has

♠ Kxxxx   ♡ xxx   ◊ Axx   ♣ xx

he should take a simple preference by bidding three hearts, knowing that it is unlikely that West will have three-card support for spades.

In auction [C] if East has a hand not better than, *e.g.*,

♠ Kxx   ♡ QJ10x   ◊ Axx   ♣ Q10x

he should pass. Since West's range is 9-12, game is not likely.

In auction [D], East may pass for penalties if he has a suitable hand such as

♠ AQJ9x   ♡ Qx   ◊ xxx   ♣ KJx

If East has a hand with which he does not wish to pass the double, he must make a bid that caters to the possibility that his partner has only 8 HCP. Thus, with a hand such as

♠ Axx   ♡ QJxxxx   ◊ x   ♣ Jxx

East should jump to three hearts rather than to four. The three heart bid is not forcing, but West will raise if he has a good fit and at least 11-12 HCP or will bid something else if he has a better hand without heart support.

See also BALANCING TWO CLUB BID.

INCREDIBLE DOUBLE

When a player who has made a weak preemptive bid and has received a raise from his partner doubles the opponent's voluntarily bid game contract, his double, if it is a penalty double, seems quite inconsistent with his prior announcement of weakness. Accordingly, some partnerships use this double, termed the "Incredible Double," to have the preempter show not a desire to penalize, but rather an absolute lack of defensive strength. The double thus suggests that a sacrifice should be taken. Doubler's partner may pass only if he has enough strength in his own hand to defeat the contract.

A preempter's double is not the Incredible Double unless three conditions are met. First, the doubler's preemptive bid must have been raised by his partner. Second, the double must be made directly over the game bid, not in the passout seat. Third, the vulnerability must be favorable.

Examples:

	North	East	South	West
[A]	1♠	2♦	Double*	3♦
	4♡	Double		
[B]	2♡	2♠	4♡	4♠
	Double			
[C]	2♡	Pass	4♡	Double
	Pass	4♠	Pass	Pass
	Double			
[D]	2♡	Pass	4♡	Double
	Pass	4♠	Double	

*negative

In each auction, the preempting side is not vulnerable; the other side is vulnerable. In auctions [A] and [B] the final double is the Incredible Double. In auction [C], North's double is not the Incredible Double because it was not made directly over the game bid. In auction [D], South's double is not incredible because South was not the preempter. South may well have a good defensive hand.

See also NEGATIVE SLAM DOUBLES; POSITIVE SLAM DOUBLES.

IMPOSSIBLE THREE NOTRUMP

The Impossible Three Notrump convention uses a bid of three notrump to suggest that the partnership sacrifice against the opponents' probable game contract. The convention is used principally when the partnership has bid one or both minor suits.

For a bid of three notrump to constitute a suggestion for sacrifice, the prior auction must make it implausible that the bidder could reasonably expect to make three notrump. Such auctions include those in which the three notrump bidder is a passed hand and his partner has opened with a preempt, and those in which the hand obviously belongs to the opponents.

For example:

North	East	South	West
1 ◇	Pass	2 ♡	3 ♣
3 ♠	3 Notrump		

The partnership may agree that if the opponents' suit is spades, the Impossible Three Notrump may also be used when the partnership's suit is hearts, as in the auction

North	East	South	West
Pass	Pass	Pass	1 ♣
1 ♡	1 ♠	2 ♡	3 ♠
3 Notrump			

Opposite an Impossible Three Notrump bid, partner should sacrifice if he has little defense and has sufficient playing strength to avoid incurring an unduly heavy penalty at the five level. With defensive strength or with a poor playing hand, he should escape at the four level.

See also INCREDIBLE DOUBLE; BIC CUE-BIDS.

BIC CUE-BIDS

The BIC Cue-Bid was devised as a concession to the wide range of hands on which preempts are made. The cue-bid is made by the partner of the preemptor after an opponent has bid a suit over the preempt. For example,

North	East	South	West
2 ◊ (weak)	2 ♡	3 ♡	

The cue-bid invites the preemptor to participate in the decision as to whether to sacrifice. The preemptor should sacrifice if he has the traditional dearth of defensive strength. He should permit the opponents to play in their game or slam if he has more defense than would normally be expected.

See also INCREDIBLE DOUBLE; IMPOSSIBLE THREE NOTRUMP.

GAMBLE DOUBLE

When a player has made a preemptive bid and his right-hand opponent later cue-bids his suit, the cue-bid usually indicates a control in the preempter's suit. Using standard methods, a double by the preempter would indicate a desire to have his suit led by partner.

The Gamble Double is a convention based on the proposition that a lead of the preempter's suit, after the cue-bid, will not be very effective. Hence it uses the double to ask the preempter's partner *not* to lead the suit of the preempt. The double thus suggests that the preempter's suit is broken and that preempter has an outside void or singleton. If the partner of the doubler is the opening leader, he should consider trying to hit the preempter's short suit, especially if he has the ace of trumps.

DOUBLE OF SPLINTER BID TO SHOW ANOTHER SUIT

A splinter bid shows a singleton or void in the suit bid. Traditionally a double of a splinter bid promises that the defender has values in that suit. This treatment has somewhat limited utility since, by hypothesis, at most one trick may be cashed in this suit by the defenders. Indeed, the lead of the suit doubled may even assist the declarer by allowing him to take early ruffs of the suit led or by establishing his own high cards in that suit.

A more modern treatment uses the double of a splinter bid to call for the lead of an unbid suit, which may be a greater source of defensive tricks. If the declaring side has bid three suits, the double calls for the lead of the only unbid suit. If only two suits have been bid, the double calls for the lead of the lower unbid suit.

VI
Two- and Three-Suited Opening Bids

MODIFIED FLANNERY RESPONSES

As originally devised, the responder's jumps to three hearts or three spades over a Flannery opening bid of two diamonds were invitations to opener to bid game with a maximum. *See* FLANNERY TWO DIAMONDS. A modification of the convention uses these responses as game-forcing bids which initiate slam exploration.

Responder's game-forcing jump to three of a major sets the suit of the jump as the trump suit. Opener is asked to describe his distribution as follows:

> four of the agreed major = four spades, five hearts, two cards in each minor suit; minimum (11-13 HCP) strength
>
> cheapest bid in the other major = four spades, five hearts, two cards in each minor; maximum (14-15 HCP) strength
>
> three notrump = four spades, five hearts, two cards in each minor; maximum strength, with a concentration of honors in the minors
>
> four clubs = four spades, five hearts, three or four clubs
>
> four diamonds = four spades, five hearts, three or four diamonds

Following opener's rebid, responder may sign off by bidding four of the agreed major suit. Any other bid by responder is a cue-bid and invites opener to cue-bid an ace or king in return.

Using this modification of the Flannery responses, responder's only way to invite a game in a major suit is to respond two notrump and, over a three club or three diamond rebid by opener (which do not define opener's strength), to bid three of the preferred major suit.

A further modification uses a three diamond response to the two diamond opening as a slam try. Responder's three diamond bid asks opener to indicate with his first rebid only whether he has maximum or minimum strength. It is used when responder does not want to explore for slam unless opener has a maximum, regardless of distribution.

Using this modification, opener rebids three hearts with a minimum, or three spades with a maximum. Opener should show a minimum even with the upper end of the point-count range if his hand looks unsuitable for slam. The influencing factors are whether his high cards are mostly aces and kings, rather than queens and jacks, and whether his high cards are concentrated in his long suits rather than his short suits. Thus, a bid of three hearts, showing a minimum, might be made with a "poor" 14 or 15 count, and a bid of three spades, showing a maximum, might be made with an appropriate 13 count. Examples:

[A] ♠ K J x x   ♡ K Q J x x   ◊ J x   ♣ K J
[B] ♠ K Q x x   ♡ A x x x x   ◊ A x x   ♣ x

Hand A, though it contains 15 HCP, is a poor hand for slam; opener should bid three hearts. In contrast, though hand B has only 13 HCP, opener should consider it a maximum and bid three spades.

If opener rebids three hearts, showing a minimum, responder signs off in four of the major suit he prefers. In this sequence, the three diamond slam try modification has allowed responder to make a slam try and sign off in game opposite a minimum opening, while giving the defenders no further information as to opener's distribution.

If opener has rebid three spades, showing a maximum, responder's next bid sets the trump suit and asks opener to reveal his minor suit distribution. Responder's bid of three notrump agrees on hearts as trumps; his bid of four clubs agrees on spades. In response to either, opener shows his distribution in steps, as follows:

First step = four spades, five hearts, three diamonds, one club
Second step = four spades, five hearts, one diamond, three clubs
Third step = four spades, five hearts, two diamonds, two clubs
Fourth step = four spades, five hearts, four diamonds, no clubs
Fifth step = four spades, five hearts, no diamonds, four clubs

After opener's bid of one of the first three steps, as in the auction

Opener	Responder
2 ◇	3 ◇
3 ♠	4 ♣
4 ♡	

responder may sign off in four of the agreed trump suit or may use an ace-asking bid such as ROMAN KEY CARD BLACKWOOD. After opener's bid of the fourth or fifth step, which takes the partnership beyond four of the agreed trump suit, responder may sign off by bidding five of the agreed suit. If opener's rebid has shown appropriate distribution, responder will of course bid the slam. For example, if the partnership held

Opener
♠ K J x x   ♡ A Q x x x   ◇ A x x x   ♣ —

Responder
♠ A Q x x   ♡ K x   ◇ K Q x x   ♣ x x x

the auction could go

Opener	Responder
2 ◇	3 ◇
3 ♠	4 ♣
4 Notrump	7 ♠

Knowing that opener considers his hand to be a maximum and that all of opener's high cards are concentrated in spades, hearts, and diamonds, responder can envision the grand slam. If opener had bid four diamonds over four clubs, showing a singleton club and three diamonds, responder would settle for six spades. And if opener had shown instead a singleton or void in diamonds, responder would realize that he had wasted values in that suit and would sign off in the minimum number of spades.

FLEXIBLE FLANNERY

As originally devised, the FLANNERY CONVENTION is a two diamond opening bid showing 11-15 HCP, with four spades and five hearts. A modification of Flannery permits opener to open two diamonds with four spades and six hearts as well.

The goal of the modification is to allow the partnership to avoid playing in a 4-3 spade fit when a 6-2 heart fit is available. When the partnership has this understanding, the responder to a Flannery opening must, if he has a weak hand with which he wishes to get out cheaply, bid two hearts. Using traditional Flannery, a responder who holds three spades and two hearts may use his judgment as to which suit to prefer.

Using Flexible Flannery, if the responder wishes to know more about opener's hand he responds two notrump. Opener's first rebids do not give any indication of the strength of his hand, but they describe his distribution as follows.

3♣ = four spades, five hearts, two cards in each minor
3♦ = four spades, five hearts, three diamonds, one club
3♡ = four spades, five hearts, one diamond, three clubs
3♠ = four spades, six hearts, no minor suit void
3NT = four spades, six hearts, minor suit void

After opener has rebid three clubs, responder may ask about opener's strength by rebidding three diamonds. Opener answers as follows:

3♡ = minimum, *i.e.*, 11-13 HCP
3♠ = maximum, *i.e.*, 14-15 HCP
3NT = maximum with concentration of honors in the minor suits

After opener has rebid three spades or three notrump directly over the two notrump response, showing four spades and six hearts, responder can bid four clubs to ask opener to disclose which of his minor suits is the longer. Opener bids four diamonds to show longer clubs, or four hearts to show longer diamonds.

EXTENDED FLANNERY

A traditional Flannery-type opening promises exactly four spades and exactly five hearts. *See* FLANNERY TWO DIAMONDS; FLANNERY TWO HEARTS. The Extended Flannery convention allows a two diamond or two heart opening with any of three major suit holdings: four spades and five hearts, four spades and six hearts, or five spades and six hearts. *See also* FLEXIBLE FLANNERY; EXTRA-SHAPE FLANNERY.

The additional distributions are accommodated by a schedule of rebids in which opener gives only a partial immediate description of his hand if he has minimum strength or semi-balanced distribution. If responder wants to know more after one of these responses, he makes a relay bid to ask for details. *See* RELAYS IN GENERAL.

Responder bids two notrump to ask opener to describe his hand. Using Extended Flannery, opener rebids as follows:

3 ♣ = minimum strength, with any distribution *other than* four spades, five hearts, two diamonds, and two clubs

3 ◇ = four spades, five hearts, two diamonds, and two clubs, with any strength

3 ♡ = four spades and six hearts, with maximum strength

3 ♠ = four spades, five hearts, and three or four diamonds, with maximum strength

3 NT = four spades, five hearts, and three or four clubs, with maximum strength

4 ♣ = five spades, six hearts, two diamonds, and no clubs, with maximum strength

4 ◇ = five spades, six hearts, two clubs, and no diamonds, with maximum strength

4 ♡ = five spades, six hearts, one diamond, and one club

After opener's rebid of three clubs, showing minimum strength, responder may bid three diamonds to ask opener to describe his distribution. Over three diamonds, opener's rebids from three hearts through four hearts show the same distributions that would have been shown by those bids immediately over two notrump. Thus, in the auction

Opener	Responder
2 ◇	2 Notrump
3 ♣	3 ◇
4 ◇	

opener has shown minimum strength, with five spades, six hearts, two clubs, and no diamonds. With maximum strength and this distribution, opener would have bid four diamonds directly over two notrump.

After opener's rebid of three diamonds over two notrump, showing four spades, five hearts, and doubletons in both minor suits, responder may bid three of either major suit to invite opener to bid game if he has a maximum. After opener's rebid of three hearts over two notrump, which shows four spades and six hearts but does not specify the minor-suit distribution, responder may bid three spades to ask for further information. Opener's responses to three spades are as follows:

3 NT = no clubs, three diamonds
4 ♣   = one club, two diamonds
4 ◇   = two clubs, one diamond
4 ♡   = three clubs, no diamonds

Opener's rebids of three spades and three notrump over two notrump reveal which of his minors is shorter but do not disclose whether the shortness is a singleton or a void. Responder may ask for clarification over either of these bids by bidding four clubs. Opener bids four diamonds if his short suit is a singleton; he bids four hearts if it is a void.

EXTRA-SHAPE FLANNERY

A modification of the FLANNERY TWO DIAMONDS convention called Extra-Shape Flannery permits the partnership to open two diamonds not only with four spades and five hearts, but also with four spades, *four* hearts, four diamonds, and a singleton club. Opener clarifies his distribution by his rebid over a two notrump response.

As with the traditional Flannery convention, responder's bid of two notrump asks opener to describe his distribution and, if he has doubletons in both minor suits, to describe his strength. In order to accommodate the 4-4-4-1 opening, the Extra-Shape Flannery rebids of three clubs and three diamonds over two notrump are revised. The three diamond rebid shows the 4-4-4-1 hand, and the three club bid becomes a two-way bid that shows either 3-1 or 1-3 in the minor suits.

The Extra-Shape Flannery schedule of rebids is as follows:

3 ♣ = four spades, five hearts, with either three clubs and one diamond or three diamonds and one club
3 ♢ = four spades, four hearts, four diamonds, and one club
3 ♡ = four spades, five hearts, two diamonds, and two clubs, with minimum strength
3 ♠ = four spades, five hearts, two diamonds, and two clubs, with maximum strength
3 NT = four spades, five hearts, four diamonds, and no clubs
4 ♣ = four spades, five hearts, no diamonds, and four clubs

If opener has rebid three clubs, showing a singleton in one of the minor suits without identifying which, responder may seek further information by bidding three diamonds. Over responder's three diamond rebid, opener bids three hearts to show a singleton diamond, or three spades to show a singleton club.

Other Responses to the Extra-Shape Flannery Opening

Most of the responses to the opening two diamond bid are natural. Two hearts and two spades are signoffs; three hearts and three spades invite game in the suit bid; four hearts and four spades are signoffs. In order to force to game and explore for slam, responder must begin by bidding two notrump.

If responder holds three spades, two hearts, and four cards in each minor suit, he may respond three clubs. This response is not forcing; opener may pass with a minimum hand and three or four clubs. A three diamond rebid by opener would be a correction of contract and would not be forcing.

Using Extra-shape Flannery, the partnership may define responder's jumps to four clubs and four diamonds as key-card asking bids, requiring opener to show how many of the five key cards (the four aces plus the king of trumps) he has. The jump to four clubs establishes hearts as trumps; the jump to four diamonds establishes spades as trumps. If the partnership uses KEY CARD BLACKWOOD, opener would show his key cards by bidding one of the following steps:

First step   = 0 or 4 key cards
Second step = 1 or 5 key cards
Third step = 2 key cards
Fourth step = 3 key cards

If the partnership uses ROMAN KEY CARD BLACKWOOD, opener's step responses would be

First step   = 0 or 3 key cards
Second step = 1 or 4 key cards
Third step = 2 or 5 key cards, without the queen of trumps
Fourth step = 2 or 5 key cards, with the queen of trumps

See also EXTENDED FLANNERY; FLEXIBLE FLANNERY; TWO DIAMOND OPENING AS MINIMUM THREE-SUITER; HEART OPENING AS MINIMUM THREE-SUITER.

TRANSFER RESPONSES TO FLANNERY

The traditional method of responding to a Flannery opening, which promises four spades and five hearts, assigns a special meaning to a three club response. That response asks opener to bid three notrump if he has the ace, king, or queen of clubs. *See* FLANNERY TWO DIAMONDS. This method leaves the partnership no way to reach a partial in clubs.

Transfer responses to Flannery openings of either two diamonds or two hearts (*see* FLANNERY TWO HEARTS) are designed to permit the partnership to stop in three clubs. The meaning of all of the original responses to the Flannery opening are retained except those of two notrump, three clubs, three diamonds, and three hearts. The new artificial responses having the following meanings.

The response of two notrump forces opener to rebid three clubs. Responder will pass if he has a weak hand with a long club suit. Or he may invite game in a major suit by bidding three hearts or three spades. If responder wishes to know opener's minor distribution, he rebids three diamonds after opener's forced three club bid. Opener replies as follows

$3\heartsuit$ = singleton diamond, three clubs
$3\spadesuit$ = singleton club, three diamonds
3NT = no singleton, *i.e.*, 4-5-2-2 distribution
$4\clubsuit$ = four clubs, void in diamonds
$4\diamondsuit$ = four diamonds, void in clubs

The response of three clubs to the Flannery opening asks opener whether he has stoppers in clubs and/or diamonds. Opener bids three diamonds to announce a stopper in one suit but not both. Responder bids three hearts to ask which; opener rebids three spades to show a club stopper, or three notrump to show a diamond stopper. If opener has stoppers in both minors, he shows them over responder's three-clubs by bidding three hearts with minimum strength or three spades with maximum strength.

The responses of three diamonds and three hearts over the Flannery opening are transfers to hearts and spades, respectively. These responses are forcing to game and show slam interest. The partnership may agree on a cue-bidding structure to follow.

There are flaws in this scheme of responding. It presents the opponents with several opportunities to make lead-directing doubles or artificial bids. More importantly, it does not permit responder to both learn opener's distribution and extend a game invitation. Given these flaws and the complexity of the conventions mechanism, it seems a high price to pay in order to be able to play in three clubs.

REVERSE FLANNERY

The Flannery Convention is an opening bid that promises four spades and five hearts. *See* FLANNERY TWO DIAMONDS; FLANNERY TWO HEARTS. "Reverse" Flannery is a conventional opening bid of two hearts to promise five spades and four hearts.

This device is used by partnerships whose bidding style is based on the canape principle of bidding short suits before long suits. *See, e.g.,* BLUE TEAM CLUB. Using the canape style, the combination of five spades and four hearts cannot easily be shown.

Since partnerships using canape style systems, such as the Blue Team system, usually have committed their two diamond opening to some other purpose, the opening used to show the "reverse" Flannery is two hearts.

ONE-TWO-THREE TWO-SUITERS

The One-Two-Three Two-Suiter convention devotes opening bids of two in a suit other than clubs (the two-club opening is strong, artificial, and forcing) to weak hands containing two long suits. The suit lengths may be 5-4, 5-5, 6-5, or 6-6. The promised strength is 2-10 points not vulnerable or 4-11 vulnerable. The name of the convention derives from the fact that, in ascending order, the three two-suited openings show one, or either of two, or any of three pairs of suits.

The Two Diamond Opening: The Majors

The two diamond opening promises both major suits. Responder may pass, or may bid two hearts or two spades as a sign-off; or he may preempt to three or four hearts or spades. A three club response is also a sign-off.

Responder's forcing bid is two notrump, asking opener to show whether he has a minimum or a maximum and, if a maximum, to show his distribution. Opener rebids three clubs with minimum strength and any distribution. Other rebids promise a maximum with the following distribution:

3 ♦ = five spades, five hearts, one diamond, two clubs
3 ♡ = four spades, five hearts, any minor suit distribution
3 ♠ = five spades, four hearts, any minor suit distribution
3NT = five spades, five hearts, two diamonds, one club
4 ♣ = five spades, five hearts, three diamonds, no clubs
4 ♦ = five spades, five hearts, no diamonds, three clubs
4 ♡ = six spades and five hearts, or five spades and six hearts

After a three club rebid by opener, showing a minimum, responder may inquire as to opener's distribution by bidding three diamonds. Opener rebids as above except that the three notrump bid is made with either two diamonds and one club, or one diamond and two clubs.

The Two Heart Opening (Two Possibilities)

The two heart opening shows a long club suit and either a spade suit or a diamond suit. Responder can bid three clubs as a sign-off, or a nonforcing three diamonds, which shows support for diamonds and a tolerance for spades. Opener should correct to three spades if that is his second suit. Or responder may bid two spades, which is not forcing if opener's second suit is spades. If his second suit is diamonds, opener will bid again; he should bid three clubs with longer or better clubs than diamonds, two notrump with longer or better diamonds.

Responder's forcing bid is two notrump. This response, which is not forcing to game, however, asks opener to show his second suit and, if it is spades, whether his strength is minimum or maximum. Opener rebids as follows

    3♣ = clubs and diamonds
    3◊ = clubs and spades with minimum strength
    3♡ = clubs and spades with maximum strength

Following any of these rebids, responder's bid of opener's higher ranking suit is not forcing.

The Two Spade Opening (Three Possibilities)

The two spade opening shows that opener's suits are either clubs and hearts, or diamonds and a major.

In order to sign off, responder bids at the three level. His bid shows some tolerance for both the suit bid and the next higher suit. Thus, a three club response shows tolerance for both minors; a three-diamond response shows tolerance for both red suits; and a three-heart response shows tolerance for both majors. In each case, opener will have length in either the suit of the response or in the next higher suit. He will pass or correct accordingly.

The only forcing response to the two spade opening is two notrump. Opener rebids as follows:

    3♣ = clubs and hearts
    3◊ = diamonds and hearts
    3♡ = diamonds and spades

Following any of these rebids, any suit bid by responder may be passed.

GORSKI TWO DIAMONDS

The Gorski Two Diamond convention uses an opening bid of two diamonds to show either a balanced hand worth 12-14 HCP with four cards in each major suit, or a FLANNERY-type hand, *i.e.*, 11-15 HCP with four spades and five hearts.

The only forcing response is two hearts. This response, which responder will rarely use with fewer than 11 HCP, is artificial and says nothing about responder's heart holding. Rather, it asks opener to disclose his precise distribution. Opener rebids as follows:

2♠ = four spades, five hearts, two diamonds, two clubs, 11-13 HCP

2NT = four spades, four hearts, either 3-2 or 2-3 in diamonds and clubs; 12-14 HCP

3♣ = four spades, five hearts, one diamond, three clubs; point count unspecified

3◇ = four spades, five hearts, three diamonds, one club; point count unspecified

3♡ = four spades, five hearts, two diamonds, two clubs; 14-15 HCP

3NT = four spades, five hearts, two diamonds, two clubs; 14-15 HCP, with high cards concentrated in the minor suits

4♣ = four spades, five hearts, four clubs

4◇ = four spades, five hearts, four diamonds

DYNAMIC TWO DIAMONDS

The Dynamic Two Diamond convention uses an opening bid of two diamonds to show a hand with 5-10 HCP and five or more cards in each major suit. Responder may sign off at two of either major, or may preempt by jumping to any level in either major. Responses of two notrump, three clubs, and three diamonds are artificial and forcing.

A response of two notrump is a relay bid, requiring opener to bid three clubs. This response is made with one of two types of hands, neither of which seeks a major suit game. First, responder may have a long club suit and wish to play the club partial; if he has this type of hand he simply passes the three club rebid.

Alternatively, responder may have a hand with which he wishes to play three notrump if opener has the maximum strength for his opening. Responder might have

$$\spadesuit A Q \qquad \heartsuit x x \qquad \diamondsuit A K Q x \qquad \clubsuit Q J 10 x x$$

With such a hand, responder bids three diamonds over opener's forced three club bid. Opener now bids three hearts with 5-7 points, or three spades with 8-10. Over three hearts, responder may pass; a bid by him of three spades would be a sign-off. If opener has a decent six-card heart suit he would probably be well advised, even with 5-7 points, to bid four hearts rather than three.

A response of three clubs to the two diamond opening asks opener to bid his better major suit. Responder may pass the rebid or raise to game.

A response of three diamonds is used when responder has a hand worth an invitation to game in a major suit. Apparently, responder's preference as between hearts and spades is undisclosed. Opener is required to bid three hearts with a hand worth 5-7 points and no compensating length values and no semi-solid suit. If opener has a maximum, *i.e.*, 8-10 points, he rebids three notrump if his major suits are of equal length and quality; or he bids four clubs with better hearts and four diamonds with better spades. Responder may pass opener's three heart bid; responder's three spade bid over three hearts by opener would be a signoff.

UNI-CLUB TWO HEART AND TWO SPADE OPENINGS

In the UNIVERSAL CLUB SYSTEM an opening bid of two hearts or two spades promises five cards in the suit bid and another, unspecified, five-card suit, with 14 or more HCP. For a Uni-Club two heart bid opener's minimum would be

$$\spadesuit x \qquad \heartsuit A K x x x \qquad \diamondsuit x x \qquad \clubsuit A K x x x$$

Apparently there is no upper limit. These openings are forcing for one round.

Responder bids as follows over the two heart or two spade opening. Holding three or more of opener's promised suit, he raises to three with 0-6 HCP. If he has a fit for opener's promised suit and 7-12 HCP, he jumps to four clubs.

Responder's bid of a new suit in response to the two-heart or two-spade opening promises a six-card suit of his own. A response of three notrump shows a solid suit with six or seven winners.

If responder lacks the wherewithal to make any of the above responses, or if he wishes to know opener's second suit, he responds two notrump. Opener rebids his second suit naturally unless his hand contains more than nine playing tricks. Opener's bid of three of his second suit is not forcing.

If opener's hand contains ten or more playing tricks, he rebids three notrump over responder's two notrump response. The three notrump call is forcing and requires responder to bid four clubs in order to permit opener to identify his second suit. Opener now rebids his second suit by bidding four of that suit unless the suit is clubs. If his second suit is clubs he rebids the suit he has opened. In this sequence, the partnership is committed to game.

UNI-CLUB TWO CLUB OPENING

In the UNIVERSAL CLUB SYSTEM, an opening bid of two clubs shows a three-suited hand worth 12-17 HCP. The short suit is diamonds. The Uni-Club two club opening is not forcing.

Responses of two hearts and two spades are nonforcing sign-off bids. A response of three clubs is preemptive.

The only forcing response is two diamonds. The two diamond bid is artificial and suggests that responder has at least a 10-point hand. It asks opener to describe his strength in steps. Opener's rebids are as follows:

$$2\heartsuit = 12\text{-}13 \text{ HCP}$$
$$2\spadesuit = 14\text{-}15 \text{ HCP}$$
$$2\text{NT} = 16\text{-}17 \text{ HCP}$$

UNI-CLUB TWO DIAMOND OPENING

In the UNIVERSAL CLUB SYSTEM, an opening bid of two diamonds shows a three-suited hand worth 16-21 HCP. Diamonds must be one of opener's suits. The Uni-Club two diamond opening is not forcing.

The only forcing response to two diamonds is two hearts. This call is artificial and asks opener to identify his short suit. Opener does so by rebidding as follows:

> 2♠ = short in spades
> 2NT = short in hearts
> 3♣ = short in clubs

Following such a rebid, responder's bid in one of opener's long suits, or his bid of two notrump over two spades, invites opener to bid game with 19-21 points.

If responder has a weak hand with length in diamonds, he passes the two diamond opening bid. In order to sign off in one of opener's other suits, responder makes the cheapest nonforcing bid in a suit in which he is willing to play. If opener is short in the suit bid by responder, he bids again; otherwise he passes.

TWO-SUIT TWO-BIDS

The Two-Suit Two-Bid convention assigns two-suited meanings to three two-level openings.

An opening bid of two clubs shows 12-19 points, including distribution, and at least five cards in each minor suit. The two club opening is not forcing. Responder may pass or may sign off in two diamonds. With interest in game, responder may bid three clubs asking opener to bid on with a maximum. Responder may create a game forcing auction by responding three diamonds over two clubs.

An opening bid of two hearts shows 12-19 points with at least five hearts and a five-card minor. Responder may pass or may bid two notrump to ask opener to bid his second suit.

An opening bid of two spades shows 12-19 points with at least five spades and another, unspecified, five-card suit. Responder may pass or may bid two notrump to seek identification of opener's second suit.

An opening bid of two diamonds is a multi-purpose strong, forcing bid. It may be made with a one-suited hand suitable for a traditional ARTIFICIAL TWO CLUB OPENING, or a two- or three-suited hand worth 20 or more points, including distribution, or a balanced hand containing 27 or more HCP.

Employing this convention the partnership may neither use weak two-bids nor ACOL TWO-BIDS. And given that the Two-Suit Two-Bid convention is devoted to hands worth an opening bid of one, its utility seems substantially lower than that of other bidding devices that accommodate one or both types of one-suited two-bids, *see, e.g.,* COMPREHENSIVE MULTICOLORED TWO-BIDS; TARTAN TWO-BIDS, or that show two-suited hands too weak to open at the one level, *see, e.g.,* PENDER TWO-BIDS; ONE-TWO-THREE TWO-SUITERS.

NOISICERP TWO DIAMOND OPENING

The Noisicerp convention is a two diamond opening showing 10-14 high card points and three four-card suits, one of which must be diamonds. The convention is intended to avoid the rebid problem resulting from a minimum one diamond opening in a system in which both a one notrump rebid and a two club rebid show extra values.

The two diamond opening is not forcing. Responder needs 11-12 points to try for game. He may pass if he has a diamond fit and a weaker hand. If he wishes to learn in which suit opener has the singleton, responder bids two notrump. Opener then identifies his singleton as follows:

3 ♣ = singleton club
3 ◇ = singleton spade
3 ♡ = singleton heart

For other possible responding actions, *see* TWO DIAMOND OPENING AS A MINIMUM THREE-SUITER; ROMAN TWO DIAMONDS; TWO-PHASE TWO NOTRUMP RESPONSE TO THREE-SUITED OPENINGS.

TWO HEART OPENING AS A MINIMUM
THREE-SUITER

Many top ranking British pairs use an opening bid of two hearts to show a hand with three four-card suits and 10-15 points. One of the three suits must be hearts; the other two suits are not disclosed by the opening bid. The two heart opening is not forcing.

Responder needs at least 11-12 points to try for game. With less, he tries to find a fit in which to play a part-score. The following schedule of responses may be used:

2 ♠	= natural, not forcing; but opener should not pass if he has a singleton spade
2 NT	= artificial, game forcing; asks opener for more information
3 ♣	= natural, not forcing; but opener should not pass if he has a singleton club
3 ◊	= natural; a signoff opposite a singleton diamond, but forcing if opener has four diamonds
3 ♡	= natural, game invitation
3 ♠	= solid spade suit and asks opener how many aces and kings he has
3 NT	= natural, signoff
4 ♣	= clubs and spades; game forcing, without slam interest
4 ◊	= diamonds and spades; game forcing, without slam interest
4 ♡	= natural, signoff
4 ♠	= clubs and diamonds; game forcing, without slam interest

Within this framework, responder's bids of two spades, three clubs, and three diamonds are natural and not forward-going. As indicated in the next section, however, in some circumstances, opener is required to rebid.

With a good two-suited hand in which hearts is not one of the long suits, responder jumps to the four level as shown above. These jumps show no interest in slam. Over four clubs or four diamonds, opener should bid game in spades if he has four spades; with a singleton spade, he bids game in the minor suit. Over the jump to four spades, opener bids game in his better minor.

If responder has game-going values but is unsure in what suit to play, or if he wishes to explore for slam, he must respond two notrump.

When responder has bid two spades or three clubs, opener should not pass unless he has four cards in the suit bid and has minimum strength. If, over a two spade response, opener has a singleton spade, or if he has four spades and better than a minimum, he rebids as follows:

2 NT = singleton spade and minimum strength
3 ♣ = singleton spade and better than minimum strength
3 ◇ = singleton club and better than minimum strength
3 ♡ = singleton diamond and better than minimum strength

Over responder's bid of three clubs in response to the two heart opening, if opener has a singleton club, or if he has four clubs and better than a minimum, he rebids as follows:

3 ◇ = singleton club and minimum strength
3 ♡ = singleton club and better than minimum strength
3 ♠ = singleton diamond and better than minimum strength
3 NT = singleton spade and better than minimum strength

After any of these rebids, responder's next bid is usually the final contract.

After responder's bid of three diamonds in response to the two heart opening, opener should pass if he has a singleton diamond. If, however, he has four diamonds, he must bid again, regardless of his strength.

Opener's Rebids After Two Notrump Response

The response of two notrump is game forcing. It asks opener to identify his singleton as follows:

3 ♣ = singleton diamond
3 ◇ = singleton club
3 ♡ = singleton spade

After opener's rebid, responder may set the final contract by bidding game in notrump or in one of the suits in which opener has shown length. Alternatively, responder may explore for slam by asking opener how many controls (ace = 2, king = 1) his hand contains or what high cards he has in a specific suit.

In order to ask about controls, responder normally bids the suit in which opener has shown a singleton. The one exception is that, in order to save space after opener's rebid of three diamonds, showing a singleton club, responder's control-asking bid is three hearts. In response to a control-asking bid, opener bids in steps as follows:

First step   = 0-2 controls
Second step   = 3 controls
Third step   = 4 controls
Fourth step   = 5 controls
Fifth step   = 6 controls
Sixth step   = 7 controls

In order to ask opener what high cards he holds in a specific suit, responder makes a bid below game in that suit. Opener responds to these suit-asking bids in steps, showing the following:

First step   = neither the ace nor the king
Second step   = ace or king, but not both, and no queen
Third step   = ace-king, or ace-queen, or king-queen, but not all three top honors
Fourth step   = ace, king, and queen

Responder may, on a given hand, make both types of asking bids. Either type asking bid may be made first, so long as the suit-asking bid is made below the level of game. For example:

[A]	Opener	Responder	[B]	Opener	Responder
	2 ♡	2 Notrump		2 ♡	2 Notrump
	3 ♣	3 ♡		3 ♣	3 ◇
	3 Notrump	4 ◇		3 Notrump	4 ♣
	4 Notrump			4 ♡	

In each auction, opener's three club rebid shows a singleton diamond. In auction A, responder's three heart rebid asks about the strength of opener's hearts; opener's bid of three notrump, the second step, shows the ace or the king. Over three notrump, responder's bid of four diamonds, opener's singleton, asks how many controls opener has. Opener's bid of four notrump, the third step, shows four controls.

In auction B, responder's rebid of three diamonds, opener's singleton, asks about opener's controls. Opener's bid of three notrump, the third step, shows four controls. Responder's bid of four clubs now asks about club strength, and opener's four heart bid, the second step, shows the ace or king.

Responder's bid of three spades directly over the two heart opening promises a solid spade suit and asks opener how many controls he has. Opener uses the six-step schedule shown in the preceding section for responding to a control-asking bid when the first response was two notrump.

After opener's control-showing response to the three spade inquiry, responder may bid a new suit to ask about opener's high cards in the new suit. Opener's responses conform to the four-step schedule shown above.

There are two respects in which responder's asking bids here differ from his asking bids after his two notrump response. First, the control-asking bid automatically precedes the suit-asking bid, since the three spade response not only shows his suit but is itself the asking bid. Second, his ensuing suit-asking bid may be above the game level. Thus, in the auction

Opener	Responder
2 ♡	3 ♠
4 ◇	4 ♡, 5 ♣, or 5 ◇

each of the final bids shown for responder would ask about opener's high cards in the suit bid.

See also ROMAN TWO CLUBS; TWO DIAMOND OPENING AS MINIMUM THREE-SUITER; EXTRA-SHAPE FLANNERY.

TWO-PHASE TWO NOTRUMP RESPONSE TO THREE-SUITED OPENINGS

When the partnership has agreed to use three-suited opening bids such as NEAPOLITAN TWO DIAMONDS or TWO DIAMONDS AS MINIMUM THREE-SUITER, it needs a way to have opener show both his strength and his singleton at a convenient level of the auction. Use of a two-phase two notrump relay may be helpful opposite such openings.

Over two notrump, opener's cheapest bid, three clubs, shows minimum strength, with four diamonds. This rebid keeps the auction low when opener's values are slim and permits responder to sign off in three diamonds. If responder does not want to sign off in three diamonds, he may make a further relay bid to learn more about opener's distribution.

Opener's next cheapest rebid over two notrump, three diamonds, specifies his distribution but not his strength. This bid shows a singleton diamond. All higher bids by opener pinpoint his distribution and promise maximum values.

The complete schedule of opener's rebids over two notrump is as follows:

3 ♣	=	minimum strength, four diamonds, singleton otherwise undisclosed
3 ♦	=	singleton diamond, strength undisclosed
3 ♥	=	singleton heart, maximum strength
3 ♠	=	singleton spade, maximum strength
3 NT	=	singleton club, maximum strength

After opener's three club rebid, responder may ask where the singleton is by bidding three diamonds. Opener's bids of three hearts and three spades show singletons in the suits bid; his bid of three notrump shows a singleton club.

VII
Offensive Preemptive Conventions

KANTAR THREE NOTRUMP

The Kantar Three Notrump convention is an opening bid of three notrump based on a solid seven or eight card major suit with no side suit aces and with at most one side suit king. Using this device, opening bids of four hearts and four spades deny solid suits. The convention is designed to remove the ambiguity of four-level major suit preempts as to suit quality and outside controls. The convention key facilitates the evaluation of slam prospects.

The responder may pass if he judges that three notrump is a better contract than four of the opener's suit. If he wants to play game in the opener's suit, the responder may bid four of what he thinks is the opener's suit (the opener will correct if the responder guesses wrong); or if the responder judges that the opener should be the declarer at four of his suit, he bids four diamonds, asking the opener simply to bid his suit.

If the responder has greater aspirations, he may make any of a number of asking bids. A four-club response over three notrump asks opener to bid a side suit in which he has a king; or otherwise to bid his long suit. With the king of clubs, the opener rebids four notrump. The responder should be sure what the opener's suit is in order to make the four club asking bid; otherwise he will find a bid of four hearts or four spades by the opener to be ambiguous. If the opener shows a side king and the responder wants to play at slam with the opener as the declarer, he jumps to six clubs, asking the opener to bid his suit.

A four notrump response to the three notrump opening asks the opener what outside queens he has. The same query may be made after the responder has bid four clubs to ask about kings. If the opener has one outside queen, he bids it; if he has two outside queens, he jumps to the six level as follows:

6♣ = queen of diamonds plus queen of other major
6◊ = queen of clubs plus queen of other major
6♡ = queen of clubs plus queen of diamonds

A response of five notrump over the three notrump opening asks the opener to bid a grand slam if his suit is good enough to play for no losers opposite a void.

If the opener and the responder hold the following hands

(Opener)
♠ A K Q J x x x   ♡ x x   ◊ Q x   ♣ x x
(Responder)
♠ x   ♡ A Q x x   ◊ A K x x x   ♣ A x x

the bidding might go —

Opener	Responder
3 Notrump	4♣ (kings?)
4♠ (no kings)	4 Notrump (queens?)
5◊ (◊ Q)	7♠

Knowing that the opener has a solid spade suit, the responder wants to bid the grand slam if the opener has either the king of hearts or the queen of diamonds. He gets to ask about each card rather than just gambling.

RUBIN OPENING TRANSFERS

A system of four-level opening transfer bids designed to distinguish between weaker and stronger preempts and to make it more difficult for the opponents to find a good sacrifice against game or slam is called Rubin Transfers. Openings of four clubs, four diamonds, and four notrump are artificial and show strength; openings of four hearts and four spades are natural and weak.

The four club opening bid promises either a hand with a long semi-solid major suit and 3½ to 4 honor tricks, or a minor suit with 2½ to 3 honor tricks and no voids.

A response of four diamonds simply asks opener to bid his suit.

A response of four hearts or four spades is a slam try.

If the responder bids five diamonds or five clubs, he shows a semi-solid suit which the opener may raise to slam if he has first-round controls in three suits.

The four diamond opening bid shows a hand with a long, strong major suit and 2½ to 3 honor tricks. If the responder has no slam interest, he bids four hearts. If the opener's suit is hearts, he will pass; if his suit is spades, he will bid four spades.

If the responder has interest in a heart slam, he responds four spades to the four diamond opening. If the responder has interest in slam no matter which suit the opener has, he can bid five clubs or five diamonds as cue-bids, or four notrump as Blackwood.

Using Rubin transfers, if the opener and the responder have the following hands:

(Opener)
♠ A K J x x x   ♡ x x   ◊ K x x   ♣ x

(Responder)
♠ Q x x   ♡ A x x   ◊ A Q x x x   ♣ A x

the bidding might go —

Opener	Responder
4 ◊	5 ♣
5 ◊	5 ♡
5 ♠	5 NT (Grand Slam Force)
7 ♠	

The four notrump opening bid shows a strong hand with long clubs or diamonds, with at least one void. If the responder has no interest in slam, he should bid five clubs.

If he holds three aces, he should bid five spades; holding all four aces, he should bid five notrump.

FOUR CLUBS AND FOUR DIAMONDS AS POWER PREEMPTS

Power Preempts are opening bids of four clubs and four diamonds to show precise strengths for four-level preempts in hearts or spades. Unlike the NAMYATS convention, which uses a four club opening to show hearts and a four diamond opening to show spades, Power Preempt openings of four clubs and four diamonds do not identify which major suit is held. *See also* KANTAR THREE NOTRUMP, RUBIN OPENING TRANSFERS. The premise of this convention is that if responder has a good hand he will be able to infer which suit opener holds, or, if his hand is weak, the initial ambiguity will be immaterial.

In the Power Preempt convention, an opening bid of four clubs shows a preempt in hearts or spades with no losers in the long suit. A four diamond opening shows a preempt in hearts or spades with a one-loser suit. In first or second seat, the four club opening denies an ace or king of a side suit; the four diamond opening may, but is not required to, include a side ace or king.

In response to either opening, responder may sign off or make an asking bid. If responder has no interest in slam in either hearts or spades, he signs off by bidding four hearts. Opener, if his suit is hearts, passes; otherwise he bids four spades, which responder passes.

If responder has interest in slam when opener's suit is spades but not when it is hearts, he bids four hearts. Opener will of course pass if his suit is hearts; but if his suit is spades, he will bid four spades, and responder may then proceed accordingly.

If responder has slam interest when opener's suit is hearts but not when the suit is spades, he responds four spades over the four club or four diamond opening. Opener must pass if his suit is spades. If his suit is hearts, he treats the four spade bid as an asking bid.

In response to either a four club or a four diamond opening, responder's bids of five of a minor suit are asking bids. Five clubs asks about clubs; five diamonds asks about diamonds. These bids are also asking bids after opener has identified his suit, *e.g.*, in the auction

Opener	Responder
4 ♣	4 ♡
4 ♠	5 ♣ or 5 ◊

As indicated, if opener's suit is hearts, a bid of four spades is also an asking bid in spades in the auction

Opener	Responder
4 ♣	4 ♠

In addition, responses in notrump are asking bids. Because the four club and four diamond openings in first or second seat have different restrictions with respect to outside strength, responder's asking bids in notrump have different meanings depending on which opening bid was used. Further, the answers to the suit asking bids differ somewhat depending on the opening.

Asking Bid Responses and Rebids Following a Four Club Opening

Since the four club opening in first or second seat denies any ace or king outside the long suit, the initial suit-asking bids ask opener only about distributional control. He responds by steps:

First step   = doubleton or longer
Second step = singleton
Third step   = void

Thereafter, if responder bids the same suit, he asks whether opener has the queen of the suit. Opener's bid of the first step over the new asking bid denies the queen; the second step shows the queen.

Opposite the four club opening, responder's bid of four notrump asks whether opener has any outside queen. Opener bids five of a suit in which he has the queen; with no outside queen, he bids his long suit. Responder's bid of five notrump directly over the four club opening asks opener whether he has extra length in his suit.

Asking bid Responses And Rebids Following a Four Diamond Opening

Opposite a four diamond opening, responder's bid of four notrump is ROMAN KEY CARD BLACKWOOD. Responder's bids of five clubs and five diamonds remain asking bids in those suits. Since the four diamond opening does not deny an ace or king outside the long suit, the four diamond opener's answers to responder's suit asking bids are as follows:

First step   = doubleton or longer
Second step = king
Third step   = singleton
Fourth step = ace
Fifth step   = void

1073

After opener bids the first step, if responder bids the same suit, he asks whether opener has third round control. Opener answers in three steps:

First step   = no third round control
Second step = doubleton
Third step   = queen

Using these methods, if the partnership held the following hands,

Opener
♠ A K J 10 x x x   ♡ x x   ◊ x x   ♣ K x
Responder
♠ Q x   ♡ A J 10   ◊ A x   ♣ A Q J x x x

the bidding might be

Opener	*Responder*
4 ◊	5 ♣
5 ♡	7 Notrump

Responder can envision a grand slam if opener has the king or a singleton club. Since opener bids the second step, showing the king, responder can count more than enough top tricks for the grand slam in notrump.

Third- and Fourth-Seat Openings

Opposite a passed hand, the requirements for a Power Preempt are slightly modified. Opener's suit must include the ace. This knowledge will help responder to decide whether to sacrifice if the opponents enter the auction. In addition, opener must have at least one outside ace or king.

Responder's new-suit responses to each opening remain asking bids. Opener's answers after either opening are those set forth above with respect to the four diamond opening.

Power Preempts as Overcalls

Power Preempts may be used not only as openings but also as overcalls when the bidding has been opened by the opponents with one of a minor suit. The responding structure remains the same.

See also ROMEX NAMYATS.

ROMEX NAMYATS

The Romex variation of the NAMYATS convention sets precise requirements for the opening bids of four clubs as a heart preempt and four diamonds as a spade preempt. For a Romex Namyats opening, opener's hand must meet certain criteria with respect to distribution, trump suit quality, losers, and controls. Romex Namyats also modifies and sets standards for certain of the responses.

Requirements for Four Club and Four Diamond Openings

The opening bid of four clubs shows a constructive preempt in hearts, and the opening bid of four diamonds shows a constructive preempt in spades. In Romex Namyats, opener's major suit must be seven, eight, or nine cards long. His hand should not contain a void. It should contain four or four and one-half "losers." In the Romex system, losers are counted within suits, as follows. In any suit shorter than three cards, a loser is counted for each card that is not the ace or king; in any suit longer than two cards, a loser is counted for any of the three top honors that are missing. No suit is deemed to have more than three losers. For purposes of Romex Namyats, the absence of the queen of opener's long suit is considered half a loser.

The Romex Namyats opener's hand must contain one or two aces and one or two of the five key cards (the four aces and the king of trump). If it has only one key card, it must have the queen of trump. Finally, the hand may not contain as many as five controls (ace = two, king = one). This limitation on controls coordinates closely with Romex's DYNAMIC ONE NOTRUMP openings.

Examples:

[A] ♠ A K J x x x x
♥ x x
♦ x
♣ K Q x

[B] ♠ A K Q x x x x x
♥ —
♦ K x
♣ x x x

[C] ♠ K x
♥ A J 10 x x x x x
♦ K x
♣ x

[D] ♠ x
♥ A K x x x x x x
♦ A
♣ x x x

Hand A is an appropriate four diamond opening. It contains four controls, four and one-half losers, one ace, and two key cards. Hand B is not an appropriate four diamond opening; though it has only four losers and fewer

1075

than five controls, it is "flawed" because it contains a void. Hand C fails to meet the requirements for a four club opening; though it has four and one-half losers, fewer than five controls, and no void, it contains only one key card and lacks the queen of trump. Hand D is inappropriate for a four club opening because it contains five controls. If the king of hearts were the queen, it would fail to meet the requirements because it would have five losers.

Responses and Rebids

In responding to Romex Namyats, responder takes into account the fact that opener has precisely four or four and one-half losers and precisely one or two key cards. In order to try for slam, responder must have at least two key cards and be able to cover three losers. If his hand does not meet these requirements, he signs off by bidding four hearts over a four club opening, or four spades over a four diamond opening. After the signoff, opener may not bid again.

If responder has at least two key cards in his own hand and has at least second round control of all side suits, he may commence slam exploration by asking opener how many key cards he has. The KEY CARD BLACKWOOD bid is the suit just above the opening bid, *i.e.*, four diamonds over four clubs, or four hearts over four diamonds.

Opener's responses to the Blackwood bid are modified to take account of the Romex Namyats requirements that he have precisely one or two key cards. His responses, in steps, are

First step = one key card, with the queen of trumps
Second step = two key cards, without the queen of trumps
Third step = two key cards, with the queen of trumps

For example, opposite a four diamond opening, if responder holds

♠ x x x   ♡ K Q   ◇ A K Q x x   ♣ A x x

he has the requisite key cards and controls, and knows that the partnership is lacking at least one, but not more than two, key cards. He would bid four hearts, Key Card Blackwood. Opener might hold, for example,

[A] ♠ K Q x x x x x   ♡ x   ◇ x   ♣ K Q x x

[B] ♠ A K J x x x x   ♡ x x   ◇ x   ♣ K Q x

With hand A, opener would bid four spades, showing one key card. Responder, knowing that the partnership was missing two key cards, would sign off at five spades. With hand B, opener would bid four notrump, showing two key cards. Responder, knowing the partnership was missing only one ace or the king of trumps, would bid six spades.

If responder has a hand with which a slam invitation is appropriate except that it lacks first or second round control of one of the side suits, he may use the Key Card LACKWOOD convention. If opener has control in the problem suit, he will show the number of key cards he has.

Following opener's disclosure of his key cards, if a grand slam is a possibility, responder makes the cheapest bid other than the trump suit. This bid asks opener to make a SPIRAL CUE-BID.

See also KEY CARD NAMYATS RESPONSES: FOUR CLUBS AND FOUR DIAMONDS AS POWER PREEMPTS.

KEY CARD NAMYATS RESPONSES

The usual responses to NAMYATS opening bids of four clubs, showing a constructive preempt in hearts, and four diamonds, showing a constructive preempt in spades, allow responder to make CONTROL ASKING BIDS in order to invite slam if opener has control of a particular side suit. One modification, Key Card Namyats, gives artificial meanings to suit responses other than four of the suit shown by the opening bid (the ''anchor'' suit). The modified responses allow the partners to collaborate in the determination of whether the partnership has sufficient trump quality, controls, and key cards (*i.e.*, the four aces plus the king of opener's suit), to bid a slam.

Key-Card-and-Control-Showing Responses

If responder has no slam interest, he bids four of the anchor suit. Any other response through five of the anchor suit is artificial, showing slam interest and revealing how many of the five key cards responder has. In addition, three of these responses identify a suit in which responder has neither first nor second round control.

After an opening bid of four clubs, responder's slam-interest bids are as follows:

    4 ◇ = 1 or 3 key cards
    4 ♠ = 2 key cards, with 2 quick losers in spades
    5 ♣ = 2 key cards, with 2 quick losers in clubs
    5 ◇ = 2 key cards, with 2 quick losers in diamonds
    5 ♡ = 2 key cards, no suit with 2 quick losers, singleton or void
            in hearts

After a four diamond opening, the slam-interest responses are:

    4 ♡ = 1 or 3 key cards
    5 ♣ = 2 key cards, with 2 quick losers in clubs
    5 ◇ = 2 key cards, with 2 quick losers in diamonds
    5 ♡ = 2 key cards, with 2 quick losers in hearts
    5 ♠ = 2 key cards, no suit with 2 quick losers, singleton or void
            in spades

After responder has shown precisely two key cards, opener often can accurately place the final contract. He signs off in five of the anchor suit in any of three circumstances: (1) when he has only one key card in his own hand (unless he also has a void); (2) when he has neither first nor second round control of a suit in which responder has shown two quick losers; or (3) when he has inadequate trump quality opposite responder's announcement of trump shortness.

If opener knows from responder's bid that the partnership has all five key cards but he remains unsure whether slam should be bid, he may, if there is room, bid a new suit below five of the anchor suit. If there is room for more than one such new-suit bid, opener bids the suit in which he has values.

If opener knows from responder's bid that the partnership should bid at least a small slam and that a grand slam is a possibility, he may try for seven in one of the following ways. If the partnership has all five key cards, opener bids five notrump. If the partnership is missing one key card but opener has a void, he bids the suit of his void above five of the anchor suit.

For example, if opener and responder held

Opener
♠ A Q J x x x x   ♡ A x x x   ◇ x x   ♣ —

Responder
♠ K x   ♡ x x   ◇ A K Q x x x   ♣ K Q x

the auction would be

Opener	Responder
4 ◇	5 ♡
6 ♣	7 ♠

Responder's five heart bid shows slam interest, two key cards, and neither first nor second round control of hearts. Opener's bid of six clubs, going beyond five of the agreed spade suit, shows grand slam interest, no more than one key card missing, and a void in clubs. Responder can infer that opener has the ace of hearts, both because the partnership is missing only one key card which must be the club ace since opener is void in clubs and responder does not have it, and because opener's continued interest in a grand slam opposite responder's announced lack of heart control implies that opener himself has first round heart control.

Rebids After Response Showing One or Three Key Cards

Responder's bid of four diamonds in response to a four club opening and his bid of four hearts in response to a four diamond opening are ambiguous, showing one or three key cards. Opener will not be sure how many key cards the partnership holds unless he himself has more than two. After this response, opener returns to four of the anchor suit unless he has either three key cards or two key cards and a void.

If opener has bid four of the anchor suit, responder bids again if he has three key cards rather than one. Responder's bids over four of the anchor suit have the same control-showing meanings they would have had if made directly over the opening bid. Thus, in this sequence

4 ♠ (when anchor suit is hearts) = 3 key cards, with 2 quick losers in spades

5 ♣ = 3 key cards, with 2 quick losers in clubs

5 ♦ = 3 key cards, with 2 quick losers in diamonds

5 ♡ (when anchor suit is hearts) = 3 key cards, no suit with 2 quick losers, singleton or void in hearts

5 ♡ (when anchor suit is spades) = 3 key cards, with 2 quick losers in hearts

5 ♠ (when anchor suit is spades) = 3 key cards, no suit with 2 quick losers, singleton or void in spades

If responder has shown one or three key cards and opener has three key cards, he rebids four notrump. If opener has two key cards and a void, he rebids the suit of the void. Thus, in the auction

Opener	Responder
4 ♣	4 ♦
4 ♠	

opener has shown two key cards plus a void in spades. If instead of four spades he had rebid five of a minor suit, he would have shown two key cards plus a void in that minor.

See also ROMEX NAMYATS; LACKWOOD.

ROTH FOUR CLUB ASKING BID AFTER PREEMPTS

Because of the benefits to be gained, players make preemptive openings on a wide range of hands. For example, depending on the vulnerability, a three heart opening may be made on

[A] ♠ —   ♡ J 10 x x x x   ◊ Q x x   ♣ x x x x
[B] ♠ x   ♡ K Q 10 x x x x ◊ x x x   ♣ x x
[C] ♠ x x   ♡ Q J x x x x x ◊ K x   ♣ x x

The Roth Four Club Asking Bid is a convention that permits the responder, after his partner has opened with a three-level preempt, to assess the partnership's prospects for slam without going past the last makeable contract.

After an opening bid of three of any suit, a response of four clubs asks opener how good his hand is; if it is not extremely weak, opener is required to indicate whether his strength lies principally in his suit or outside. Opener's answers to the four club inquiry are as follows:

4 ◊ = very weak hand, with preempt suit headed by less than king and queen

4 ♡ = preempt suit headed by two of the top three honors

4 ♠ = good hand with one or two honors outside of suit; preempt suit headed by less than king and queen

4 NT = solid preempt suit

After hearing opener's rebid, responder is usually able to place the final contract. His further bids are largely natural. His bid of a new suit is a signoff in that suit. A bid of four notrump after opener's rebid of four spades, may be used as BLACKWOOD.

See also KEY CARD FOUR CLUBS AFTER PREEMPTS; KEY CARD GERBER.

GAMBLING TWO NOTRUMP OPENING

The use of a two notrump opening as a gambling bid showing a long minor suit allows opener to distinguish among minor suit preempts of varying types. Responder is then better able to determine whether or not the partnership should attempt a three notrump contract.

The Gambling Two Notrump opening promises a long, solid minor suit, with one side suit stopped. Opening bids of three clubs and three diamonds promise long, solid suits with no outside stopper. (*See* GAMBLING THREE NOTRUMP OPENING, which is ambiguous because it may be used with either one or no outside stopper.) An opening bid of three notrump shows a nonsolid minor suit with no outside strength. *See* THREE NOTRUMP AS WEAK MINOR PREEMPT.

Examples:

[A]	♠ x x	♡ x x·	◊ A K Q x x x x	♣ K x
[B]	♠ x x	♡ x x	◊ A K Q x x x x	♣ x x
[C]	♠ x x	♡ x x	◊ K Q J x x x x	♣ x

With hand [A], opener would bid two notrump; with hand [B], three diamonds, with hand [C] three notrump. There is no way, however, to make an ordinary three-level-type preempt in a minor suit on a hand such as [C] with one fewer diamond.

Opposite the Gambling two notrump opening, responder may pass, gambling that exactly two notrump will be made.

If responder wishes to play in three of opener's suit, he bids three clubs, over which opener will pass if his suit in clubs or bid three diamonds if that is his suit. If responder wishes to preempt to the five level, he jumps to five clubs, over which opener passes if his suit is clubs or bids five diamonds if it is diamonds.

If responder has two suits stopped and wishes to explore the wisdom of a three notrump contract, he responds three diamonds, asking opener to bid the side suit in which he has a stopper. Opener's bid of three hearts or three spades shows a stopper in the suit bid; a rebid of three notrump shows that the stopper is in his other minor. If responder now knows that the partnership has all suits stopped, he may make three notrump the final contract, either by passing if that has been opener's rebid, or by bidding it himself. If he knows that there is no stopper in one suit, he may retreat to four or five of opener's presumed suit.

If responder wishes to know whether opener's outside stopper is an ace, he may bid four clubs, which is the GERBER convention.

GAMBLING THREE CLUB OPENING

The Gambling Three Club convention is designed to allow opener to distinguish between preempts in which his suit is solid and those in which it is not. The three club opening does not identify the suit of the preempt but promises that the suit is at least seven cards long and is headed by the ace, king, and queen. The bid denies any outside ace or king. For example:

♠ x x   ♡ x   ◊ A K Q x x x x   ♣ x x x

If responder has stoppers in three suits he may bid three notrump. A response of three hearts asks opener to bid his long suit; opener's rebid may be passed.

A response of three diamonds is game forcing and asks opener to bid a suit in which he has a singleton or void. With no singleton or void, opener simply makes the cheapest bid in his long suit. To respond three diamonds responder must have sufficient strength in three suits to know which is opener's long suit.

If opener has shown shortness over the three diamond response, responder may, if he has a suitable fitting hand, jump to slam in opener's inferred suit; or he may jump to five notrump to ask opener either to bid a grand slam if his shortness is a void, or to bid the small slam if his shortness is a singleton.

If opener and responder held

     (Opener)
     ♠ x x   ♡ A K Q x x x x   ◊ x x x   ♣ x
     (Responder)
     ♠ A K Q x   ♡ J x x   ◊ A K   ♣ Q x x x

the auction might go

Opener	Responder
3♣	3◊
4♣	5 Notrump
6♡	

If opener's black-suit holdings were reversed, he would bid three spades over three diamonds, and responder would lose interest in slam. If, instead of three diamonds and one club, opener had two cards in each suit, he would rebid three hearts, and responder would raise to four hearts.

POINTED PREEMPTS

The Pointed Preempt convention uses artificial opening bids of two diamonds and two spades to assist opener in giving greater definition to the trick-taking potential of his preemptive bids. The two heart opening may be used to show a multi-suited hand worth an opening bid. *See, e.g.,* FLANNERY TWO HEARTS.

Openings at the three level are natural preempts showing one-suited hands containing 5 to 6 playing tricks.

An opening bid of two spades is artificial, and shows a one-suited hand containing 6½ to 7½ playing tricks. The suit need not be spades. The two-spade opening forces responder to bid two notrump. Thereafter, opener's rebid of a suit at the three level shows his long suit and indicates that the suit is not solid. With a solid suit, opener rebids three notrump.

An opening bid of two diamonds is artificial and shows either a weak two-bid in hearts or spades, or a hand containing 8-9 playing tricks, or a 22-26 point hand with a five-card suit and no second suit. Responder proceeds as follows. He bids two hearts if he has a hand with which he would have passed a weak two-bid in hearts. He bids two spades if he has a hand with which he would have invited game opposite a weak-two opening in hearts but would have passed a weak two spade opening. This response promises at least two honor tricks and at least 11 HCP. If opener has the weak two-heart hand, he rebids two notrump over two spades.

If opener rebids a suit at the three or four level after a response of two hearts or two spades, he shows an 8-9 trick playing hand. The suit he bids is his long suit.

If responder has a hand with two honor tricks and either a six-card or longer minor suit, or support for both majors, he may bid two notrump as the MCCABE ADJUNCT. This response forces opener to rebid three clubs if he has the weak two-bid type hand. Responder may pass three clubs, or bid three diamonds to play, or may bid three hearts to invite opener to bid game in his major suit, whichever it is.

A three-club response to the two diamond opening shows a strong hand, but does not indicate that responder has support for either major suit. Opener is required to transfer into his long suit as follows:

$3\diamondsuit$ = transfer to hearts
$3\heartsuit$ = transfer to spades
$3\spadesuit$ = transfer to diamonds
3NT = transfer to clubs

Over opener's rebid, any bid by responder in a suit other than opener's long suit is a slam try showing either a long suit or a cue-bid. Opener should, in return, cue-bid a side ace or a king if he has one.

If opener has the 5-3-3-2 hand worth 22 or more points, over a two-heart response he rebids two notrump with 22-24 HCP, or three notrump with 25-26 HCP. Following the two notrump rebid, responder and opener bid their suits naturally; a three club rebid by responder is not the STAYMAN convention.

PREEMPTIVE OPENING TRANSFER

The Preemptive Opening Transfer convention requires that an opening preemptive bid be made in the suit below the opener's long suit. With a suitable hand, responder may bid three notrump to play. The transfer has the advantage of allowing the partner of the preempter, whose hand pattern and strength may remain undisclosed, to become the declarer.

With no interest in a slam or a three notrump contract, responder simply bids the long suit shown by the opening bid. If the preempt has been at the three level, responder may either make a nonjump bid in opener's suit if he would have passed a natural preempt in the suit; or he may jump in opener's suit if he would have raised a natural preempt.

If responder has interest in exploring for game or slam, he may bid a new suit. This bid asks opener if he has an ace. If he has no ace, opener is to bid notrump. If he has an ace, opener bids his cheapest control, *i.e.*, ace, king, singleton, or void. If responder now bids opener's long suit at any level or game in notrump, opener should not bid again. If, instead, responder cue-bids, opener should show another control if he has one. For example, in the auction

Opener	Responder
3♣	3♡
3♠	

if responder bids three notrump or four diamonds, responder must pass. If, instead, responder bids, for example, four clubs, opener must show another control if he has one. If he has no other, he must bid four notrump.

Making the denial in notrump enables responder to be the declarer in the eventual diamond contract. This is fine, of course, if the hand will be played in opener's suit. But if responder wants to explore for slam and then decides not to play slam, if he chooses to play in a game in notrump rather than in opener's suit, opener will usually end up the declarer.

TWO NOTRUMP AS WEAK MINOR PREEMPT

Some partnerships agree to use an opening bid of two notrump to show a hand of preemptive strength with a long minor suit. The minor suit is unspecified. Use of two notrump as the opening bid with such hands allows the partnership to explore for game in a major suit while preserving the possibility of playing at the three level on hands when game is not a good prospect. Generally, the convention is not used in fourth seat.

In response to the two notrump opening, if responder has no interest in game in a major suit, he signs off by bidding three clubs. If responder has support for both minors, he may bid four clubs as a preempt or four diamonds as a game force. After responder's bid of three or four clubs, opener passes if clubs is his suit, or corrects to diamonds if diamonds is his suit. After responder's game-forcing bid of four diamonds, opener bids five diamonds if that is his suit. If his suit is clubs, he bids four notrump. This permits responder to bid five clubs, making the strong hand the declarer.

If responder is interested in a major suit game and has a six-card or longer suit, he may bid his suit naturally at the three level. His bids of three hearts and three spades are not forcing. If responder has game-invitational strength with at least five cards in each major, he makes an artificial response of three diamonds. After responder's bid of three diamonds, if opener has three-card or longer support for a major, he bids it. If he cannot support one of the majors, he bids his minor.

The complete schedule of responder's bids is as follows:

3 ♣	=	signoff in opener's minor
3 ◇	=	artificial and forcing, with at least five-five in hearts and spades
3 ♡	=	at least six hearts, invites game
3 ♠	=	at least six spades, invites game
3 NT	=	natural signoff
4 ♣	=	preemptive, with support for both minor suits
4 ◇	=	game forcing in opener's suit
4 ♡	=	natural signoff
4 ♠	=	natural signoff

See also GAMBLING TWO NOTRUMP; PREEMPTIVE OPENING TRANSFER; TWO-UNDER PREEMPTS.

TWO-UNDER PREEMPTS

The Bergen-Cohen Two-Under Preempt convention uses several opening bids at the two and three levels as artificial preempts. The opening bid is made in the denomination that ranks two steps below opener's long suit.

This convention makes the intermediate suit, *i.e.*, the suit that ranks between the artificial opening bid and the suit promised, available for a game try by responder, while allowing the partnership to sign off cheaply when opener has minimum values for his preempt. It may also have the advantage, when opener has more than minimum values, of making the strong hand the declarer and concealing his hand from the defenders.

The Preempts

Using this convention, the opening preemptor generally makes the bid that ranks two steps below his long suit. For example, a two diamond opening shows a weak two bid in spades; a two spade opening shows a three-level preempt in clubs; a three diamond opening shows a three-level preempt in spades. The exceptions to the two-under principle are, first, that, since an opening two club bid is used as the strong, artificial forcing opening, two clubs is not available to show a weak two bid in hearts; thus, the two heart opening is natural. Second, though spades ranks two steps under clubs, a four-level preempt in clubs is shown by a three heart opening; this allows the partnership to land in three notrump when either opener or responder has maximum values.

The complete schedule of two-under preempts is as follows:

2 ◇	=	weak two bid in spades
2 ♠	=	three-level preempt in clubs
2 NT	=	three level preempt in diamonds
3 ♣	=	three-level preempt in hearts
3 ◇	=	three-level preempt in spades
3 ♡	=	four-level preempt in clubs
3 NT	=	four-level preempt in diamonds

A three spade opening bid is not used as a two-under preempt. Rather, it is used to show a hand with a long solid minor suit and no outside aces or kings, *i.e.*, a hand that might otherwise be opened with a GAMBLING THREE NOTRUMP. Using a bid other than three notrump to show this hand allows the responder to become the declarer, which will likely provide advantages on the opening lead and during the play since the location of responder's high cards will remain concealed.

In addition, some partnerships decline to use the two notrump opening as a diamond preempt, preferring instead to use that opening naturally. *But see* KOKISH RELAY. If the two notrump bid is used naturally, the only available preempt in diamonds, in the two-under convention, is three notrump.

Opposite a two-under preempt, responder may sign off by bidding the suit promised by the opening. In order to invite game, he bids the suit that ranks next above the artificial opening.

In general, opener makes the cheapest possible bid over the game invitation to show that he has minimum values for his preempt. With a maximum he makes a higher bid, and that bid gives information about his distribution. Precise sequences are set out in the sections below.

Rebids After the Two Diamond Opening and a Two Heart Response

The two diamond opening shows a weak two bid in spades. If responder makes a game try by bidding two hearts, opener bids two spades to show a minimum hand. Any other bid shows a maximum. His bid of two notrump shows a maximum with three or four hearts, but it does not disclose how many spades he holds. Higher bids focus on the length and strength of opener's spade suit. The complete schedule of the two diamond opener's rebids is as follows.

2 ♠	=	minimum
2 NT	=	maximum with three or four hearts
3 ♣	=	maximum with a five-card spade suit
3 ◊	=	maximum with a weak six-card spade suit
3 ♡	=	maximum with a fair six-card spade suit
3 ♠	=	maximum with a good six-card spade suit
3 NT	=	solid six-card spade suit

After opener's two notrump rebid, showing three or four hearts, responder may bid three clubs to ask about opener's precise major-suit distribution. Opener answers as follows:

3 ◊	=	five spades, three hearts
3 ♡	=	five spades, four hearts
3 ♠	=	six spades, three hearts
3 NT	=	six spades, four hearts

Rebids After the Three-Level Preempts in Clubs and Diamonds

The two spade opening shows a three-level preempt in clubs. After responder's artificial game try of two notrump, opener rebids three clubs to show minimum strength. His higher rebids show maximum strength and indicate whether he has three or more cards in a major suit. In showing major suit length, opener bids artificially; if the hand is to be played in a major suit, this will enable responder, who has the stronger hand, to be the declarer.

The two spade opener's rebids over two notrump are as follows:

> 3 ♣ = minimum
> 3 ♢ = maximum with a four-card major
> 3 ♡ = maximum with three spades
> 3 ♠ = maximum with three hearts
> 3 NT = maximum with no three- or four-card major

After opener's three diamond bid, showing a four-card major, responder may bid three hearts to ask which. Opener bids three spades to show four hearts; he bids three notrump to show four spades.

The responding scheme after a two notrump opening, showing diamonds, is similar. After responder bids three clubs to invite game, opener's rebids are:

> 3 ♢ = minimum
> 3 ♡ = maximum with three or four spades
> 3 ♠ = maximum with three or four hearts
> 3 NT = maximum with no three- or four-card major

Auctions After Three-Level Preempts in Hearts and Spades

After a three club opening, showing a three-level preempt in hearts, responder bids three diamonds to invite game, and opener rebids as follows:

> 3 ♡ = minimum
> 3 ♠ = maximum with six hearts
> 3 NT = maximum with seven hearts

Similarly, after a three diamond opening, which shows a three-level preempt in spades, and a three heart response inviting game, opener's rebids are:

3 ♠   = minimum
3 NT = maximum with six-card suit
4 ♣   = maximum with seven-card suit

Rebids After Four-Level Minor Suit Preempts

The only deviation from the principle that opener rebids as cheaply as possible with minimum values occurs when the opening bid was three hearts, showing a four-level preempt in clubs. After responder's three spade game try, opener rebids three notrump with a maximum and four clubs with a minimum. This enables the partnership to stop in three notrump when opener has maximum values.

After a three notrump opening, showing a four-level preempt in diamonds, and a four club response inviting game, opener rebids four diamonds to show a minimum. Any higher bid shows a maximum and discloses how many key cards (the four aces and the king of diamonds) he holds. Since he promises a maximum, he is presumed to hold at least one key card; since he has preempted, he is presumed to hold no more than two. His key-card showing responses are:

4 ♡   = maximum, one key card, without the queen of diamonds
4 ♠   = maximum, one key card, with the queen of diamonds
4 NT = maximum, two key cards, without the queen of diamonds
5 ♣   = maximum, two key cards, with the queen of diamonds

See also PREEMPTIVE OPENING TRANSFER.

VIII

Conventions for the Defenders

RUSINOW LEADS AGAINST NOTRUMP

The RUSINOW LEAD convention, which requires the opening leader to lead the lower of touching honors, traditionally has been used only against suit contracts. The partnership may agree to use these leads against notrump contracts with holdings other than ace-king in order to clarify all honor leads.

When the partnership is using these methods, the only honor sequence from which the opening leader does not lead the second highest of his touching honors is the ace-king. If his suit is not solid or semi-solid, the opening leader leads the ace from ace-king. In response to the ace lead, third hand should give an ATTITUDE SIGNAL.

The lead of the king is used when the suit is solid or when the leader has a semi-solid holding missing the queen, jack, or ten. For example, A K Q J x , A K J 10 x , K Q 10 9 x , K Q J 9 , or K J 10 9 x x. The lead of the king from these holdings suggests that third hand take one of three actions. If he has the ace, he should overtake the king and return the suit. If he does not have the ace but does have the queen, jack, or ten, he should unblock that card. If he has no honor in the suit, he should give a COUNT SIGNAL.

The lead of the queen promises the king. This lead asks third hand to encourage if he holds the ace or the jack; it does not ask him to unblock.

The lead of the jack promises the queen and normally denies any higher honor. Third hand signals normally.

The lead of the ten promises the jack; the lead of the nine promises the ten. When either of these leads is made, the leader may also hold the ace or king. If the opening leader's suit is headed by the nine, he should lead the second highest card.

With some interior sequences, the opening leader should ignore the Rusinow principle and lead the top of the sequence in order to help his partner realize that the suit will be established if he returns it. For example, from A Q J 9 x , the conventional lead would be the jack. Since the jack is also led from Q J 10 x x , third hand would not know who had the ace when declarer won the king; thus, he might be unsure whether to return this suit or to switch to another. If the queen is led instead, however, ostensibly showing the king, third hand should not long be in the dark: either he will have that card or dummy or declarer will produce it. Thus alerted that the opening lead has been antisystemic, third hand should infer that if he returns the suit, it will be established.

Similarly, from A Q 10 9 x , the ten should be led. Either third hand will hold the jack or that card will surface from dummy or declarer, and third hand will again reason that the suit can be established if he returns it.

See also JOURNALIST HONOR LEADS AGAINST NOTRUMP; JACK, TEN OR NINE TO SHOW 0 OR 2 HIGHER HONORS.

SMITH ECHO

The Smith Echo is a suit-preference signal used against notrump contracts. The purpose of the echo, by either defender, is to indicate his desire to have his partner continue the suit led on opening lead. A defender's failure to echo suggests that his partner should shift to another suit.

The Smith signal is not given on the opening trick but rather is given during the declarer's subsequent run of a long suit in his own hand or in dummy (the "surrogate" suit). When declarer runs the surrogate suit, if the partner of the opening leader believes (a) that the opening lead was a favorable one for the defending side, and (b) that it is safe for his partner to lead the suit again, he plays high-low in declarer's suit. This echo suggests that, when the defense gains the lead again, the suit led on opening lead should be continued. When a defender instead plays low-high, he indicates that, from his hand, it appears that his partner should not continue the suit originally led but should switch to another suit. The reason for the shift suggestion may be that another suit is likely to have greater potential for producing defense tricks. Or, if the discouraging signal is given by third hand, the reason may be his perception that continuation of the suit by the opening leader may cost a trick and that the continuation should come instead from third hand.

For example, suppose West's opening lead was a low spade from A 10 x x x, and dummy held ♠ x x, East played the jack, and declarer the king. On regaining the lead, West would like to continue with a low spade if East started with ♠ Q J x, but not if he started with ♠ J x x. If declarer proceeds to run a long suit and the defenders have agreed to use the Smith Echo, East should play a high card followed by a lower card in declarer's suit if he has the queen of spades. He should play a low card followed by a higher card if he does not have the queen of spades and has another suit he would like West to lead instead.

When the partnership has agreed to use Smith Echoes, they may apply to the opening leader as well as to his partner. Suppose, for example, West's opening lead is the jack of hearts, promising zero or two higher cards in the suit, *see* JACK, TEN OR NINE TO SHOW 0 OR 2 HIGHER HONORS, and East has no honors in the suit. If dummy has ♡ K x and the trick is won with the king, the lead will remain ambiguous to East. If declarer proceeds to run a long suit, West may play high-low in that suit to indicate that he wants hearts continued if East gets the lead. He would play low-high to ask East to shift.

Use of the Smith Echo is not compatible with other types of signals in the suit being run by declarer. Thus, agreement to use this convention means that when declarer is running a long suit, the defenders cannot give COUNT SIGNALS to indicate the number of cards they hold in that suit. Nor can they give the traditional SUIT PREFERENCE SIGNALS by means of their carding in that suit.

Note that the Smith Echo is not used when declarer is not running his suit but is attempting to knock out a defender's stopper. In the latter instance, the defender who does not hold the stopper should usually attempt to give his partner a count signal in order to permit partner to hold up the stopper just long enough to prevent declarer's use of the long suit. For example:

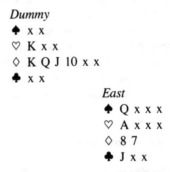

Dummy
♠ x x
♡ K x x
◇ K Q J 10 x x
♣ x x

East
♠ Q x x x
♡ A x x x
◇ 8 7
♣ J x x

West has led a low club against three notrump, and declarer has won East's jack with the king. When declarer leads a low diamond to the king and continues with the queen, East should play the eight first, followed by the seven, telling West that East has an even number of diamonds so that West, if he holds ◇ A x x, may intelligently win the second round of the suit. If, however, declarer has played the ace of diamonds and is running the suit, East should play the seven of diamonds and then the eight, telling his partner that the jack was his highest club.

Reverse Smith Echo

Some partnerships have agreed to reverse the meanings of the echo and non-echo. For these partnerships, a defender's high-low signal in the long suit run by declarer discourages partner from continuing the suit of the opening lead; a low-high signal encourages.

See also CINCINNATI CARDING.

CINCINNATI CARDING

Using standard carding methods, on the opening lead of an honor card, third hand generally follows suit with a high card to indicate that he wants the suit continued, or with a low card to ask partner to shift. His play of the low card does not indicate to which suit the shift is desired. *See* AT-TITUDE SIGNALS.

Cincinnati carding provides the defenders with a method of signaling that usually allows the partner of the opening leader both to discourage continuation of the suit and to indicate which shift is desired.

Attitude and Suit Preference Signals on Opening Lead

The Cincinnati method uses UPSIDE-DOWN SIGNALS to show attitude on opening lead. Thus, third hand's play of a low card encourages continuation of the suit. In addition, on the theory that more often than not third hand will have both a high odd card and a high even card with which to signal, this convention uses ODD-EVEN DISCARDS to give SUIT PREFERENCE SIGNALS. Using Cincinnati signals, therefore, when third hand wants a shift, he plays a high odd-numbered card if he wants a shift to the higher ranking suit; he plays a high even-numbered card if he wants a shift to the lower ranking suit.

Three-Stage Count Signals in a Surrogate Suit

Another facet of Cincinnati signaling allows one defender to give count signals that may assist his partner in counting the hand as a whole. When declarer is playing a suit as to which a defender has no need to signal his count or attitude, and which he need not use to give a suit preference signal, if the defender is following with cards that are essentially equals, he may make his first three plays in an order that gives count in another suit.

Excluding the suit being played by declarer (the "surrogate" suit), there are three suits as to which the signaler may communicate his count. The signaling defender's first play identifies the suit in which his next two plays will give count (the "target" suit). He plays the highest of his three cards first to say that his ensuing count signal will focus on the highest of the other suits; his play of the middle card first says the target suit is the middle suit; his play of the lowest of the three cards first means that the target suit is the lowest suit. The signaler's partner often will not be sure until the second or third round of the surrogate suit which suit is the target of the count signals.

After first playing the card that corresponds to the target suit, the signaler then gives an upside-down count signal. That is, he plays his next two cards in high-low order to show an odd number of cards in the target suit; he plays low-high in order to show an even number.

For example, if the surrogate suit is hearts, the signaler may indicate how many cards he has in spades, diamonds, or clubs. If he holds 9 8 6 in hearts, his signals would have the following meanings:

Order of play	Target Suit	Count
9, 8, 6	spades	odd
8, 9, 6	diamonds	odd
6, 9, 8	clubs	odd
9, 6, 8	spades	even
8, 6, 9	diamonds	even
6, 8, 9	clubs	even

Once the signaler's partner knows the signaler's count in the surrogate suit and one other suit, he usually will be able to deduce needed information as to declarer's entire distribution.

Single-Stage Surrogate Signaling

On some hands, the defenders do not have the luxury of playing three rounds of a suit in order to identify and give a count signal in a side suit. On a hand where both defenders can recognize that there is a key suit to be counted, as where dummy has a suit headed by the king and queen and has no side entry, a defender may be able to start a count signal in the surrogate suit immediately.

For an immediate signal to be given in the surrogate suit, it must be clear to both defenders that no count or attitude signal is needed with respect to the surrogate suit, and that the suit need not be used to give a suit preference signal. It must also be clear that the defender has no other need to play his cards in any particular order, *e.g.*, to force a high card from the hand of declarer or dummy. Ordinarily, the trump suit makes an appropriate surrogate suit, assuming no trump echo is needed.

See also BETHE SIGNALS; SMITH ECHO.

SECOND-ROUND COUNT SIGNALS

Second-round count signals are a variety of ODD-EVEN SIGNALS, used on the second round of a suit or at the defender's first discarding opportunity, to permit each defender to indicate how many cards he has in the suit led on opening lead. The goal is to permit each defender to know how many cards declarer has in the suit led. This knowledge enables the defenders to determine whether the suit must be led through the declarer's hand in order not to lose an unnecessary trick.

Using this convention, the defender who continues the suit plays an even-numbered card if he began with an even number of cards in the suit led; he plays an odd-numbered card if he began with an odd number of cards in that suit. If either defender has an opportunity to discard before the suit of the opening lead is continued, and if he can afford to part with a card of the suit led, he may give his odd-even signal in discarding.

For example, if West led a diamond and East originally held ◇ Q 8 5 3 and played the queen, the next diamond East would play would be the 8. If his original holding had been Q 8 3, his next play would be the 3.

If the signaling defender began with an even number of cards in the suit but does not have an even-numbered card, he plays a high odd card on the second round of the suit (or on his first discard of the suit), and thereafter plays a lower card.

See also SMITH ECHO; BETHE SIGNALS.

BETHE SIGNALS

Bethe Signals enable third hand, in certain circumstances, to give both a count signal and a suit-preference signal simultaneously in following to the opening lead. The conditions under which such a signal may be given are strictly circumscribed. First, the lead must be in a suit in which third hand is known to have six or more cards, but whose length is otherwise unspecified. Second, either the lead is a card that is about to hold the trick, or the card played by dummy will hold the trick, or declarer will win the trick without the signaler's having to play an honor.

If these conditions are met, a Bethe signal may be given. In order to show how many cards he has in the suit led, third hand plays an even-numbered card if he has an even number of cards; he plays an odd-numbered card if he has an odd number of cards. In order to give the suit preference signal, third hand plays a high card to ask the opening leader to shift to the higher ranking side suit; he plays a low card to ask the leader to shift to the lower side suit. If third hand wants the opening leader to continue the suit led, he plays a middle card.

For example, if the opening lead against a diamond contract were the ace of spades and third hand held ♠ J 9 8 6 3 2, he would play the six if he wanted the suit continued. If he wanted a shift, he would play the eight to ask for a shift to hearts, or the two to ask for a shift to spades.

See also SECOND-ROUND COUNT SIGNALS; CINCINNATI CARDING.

EXTENDED TRUMP ECHO

The TRUMP ECHO, a high-low signal in the trump suit to show an odd number of trumps, is normally used to alert the partner of the echoer that the echoer is interested in obtaining a ruff. Some partnerships have widened the use of this signal to show simply an urgent interest in having a side suit led.

This extension allows a defender to give the trump echo either when he has three trumps and desires to ruff a side suit, or when he has as few as two trumps and wishes his partner to lead a side suit in which he has trick-taking strength. The extension is useful for occasion when the defender has no opportunity to make a vigorous signal in a side suit.

ENCRYPTED SIGNALS

A danger inherent in the defender's use of length or attitude signals is that the declarer, as well as the signal's partner, may obtain the information transmitted. An esoteric convention designed to conceal from declarer the nature of the defenders' signals and as well to take advantage of the benefits of UPSIDE DOWN SIGNALS is called encrypted signaling.

The code depends on the locations of the odd-numbered cards in a given suit, *i.e.*, the three, five, seven, and nine. When declarer has ruffed a suit in his hand or otherwise failed to follow suit, the defenders, but often not the declarer, know the distribution of that suit between the two defending hands. The defenders may agree that a defender who originally held an odd number of odd-spot cards in that suit, will use upside-down signals in all subsequent signaling; a defender who originally held an even number of odd-spot cards will use standard signaling.

Unless the three, five, seven, and nine of the key suit have all appeared early, only the defenders will know which of them is using which method of signaling.

Example

[A] ♠ A K 7 6 2   ♡ J x   ◊ K Q 9 5   ♣ x x

If hand [A] belongs to one of the defenders and spades are led and played until the declarer ruffs, the playing holding hand [A] would thereafter use upside down signals in all suit signaling. If, however, diamonds were the first suit in which declarer failed to follow, the player holding hand [A] would thereafter use traditional signaling.

Use of this convention may result, on a given hand, in both partners using upside down signals, if both originally held an odd number of odd-spot cards in the first suit to which declarer fails to follow; or it may result in both using standard signaling, if both originally held an even number of odd-spot cards in that suit; or it may result in one partner using one method and one partner using the other.

Declarer will be able to deduce, from the number of odd-spot cards in the key suit originally held by his hand and dummy, that both opponents are to use the same methods (*i.e.*, either both standard or both upside down) or that they are to use different methods. Since there are a total of four odd-spot cards, if the declaring side originally held an even number, so did the defending side; and if the defending side held an even number, both defenders will use the same signaling method. If the declaring side originally held an odd number, so did the defending side, and the defenders will be using different methods. But the available information will not tell declarer which method both defenders are using if they are using the same; or if they are using different methods, which defender is using which method.

Index

1110

50 HIGHLY-RECOMMENDED TITLES

**CALL TOLL FREE 1-800-274-2221
IN THE U.S. & CANADA TO ORDER ANY OF
THEM OR TO REQUEST OUR
FULL-COLOR 64 PAGE CATALOG OF
ALL BRIDGE BOOKS IN PRINT,
SUPPLIES AND GIFTS.**

FOR BEGINNERS
#0300 Future Champions' Bridge Series 9.95
#2130 Kantar-Introduction to Declarer's Play 7.00
#2135 Kantar-Introduction to Defender's Play 7.00
#0101 Stewart-Baron-The Bridge Book 1 .... 9.95
#1101 Silverman-Elementary Bridge
    Five Card Major Student Text 4.95
#0660 Penick-Beginning Bridge Complete 9.95
#0661 Penick-Beginning Bridge Quizzes 6.95
#3230 Lampert-Fun Way to Serious Bridge 10.00

FOR ADVANCED PLAYERS
#2250 Reese-Master Play 4.95
#1420 Klinger-Modern Losing Trick Count 13.95
#2240 Love-Bridge Squeezes Complete 5.95
#0103 Stewart-Baron-The Bridge Book 3 .... 9.95
#0740 Woolsey-Matchpoints 14.95
#0741 Woolsey-Partnership Defense 12.95
#1702 Bergen-Competitive Auctions 9.95
#0636 Lawrence-Falsecards 9.95

BIDDING — 2 OVER 1 GAME FORCE
#4750 Bruno & Hardy-Two-Over-One Game Force:
    An Introduction 9.95
#1750 Hardy-Two-Over-One Game Force 14.95
#1790 Lawrence-Workbook on the Two Over One System 11.95
#4525 Lawrence-Bidding Quizzes Book 1 .... 13.95

Prices subject to change without notice.

DEFENSE

#0520 Blackwood-Complete Book of Opening Leads 17.95
#3030 Ewen-Opening Leads 15.95
#0104 Stewart-Baron-The Bridge Book 4 .... 7.95
#0631 Lawrence-Dynamic Defense 11.95
#1200 Woolsey-Modern Defensive Signalling 4.95

FOR INTERMEDIATE PLAYERS

#2120 Kantar-Complete Defensive Bridge 20.00
#3015 Root-Commonsense Bidding 14.00
#0630 Lawrence-Card Combinations 12.95
#0102 Stewart-Baron-The Bridge Book 2 .... 9.95
#1102 Silverman-Intermediate Bridge Five
      Card Major Student Text 4.95
#0575 Lampert-The Fun Way to Advanced Bridge 11.95
#0633 Lawrence-How to Read Your Opponents' Cards 9.95
#3672 Truscott-Bid Better, Play Better 11.00
#1765 Lawrence-Judgment at Bridge 9.95

PLAY OF THE HAND

#2150 Kantar-Test your Bridge Play, Vol. 1 .... 7.00
#3675 Watson-Watson's Classic Book on
      the Play of the Hand 12.00
#1932 Mollo-Gardener-Card Play Technique 12.95
#3009 Root-How to Play a Bridge Hand 12.00
#1104 Silverman-Play of the Hand as
      Declarer and Defender 4.95
#2175 Truscott-Winning Declarer Play 10.00
#3803 Sydnor-Bridge Made Easy Book 3 .... 6.00

CONVENTIONS

#2115 Kantar-Bridge Conventions 10.00
#0610 Kearse-Bridge Conventions Complete 29.95
#3011 Root-Pavlicek-Modern Bridge Conventions 15.00
#0240 Championship Bridge Series (All 36) 25.95

DUPLICATE STRATEGY

#1600 Klinger-50 Winning Duplicate Tips 12.95
#2260 Sheinwold-Duplicate Bridge 3.95

FOR ALL PLAYERS

#3889 Darvas & de V. Hart-Right Through The Pack 12.95
#0790 Simon: Why You Lose at Bridge 11.95
#4850 Encyclopedia of Bridge, Official (ACBL) 39.95

Andersen THE LEBENSOHL CONVENTION COMPLETE .... $ 6.95
Baron THE BRIDGE PLAYER'S DICTIONARY $19.95
Bergen BETTER BIDDING WITH BERGEN,
    Vol. I, Uncontested Auctions $11.95
Bergen BETTER BIDDING WITH BERGEN,
    Vol. II, Competitive Auctions .... $ 9.95
Blackwood COMPLETE BOOK OF OPENING LEADS $17.95
Blackwood-Hanson PLAY FUNDAMENTALS .... $ 6.95
Boeder THINKING ABOUT IMPS $12.95
Bruno-Hardy 2 OVER 1 GAME FORCE: AN INTRODUCTION .... $ 9.95
Darvas & De V. Hart RIGHT THROUGH THE PACK $12.95
DeSerpa THE MEXICAN CONTRACT .... $ 5.95
Eber & Freeman HAVE I GOT A STORY FOR YOU .... $ 7.95
Feldheim FIVE CARD MAJOR BIDDING IN
    CONTRACT BRIDGE $12.95
Flannery THE FLANNERY 2 DIAMOND OPENING .... $ 7.95
Goldman ACES SCIENTIFIC .... $ 9.95
Goldman WINNERS AND LOSERS AT THE
    BRIDGE TABLE .... $ 3.95
Groner DUPLICATE BRIDGE DIRECTION $14.95
Hardy
    COMPETITIVE BIDDING WITH TWO SUITED HANDS .... $ 9.95
    TWO-OVER-ONE GAME FORCE $14.95
    TWO-OVER-ONE GAME FORCE QUIZ BOOK $11.95
Harris BRIDGE DIRECTOR'S COMPANION (3rd Edition) $19.95
Kay COMPLETE BOOK OF DUPLICATE BRIDGE $14.95
Kearse BRIDGE CONVENTIONS COMPLETE $29.95
Kelsey COUNTDOWN TO BETTER BRIDGE .... $ 9.95
Kelsey THE TRICKY GAME $11.95
Lampert THE FUN WAY TO ADVANCED BRIDGE $11.95
Lawrence
    CARD COMBINATIONS $12.95
    COMPLETE BOOK ON BALANCING $11.95
    COMPLETE BOOK ON OVERCALLS $11.95
    DYNAMIC DEFENSE $11.95
    FALSECARDS .... $ 9.95
    HAND EVALUATION $11.95
    HOW TO READ YOUR OPPONENTS' CARDS .... $ 9.95
    JUDGMENT AT BRIDGE .... $ 9.95
    PARTNERSHIP UNDERSTANDINGS .... $ 4.95
    PLAY BRIDGE WITH MIKE LAWRENCE $11.95
    PLAY SWISS TEAMS WITH MIKE LAWRENCE .... $ 7.95
    WORKBOOK ON THE TWO OVER ONE SYSTEM $11.95

Lawrence & Hanson WINNING BRIDGE INTANGIBLES	$ 4.95
Lipkin INVITATION TO ANNIHILATION	$ 8.95
Michaels & Cohen 4-3-2-1 MANUAL	$ 2.95
Penick BEGINNING BRIDGE COMPLETE	$ 9.95
Penick BEGINNING BRIDGE QUIZZES	$ 6.95
Powell TICKETS TO THE DEVIL	$ 5.95
Reese & Hoffman PLAY IT AGAIN, SAM	$ 7.95
Rosenkranz	
BRIDGE: THE BIDDER'S GAME	$12.95
TIPS FOR TOPS	$ 9.95
MORE TIPS FOR TOPS	$ 9.95
TRUMP LEADS	$ 7.95
OUR MAN GODFREY	$10.95
Rosenkranz & Alder BID TO WIN, PLAY FOR PLEASURE	$11.95
Rosenkranz & Truscott BIDDING ON TARGET	$10.95
Silverman	
ELEMENTARY BRIDGE FIVE CARD MAJOR STUDENT TEXT	$ 4.95
INTERMEDIATE BRIDGE FIVE CARD MAJOR STUDENT TEXT	$ 4.95
ADVANCED & DUPLICATE BRIDGE STUDENT TEXT	$ 4.95
PLAY OF THE HAND AS DECLARER	
& DEFENDER STUDENT TEXT	$ 4.95
Simon	
CUT FOR PARTNERS	$ 9.95
WHY YOU LOSE AT BRIDGE	$11.95
Stewart & Baron	
THE BRIDGE BOOK, Vol. 1, Beginning	$ 9.95
THE BRIDGE BOOK, Vol. 2, Intermediate	$ 9.95
THE BRIDGE BOOK, Vol. 3, Advanced	$ 9.95
THE BRIDGE BOOK, Vol. 4, Defense	$ 7.95
Thomas SHERLOCK HOLMES, BRIDGE DETECTIVE	$ 9.95
Von Elsner	
CRUISE BRIDGE	$ 5.95
EVERYTHING JAKE WITH ME	$ 5.95
THE BEST OF JAKE WINKMAN	$ 5.95
THE JAKE OF HEARTS	$ 5.95
Woolsey	
MATCHPOINTS	$14.95
MODERN DEFENSIVE SIGNALLING	$ 4.95
PARTNERSHIP DEFENSE	$12.95
World Bridge Federation APPEALS COMMITTEE DECISIONS	
from the 1994 NEC WORLD CHAMPIONSHIPS	$ 9.95